Data Structures
Using Java™

Data Structures Using Java™

Yedidyah Langsam
Moshe J. Augenstein
Aaron M. Tenenbaum

Brooklyn College of The City University of New York

PEARSON
Prentice
Hall

Upper Saddle River, New Jersey 07458

Library of Congress Cataloging-in-Publication Data
CIP DATA AVAILABLE.

Vice President and Editorial Director, ECS: *Marcia Horton*
Executive Editor: *Petra Recter*
Vice President and Director of Production and Manufacturing, ESM: *David W. Riccardi*
Executive Managing Editor: *Vince O'Brien*
Assistant Managing Editor: *Camille Trentacoste*
Production Editor: *Irwin Zucker*
Manufacturing Manager: *Trudy Pisciotti*
Manufacturing Buyer: *Lisa McDowell*
Director of Creative Services: *Paul Belfanti*
Creative Director: *Carole Anson*
Art Director: *Jayne Conte*
Cover Designer: *Bruce Kenselaar*
Cover Art: *Gennady Kurbat; Getty Images Inc.—Illustration Works, Inc.*
Executive Marketing Manager: *Pamela Shaffer*
Marketing Assistant: *Barrie Reinhold*

 © 2003 Pearson Education, Inc.
Pearson Prentice Hall
Upper Saddle River, New Jersey 07458

The author and publisher of this book have used their best efforts in preparing this book. These efforts include the development, research, and testing of the theories and programs to determine their effectiveness. The author and publisher make no warranty of any kind, expressed or implied, with regard to these programs or the documentation contained in this book. The author and publisher shall not be liable in any event for incidental or consequential damages in connection with, or arising out of, the furnishing, performance, or use of these programs.

Java is a trademark of Sun Microsystems, Inc.

Printed in the United States of America

10 9 8 7 6 5 4 3 2 1

ISBN 0-13-047721-4

Pearson Education Ltd., *London*
Pearson Education Australia Pty. Ltd., *Sydney*
Pearson Education Singapore Pte. Ltd.
Pearson Education North Asia Ltd. *Hong Kong*
Pearson Education Canada Inc., *Toronto*
Pearson Educación de Mexico, S.A. de C.V.
Pearson Education—Japan, Inc., *Tokyo*
Pearson Education—Malaysia Pte. Ltd.
Pearson Education Inc., *Upper Saddle River, New Jersey*

Dedication

*To Shoshanah Binah, Tziyonah Miriam, Tziporah Avigayil, Shmuel David,
and my wife, Vivienne*

YL

*To Pinny, Chesky, Ephraim, Rifky, Sora Malka, Reuven,
Chaya, and, of course, Gail*

MA

To Sara, Betzalel, and, of course, Miriam

AT

Contents

CHAPTER 8   Graphs and their Applications   **521**

Preface

This text is designed for a two-semester course in data structures and programming. For several years, we have taught a course in data structures to students who have completed a semester course in high-level language programming. We found that a considerable amount of time was spent in teaching programming techniques because the students did not have sufficient background in programming and were unable to implement abstract structures on their own. The brighter students eventually caught on. The weaker students never did. Based on this experience, we have reached the firm conviction that a first course in data structures must go hand-in-hand with a second course in programming. This text is a product of that conviction.

The text introduces abstract concepts, shows how they are useful in problem solving, and then shows how the abstractions can be made concrete by using a programming language. Equal emphasis is placed on both the abstract and concrete versions of concepts, so that the students learn about the concept itself, its implementation, and its application. The language used in this text is Java. Java is well suited to such a course because it contains the control structures necessary to make programs readable and allows basic data structures, such as stacks, linked lists, and trees, to be implemented in a variety of ways. This allows students to appreciate the choices and tradeoffs that face a programmer in a real situation. Java is widely used on many different computers and continues to grow in popularity. The fact that Java is object-oriented allows students to go more easily from abstractions to implementations.

The only prerequisite for students using this text is a one-semester course in programming. Students who have had a course in programming using another language can use this text together with an elementary Java text. Chapter 1 provides the information necessary for such students to acquaint themselves with Java.

Chapter 1 is an introduction to data structures. Section 1.1 introduces abstract data structures and implementations. Sections 1.2 and 1.3 introduce arrays and classes in Java. Chapter 2 discusses stacks and their Java implementation. Since the stack is the first new data structure introduced, considerable discussion of the pitfalls of implementing it is included. Section 2.3 introduces postfix, prefix, and infix notations. Chapter 3 covers recursion, its applications, and its implementation. Chapter 4 introduces queues, priority queues, and linked lists and their implementations, using arrays of available nodes as well as dynamic storage. Chapter 5 discusses trees, Chapter 6 introduces **O** notation and covers sorting, and Chapter 7 covers both internal and external searching. Chapter 8 introduces graphs, and chapter 9 discusses storage management.

A one-semester course in data structures consists of section 1.1, chapters 2–7, and sections 8.1, 8.2, and part of 8.4. Parts of chapters 3, 6, 7, and 8 can be omitted if time is pressing.

This text covers the following knowledge units as described in the report *Computing Curricula* 2001 of the ACM/IEEE-CS Joint Curriculum Task Force: PF2 (Algorithms and problem-solving), PF3 (Fundamental data-structures), PF4 (Recursion), DS5 (Graphs and trees), AL1 (Basic Algorithmic analysis), AL3 (Fundamental computing algorithms), and PL6 (Object-oriented programming). The book can be used for the following courses of that curriculum: CS 103I (Data Structures and Algorithms); CS 112I (Data Abstraction); CS103O (Algorithms and Data Structures); as a supplement to CS 112O (Object-Oriented Design and Methodology); CS 102B (Algorithms and Programming Techniques) and CS 103B (Principles of Object-Oriented Design); and as a supplement to CS 112A (Programming Methodology).

Algorithms are presented as intermediaries between English-language descriptions and Java programs. They are written in Java style interspersed with English. These algorithms allow the reader to focus on the method used to solve a problem without concern about declaration of variables and the peculiarities of real language. In transforming an algorithm in to a program, we introduce these issues and point out the pitfalls that accompany them. We distinguish between algorithms and programs by presenting the former in italics and the latter in roman.

Most of the concepts in the text are illustrated by several examples. Some of these examples are important topics in their own right (e.g., postfix notation, multiword arithmetic) and may be treated as such. Other examples illustrate different implementation techniques (e.g., sequential storage of trees). Instructors are free to cover as many or as few of these examples as they wish. Examples may also be assigned to students as independent reading. It is anticipated that all the examples will not be covered in sufficient detail within the confines of a one- or two-semester course. At the stage of a student's development for which the text is designed, it is more important to cover several examples in great detail than to cover a broad range of topics cursorily.

Several additional supplementary materials are available to the instructor. These include chapter objectives and slides of all the figures in the text; solutions (and, when applicable, working code) to the end-of-chapter exercises; working versions of all the code in the text; and approximately one thousand additional exercises to supplement the exercises at the end of each chapter.

All the programs and algorithms in this text have been tested and debugged. The programs given in this book were developed using the Sun™ Java 2 Standard Edition SDK available at *http://java.sun.com/j2se/*. Readers are encouraged to download the Sun™ Java 2 Platform as well as the associated documentation in order to develop their own programs. The Forte for Java™, release 3.0, Community Edition IDE may also be useful and is freely available at the aforementioned site. We wish to thank Shalva S. Landy and Edward Mardakhaev for their invaluable assistance in this task. Their zeal for the task was above and beyond the call of duty, and their suggestions were always valuable. Of course, any errors that remain are the sole responsibility of the authors.

The exercises vary widely in type and difficulty. Some are drill exercises to ensure comprehension of topics in the text. Others involve modifications of programs or algorithms presented in the text. Still others introduce new concepts and are quite challenging.

Often, a group of successive exercises includes the complete development of a new topic that can be used as the basis for a term project or an additional lecture. The instructor should take care in assigning exercises to ensure that they are suitable to the level of the students. We consider it imperative for students to be assigned from five to twelve (depending on difficulty) programming projects per semester. The exercises contain several projects of this type.

We would like to thank Sarita Setton-Bakst, Alexander Kaplan, Shalva S. Landy, Marina Marchenko, Edward Mardakhaev, Amani Saleh, Boris Sery, and Nechama Stern for their invaluable assistance.

The authors would like to thank Vivienne Esther Langsam for helping us complete the index in the face of a fast approaching deadline.

We would like thank the editors and staff at Prentice Hall and especially the reviewers for their helpful comments and suggestions.

Finally, we thank our wives, Vivienne Langsam, Gail Augenstein, and Miriam Tenenbaum, for their advice and encouragement during the long and arduous task of producing such a book, and our children and grandchildren, who make it all worthwhile.

YEDIDYAH LANGSAM

MOSHE AUGENSTEIN

AARON M. TENENBAUM

CHAPTER 1

Introduction to Data Structures

A computer is a machine that manipulates information. The study of computer science includes the study of how information is organized in a computer, how it can be manipulated, and how it can be utilized. Thus it is exceedingly important for a student of computer science to understand the concepts of information organization and manipulation.

1.1 INFORMATION AND MEANING

If computer science is fundamentally the study of information, the first question that arises is: what is information? Unfortunately, although the concept of information is the bedrock of the entire field, this question cannot be answered precisely. In this sense, the concept of information in computer science is similar to the concepts of point, line, and plane in geometry: they are all undefined terms about which statements can be made but which cannot be explained in terms of more elementary concepts.

In geometry, it is possible to talk about the length of a line despite the fact that the concept of a line is itself undefined. The length of a line is a measure of quantity. Similarly, in computer science, we can measure quantities of information. The basic unit of information is the *bit*, whose value asserts one of two mutually exclusive possibilities. For example, if a light switch can be in one of two positions but not in both simultaneously, the fact that it is either in the "on" position or the "off" position is one bit of information. If a device can be in more than two possible states, then the fact that it is in a particular state is more than one bit of information. For example, if a dial has eight possible positions, then the fact that it is in position four rules out seven other possibilities, whereas the fact that a light switch is on rules out only one other possibility.

Another way of thinking of this phenomenon is as follows. Suppose we had only two-way switches, but could use as many of them as we needed. How many switches would be necessary to represent a dial with eight positions? Clearly, one switch can represent only two positions (see Figure 1.1.1a). Two switches can represent four different

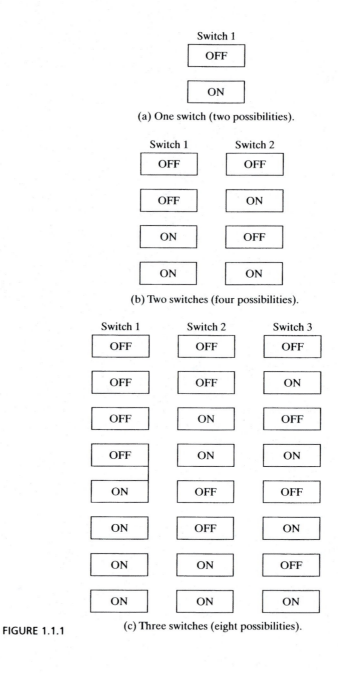

Switch 1

| OFF |

| ON |

(a) One switch (two possibilities).

Switch 1	Switch 2
OFF	OFF
OFF	ON
ON	OFF
ON	ON

(b) Two switches (four possibilities).

Switch 1	Switch 2	Switch 3
OFF	OFF	OFF
OFF	OFF	ON
OFF	ON	OFF
OFF	ON	ON
ON	OFF	OFF
ON	OFF	ON
ON	ON	OFF
ON	ON	ON

FIGURE 1.1.1   (c) Three switches (eight possibilities).

positions (Figure 1.1.1b), and three switches are required to represent eight different positions (Figure 1.1.1c). In general, n switches can represent 2^n different possibilities.

The binary digits 0 and 1 are used to represent the two possible states of any bit (in fact, the word "bit" is a contraction of the words "binary digit"). Given n bits, a string of n ones and zeros is used to represent their settings. For example, the string 101011 represents six switches, the first of which is "on" (one), the second of which is "off" (zero), the third on, the fourth off, and the fifth and sixth on.

We have seen that three bits are sufficient to represent eight possibilities. The eight possible configurations of these three bits (000, 001, 010, 011, 100, 101, 110, and 111) can be used to represent the integers 0 through 7. However, there is nothing intrinsic about these bit settings that implies that a particular setting represents a particular integer. Any assignment of integer values to bit settings is equally valid as long as no two integers are assigned to the same bit setting. Once such an assignment has been made, a particular bit setting can be unambiguously interpreted as a specific integer. Let us examine several widely used methods for interpreting bit settings as integers.

Binary and Decimal Integers

The most widely used method for interpreting bit settings as nonnegative integers is the **_binary number system_**. In this system each bit position represents a power of 2. The rightmost bit position represents 2^0, which equals 1, the next position to the left represents 2^1, which is 2, the next bit position represents 2^2, which is 4, and so on. An integer is represented as a sum of powers of 2. A string of all zeros represents the number 0. If a 1 appears in a particular bit position, then the power of 2 represented by that bit position is included in the sum, but if a 0 appears, then that power of 2 is not included in the sum. For example, the group of bits 00100110 has ones in positions 1, 2, and 5 (counting from right to left with the rightmost position counted as position 0). Thus 00100110 represents the integer $2^1 + 2^2 + 2^5 = 2 + 4 + 32 = 38$. Under this interpretation, any string of bits of length n represents a unique nonnegative integer between 0 and $2^n - 1$, and any nonnegative integer between 0 and $2^n - 1$ can be represented by a unique string of bits of length n.

There are two widely used methods for representing negative binary numbers. In the first method, called **_ones complement notation_**, a negative number is represented by changing each bit in its absolute value to the opposite bit setting. For example, since 00100110 represents 38, 11011001 is used to represent -38. This means that the leftmost bit of a number is no longer used to represent a power of 2, but is reserved for the sign of the number. A bit string starting with a 0 represents a positive number, while a bit string starting with a 1 represents a negative number. Given n bits, the range of numbers that can be represented is $-2^{(n-1)} + 1$ (a 1 followed by $n - 1$ zeros) to $2^{(n-1)} - 1$ (a 0 followed by $n - 1$ ones). Note that under this representation, there are two representations for the number 0, a "positive 0" consisting of all zeros, and a "negative 0" consisting of all ones.

The second method of representing negative binary numbers is called **_twos complement notation_**. In this notation, 1 is added to the ones complement representation of a negative number. For example, since 11011001 represents -38 in ones complement notation, 11011010 is used to represent -38 in twos complement notation. Given n bits, the range of numbers that can be represented is $-2^{(n-1)}$ (a 1 followed by $n-1$ zeros) to $2^{(n-1)} - 1$ (a 0 followed by $n-1$ ones). Note that $-2^{(n-1)}$ can be represented in twos complement notation but not in ones complement notation. However, its absolute value, $2^{(n-1)}$, cannot be represented in either notation using n bits. Note also that there is only one representation for the number 0 using n bits in twos complement notation. To see this, consider 0 using eight bits: 00000000. The ones complement is 11111111, which is negative 0 in that notation. Adding one to produce the twos complement form yields 100000000, which is nine bits long. Since only eight bits are allowed, the leftmost bit (or "overflow") is discarded, leaving 00000000 as minus 0.

The binary number system is by no means the only method by which bits can be used to represent integers. For example, a string of bits may be used to represent integers in the decimal number system, as follows. Four bits can be used to represent a decimal digit between 0 and 9 in the binary notation described above. A string of bits of arbitrary length may be divided into consecutive sets of four bits where each set represents a decimal digit. The string then represents the number that is formed by those decimal digits in conventional decimal notation. For example, in this system, the bit string 00100110 is separated into two strings of four bits each: 0010 and 0110. The first of these represents the decimal digit 2, and the second represents the decimal digit 6, so that the entire string represents the integer 26. This representation is called **binary coded decimal**.

One important feature of the binary coded decimal representation of nonnegative integers is that not all bit strings are valid representations of a decimal integer. Four bits can be used to represent one of sixteen different possibilities since there are sixteen possible states for a set of four bits. However, in the binary coded decimal integer representation, only ten of those sixteen possibilities are used. That is, codes such as 1010 and 1100, whose binary values are ten or larger, are invalid in a binary coded decimal number.

Real Numbers

The usual method used by computers to represent real numbers is **floating-point notation**. There are many varieties of floating-point notation, and each has individual characteristics. The key concept is that a real number is represented by a number, called a **mantissa**, times a **base** raised to an integer power, called an **exponent**. The base is usually fixed, and the mantissa and exponent vary to represent different real numbers. For example, if the base is fixed at 10, the number 387.53 could be represented as 38753×10^{-2}. (Recall that 10^{-2} is .01.) The mantissa is 38753, and the exponent is -2. Other possible representations are $.38753 \times 10^3$ and 387.53×10^0. We choose the representation in which the mantissa is an integer with no trailing zeros.

In the floating-point notation that we describe (which is not necessarily implemented on any particular machine exactly as described), a real number is represented by a 32-bit string consisting of a 24-bit mantissa followed by an 8-bit exponent. The base is fixed at 10. Both the mantissa and the exponent are twos complement binary integers. For example, the 24-bit binary representation of 38753 is 000000001001011101100001, and the 8-bit twos complement binary representation of -2 is 11111110; so the representation of

387.53 is 00000000100101110110000111111110. Other real numbers and their floating point representations are:

0	00000000000000000000000000000000
100	00000000000000000000000100000010
.5	00000000000000000000010111111111
.000005	00000000000000000000010111111010
12000	00000000000000000000110000000011
−387.53	11111111011010001001111111111110
−12000	11111111111111111111010000000011

The advantage of floating-point notation is that it can be used to represent numbers with extremely large or extremely small absolute values. For example, in the notation presented above, the largest number that can be represented is $(2^{23-1}) \times 10^{127}$, which is a very large number indeed. The smallest positive number that can be represented is 10^{-128}, which is quite small. The limiting factor on the precision with which numbers can be represented on a particular machine is the number of significant binary digits in the mantissa. Not every number between the largest and the smallest can be represented. Our representation allows only twenty-three significant bits. Thus a number such as 10 million and 1, which requires twenty-four significant binary digits in the mantissa, would have to be approximated by 10 million (1×10^7), which only requires one significant digit.

Character Strings

As we all know, information is not always interpreted numerically. Items such as names, job titles, and addresses must also be represented in some fashion by a computer. To enable the representation of such nonnumeric objects, still another method of interpreting bit strings is necessary. Such information is usually represented in character string form. For example, in some computers, the eight bits 00100110 are used to represent the character '&'. A different eight-bit pattern is used to represent the character 'A', another to represent 'B', another to represent 'C', and still another for each character that has a representation in a particular machine. A Russian machine uses bit patterns to represent Russian characters, whereas an Israeli machine uses bit patterns to represent Hebrew characters.

If eight bits are used to represent a character, up to 256 different characters can be represented, because there are 256 different eight-bit patterns. If the string 11000000 is used to represent the character 'A', and 11000001 is used to represent the character 'B', then the character string "AB" would be represented by the bit string 1100000011000001. In general, a character string is represented by the concatenation of the bit strings that represent the individual characters of the string. One common 8-bit pattern is known as the extended ASCII code (American Standard Code for Information Interchange).

In order to be able to represent a greater number of characters, Java has adopted an international 16-bit-based code known as ***Unicode UTF-16***. Using sixteen bits allows for up to 2^{16}, or 65,536, characters to be represented.

As in the case of integers, there is nothing intrinsic about a particular bit string that makes it suitable for representing a specific character. The assignment of bit strings to characters may be entirely arbitrary, but it must be adhered to consistently. It may be that some convenient rule is used in assigning bit strings to characters. For example, two bit strings may be assigned to two letters so that the one with a smaller binary value is assigned to the letter that comes earlier in the alphabet. However, such a rule is merely a convenience; it is not mandated by any intrinsic relation between characters and bit strings. In fact, computers even differ over the number of bits used to represent a character. Some computers use seven bits (and therefore allow only up to 128 possible characters), some use eight (up to 256 characters), some use ten (up to 1024 possible characters), while the Java Virtual Machine uses sixteen (up to 65,536). The number of bits necessary to represent a character in a particular computer is called the *byte size*, and a group of bits of that number is called a *byte*.

Note that using sixteen bits to represent a character means that 65,536 possible characters can be represented. It is not very often that one finds a computer that uses so many different characters (although it is conceivable for a computer to include upper- and lower-case letters, special characters, international alphabets, italics, boldface, and other type characters), so that many of the 16-bit codes are not used to represent characters.

Thus we see that information itself has no meaning. Any meaning can be assigned to a particular bit pattern, as long as it is done consistently. It is the interpretation of a bit pattern that gives it meaning. For example, the bit string 00100110 can be interpreted as the number 38 (binary), the number 26 (binary coded decimal), or the character '&' (ASCII). A method of interpreting a bit pattern is often called a *data type*. We have presented several data types: binary integers, binary coded decimal non-negative integers, real numbers, and character strings. The key questions are how to determine what data types are available to interpret bit patterns and what data type to use in interpreting a particular bit pattern.

Hardware and Software

The *memory* (also called *storage* or *core*) of a computer is simply a group of bits (switches). At any instant of the computer's operation, any particular bit in memory is either 0 or 1 (off or on). The setting of a bit is called its *value* or its *contents*.

The bits in a computer memory are grouped together into larger units such as bytes. In some computers, several bytes are grouped together into units called *words*. Each unit (byte or word, depending on the machine) is assigned an *address*; that is, a name identifying a particular unit among all the units in memory. This address is usually numeric, so that we may speak of byte 746 or word 937. An address is often called a *location*, and the contents of a location are the values of the bits that make up the unit at that location.

Every computer has a set of "native" data types. This means that it is constructed with a mechanism for manipulating bit patterns consistent with the objects they represent. For example, suppose a computer contains an instruction to add two binary integers and place their sum at a given location in memory for subsequent use. Then there is a mechanism built into the computer to:

1. Extract operand bit patterns from two given locations.
2. Produce a third bit pattern representing the binary integer that is the sum of the two binary integers represented by the two operands.
3. Store the resultant bit pattern at a given location.

The computer "knows" that the bit patterns at the given locations are to be inter-preted as binary integers because the hardware that executes that particular instruction is designed to do so. This is akin to a light "knowing" that it is to be on when the switch is in a particular position.

If the same machine also has an instruction to add two real numbers, then there is a separate built-in mechanism to interpret operands as real numbers. Two distinct in-structions are necessary for the two operations, and each instruction carries within itself an implicit identification of the types of its operands as well as their explicit locations. Therefore, it is the programmer's responsibility to know which data type is contained in each location that is used. It is the programmer's responsibility to choose between using an integer or real addition instruction to obtain the sum of two numbers.

A high-level programming language aids in this task considerably. For example, if a Java programmer declares

```
int x, y;
float a, b;
```

space is reserved at four locations for four different numbers. These four locations may be referenced by the ***identifiers*** x, y, a, and b. An identifier is used instead of a numeri-cal address to refer to a particular memory location because of its convenience for the programmer. The contents of the locations reserved for x and y will be interpreted as integers, while the contents of a and b will be interpreted as floating point numbers. The compiler that is responsible for translating Java programs into machine language will translate the "+" in the statement

```
x = x + y;
```

into integer addition, and will translate the "+" in the statement

```
a = a + b;
```

into floating point addition. An operator such as "+" is really a ***generic*** operator be-cause it has several different meanings depending on its context. The compiler relieves the programmer of specifying the type of addition that must be performed by examin-ing the context and using the appropriate version.

It is important to recognize the key role played by declarations in a high-level lan-guage. It is by means of declarations that the programmer specifies how the contents of the computer memory are to be interpreted by the program. In doing this, a declaration specifies how much memory is needed for a particular entity, how the contents of that memory are to be interpreted, and other vital details. Declarations also specify to the compiler exactly what is meant by the operation symbols that are subsequently used.

Concept of Implementation

Thus far, we have been viewing data types as a method of interpreting the memory contents of a computer. The set of native data types that a particular computer can sup-port is determined by what functions have been wired into its hardware. However, we can view the concept of "data type" from a completely different perspective; not in terms of what a computer can do, but in terms of what the user wants done. For example, if one wishes to obtain the sum of two integers, one does not care very much about the detailed mechanism by which that sum will be obtained. One is interested in manipulating the mathematical concept of an "integer," not in manipulating hardware bits. The hardware of the computer may be used to represent an integer and is useful only insofar as the representation is successful.

Once the concept of "data type" is divorced from the hardware capabilities of the computer, a limitless number of data types can be considered. A data type is an abstract concept defined by a set of logical properties. Once an abstract data type is defined and the legal operations involving it are specified, we may *implement* that data type (or a close approximation to it). An implementation may be a *hardware implementation* in which the circuitry necessary to perform the required operations is designed and constructed as part of a computer. Or it may be a *software implementation* in which a program consisting of already existing hardware instructions is written to interpret bit strings in the desired fashion and to perform the required operations. Thus, a software implementation includes a specification of how an object of the new data type is represented by objects of previously existing data types, as well as a specification of how such an object is manipulated in conformance with the operations defined for it.

Often a particular machine may be entirely simulated through software. A computer that is completely simulated by software, known as a *virtual machine*, may be implemented on any number of actual hardware platforms. Programs that are written for the virtual machine will run on any computer for which the virtual machine has been implemented. This is the approach taken by Java, which contributes to the high degree of portability of Java applications. Throughout the remainder of this text, the term "implementation" is used to mean "software implementation."

Example

We illustrate these concepts with an example. Suppose the hardware of a computer contains an instruction

```
MOVE (source, dest, length)
```

that copies a character string of *length* bytes from an address specified by *source* to an address specified by *dest*. (We present hardware instructions and locations using uppercase letters. The length must be specified by an integer. *source* and *dest* can be specified by identifiers that represent storage locations.) An example of this instruction is MOVE(a, b, 3), which copies the three bytes starting at location a to the three bytes starting at location b.

Note the different roles played by the identifiers a and b in this operation. The first operand of the MOVE instruction is the contents of the location specified by the identifier a. The second operand, however, is not the contents of location b, since they are irrelevant to the execution of the instruction. Rather, the location itself is the operand, since the location specifies the destination of the character string. Although an identifier always stands for a location, it is common for an identifier to be used to reference the contents of that location. It is always apparent from the context whether an identifier is referencing a location or its contents. The identifier appearing as the first operand of a MOVE instruction refers to the contents of memory, while the identifier appearing as the second operand refers to a location.

We also assume that the computer hardware contains the usual arithmetic and branching instructions, which we indicate by using Java-like notation. For example, the instruction

```
z = x + y;
```

interprets the contents of the bytes at locations x and y as binary integers, adds them, and inserts the binary representation of their sum into the byte at location z. (We do not operate on integers greater than one byte in length and ignore the possibility of overflow.) Here again, x and y are used to reference memory contents, while z is used to reference a memory location, but the proper interpretation is clear from the context.

Sometimes, it is desirable to add a quantity to an address to obtain another address. For example, if a is a location in memory, we might want to reference the location 4 bytes beyond a. We cannot refer to this location as $a + 4$ because that notation is reserved for the integer contents of location a plus 4. We therefore introduce the notation $a[4]$ to refer to this location. We also introduce the notation $a[x]$ to refer to the address given by adding the binary integer contents of the byte at x to the address a.

The MOVE instruction requires the programmer to specify the length of the string to be copied. Thus, its operand is a fixed-length character string (i.e., the length of the string must be known). A fixed-length string and a byte-sized binary integer may be considered native data types of this particular machine.

Suppose we wished to implement varying-length character strings on this machine. That is, we want to enable programmers to use the instruction

```
MOVEVAR(source, dest)
```

to move a character string from location *source* to location *dest* without being required to specify any length.

To implement this new data type, we must first decide on how it is to be represented in the memory of the machine and then indicate how that representation is to be manipulated. Clearly, it is necessary to know how many bytes must be moved in order to execute the instruction. Since the MOVEVAR operation does not specify the number, it must be contained within the representation of the character string itself. A varying-length character string of length l may be represented by a contiguous set of $l + 1$ bytes ($l < 65{,}536$). The first byte contains the binary representation of the length l, and the remaining bytes contain the representations of the characters in the string. Representations of three such strings are illustrated in Figure 1.1.2 (Note that the digits 5 and 9 in these figures do not stand for the bit patterns representing the characters '5' and '9' but for the patterns 00000000 00000101 and 00000000 00001001 [assuming sixteen bits per character], which represent the integers five and nine. Similarly, 14 in Figure 1.1.2c stands for the bit pattern 00000000 00001110. Note also that this representation may be different from the way character strings are actually implemented in Java.)

The program to implement the MOVEVAR operation can be written as follows (i is an auxiliary memory location):

```
MOVE(source, dest, 1);
for (i = 1; i < dest; i++)
MOVE(source[i], dest[i], 1);
```

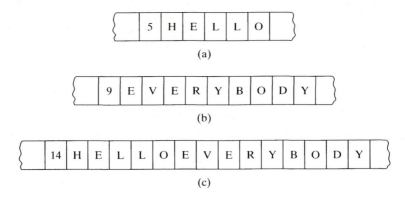

FIGURE 1.1.2 Varying-length character strings.

Similarly, we can implement an operation CONCATVAR(c_1, c_2, c_3) to concatenate two varying-length character strings at locations c_1 and c_2 and place the result at c_3. Figure 1.1.2c illustrates the concatenation of the two strings in Figures 1.1.2a and b:

```
// move the length
z = c1 + c2;
MOVE(z, c3, 1);
// move the first string
for (i = 1; i <= c1; MOVE(c1[i], c3[i], 1)
  ;
// move the second string
for (i = 1; i <= c2) {
  x = c1 + i;
  MOVE(c2[i], c3[x], 1);
}
```

However, once the operation MOVEVAR has been defined, CONCATVAR can be implemented using MOVEVAR as follows:

```
MOVEVAR(c2, c3[c1]);        // move the second string
MOVEVAR(c1, c3);            // move the first string
z = c1 + c2;                // update the length of the result
MOVE(z, c3, 1);
```

Figure 1.1.3 illustrates phases of this operation on the strings of Figure 1.1.2. Although this latter version is shorter, it is not really more efficient, since all the instructions used in implementing MOVEVAR are performed each time it is used.

The statement $z = c_1 + c_2$ in both of the above algorithms is of particular interest. The addition instruction operates independently of the use of its operands (in this case, parts of varying-length character strings). The instruction is designed to treat its operands as single-byte integers regardless of any other use that the programmer has

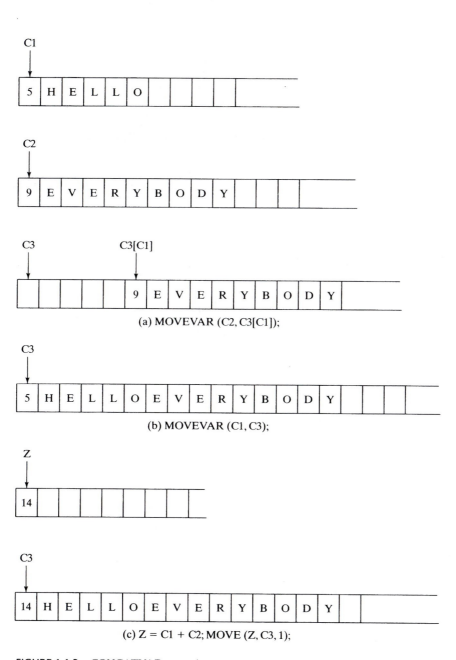

(a) MOVEVAR (C2, C3[C1]);

(b) MOVEVAR (C1, C3);

(c) Z = C1 + C2; MOVE (Z, C3, 1);

FIGURE 1.1.3 CONCATVAR operations.

for them. Similarly, the reference to $c3[c1]$ is to the location whose address is given by adding the contents of the byte at location $c1$ to the address $c3$. Thus the byte at $c1$ is treated as holding a binary integer, although it is also the start of a varying-length character string. This illustrates the fact that a data type is a method of treating the contents of memory and that those contents have no intrinsic meaning.

Note that this representation of varying-length character strings allows only strings whose length is less than or equal to the largest binary integer that fits into a single byte. If a byte is sixteen bits, this means that the largest such string is 65,535 (i.e., $2^{16} - 1$) characters long. To allow for longer strings, a different representation must be chosen and a new set of programs must be written. If we use this representation of varying-length character strings, then the concatenation operation is invalid if the resulting string is more than 65,535 characters long. Since the result of such an operation is undefined, a wide variety of actions can be implemented if that operation is attempted. One possibility is to use only the first 65,535 characters of the result. Another possibility is to ignore the operation entirely and not move anything to the result field. There is also the choice of printing a warning message or of assuming that the user wants to achieve whatever result the implementer decides on.

As was pointed out earlier, there may be several different ways of implementing an abstract data type. For example, the C language uses an entirely different implementation of character strings that avoids this limitation on the length of the string. In C, all strings are terminated by the special character '\0'. This character, which never appears within a string, is automatically placed by the C compiler at the end of every string. Since the length of the string is not known in advance, all string operations must proceed one character at a time until '\0' is encountered.

The algorithm to implement the MOVEVAR operation, under this implementation can be written as follows:

```
i = 0;
while (source[i] != '\0') {
    MOVE(source[i], dest[i], 1);
    i++;
}
dest[i] = '\0';        //terminate the destination string with '\0'
```

To implement the concatenation operation, CONCATVAR($c1$, $c2$, $c3$) we may write

```
i = 0;
// move the first string
while (c1[i] != '\0') {
    MOVE(c1[i], c3[i], 1);
    i++;
}
// move the second string
j = 0;
while (c2[j] != '\0')
    move(c2[j++], c3[i++], 1);
// terminate the destination string with a '\0'
c3[i] = '\0';
```

A disadvantage of the C implementation of character strings is that the length of a character string is not readily available without advancing through the string one character at a time until '\0' is encountered. This is more than offset by the advantage of not having an arbitrary limit placed on the length of the string.

It is important to note that implementation details are often hidden from the user. This is the approach used by the Java language. The implementer of the Java *String* class (or any other class, for that matter) need only publish the behavior of the class via its set of supported methods—the internal implementation is of no concern or use to the user of the class. Furthermore, this approach to language design leaves it open to the class implementer to select the exact representation to be used. One Java implementation could use null-terminated character arrays, a second could use a length field, and a third could use some other representation entirely.

Once a representation has been chosen for objects of a particular data type, and routines have been written to operate on those representations, the programmer is free to use that data type to solve problems. The original hardware of the machine plus the programs for implementing more complex data types than those provided by the hardware can be thought of as a "better" machine than the one consisting of the hardware alone. The programmer of the original machine need not worry about how the computer is designed and what circuitry is used to execute each instruction. The programmer need know only what instructions are available and how they can be used. Similarly, the programmer who uses the "extended" machine (which consists of hardware and software), or "virtual computer," as it is sometimes known, need not be concerned with the details of how various data types are implemented. All the programmer needs to know is how they can be manipulated.

Abstract Data Types

A useful tool for specifying the logical properties of a data type is the ***abstract data type***, or ***ADT***. Fundamentally, a data type is a collection of values and a set of operations on those values. The collection and the operations form a mathematical construct that may be implemented using a particular hardware or software data structure. The term "abstract data type" refers to the basic mathematical concept that defines the data type.

In defining an abstract data type as a mathematical concept, we are not concerned with space or time efficiency. Those are implementation issues. In fact, the definition of an ADT is not concerned with implementation details at all. It may not even be possible to implement a particular ADT on a particular piece of hardware or using a particular software system. For example, we have already seen that the ADT *integer* is not implementable in full generality. Nevertheless, by specifying the mathematical and logical properties of a data type or structure, the ADT is a useful guideline to implementers and a useful tool to programmers who wish to use the data type correctly.

There are a number of methods for specifying an ADT. The method we use is semiformal and borrows heavily from Java notation but extends it where necessary. To illustrate the concept of an ADT and our specification method, consider the ADT *RATIONAL*, which corresponds to the mathematical concept of a rational number. The operations we define on rational numbers are creation of a rational number from two integers, addition, multiplication, and testing for equality. The following is an initial specification of this ADT:

```
abstract class RATIONAL <integer, integer> {
  // value definition
  condition RATIONAL[1] != 0;

  // method definition
abstract RATIONAL makeRational(int a, int b)
precondition    b != 0;
postcondition   makeRational[0] == a;
                makeRational[1] == b;

abstract RATIONAL add(RATIONAL a, RATIONAL b)    // written a + b
postcondition   add[1] == a[1] * b[1];
                add[0] == a[0] * b[1] + b[0] * a[1];

abstract RATIONAL mult(RATIONAL a, RATIONAL b)    // written a * b
postcondition   mult[0] == a[0] * b[0];
                mult[1] == a[1] * b[1];

abstract boolean equals(RATIONAL a, RATIONAL b)  // written a == b
postcondition equals == (a[0]*b[1] == b[0]*a[1]);
}
```

An ADT consists of two parts: a value definition and a method definition. The value definition defines the collection of values for the ADT and consists of two parts: a definition clause and a condition clause. For example, the value definition for the ADT *RATIONAL* states that a *RATIONAL* value consists of two integers, where the second does not equal zero. Of course, the two integers that comprise a rational number are the numerator and the denominator. We use array notation (square brackets) to indicate the parts of an abstract type.

The keywords ***abstract class*** introduce a value definition, and the keyword ***condition*** is used to specify any conditions on the newly defined type. In this definition, the condition specifies that the denominator may not be zero. The definition clause is required, but the condition clause may not be necessary for every ADT.

Immediately following the value definition comes the method specification. Each method is defined as an abstract function with three parts: a header, the optional preconditions, and the postconditions. For example, the method definition of the ADT *RATIONAL* includes the methods of creation (*makeRational*), addition (*add*), and multiplication (*mult*), as well as a test for equality (*equal*). Let us consider the specification for multiplication first, since it is the simplest. It contains a header and postconditions, but no preconditions.

```
abstract RATIONAL mult(RATIONAL a, RATIONAL b)    // written a * b
postcondition   mult[0] == a[0] * b[0];
                mult[1] == a[1] * b[1];
```

The header of this definition is the first line, which is just like a Java method header. The keyword ***abstract*** indicates that this is not a Java method but an ADT method definition.

The comment beginning with the new keyword ***written*** indicates an alternative way of writing the method.

The postcondition specifies what the method does. In a postcondition, the name of the method (in this case, *mult*) is used to denote the result of the operation. Thus, *mult*[0] represents the numerator of the result, and *mult*[1] the denominator of the result. That is, it specifies what conditions become true after the operation is executed. In this example, the postcondition specifies that the numerator of the result of a rational multiplication equals the integer product of the numerators of the two inputs, and that the denominator equals the integer products of the two denominators.

The specification for addition (ADD) is straightforward and simply states that

$$\frac{a0}{a1} + \frac{b0}{b1} = \frac{a0 \times b1 + a1 \times b0}{a1 \times b1}$$

The creation operation (*makeRational*) creates a rational number from two integers and contains the first example of a precondition. In general, preconditions specify any restrictions that must be satisfied before the operation can be applied. In this example, the precondition states that *makeRational* cannot be applied if its second parameter is 0.

The specification for equality (*equal*) is more significant and conceptually more complex. In general, any two values in an ADT are "equal" if and only if the values of their components are equal. Indeed, it is usually assumed that an equality (and inequality) method exists and is defined that way, so that no explicit equal method definition is required. The assignment method (setting the value of one object to the value of another) is another example of a method that is often assumed for an ADT and is not specified explicitly.

However, for some data types, two values with unequal components may be considered equal. Indeed, such is the case with rational numbers, where, for example, the rational numbers 1/2, 2/4, 3/6, and 18/36 are all equal despite the inequality of their components. Two rational numbers are considered equal if their components are equal when the numbers are reduced to lowest terms (i.e., when their numerators and denominators are both divided by their greatest common divisor). One way of testing for rational equality is to reduce the two numbers to lowest terms and then test for equality of numerators and denominators. Another way of testing for rational equality is to check whether the cross-products (i.e., the numerator of one times the denominator of the other) are equal. This is the method that we used in specifying the abstract *equal* method.

The abstract specification illustrates the role of an ADT as a purely logical definition of a new data type. As collections of two integers, two ordered pairs are unequal if their components are not equal; yet as rational numbers, they may be equal. It is unlikely that any implementation of rational numbers would implement a test for equality by actually forming the cross-products; they might be too large to represent as machine integers. Most likely, an implementation would first reduce the inputs to lowest terms and then test for component equality. Indeed, a reasonable implementation would insist that *makeRational*, *add*, and *mult* only produce rational numbers in lowest terms. However, mathematical definitions such as abstract data type specifications need not be concerned with implementation details.

In fact, the realization that two rationals can be equal even if they are componentwise unequal forces us to rewrite the postconditions for *makeRational*, *add*, and *mult*. That is, if

$$\frac{m0}{m1} == \frac{a0}{a1} \times \frac{b0}{b1}$$

it is not necessary that $m0$ equal $a0 * b0$ and that $m1$ equal $a1 * b1$, only that $m0 * a1 * b1$ equal $m1 * a0 * b0$. A more accurate ADT specification for *RATIONAL* is the following:

```
abstract class RATIONAL <integer, integer> {
  // value definition
  condition RATIONAL[1] != 0;

  // method definition
  abstract boolean equals(RATIONAL a, RATIONAL b) // written a == b
  postcondition equals == (a[0]*b[1] == b[0]*a[1]);

  abstract RATIONAL makeRational(int a, int b)      // written [a, b]
  precondition    b != 0;
  postcondition   makeRational[0]*b == a*makeRational[1];

  abstract RATIONAL add(RATIONAL a, RATIONAL b)    // written a + b
  postcondition   add == [a[0]*b[1] + b[0]*a[1], a[1]*b[1]];

  abstract RATIONAL mult(RATIONAL a, RATIONAL b)   // written a * b
  postcondition   mult == [a[0]*b[0], a[1]*b[1]];
}
```

Here, the *equals* method is defined first and the method $==$ is extended to rational equality using the **written** clause. That operator is then used to specify the results of subsequent rational methods (*add* and *mult*).

The result of the *makeRational* operation on the integers a and b produces a rational that equals a/b, but the definition does not specify the actual values of the resulting numerator and denominator. The specification for *makeRational* also introduces the notation $[a, b]$ for the rational formed from integers a and b, and this notation is then used in defining *add* and *mult*.

The definitions of *add* and *mult* specify that their results equal the unreduced results of the corresponding operation, but the individual components are not necessarily equal.

Note, again, that in defining these methods we are not specifying how they are to be computed, only what their result must be. How they are computed is determined by their implementation, not by their specification.

Sequences as Value Definitions

In developing the specifications for various data types, we often use set-theoretic notation to specify the values of an ADT. In particular, it is helpful to use the notation of mathematical sequences that we now introduce.

A ***sequence*** is simply an ordered set of elements. A sequence S is sometimes written as the enumeration of its elements, such as

$$S = \ <s_0, s_1, \ldots, s_{n-1}>$$

If S contains n elements, then S is said to be of length n. We assume the existence of a length method *length* such that *S.length*() is the length of the sequence S. We also assume the methods *S.first*(), which returns the value of the first element of S (s_0 in the example above), and *S.last*(), which returns the value of the last element of S (s_{n-1} in the example above). There is a special sequence of length zero, called *nullSeq*, that contains no elements. *nullSeq.first*() and *nullSeq.last*() are undefined.

We wish to define an ADT *sequence1* whose values are sequences of elements. If the sequences can be of arbitrary length and consist of elements all of which are of the same type, *type*, then *sequence1* can be defined by

```
abstract class <<type> sequence1 { ... }
```

Alternatively, we may wish to define an ADT *sequence2* whose values are sequences of fixed length whose elements are of specific types. In such a case, we would specify the definition

```
abstract class <<type0, type1, type2, ..., typen> sequence2 { ... }
```

Of course, we may want to specify a sequence of fixed length, all of whose elements are of the same type. We could then write

```
abstract class <<type, n> sequence3 { ... }
```

In this case *sequence3* represents a sequence of length n, all of whose elements are of type *type*.

For example, using the foregoing notation we could define the following types:

```
abstract class <<int> intSeq { ... }
                          // sequence of integers of any length

abstract class <<int, char, float> seq3 { ... }
                          // sequence of length 3 consisting of
                          // an integer, a character, and a
                          // floating-point number

abstract class <<int, 10> intSeq { ... }
                          // sequence of 10 integers

abstract class <<, 2> pair { ... }
                          // arbitrary sequence of length 2
```

Two sequences are *equal* if each element of the first is equal to the corresponding element of the second. A ***subsequence*** is a contiguous portion of a sequence. If S is a sequence, then the method *S.sub(i,j)* refers to the subsequence of S starting at position i in S and consisting of j consecutive elements. Thus if T equals *S.sub(i,k)*, then T is the sequence $<t_0, t_1, \ldots, t_{k-1}>$, $t_0 = s_i$, $t_1 = s_{i+1}$, $\ldots$, $t_{k-1} = s_{i+k-1}$. If i is not between 0 and $S.length() - k$, then *S.sub(i,k)* is defined as *nullSeq*.

The concatenation of two sequences, written $S + T$, is the sequence consisting of all the elements of S followed by all the elements of T. It is sometimes desirable to specify the insertion of an element in the middle of a sequence. $S.place(i,x)$ is defined as the sequence S with the element x inserted immediately following position i (or into the first element of the sequence if i is -1). All subsequent elements are shifted by one position. That is, $S.place(i,x)$ equals $S.sub(0,i) + <x> + S.sub(i + 1, S.length() - i - 1)$.

Deletion of an element from a sequence can be specified in one of two ways. If x is an element of sequence S, then $S - <x>$ represents the sequence S without all occurrences of element x. The sequence $S.delete(i)$ is equal to S with the element at position i deleted. *delete* can also be written in terms of other methods as $S.sub(0,i - 1) + S.sub(i + 1, S.length() - i - 1)$.

ADT for Varying-Length Character Strings

As an illustration of the use of sequence notation in defining an ADT, we develop an ADT specification for the varying-length character string. There are four basic methods (aside from equality and assignment) normally included in systems that support such strings:

length	a method that returns the current length of the string
concat	a method that returns the concatenation of its two input strings
substring	a method that returns a substring of a given string
indexOf	a method that returns the first position of one string as a substring of another.

```
abstract class STRING << char >> {
  abstract int length(STRING s)
  postcondition length == s.length();

  abstract STRING concat(STRING s1, STRING s2)
  postcondition   concat == s1 + s2;

  abstract STRING substring(STRING s1, int i, int j)
  precondition   0 <= i < s1.length();
                 0 <= j <= s1.length() - i;
  postcondition substring == s1.sub(i, j);

  abstract int indexOf(STRING s1, STRING s2)
  postcondition   // lastPos = s1.length() - s2.length()
                  (indexOf == -1 && for (i = 0; i <= lastPos; i++)
                  (s2 != s1.sub(i, s2.length())))))
                  ||
                (indexOf >= 0 && indexOf <= lastPos
                        && s2 == str1.sub(indexOf, s2.length())
                        && for (i = 1; i < indexOf; i++)
                              (s2 != s1.sub(i, s2.length()))))
}
```

The postcondition for *indexOf* is complex and introduces some new notation, so we review it here. First, note that the content of the initial comment has the form of a Java assignment statement. This merely indicates that we wish to define the symbol *lastPos* as representing the value of $s1.length() - s2.length()$ for use in the postcondition to simplify the appearance of the condition. Here, *lastPos* represents the maximum possible value of the result (i.e., the last position of *s1* where a substring whose length equals that of *s2* can start). *lastPos* is used twice the postcondition. The longer expression *s1.length()* − *s2.length* could have been used in both cases, but we choose to use a more compact symbol (*lastPos*) for clarity.

The postcondition itself states that one of two conditions must hold. The two conditions, which are separated by the ‖ operator, are:

1. The method's value (*indexOf*) is −1, and *s2* does not appear as a substring of *s1*.
2. The method's value is between 0 and *lastPos*, *s2* does appear as a substring of *s1* beginning at the method value's position, and *s2* does not appear as a substring of *s1* in any earlier position.

Note the use of a pseudo-*for* loop in a condition. The condition

```
for (i = x; i <= y; i++)
    (condition(i))
```

is true if *condition*(i) is true for all i from x to y inclusive. It is also true if $x > y$. Otherwise, the entire *for*-condition is false.

Data Types in Java

The Java language contains eight ***primitive data types***: *boolean, char, byte, short, int, long, float*, and *double*. We have already seen how integers, floats, and characters can be implemented in hardware. A *boolean* variable occupies a single bit and may be only be assigned the values ***true*** or ***false***. As discussed earlier in this section, variables of type *char* may contain any character represented by sixteen bits (using Unicode UTF-16). Four of these types are used to represent the ***integral*** types:

Type	Size	Value
byte	8 bits	−128 to 127
short	16 bits	−32,768 to 32,767
int	32 bits	−2,147,483,648 to 2,147,483,647
long	64 bits	−9,223,372,036,854,775,808 to 9,223,372,036,854,775,807

float and *double* variables are used to represent ***floating-point*** numbers occupying thirty two and sixty four bits respectively. Several special values (and constants) are defined, including positive infinity (POSITIVE_INFINITY), negative infinity (NEGATIVE_INFINITY), and not-a-number (NaN). These may be the result of certain floating-point operations and are defined as part of the IEEE 754 floating-point standard used by the Java language. *float* variables have a precision of eight decimal digits, while *double* carries a precision of seventeen decimal digits.

Type	Size	Max Value	Min Value
float	32 bits	$\pm 3.40282347E+38$	$\pm 1.40239846E-45$
double	64 bits	$\pm 1.79769313486231570E+308$	$\pm 4.94065645841246544E-324$

A variable declaration in Java specifies two things. First, it specifies the amount of storage that must be set aside for objects declared with that type. For example, a variable of type *int* must have enough space to hold the largest possible integer value. Second, it specifies how data represented by strings of bits are to be interpreted. The same bits at a specific storage location can be interpreted as an integer of a floating-point number, yielding two completely different numeric values.

A variable declaration specifies that storage is to be set aside for an object of the specified type, and that the object at that storage location can be referenced with the specified variable identifier.

Objects and Java

A Java programmer can think of the Java language as defining a new machine with its own capabilities, data types, and operations. The user can state a problem solution in terms of the more useful Java constructs rather than in terms of lower-level machine language constructs. Thus problems can be solved more easily because a larger set of tools is available.

Java is an ***object-oriented*** language. Recall that when we defined the ADT *RATIONAL* it was necessary to describe its behavior in terms of both of its data components and its method components. Thus we specified that a rational number consists of a numerator and denominator, as well as a series of methods, such as *add*, *mult*, and *equal*. Such a definition is known in Java as a ***class.*** A class is a collection of data, which may be of both primitive and non-primitive type, and methods that operate on the data. A particular instance of a class (i.e., data interpreted according to the definition of the class) is known as an ***object***. In Section 1.3 we define the *Rational* class and illustrate how it may be used to process rational numbers.

As a simple example of the use of a class, consider an application that processes geometric figures such as circles. In order to specify a circle, we need to specify the x and y coordinates of its center as well as its radius. Using the constant π, we may calculate its area and circumference. We can think of a circle as a collection of the data representing its center and radius, π, and methods to calculate the area and circumference. We adopt the Java convention that class names begin with a capital letter, variables begin with a lower-case letter, and constants are written with all capital letters. The *Circle* class may thus be defined by

```java
public class Circle {
  float x, y;
  double radius;

  public double circumference () {
      return 2 * Math.PI * radius;
  } // end circumference method

  public double area () {
      return Math.PI * radius * radius;
  } // end area method
} // end Circle class
```

Once the *Circle* class has been defined, individual instances of the *Circle* class, known as ***objects of the class***, may be created by writing

```
Circle c = new Circle();
```

In this declaration, the variable *c* is declared to be a reference to an object of the *Circle* class. The ***new*** keyword causes a new instance of a *Circle* object to be created and a reference to it is placed in the variable *c*. A reference may be thought of as a location. That is, the contents of the location named *c* contain the location of an object whose type is *Circle*. Often variables of a class are declared, without having them refer to a specific object of the class. Thus the statement

```
Circle c1, c2;
```

declares *c*1 and *c*2 to be variables of the *Circle* class without any objects of the class being created. *c*1 and *c*2 have not been initialized with location (reference) values.

Value and Reference Semantics

An important distinction must be made between the Java primitive types described above and the ***nonprimitive*** types: *Arrays* and *Objects*. Upon assigning a value to a primitive type, a copy of the value stored in the variable appearing on the right side of the assignment operator is assigned to the variable that appears to the left of the assignment operator. Similarly, when passing a primitive argument to a parameter of a method, a copy of the original value is stored at the location represented by the parameter. This behavior is often referred to as a ***call by value***.

A nonprimitive type, however, contains a reference to the object being assigned rather than the object itself. It is therefore quite possible that two nonprimitive variables refer to the same object. Assume the following sequence of statements:

```
Circle c1, c2;            // Define c1 and c2 to be reference
                          // variables to Circle objects

c1 = new Circle();        // Assign a reference to a newly
                          // instantiated object of the Circle
                          // class to the variable c1

c1.x = 0;                 // Initialize the data components of the
c1.y = 0;                 // Circle object referenced by c1
c1.radius = 1;

c2 = c1;                  // c2 and c1 refer to the same object

c2.radius = 10;           // The radius of the object referred to by
                          // both c1 and c2 is now 10.
```

Now compare this with the following statements involving primitive types:

```
int x, y;                 // Declare x and y to be variables which
                          // can contain integer values
```

```
y = 0;                    // Place the value 0 into the storage
                          // allocated for the variable y

x = y;                    // Copy the value in the variable y into
                          // the variable x

y = 1;                    // Place the value 1 into the storage
                          // allocated for the variable y.
                          // x retains the value 0
```

Nonprimitive variables are often said to have **reference** behavior, and primitive values are said to exhibit **value** behavior.

An exception to the reference behavior of Java objects occurs when passing parameters to methods. All parameters are passed to a Java method by value. That is, the values being passed are copied into the parameters of the called method at the time the method is invoked. This is true even for reference variables. The parameter is initially a copy of the reference that refers to the same object as the argument sent to the method when it is called. When a new value is assigned to the parameter, the parameter is changed to reference the new value, but the value of the original argument reference remains unchanged. If the value of a parameter is changed within the method, the value in the calling application is not changed.

For example, consider the following application segment and method (the line numbers are for reference only):

```
1    int x = 5;
2    System.out.println("\n" + x);
3    method(x);
4    System.out.println("\n" + x);
     ...
5    void method(int y) {
6        ++y;
7        System.out.println("\n" + y);
8    } // end method
```

Line 2 prints 5 and then line 3 invokes *method*. The value of *x*, which is 5, is copied into *y*, and *method* begins execution. Line 7 then prints 6 and *method* returns. However when line 6 incremented the value of *y*, the value of *x* remained unchanged. Thus line 4 prints 5. *x* and *y* refer to two different variables that happen to have the same value at the beginning of *method*. *y* can change independently of *x*. This is true even for the case in which *x* and *y* refer to objects. In summary, parameters that are changed within a method may never modify their arguments.

Data Structures and Java

The study of data structures involves two complementary goals. The first goal is to identify and develop useful mathematical entities and operations and to determine what classes of problems can be solved by using them. The second goal is to determine representations for those abstract entities and to implement the abstract operations on the concrete representations. The first of these goals views a high-level data type as a tool that can be used to solve other problems, while the second views the implementation of such a data type as a problem to be solved using already existing data types. In determining representations for abstract entities, we must be careful to specify what facilities are available for constructing such representations. For example, it must be stated whether the full Java language is available or we are restricted to the hardware facilities of a particular machine.

In Sections 1.2 and 1.3 we examine several data structures that already exist in Java: the array, the string, and the class. We describe the facilities that are available in Java for utilizing these structures. We also focus on the abstract definitions of these data structures and how they can be useful in problem solving. Finally, we examine how they could be implemented if Java were not available (although a Java programmer can simply use the data structures as defined in the language without being concerned about most of these implementation details).

In the remainder of the book, we develop more complex data structures and show their usefulness in problem solving. We also show how to implement these data structures using the data structures that are already available in Java. Since the problems that arise in the course of attempting to implement high-level data structures are quite complex, this will also allow us to investigate the Java language more thoroughly and to gain valuable experience in its use.

Often, no implementation, hardware or software, can model a mathematical concept completely. For example, it is impossible to represent arbitrarily large integers on a computer because the size of such a machine's memory is finite. Thus it is not the data type "integer" that is represented by the hardware but rather the data type "integer between x and y", where x and y are the smallest and largest integers representable by that machine.

It is important to recognize the limitations of a particular implementation. Often it will be possible to present several implementations of the same data type, each with its own strengths and weaknesses. One particular implementation may be better than another for a specific application, and the programmer must be aware of the possible tradeoffs that might be involved.

One important consideration in any implementation is its efficiency. In fact, the reason that the high-level data structures we discuss are not built into Java is the significant overhead they would entail. There are languages of significantly higher level than Java that have many of these data types already built into them, but many of these are inefficient and thus are not in widespread use.

Efficiency is usually measured by two factors: time and space. If an application is heavily dependent on manipulating high-level data structures, then the speed at which those manipulations can be performed will be the major determinant of the speed of the entire application. Similarly, if a program uses a large number of such structures, then an implementation that uses an inordinate amount of space to represent the data structure will be impractical. Unfortunately, there is usually a tradeoff between these two efficiencies, so that an implementation that is fast uses more storage than one that is slow. The choice of implementation in such cases involves a careful evaluation of the tradeoffs among the various possibilities.

EXERCISES

1.1.1   In the text, an analogy is made between the length of a line and the number of bits of information in a bit string. In what ways is this analogy inadequate?

1.1.2   Determine what hardware data types are available on the computer at your particular installation and what operations can be performed on them.

1.1.3   Prove that there are 2^n different settings for n two-way switches. Suppose we wanted to have m settings. How many switches would be necessary?

1.1.4   Interpret the following bit settings as binary positive integers, binary integers in twos complement, and binary coded decimal integers. If a setting cannot be interpreted as a binary coded decimal integer, explain why.

    a. 10011001

    b. 1001

    c. 000100010001

    d. 01110111

    e. 01010101

    f. 100000010101

1.1.5   Write Java methods *add*, *subtract*, and *multiply* that read two strings of 0s and 1s representing binary nonnegative integers and print the string representing their sum, difference, and product respectively.

1.1.6   Assume a ternary computer in which the basic unit of memory is a "trit" (ternary digit) rather than a bit. A trit can have three possible settings (0, 1, and 2) rather than just two (0 and 1). Show how nonnegative integers can be represented in ternary notation using trits by a method analogous to binary notation using bits. Is there any nonnegative integer that can be represented using ternary notation and trits that cannot be represented using binary notation and bits? Are there any that can be represented using bits that cannot be represented using trits? Why are binary computers more common than ternary computers?

1.1.7   Write a Java applet to read a string of 0s and 1s representing a positive integer in binary and to print a string of 0s, 1s, and 2s representing the same number in ternary notation (see the preceding exercise). Write another Java applet to read a ternary number and print the equivalent in binary.

1.1.8   Write an ADT specification for complex numbers $a + bi$, where $abs(a + bi)$ is $sqrt(a^2 + b^2)$, $(a + bi) + (c + di)$ is $(a + c) + (b + d)i$, $(a + bi)*(c + di)$ is $(a*c - b*d) + (a*d + b*c)i$, and $-(a + bi)$ is $(-a) + (-b)i$.

1.2   ARRAYS, STRINGS, AND VECTORS IN JAVA

In this section and the next, we examine several data structures that are an invaluable part of the Java language. We will see how to use these structures and how they can be implemented. These structures are **composite** or **structured** data types; that is, they are made up of simpler data structures that exist in the language. The study of these data structures involves an analysis of how simple structures combine to form the composite and how to extract a specific component from the composite. We expect that you have already seen these data structures in an introductory Java programming course and are aware of how they are defined and used in Java. In these sections, therefore, we will not dwell on the many details associated with these structures but instead will highlight those features that are interesting from a data structure point of view.

The first of these data types is the ***array***. The simplest form of an array is a ***one-dimensional array*** that may be defined abstractly as a finite ordered set of homogeneous elements. By "finite" we mean that there is a specific number of elements in the array. This number may be large or small, but it must exist. By "ordered" we mean that the elements of the array are arranged so that there is a zeroth, first, second, third, etc. By "homogeneous" we mean that all the elements in the array must be of the same type. For example, an array may contain all integers or all characters but not both. A Java array may also contain references to Java objects.

However, specifying the form of a data structure does not completely describe the structure. We must also specify how the structure is accessed. For example, the Java declaration

```
type a[ ] = new type[100];
```

creates an array of one hundred items of type *type* and initializes each item to the default value for that type (0 for ***int***, the null character for ***char***, ***false*** for ***boolean***, 0.0 for ***float*** and ***double***, and ***null*** for objects). The variable *a* is a reference to the newly created array. Alternatively, one may declare an array by specifying a series of intial values. For example, the declaration

```
char b[ ] = {'a', 'b', 'c', 'd', 'e'};
```

creates a reference variable *b* which refers to an array of five characters initialized with the characters 'a', 'b', 'c', 'd', 'e'.

The two basic operations that access an array are ***extraction*** and ***storing***. The extraction operation is a method that accepts an array, *a*, and an index, *i*, and returns an element of the array. In Java, the result of this operation is denoted by the expression $a[i]$. The storing operation accepts an array, *a*, an index, *i*, and an element, *x*. In Java, this operation is denoted by the assignment statement $a[i] = x$. The operations are defined by the rule that after the assignment statement has been executed, the value of $a[i]$ is the value of *x*.

The smallest element of an array's index is called its ***lower bound*** and in Java is always zero, while the highest element is called its ***upper bound***. If *lower* is the lower bound of an array and *upper* the upper bound, the number of elements in the array, called its ***length*** or ***range***, is given by $upper - lower + 1$. For example, in the array *a* declared above, the lower bound is 0, the upper bound is 99, and the length is 100. The length of any array in Java may be obtained by appending *.length* to its name. For example, in the array *b* declared above, the value of *b.length* is 5.

An important feature of a Java array is that once an array has been declared, neither the upper bound nor the lower bound (and hence the range as well) may be changed during a program's execution. The lower bound is always fixed at 0, and the upper bound is fixed at the time the array is created. It is important to distinguish between an array reference and the array itself. An array, once created, is fixed in size, but an array reference may refer to different arrays throughout an application. For example, suppose a programmer were to write

```
double x[ ];            // Creates a reference variable x, which
                        // may later be used to refer to an array
                        // containing double elements.
x = new double[10];     // Creates an array of 10 double elements
                        // referenced by the variable x.
x = new double[50];     // Creates an array of 50 double elements
                        // referenced by the variable x. The
                        // previous array of 10 double elements
                        // is no longer accessible.
```

One very useful technique is to use the *length* construct, which produces the size of an array, to minimize the work needed when an array size is changed. For example, consider the following application segment to declare and initialize an array of characters to the capital letters of the English alphabet (65 is the numeric value of the bits representing the letter 'A' in Unicode):

```
char c[ ] = new char[26];
for (int i = 0; i<26; i++)
    c[i] = (char) (65+i);
```

In order to change the array to a larger (or smaller) size, the constant 26 must be changed in two places: once in the declarations and once in the *for* statement. Consider the following equivalent alternative:

```
char c[ ] = new char[26];
for (int i = 0; i< c.length; i++)
    c[i] = (char) (65+i);
```

Now, only a single change in the array size is needed to change the upper bound.

The Array as an ADT

We can represent an array as an abstract data type with a slight extension of the conventions and notation discussed earlier. We assume the method *type(arg)*, which returns the type of its argument *arg*. In fact, if *arg* is a Java object, we can get its class (which is its type) by *arg.getClass()*. However, we cannot do this for primitive variables such as integers, booleans, and so on. Since we are not concerned here with implementation, but rather with specification, the use of such a function is permissible.

Let *ARRTYPE(ub, elType)* denote the ADT corresponding to the Java array type *elType array[ub]*. This is our first example of a parameterized ADT, in which the precise ADT is determined by the values of one or more parameters. In this case, *ub* and *elType* are the parameters; note that *elType* is a type indicator, not a value. We may now view any one-dimensional array as an entity of the type *ARRTYPE*. For example,

ARRTYPE(10, *int*) would represent the type of the array in the designator *int* [10]. We may now view any one-dimensional array as an entity of the type *ARRTYPE*. The specification follows:

```
abstract class <<elType, ub>> ARRTYPE(ub, elType) {
  condition type(ub) == int;

  abstract elType extract(a, i)              // written a[i]
  ARRTYPE(ub, elType) a;
  int i;
  precondition 0 <= i < ub;
  postcondition extract == aᵢ

  abstract store(a, i, elt)                  // written a[i] = elt
  ARRTYPE (ub, elType) a;
  int i;
  elType elt;
  precondition 0 <= i < ub;
  postcondition a[i] == elt;
}
```

The *store* operation is our first example of an operation that modifies one of its parameters, in this case the array *a*. This is indicated in the postcondition by specifying the value of the array element to which *elt* is being assigned. The postcondition states that when the *store* operation is completed, the result of the *extract* operation applied to *a* and *i* (which is written *a*[*i*]) equals the value of *elt*. Unless a modified value is specified in a postcondition, we assume that all the parameters retain the same value after the operation is applied in a postcondition as before. It is not necessary to specify that such values remain unchanged. Thus, in this example, all the array elements other than the one to which *elt* is assigned retain the same values.

Note that once the operation *extract* has been defined together with its bracket notation *a*[*i*], that notation can be used in the postcondition for the subsequent *store* operation specification. Within the postcondition of *extract*, however, subscripted sequence notation must be used because the array bracket notation itself is being defined.

Using One-Dimensional Arrays

A one-dimensional array is used when it is necessary to keep a large number of items in memory and reference them in a uniform manner. Let us see how these two requirements apply to practical situations.

Suppose we wish to generate one hundred random integers between 1 and 100, find their average, and determine by how much each integer deviates from that average. The following application accomplishes this:

```
public class Average {
  public static void main(String[ ] args) {
    int num[ ] = new int[100];          // array of numbers
    int total;                          // sum of the numbers
    int avg;                            // average of the numbers
    int diff;                           // difference between each
                                        // number and the average
```

```
        total = 0;
        for (int i = 0; i < num.length; i++) {
          // Generate random numbers from 1 to 100
          // place the numbers into the array, and add them
          num[i] = 1 + (int) Math.round((99.0 * Math.random()));
          total += num[i];
        }
        avg = total / num.length;                // compute the average
        System.out.println("number difference"); // print heading

        // print each number and its difference
        for (int i = 0; i < num.length; i++) {
            diff = num[i] - avg;
            System.out.println("" + num[i] + " " + diff + "\n");
        }
      System.out.println("average is: " + avg);
    } // end main method
  } // end Average class
```

This application uses two groups of one hundred numbers. The first group is the set of random integers and is represented by the array *num*, and the second group is the set of differences that are the successive values assigned to the variable *diff* in the second loop. Here a question arises: Why is an array used to hold all the values of the first group simultaneously, but only a single variable to hold one value at a time of the second group?

The answer is quite simple. Each difference is computed and printed and is never needed again. Thus the variable *diff* can be reused for the difference of the next integer and the average. However, the original integers that are the values of the array *num* must all be kept in memory. Although each can be added into *total* as it is input, it must be retained until after the average is computed in order for the program to compute the difference between it and the average. Therefore, an array is used.

Of course, one hundred separate variables could have been used to hold the integers. The advantage of an array, however, is that it allows the programmer to declare only a single identifier and yet obtain a large amount of space. Furthermore, in conjunction with the *for* loop, it also allows the programmer to reference each element of the group in a uniform manner instead of having to code a series of statements such as

```
num0  = 1 + (int) (99.0 * Math.random());
num1  = 1 + (int) (99.0 * Math.random());
num2  = 1 + (int) (99.0 * Math.random());
          ...
num99 = 1 + (int) (99.0 * Math.random());
```

A particular element of an array may be retrieved through its index. For example, suppose a company is using an applet where an array is declared by

```
int sales[ ] = new int[10];
```

The array will hold sales figures for a ten-year period. Suppose that two input fields, *input*1 and *input*2, are placed on the applet: the first contains an integer from 0 to 9 representing a year, and the second contains the sales figure for that year. It is desired to read the sales figure into the appropriate element of the array. This can be accomplished by executing the statements

```
yr = Integer.parseInt(input1.getText());
sales[yr] = Integer.parseInt(input2.getText());
```

within the action method of the applet. In this statement, a particular element of the array is accessed directly by using its index. Consider the situation if ten variables $s0, s1, \ldots, s9$ had been declared. Then, even after executing $yr = Integer.parseInt(input1.getText())$ to set yr to the integer representing the year, the sales figure could not be read into the proper variable without coding something like:

```
switch (yr) {
    case 0:        s0 = Integer.parseInt(input2.getText());    break;
    case 1:        s1 = Integer.parseInt(input2.getText());    break;
        .
        .
        .
    case 9:        s9 = Integer.parseInt(input2.getText());    break;
}
```

This is bad enough with ten elements—imagine the inconvenience if there were a hundred or a thousand.

Implementing One-Dimensional Arrays

A one-dimensional array can be implemented easily. The Java declaration

```
int b[ ] = new int[100];
```

reserves one hundred successive memory locations, each large enough to contain a single integer. We call the address of the first of these locations the **base address** of the array b, and we denote it by $base(b)$. Suppose that the size of each individual element of the array is $esize$. Then a reference to the element $b[0]$ is to the element at location $base(b)$, a reference to $b[1]$ is to the element at $base(b) + esize$, a reference to $b[2]$ is to the element $base(b) + 2*esize$. In general, a reference to $b[i]$ is to the element at location $base(b) + i*esize$. Thus it is possible to reference any element in the array, given its index.

In Java, all elements of any particular array have the same fixed, predetermined size. Some programming languages, however, allow arrays of objects of differing sizes. For example, a language might allow arrays of varying-length character strings. In such cases, the above method cannot be used to implement the array. This is because this method of calculating the address of a specific element of the array depends upon knowing the fixed size $esize$ of each preceding element. If not all of the elements have the same size, a different implementation must be used.

One method of implementing an array of varying-sized elements is to reserve a contiguous set of memory locations, each of which holds a reference to another location. The contents of each such memory location is the address of the varying-length array element in some other portion of memory. For example, Figure 1.2.1a illustrates an array of five varying-length character strings under the two implementations of

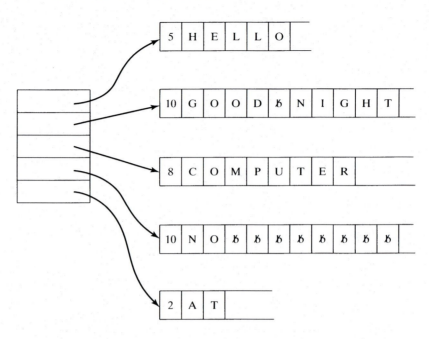

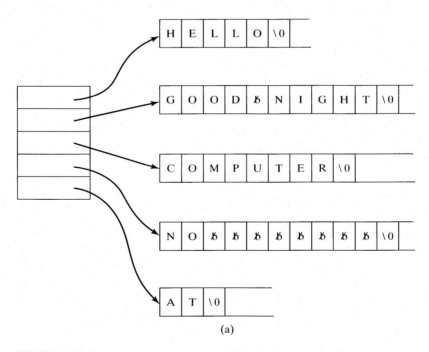

(a)

FIGURE 1.2.1   Implementations of an array of varying-length strings.

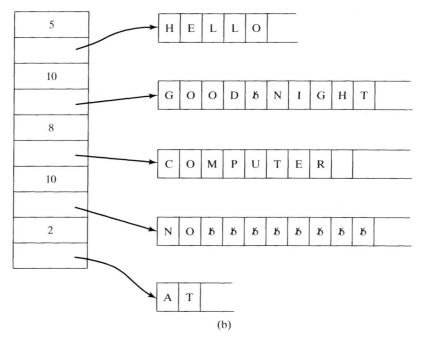

(b)

FIGURE 1.2.1 (*Continued*)

varying-length integers presented in Section 1. The arrows in the diagram indicate the addresses of other portions of memory. The character 'ƀ' indicates a blank.

Since the length of each address is fixed, the location of the address of a particular element can be computed in the same way that the location of a fixed-length element was computed in the previous examples. Once this location is known, its contents can be used to determine the location of the actual array element. This, of course, adds an extra level of indirection to referencing an array element by involving an extra memory reference, which in turn decreases efficiency. However, this is a small price to pay for the convenience of being able to maintain such an array.

A similar method for implementing an array of varying-sized elements is to keep all the fixed-length portions of the elements in the contiguous array area, in addition to keeping the address of the varying-length portion in the contiguous area. For example, in the implementation of varying-length character strings presented in the previous section, each such string contains a fixed-length portion (a 1-byte length field) and a variable-length portion (the character string itself). One implementation of an array of varying-length character strings keeps the length of the string together with the address, as shown in Figure 1.2.1b. The advantage of this method is that those parts of an element that are of fixed length can be examined without an extra memory reference. For example, a method to determine the current length of a varying-length character string can be implemented with a single memory lookup. The fixed-length information for an array element of varying length stored in the contiguous memory area of the array is often called a ***header***.

Arrays as Parameters

Every parameter of a Java method must be declared within the method. However, the size of a one-dimensional array parameter is only specified in the main program. This is because new storage is not allocated for an array parameter in Java. Rather, the parameter refers to the original array that was allocated in the main program. For example, consider the following method to compute the average of the elements of an array:

```
public double avg(double a[ ]) {
   double sum = 0;

     for (int i = 0; i < a.length; i++)
        sum += a[i];
   return sum / a.length;
}
```

In the main application, we might have written

```
public static final int ARANGE = 100;
double a[ ] = new double[ARANGE];

   ...
average = avg(a);
```

Note that the length of the array is not passed to the method—the length of the array may always be obtained by using *length*.

Since an array variable in Java is a reference to the actual storage locations currently allocated for the array, array parameters are passed ***by reference*** rather than by value. That is, unlike simple variables that are passed by value, an array's contents are not copied when it is passed as a parameter in Java. Instead, a reference to the array is passed. If a calling method contains the call *method(a)*, where *a* is an array and the method *method* has the header

```
public int method(int b[ ])
```

then the statement

```
b[i] = x;
```

inside *method* modifies the value of *a*[*i*] inside the calling method. *b* inside *method* references the same array of locations as *a* in the calling function.

Passing an array by reference rather than by value is more efficient in both time and space. The time that would be required to copy an entire array on invoking a function is eliminated. Also, the space that would be needed for a second copy of the array in the called function is reduced to space for only a single pointer variable.

Two-Dimensional Arrays

The component type of an array can be another array. For example, we may define

```
int a[ ] = new int [3][5];
```

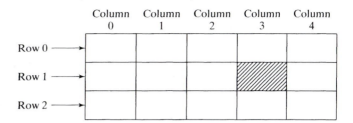

FIGURE 1.2.2   Two-dimensional arrays.

This defines a new array containing three elements. Each of these elements is itself an array containing five integers. Figure 1.2.2 illustrates such an array. An element of this array is accessed by specifying two indices: a row number and a column number. For example, the element that is darkened in Figure 1.2.2 is in row 1 and column 3 and may be referenced as $a[1][3]$. Such an array is called a **two-dimensional** array. The number of rows or columns is called the **range** of the dimension. In the array a above, the range of the first dimension is 3 and the range of the second dimension is 5. Thus the array a has three rows and five columns.

A two-dimensional array clearly illustrates the differences between a **logical** and a **physical** view of data. A two-dimensional array is a logical data structure that is useful in programming and problem solving. For example, such an array is useful in describing an object that is physically two-dimensional, such as a map or a checkerboard. It is also useful in organizing a set of values that are dependent upon two inputs. For example, a program for a department store that has twenty branches each of which sells thirty items might include a two-dimensional array declared by

```
int sales[ ][ ] = new int[20][30];
```

Each element $sales[i][j]$ represents the amount of item j sold in branch i.

However, although it is convenient for the programmer to think of the elements of such an array as being organized in a two-dimensional table, and programming languages do indeed include facilities for treating them as a two-dimensional array, the hardware of most computers has no such facilities. An array must be stored in the memory of a computer, and that memory is usually linear. By this we mean that the memory of a computer is essentially a one-dimensional array. A single address (which may be viewed as a subscript of a one-dimensional array) is used to retrieve a particular item from memory. In order to implement a two-dimensional array, it is necessary to develop a method of ordering its elements in a linear fashion and of transforming a two-dimensional reference to the linear representation.

One method of representing a two-dimensional array in memory is the **row-major** representation. Under this representation, the first row of the array occupies the first set of memory locations reserved for the array, the second row occupies the next set, and so forth. There may also be several locations at the start of the physical array that serve as a header and contain the upper and lower bounds of the two dimensions. (This header should not be confused with the headers discussed earlier. This header is for the entire array, whereas the headers mentioned earlier are headers for the individual array

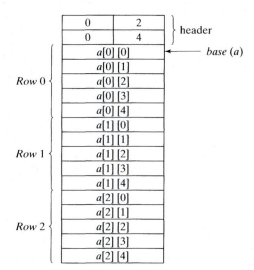

FIGURE 1.2.3   Representing a two-
dimensional array.

elements.) Figure 1.2.3 illustrates the row-major representation of the two-dimensional array *a* declared above and illustrated in Figure 1.2.2. Alternatively, the header need not be contiguous to the array elements, but could instead contain the address of the first element of the array. Additionally, if the elements of the two-dimensional array are variable-length objects, the elements of the contiguous area could themselves contain the addresses of those objects in a form similar to those of Figure 1.2.1 for linear arrays.

Let us suppose that a two-dimensional integer array is stored in row-major sequence, as in Figure 1.2.3, and let us suppose that, for an array *ar*, *base*(*ar*) is the address of the first element of the array. That is, if *ar* is declared by

```
int ar[ ][ ] = new int[r1][r2];
```

where *r*1 and *r*2 are the ranges of the first and second dimensions respectively, then *base*(*ar*) is the address of *ar*[0][0]. We also assume that *esize* is the size of each element in the array. Let us calculate the address of an arbitrary element, *ar*[*i*1][*i*2]. Since the element is in row *i*1, its address can be calculated by computing the address of the first element of row *i*1 and adding the quantity *i*2*esize (this quantity represents how far into row *i*1 the element at column *i*2 is). But in order to reach the first element of row *i*1 (i.e., the element *ar*[*i*1][0]), it is necessary to pass through *i*1 complete rows each of which contains *r*2 elements (since there is one element from each column in each row), so that the address of the first element of row *i*1 is at *base*(*ar*) + *i*1**r*2*esize. Therefore, the address of *ar*[*i*1][*i*2] is at

```
base(ar) + i1 * r2 + i2 * esize
```

As an example, consider the array *a* of Figure 1.2.2 whose representation is illustrated in Figure 1.2.3. In this array, *r*1 = 3, *r*2 = 5, and *base*(*a*) is the address of *a*[0][0]. Let us also suppose that each element of the array requires a single unit of storage, so that

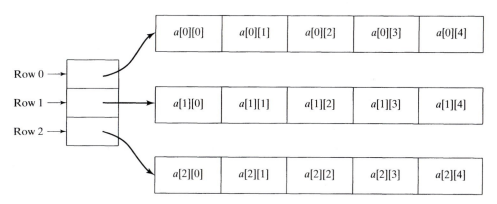

FIGURE 1.2.4   Alternative implementation of a two-dimensional array.

esize equals 1. (This is not necessarily true, because *a* was declared as an array of integers, and an integer may need more than one unit of memory on a particular machine. For simplicity, however, we accept this assumption.) Then the location of *a*[2][4] can be computed by

```
base[a] + 2*5 + 4*1
```

that is,

```
base(a) + 14
```

You may confirm the fact that *a*[2][4] is fourteen units past *base*(*a*) in Figure 1.2.3.

Another possible implementation of a two-dimensional array is as follows. An array *ar* declared with upper bounds *u*1 and *u*2 consists of *u*1 one-dimensional arrays. The first is an array *ap* of *u*1 pointers. The *i*th element of *ap* is a pointer to a one-dimensional array whose elements are the elements of the two-dimensional array *ar*. For example, Figure 1.2.4 illustrates such an implementation for the array *a* of Figure 1.2.2, where *u*1 is 3 and *u*2 is 5.

To reference *ar*[*i*][*j*], the array *ar* is first accessed to obtain the pointer *ar*[*i*]. The array at that pointer location is then accessed to obtain *a*[*i*][*j*].

This second implementation is the simpler and most straightforward of the two. However, the *u*1 arrays *ar*[0] through *ar*[*u*1 − 1] would usually be allocated contiguously, with *ar*[0] immediately followed by *ar*[1], and so on. The first implementation avoids allocating the extra pointer array, *ap*, and computing the value of an explicit pointer to the desired row array. It is therefore more efficient in both space and time.

Multidimensional Arrays

Java also allows arrays with more than two dimensions. For example, a three-dimensional array may be declared by

```
int b[ ][ ][ ] = new int[3][2][4];
```

and is illustrated in Figure 1.2.5a. An element of this array is specified by three subscripts, such as *b*[2][0][3]. The first subscript specifies a plane number, the second subscript, a row number, and the third, a column number. Such an array is useful when

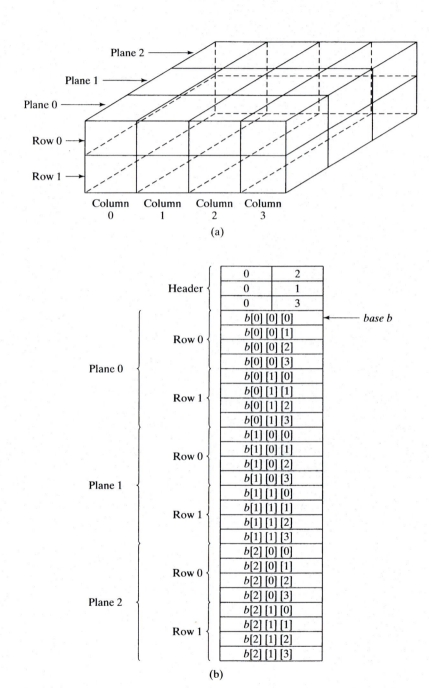

FIGURE 1.2.5   Three-dimensional array.

a value is determined by three inputs. For example, an array of temperatures might be indexed by latitude, longitude, and altitude.

For obvious reasons, the geometric analogy breaks down when we go beyond three dimensions. However, Java does allow an arbitrary number of dimensions. For example, a six-dimensional array may be declared by

```
int c[ ][ ][ ][ ][ ][ ] = new int[7][15][3][5][8][2];
```

Referencing an element of this array would require six subscripts, such as $c[2][3][0][1][6][1]$. The number of different subscripts that are allowed in a particular position (the range of a particular dimension) equals the upper bound of that dimension. The number of elements in an array is the product of the ranges of all its dimensions. For example, the array b above contains $3*2*4 = 24$ elements, while the array c contains $7*15*3*5*8*2 = 25{,}200$ elements.

The row-major representation of arrays can be extended to arrays of more than two-dimensions. Figure 1.2.5b illustrates the representation of the array b of Figure 1.2.5a. The elements of the six dimensional array c described above are ordered as follows:

```
C[0][0][0][0][0][0]
C[0][0][0][0][0][1]
C[0][0][0][0][1][0]
C[0][0][0][0][1][1]
C[0][0][0][0][2][0]
    ...
    ...
C[6][14][2][4][5][0]
C[6][14][2][4][5][1]
C[6][14][2][4][6][0]
C[6][14][2][4][6][1]
C[6][14][2][4][7][0]
C[6][14][2][4][7][1]
```

That is, the last subscript varies most rapidly, and a subscript is not increased until all possible combinations of the subscripts to its right have been exhausted. This is similar to the odometer (mileage indicator) of a car, where the rightmost digit changes most rapidly.

What mechanism is needed to access an element of an arbitrary multidimensional array? Suppose that ar is an n-dimensional array declared by:

```
int ar[ ][ ]...[ ] = new int[r1][r2]...[rn];
```

and stored in row-major order. Each element of ar is assumed to occupy $esize$ storage locations, and $base(ar)$ is defined as the address of the first element of the array (i.e., $ar[0][0]\ldots[0]$). Then, to access the element

```
ar[i1][i2]...[in];
```

it is first necessary to pass through $i1$ complete "hyper-planes," each consisting of $r2*r3*\ldots*rn$ elements, to reach the first element of ar whose first subscript is $i1$. Then it is necessary to pass through an additional $i2$ groups of $r3*r4*\ldots*rn$ elements in order to reach the first element of *ar* whose first two subscripts are *i*1 and *i*2, respectively. A similar process must be carried out through the other dimensions until the first element whose first $n-1$ subscripts match those of the desired element is reached. Finally, it is necessary to pass through *in* additional elements to reach the element desired.

Thus the address of *ar*[*i*1][*i*2]...[*in*] may be written as *base*(*ar*) + *esize**[*i*1**r*2* ...*rn + *i*2**r*3*...*rn + ... + (*i*(*n* − 1)*rn + *in*)], which can be evaluated more efficiently by using the equivalent formula:

```
base(ar) + esize * [in + rn * (i(n - 1) + r(n - 1)
* (... + r3 * (i2 + r2 * i1) ...) ) ]
```

This formula may be evaluated by the following algorithm that computes the address of the array element and places it into *addr* (assuming arrays *i* and *r* of size *n* to hold the indices and the ranges, respectively):

```
offset = 0;
for (j = 0; j < n; j++)
   offset = r[j] * offset + i[j];
addr = base(ar) + esize * offset;
```

Character Strings in Java

It is tempting to think of a string as a one-dimensional array of characters. Although a Java string shares several common characteristics with a Java array, a string in Java is actually an instance of the Java *String* class. A string constant or **literal** is denoted by any set of characters included in double quote marks. Various escape sequences can be used to represent special characters within a string: \n for a new-line character, \t for a tab character, \b for a backspace character, \" for the double quote character, \\ for the backslash character, \' for the single quote character, \r for the carriage return character, and \f for the form feed character. Thus, for example, "I DON\'T KNOW\n" represents the string I DON'T KNOW followed by the new-line character.

The method *length* may be used to obtain the length of a string. For example, suppose a programmer declares

```
String s1, s2;
s1 = new String ("HELLO THERE");
s2 = new String ("I DON\'T KNOW HIM");
```

then s1.*length*() is 11, and s2.*length*() is 16 (the **escape sequence** \' represents the single quote character).

The compiler creates a new *String* object each time it encounters a string literal. Thus the statement

```
s1 = "HELLO THERE";
```

has the same effect as the declaration of *s*1 shown above.

It is important to note that all strings in Java are immutable; that is, once a string is created, there is no way to change it. (Objects of a related class, *StringBuffer*, may be modified.) Recall that nonprimitive variables in Java are actually references to the object being assigned. Thus assigning one string variable to another sets both variables pointing to the identical string. For example,

```
String s1, s2;
s1 = "HELLO THERE";    // s1 refers to a newly created String object
s2 = s1;               // s1 and s2 refer to the identical String
                       // object
```

In order to determine whether or not two *String* variables refer to the same *String* object, we make use of the logical==operator. It is quite possible that two strings appear to be identical and yet are different. Consider the following statements:

```
String s1, s2;
s1 = "HELLO THERE";    // s1 refers to a newly created String object
s2 = "HELLO THERE";    // s2 refers to a newly created String
                       // object
```

The Boolean expression *s*1==*s*2 is ***false*** because *s*1 and *s*2 refer to different *String* objects. In order to compare two different *String* objects for equality, we may use the *String* method *equals*. The *String* method *compareTo* compares two strings lexicographically (i.e., in alphabetic order; for nonalphabetic characters, the UNICODE representation order is used). The *String* method *compareTo* returns 0 if the strings are lexicographically the same, a negative number if the string that invoked the *compareTo* method is lexicographically less than its parameter, and a positive number if the string that invoked the *compareTo* method is lexicographically greater than its parameter. The table below summarizes these relationships.

```
String s1, s2, s3, s4;
s1 = "HELLO THERE";
s2 = "HELLO THERE";
s3 = "GOOD BYE";
s4 = s1;
```

Expression	Value
s1==s2	false
s1==s4	true
s1.equals(s2)	true
s1.equals(s3)	false
s1.equals(s4)	true
s1.compareTo(s2)	0
s1.compareTo(s3)	Positive value
s3.compareTo(s1)	Negative value

To illustrate the immutability of strings and the fact that a string variable merely contains a reference to an actual string of characters, consider the following example. The lines are numbered for reference.

1. String s1 = "HELLO";
2. String s2 = "BYE";

3. String s3 = "GOOD";
4. s1 = s3;
5. s3 = s3 + s2;

Statements 1–3 set up three variables, *s*1, *s*2, and *s*3, and initialize them to reference newly allocated strings of characters, as shown in Figure 1.2.6a. Statement 4 results in Figure 1.2.6b. *s*1 and *s*3 now both reference the storage allocated for *s*3. Since nothing references the string "HELLO" any longer, that storage is ripe for garbage collection. Statement 5 creates new storage for "GOODBYE" and resets the reference in *s*3; the string "GOOD" is now only referenced by *s*1, it is not modified by the addition of "BYE". See Figure 1.2.6c.

Character String Operations

The Java *String* class implements a wide variety of methods operating on character strings. In addition to the *equals, compareTo*, and *length* methods presented earlier, the following methods are often used in this text. The reader is urged to consult a Java reference for other useful *String* methods.

- *str.charAt(int)*   Returns the character at the specified index, *int*, of string *str*.
- *str1.concat(str2)*   Concatenates *str2* to the end of *str1*.
                             Equivalent to *str1* = *str1* + *str2*;
- *str1.indexOf(str2)*   Returns the index within *str1* of the first occurrence of *str2*.
- *str1.indexOf(str2, int)* Returns the index within *str1* of the first occurrence of *str2*, starting at the specified index.
- *valueOf(boolean)*   Returns the *String* representation of the Boolean argument.
- *valueOf(char[ ])*   Returns the *String* representation of the *char array* argument.
- *valueOf(char[ ], int, int)* Returns the *String* representation of a specific subarray of the *char array* argument. The second parameter represents the initial offset into the value of the string, and the third parameter represents the length of the value of the string.
- *valueOf(double)*   Returns the *String* representation of the *double* argument.
- *valueOf(float)*   Returns the *String* representation of the *float* argument.
- *valueOf(int)*   Returns the *String* representation of the *int* argument.
- *valueOf(long)*   Returns the *String* representation of the *long* argument.

Vectors in Java

The **vector** is one of the most useful of the so-called **container** classes that are available to the Java programmer. In many ways a vector is similar to an array, with two significant exceptions. First, unlike an array, a vector can grow and shrink automatically as items are inserted and deleted. Second, while an array, as a feature of the Java language,

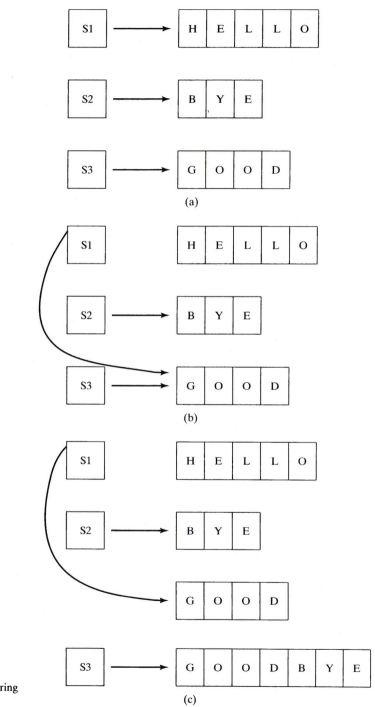

FIGURE 1.2.6   String assignments.

can contain elements of any type, vectors, because defined in the *java.util* package, may only contain elements of type *Object*, which we introduce in Section 1.3. We defer discussion of vectors to the end of the next section

EXERCISES

1.2.1 a. The ***median*** of an array of numbers is the element *m* of the array such that half the remaining numbers in the array are greater than or equal to *m*, and half are less than or equal to *m*, if the number of elements in the array is odd. If the number of elements is even, then the median is the average of the two elements *m*1 and *m*2 such that half the remaining elements are greater than or equal to *m*1 and *m*2, and half the elements are less than or equal to *m*1 and *m*2. Write a Java method that accepts an array of numbers and returns the median of the numbers in the array.

 b. The ***mode*** of an array of numbers is the number *m* in the array that is repeated most frequently. If more than one number is repeated with equal maximal frequency, then there is no mode. Write a Java method that accepts an array of numbers and returns the mode or an indication that the mode does not exist.

1.2.2 Write a Java application that can do the following: Read a group of temperature readings (a reading consists of two numbers, an integer between −90 and 90 representing the latitude at which the reading was taken and the observed temperature at that latitude). Print a table consisting of each latitude and the average temperature at that latitude. If there are no readings at a particular latitude, print "NO DATA" instead of an average. Then print the average temperature in the northern and southern hemispheres (the northern consists of latitudes 1 through 90, and the southern, of latitudes −1 through −90). (This average temperature should be computed as the average of the averages, not the average of the original readings.) Also determine which hemisphere is warmer. In making the determination, take the average temperatures in all latitudes of each hemisphere for which there are data for both that latitude and the corresponding latitude in the other hemisphere. (For example, if there are data for latitude 57 but not for latitude −57, then the average temperature for latitude 57 should be ignored in determining which hemisphere is warmer.)

1.2.3 Write an application for a chain of twenty department stores, each of which sells ten different items. Every month, each store manager submits a data card for each item consisting of a branch number (from 1 to 20), an item number (from 1 to 10), and a sales figure (less than $100,000) representing the amount of sales for that item in that branch. However, some managers may not submit cards for some items (e.g., not all items are sold in all branches). Write a Java application that reads these data cards and prints a table with twelve columns. The first column should contain the branch numbers from 1 to 20 and the word "TOTAL" in the last line. The next ten columns should contain the sales figures for each of the ten items for each of the branches, with the total sales of each item in the last line. The last column should contain the total sales of each of the twenty branches for all items, with the grand total sales figure for the chain in the lower right-hand corner. Each column should have an appropriate heading. If no sales were reported for a particular branch and item, assume zero sales. Do not assume that your input is in any particular order.

1.2.4 Show how a checkerboard can be represented by a Java array. Show how to represent the state of a game of checkers at a particular instant. Write a Java method that accepts an array representing such a checkerboard and prints all possible moves that black can make from that position.

1.2.5 Write a method *printArray(a)* that accepts an *m* by *n* array *a* of integers and prints the values of the array on several pages as follows: Each page is to contain fifty rows and twenty columns of the array. Headings "COL 0", "COL 1", and so on, should be printed along the top of each page, and headings "ROW 0", "ROW 1", and so on, along the left margin of each page. The array should be printed by subarrays. For example, if *a* were a 100 by 100 array, the first page contains $a[0][0]$ through $a[49][19]$, the second page contains $a[0][20]$ through $a[49][39]$, the third page contains $a[0][40]$ through $a[49][59]$, and so on, until the fifth page contains $a[0][80]$ through $a[49][99]$, the sixth page contains $a[50][0]$ through $a[99][19]$, and so on. The entire printout occupies ten pages. If the number of rows is not a multiple of 50, or the number of columns is not a multiple of 20, the last pages of the printout should contain fewer than one hundred numbers.

1.2.6 Assume that each element of an array *a* stored in row-major order occupies four units of storage. If *a* is declared by each of the following, and the address of the first element of *a* is 100, find the address of the indicated array element:

a. **int** a[ ] = **new int**[100];   address of   a[10]
b. **int** a[ ] = **new int**[200];   address of   a[100]
c. **int** a[ ][ ] = **new int**[10][20];   address of   a[0][0]
d. **int** a[ ][ ] = **new int**[10][20];   address of   a[2][1]
e. **int** a[ ][ ] = **new int**[10][20];   address of   a[5][1]
f. **int** a[ ][ ] = **new int**[10][20];   address of   a[1][10]
g. **int** a[ ][ ] = **new int**[10][20];   address of   a[2][10]
h. **int** a[ ][ ] = **new int**[10][20];   address of   a[5][3]
i. **int** a[ ][ ] = **new int**[10][20];   address of   a[9][19]

1.2.7 Write a Java method *listOff* that accepts two one-dimensional array parameters of the same size: *range* and *sub*. *range* represents the range of an integer array. For example if the elements of *range* are

    3   5   10   6   3

range represents an array *a* declared by

```
int a[ ][ ][ ][ ][ ] = new int[3][5][10][6][3];
```

The elements of *sub* represent subscripts to the above array. If $sub[i]$ does not lie between 0 and $range[i] - 1$, then all the subscripts from the *i*th onwards are missing. In the above example, if the elements of *sub* are

    1   3   1   2   3

sub represents the one-dimensional array $a[1][3][1][2]$. The method *listOff* should print the offsets from the base of the array *a* represented by *range* of all the elements of *a* that are included in the array (or the offset of the single element if all the subscripts are within bounds) represented by *sub*. Assume that the size (*esize*) of each element of *a* is 1. In the foregoing example, *listOff* would print the values 4, 5, and 6.

1.2.8   a.   A *lower triangular* array *a* is an *n* by *n* array in which $a[i][j] == 0$ if $i < j$. What is the maximum number of nonzero elements in such an array? How can these elements be stored sequentially in memory? Develop an algorithm for accessing $a[i][j]$ where $i >= j$. Define an *upper triangular* array in an analogous manner, and do the same as above for such an array.

   b.   A *strictly lower triangular array* *a* is an *n* by *n* array in which $a[i][j] == 0$ if $i <= j$. Answer the questions in part (a) for such an array.

   c.   Let *a* and *b* be two *n* by *n* lower triangular arrays. Show how an *n* by *n* + 1 array *c* can be used to contain the nonzero elements of the two arrays. Which elements of *c* represent the elements $a[i][j]$ and $b[i][j]$, respectively?

   d.   A *tridiagonal* array *a* is an *n* by *n* array in which $a[i][j] == 0$ if the absolute value of $i - j$ is greater than 1. What is the maximum number of nonzero elements in such an array? How can these elements be stored sequentially in memory? Develop an algorithm for accessing $a[i][j]$ if the absolute value of $i - j$ is 1 or less. Do the same for an array *a* in which $a[i][j] == 0$ if the absolute value of $i - j$ is greater than *k*.

1.2.9   Write a Java method *numOccur* that accepts two strings and returns the number of times the second occurs as a substring of the first.

1.2.10   Write a Java method *reverse* that accepts a string *s*1 and returns the string *s*2 consisting of the reversal of *s*1 (i.e., the last character of *s*1 is the first character of *s*2, the next-to-last character of *s*1 is the second character of *s*2, and so on).

1.3   CLASSES AND OBJECTS IN JAVA

In this section, we introduce the concept of Java classes. We assume that you are familiar with basic object-oriented programming concepts from an introductory course. We review some highlights of this approach to programming and point out some interesting and useful features needed for a more general study of data structures.

Object-oriented programming (OOP) and design is a comparatively new paradigm in computer science that has slowly become the predominant method of software development. The basic concept of object orientation is to view data rather than procedure as the central focus of problem solution. Under this approach, applications model the problem at hand by describing each object in terms of a class that defines its contents and capabilities.

A *class* embodies the concept of an abstract data type by defining both the set of values of a given type and the set of operations that can be performed on them. A variable of a class type is known as an *object*, and the operations on it are called *methods*. When one object *A* invokes a method *m* on another object *B*, we sometimes say "*A* is sending message *m* to *B*." *B* is viewed as receiving the message and carrying out a transformation in response to it.

To illustrate these concepts, let us assume that a programmer wishes to describe a student attending a university. Typically, we would need to keep track of the student's identification number, name, grade point index, number of credits, and date of admittance. In addition, we would often wish to print the student's grade point average and determine whether or not the student has the minimum number of credits necessary for graduation. Consider the following declaration:

```
public class Student {
  static final int GRADUATION = 120;
  static int totalStudents = 0;

  String idNumber;
  String firstName, lastName;
  double gpIndex;
  int credits;
  Date dateAdmitted;

  public boolean readyToGraduate () {
      return credits >= GRADUATION ? true: false ;
  } // end readyToGraduate method

  public void printGPIndex () {
      System.out.println("Grade Point Average is " + gpIndex);
  } // end printGPIndex method

  public static void printTotalStudents() {
      System.out.println("The total number of students is " +
      totalStudents);
  } // end printTotalStudents method

  ...         // other class methods

} // end Student class
```

The *Student* class defined above includes data elements, or **members,** of the class: *GRADUATION*, *totalStudents*, *idNumber*, *firstName*, *gpIndex*, *credits*, and *dateAdmitted*; as well as class methods: *readyToGraduate*, *printGPIndex*, and *printTotalStudents*. Note that *dateAdmitted* is defined in terms of the *Date* class. We leave the definition of the *Date* class as an exercise for the reader. Now suppose that an application contains the declaration

```
Student person1 = new Student();
Student person2 = new Student();
```

person1 and *person2* are reference variables that refer to newly created **instances** of objects of the *Student* class. *idNumber*, *firstName*, *gpIndex*, *credits*, and *dateAdmitted* are known as **instance variables** because each object of the class, namely *person*1 and *person*2, has its own copy of these variables. On the other hand, the *static* keyword specifies that *GRADUATION* and *totalStudents* are common to the entire class. Such variables are known as **class variables**. The *final* keyword indicates that *GRADUATION* is a class constant and may not be assigned another value.

An object's instance variables may be assigned values by writing statements like the one shown below.

```
person1.gpIndex = 4.0;
```

We may think of this statement as representing a message to the object referred to by *person*1 to set its *gpIndex* to 4.0.

Similarly, *ReadyToGraduate* and *printGPIndex* are known as ***instance methods*** because each object of the *Student* class invokes these methods on its own instance variables. Specifying

```
person1.printGPIndex ();
```

prints the value contained in the *gpIndex* referred to by *person*1, while

```
person2.printGPIndex ();
```

prints the value contained in the *gpIndex* of the *person*2 object. By analogy to class variables, the ***static*** keyword in the header of the *printTotalStudents* method indicates that *printTotalStudents* is a ***class method***. Class methods are invoked by reference to the class (in this case *Student*). Thus, to print the total number of instantiated student objects we would write

```
Student.printTotalStudents();
```

A class method cannot reference a nonstatic data member of a class, because nonstatic data methods have individual values for each object of the class, whereas a static data member has a single value for the entire class.

Constructors

Each time a new object is created, Java automatically initializes all instance variables to their default values. **int**, **byte**, **short**, **long**, **float**, and **double** are initialized to 0, **char** to \u0000, **boolean** to **false**, and *String* to **null**.

Often it is desirable to instantiate an object with specific initial values. A ***constructor*** is a special method of a class that is invoked whenever an object of that class is created. A constructor is always named with the same name as the class itself. In our example above, a constructor is not specified; therefore, the ***default constructor*** is used and each of the object's instance variables is given its appropriate default initial value.

The class variable *totalStudents* is initialized to zero when the class is first accessed. Whenever an object of the class is created, it would be reasonable to increment this counter. This can be accomplished by including the following constructor in the class definition:

```
public Student() {
   totalStudents++;
} // end constructor
```

The constructor *Student* is invoked each time a new object is created.

Suppose we also wanted to initialize an object with a student's first and last names. We could define another constructor method for the *Student* class:

```
public Student(String first, String last) {
   firstName = first;
   lastName = last;
   totalStudents++;
} // end constructor
```

This constructor is invoked whenever a statement of the form

```
Student person3 = new Student("Boris", "Sery");
```

is used. The string arguments are passed to the constructor and assigned to the newly created object's instance variables.

The reader will note that we have defined two methods that have the same name but different numbers of parameters. Such methods are said to be **overloaded**. That is, the same method name, in this case the class constructor, can apply to different methods if their parameters are of different types. There is no limit to the number of overloaded methods or constructors that may be defined. The compiler chooses the constructor that matches the arguments provided when the object is created. Overloaded methods are useful whenever the programmer wishes to accomplish the same basic tasks but with different numbers or types of parameters.

Representing Other Data Structures

Throughout the remainder of this text, classes are used to represent more complex data structures. Aggregating data and methods into a class is useful because it enables us to group objects within a single entity and to name each object appropriately according to its function.

As examples of how classes can be used in this fashion, let us consider the problem of representing rational numbers.

Rational Numbers

In Section 1.1 we presented an ADT for rational numbers. Recall that a ***rational number*** is any number that can be expressed as the quotient of two integers. Thus 1/2, 3/4, 2/3, and 2 (i.e., 2/1) are all rational numbers, but $\sqrt{2}$ and π are not. A computer usually represents a rational number by its decimal approximation. If we instruct the computer to print 1/3, it responds with .333333. Although this is close enough (the difference between .333333 and one-third is only one third of a million), it is not exact. If we were to ask for the value of 1/3 + 1/3, the result would be .666666 (which equals .333333 + .333333), while the result of printing 2/3 might be .666667. This would mean that the result of the test 1/3 + 1/3 == 2/3 would be false! In most instances, the decimal approximation is good enough, but sometimes it is not. It is therefore desirable to implement a representation of rational numbers for which exact arithmetic can be performed.

How can we represent a rational number exactly? Since a rational number consists of a numerator and a denominator, we can represent a rational number by defining a *Rational* class, as follows:

```
public class Rational {

  private long numerator, denominator;
  public Rational() {
       numerator = 0;
       denominator = 1;
  }
```

```
   public Rational (long i) {
        numerator = i;
        denominator = 1;
   }

   public Rational (long num, long denom) {
                              // We will modify this definition shortly
     numerator = num;
     denominator = denom;
   }

   // class methods to be developed below
   private Rational reduce () {        …

   public boolean equals(Rational rat) {        …

   public Rational multiply(Rational rat) {        …

   public Rational add(Rational rat) {        …

   public Rational divide(Rational rat) {        …

   public String toString() {        …

} // end Rational class
```

Then, when we declare an object to be a *Rational*, the appropriate constructor is invoked. The operator ***new*** in Java allocates a new object of the given type and returns a reference to it. When ***new*** is called, the constructor is invoked automatically. Thus the statement

```
Rational r = new Rational ();
```

declares a reference variable to an object of the *Rational* class, allocates a new object of the *Rational* class, initializes it to the rational zero (0/1) (since that is what the constructor *Rational* with no parameters does), and sets *r* pointing to it. The declaration

```
Rational r = new Rational (3)
```

sets *r* to the rational 3/1, since it invokes the second version of the constructor. Finally, the declaration

```
Rational r = new Rational (2, 5)
```

sets *r* to the rational 2/5, invoking the third version of *Rational*, with two parameters.

The instance variables *numerator* and *denominator* and the method *reduce* are ***private***. That is, they can be referenced only from within the methods of the *Rational* class. The methods *equals, multiply, add, divide*, and *toString*, by contrast, are ***public***. This means they can be referenced outside the methods of the *Rational* class.

The reasons for doing this are simple. We do not want "outsiders" manipulating either the *numerator* or *denominator* member. They are merely a way of implementing a rational number and are to be used solely for that purpose. An external method manipulates a *Rational*; only within the internal methods of *Rational* should we be able to access *numerator* and *denominator*. Similarly, the method *reduce* is a method to reduce the internal representation of the *Rational* (i.e., the numerator and denominator) to lowest terms. We intend to use *reduce* to ensure that every rational number is kept in lowest terms. The outside world has no cause to call *reduce*. Every method that manipulates the internal numerator and denominator (i.e., *equals, add, multiply*, and *divide*) is a member of the *Rational* class and will automatically ensure that the resulting number is in reduced form by calling *reduce*. We will see this when we present the implementations of these methods. There is no need for anyone else to call *reduce*, and therefore *reduce* is defined as private.

On the other hand, the methods *equals, add, multiply, divide*, and *toString* are public. These functions form the public interface for the *Rational* class. That is, they are the methods by which the outside world can manipulate and use objects of type *Rational*. The ability to restrict access to certain members of the class to methods of the class itself is known as ***information hiding***.

We now turn our attention to the implementation of the class methods. You might think that we are now ready to define rational number arithmetic for our new representation, but there is one significant problem. Suppose we defined two rational numbers *r*1 and *r*2 and gave them values. How can we test whether the two numbers are the same? Perhaps you might want to code

```
if (r1.numerator == r2.numerator && r1.denominator == r2.denominator)
   ...
```

That is, if both numerators and denominators are equal, then the two rational numbers are equal. However, it is possible for both numerators and denominators to be unequal, yet the two rational numbers are the same. For example, the numbers 1/2 and 2/4 are indeed equal although their numerators (1 and 2) as well as their denominators (2 and 4) are unequal. We therefore need a new way of testing equality under our representation.

Well, why are 1/2 and 2/4 equal? The answer is that they both represent the same ratio. One out of two and two out of four are both one-half. In order to test rational numbers for equality, we must first reduce them to lowest terms. Once both numbers have been reduced to lowest terms, we can then test for equality by simple comparison of their numerators and denominators.

Define a ***reduced rational number*** as a rational number for which there is no integer that evenly divides both the denominator and numerator. Thus 1/2, 2/3, and 10/1 are all reduced, while 4/8, 12/18, and 15/6 are not. In our example, 2/4 reduced to lowest terms is $\frac{1}{2}$, so the two rational numbers are equal.

A procedure known as Euclid's algorithm can be used to reduce any fraction of the form *numerator/denominator* into its lowest terms. This procedure may be outlined as follows:

1. Let *a* be the larger of the *numerator* and *denominator*, and let *b* be the smaller.
2. Divide *b* into *a*, finding a quotient *q* and a remainder *r* (i.e., $a = q*b + r$).
3. Set $a = b$ and $b = r$.
4. Repeat steps 2 and 3 until *b* is zero.
5. Divide both the *numerator* and the *denominator* by the value of *a*.

As an illustration, let us reduce 1032/1976 to its lowest terms.

step 0	*numerator* = 1032		*denominator* = 1976	
step 1	*a* = 1976	*b* = 1032		
step 2	*a* = 1976	*b* = 1032	*q* = 1	*r* = 944
step 3	*a* = 1032	*b* = 944		
step 4 and 2	*a* = 1032	*b* = 944	*q* = 1	*r* = 88
step 3	*a* = 944	*b* = 88		
step 4 and 2	*a* = 944	*b* = 88	*q* = 10	*r* = 64
step 3	*a* = 88	*b* = 64		
step 4 and 2	*a* = 88	*b* = 64	*q* = 1	*r* = 24
step 3	*a* = 64	*b* = 24		
step 4 and 2	*a* = 64	*b* = 24	*q* = 2	*r* = 16
step 3	*a* = 24	*b* = 16		
step 4 and 2	*a* = 24	*b* = 16	*q* = 1	*r* = 8
step 3	*a* = 16	*b* = 8		
step 4 and 2	*a* = 16	*b* = 8	*q* = 2	*r* = 0
step 3	*a* = 8	*b* = 0		
step 5	1032/8 = 129		1976/8 = 247	

Thus 1032/1976 in lowest terms is 129/247.

Let us write a method to reduce a rational.

```
private Rational reduce () {
   long a, b, remainder;
   if (numerator > denominator) {
        a = numerator;
        b = denominator;
   }
   else {
        a = denominator;
        b = numerator;
   }
   while (b != 0) {
        remainder = a % b;
        a = b;
        b = remainder;
   }
   return new Rational(numerator / a, denominator / a);
} // end reduce method
```

Using the method *reduce*, we can write another method *equals* that determines whether or not two rational numbers *r1* and *r2* are equal. If they are, the method returns ***true***; otherwise, the method returns ***false***.

```
public boolean equals(Rational rat) {
        Rational r1, r2;
        r1 = reduce();
        r2 = rat.reduce();
        if (r1.numerator == r2.numerator && r1.denominator ==
            r2.denominator)
                return true;
        else
                return false;
} // end equals method
```

Note, at this point we may want to redefine the constructor *Rational(**long** num,* ***long** denom*) to produce only rationals in reduced form. That is, it produces the rational number in reduced form that is equal to *num/denom*, as follows:

```
public Rational (long num, long denom) {
  long a, b, rem;

  if (num > denom) {
    a = num;
    b = denom;

  }
  else {
    a = denom;
    b = num;
  }
  while (b != 0) {
    rem = a % b;
    a = b;
    b = rem;
  }
  numerator = num / a;
  denominator = denom / a;
} // end Rational constructor
```

In this way, we are sure that all rationals produced by the constructors are in reduced form. We have to make sure that all other routines producing rationals (e.g. *add, multiply*) also produce rationals in reduced form. We can then assume that every *Rational* is in reduced form.

We may now write methods to perform arithmetic on rational numbers. We present a first try at a method to multiply two rationals.

```
public Rational multiply(Rational rat) {
    return  new  Rational(numerator  *  rat.numerator,  denominator  *
    rat.denominator);
} // end multiply method
```

In this method, two reduced rationals a/b and c/d, are multiplied by computing $(a*c)/(b*d)$. However, in this method, there is the danger that the product of the two numerators and two denominators may be too large even for a ***long*** variable. We would like the products to be as small as possible. The solution is to reduce a/d and c/b. In that way, since we assume that the input rationals a/b and c/d are in reduced form, we are certain that $a*c$ has no terms in common with $b*d$ and that the products are as small as possible.

Here is the method *multiply* implementing these ideas:

```
public Rational multiply(Rational rat) {
  Rational r1, r2;

  r1 = new Rational(numerator, rat.denominator);
  r2 = new Rational (rat.numerator, denominator);
  return new Rational(r1.numerator * r2.numerator,
                                  r1.denominator * r2.denominator);
} // end multiply method
```

The method *divide* simply multiplies by a reciprocal.

```
public Rational divide(Rational rat) {
  Rational rn1;

  rn1 = new Rational(rat.denominator, rat.numerator);
  return  multiply(rn1);
} // end divide method
```

The method *equals* assumes that both rationals being tested for equality are in reduced form.

```
public boolean equals(Rational rat) {
  if (numerator == rat.numerator && denominator == rat.denominator)
    return true;
  else
    return false;
} // end equals method
```

Just as with the *multiply* method, to add two rational numbers we could first reduce each to lowest terms, then multiply the two denominators to produce a resulting denominator, then multiply each numerator by the denominator of the other rational number and add the two products to produce the numerator. The result can then be reduced to lowest terms. However, this too entails the danger that the product of the two denominators may be too large even for a ***long*** variable.

Instead, we use the following algorithm to add a/b to c/d. We assume that the value $rden(x, y)$ denotes the denominator of x/y reduced to lowest terms:

```
k = rden(b, d);
denom = b*k;                     // the resulting denominator
num = a*k +c*(denom / d);        // the resulting numerator
```

num is the numerator of the sum, *denom* is the denominator. We leave it as an exercise to show that this algorithm is correct.

Implementing this algorithm in the context of the *Rational* class provides the following definition of the method *add*:

```
public Rational add(Rational r) {
    Rational rn1;
    long k, denom, num;

    // implement the line k = rden(b, d); of the algorithm
    rn1 = new Rational(denominator, rat.denominator);
    k = rn1.denominator;

    // compute the denominator of the result;
    // algorithm line denom = b*k;

    denom = denominator * k;
    // compute the numerator of the result
    // algorithm line num = a*k + c*a(denom/r.denominator);
    num = numerator * k + rat.numerator * (denom/rat.denominator);
    // form a Rational from the result and reduce the result to
    // lowest terms

    return rn1 = new Rational(num, denom);
} // end add method
```

Most Java classes provide a method *toString* that converts an object to an appropriate *String* object suitable for printing. To implement the method *toString* we first must decide on a format for the output. A reasonable format might be to print the numerator followed by a slash followed by the denominator. We adopt this format in the routine below:

```
public String toString() {
    return numerator + "/" + denominator;
} // end toString method
```

Using the class *Rational*

The Java language provides two mechanisms for executing programs: ***applications*** and ***applets***. Applications are classes that are designed to be self-standing. Each application class contains a method of the form:

```
public static void main(String[ ] args) … {
} // end main method
```

which is invoked by the Java interpreter. Statements contained in the *main* method are executed sequentially. Upon reaching the last statement in the method, control is returned to the operating system and the application terminates. Applications may invoke other methods, call upon other classes, read and write to files, and perform any operation defined by the Java language specification.

Often, however, it is desired to invoke programs in the context of a ***browser***. These programs, known as applets, are frequently downloaded from the Internet, and their origin may not be known. Security is often a prime concern. The Java language provides a mechanism by which applets are constrained to function within the confines of the *sandbox*, from which they can do no harm to the local environment. The most important restriction on an applet is that it has no access to the local file system. The reader is urged to consult a Java reference text for additional restrictions placed upon applets.

Applets are invoked when the browser encounters an HTML statement containing the *applet* tag. The *applet* tag may optionally contain *height* and *width* parameters that control the amount of space on the browser page allocated to the applet.

```
<applet code=appletClass height = x width = y> </applet>
```

Applets are often ***event-driven***, that is, they react to external events, such as mouse clicks, system events, and other forms of user-computer interaction. The browser invokes the applet, which in turn invokes the methods defined by the programmer. Many methods defined in the *java.applet* package are designed to allow the applet to interact with the user. Java's *abstract windowing toolkit* (AWT) provides a powerful framework for working with graphics in a windows environment. A graphical user interface, or ***gui***, may be designed by using the methods present in the *java.awt* and *java.awt.event* packages.

In the following example, we illustrate the use of the *Rational* class by means of an applet designed to display the user interface shown in Figure 1.3.1. Although the reader should be familiar with the basics of applet programming before continuing with the following example, detailed knowledge of Java applet programming is not necessary for an understanding of data structures.

We want to write an applet that allows the user to input two rational numbers, select the arithmetic operation from the keyboard, and indicate that the computation

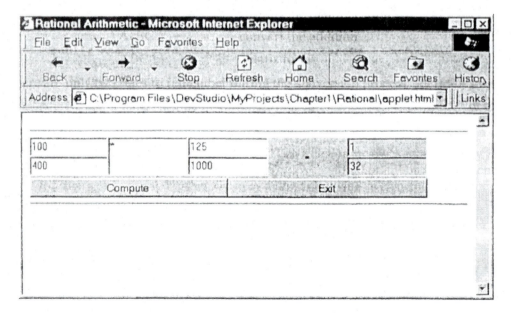

FIGURE 1.3.1   An applet displaying the result of the ***RationalApplet class***.

should be performed by means of a mouse click. The applet class, which we will call *RationalApplet*, may be invoked by the following HTML code:

```
<html>
  <head>
      <title>Rational Arithmetic</title>
  </head>
  <body>
      <hr>
      <applet code=RationalApplet height=75 width = 500> </applet>
      <hr>
  </body>
</html>
```

The *RationalApplet* class consists of three methods:

1. *init* is responsible for laying out the graphical user interface and is invoked when the applet is initilized by the browser.
2. *addButton* is responsible for instantiating a new mouse button and assigning an action to be performed when a mouse click is detected.
3. *actionPerformed* is responsible for performing the appropriate arithmetic operation as input by the user.

The applet is as follows:

```
import java.io.IOException;
import java.applet.*;
import java.awt.*;
import java.awt.event.*;
import java.util.*;

public class RationalApplet extends Applet implements
ActionListener {
   private TextField num1numerator, num1denominator;
   private TextField num2numerator, num2denominator;
   private TextField ansnumerator, ansdenominator;
   private TextField operation;

   public void init() {
     setLayout(new BorderLayout());

     Panel p1=new Panel();
     p1.setLayout(new GridLayout(2,1));

     num1numerator=new TextField("",8);
     num1numerator.setEditable(true);
     p1.add(num1numerator, "North");

     num1denominator = new TextField("",8);
     num1denominator.setEditable(true);
     p1.add(num1denominator, "South");
```

```
    Panel p2=new Panel();
    p2.setLayout(new GridLayout(2,1));

    num2numerator=new TextField("",8);
    num2numerator.setEditable(true);
    p2.add(num2numerator, "North");

    num2denominator = new TextField("",8);
    num2denominator.setEditable(true);
    p2.add(num2denominator, "South");

    Panel p3=new Panel();
    p3.setLayout(new GridLayout(1,1));

    operation=new TextField("", 2);
    p3.add(operation,"Center");

    Panel p4=new Panel();
    p4.setLayout(new GridLayout(1,1));

    Label l=new Label("=",Label.CENTER);
    p4.add(l,"Center");

    Panel p5=new Panel();
    p5.setLayout(new GridLayout(2,1));

    ansnumerator=new TextField("",8);
    ansnumerator.setEditable(false);
    p5.add(ansnumerator, "North");

    ansdenominator = new TextField("",8);
    ansdenominator.setEditable(false);
    p5.add(ansdenominator, "South");

    Panel p=new Panel();
    p.setLayout(new GridLayout(1,5));
    p.add(p1);
    p.add(p3);
    p.add(p2);
    p.add(p4);
    p.add(p5);
    add(p, "North");

    Panel mainpanel=new Panel();
    mainpanel.setLayout(new GridLayout(1,2));
    addButton(mainpanel,"Compute");
    addButton(mainpanel,"Exit");
    add (mainpanel, "South");
} // end init method

public void addButton(Container c, String s) {
    Button b=new Button(s);
    c.add(b);
    b.addActionListener(this);
} // end addButton method
```

```
public void actionPerformed(ActionEvent evt) {
    Rational result=new Rational();
    String s = evt.getActionCommand();
    if (s.equals("Compute")) {
        Rational r1 = new Rational(Long.parseLong(num1numerator.
        getText()),
                    Long.parseLong(num1denominator.getText()));
        Rational r2 = new
        Rational(Long.parseLong(num2numerator.getText()),
                    Long.parseLong(num2denominator.getText()));
        char operator=(operation.getText()).charAt(0);
        switch (operator) {
          case '+':    result = r1.add(r2);        break;
          case '*':    result = r1.multiply(r2);   break;
          case '/':    result = r1.divide(r2);     break;
          default:     System.out.println("Undefined operation");
        }
        String str = result.toString();
        int i = str.indexOf("/");
        ansnumerator.setText(str.substring(0,i));
        ansdenominator.setText(str.substring(i + 1));
    }
    else {
        System.exit(0);
    }
} // end actionPerformed method
} // end RationalApplet class
```

Allocation of Storage and Scope of Classes

Until now we have been concerned with the declaration of variables, that is, the description of a variable's type or attribute and the methods that manipulate them. Two important questions, however, remain to be answered. At what point is a class or object (and its data members) associated with actual storage (i.e., *storage allocation*)? At what point in a program may a particular class or object (and its data members) be referenced (i.e., *scope* or *visibility* of classes)?

In the previous section we distinguished between instance variables, which "belong" to each instance of the class, and class variables, which are "common" to the entire class. In Java, class variables (i.e., those with the *static* modifier) are automatically allocated storage at the time that the class is first loaded. If initial values are provided, they are assigned to the variables at the time of creation; otherwise the class variables are initialized to their default values. Instance variables, on the other hand, are allocated storage each time a new object is created. The programmer creates a new object (and associates storage with the object's variables) each time the *new* keyword is invoked. At that time the default class constructor is invoked and the object's variables are assigned their initial values. As we have seen, the programmer may override the default constructor with one or more class constructors that may be used to initialize the object and its data members. If more than one constructor is defined, the *parameter signature* is used to choose among them.

It is also possible to define a ***static initializer*** to initialize class variables. The static initializer is invoked only the first time any object of that class comes into existence. The programmer may specify any number of initial actions that are invoked at the time that the class is first loaded by preceding them with the ***static*** keyword. Static initializers have the form:

```
static {          // static initializer
  ...
} // end initializer
```

We consider static initializers further in Chapter 4.

Recall from Section 1.1 that Java always passes arguments to parameters of a method by a "call by value" mechanism. Storage for parameters declared within a method are allocated storage when the method is invoked. When the method terminates, storage assigned to those variables is deallocated. These parameters exist only as long as the method is active. Thus any change made to the parameter within the method does not affect the argument's initial value.

Once storage is allocated for a class or object, it remains allocated until the Java interpreter determines that it is no longer needed. At that time, a process known as ***garbage collection*** reclaims, or deallocates, the storage so that it may be reused. The allocation and deallocation of storage runs automatically in the background, freeing the programmer from having to worry about the details of the storage allocation process.

We now turn to the second of our questions, namely, the scope or visibility of an object. ***Encapsulation***, which is the ability to restrict access to certain members of the class to methods of the class itself, is an important component of modern programming. Were it not for the ability to restrict access to variables, it would be possible for programmers to inadvertently change the value of a class member by assigning a value to a similarly named variable. Such errors, known as ***side-effect*** errors, are very difficult to correct. Furthermore, programmers often wish to hide the details of the implementation of a class from other classes that may use it. This allows the programmer to change the implementation without having to worry that other classes that refer to it will "break" under the new implementation.

The Java language provides three keywords that allow the programmer to limit or extend the visibility of a class, its methods, and its data members: ***public, private***, and ***protected***. If the keywords are not specified, the class (or its methods and data members) is said to have ***package visibility***. In order to understand how these concepts are applied, we first discuss the organization of a Java class and its relationship to the file and directory in which it is defined as well as its relationship to other classes.

A class is usually defined in a file having the same name as the class. Thus a class named *ClassA* might be defined in a file named *ClassA.java* (*ClassA.class* after it is compiled). All classes defined in the same directory are said to be in the same ***default package***. It is often useful for one class to be able to refer to a group of related classes that reside in a different directory. In such cases, the package is given a name. Each class of the package is placed in the same directory as other classes of the package and is prefaced by a header that identifies the name of the package. For example, suppose it was desired to define a package *packageA* which consists of two related classes: *ClassB* and *ClassC*. *ClassB* and *ClassC* would both begin with the statement

    package packageA;

and would be stored in a directory called *packageA*. If *ClassA* wanted to refer to the methods and data members of the classes defined in *packageA*, it would begin with the statement

    import packageA.*;

in which the asterisk specifies that all classes of the package should be imported. The ability to import classes allows a programmer to make use of the large number of pre-defined classes provided by the Java language. In addition, the use of packages allows the Java programmer to organize a large number of classes by function and facilitates the reuse of code.

In Section 2.3 we use the concept of inheritance in which one or more independently defined classes are said to *inherit* the methods and data elements of the class upon which they are based. Such classes are known as *subclasses* and can be identified by the use of the keyword *extends*. For example, if *ClassD* wished to inherit the methods and data members of *ClassA* (in order to extend the capabilities of *ClassA*), it would begin with the header

    public class ClassD **extends** ClassA {

ClassA is known as the *superclass* of *ClassD*. The reader is urged to review the concept of inheritance before proceeding.

Ordinarily, only one class is defined per file. Java 1.1 extended the Java language by allowing classes to be nested within other classes. Such *inner classes* are used as auxiliaries, or "helpers," by their container classes and are not intended for use by other "top-level" classes. During compilation, the Java compiler locates each inner class and creates a separate *.class* file.

To summarize, the organizational structure of a Java application or applet consists of packages, classes, subclasses, and inner classes; and four visibility categories: public, private, protected, and package. A private method or member may only be referenced from within the class in which it is declared. No other class may access the private methods or members of another, nor are they inherited by any subclass that extends the class in which they are declared. Public elements, on the other hand, are visible to any class that wishes to use them. Protected methods and members are visible to all classes within a package, but may not be accessed by classes that lie outside the package. Protected methods are also visible to subclasses of the class in which they are defined, even if those classes are not in the same package. By default, (i.e., if neither *public, private*, nor *protected* is specified), the methods and members have package visibility, that is, they are visible only within the package in which they are defined and may not be used by classes or even subclasses that are defined outside the package.

To illustrate these rules, consider the following application (the numbers to the left of each line are for reference purposes). Figure 1.3.2 illustrates the directory structure of the files in which the various classes are defined.

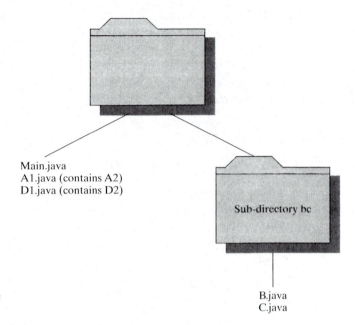

Main.java
A1.java (contains A2)
D1.java (contains D2)

Sub-directory bc

FIGURE 1.3.2   File layout for scope example.

B.java
C.java

```
// source Main.java

1    import bc.*;
2    public class Main {
3        public static void main (String[ ] args) {
4            A1 a1main = new A1();
5            a1main.print();
6            System.out.print(a1main.x + "   ");
7            System.out.print(a1main.y + "   ");
8            System.out.println(a1main.z);
9            A1.A2 a2main = new A1.A2();
10           a2main.print();
11           bc.B bmain = new bc.B();
12           bmain.print();
13           bc.C cmain = new bc.C();
14           cmain.print();
15           System.out.print(cmain.x + "   ");
16           System.out.print(cmain.y + "   ");
17           System.out.println(cmain.z);
18           D2 d2main = new D2();
19           d2main.println();
20       } // end main
21    } // end class Main

// end of source Main.java
```

```java
// source A1.java

22  public class A1 {
23      public static int x, y, z;
24      private static int a, b;

25      public A1() {
26          x = 1;
27          y = 2;
28          z = 3;
29          a = 1;
30          b = 2;
31      } // end constructor A1

32      public void print() {
33          System.out.print(x + "   ");
34          System.out.print(y + "   ");
35          System.out.print(z + "   ");
36          System.out.print(a + "   ");
37          System.out.println(b + "   ");
38      } // end print
39      public static class A2 {
40          private int a, b;

41          public A2() {
42              a = 4;
43              b = 5;
44          } // end constructor A2

45          public void print() {
46              System.out.print(A1.x + "   ");
47              System.out.print(A1.y + "   ");
48              System.out.print(A1.z + "   ");
49              System.out.print(A1.a + "   ");
50              System.out.println(A1.b);
51              System.out.print(a + "   ");
52              System.out.println(b);
53          } // end print
54      }  // end inner class A2
55  }  // end outer class A1

// end of source A1.java

// source D1.java

56  public class D1 {
57      protected int n;
58  } // end class D1

// end source of D1.java
```

```
// source D2.java

59   class D2 extends D1 {
60          public D2() {
61               n = 3;
62          } // end constructor D2

63          public void println() {
64               System.out.println(n);
65          } // end println
66   } // end class D2
```

```
// end of source D2.java
```

```
// subdirectory bc
```

```
// source B.java

67        package bc;
68        public class B {
69           int b;

70           public B() {
71               b = 7;
72           } // end constructor B

73           public void print() {
74               System.out.println(b);
75           } // end print
76        } // end class B
```

```
// end of source B.java
```

```
// source C.java

77   package bc;
78   public class C {
79          public int x, y, z;
80          B bnum = new B();

81          public C() {
82               x = 10;
83               y = 20;
84               z = 30;
85          } // end constructor C

86          public void print() {
87               System.out.print(x + "   ");
88               System.out.print(y + "   ");
89               System.out.println(z);
90               System.out.println(bnum.b);
91          } // end print
92   } // end class C
```

```
// end of source C.java
```

Execution of the application yields the following results:

```
a   1  2  3  1  2       // public variables x, y, z and private
                        // variables a, b are printed by using the
                        // print method of class A1
b   1  2  3             // public variables x, y, z are printed by main
c   1  2  3  1  2       // public variables x, y, z and private
                        // variables a, b of class A1 are printed by
                        // inner class A2
d   4  5                // public variables a, b of inner class A2 are
                        // printed by class A2
e   7                   // package variable b is printed by class B
f   10  20  30          // public variables x, y, z are printed by
                        // class C
g   7                   // package variable b of class B is printed by
                        // class C
h   10  20  30          // public variables x, y, z of class C are
                        // printed by main
i   3                   // protected variable n created by class D1 is
                        // printed by class D2 extending D1
```

Let us trace through the application. Execution begins with line 1, in which the *Main* class imports all the public methods and data members of *package bc*. Note that *package bc*, defined in lines 67–90, is in a subdirectory of the current directory called *bc* (see Figure 1.3.2) and contains classes *B* and *C*. Both class *B* and class *C* are members of *package bc*, because they are identified as members of the package in lines 67 and 77, respectively.

Execution then continues at line 2, which defines the class *Main*. Every application must have one *Main* class containing a *main* method (line 4) that marks the entry point into the application. The method *main* defines an object *a1main* of the class *A1* and instantiates the object by invoking its constructor (lines 25–31), allocating storage for its data members in line 4. Examination of the definition of class *A1* (lines 22–55) reveals three **public** data members [*x, y, z* (line 23)] and two **public** methods [constructor *A1* (lines 25–31) and *print* (lines 32–38)] which will be available to all classes that wish to use them. The **private** data members, [*a* and *b* (line 24)] will only be available to the methods of their own class. Class *A1* also contains an inner class, *A2* (lines 39–54), which will be discussed later.

The *main* method then invokes the *print* method of class *A1* (line 5), resulting in the output shown on line a. Since this *print* method is defined as **public** (line 32), it may be called by any method in the application, including the *main* method. Because data members *x, y,* and *z* are **public**, they may be printed either by the *print* method of class *A1* (line 5) or by the *print* (lines 6 and 7) and *println* (line 8) methods of the default *System.out* object (output line b). However, **private** data members *a* and *b* may only be accessed through the methods of the class in which they are defined.

Line 9 then defines a new object *a2main* of the inner class *A2* (lines 39–54) and instantiates the object by invoking its constructor (lines 41–44). Inner classes are hidden within the outer class and are only accessible through the outer class. The **static** keyword (line 39) restricts class *A2* from directly accessing any of the data members of the outer class *A1*. Once the *main* method has created an object (*a2main*) of the *A2* class, its public methods may be used. Line 10 then calls upon the ***public*** *print* method of *A*2 to print the ***public*** variables *x*, *y*, *z*, and the ***private*** variables *a*, *b* of its outer class *A*1 (output line c) and its own ***private*** variables *a* and *b*, producing the output of line d. Note that when the *print* method of *A*2 refers to the variables *a* and *b* without specifying a class, it refers to the data members of *A*2, while under the same circumstances, the *print* method of *A*1 refers to the *a* and *b* of *A*1.

Line 11 of *main*, referring to the package *bc*, defines a new object *cmain* of the class *B*, thus instantiating an integer variable *b* with an initial value of 7 by invoking its constructor (lines 70–72). Class *B*'s *print* method (lines 73–75) is invoked on line 12, resulting in output line e.

Note that variable *b* of class *B* is declared to be neither ***public*** nor ***private*** (line 69). Therefore, *b* has package visibility and is accessible to all classes in the package.

Execution then continues with line 13, which defines a new object *cmain* of the class *C*. When *cmain* is instantiated, a new object *bnum* of class *B* is created within class *C* (line 80), which upon creation invokes *B*'s constructor (line 70–72). Class *C*'s constructor (lines 81–85) is also invoked, thus initializing the ***public*** variables *x*, *y* and *z*. Of course, these variables *x*, *y*, and *z* belong to the object *cmain*, and should not be confused with the variables *x*, *y*, and *z* which belong to *a*1*main*. Line 14 then invokes the ***public*** *print* method of class *C*, resulting in output lines f and g. Note that *C*'s *println* may access *bnum.b* (line 90) because both *B* and *C* are in the same package and *b* has package visibility. Lines 15, 16, and 17 use the default *System.out.print* and *System.out.println* to print the *cmain* ***public*** variables *x*, *y*, and *z*, resulting in output line h.

Returning to line 18 of the *main* method, a new object *d2main* of class *D*2 is created. Since class *D*2 ***extends*** class *D*1 (line 59), class *D*2 inherits all of *D*'s methods and data members. The subclass *D*2 behaves as if all of the methods and data members of *D*1 were defined within it. Therefore, when the constructor for *D*2 (lines 60–62) is invoked at the time of the creation of *d2main*, the variable *n* of the *D*1 class is initialized. *n* is ***protected*** (line 57) and thus is available to all subclasses and package members of the class in which it is created. Finally, line 19 of the *main* method invokes *D*2.*println*, resulting in output line i.

Vectors in Java

One of the major limitations of arrays is their static nature. Once an array is created it is of a fixed size. Thus the programmer is often faced with the following dilemma: If the amount of storage necessary for the application has been overestimated, the array, once created, may contain a significant amount of wasted storage; on the other hand, if the amount of required storage is underestimated, a new array of larger size will have to be created, and all the information from the first array will need to be copied over to the second array. The *java.util* package addresses these issues by defining an object known as a ***vector*** that can change its size dynamically.

In order to illustrate how a vector is used, we will revisit the *Student* class described earlier in this section. We repeat here, for the reader's convenience, the definition of this class.

```
public class Student {
    static final int GRADUATION = 120;
    static int totalStudents = 0;
```

```
        String idNumber;
        String firstName, lastName;
        double gpIndex;
        int credits;
        Date dateAdmitted;
    ...         // other class methods
} // end Student class
```

Suppose it was desired to store information on a number of students. Since the number of students will change from semester to semester, it is appropriate to store the students' information in a vector. A vector *classRecords*, with an initial capacity of twenty-five student records, may be defined by:

```
Vector classRecords = new Vector(25);
```

This defines a vector which has the potential of holding up to twenty-five records. However, unlike an array, if you attempt to add a twenty-sixth member, the vector will automatically double in size (with room for a total of fifty records). Should you once again exceed the vector's capacity by attempting to insert a fifty-first record, the vector will once again double its size (with room for a total of one hundred records), and so on. In general, a vector *v* may be defined by the statement:

```
Vector v = new Vector(m, n);
```

where *m* represents the amount of initial storage, and *n* represents the amount of storage that is added to the vector when its current size is exceeded. If *n* is omitted, the vector doubles in size; if both *m* and *n* are omitted, a vector with the potential for ten objects is created by default. The current size of a vector may be obtained by using the *v.size* method. Vectors, like arrays, are indexed from zero to *v.size*() - 1.

In order to insert an object into a vector, the *add* method of the *Vector* class is used. For example, using the *Student* class constructor presented earlier in this section, the statements

```
        classRecords.add(new Student("Boris", "Sery"));
        classRecords.add(new Student("Edward", "Mardakhaev"));
        classRecords.add(new Student("Marina", "Marchenko"));
```

would add three students into the first three positions of the *classRecords* vector. It is also possible to insert an object into the middle of a vector. Thus the statement

```
        classRecords.add(1, new Student("Shalva", "Landy"));
```

would add the student whose name is "Shalva Landy" to position one of the *classRecords* vector, shifting the remaining elements up.

An object may be removed from a vector by invoking the *remove* method. Thus the statement

```
        Student s = (Student) classRecords.remove(2);
```

would remove the student whose name is "Edward Mardakhaev" from the vector, shifting the remaining elements down by one, and assigning the object returned by the *remove* method to the variable *s*. Note that the object must be cast as an object of the

Student class before it is assigned to the variable *s*. This is because a vector can only contain items of the *Object* class, and *Objects* must be cast into a compatible type before they may be assigned to a class object.

Java 2 added the *v.get(i)* and *v.set(i, x)* methods to the *Vector* class. The *get* method retrieves the object stored in location *i* of vector *v* without removing it from the vector. It should be noted that the *set* method overwrites the contents of location *i* with the object *x*, while the *add* method inserts object *x* at the specified location, shifting all items in the vector up to make room for the newly inserted item.

Unlike an array, vector elements do not exist until objects are added to the vector. Thus, assuming the sequence of statements above, the statement

```
classRecords.add(10, new Student("Alexander", "Kaplan"));
```

yields an "*ArrayIndexOutOfBoundsExeception* 10 > 3", since the vector *classRecords* currently contains only three elements. The *setSize(n)* method allows the programmer to set the size of the vector to *n* elements. If *n* is greater than the current size of the vector, this method increases the vector to size *n*, setting the additional elements to ***null***. If *n* is less than the current size of the vector, the vector is trimmed to size *n*, and the elements that were above the $(n-1)^{th}$ position are discarded. Thus the statements:

```
classRecords.setSize(15);
classRecords.add(10, new Student("Alexander", "Kaplan"));
```

would set the size of the *classRecords* vector to fifteen, then increase the size to sixteen, inserting "Alexander Kaplan" in the vector at index ten, and setting the objects in index three through nine and eleven through fifteen to ***null***.

The reader is urged to consult the Java documentation in order to learn about the other vector methods defined in the *java.util* package.

EXERCISES

1.3.1   Implement complex numbers, as specified in Exercise 1.1.8, using structures with real and complex parts. Write routines to add, multiply, and negate such numbers.

1.3.2   Suppose a real number is represented by a Java class, such as:

```
public class Real {
    private long left, right;
...
```

where *left* and *right* represent the digits to the left and right of the decimal point, respectively. If *left* is a negative integer, then the represented real number is negative.

a.   Write a routine to input a real number, and create an object representing that number.

b.   Write a function that accepts such a structure and returns the real number represented by it.

c.   Write routines *add*, *subtract*, and *multiply* that accept two such structures, and set the value of a third structure to represent the number that is the sum, difference, and product, respectively, of the two input records.

1.3.3   Assume two arrays, one of student records, the other of employee records. Each student record contains members for a last name, first name, and grade point index. Each employee record contains members for a last name, first name, and salary. Both arrays are ordered in alphabetical order by last name and first name. Two records with the same last name/first name do not appear in the same array. Write a Java method to give a 10 percent raise to every employee who has a student record and whose grade point index is higher than 3.0.

1.3.4   Write a method as in the preceding exercise, but assume that the employee and student records are kept in a vector rather than in two ordered arrays.

1.3.5   Write a method as in Exercise 1.3.3, but assuming that the employee and student records are kept in two ordered external files rather than in two ordered arrays.

1.3.6   Using the rational number representation given in the text, write routines to add, subtract, and divide such numbers.

1.3.7   Write a method *negate* for the class *Rational* that returns the negative of a rational number.

1.3.8   The text presents a method *equals* that determines whether or not two rational numbers $r1$ and $r2$ are equal by first reducing $r1$ and $r2$ to lowest terms and then testing for equality. An alternative method would be to multiply the denominator of each by the numerator of the other and testing the two products for equality. Write a method *equal2* to implement this algorithm. Which of the two methods is preferable?

1.3.9   Define a class *NewString* that represents a string by a length and a reference to an array of characters.

   a. Write a constructor for *NewString* that allocates appropriate storage for it and initializes it to a given Java string.

   b. Write a constructor for *NewString* that allocates storage of a given size for the string but does not initialize its characters.

   c. Write a method *concat* that concatenates one *NewString* with another.

1.3.10 Implement a class *NewString*, as in the previous exercise, using a vector.

CHAPTER 2

The Stack

The stack is one of the most useful concepts in computer science. In this chapter, we shall examine this deceptively simple data structure and see why it plays such a prominent role in the areas of programming and programming languages. We shall define the abstract concept of a stack and show how it can be made into a concrete and valuable tool in problem solving.

2.1 DEFINITION AND EXAMPLES

A *stack* is an ordered collection of items into which new items may be inserted and from which items may be deleted at one end, called the *top* of the stack. We can picture a stack as in Figure 2.1.1.

Unlike an array, the definition of a stack provides for the insertion and deletion of items, and thus a stack is a dynamic, constantly changing object. The question therefore arises, how does a stack change? The definition specifies that a single end of the stack is designated as the stack top. New items may be put on top of the stack (in which case the top of the stack moves upwards to correspond to the new highest element) or items which are at the top of the stack may be removed (in which case the top of the stack moves downwards to correspond to the new highest element). To answer the question "which way is up?" we must decide which end of the stack is designated as its

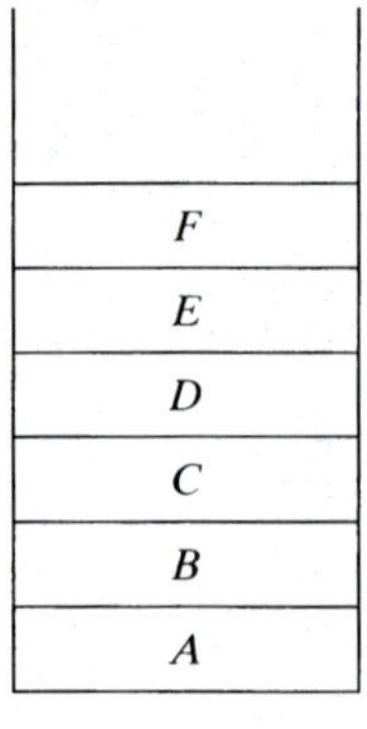

FIGURE 2.1.1 Stack containing stack terms.

68

top—that is, at which end items are added or deleted. By drawing Figure 2.1.1 so that F is physically higher on the page than all the other items in the stack, we imply that F is the current top element of the stack. If any new items are added to the stack, they are placed on top of F, and if any items are deleted, F is the first to be deleted. This is also indicated by the vertical lines that extend past the items on the stack in the direction of the stack top.

Figure 2.1.2 is a motion picture of a stack as it expands and shrinks with the passage of time. Figure 2.1.2(a) shows the stack as it exists at the time of the snapshot in Figure 2.1.1. In Figure 2.1.2(b), item G is added to the stack. According to the definition, there is only one place on the stack where it can be placed—the top. The top element on the stack is now G. As the motion picture progresses through frames c, d, and e, items $H, I,$ and J are successively added onto the stack. Note that the last item inserted (in this case J) is at the top of the stack. Beginning with frame f, however, the stack begins to shrink, as first J, then $I, H, G,$ and F are successively removed. At each point, the top element is removed, since a deletion can be made only from the top. Item G could not be removed from the stack before items $J, I,$ and H were gone. This illustrates the most important attribute of a stack, that the last element inserted is the first element deleted. Thus J is deleted before I because J was inserted after I. For this reason a stack is sometimes called a last-in, first-out (or LIFO) list.

Between frames j and k, the stack has stopped shrinking and begins to expand again as item K is added. However, this expansion is short-lived, as the stack then shrinks to only three items in frame n.

Note that there is no way to distinguish between frame a and frame i by looking at the stack's state at the two instances. In both cases, the stack contains the identical items in the same order and has the same stack top. No record is kept on the stack of the fact that four items had been pushed and popped in the meantime. Similarly, there is no way to distinguish between frames d and f or j and l. If a record is needed of the intermediate items having been on the stack, it must be kept elsewhere; it does not exist within the stack itself.

In fact, we have actually taken an extended view of what is really observed in a stack. The true picture of a stack is given by a view from the top looking down, rather than from a side looking in. Thus, in Figure 2.1.2, there is no perceptible difference between frames h and o. In each case the element at the top is G. While the stack at h and the stack at o are not equal, the only way to determine this is to remove all the elements on both stacks and compare them individually. While we have been looking at cross-sections of stacks to make our understanding clearer, it should be noted that this is an added liberty and there is no real provision for taking such a picture.

Primitive Operations

The two changes which can be made to a stack are given special names. When an item is added to a stack, it is **pushed** onto the stack, and when an item is removed, it is **popped** from the stack. Given a stack s, and an item i, performing the operation $s.push(i)$ adds the item i to the top of stack s. Similarly, the operation $s.pop()$ removes the top element and returns it as a method value. Thus the assignment operation

```
i = s.pop();
```

removes the element at the top of s and assigns its value to i.

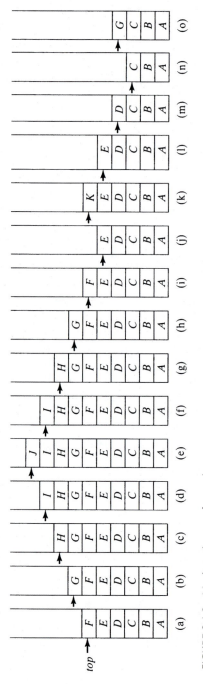

FIGURE 2.1.2   Motion picture of a stack.

70

For example, if *s* is the stack in Figure 2.1.2, we performed the operation *s.push*(*G*) in going from frame (a) to frame (b). We then performed, in turn, the operations

```
s.push(H);      (frame (c))
s.push(I);      (frame (d))
s.push(J);      (frame (e))
s.pop();        (frame (f))
s.pop();        (frame (g))
s.pop();        (frame (h))
s.pop();        (frame (i))
s.pop();        (frame (j))
s.push(K);      (frame (k))
s.pop();        (frame (l))
s.pop();        (frame (m))
s.pop();        (frame (n))
s.push(G);      (frame (o))
```

Because of the push operation which adds elements to a stack, a stack is sometimes called a ***pushdown list***.

There is no upper limit on the number of items that may be kept on a stack, since the definition does not specify how many items are allowed in the collection. Pushing another item onto a stack merely produces a larger collection of items. However, if a stack that contains a single item is popped, the resulting stack contains no items and is called an ***empty stack***. Although the *push* operation is applicable to any stack, the *pop* operation cannot be applied to an empty stack because such a stack has no elements to pop. Therefore, before applying the *pop* operator to a stack, we must ensure that the stack is not empty. The operation *s.empty*() determines whether or not a stack *s* is empty. If the stack is empty, *empty* returns the value *true*; otherwise it returns the value *false*.

Another operation that can be performed on a stack is to determine what the top item is without removing it. This operation is written *s.peek*() and returns the top element of stack *s* without changing the stack. The operation *peek* is not really a new operation, since it can be decomposed into a pop and a push.

```
i = s.peek();
```

is equivalent to

```
i = s.pop();
s.push(i);
```

Like the operation *pop*, *peek* is not defined for an empty stack. The result of an illegal attempt to pop or access an item from an empty stack is called ***underflow***. Underflow can be avoided by ensuring that *s.empty*() is false before attempting the operation *s.pop*() or *s.peek*().

Example

Now that we have defined a stack and have indicated the operations that can be performed on it, let us see how we may use the stack in problem-solving. Consider a mathematical expression that includes several sets of nested parentheses; for example,

$$7 - ((X*((X + Y)/(J - 3)) + Y)/(4 - 2.5))$$

and we want to ensure that the parentheses are nested correctly. That is, we want to check that:

1. There are an equal number of right and left parentheses.
2. Every right parenthesis is preceded by a matching left parenthesis.

Expressions such as

$$((A + B)   \text{or}   A + B($$

violate condition 1, while

$$)A + B(-C   \text{or}   (A + B)) - (C + D$$

violate condition 2.

To solve this problem, think of each left parenthesis as opening a scope and each right parenthesis as closing a scope. The ***nesting depth*** at any particular point in an expression is the number of scopes that have been opened but not yet closed at that point. This is the same as the number of left parentheses encountered whose matching right parentheses have not yet been encountered. Let us define the ***parenthesis count*** at a particular point in an expression as the number of left parentheses minus the number of right parentheses that have been encountered in scanning the expression from its left end up to that particular point. If the parenthesis count is nonnegative, then it is the same as the nesting depth. The two conditions that must hold if the parentheses in an expression form an admissible pattern are as follows:

1. The parenthesis count at the end of the expression is 0. This implies that no scopes have been left open or that exactly as many right parentheses as left parentheses have been found.
2. The parenthesis count at each point in the expression is nonnegative. This implies that no right parenthesis is encountered for which a matching left parenthesis was not previously encountered.

In Figure 2.1.3, the count at each point in each of the previous five strings is given directly below that point. Since only the first string meets the two conditions listed above, it is the only one of the five with a correct parentheses pattern.

Let us now change the problem slightly and assume that three different types of scope delimiters exist. These types are indicated by parentheses ((and)), brackets ([and]), and braces ({and}). A scope ender must be of the same type as its scope opener. Thus strings such as

$$(A + B], [(A + B]), \{A - (B]\}$$

are illegal.

$$7 - (\ (\ X * (\ (X + Y\ )\ /\ (\ J - 3\ )\ )\ ) + Y\ )\ /\ (\ 4 - 2.5\ )\ )$$
0 0 1 2 2 2 3 4 4 4 4 3 3 4 4 4 4 3 2 2 2 1 1 2 2 2   2 1 0

$$(\ (\ A + B\ )$$
1 2 2 2 2 1

$$A + B\ ($$
0 0 0 1

$$)\quad A\ +\ B\ (\ - C$$
−1   −1 −1 −1 0 0 0

FIGURE 2.1.3 Parentheses count
at various points of strings.

$$(\ A + B\ )\quad)\ -\ (\ C + D$$
1 1 1 1 0 −1 −1 0 0 0 0

It is necessary to keep track not only of how many scopes have been opened, but also of their types. This information is needed because when a scope ender is encountered, we must know the symbol with which the scope was opened in order to ensure that it is being closed properly.

A stack may be used to keep track of the types of scopes encountered. Whenever a scope opener is encountered, it is pushed onto the stack. Whenever a scope ender is encountered, the stack is examined. If the stack is empty, then the scope ender does not have a matching opener and therefore the string is invalid. If, however, the stack is non-empty, we pop the stack and check whether the popped item corresponds to the scope ender. If a match occurs, we continue. If it does not, then the string is invalid. When the end of the string is reached, the stack must be empty; otherwise one or more scopes have been opened which have not been closed and the string is invalid. The algorithm for this procedure is outlined below. Figure 2.1.4 shows the state of the stack after reading in parts of the string $\{x + (y - [a + b]) * c - [(d + e)]\}/(h - (j - (k - [l - n])))$.

```
valid = true;             // assume the string is valid
s = the empty stack;
while (we have not read the entire string) {
      read the next symbol (symb) of the string;
      if (symb == '(' || symb == '[' || symb == '{')
            s.push(symb);

      if (symb == ')' || symb == ']' || symb == '}')
            if (s.empty())
                  valid = false;
            else {
                  i = s.pop();
                  if (i is not the matching opener of symb)
                        valid = false;
            } // end else
} // end while
if (!s.empty())
      valid = false;
if (valid)
      System.out.println("the string is valid");
else
      System.out.println("the string is invalid");
```

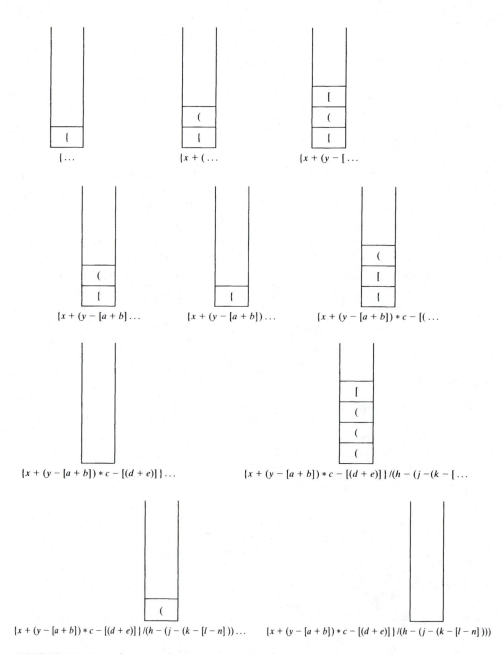

FIGURE 2.1.4   Parentheses stack at various stages of processing.

Let us see why the solution to this problem calls for the use of a stack. The last scope to be opened must be the first to be closed. This is simulated by a stack where the last element arriving is the first to leave. Each item on the stack represents a scope that has been opened but has not yet been closed. Pushing an item onto the stack corresponds to opening a scope, and popping an item from the stack corresponds to closing a scope, leaving one less scope open.

Note the correspondence between the number of elements on the stack in this example and the parenthesis count in the previous example. When the stack is empty (parenthesis count equals 0) and a scope ender is encountered, an attempt is being made to close a scope which has never been opened, so that the parenthesis pattern is invalid. In the first example, this is indicated by a negative parenthesis count, and in the second example by an inability to pop the stack. The reason a simple parenthesis count is inadequate for the second example is that we must keep track of the actual scope openers. This can be done by the use of a stack. Note also that at any point we examine only the element at the top of the stack. The configuration of parentheses below the top element is irrelevant while examining this top element. It is only after the top element has been popped that we concern ourselves with subsequent elements on a stack.

In general, a stack can be used in any situation that calls for a last-in, first-out discipline or that displays a nesting pattern. We shall see more examples of the use of stacks in the remaining sections of this chapter and, indeed, throughout the text.

The Stack as an Abstract Data Type

The representation of a stack as an abstract data type is straightforward. We use *eltype* to denote the type of the stack element and parameterize it with *eltype*.

```
abstract class <<eltype> STACK(eltype) {
    abstract STACK(eltype) s.empty()
    postcondition       empty == (s.length() == 0);

    abstract eltype STACK(eltype) s.pop()
    precondition        s.empty() == FALSE;
    postcondition       pop == s'.first();
                        s == s'.sub(1, s'.length() - 1);

    abstract STACK(eltype) s.push(eltype elt)
    postcondition       s == <elt> + s';
}
```

EXERCISES

2.1.1   Use the operations *push, pop, peek,* and *empty* to construct operations which do each of the following:

   a. Set *i* to the second element from the top of the stack, leaving the stack without its top two elements.

   b. Set *i* to the second element from the top of the stack, leaving the stack unchanged.

    c. Given an integer n, set i to the nth element from the top of the stack, leaving the stack without its top n elements.

    d. Given an integer n, set i to the nth element from the top of the stack, leaving the stack unchanged.

    e. Set i to the bottom element of the stack, leaving the stack empty.

    f. Set i to the bottom element of the stack, leaving the stack unchanged. (Hint: use another, auxiliary stack.)

    g. Set i to the third element from the bottom of the stack.

2.1.2 Simulate the action of the algorithm in this section for each of the following strings by showing the contents of the stack at each point.

    a. $(A + B\})$

    b. $\{[A + B] - [(C - D)]$

    c. $(A + B) - \{C + D\} - [F + G]$

    d. $((H) * \{([J + K])\})$

    e. $(((A))))$

2.1.3 Write an algorithm to determine whether an input character string is of the form

        x C y

where x is a string consisting of the letters 'A' and 'B' and y is the reverse of x (i.e., if x = "ABABBA" then y must equal "ABBABA"). At each point you may read only the next character in the string.

2.1.4 Write an algorithm to determine whether an input character string is of the form

        a D b D c D ... D z

where each string $a, b, \ldots, z$ is of the form of the string defined in Exercise 3. (Thus a string is in the proper form if it consists of any number of such strings separated by the character 'D'.) At each point you may read only the next character in the string.

2.1.5 Design an algorithm that does not use a stack to read a sequence of *push* and *pop* operations and determine whether or not underflow occurs on some *pop* operation. Implement the algorithm as a Java program.

2.1.6 What set of conditions is necessary and sufficient for a sequence of *push* and *pop* operations on a single stack (initially empty) to leave the stack empty and not cause underflow? What set of conditions is necessary for such a sequence to leave a nonempty stack unchanged?

2.2   REPRESENTING STACKS IN JAVA

Before programming a problem solution that uses a stack, we must decide how to represent a stack using the data structures that exist in our programming language. As we shall see, there are several ways to represent a stack in Java. We now consider the simplest of these. Throughout this text, you will be introduced to other possible representations. Each of them, however, is merely an implementation of the concept introduced in Section 1 of this chapter. Each has advantages and disadvantages in terms of how close it comes to mirroring the abstract concept of a stack and how much effort must be made by the programmer and the computer in using it.

A stack is an ordered collection of items, and Java already contains a data type which is an ordered collection of items—the array. Whenever a problem solution calls for use of a stack, therefore, it is tempting to begin a program by declaring a variable *stack* as an array. However, a stack and an array are two entirely different things. The number of elements in an array is fixed and is assigned by the declaration for the array. In general, the user cannot change this number. A stack, on the other hand, is fundamentally a dynamic object whose size is constantly changing as items are popped and pushed.

However, although an array cannot be a stack, it can be the home of a stack. That is, an array can be declared large enough for the maximum size of the stack. During the course of program execution, the stack can grow and shrink within the space reserved for it. One end of the array is the fixed bottom of the stack, while the top of the stack constantly shifts as items are popped and pushed. Thus another field is needed which, at each point during program execution, keeps track of the current position of the top of the stack.

A stack in Java may therefore be declared as a class containing two variables: an array to hold the elements of the stack, and an integer to indicate the position of the current stack top within the array. This may be done for a stack of integers by the declarations:

```
public class Stack {
  private final int STACKSIZE = 100;
  private int top;
  private int[] items;

  // stack methods to go here

} // end class Stack
```

Once this has been done, an actual stack object *s* may be declared by:

```
Stack s = new Stack();
```

Each time a new stack object is created, the class constructor is invoked.

```
public Stack() {
  items = new int[STACKSIZE];
  top = -1;
} // end constructor
```

Here, we assume that the elements of the stack *s* contained in the array *items* are integers and that the stack will at no time contain more than *STACKSIZE* integers. In this example *STACKSIZE* is set to 100 to indicate that the stack can contain 100 elements (*items*[0] through *items*[99]).

There is, of course, no reason to restrict a stack to contain only integers; *items* could just as easily have been declared as *items* = *new float* [*STACKSIZE*] or *items* = *new char* [*STACKSIZE*], or of whatever other class we might wish to give to the elements of the stack. As we will see later on in this chapter, should the need arise, a stack can contain objects of different types by using the Java vector class.

For simplicity, we assume, in the remainder of this section, that a stack is declared to have only homogeneous elements (so that vectors are not necessary). The identifier *top* must always be declared as an integer, since its value represents the position within the array *items* of the topmost stack element. Therefore, if the value of *top* is 4, there are five elements on the stack: *items*[0], *items*[1], *items*[2], *items*[3], and *items*[4]. When the stack is popped, the value of *top* is changed to 3 to indicate that there are now only four elements on the stack and that *items*[3] is the top element. On the other hand, if a new object is pushed onto the stack, the value of *top* must be increased by 1 to 5 and the new object inserted into *items*[5].

The empty stack contains no elements and therefore can be indicated by *top* equaling −1. In order to initialize a stack *s* to the empty state, the stack constructor *Stack* instantiates an integer array *items* of *STACKSIZE* elements and executes *top* = −1.

To determine, during the course of execution, whether or not a stack is empty, the condition *top* == −1 may be tested in an *if* statement, as follows:

```
if (top == -1)
        // stack is empty
else
        // stack is not empty
```

This test corresponds to the operation *s.empty*() that was introduced in Section 1. We may therefore write a method that returns *true* if the stack is empty and *false* if it is not empty, as follows:

```
public boolean empty() {
    if (top == -1)
                return true;
    else
                return false;
} // end empty
```

Once this method exists, a test for the empty stack is implemented by the statement

```
if (s.empty())
        // stack is empty
else
        // stack is not empty
```

You may wonder why we bother to define the method *empty* when we could just as easily have defined the variables *top* and *items* to be *public* and write *if(s.top* == −1) each time that we want to test for the empty condition. The answer is that we wish to make our programs more comprehensible and to make the use of a stack independent of its implementation. The Java language implements the concept of **information hiding**, restricting access to certain variables and methods of a class to methods of the class itself. By defining the variables *top* and *items* to be **private**, we indicate that they may only be referenced from within methods of the class *Stack*. The *empty* method, by contrast, is **public**. This means that it can be referenced by any program which includes the *Stack* class. Once we understand the stack concept, the phrase "*s.empty*()" is more meaningful than the phrase "*s.top* $== -1$". If we should later introduce a better implementation of a stack so that "*s.top* $== -1$" becomes meaningless, we would have to change every reference to the identifier *s.top* throughout the entire program. On the other hand, the phrase "*s.empty*()" would retain its meaning, since it is an inherent attribute of the stack concept rather than of an implementation of that concept. All that would be required to revise a program to accommodate a new implementation of the stack would be a possible revision of the declaration of the variables in the class definition and the rewriting of the method *empty*.

Aggregating the set of implementation-dependent trouble spots into small, easily identifiable units is an important method of making a program more understandable and modifiable. This concept is known as ***modularization***, in which individual methods are isolated into low-level ***modules*** whose properties are easily verifiable. These low-level modules can then be used by more complex routines which do not have to concern themselves with the details of the low-level modules, but only with their function. The complex routines may then themselves be viewed as modules by still higher level routines which use them independently of their internal details.

Programmers should always be concerned with the readability of the code they produce. A small amount of attention to clarity will save a large amount of time in debugging. Large and medium-sized programs will almost never be correct the first time they are run. If precautions are taken when a program is written to ensure that it is easily modifiable and comprehensible, the total time needed to get the program to run correctly is reduced sharply. For example, the *if* statement in the *empty* method could be replaced by the shorter, more efficient statement

```
return top == -1;
```

This statement is precisely equivalent to the longer statement

```
if (top == -1)
        return true;
    else
        return false;
```

This is because the value of the expression *top* $== -1$ is *true* if and only if the condition *top* $== -1$ is *true*. However, someone who reads a program will probably be much more comfortable reading the *if* statement. Often you will find that if you use "tricks" of the language in writing programs, you will be unable to decipher your own programs after putting them aside for a day or two.

While it is true that the Java programmer is often concerned with economy of code, it is also important to consider the time that will no doubt be spent in debugging. The mature professional (whether in Java or in any other language) is constantly concerned with the proper balance between code economy and code clarity.

Implementing the *pop* Operation

The possibility of underflow must be considered in implementing the *pop* operation, since the user may inadvertently attempt to pop an element from an empty stack. Of course, such an attempt is illegal and should be avoided. However, if such an attempt is made, the user should be informed of the underflow condition. We therefore introduce a method *pop* that performs the following three actions:

1. If the stack is empty, print a warning message and halt execution.
2. Remove the top element from the stack.
3. Return this element to the calling program.

We assume that the stack consists of integers. Of course, if the stack consists of some other type or object, the type of the *pop* method must be changed accordingly.

```
public int pop() {
        if (empty()) {
                System.out.println("Stack underflow");
                System.exit(1);
        }
        return items[top--];
} // end pop
```

Let us look at the *pop* method more closely. If the stack is not empty, the top element of the stack is retained as the returned value. This element is then removed from the stack by the expression *top*--. Assume that *top* equals 87 when the *pop* method is invoked; that is, there are eighty-eight items on the stack. The value of *items*[87] is returned and the value of *top* is changed to 86. Note that *items*[87] still retains its old value; the array *items* is not changed by the call to *pop*. However, the stack is modified, since it now contains only eighty-seven elements rather than eighty-eight. Recall that an array and a stack are two different objects. The array only provides a home for the stack. The stack itself contains only those elements between the zeroth element of the array and the *top*th element. Thus, reducing the value of *top* by 1 effectively removes an element from the stack. This is true despite the fact that *items*[87] retains its old value.

In order to use the *pop* method, the programmer can declare *int x* and write:

```
x = s.pop();
```

x then contains the value popped from the stack. If the intent of the *pop* operation is not to retrieve the element on the top of the stack, but only to remove it from the stack, the programmer can simply write:

```
s.pop();
```

which will pop the stack and discard the value that was removed from the stack. Of course, the programmer should ensure that the stack is not empty when the *pop* method is invoked. If the programmer is unsure of the state of the stack, its status may be determined by coding

```
if (!s.empty())
    x = s.pop();
else
    // take remedial action
```

If the programmer unwittingly invokes *pop* with an empty stack, the function prints the error message *stack underflow* and execution halts. Although this is an unfortunate state of affairs, it is far better than what would occur if the *if* statement in the *pop* method was omitted entirely. In that case, the value of *top* would be −1 and an attempt would be made to access the nonexistent element *items*[−1].

A programmer should always provide for the almost certain possibility of error. This can be done by including diagnostics that are meaningful in the context of the problem. By doing so, the programmer is able to pinpoint the source of any error that occurs and immediately take corrective action.

Testing for Exceptional Conditions

In the context of a given problem, it may not be necessary to halt execution immediately upon the detection of underflow. Instead, it might be more desirable for the *pop* method to signal the calling program that an underflow has occurred. Upon detecting this signal, the calling routine can take corrective action. Let us call the method that pops the stack and returns an indication as to whether underflow has occurred, *popAndTest*. If *popAndTest* is applied to a stack which is empty, a Boolean variable, let us call it *underflow*, is set to *true*. If the stack is not empty, *underflow* is set to *false* and the value at the top of the stack is popped from the stack and returned to the calling routine. Unlike the *pop* method, the *popAndTest* method must therefore be able to return two values. Since simple variable parameters in Java are always passed by value, there is no way to modify the values of simple variable arguments that are passed to a method. When using the *return* statement, Java methods may only return a single variable or object. Consequently we must define a utility class, *PopAndTestResult*, representing an object containing both values (the underflow status and the popped value) that must be returned by the *popAndTest* method.

```
class PopAndTestResult {
    public boolean underflow;
    public int value;

    PopAndTestResult(boolean u) {
        underflow = u;
    } // end constructor

    PopAndTestResult(boolean u, int v) {
        underflow = u;
        value = v;
    } // end constructor
} // end class popAndTestResult
```

The *popAndTest* method may then be written as:

```
public PopAndTestResult popAndTest() {
    if (empty())
            return new PopAndTestResult(true);
    else
```

```
                    return new PopAndTestResult(false, items[top--]);
    } // end popAndTest
```

In the calling program the programmer would write:

```
    // Declare an object to hold the result
    PopAndTestResult result;

    result = s.popAndTest();
    if (result.underflow)
        // take corrective action; result.value is undefined
    else
        // use value of result.value
```

When using the *popAndTest* method on an empty stack, it would be meaningless to refer to the contents of the *value* field of the *result* object. Thus two *PopAndTestResult* constructors are provided. Java allows method names to be **overloaded**. That is, the same method name can apply to different methods if their parameter **signatures** are of different types or number. The Java compiler automatically chooses the appropriate constructor based upon the parameters sent to the constructor at the time at the object is created.

Implementing the *Push* Operation

Let us now examine the *push* operation. It may seem as if this operation would be quite easy to implement using the array representation of a stack. A first attempt at a *push* method might be the following:

```
    public void push(int x) {
        items[++top] = x;
    } // end push
```

This routine makes room for the item *x* to be pushed onto the stack by incrementing *top* by 1, and then inserts *x* into the array *items*.

The routine directly implements the *push* operation introduced in the last section. Yet, as it stands, it is quite incorrect. It allows a subtle error to creep in, caused by using the array representation of the stack. Recall that a stack is a dynamic structure that is constantly allowed to grow and shrink and thus change its size. An array, on the other hand, is a fixed object of predetermined size. Thus it is quite conceivable that a stack may outgrow the array that was set aside to contain it. This occurs when the array is full; that is, when the stack contains as many elements as the array and an attempt is made to push yet another element onto the stack. The result of such an attempt is called an **overflow**.

Assume that the array *items* is full and that the Java *push* routine is called. Remember that the first array position is 0 and the arbitrary size (*STACKSIZE*) chosen for the array *items* is 100. The full array is then indicated by the condition $top == 99$, so that position 99 (the hundredth element of the array) is the current top of the stack.

When *push* is called, *top* is increased to 100 and an attempt is made to insert *x* into *items*[100]. Of course, since the upper bound of *items* is 99, this attempt at insertion results in an unpredictable error depending on the contents of the memory location following the last array position. An error message may be produced that is unlikely to relate to the cause of the error.

The *push* procedure must therefore be revised to read as follows:

```java
public void push(int x) {
   if (top == STACKSIZE - 1) {
         System.out.println("Stack Overflow");
         System.exit(1);
   }
      items[++top] = x;
} // end push
```

Here, we check whether the array is full before attempting to push another element onto the stack. The array is full if $top == STACKSIZE - 1$.

You should again note that if and when overflow is detected in *push*, execution halts immediately after an error message is printed. This action, as in the case of *pop*, may not be the most desirable. It might, in some cases, make more sense for the calling routine to invoke the *push* method with the instructions:

```java
if (s.pushAndTest(x))
   // overflow has been detected, x was not
   // pushed on stack. take remedial action.
else
   // x was successfully pushed on the stack
   // continue processing.
```

This allows the calling program to proceed after the call to *pushAndTest* whether or not overflow was detected. The method *pushAndTest* is left as an exercise for the reader.

Although the overflow and underflow conditions are treated similarly in *push* and *pop*, there is a fundamental difference between them. Underflow indicates that the *pop* operation cannot be performed on the stack and may indicate an error in the algorithm or the data. No other implementation or representation of the stack will cure the underflow condition. Rather, the entire problem must be rethought. (Of course, an underflow might occur as a signal for ending one process and beginning another. But in such a case, the *empty* method should be used before the *pop* method is invoked.)

Overflow, however, is not a condition that is applicable to a stack as an abstract data structure. Abstractly, it is always possible to push an element onto a stack. A stack is just an ordered set, and there is no limit to the number of elements that such a set can contain. The possibility of overflow is introduced when a stack is implemented by an array with only a finite number of elements, thereby prohibiting the growth of the stack beyond that number. It may very well be that the algorithm the programmer used is correct, just that the implementation of the algorithm did not anticipate that the stack would become so large. Thus, in some cases, an overflow condition can be corrected by changing the value of the constant *STACKSIZE* so that the array field *items* contains more elements. There is no need to change the methods *pop* or *push*, because they refer to whatever data structure was declared for the object *stack* in the program declarations. *push* also refers to the constant *STACKSIZE*, rather than to the actual value 100.

However, more often than not, an overflow does indicate an error in the program that cannot be attributed to a simple lack of space. The program may be in an infinite loop where items are constantly being pushed onto the stack and nothing is ever popped. Thus the stack will outgrow the array bound no matter how high it is set. The programmer should always check that this is not the case before indiscriminately raising the array bound. Often, the maximum stack size can be determined easily from the program and its inputs, so that if the stack does overflow, there is probably something wrong with the algorithm which the program represents.

Let us now look at our last operation on stacks, *s.peek*(), which returns the top element of a stack without removing it from the stack. As noted in the last section, *peek* is not really a primitive operation because it can be decomposed into the two operations:

```
x = s.pop();
s.push(x);
```

However, this is a rather awkward way to retrieve the top element of a stack. Why not ignore the decomposition noted above and directly retrieve the proper value? Of course, a check for the empty stack and underflow must then be explicitly stated, since the test is no longer handled by a call to *pop*.

We present a Java method *peek* for a stack of integers, as follows:

```java
public int peek() {
  if (empty()) {
      System.out.println("Stack underflow");
      System.exit(1);
  }
  return items[top];
} // end peek
```

You may wonder why we bother writing a separate method *peek* when a reference to *items*[*top*] would serve just as well. There are several reasons for this. First, the routine *peek* incorporates a test for underflow so that no mysterious error occurs if the stack is empty. Second, it allows the programmer to use a stack without worrying about its internal makeup. *items* and *top* are private to the stack class and cannot be accessed outside of a method of that class. Third, if a different implementation of a stack is introduced, the programmer need not comb through all of the places in the program that refer to *items*[*top*] in order to make the references compatible with the new implementation. Only the *peek* method would need to be changed.

EXERCISES

2.2.1   Write Java methods that use the routines presented in this chapter to implement the operations of Exercise 2.1.1.

2.2.2   Given a sequence of *push* and *pop* operations and an integer representing the size of an array in which a stack is to be implemented, design an algorithm to determine whether or not overflow occurs. The algorithm should not use a stack. Implement the algorithm as a Java program.

2.2.3   Implement the algorithms in Exercises 2.1.3 and 2.1.4 as Java programs.

2.2.4   Show how to implement a stack of integers in Java by using an array $s = new\ int\ [STACKSIZE]$ where $s[0]$ is used to contain the index of the top element of the stack, and where $s[1]$ through $s[STACKSIZE - 1]$ contain the elements on the stack. Write the class *stack* including the methods *pop*, *push*, *empty*, and for this implementation.

2.2.5   Implement a stack in Java in which each item on the stack is a varying number of integers. Choose a Java data structure for such a stack and design *push* and *pop* methods for it.

2.2.6   Consider a language that does not have arrays but does have stacks as a data type. That is, one can declare

```
stack s;
```

and the *push*, *pop*, *empty*, and *peek* operations are defined. Show how a one-dimensional array can be implemented by using these operations on two stacks.

2.2.7   Design a method for keeping two stacks within a single linear array $s[SPACESIZE]$ so that neither stack overflows until all of memory is used and an entire stack is never shifted to a different location within the array. Write Java methods *push*1, *push*2, *pop*1, and *pop*2 to manipulate the two stacks. (Hint: the two stacks grow toward each other.)

2.2.8   The Bashemin Parking Garage contains a single lane that holds up to ten cars. There is only a single entrance/exit to the garage at one end of the lane. If a customer arrives to pick up a car and it is not the one nearest the exit, all the cars blocking its path have to be moved out, his car is then driven out, and the other cars are then returned in the same order they were in originally. Write a program that processes a group of input lines. Each input line contains an 'A' for arrival or 'D' for departure, and a license plate number. Cars are assumed to arrive and depart in the order specified by the input. The program should print a message whenever a car arrives or departs. When a car arrives, the message should specify whether or not there is room for the car in the garage. If there is no room, the car leaves without entering the garage. When a car departs, the message should include the number of times that the car was moved out of the garage to allow other cars to depart.

2.3   EXAMPLE: INFIX, POSTFIX, AND PREFIX

Basic Definitions and Examples

This section examines a major application that illustrates the different types of stacks and the various operations and functions defined upon them. The example is also an important topic of computer science in its own right.

Consider the sum of A and B. We think of applying the *operator* "+" to the *operands* A and B and write the sum as $A + B$. This representation is called *infix*. There are two alternative notations for expressing the sum of A and B using the symbols A, B, and +. These are:

+A B   prefix

A B+   postfix

The prefixes "pre-", "post-", and "in-" refer to the relative position of the operator with respect to the two operands. In prefix notation the operator precedes the two operands, in postfix notation the operator follows the two operands, and in infix notation the operator is between the two operands. The prefix and postfix notations are not really as awkward to use as they might first appear. For example, a Java method to return the sum of the two arguments A and B is invoked by *add(A, B)*. The operator *add* precedes the operands A and B.

Let us now consider some additional examples. The evaluation of the expression $A + B * C$, as written in standard infix notation, requires knowledge of which of the two operations, + or *, is to be performed first. In the case of + and * we "know" that multiplication is to be done before addition (in the absence of parentheses to the contrary). Thus $A + B * C$ is interpreted as $A + (B * C)$ unless otherwise specified. We say that multiplication takes *precedence* over addition. Suppose we want to rewrite $A + B * C$ in postfix. Applying the rules of precedence, we first convert the portion of the expression that is evaluated first, namely the multiplication. By doing this conversion in stages we obtain:

A + (B * C)	parentheses for emphasis
A + (BC *)	convert the multiplication
A(BC *)+	convert the addition
ABC *+	postfix form

There are only two rules to remember during the conversion process: operations with the highest precedence are converted first, and after a portion of the expression has been converted to postfix, it is to be treated as a single operand. Consider the same example with the precedence of operators reversed by the deliberate insertion of parentheses.

(A + B) * C	infix form
(AB+) * C	convert the addition
(AB+)C *	convert the multiplication
AB + C *	postfix form

In this example, the addition is converted before the multiplication because of the parentheses. In going from $(A + B) * C$ to $(AB+) * C$, A and B are the operands and + is the operator. In going from $(AB+) * C$ to $(AB+)C *$, $(AB+)$ and C are the operands and * is the operator. The rules for converting from infix to postfix are simple, providing you know the order of precedence.

We consider five binary operations: addition, subtraction, multiplication, division, and exponentiation. The first four are available in Java and are denoted by the usual operators +, −, *, and /. The fifth, exponentiation, is represented by the operator $. The value of the expression $A \$ B$ is A raised to the B power, so that $3 \$ 2$ is 9. For these binary operators the following is the order of precedence (highest to lowest):

Exponentiation

Multiplication/Division

Addition/Subtraction

When unparenthesized operators of the same precedence are scanned, the order is assumed to be left to right except in the case of exponentiation, where the order is assumed to be from right to left. Thus $A + B + C$ means $(A + B) + C$ while $A \$ B \$ C$ means $A \$ (B \$ C)$. By using parentheses we can override the default precedence.

We give the following additional examples of converting from infix to postfix. Be sure that you understand each of these examples (and can do them on your own) before proceeding to the remainder of this section.

Infix	Postfix
A + B	AB+
A + B − C	AB + C −
(A + B) * (C − D)	AB + CD−*
A $ B * C − D + E / F/(G + H)	AB $ C * D − EF / GH +/+
((A + B) * C − (D − E)) $ (F + G)	AB + C * DE − − FG + $
A − B/(C * D $ E)	ABCDE $ */ −

The precedence rules for converting an expression from infix to prefix are identical. The only change from postfix conversion is that the operator is placed before the operands rather than after them. We present the prefix forms of the above expressions. Again, you should attempt to make the transformations on your own.

Infix	Prefix
A + B	+AB
A + B − C	−+ABC
(A + B) * (C − D)	* + AB − CD
A $ B * C − D + E / F/(G + H)	+ − * $ ABCD // EF + GH
((A + B) * C − (D − E)) $ (F + G)	$ − * + ABC − DE + FG
A − B/(C * D $ E)	−A / B * C $ DE

Note that the prefix form of a complex expression is not the mirror image of the postfix form, as can be seen from the second of the examples above, $A + B - C$. We will henceforth consider only postfix transformations and leave to the reader as exercises most of the work involving prefix.

One point immediately obvious about the postfix form of an expression is that it requires no parentheses. Consider the two expressions $A + (B * C)$ and $(A + B) * C$. While the parentheses in one of the two expressions are superfluous [by convention

$A + B * C = A + (B * C)]$, the parentheses in the second expression are necessary to avoid confusion with the first. The postfix forms of these expressions are:

Infix	Postfix
A + (B * C)	ABC * +
(A + B) * C	AB + C *

There are no parentheses in either of the two transformed expressions. The order of the operators in the postfix expressions determines the actual order of operations in evaluating the expression, making the use of parentheses unnecessary.

In going from infix to postfix we sacrifice the ability to note at a glance the operands associated with a particular operator. We gain, however, an unambiguous form of the original expression without the use of cumbersome parentheses. In fact, the postfix form of the original expression might look simpler were it not for the fact that it appears difficult to evaluate. For example, how do we know that if $A = 3$, $B = 4$, and $C = 5$ in the examples above, we have 345 * + equals 23 and 34 + 5 * equals 35?

Evaluating a Postfix Expression

The answer to this question lies in the development of an algorithm for evaluating expressions in postfix. Each operator in a postfix string refers to the previous two operands in the string. (Of course, one of these two operands may itself be the result of applying a previous operator.) Suppose that each time we read an operand we push it onto a stack. When we reach an operator, its operands will be the top two elements on the stack. We can then pop these two elements, perform the indicated operation on them, and push the result on the stack so that it will be available for use as an operand of the next operator. The following algorithm evaluates an expression in postfix using this method.

```
opndstk = the empty stack;
// scan the input string reading one element at a time into symb
while (not end of input) {
  symb = next input character;
  if (symb is an operand)
        opndstk.push(symb);
  else {
        // symb is an operator
        opnd2 = opndstk.pop();
        opnd1 = opndstk.pop();
        value = result of applying symb to opnd1 and opnd2;
        opndstk.push(value);
  } // end else
} // end while
return(opndstk.pop());
```

Let us now consider an example. Suppose we are asked to evaluate the following postfix expression:

$$6 \quad 2 \quad 3 \quad + \quad - \quad 3 \quad 8 \quad 2 \quad / \quad + \quad * \quad 2 \quad \$ \quad 3 \quad +$$

We show the contents of the stack *opndstk* and the variables *symb, opnd1, opnd2,* and *value* after each successive iteration of the loop. The top of *opndstk* is to the right.

symb	opnd1	opnd2	value	opndstk
6				6
2				6,2
3				6,2,3
+	2	3	5	6,5
−	6	5	1	1
3	6	5	1	1,3
8	6	5	1	1,3,8
2	6	5	1	1,3,8,2
/	8	2	4	1,3,4
+	3	4	7	1,7
*	1	7	7	7
2	1	7	7	7,2
$	7	2	49	49
3	7	2	49	49,3
+	49	3	52	52

Each operand is pushed onto the operand stack as it is encountered. Therefore, the maximum size of the stack is the number of operands that appear in the input expression. However, in dealing with most postfix expressions, the actual size of the stack needed is less than this theoretical maximum, since an operator removes operands from the stack. In the previous example, the stack never contained more than four elements despite the fact that eight operands appeared in the postfix expression.

Program to Evaluate a Postfix Expression

There are a number of questions we must consider before we can actually write a program to evaluate an expression in postfix notation. A primary consideration, as in all programs, is to define precisely the form and the restrictions, if any, on the input. Usually the programmer is presented with the form of the input and is required to design a program to accommodate the given data. On the other hand, we are in the fortunate position of being able to choose the form of our input. This enables us to construct a program that is not overburdened with transformation problems that overshadow the actual intent of the routine. Had we been confronted with data in a form that is awkward and cumbersome to work with, we could have relegated the transformations to various functions and used the output of these functions as input to our primary routine. In the "real world," recognition and transformation of input are a major concern.

Let us assume in this case that each input line is in the form of a string of digits and operator symbols. We assume that operands are single nonnegative digits, e.g. $0, 1, 2, \ldots, 8, 9$. For example, an input line might contain $345*+$ in the first five columns, followed by an end-of-line character ('\n'). We would like to write a program that reads input lines of this format, as long as there are any remaining, and prints for each line the original input string and the result of the evaluated expression.

Since the symbols are read as characters, we must find a method to convert the operand characters to numbers and the operator characters to operations. For example, we must have a method for converting the character '5' to the number 5 and the character '+' to the addition operation.

The conversion of a character to an integer can be handled easily in Java, using the *Character.digit* method. If c is a single-digit character, then the expression *Character.digit*$(c, 10)$ yields its numerical value in base 10. To implement the operation corresponding to an operator symbol, we use a method *oper* that accepts the character representation of an operator and two operands as input parameters, and returns the value of the expression obtained by applying the operator to the two operands. The body of the method will be presented shortly.

Our program consists of the definition of a class *Postfix* which implements a postfix string as well as methods for computing its value. We assume that a class *DoubleStack* representing a stack of ***double***s, with the methods *push* and *pop* and a constructor that creates an empty stack, has already been defined.

```
public class Postfix {
  public static void main(String[] args) throws IOException {
      String expr;

      System.out.println("Enter a postfix string: ");
      expr = readString();
      System.out.println("The original postfix expression is " + expr);
      System.out.println("Its value is " + eval(expr));
  } // end main

  public static String readString() throws IOException {
      char[] charArray = new char[80];
      int position = 0;
      char c;

      while ((c = (char) System.in.read()) != '\n')
          charArray[position++] = c;
      return   String.copyValueOf(charArray,0,position-1);
  } // end readString

  public static double eval(String expr) {
      char c;
      int position;
      double opnd1, opnd2, value;

      DoubleStack opndstk = new DoubleStack();
```

```
    for (position = 0; position < expr.length(); position++) {
        c = expr.charAt(position);
        if (Character.isDigit(c))
            // operand--convert the character representation of
            // the digit into double and push it into the
            // stack
            opndstk.push((double) Character.digit(c, 10));
        else {
            // operator
            opnd2 = opndstk.pop();
            opnd1 = opndstk.pop();
            value = oper(c, opnd1, opnd2);
            opndstk.push(value);
        } //end else
    } // end for
    return opndstk.pop();
} // end eval
public static double oper(char symb, double op1, double op2) {
    double value = 0;
    switch (symb) {
        case '+' : value = op1 + op2;                    break;
        case '-' : value = op1 - op2;                    break;
        case '*' : value = op1 * op2;                    break;
        case '/' : value = op1 / op2;                    break;
        case '$' : value = Math.pow(op1, op2);           break;
        default  : System.out.println("illegal operator:"
                    + symb);
                     System.exit(1);
    } // end switch
    return value;
} // end oper
} // end class Postfix
```

readString, invoked by the *main* method, is responsible for reading in characters from the keyboard, one at a time, into an array of characters. Input is terminated when the *System.in.read*() method encounters a carriage return. The *readString* method then creates a string object by invoking the *copyValueOf(array, n, m)* method, defined in the *String* class, from the characters in the *array* starting with character *n* through character *m*.

The main part of the program is, of course, the method *eval*, presented above. This method is merely the Java implementation of the evaluation algorithm, taking into account the specific environment and format of the input data and calculated outputs. *eval* invokes a method *isDigit* defined in the *Character* class which determines whether or not its argument is an operand. The declaration for a stack makes use of the *Stack* class defined in the previous section, suitably modified so that it may contain a stack of *double*. All of the methods (i.e., *pop*, *push*, and *empty*) that constitute the *DoubleStack* class are available to our program.

The method *oper* checks that its first argument is a valid operator and, if it is, determines the results of its operation on the next two arguments. For exponentiation, we make use of the *pow(op1, op2)* method defined in the *Math* class.

Limitations of the Program

Before we leave the program, we should note some of its deficiencies. Understanding what a program cannot do is as important as knowing what it can do. It should be obvious that attempting to use a program to solve a problem for which it was not intended will lead to chaos. Worse still is the case where an attempt is made to solve a problem with an incorrect program only to have the program produce incorrect results without the slightest trace of an error message. In these cases the programmer has no indication that the results are wrong, and may therefore make faulty judgments based on the results. For this reason, it is important for the programmer to understand the limitations of the program.

A major criticism of this program is that it does nothing in terms of error detection and recovery. If the data on each input line represent a valid postfix expression, then the program works. Suppose, however, that one input line has too many operators or operands or that they are not in the proper sequence. These problems could come about as a result of someone innocently using the program on a postfix expression that contains two-digit numbers, yielding an excessive number of operands. Or perhaps the user of the program is under the impression that the program handles negative numbers and they are to be entered with the minus sign, the same sign used to represent subtraction. These minus signs are treated as subtraction operators, resulting in an excess number of operators. Depending on the specific type of error, the computer may take one of several actions (e.g., halt execution, print erroneous results).

Suppose that at the final statement of the program, the stack *opndstk* is not empty. We get no error messages (because we asked for none) and *eval* returns a numerical value for an expression that was probably incorrectly stated in the first place. Suppose one of the calls to the *pop* method raises the *underflow* condition. Since we did not use the *popAndTest* method to pop elements from the stack, the program halts. This seems unreasonable, because faulty data on one line should not prevent the processing of additional lines. By no means are these the only problems that could arise. As exercises, you may wish to write programs that accommodate less restrictive inputs and some others that detect some of the errors listed above.

Converting an Expression from Infix to Postfix

We have thus far presented routines to evaluate a postfix expression. Although we have discussed a method for transforming infix to postfix, we have not as yet presented an algorithm for doing so. It is to this task that we now direct our attention. Once such an algorithm has been constructed, we will have the capability of reading an infix expression and evaluating it by converting it to postfix and then evaluating the postfix expression.

In our previous discussion, we mentioned that expressions within innermost parentheses must be converted to postfix so that they can be treated as single operands. In this fashion, parentheses can be successively eliminated until the entire expression is converted. The last pair of parentheses to be opened within a group of parentheses encloses the first expression in the group to be transformed. This last-in first-out behavior should immediately suggest the use of a stack.

Consider the two infix expressions $A + B * C$ and $(A + B) * C$ and their respective postfix versions, $ABC * +$ and $AB + C *$. In each case the order of the operands is the same as the order of the operands in the original infix expressions. In scanning the first expression, $A + B * C$, the first operand A can be inserted immediately into the postfix expression. Clearly the $+$ symbol cannot be inserted until its second operand, which has not yet been scanned, is inserted. Therefore, it must be stored away to be retrieved and inserted in its proper position. When the operand B is scanned, it is inserted immediately after A. Now, however, two operands have been scanned. What prevents the symbol $+$ from being retrieved and inserted? The answer is, of course, the $*$ symbol that follows, which has precedence over $+$. In the case of the second expression, the closing parenthesis indicates that the $+$ operation should be performed first. Remember that in postfix, unlike infix, the operator that appears earlier in the string is the one that is applied first.

Since precedence plays such an important role in transforming infix to postfix, let us assume the existence of a method, *precedence*(*op*1, *op*2), where *op*1 and *op*2 are characters representing operators. This function returns *true* if *op*1 has precedence over *op*2 when *op*1 appears to the left of *op*2 in an infix expression without parentheses. Otherwise *precedence*(*op*1, *op*2) returns *false*. For example, *precedence*('*', '+') and *precedence*('+', '+') are *true*, whereas *precedence*('+', '*') is *false*.

Let us now present an outline of an algorithm to convert an infix string without parentheses into a postfix string. Since we assume no parentheses in the input string, precedence is the only governor of the order in which operators appear in the postfix string. (The line numbers that appear in the algorithm will be used for future reference.)

```
1    opstk = the empty stack;
2    while (not end of input) {
3            symb = next input character;
4            If (symb is an operand)
                    add symb to the postfix string
5            else {
6                    while(!opstk.empty() &&
                            precedence(opstk.peek(), symb)) {
7                            topsymb = opstk.pop();
8                            add topsymb to the postfix string;
                    } // end while
9                    push(opstk, symb);
            } // end else
    } // end while
    // output any remaining operators
10   while(!opstk.empty()) {
11           topsymb = opstk.pop();
12           add topsymb to the postfix string;
    } // end while
```

Simulate the algorithm with such infix strings as "$A * B + C * D$" and "$A + B * C \ \$ \ D \ \$ \ E$" [where '\$' represents exponentiation, and *precedence*('\$', '\$') equals *false*] to convince yourself that it is correct. Note that at each point of the simulation, any operator on the stack has a lower precedence than all the operators above it. This is because the initial empty stack trivially satisfies this condition, and an operator is pushed onto the stack (line 9) only if the operator currently on top of the stack has a lower precedence than the incoming operator.

How must this algorithm be modified in order to accommodate parentheses? The answer, surprisingly, is not very much. When an opening parenthesis is read, it must be pushed onto the stack. This can be done by establishing the convention that *precedence*(*op*, '(') equals *false* for any operator symbol *op* other than a right parenthesis. In addition, we define *precedence*('(', *op*) to be *false* for any operator symbol *op*. [The case of *op*== ')' will be discussed shortly.] This ensures that an operator symbol appearing after a left parenthesis is pushed onto the stack.

When a closing parenthesis is read, all the operators up to the first opening parenthesis must be popped from the stack into the postfix string. This can be done by defining *precedence*(*op*, ')') as *true* for all operators *op* other than a left parenthesis. Special action must be taken when these operators have been popped off the stack and the opening parenthesis is uncovered. The opening parenthesis must be popped off the stack, and it and the closing parenthesis discarded rather than placed in the postfix string or on the stack. Let us set *precedence*('(', ')') to *false*. This ensures that upon reaching an opening parenthesis, the loop beginning at line 6 is skipped so that the opening parenthesis is not inserted into the postfix string. Execution therefore proceeds to line 9. However, since the closing parenthesis should not be pushed onto the stack, line 9 is replaced by the statement

```
9     if (opstk.empty() || symb != ')')
              opstk.push(symb);
      else // pop the open parenthesis and discard it
              topsymb = opstk.pop();
```

With the above conventions for the *precedence* method and the revision to line 9, the algorithm can be used to convert any infix string to postfix. We summarize the precedence rules for parentheses:

```
precedence('(',op) = false       for any operator op
precedence(op,'(') = false       for any operator op other than ')'
precedence(op,')') = true        for any operator op other than '('
precedence(')',op) = undefined   for any operator op (an attempt to
                                 compare  the  two  indicates  an
                                 error).
```

We illustrate this algorithm on some examples:

Example 1: $A + B * C$

The contents of *symb*, the postfix string, and *opstk* are shown after scanning each symbol. *opstk* is shown with its top to the right.

	symb	*postfix string*	*opstk*
1	A	A	
2	+	A	+
3	B	AB	+
4	*	AB	+*
5	C	ABC	+*
6		ABC*	+
7		ABC* +	

Lines 1, 3, and 5 correspond to the scanning of an operand, so the symbol (*symb*) is immediately placed on the postfix string. In line 2 an operator is scanned and the stack is found to be empty, so the operator is placed on the stack. In line 4 the precedence of the new symbol (*) is greater than the precedence of the symbol on the top of the stack (+), so the new symbol is pushed onto the stack. In steps 6 and 7 the input string is empty, so the stack is popped and its contents placed on the postfix string.

Example 2: $(A + B) * C$

symb	*postfix string*	*opstk*
(		(
A	A	(
+	A	(+
B	AB	(+
)	AB +	
*	AB +	*
C	AB + C	*
	AB + C*	

In this example, when the right parenthesis is encountered the stack is popped until a left parenthesis is encountered, at which point both parentheses are discarded. By using parentheses to force an order of precedence different than the default, the order of appearance of the operators in the postfix string is different than in example 1.

Example 3: $((A - (B + C)) * D) \$ (E + F)$

symb	postfix string	opstk
(		(
(		((
A	A	((
–	A	((–
(	A	((–(
B	AB	((–(
+	AB	((–(+
C	ABC	((–(+
)	ABC +	((–
)	ABC + –	(
*	ABC + –	(*
D	ABC + – D	(*
)	ABC + – D *	
$	ABC + – D *	$
(	ABC + – D *	$ (
E	ABC + – D * E	$ (
+	ABC + – D * E	$ (+
F	ABC + – D * EF	$ (+
)	ABC + – D * EF +	$
	ABC + – D * EF + $	

Why does the conversion algorithm seem so involved, whereas the evaluation algorithm seems so simple? The answer is that the former converts from one order of precedence (governed by the *precedence* method and the presence of parentheses) to the natural order (i.e., the operation to be executed first appears first). Because of the many combinations of elements at the top of the stack (if it is not empty) and possible incoming symbols, a large number of statements are necessary to ensure that every possibility is covered. In the latter algorithm, on the other hand, the operators appear in precisely the order they are to be executed. For this reason, the operands can be stacked until an operator is found, at which point the operation is performed immediately.

The motivation behind the conversion algorithm is the desire to output the operators in the order in which they are to be executed. In solving this problem by hand, we could follow vague instructions that require us to convert from the inside out. This works very well for humans doing a problem with pencil and paper (if they do not become confused or make a mistake). However, a program or an algorithm must be more precise in its instructions. We cannot be sure that we have reached the innermost parentheses or the operator with the highest precedence until additional symbols have been scanned. At that time, we must backtrack to some previous point.

Rather than backtrack continuously, we make use of the stack to "remember" the operators encountered previously. If an incoming operator is of greater precedence than the one on top of the stack, then this new operator is pushed onto the stack. This means that when all the elements in the stack are finally popped, the new operator will precede the former top in the postfix string (which is correct since it has higher precedence). If, on the other hand, the precedence of the new operator is less than that of the top of the stack, then the operator at the top of the stack should be executed first. Therefore the top of the stack is popped and the incoming symbol is compared with the new top, and so on. Parentheses in the input string override the order of operations. Thus, when a left parenthesis is scanned, it is pushed on the stack. When its associated right parenthesis is found, all the operators between the two parentheses are placed on the output string, because they are to be executed before any operators appearing after the parentheses.

Program to Convert an Expression from Infix to Postfix

There are two things that we must do before we actually start writing a program. The first is to define precisely the format of the input and output. The second is to construct, or at least define, the routines that the main routine depends upon. We assume that the input consists of strings of characters, one string per input line. The end of each string is signaled by the occurrence of an end-of-line character ('\n'). For the sake of simplicity, we assume that all operands are single-character letters or digits. All operators and parentheses are represented by themselves, and '$' represents exponentiation. The output is a character string. These conventions make the output of the conversion process suitable for the evaluation process, provided that all the single-character operands in the initial infix string are digits.

In transforming the conversion algorithm into a program, we make use of a stack of characters *charStack*, including the methods *empty, pop, push*, and *popAndTest* and a constructor to create an empty stack. In order to create a *String* object, we make use of the *readString* method presented earlier. We also make use of a method *isOperand* that returns *true* if its argument is an operand and *FALSE* otherwise. This simple method is left to the reader.

Similarly, the *precedence* method is left to the reader as an exercise. It accepts two single-character operator symbols as arguments and returns *true* if the first has precedence over the second when it appears to the left of the second in an infix string, and *false* otherwise. The method should, of course, incorporate the parentheses conventions previously introduced.

All of these methods are incorporated into a class *Infix* which may be used to process a series of characters representing an infix expression. The class contains the methods described above as well as the conversion method *postfix* and a *main* method that calls it. The *main* method reads a line containing an expression in infix, calls the routine *postfix*, and prints the postfix string. The body of the class follows:

```
public class Infix {
  public final static int MAXCOLS = 80;
  public static void main(String[] args) throws IOException {
        String infix;
        System.out.println("Enter an infix string: ");
        infix = readString();
```

```
                    System.out.println("The original infix expression is " +
                    infix);
                    System.out.println("In postfix it is " + postfix(infix));
          } // end main
       public static String postfix(String infix) {
              int position, outpos = 0;
              char symb, topsymb = '+';
              char[] postr = new char[MAXCOLS];
              charStack opstk = new charStack();
              PopAndTestResult result;
              for (position = 0; position < infix.length(); position++) {
                    symb = infix.charAt(position);
                    if (isOperand(symb))
                           postr[outpos++] = symb;
                    else {
                         result = opstk.popAndTest();
                         if (!result.underflow)
                             topsymb = result.value;
                         while (!result.underflow && precedence(topsymb, symb)){
                                postr[outpos++] = topsymb;
                                result = opstk.popAndTest();
                                if (!result.underflow)
                                       topsymb = result.value;
                         } // end while
                         if (!result.underflow)
                                opstk.push(topsymb);
                         if (result.underflow || (symb != ')'))
                                opstk.push(symb);
                         else
                                topsymb = opstk.pop();
                    } // end else
              } // end for
            while (!opstk.empty())
                    postr[outpos++] = opstk.pop();
            return  String.copyValueOf(postr,0,outpos);
       } // end postfix
     public static String readString() throws IOException {
          // presented earlier
     public static boolean isOperand(char symb) {
          // left for the reader
     public static boolean precedence(char op1, char op2) {
          // left for the reader
 } // end class Infix
```

The program has one major flaw, in that it does not check whether the input string is a valid infix expression. In fact, it would be instructive for you to examine the operation of this program when it is presented with a valid postfix string as input. As an exercise you are asked to write a program that checks whether or not an input string is a valid infix expression.

We can now write a method to read an infix string and compute its numerical value. If the original string consists of single-digit operands with no letter operands, the following method reads the original string and prints its value.

```
public static void main(String[] args) throws IOException {
    String instring, poststring;
    System.out.println("Enter an infix string: ");
    instring = readString();
    System.out.println("The original infix expression is " + instring);
    poststring = postfix(instring);
    System.out.println("In postfix it is " + poststring);
    System.out.println("Its value is " + eval(poststring));
} // end main
```

The class that calls this method will reference both the *CharStack* class and the *DoubleStack* class because *postfix* uses a stack of character (*char*) operators (i.e., *opstk*), while *eval* uses a stack of *double* operands (i.e., *opndstk*). The appropriate stack-manipulation routines (*pop*, *push*, etc.) will be automatically be invoked depending on the type of the stack object being referenced. As we will soon see, it is possible to declare a stack that can contain objects of varying types.

Most of our attention in this section has been devoted to transformations involving postfix expressions. An algorithm to convert an infix expression into postfix scans characters from left to right, stacking and unstacking as necessary. If it were necessary to convert from infix to prefix, the infix string could be scanned from right to left and the appropriate symbols entered in the prefix string from right to left. Since most algebraic expressions are read from left to right, postfix is a more natural choice.

The programs above are by no means comprehensive or unique. They are merely indicative of the types of routines one could write to manipulate and evaluate postfix expressions. There are many variations of these routines that are equally acceptable. Some of the early high-level language compilers used routines such as *eval* and postfix to handle algebraic expressions. Since that time, more sophisticated techniques have been developed to handle these problems.

EXERCISES

2.3.1   Transform each of the following expressions to prefix and postfix.

   a. $A + B - C$

   b. $(A + B) * (C - D) \$ E * F$

   c. $(A + B) * (C \$ (D - E) + F) - G$

   d. $A + (((B - C) * (D - E) + F)/G) \$ (H - J)$

2.3.2   Transform each of the following prefix expressions to infix.

   a. $+ - ABC$

   b. $+ A - BC$

   c. $++A - *\$ BCD/ + EF*GHI$

   d. $+-\$ ABC * D ** EFG$

2.3.3 Transform each of the following postfix expressions to infix.

   a. $AB + C -$

   b. $ABC + -$

   c. $AB - C + DEF -+ \$$

   d. $ABCDE-+ \$*EF* -$

2.3.4 Apply the evaluation algorithm in the text to evaluate the following postfix expressions. Assume $A = 1, B = 2, C = 3$.

   a. $AB + C - BA + C\$ -$

   b. $ABC + *CBA -+ *$

2.3.5 Modify the *eval* method to accept as input a character string of operators and operands representing a postfix expression and to create the fully parenthesized infix form of the original postfix. For example, $AB+$ would be transformed into $(A + B)$, and $AB + C -$ would be transformed into $((A + B) - C)$.

2.3.6 Write a single program combining the features of *eval* and *postfix* to evaluate an infix string. Use two stacks, one for operands and the other for operators. Do not first convert the infix string to postfix and then evaluate the postfix string; instead, evaluate as you go along.

2.3.7 Write a *prefix* method to accept an infix string and create the prefix form of that string, assuming that the string is read from right to left and that the prefix string is created from right to left.

2.3.8 Write a Java program to convert

   a. a prefix string to postfix.

   b. a postfix string to prefix.

   c. a prefix string to infix.

   d. a postfix string to infix.

2.3.9 Write a Java method *reduce* that accepts an infix string and forms an equivalent infix string with all superfluous parentheses removed. Can this be done without using a stack?

2.3.10 Assume a machine that has a single register and six instructions.

LD	A	places the operand A into the register
ST	A	places the contents of the register into the variable A
AD	A	adds the contents of the variable A to the register
SB	A	subtracts the contents of the variable A from the register
ML	A	multiplies the contents of the register by the variable A
DV	A	divides the contents of the register by the variable A

Write a program that accepts a postfix expression containing single-letter operands and the operators $+, -, *$, and $/$ and prints a sequence of instructions to evaluate the expression and leave the result in the register. Use variables of the form

TEMPn as temporary variables. For example, using the postfix expression $ABC*+DE-/$ should print the following:

```
LD      B
ML      C
ST      TEMP1
LD      A
AD      TEMP1
ST      TEMP2
LD      D
SB      E
ST      TEMP3
LD      TEMP2
DV      TEMP3
ST      TEMP4
```

2.4   STACK OF OBJECTS OF VARYING TYPES

There are a number of drawbacks to the simple array implementation of stacks that we presented in the previous two sections. First, although two stacks are used in the complete solution (a stack of operators in the *postfix* routine and a stack of operands in the *eval* routine), only a single stack is used at any one time. Nevertheless, two separate stacks must be declared. It would be nicer if a single stack could be declared and used for both purposes.

Second, because the stacks are not of the same type, it is necessary to declare them separately. And with the separate declarations, it is necessary to provide separate sets of primitive routines (i.e., *push, pop, empty*, etc.). This, in turn, implies that when the implementation of a stack is to be changed to a different underlying data structure, it must be changed for each type of stack that we have created.

It would be more efficient if we could design a system around a stack of indeterminate type on which the primitive routines could be defined. We would then create instances of such a stack as necessary. This would eliminate the need to create separate classes.

Java, being a true object-oriented language, provides us with the tools to create and manipulate an object of indeterminate type. The reader will recall that all objects in Java are said to be derived from the superclass *Object*. With the exception of the primitive types, *int, double, char,* or *boolean*, an object of any type may be stored in an object of type *Object*. In order to allow primitive values to also be part of an object, Java provides the programmer with a series of **wrapper** classes (*Integer, Double, Character, Boolean,* etc.), defined in the *java.lang* package, that may be used to contain (or wrap) the primitive types. That is, an object of type *Integer* contains a single data element of type *int*, an object of type *Double* contains a single data element of type *double*, and so on. It is the programmer's responsibility to wrap any primitive types in the appropriate wrapper and "unwrap" the item extracted from the data structure prior to assigning it to a variable of primitive type. For example, when pushing a variable *x*, declared by:

```
int x;
```

it is first necessary to wrap *x*, which is of type *int*, in an object of type *Integer*. This may be done by creating an object of type *Integer* and using its constructor method before pushing it into the stack using the *push* method of the *Stack* class:

```
s.push(new Integer(x));
```

Similarly, when using the *pop* method of the *Stack* class, it is necessary to first cast the reference to *Object* into a reference to the *Integer* object. Once this has been done, the *intValue* method of the *Integer* class may be used to extract the value wrapped within the item originally pushed into the stack. These two operations may be combined by writing:

```
x = ((Integer) s.pop()).intValue();
```

Using an *Object* allows the programmer to define the features of a data structure without reference to a particular type, with the method using the data structure being responsible for properly interpreting the object placed on the data structure. We now present a complete *ObjectStack* class followed by a short method illustrating its use.

```java
public class ObjectStack {
  private final int STACKSIZE = 100;
  private int top;
  private Object[] items;

  public ObjectStack() {
      items = new Object[STACKSIZE];
      top = -1;
  } // end constructor

  public boolean empty() {
      if (top == -1)
              return true;
      return false;
  } // end empty

  public void push(Object x) {
      if (top > STACKSIZE - 1) {
              System.out.println("Stack Overflow");
              System.exit(1);
      }
      items[++top] = x;
  } // end push

  public Object pop() {
      if (empty()) {
              System.out.println("Stack underflow");
              System.exit(1);
      }
      return items[top--];
  } // end pop

  public PopAndTestResult popAndTest() {
      if (empty())
              return new PopAndTestResult(true);
```

```
        else
                return new PopAndTestResult(false, items[top--]);
    } // end popAndTest

    public Object peek() {
        if (empty()) {
            System.out.println("Stack underflow");
            System.exit(1);
        }
        return items[top];
    } // end peek

} // end class Stack

class PopAndTestResult {
    public boolean underflow;
    public Object value;

    PopAndTestResult(boolean u) {
        underflow = u;
    } // end constructor

    PopAndTestResult(boolean u, Object v) {
        underflow = u;
        value = v;
    } // end constructor
} // end class PopAndTestResult
```

As an example of the use of an *ObjectStack*, consider the following example. Assume a class defined as follows:

```
public class ClassA {
    private double value;
    private char character;

    public ClassA(double v, char c) {
        value = v;
        character = c;
    } // end constructor

    public void println() {
        System.out.println(" " + value + " " + character);
    }
} // end ClassA class
```

The following application illustrates how both *ClassA* objects and integers wrapped in an ***Integer*** object may be contained within a single stack.

```
public class SampleObjectStack {
    public static void main(String[] args) {
        // Define and declare a new stack of objects
        ObjectStack s = new ObjectStack();
```

```
// Use the stack to hold Integer objects
int x;
System.out.println(s.empty());
for (int i = 0; i < 10; i++)
        // create an Integer Object
        s.push(new Integer(i));
System.out.println("Result of peek = " + s.peek());
while (!s.empty()) {
        System.out.println("Stack is not empty");
        // extract the int from the Integer object
        x = ((Integer) s.pop()).intValue();
        System.out.println(" " + x);
}
System.out.println("Stack is empty");

// Use the same stack to hold ClassA objects
ClassA a;
System.out.println(s.empty());
for (int i = 65; i < 91; i++) {          // (char) 65 through
        // (char) 91 are the characters 'A' through 'Z'
        a = new ClassA(i, (char) i);
        s.push(a);
}
while (!s.empty()) {
        System.out.println("Stack is not empty");
        a = (ClassA) s.pop();
        a.println();
}
System.out.println("Stack is empty");
} // end main method
} // end SampleObjectClass
```

Stacks in Java Using Vectors

One additional drawback of our stack implementation is its reliance on a fixed-size array. Often the programmer does not know in advance the size of the stack, which leads to either under- or overestimation of the amount of storage allocated to the stack.

The *java.util* package contains a number of classes implementing the so-called **container** types. These classes are very useful to the programmer, since they allow a number of different objects to be referred to by a single entity. One of the most useful classes defined in this package is known as a **Vector**. A vector is in many ways like an array, with two major exceptions. Unlike an array, which is fixed in size, the vector class provides a data structure that may change dynamically in size in response to an application's changing storage requirements. Left to its own devices, a vector will grow on its own as items are added. Although we do not discuss this aspect of vectors in detail, the reader should consult the Java documentation in order to choose one of the many alternative methods defined in this class for changing a vector's size.

Of far greater importance, a vector is designed to store references to *Objects*.

Note, however, that only objects may be referenced by vectors. Thus items of primitive type, such as *int, double, char*, or *boolean*, may not be directly referenced by a vector. As we explained earlier, in order to get around this restriction, Java provides the programmer with a series of **wrapper** classes, defined in the *java.lang* package (*Integer, Double, Character, Boolean*, etc.), that may be used to contain (or wrap) the primitive types. It is the programmer's responsibility to provide some way to figure out what kind of object is actually stored at each position of the vector and to make sure that the use of a method is consistent with what has been placed at that location. This may often be accomplished by storing an identifying field as part of each object whose value indicates the type of object currently in use.

We now present a complete implementation of the *VectorStack* class.

```java
import java.util.Vector;
public class VectorStack {
  private int top;
  private Vector items;

  public VectorStack() {
        items = new Vector();
        top = -1;
  } // end constructor

  public boolean empty() {
        if (top == -1)
                return true;
        return false;
  } // end empty

  public void push(Object x) {
        items.add(++top, x);
  } // end push

  public Object pop() {
        if (empty()) {
                System.out.println("Stack underflow");
                System.exit(1);
        }
        return items.remove(top--);
  } // end pop

  public PopAndTestResult popAndTest() {
        if (empty())
                return new PopAndTestResult(true);
        else
                return new PopAndTestResult(false, items.remove(top--));
  } // end popAndTest

  public Object peek() {
     if (empty()) {
                System.out.println("Stack underflow");
                System.exit(1);
     }
```

```
            return items.get(top);
    } // end peek
} // end Stack class

class PopAndTestResult {
    public boolean underflow;
    public Object value;

  PopAndTestResult(boolean u) {
      underflow = u;
  } // end constructor

  PopAndTestResult(boolean u, Object v) {
      underflow = u;
      value = v;
  } // end constructor
} // end PopAndTestResult class
```

Dealing with Heterogeneous Data

Thus far, the stacks we have seen have always contained homogeneous elements; that is, all the elements of a stack at any one time were all of the same type. Thus, when we popped an element from a stack, we always knew what type the element was, even if it was wrapped in an *Object*.

Sometimes, however, we want objects of different types on a stack. One way of handling this is by having all the different-typed objects derive from a single type object that contains within it the type of the object within.

For example, consider an insurance company that offers three kinds of policies: life, auto, and home. A policy number identifies each insurance policy, of whatever kind. For all three types of insurance, it is necessary to have the policyholder's name, policy number, the amount of insurance, and the monthly premium payment. A class *Insurance* may be defined to hold the data common to each of the three kinds of insurance, as follows:

```
public class Insurance {
  protected final int LIFE = 1;
  protected final int AUTO = 2;
  protected final int HOME = 3;

  protected int kind;                     // LIFE, AUTO, or HOME
  protected int polnumber;
  protected double amount;
  protected double premium;
  protected String name;

  public int getKind() {
      return kind;
  } // end getKind

  public String getName() {
      return name;
  } // end getName

  public String policyType() {
      if (kind == LIFE)
              return "LIFE";
```

```
    else if (kind == AUTO)
            return "AUTO";
    else  if (kind == HOME)
            return "HOME";
    else {
            System.out.println("Invalid Insurance Type");
            System.exit(1);
            return "";
    }

} // end policyType

// other methods to process generic insurance policies

} // end Insurance
```

The member *kind* is used to distinguish among the three types of insurance. If its value is LIFE (1), then the class holds a life insurance policy; if AUTO (2), an auto insurance policy; and if HOME (3), a home insurance policy. The *policyType* and *getKind* methods may be applied to a variable of type *Insurance* in order to determine which type of policy it represents. Of course additional methods (e.g., *getName*, as shown above) would be defined to process the information contained in an object of type *Insurance.*

In addition to the information common to all three types of insurance, there are several items that may be unique to a specific insurance policy. Thus for auto and home insurance policies, a deductible amount is needed. For a life insurance policy, the insured's birth date and beneficiary are needed. For an auto insurance policy, a license number, state, car model, and year are required. For a homeowner's policy, an indication of the age of the house is required. Thus the *Insurance* class may be extended by defining three additional classes, *LifeInsurance*, *AutoInsurance*, and *HomeInsurance*:

```
public class LifeInsurance extends Insurance {
  private String beneficiary;
  private int yearBorn;

  public void setLife(int polnumber, String name, double amount,
                              double premium, String b, int y) {
        kind = LIFE;
        this.polnumber = polnumber;
        this.name = name;
        this.amount = amount;
        this.premium = premium;
        beneficiary = b;
        yearBorn = y;
  } // end setHome

  public String getBenefic() {
        return beneficiary;
  } // end getBenefic

  public int getYear() {
        return yearBorn;
  } // end getYear
```

```
    // other methods to process life insurance policies

} // end LifeInsurance

public class AutoInsurance extends Insurance {
  private double autoDeduct;
  private String license;
  private String state;
  private String model;
  private int year;

  public void setAuto(int polnumber, String name, double amount,
     double premium, double d, String l, String s, String m, int y) {
        kind = AUTO;
        this.polnumber = polnumber;
        this.name = name;
        this.amount = amount;
        this.premium = premium;
        autoDeduct = d;
        license = l;
        state = s;
        model = m;
        year = y;
  } // end setAuto

  public double getDeduct() {
        return autoDeduct;
  } // end getDeduct

  public String getLicense() {
        return license;
  } // end getLicense

  public String getState() {
        return state;
  } // end getState;

  public String getModel() {
        return model;
  } // end getModel;

  public int getYear() {
        return year;
  } // end getYear

  // other methods to process auto insurance policies

} // end AutoInsurance

public class HomeInsurance extends Insurance {
  private double homeDeduct;
  private int yearBuilt;
  public void setHome(int polnumber, String name, double amount,
                              double premium, double h, int y) {
        kind = HOME;
```

```
        this.polnumber = polnumber;
        this.name = name;
        this.amount = amount;
        this.premium = premium;
        homeDeduct = h;
        yearBuilt = y;
    } // end setHome

    public double getDeduct() {
        return homeDeduct;
    } // end getDeduct

    public int getYear() {
        return yearBuilt;
    } // end getYear

    // other methods to process home insurance policies

} // end HomeInsurance
```

Through the process of ***inheritance***, by specifying that these classes ***extend*** *Insurance*, all the members and methods of the *Insurance* class are also available to variables which are declared to be of type *LifeInsurance*, *AutoInsurance*, and *HomeInsurance*. Note that the members of the *Insurance* class are declared to be ***protected***. This makes them available to all the subclasses that may extend the *Insurance* class, yet protects them from being accessed from outside of the *Insurance* class hierarchy. Also note that the *setLife*, *setAuto*, and *setHome* methods make use of the ***this*** reference keyword. This is necessary because the variables on the left-hand side of the assignment statements refer to an object of the class itself, while those on the right of the assignment statement, although of the same name, refer to parameters of the method. Whenever there is ambiguity about which variable the identifier refers to, the *this* reference keyword may be used to specify a variable of the class itself.

A program wishing to use these classes may then declare an object of these types and manipulate them using the appropriate methods of each class.

```
AutoInsurance    policy1 = new AutoInsurance();
HomeInsurance    policy2 = new HomeInsurance();
LifeInsurance    policy3 = new LifeInsurance();

policy1.setAuto(1111, "Tom Sawyer", 1000.00, 200.00, 500,
                                    "EMT-1", "NY", "Chevy", 1996);
policy2.setHome(2222, "Huck Finn", 2000.00, 100.00, 500, 1940);
policy3.setLife(3333, "Becky", 5000.00, 100, "Tom Sawyer", 1950);
System.out.println("Kind = " + policy1.policyType() + " Name = " +
                policy1.getName() + " Deductible = " +
                policy1.getDeduct());
System.out.println("Kind = " + policy2.policyType() + " Name = " +
                policy2.getName() +   " Deductible = " +
                policy2.getDeduct());
System.out.println("Kind = " + policy3.policyType() + "  Name = " +
                policy3.getName() +   " Beneficiary =" +
                policy3.getBenefic());
```

The *getName* method may be used by all three policy types became it is a member of the superclass *Insurance*. Although the *getDeduct* method is defined for both the *AutoInsurance* and *HomeInsurance* classes, when it is invoked Java automatically uses the appropriate method for that object. It would, of course, be illegal to use the *getBenefic* method on either *policy1* or *policy2*, since that method is not defined for objects of the *AutoInsurance* and *HomeInsurance* classes.

Now suppose an insurance agent wished to maintain a list of the various policies that have been sold. In order to maintain a list of objects of different classes, a variable of type *Vector* would be defined. Since the *Vector* class is defined in the *java.util* package, it must be imported into our program before it may be referenced.

```
import java.util.*;
```

For example, the vector *policies*, declared by

```
Vector policies = new Vector();
```

may contain life, auto, and home insurance policies. Of course there is nothing to stop the programmer from inserting an object of a totally unrelated type into this vector. However, by carefully designing the methods used to insert items into the vector, the programmer can ensure that it will only reference appropriate objects. Elements are added to the end of the vector, increasing its size by 1, using the **addElement(object)** method. Thus, if you wished to insert *policy1*, *policy2*, and *policy3* objects, defined earlier, into the *policies* vector, you could write:

```
policies.addElement(policy1);
policies.addElement(policy2);
policies.addElement(policy3);
```

Each time the *addElement* method is invoked, it inserts a reference to its argument into the end of the vector. Should the vector be full, it automatically expands to make room available for the newly inserted objects. In order to determine the number of items currently referenced by a vector, the **size()** method is used.

It is also possible to insert an object in a specific position of a vector by invoking the **insertElementAt(object, n)** method, where *n* specifies the position of the vector where the object is inserted. This method makes room for the new object by shifting all elements from position *n* onward one position higher in the vector. Thus, if a vector contains elements in positions 0, 1, 2, 3, and 4, *insertElementAt(object, 3)* inserts *object* in position 3, moves the object formerly in position 3 to position 4, and the object formerly in position 4 to the newly created position 5. Alternatively, the **setElementAt(object, n)** method replaces the element at position *n* of the vector with the reference to *object*.

The **elementAt(i)** method is used to access an element of a vector. Since the vector contains only references to objects, rather than the objects themselves, it is necessary to **cast** the reference into the appropriate type. Suppose it is desired to print the information about each of the insurance policies referenced by the *policies* vector. This can be done as follows:

```
AutoInsurance    autoPolicy;
HomeInsurance    homePolicy;
LifeInsurance    lifePolicy;
```

```
for (int i = 0; i < policies.size(); i++) {
    System.out.println("Policy Type = " +
                (((Insurance) policies.elementAt(i)).policyType());

    switch (((Insurance) policies.elementAt(i)).getKind()) {
      case LIFE: lifePolicy = (LifeInsurance) policies.elementAt(i);
             System.out.println("Name = " + lifePolicy.getName()+
                   " Beneficiary = " + lifePolicy.getBenefic());
             break;

      case AUTO: autoPolicy = (AutoInsurance) policies.elementAt(i);
             System.out.println("Name = " + autoPolicy.getName() +
                   " Deductible = " + autoPolicy.getDeduct());
             break;

      case HOME: homePolicy = (HomeInsurance) policies.elementAt(i);
             System.out.println("Name = " + homePolicy.getName() +
                   " Deductible = " + homePolicy.getDeduct());
             break;

    } // end case
} // end for
```

The reader is encouraged to investigate the many other vector methods defined in the *java.util* package. The reader is also asked, as an exercise, to define a stack of insurance policies implemented by a vector.

The *Class* Class and the *java.lang.reflect* Package

In the previous example, it was necessary for the programmer to dedicate a member (*kind*) of the parent class, *Insurance*, to distinguish among the three types of insurance. However, it is not really necessary to keep a special extra member to do this. The Java runtime system maintains information about all runtime objects. Information on a class is kept in objects of a special class named *Class*. The programmer may access this information using this class. Using the methods defined in the *java.lang.reflect* package, an application may query the runtime system in order to identify properties of the class. Two methods, in particular, may be used to identify the class to which a particular object belongs.

In order to illustrate these ideas, consider the following example. Suppose a bank wishes to maintain a complete record of transactions on a given account, with the possibility of rolling back the transactions to any given point. Also suppose that there are two types of transactions which the bank tracks: ordinary transactions (e.g., deposits and withdrawals) and designated transactions (e.g., direct deposits, automatic debits). Ordinary transactions may be represented by a ***double*** (positive numbers represent a deposit, and negative amounts represent withdrawals). Designated deposits include both an amount and a ***string*** designation.

While an ordinary transaction item may be declared as

```
double amount;
```

a designated transaction will be declared as

```
public class DesignatedTransaction {
  private double amount;
  private String designation;

  public DesignatedTransaction(double a, String d) {
      amount = a;
      designation = d;
  } // end constructor

  public void println() {
      System.out.println(" " +  designation + " "  + amount);
  }
} // end DesignatedTransaction class
```

Because rolling back a transaction represents a LIFO behavior, we decide to store the transactions on a stack. However, our stack must accommodate both ordinary and designated transactions. We therefore choose to implement a heterogeneous *ObjectStack*, as shown in the first part of this section. Of course it will be necessary to identify whether an object popped from the stack represents an ordinary or designated transaction. We may dynamically use the methods of the *Class* class to discover what type of transaction the object represents. The following application illustrates these ideas:

```
import java.lang.reflect.*;     // To use the Java class Class

public class BankTransactions {
  public static void main(String[] args) {
      // Define and declare a stack of objects
      ObjectStack stack = new ObjectStack();

      double amount;
      DesignatedTransaction transaction;

      // To determine the class object in use.
      Object o;
      Class c;
      String s;

      // Create a Double object and push it on the stack
      amount = 1000.00;
      stack.push(new Double(amount));

      // Create a DesignatedTransaction object and push it on
      // the stack
      transaction = new DesignatedTransaction(5000.00,
                  "Direct Deposit");
      stack.push(transaction);

      while (!stack.empty()) {
              // Use the reflection methods to get the name of
              // the referenced class. In the code below, o.getClass
```

```
              // returns the Class object associated with o's
              // class, and c.getName returns a String containing
              // the name of the class represented by c.
              o = stack.pop();
              c = o.getClass();
              s = c.getName();
              if ("DesignatedTransaction".equals(s)) {
                     transaction =  (DesignatedTransaction) o;
                     transaction.println();
              }
              else if ("java.lang.Double".equals(s)) {
                     amount = ((Double) o). doubleValue();
                     System.out.println(" " + amount);
              }
       }
   } // end main method
 } // end BankTransactions class
```

When the stack is popped, we do not know whether the object belongs to the class *Double* or the class *DesignatedTransaction*. Thus we use the reference *o*, which is of (generic) type *Object*, to refer to the popped object. The *getClass* method places a reference to the class referred to by *o* into the *Class* reference *c*. Once this has been done, the *Class* method *getName* is used to identify the class referred to by *o* by returning a *String* containing its name.

Class is called the **reflector class**. The advantage of the reflector class is twofold. First, we no longer need to dedicate a member of the parent class to identify the class. Second, we gain the flexibility to add new classes (e.g., *BankFeeTransaction*) without having to modify, or even know, the details of existing transactions. A new class may be added and the code to handle it may be programmed without interfering with any other classes.

There are many other reflection methods (e.g., *getMethods*, *getConstructors*, *getParameterTypes*) that may be used by the programmer to determine the properties of a class. The reader is urged to consult with a Java reference in order to learn more about these powerful methods.

The Predefined *Stack* Class

Just as we extended the *Insurance* class by defining the various subclasses discussed above, the *java.util* package contains a subclass of *Vector* called **Stack**. Since it is derived from *Vector*, the *Stack* class is a container class that may contain references to any object. However, because it is a subclass of *Vector*, it may not reference a primitive type and requires the programmer to use the wrapper classes, *Integer*, *Double*, *Character*, *Boolean*, etc., in order to contain (or wrap) the primitive types. As with the *Vector* class, when using the *Stack* class the programmer is responsible for keeping track of the type of object popped from the stack. The *Stack* class defines the methods **empty**, **peek**, **pop**, and **push**, which are identical to those defined in Section 1, except that they use a vector rather than an array.

Let us now consider how we might use the Java *Stack* class to implement our previous example: accepting an infix string, converting it to a postfix string (using a stack of operators), and then evaluating the postfix string (using a stack of operands). Most of the methods used by this implementation are identical with those developed earlier in this section.

Unfortunately, the *popAndTest* method is not defined for the Java *Stack* class. We could, of course, create our own subclass of *Stack* in which the *popAndTest* method is defined. However, since the *popAndTest* method is only used in two places, we choose to perform the *popAndTest* explicitly by performing the test inline.

First we have to import *java.util.* A stack to hold the operators is then created by defining an object *opstk* as

```
Stack opstk = new Stack();
```

while a stack to hold the operands is created by defining an object *opndstk* as

```
Stack opndstk = new Stack();
```

As with all objects of container classes, these stacks may contain objects of any type except the primitive types. Thus, when pushing a *symb* into the *opstk*, it is first necessary to wrap the *symb*, which is of type *char*, in an object of type *Character*. This is done by creating an object of type *Character*, initializing it using its constructor method, and then pushing it onto the stack using the *push* method of the *Stack* class:

```
Character item = new Character(symb);
opstk.push(item);
```

Since a Java *Stack* consists of references to items of type *Object*, it is necessary, when using the *pop* method of the *Stack* class, to first cast the reference to *Object* into a reference to a *Character* object. Once this is done, one may use the ***charValue*** method of the *Character* class in order to extract the *topsymb* which was wrapped within the item originally pushed onto the stack. These two operations may be combined by writing:

```
topsymb = ((Character) opstk.pop()).charValue();
```

In our original algorithm, our operand stack, *opndstk*, consists of a stack of integers of primitive type *double*. Thus, when pushing a digit of type *char* onto the *opndstk*, it is necessary to convert it into the primitive type *double* by using the ***digit(char, int)*** method, which returns the integer value of the character digit using the radix specified by the second parameter. It may then be converted into a wrapper object of type *Double* and pushed into the stack using the *push* method of the Java *Stack* class. The entire sequence of operations may be written as:

```
Double value = new Double((double) Character.digit(c, 10));
opndstk.push(value);
```

The stack is popped by casting the reference to *Object* into a reference to a *Double* object and using the ***doubleValue*** method of the *Double* class to extract the operand from its container class:

```
opnd1 = ((Double) opndstk.pop()).doubleValue();
```

If the original string consists of single-digit operands with no letter operands, the following program reads the original string and prints its value:

```java
import java.util.*;                           // To use Stack class

public class Evaluate {
  public final static  int MAXCOLS = 80;

  public static void main(String[] args) throws IOException {

        String instring, poststring;

        System.out.println("Enter an infix string: ");
        instring = readString();
        System.out.println("The original infix expression is " +
        instring);
        poststring = postfix(instring);
        System.out.println("In postfix it is " + poststring);
        System.out.println("Its value is " + eval(poststring));
  } // end main

  public static String postfix(String infix) {

        int position, outpos = 0;
        char symb, topsymb = '+';
        boolean wasEmpty = true;
        char[] postr = new char[MAXCOLS];

        Stack opstk = new Stack();

        for (position = 0; position < infix.length(); position++) {
                symb = infix.charAt(position);
                if (isOperand(symb))
                        postr[outpos++] = symb;
                else {
                        // popAndTest
                        if (!opstk.empty()) {
                                wasEmpty = false;
                                topsymb = ((Character)
                                opstk.pop()).charValue();
                        }
                    else
                        wasEmpty = true;
                while (!wasEmpty && precedence(topsymb, symb)) {
                        postr[outpos++] = topsymb;
                        // popAndTest
                        if (!opstk.empty()) {
                                wasEmpty = false;
                                topsymb = ((Character)
                                        opstk.pop()).charValue();
                        }
                        else
                                wasEmpty = true;
                } // end while
```

```
              if (!wasEmpty) {
                      Character item = new Character(topsymb);
                      opstk.push(item);
              }
              if (wasEmpty || (symb != ')')) {
                      Character item = new Character(symb);
                      opstk.push(item);
              }
              else
                  topsymb = ((Character) opstk.pop()).charValue();
              } // end else
      } // end for

      while (!opstk.empty()) {
          postr[outpos++] = ((Character) opstk.pop()).charValue();
      }
      return  String.copyValueOf(postr,0,outpos);

} // end postfix

public static double eval(String expr) {

      char c;
      int position;
      double opnd1, opnd2;

      Stack opndstk = new Stack();

      for (position = 0; position < expr.length(); position++) {
              c = expr.charAt(position);
              if (Character.isDigit(c)) {
                      // operand-- convert the character
                      // representation of the digit into double
                      // and push it into the stack
                      Double value = new Double
                              ((double) Character.digit(c, 10));
                      opndstk.push(value);
              }
              else {
                  // operator
                  opnd2 = ((Double) opndstk.pop()).doubleValue();
                  opnd1 = ((Double) opndstk.pop()).doubleValue();
                  Double value = new Double(oper(c, opnd1, opnd2));
                  opndstk.push(value);
              } // end else
      } // end for
      return ((Double) opndstk.pop()).doubleValue();
} // end eval

public static String readString() throws IOException {

      // presented earlier
```

```
    public static boolean isOperand(char symb) {

        // left to the reader

    public static boolean precedence(char op1, char op2) {

        // left to the reader

    public static double oper(char symb, double op1, double op2) {

        // presented earlier
    } // end class Evaluate
```

One point regarding the above program needs to be discussed. Both the ***postfix*** and the ***eval*** methods use a container which is an instance of type ***Stack***. Although each method only places an object of a single type into the stack (i.e., ***postfix*** pushes and pops only characters, while ***eval*** pushes and pops only integers), there is nothing to stop a programmer from using the stack to hold objects of both ***Character*** and ***Double*** (as well as any other object) simultaneously. However, when popping the stack it would then be necessary to determine which type of object is being popped. Often, it is easier to use a different stack for each type of object than to use a single stack of objects of varying types.

Finally, what happens to all the wrapper objects created each time we wished to push an object into the stack? As with all objects created in Java, the Java system performs automatic garbage collection if it can determine that there are no more references to that object. However, should there be a large number of items to be pushed into the stack, the number of container objects that were created but no longer used might well accumulate to dangerous levels. In order to mark these references for garbage collection, the programmer would set them to ***null*** as soon as they have been pushed into the stack. Thus the push sequence in the ***postfix*** method would be written as

```
Character item = new Character(topsymb);
opstk.push(item);
item = null;
```

Eventually the Java garbage collector would reclaim the memory used for these objects. (The programmer could also force garbage collection by invoking the garbage collector explicitly using the ***gc*** method of the ***System*** class.)

EXERCISES

2.4.1 Using the *Insurance* class defined in the text, write an application to read in a list of insurance policies, form them into a vector, and then increase the premium on all home and life insurance policies by 10 percent, the premium on all auto insurance policies by 5 percent, the amount of all policies by 7 percent, the deductible of all auto policies by 5 percent, and the deductible of all home policies by 10 percent. Then print out all the new values.

2.4.2 Write a definition of a class representing a stack of *Insurance* objects implemented as a vector. Write a *main* method that reads in all the data pertinent to a particular insurance policy (including the data unique to a home, life, or auto policy) and pushes an *Insurance* object with all the data onto the stack. When there is no more input, the method should pop one element of the stack at a time and print all of its content.

2.4.3 Write an application, *RollBack*, that reads in a series of transactions as described in the text, maintains a running balance, and prints a line-by-line log of the transactions as they are rolled back.

2.4.4 Modify the *RollBack* application in Exercise 2.4.3, to include a new transaction type, *BankFeeTransaction*. *BankFeeTransaction* contains an amount, a designation, and the date on which it was applied.

2.4.5 Rewrite the **postfix** and **eval** methods so that they use a single stack, using the Java **Stack** class that stores elements of different types.

2.4.6 Rewrite Exercises 2.2.3, 2.2.5, and 2.2.8, using the Java **Stack** class.

C H A P T E R   3

Recursion

This chapter introduces recursion, a very powerful programming tool that is often misunderstood by beginning students of programming. We define recursion, introduce its use in Java, and present several examples. We also examine an implementation of recursion using stacks. Finally, we discuss the advantages and disadvantages of using recursion in problem solving.

3.1   RECURSIVE DEFINITION AND PROCESSES

Many objects in mathematics are defined by presenting a process to produce the object. For example, π is defined as the ratio of the circumference of a circle to its diameter. This is equivalent to the set of instructions: obtain the circumference of a circle and its diameter, divide the former by the latter, and call the result π. Clearly, the process specified must terminate with a definite result.

Factorial Function

Another example of a definition specified by a process is that of the factorial function, which plays an important role in mathematics and statistics. Given a positive integer n, *n factorial* is defined as the product of all integers between n and 1. For example, 5 factorial equals $5 * 4 * 3 * 2 * 1 = 120$, and 3 factorial equals $3 * 2 * 1 = 6$. 0 factorial is defined as 1. In mathematics, the exclamation mark (!) is often used to denote the factorial function. We may therefore write the definition of this function as follows:

```
n! = 1                              if n = 0
n! = n * (n - 1) * (n - 2) * … * 1  if n > 0
```

The three dots are really a shorthand for all the numbers between $n - 3$ and 2 multiplied together. In order to avoid this shorthand in the definition of $n!$, we would have to list a formula for $n!$ for each value of n separately, as follows:

```
0! = 1
1! = 1
```

```
2! = 2 * 1
3! = 3 * 2 * 1
4! = 4 * 3 * 2 * 1
.....
```

Of course, we cannot hope to list a formula for the factorial of very integer. In order to define the function precisely without using shorthand or an infinite set of definitions, we present an algorithm that accepts an integer n and returns the value of $n!$.

```
prod = 1;
for (x = n; x > 0; x--)
     prod = prod * x;
return prod;
```

Such an algorithm is called **iterative** because it calls for the explicit repetition of some process until a certain condition is met. This algorithm can be translated readily into a Java method that returns $n!$ when n is input as a parameter. An algorithm may be thought of as a program for an "ideal" machine without any of the practical limitations of a real computer and may therefore be used to define a mathematical function. A Java method, however, cannot serve as the mathematical definition of the factorial function because of such limitations as precision and the finite size of a real machine.

Let us look more closely at the definition of $n!$ that lists a separate formula for each value of n. We may note, for example, that 4! equals 4 * 3 * 2 * 1, which equals 4 * 3!. In fact, for any $n > 0$, we see that $n!$ equals $n * (n - 1)!$. Multiplying n by the product of all integers from $n - 1$ to 1 yields the product of all integers from n to 1. We may therefore define:

```
0! = 1
1! = 1 * 0!
2! = 2 * 1!
3! = 3 * 2!
4! = 4 * 3!
   ...
```

or, using the mathematical notation used earlier:

```
n! = 1            if n == 0
n! = n * (n - 1)!  if n > 0.
```

This definition may appear quite strange, since it defines the factorial function in terms of itself. It seems to be a circular definition and totally unacceptable until we realize that the mathematical notation is only a concise way of writing out the infinite number of equations necessary to define $n!$ for each n. 0! is defined directly as 1. Once 0! has been defined, defining 1! as 1 * 0! is not circular at all. Similarly, once 1! has been defined, defining 2! as 2 * 1! is equally straightforward. It may be argued that the latter notation is more precise than the definition of $n!$ as $n * (n - 1) * \ldots * 1$ for $n > 0$ because it does not resort to three dots to be filled in by the hopefully logical intuition of the reader. Such a definition, which defines an object in terms of a simpler case of itself, is called a ***recursive definition***.

Let us see how the recursive definition of the factorial function may be used to evaluate 5!. The definition states that 5! equals 5 * 4!. Thus, before we can evaluate 5!, we must first evaluate 4!. Using the definition once more, we find that 4! = 4 * 3!. Therefore, we must evaluate 3!. Repeating this process, we have:

```
1  5! = 5 * 4!
2        4! = 4 * 3!
3               3! = 3 * 2!
4                     2! = 2 * 1!
5                           1! = 1 * 0!
6                                 0! = 1
```

Each case is reduced to a simpler case until we reach the case of 0!, which is defined directly as 1. At line (6) we have a value that is defined directly and not as the factorial of another number. We may therefore backtrack from line (6) to line (1), returning the value computed in one line to evaluate the result of the previous line. This produces:

```
6'   0! = 1
5'   1! = 1 * 0! = 1 * 1 = 1
4'   2! = 2 * 1! = 2 * 1 = 2
3'   3! = 3 * 2! = 3 * 2 = 6
2'   4! = 4 * 3! = 4 * 6 = 24
1'   5! = 5 * 4! = 5 * 24 = 120
```

Let us attempt to incorporate this process into an algorithm. Again, we want the algorithm to input a nonnegative integer n and to compute in a variable *fact* the nonnegative integer that is n factorial.

```
1 if (n == 0)
2        fact = 1;
3 else {
4        x = n - 1;
5        find the value of x!. Call it y;
6        fact = n * y;
7 } // end else
```

This algorithm exhibits the process used to compute $n!$ by the recursive definition. The key to the algorithm is, of course, line 5, where we are told to "find the value of $x!$." This requires re-executing the algorithm with input x, since the method for computing the factorial function is the algorithm itself. To see that the algorithm eventually halts, note that x equals $n - 1$ at the start of line 5. Each time the algorithm is executed, its input is one less than the preceding time, so (since the original input n was a nonnegative integer) 0 is eventually input to the algorithm. At that point, the algorithm simply returns 1. This value is returned to line 5, which asked for the evaluation of 0!. The multiplication of y (which equals 1) by n (which equals 1) is then executed and the result is returned. This sequence of multiplications and returns continues until the original $n!$ has been evaluated. In the next section, we will see how to convert this algorithm into a Java program.

Of course, it is much simpler and more straightforward to use the iterative method for evaluation of the factorial function. We present the recursive method as a simple example to introduce recursion, not as a more effective method of solving this particular problem. Indeed, all the problems in this section can be solved more efficiently by iteration. However, later in this chapter and in subsequent chapters, we will come across examples that are more easily solved by recursive methods.

Multiplication of Natural Numbers

Another example of a recursive definition is the definition of multiplication of natural numbers. The product $a * b$, where a and b are positive integers, may be defined as a added to itself i times. This is an iterative definition. An equivalent recursive definition is:

```
a * b = a                if b == 1
a * b = a * (b - 1) + a    if b > 1.
```

To evaluate $6 * 3$ by this definition, we first evaluate $6 * 2$ and then add 6. To evaluate $6 * 2$, we first evaluate $6 * 1$ and add 6. But $6 * 1$ equals 6 by the first part of the definition. Thus

```
6 * 3 = 6 * 2 + 6 = 6 * 1 + 6 + 6 = 6 + 6 + 6 = 18.
```

The reader is urged to convert the above definition to a recursive algorithm as a simple exercise.

Note the pattern that exists in recursive definitions. A simple case of the term to be defined is defined explicitly (in the case of factorial, 0! was defined as 1; in the case of multiplication, $a * 1 = a$). The other cases are defined by applying some operation to the result of evaluating a simpler case. Thus $n!$ is defined in terms of $(n - 1)!$ and $a * b$ in terms of $a * (b - 1)$. Successive simplifications of any particular case must eventually lead to the explicitly defined trivial case. In the case of the factorial function, successively subtracting 1 from n eventually yields 0. In the case of multiplication, successively subtracting 1 from b eventually yields 1. If this were not the case, the definition would be invalid. For example, if we defined

```
n! = (n + 1)!/(n + 1)
```

or

```
a * b = a * (b + 1) - a
```

we would be unable to determine the value of 5! or $6 * 3$. (You are invited to attempt to determine these values using the above definitions.) This is true despite the fact that the two equations are valid. Continually adding 1 to n or b does not eventually produce an explicitly defined case. Even if 100! was defined explicitly, how could the value of 101! be determined?

Fibonacci Sequence

Let us examine a less familiar example. The **Fibonacci sequence** is the sequence of integers:

$$0, 1, 1, 2, 3, 5, 8, 13, 21, 34, \ldots$$

Each element in this sequence is the sum of the two preceding elements (e.g., $0 + 1 = 1, 1 + 1 = 2, 1 + 2 = 3, 2 + 3 = 5, \ldots$). If we let $fib(0) = 0, fib(1) = 1$, etc., then we may define the Fibonacci sequence by the following recursive definition:

```
fib(n) = n                    if n == 0 or n == 1
fib(n) = fib(n - 2) + fib(n - 1)  if n >= 2
```

To compute $fib(6)$, for example, we may apply the definition recursively to obtain:

```
fib(6) = fib(4) + fib(5) = fib(2) + fib(3) + fib(5) =
fib(0) + fib(1) + fib(3) + fib(5) = 0 + 1 + fib(3) + fib(5) =
1 + fib(1) + fib(2) + fib(5) =
1 + 1 + fib(0) + fib(1) + fib(5) =
2 + 0 + 1 + fib(5) =
3 + fib(3) + fib(4) =
3 + fib(1) + fib(2) + fib(4) =
3 + 1 + fib(0) + fib(1) + fib(4) =
4 + 0 + 1 + fib(2) + fib(3) =
5 + fib(0) + fib(1) + fib(3) =
5 + 0 + 1 + fib(1) + fib(2) =
6 + 1 + fib(0) + fib(1) =
7 + 0 + 1 = 8
```

Note that the recursive definition of the Fibonacci numbers differs from the recursive definitions of the factorial function and multiplication. The recursive definition of *fib* refers to itself twice. For example, $fib(6) = fib(4) + fib(5)$, so that in computing $fib(6)$, *fib* must be applied recursively twice. However, the computation of $fib(5)$ also involves determining $fib(4)$, so that a great deal of computational redundancy occurs in applying the definition. In the above example, $fib(3)$ is computed three separate times. It would be much more efficient to "remember" the value of $fib(3)$ the first time it is evaluated and reuse it each time it is needed. An iterative method of computing $fib(n)$ such as the following is much more efficient:

```
if (n <= 1)
    return n;
lofib = 0;
hifib = 1;
for (i = 2; i <= n; i++) {
    x = lofib;
    lofib = hifib;
    hifib = x + lofib;
} // end for
return hifib;
```

Compare the number of additions (not including increments of the index variable *i*) that are performed in computing *fib*(6) by this algorithm and by using the recursive definition. In the case of the factorial function, the same number of multiplications must be performed in computing *n*! by the recursive and iterative methods. The same is true of the number of additions in the two methods of computing multiplication. However in the case of the Fibonacci numbers, the recursive method is far more expensive than the iterative. We shall have more to say about the relative merits of the two methods in a later section.

Binary Search

You may have received the erroneous impression that recursion is a very handy tool for defining mathematical functions but has no influence in more practical computing activities. The next example illustrates an application of recursion to one of the most common activities in computing: searching.

Consider an array of elements in which objects have been placed in some order. For example, a dictionary or a telephone book may be thought of as an array whose entries are in alphabetical order. A company payroll file may be in the order of employees' social security numbers. Suppose such an array exists and we wish to find a particular element in it. For example, we wish to look up a name in a telephone book, a word in a dictionary, or an employee in a personnel file. The process used to find such an entry is called a *search*.

Since searching is such a common activity in computing, it is desirable to find an efficient method for performing it. Perhaps the crudest search method is the *sequential* or *linear* search, in which each item of the array is examined in turn and compared to the item being searched for until a match occurs. If the list is unordered and haphazardly constructed, a linear search may be the only way to find anything in it (unless, of course, the list is first rearranged). However, you would never use this method in looking up a name in a telephone book. Rather, you would open the book to a random page and examine the names on it. Since the names are ordered alphabetically, the examination would determine whether the search should proceed in the first or second half of the book.

Let us apply this idea to searching an array. If the array contains only one element, the problem is trivial. Otherwise, compare the item being searched for with the item at the middle of the array. If they are equal, the search has been completed successfully. If the middle element is greater than the item being searched for, the search process is repeated in the first half of the array (since if the item appears anywhere, it must appear in the first half); otherwise, the process is repeated in the second half. Note that each time a comparison is made, the number of elements yet to be searched is cut in half. For large arrays, this method is superior to a sequential search in which each comparison reduces the number of elements yet to be searched by only one. Because of the division of the array to be searched into two equal parts, this search method is called a *binary search*.

Note that we have quite naturally defined a binary search recursively. If the item being searched for is not equal to the middle element of the array, the instructions are to search a subarray using the same method. Thus the search method is defined in terms of itself with a smaller array as input. We are sure that the process will terminate because the input arrays become smaller and smaller, and a search of a one-element array is defined nonrecursively, since the middle element of such an array is its only element.

We now present a recursive algorithm to search a sorted array a for an element x between $a[low]$ and $a[high]$. The algorithm returns an *index* of a such that $a[index]$ equals x if such an *index* exists between *low* and *high*. If x is not found in that portion of the array, *binsrch* returns -1 (in Java, no element $a[-1]$ can exist).

```
1   if (low > high)
2       return -1;
3   mid = (low + high) / 2;
4   if (x == a[mid])
5       return mid;
6   if (x < a[mid])
7       search for x in a[low] to a[mid - 1];
8   else
9       search for x in a[mid + 1] to a[high];
```

Since the possibility of an unsuccessful search is included (i.e., the element may not exist in the array), the trivial case has been altered somewhat. A search on a one-element array is not defined directly as the appropriate index. Instead that element is compared to the item being searched for. If the two items are not equal, the search continues in the "first" or "second" half—each of which contains no elements. This case is indicated by the condition *low > high*, and its result is defined directly as -1.

Let us apply this algorithm to an example. Suppose the array a contains the elements $1, 3, 4, 5, 17, 18, 31, 33$ in that order, and we wish to search for 17 (i.e., x equals 17) between item 0 and item 7 (i.e., *low* is 0, *high* is 7). Applying the algorithm, we have

Line 1: Is *low > high?* It is not, so execute line 3.

Line 3: $mid = (0 + 7)/2 = 3$.

Line 4: Is $x==a[3]$? 17 is not equal to 5, so execute line 6.

Line 6: Is $x < a[3]$? 17 is not less than 5, so perform the else clause at line 8.

Line 9: Repeat the algorithm with $low = mid + 1 = 4$ and $high = high = 7$, i.e., search the upper half of the array.

Line 1: Is $4 > 7$? No, so execute line 3.

Line 3: $mid = (4 + 7)/2 = 5$.

Line 4: Is $x==a[5]$? 17 does not equal 18, so execute line 6.

Line 6: Is $x < a[5]$? Yes, since $17 < 18$, so search for x in $a[low]$ to $a[mid - 1]$.

Line 7: Repeat the algorithm with $low = low = 4$ and $high = mid - 1 = 4$. We have isolated x between the **fourth** and the **fourth** elements of a.

Line 1: Is $4 > 4$? No, so execute line 3.

Line 3: $mid = (4 + 4)/2 = 4$.

Line 4: Since $a[4] == 17$, return $mid = 4$ as the answer. 17 is indeed the fourth element of the array.

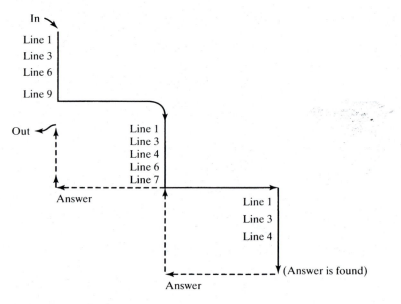

FIGURE 3.1.1 Diagrammatic representation of the binary search algorithm.

Note the pattern of calls to and returns from the algorithm. A diagram tracing this pattern appears in Figure 3.1.1. The solid arrows indicate the flow of control through the algorithm and the recursive calls. The dotted lines indicate returns. Since there are no steps to be executed in the algorithm after line 7 or 8, the returned result is returned intact to the previous execution. Finally, when control returns to the original execution, the answer is returned to the caller.

Let us examine how the algorithm searches for an item that does not appear in the array. Assume the array a as in the previous example, and assume that it is searching for an x that equals 2.

Line 1: Is $low > high$? 0 is not greater than 7, so execute line 3.

Line 3: $mid = (0 + 7)/2 = 3$.

Line 4: Is $x==a[3]$? 2 does not equal 5, so execute line 6.

Line 6: Is $x < a[3]$? Yes, $2 < 5$, so search for x in $a[low]$ to $a[mid - 1]$.

Line 7: Repeat the algorithm with $low = low = 0$ and $high = mid - 1 = 2$. If 2 appears in the array, it must appear between $a[0]$ and $a[2]$ inclusive.

Line 1: Is $0 > 2$? No, execute line 3.

Line 3: $mid = (0 + 2)/2 = 1$.

Line 4: Is $2==a[1]$? No, execute line 6.

Line 6: Is $2 < a[1]$? Yes, since $2 < 3$. Search for x in $a[low]$ to $a[mid - 1]$.

Line 7: Repeat the algorithm with $low = low = 0$ and $high = mid - 1 = 0$. If x exists in a, it must be the first element.

Line 1: Is $0 > 0$? No, execute line 3.

Line 3: *mid* = (0 + 0)/2 = 0.

Line 4: Is 2==*a*[0]? No, execute line 6.

Line 6: Is 2 < *a*[0]? 2 is not less than 1, so perform the else clause at line 8.

Line 9: Repeat the algorithm with *low* = *mid* + 1 = 1 and *high* = *high* = 0.

Line 1: Is *low* > *high*? 2 is greater than 1, so −1 is returned. The item 2 does not exist in the array.

Properties of Recursive Definitions or Algorithms

Let us summarize what is involved in a recursive definition or algorithm. In order to be correct, a recursive algorithm must not generate an infinite sequence of calls on itself. Clearly, any algorithm that does generate such a sequence can never terminate. For at least one argument or group of arguments, a recursive function *f* must be defined in terms that do not involve *f*. There must be a "way out" of the sequence of recursive calls. In the examples in this section, the nonrecursive portions of the definitions were:

```
factorial:        0! = 1
multiplication:   a * 1 = a
Fibonacci seq.:   fib(0) = 0;    fib(1) = 1
binary search:    if (low > high)
                        return -1;
                  if (x == a[mid])
                        return mid;
```

No recursive function can be computed without a nonrecursive exit of this kind. Every instance of a recursive definition or invocation of a recursive algorithm must eventually reduce to a manipulation of one or more simple nonrecursive cases.

EXERCISES

3.1.1   Write an iterative algorithm to evaluate *a* * *b* by using addition, where *a* and *b* are nonnegative integers.

3.1.2   Write a recursive definition of *a* + *b*, where *a* and *b* are nonnegative integers, in terms of the successor method *succ* defined as:

```
succ(int x) {
      return x++;
} // end succ
```

3.1.3   Let *a* be an array of integers. Present recursive algorithms to compute:

a. the maximum element of the array

b. the minimum element of the array

c. the sum of the elements of the array

d. the product of the elements of the array

e. the average of the elements of the array

3.1.4 Evaluate each of the following, using both the iterative and recursive definitions:

a. 6!

b. 9!

c. 100 * 3

d. 6 * 4

e. fib(10)

f. fib(11)

3.1.5 Assume that an array of ten integers contains the elements

$$1, 3, 7, 15, 21, 22, 36, 78, 95, 106$$

Use the recursive binary search to find each of the following items in the array

a. 1

b. 20

c. 36

3.1.6 Write an iterative version of the binary search algorithm. (*Hint*: modify the values of *low* and *high* directly.)

3.1.7 Ackerman's function is defined recursively on the nonnegative integers as follows:

$$a(m, n) = n + 1 \qquad \text{if } m == 0$$
$$a(m, n) = a(m - 1, 1) \qquad \text{if } m \neq 0, n == 0$$
$$a(m, n) = a(m - 1, a(m, n - 1)) \quad \text{if } m \neq 0, n \neq 0$$

a. Using the above definition, show that $a(2, 2)$ equals 7.

b. Prove that $a(m, n)$ is defined for all nonnegative integers m and n.

c. Can you find an iterative method of computing $a(m, n)$?

3.1.8 Count the number of additions necessary to compute $fib(n)$ for $0 \leq n \leq 10$ by the iterative and recursive methods. Does a pattern emerge?

3.1.9 If an array contains n elements, what is the maximum number of recursive calls made by the binary search algorithm?

3.2   RECURSION IN JAVA

Factorial in Java

The Java language allows a programmer to write methods that call themselves. Such routines are termed **_recursive_**.

The recursive algorithm to compute *n*! may be directly translated into a Java method as follows:

```
public long fact(int n) {
  int x;
  long y;
```

```
    if (n == 0)
      return 1;
    x = n - 1;
    y = fact(x);
    return n * y;
} // end fact
```

In the statement $y = fact(x)$; the method *fact* calls itself. This is the essential ingredient of a recursive routine. The programmer assumes that the method being computed has already been written and uses it in its own definition. However, the programmer must ensure that this does not lead to an endless series of calls.

Let us examine the execution of this method when it is called by another program. For example, suppose an applet contains the statement

```
output.setText(Long.toString(fact(4)));
```

When the calling applet calls *fact*, the parameter n is set equal to 4. Since n is not $0, x$ is set equal to 3. At this point, *fact* is called a second time with an argument of 3. Therefore, the method *fact* is reentered and the local variables (x and y) and parameter (n) of the block are reallocated. Since execution has not yet left the first call of *fact*, the first allocation of these variables remains. Thus two generations of each of these variables are in existence simultaneously. Only the most recent copy of these variables can be referenced from any point within the second execution of *fact*.

In general, each time the method *fact* is entered recursively, a new set of local variables and parameters is allocated, and only this new set may be referenced within that call of *fact*. When a return from *fact* to a point in a previous call takes place, the most recent allocation of these variables is freed and the previous copy is reactivated. This previous copy is the one that was allocated upon the original entry to the previous call and is local to that call.

This description suggests the use of a stack to keep the successive generations of local variables and parameters. The stack is maintained by the Java system and is invisible to the user. Each time a recursive method is entered, a new allocation of its variables is pushed on top of the stack. Any reference to a local variable or parameter is through the current top of the stack. When the method returns, the stack is popped, the top allocation is freed, and the previous allocation becomes the current stack top to be used for referencing local variables. This mechanism is examined more closely in Section 4, but for now, let us see how it is applied in computing the factorial method.

Figure 3.2.1 contains a series of snapshots of the stacks for the variables n, x, and y as execution of the *fact* method proceeds. Initially, the stacks are empty, as illustrated by Figure 3.2.1a. After the first call on *fact* by the calling applet, the situation is as shown in Figure 3.2.1b, with n equal to 4. The variables x and y are allocated but not initialized. Since n does not equal 0, x is set to 3 and *fact*(3) is called (Figure 3.2.1c). The new value of n does not equal 0, so x is set to 2, and *fact*(2) is called (Figure 3.2.1d).

This continues until n equals 0 (Figure 3.2.1f). At this point, the value 1 is returned from the call to *fact*(0). Execution resumes from the point at which *fact*(0) was called, which is the assignment of the returned value to the copy of y declared in *fact*(1). This is illustrated by the status of the stack shown in Figure 3.2.1g, where the variables allocated for *fact*(0) have been freed and y is set to 1.

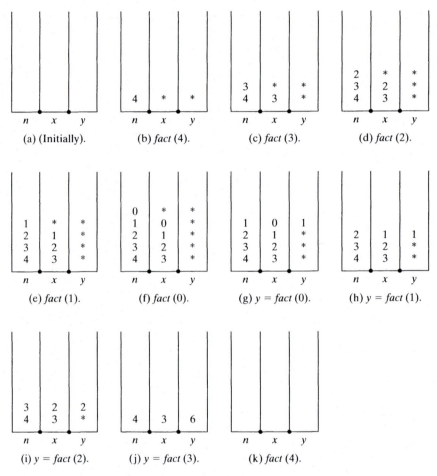

FIGURE 3.2.1   Stack at various times during execution. (An asterisk indicates an uninitialized value.)

The statement *return n * y* is then executed, multiplying the top values of *n* and *y* to obtain 1, and returning this value to *fact*(2) (Figure 3.2.1h). This process is repeated twice more, until finally the value of *y* in *fact*(4) equals 6 (Figure 3.2.1j). The statement *return n * y* is executed one more time. The product 24 is returned to the calling class, where it is displayed on the applet by the statement

```
output.setText(Long.toString(fact(4)));
```

(The *toString* method converts the result, which is of type *long*, into a *string* so that it may be sent to the *setText* method for placement on the *output* field of the applet. Both methods may be imported from the *java.awt.** package. *output* is of type *label*.)

Note that each time a recursive routine returns, it returns to the point immediately following the point from which it was called. Thus, the recursive call to *fact*(3) returns to the assignment of the result to *y* within *fact*(4), but the recursive call to *fact*(4) returns to the method which displays the result on the applet.

Let us transform some of the other recursive definitions and processes from the previous section into recursive Java programs. It is difficult to conceive of a Java programmer writing a function to compute the product of two positive integers in terms of addition, since an asterisk performs the multiplication directly. Nevertheless, such a function can serve as another illustration of recursion in Java. Following closely the definition of multiplication in the previous section, we may write:

```java
public long mult(long a, long b) {
   return b == 1 ? a : mult(a, b - 1) + a;
} // end mult
```

Note how similar this method is to the recursive definition in the last section. We leave it as an exercise for you to trace through the execution of this method when it is called with two positive integers. The use of stacks is a great aid in the tracing process.

This example illustrates that a recursive method may invoke itself even within a statement assigning a value to the function. Similarly, we could have written the recursive *fact* function more compactly as:

```java
public long fact(long n) {
   return n == 0 ? 1 : n * fact(n - 1);
} // end fact
```

This compact version avoids the explicit use of local variables x (to hold the value of $n - 1$) and y (to hold the value of *fact*(x)). However, temporary locations are set aside anyway for these two values upon each invocation of the function. These temporaries are treated just like any explicit local variable. Thus, in tracing the action of a recursive routine, it may be helpful to declare all temporary variables explicitly. See if it is any easier to trace the following more explicit version of *mult*:

```java
public long mult(long a, long b) {
   long c, d, sum;

   if (b == 1)
       return a;
   c = b - 1;
   d = mult(a, c);
   sum = d + a;
   return sum;
} // end mult
```

Another point worth noting is that it is very important to check the validity of input parameters in a recursive routine. For example, let us examine the execution of the *fact* method when it is invoked by a statement such as

```java
output.setText(Long.toString(fact(-1)));
```

Of course, the *fact* method is not designed to produce a meaningful result for negative input. However, one of the most important things for programmers to learn is that every method will inevitably be presented at some time with invalid input, and unless provision is made for this, the resultant error may be very difficult to trace.

For example, when −1 is passed as a parameter to *fact* so that *n* equals −1, *x* is set to −2 and −2 is passed to a recursive call on *fact*. Another set of *n*, *x*, and *y* is allocated, *n* is set to −2, and *x* becomes −3. This process continues until the program either runs out of time or space or the value of *x* becomes too small. No message indicating the true cause of the error is produced.

If *fact* were originally called with a complicated expression as its argument, and the expression erroneously evaluated to a negative number, a programmer might spend hours searching for the cause of the error. The problem can be remedied by revising the *fact* method to check its input explicitly, as follows:

```
public long fact(long n) throws NegativeFactorialException {

    long x, y;
    if (n < 0)
            throw new NegativeFactorialException();
    if (n == 0)
            return 1;
    x = n - 1;
    y = fact(x);
    return n * y;
} // end fact
```

NegativeFactorialException may be defined as a public class which extends the *java.lang.IllegalArgumentException*. It would be caught by the applet displaying, in turn, an appropriate error message.

Similarly, the method *mult* must guard against a nonpositive value in the second parameter.

The Fibonacci Numbers in Java

We now turn our attention to the Fibonacci sequence. A Java program to compute the *n*th Fibonacci number can be modeled closely on the recursive definition:

```
public long fib(long n) throws NegativeFibonacciException {
    long x, y;
    if (n < 0)
            throw new NegativeFibonacciException();
    if (n <= 1)
            return n;
    x = fib(n - 1);
    y = fib(n - 2);
    return x + y;
} // end fib
```

Let us trace through the action of this function in computing the sixth Fibonacci number. You may compare the action of the routine with the manual computation we performed in the last section to compute *fib*(6). The stacking process is illustrated in Figure 3.2.2. When the program is first called, the variables *n*, *x*, and *y* are allocated, and *n* is set to 6 (Fig. 3.2.2a). Since *n* > 1, *n* − 1 is evaluated and *fib* is called recursively.

(a)

n	x	y
6	*	*

(b)

n	x	y
5	*	*
6	*	*

(c)

n	x	y
4	*	*
5	*	*
6	*	*

(d)

n	x	y
3	*	*
4	*	*
5	*	*
6	*	*

(e)

n	x	y
2	*	*
3	*	*
4	*	*
5	*	*
6	*	*

(f)

n	x	y
1	*	*
2	*	*
3	*	*
4	*	*
5	*	*
6	*	*

(g)

n	x	y
2	1	*
3	*	*
4	*	*
5	*	*
6	*	*

(h)

n	x	y
0	*	*
2	1	*
3	*	*
4	*	*
5	*	*
6	*	*

(i)

n	x	y
2	1	0
3	*	*
4	*	*
5	*	*
6	*	*

(j)

n	x	y
3	1	*
4	*	*
5	*	*
6	*	*

(k)

n	x	y
1	*	*
3	1	*
4	*	*
5	*	*
6	*	*

(l)

n	x	y
3	1	1
4	*	*
5	*	*
6	*	*

(m)

n	x	y
4	2	*
5	*	*
6	*	*

(n)

n	x	y
2	*	*
4	2	*
5	*	*
6	*	*

(o)

n	x	y
1	*	*
2	*	*
4	2	*
5	*	*
6	*	*

(p)

n	x	y
0	*	*
2	1	*
4	2	*
5	*	*
6	*	*

(q)

n	x	y
2	1	0
4	2	*
5	*	*
6	*	*

(r)

n	x	y
4	2	1
5	*	*
6	*	*

(s)

n	x	y
5	3	*
6	*	*

(t)

n	x	y
3	*	*
5	3	*
6	*	*

FIGURE 3.2.2 The recursion stack of the Fibonacci function.

A new set of n, x, and y is allocated, and n is set to 5 (Fig. 3.2.2b). This process continues (Figs. 3.2.2c–f) with each successive value of n being 1 less than its predecessor, until fib is called with n equal to 1. The sixth call to fib returns 1 to its caller so the fifth allocation of x is set to 1 (Fig. 3.2.2g).

The next sequential statement $y = fib(n - 2)$ is then executed. The value of n that is used is the most recently allocated one, which is 2. Thus we again call on fib with an argument of 0 (Fig. 3.2.2h). The value of 0 is immediately returned, so that y in $fib(2)$ is set to 0 (Fig. 3.2.2i). Since each recursive call results in a return to the point of call, the call of $fib(1)$ returns to the assignment to x, while the call of $fib(0)$ returns to the assignment to y. The next statement to be executed in $fib(2)$ is the statement that returns

$x + y = 1 + 0 = 1$ to the statement that calls $fib(2)$ in the generation of the function calculating $fib(3)$. This is the assignment to x, so that x in $fib(3)$ is given the value $fib(2) = 1$ (Fig. 3.2.2j). The process of calling and pushing and returning and popping continues until finally the routine returns to the main program for the last time, with the value 8. Figure 3.2.2 shows the stack up to the point where $fib(5)$ calls on $fib(3)$ so that its value can be assigned to y. The reader is urged to complete the picture by drawing the stack states for the remainder of the program execution.

This program illustrates that a recursive routine may call itself a number of times with different arguments. In fact, as long as a recursive routine uses only local variables, the programmer can use the routine just the same as any other and can assume that it will perform its function and produce the desired value. There is no need to worry about the underlying stacking mechanism.

The Binary Search in Java

Let us now present a Java program for a binary search. A method to do this accepts a sorted array a and an element x as input and returns the index i in a such that $a[i]$ equals x, or -1 if no such i exists. Thus the method *binsrch* might be invoked in a statement such as

```
i = binsrch(a, x)
```

However, in looking at the binary search algorithm in Section 3.1 as a model for a recursive Java method, we note that two other parameters are passed in the recursive calls. Lines 7 and 9 of the algorithm call for a binary search on only part of the array. Thus, in order for the method to be recursive, the bounds between which the array is to be searched must also be specified. The method is written as follows:

```
public int binsrch(int a[], int x, int low, int high)  {
    int mid;

    if (low > high)
        return -1;
    mid = (low+high) / 2;
    return x == a[mid] ? mid : x < a[mid] ?
                                    binsrch(a, x, low, mid-1)  :
                                    binsrch(a, x, mid+1, high) ;
} // end binsrch
```

When *binsrch* is invoked by another method to search for x in a sorted array declared by

```
int a[arraySize];
```

of which the first n elements are occupied, it is called by the statement

```
i = binsrch(a, x, 0, n - 1);
```

You are urged to trace the execution of this routine and follow the stacking and unstacking using the example from the preceding section, where a is an array of eight elements ($n = 8$) containing 1, 3, 4, 5, 17, 18, 31, 33 in that order. The value being searched for is 17 (x equals 17). Note that the array a is stacked for each recursive call. The values of *low* and *high* are, respectively, the lower and upper bounds of the array a.

In the course of tracing through the *binsrch* routine, you may have noticed that the values of the two parameters *a* and *x* do not change throughout its execution. Each time that *binsrch* is called, the same array is searched for the same element; it is only the upper and lower bounds of the search that change. It therefore seems wasteful to stack and unstack these two parameters each time the method is called recursively.

One solution is to rewrite the *binsrch* method so that the parameters *a* and *x* are not defined within its header. Since *a* and *x* are not defined within the *binsrch* method, they are said to be global variables, which enables *binsrch* to access *a* and *x* without allocating additional space for them.

The method may then be invoked by a statement such as

```
i = binsrch(0, n-1);
```

In this case, all references to *a* and *x* are to the global allocations of *a* and *x* declared at the beginning of the class. All multiple allocations and freeings of space for these parameters are eliminated.

We may rewrite the *binsrch* function as follows:

```
public int binsrch(int low, int high)  {
   int mid;

   if (low > high)
        return -1;
   mid = (low + high) / 2;
   return x == a[mid] ? mid : x < a[mid] ?
                                   binsrch(low, mid-1)   :
                                   binsrch(mid+1, high);
} // end binsrch
```

Using this scheme, the variables *a* and *x* are not passed with each recursive call to *binsrch*. *a* and *x* do not change their values and are not stacked. The programmer wishing to make use of *binsrch* in a program only needs to pass the parameters *low* and *high*. The method could be invoked with a statement such as

```
i = binsrch(low, high);
```

Recursive Chains

A recursive function need not call itself directly. Rather, it may call itself indirectly, as in the following example:

```
a(formal parameters) {          b(formal parameters) {
         .                              .
         .                              .
         .                              .
   b(arguments);                   a(arguments);
         .                              .
} // end a                        } // end b
```

In this example, method *a* calls *b*, which may in turn call *a*, which may again call *b*. Thus both *a* and *b* are recursive, since they indirectly call on themselves. However, the fact that they are recursive is not evident from examining the body of either of the methods individually. The method *a* seems to be calling a separate method *b*, and it is impossible to determine, by examining *a* alone, that it may call itself indirectly.

More than two methods may participate in a **recursive chain**. Thus a method *a* may call *b*, which calls *c* ..., which calls *z*, which calls *a*. Each method in the chain may potentially call itself and is therefore recursive. Of course, the programmer must ensure that such a program does not generate an infinite sequence of recursive calls.

Recursive Definition of Algebraic Expressions

As an example of a recursive chain, consider the following recursive group of definitions:

1. An **expression** is a *term* followed by a *plus sign* followed by a *term*, or a *term* alone.
2. A **term** is a *factor* followed by an *asterisk* followed by a *factor*, or a *factor* alone.
3. A **factor** is either a *letter* or an *expression* enclosed in *parentheses*.

Before looking at some examples, note that none of the above three items is defined directly in terms of itself. However, each is defined in terms of itself indirectly. An expression is defined in terms of a term, a term in terms of a factor, and a factor in terms of an expression. Similarly, a factor is defined in terms of an expression, which is defined in terms of a term, which is defined in terms of a factor. Thus the entire set of definitions forms a recursive chain.

Let us now give some examples. The simplest form of a factor is a letter. Thus *A*, *B, C, Q, Z, M* are all factors. They are also terms, because a term may be a factor alone. They are also expressions, because an expression may be a term alone. Since *A* is an expression, (*A*) is a factor and therefore a term as well as an expression. *A* + *B* is an example of an expression that is neither a term nor a factor. (*A* + *B*), however, is all three. *A* * *B* is a term and therefore an expression, but it is not a factor. *A* * *B* + *C* is an expression that is neither a term nor a factor. *A* * (*B* + *C*) is a term and an expression but not a factor.

Each of the above examples is a valid expression. This can be shown by applying the definition of an expression to each of them. Consider, however, the string *A* + * *B*. It is neither an expression, term, nor factor. It would be instructive for you to attempt to apply the definitions of expression, term, and factor to see that none of them describe the string *A* + * *B*. Similarly, (*A* + *B* *)C* and *A* + *B* + *C* are not valid expressions according to the preceding definitions.

Let us write a program that reads and prints a character string and then prints "valid" if it is a valid expression and "invalid" if it is not. We begin by defining a class *expression* that contains methods for recognizing expressions, terms, and factors. An object of this class consists of a variable *str* which contains the input character string, and an integer *pos* whose value is the position in *str* from which we last obtained a character. A helper method, *getsymb*, is used to return the next character to be examined. If *pos* < *str.length*(), then *getsymb* returns the character located at *pos* and increments *pos* by 1. If *pos* >= *str.length*(), then *getsymb* returns a blank. Helper methods like *getsymb* are usually declared to be *private* because they are designed to be used only by other methods of that class.

The class constructor *expression* receives a string from the calling applet, copies the string in *str*, and initializes *pos* to zero.

The method that recognizes an expression is called *expr*. It returns *true* if a valid expression begins at position *pos* of *str* and *false* otherwise. It also resets *pos* to the position following the longest expression it can find.

The methods *factor* and *term* are much like *expr* except that they are responsible for recognizing factors and terms respectively. They also reposition *pos* to the position following the longest factor or term they can find within the string *str*. In order to determine whether the specified character is a letter, *factor* uses a method *isLetter(char)* which is defined in the class *Character*.

The code for these methods adheres closely to the definitions given earlier. Each of the methods attempts to satisfy one of the criteria for the entity being recognized. If one of these criteria is satisfied, then *true* is returned. If none of these criteria are satisfied, then *false* is returned. The entire expression is then declared to be valid or not valid by the method *valid*.

```java
public class Expression  {
   String str;
   int pos;

   public Expression(String input) {
      pos = 0;
      str = new String(input);
   } // end Expression

   public boolean expr() {
      // look for a term
      if (!term())
         return false;
      // We have found a term; look at the next symbol
      if (getsymb() != '+') {
         // We have found the longest expression (a single term).
         // Reposition pos so it refers to the last position of
         the expression.
         pos-;
         return true;
      } // end if
      // At this point, we have found a term and a plus sign.
      // We must look for another term.
      return term();
   } // end expr

   public boolean term() {
      if (!factor())
         return false;
      if (getsymb() != '*') {
         pos--;
         return true;
      } // end if
      return factor();
   } // end term
```

```
public boolean factor() {
    char c;

    if ((c = getsymb()) != '(')
        return Character.isLetter(c);
    return expr() && getsymb() == ')';
} // end factor

private char getsymb() {
    char c;

    if (pos < str.length())
        c = str.charAt(pos);
    else
        c = ' ';
    pos++;
    return c;
} // end getsymb

public boolean valid() {
    if (expr() && pos >= str.length())
        return true;
    else
        return false;
} // end valid

} // end Expression class
```

All three primary methods of the class are recursive because each may call itself indirectly. For example, if you trace through the actions of the program for the input string "$(a * b + c * d) + (e * (f) + g)$", you will find that each of the methods *expr*, *term*, and *factor* calls on itself.

Having described the class *Expression*, we can write the applet that places the results on the browser.

```
// An applet to determine whether an algebraic expression is
valid or not
import java.awt.*;
import java.applet.Applet;

public class AlgebraicExpression extends Applet {
    Label prompt1, prompt2;        // labels the input and output
                                   // values
    TextField input1, output1;     // input and output the value
    Expression str;
    // setup applet gui
    public void init() {

        prompt1 = new Label("Enter an algebraic expression");
        prompt2 = new Label("The expression is");
        input1 = new TextField(30);
```

```
    output1 = new TextField(30);
    output1.setEditable(false);

    add(prompt1);                  // place i/o fields on applet
    add(input1);
    add(prompt2);
    add(output1);
} // end init

// process the user's input
public boolean action(Event e, Object o){

    str = new Expression(o.toString());   // get expression
    showStatus("Calculating...");         // display result
    if (str.valid)
        output1.setText("valid");
    else
        output1.setText("invalid");
    showStatus("Done.");
    return true;
} // end action

} // end class AlgebraicExpression
```

EXERCISES

3.2.1   Determine what the following recursive Java method computes. Write an iterative method to accomplish the same purpose.

```
public int method(int n) {
    if (n == 0)
        return 0;
    return n + method(n-1);
} // end method
```

3.2.2   The Java expression m % n yields the remainder of m upon division by n. Define the **greatest common divisor** (**gcd**) of two integers x and y by:

```
gcd(x, y) = y                  if (y <= x && x % y == 0)
gcd(x, y) = gcd(y, x)          if (x < y)
gcd(x, y) = gcd(y, x % y)      otherwise
```

Write a recursive Java method to compute $gcd(x, y)$. Find an iterative method for computing this function.

3.2.3   Let $comm(n, k)$ represent the number of different committees of k people that can be formed, given n people from whom to choose. For example, $comm(4, 3) = 4$, since given four people A, B, C, and D there are four possible three-person committees: ABC, ABD, ACD, and BCD. Prove the identity:

```
comm(n, k) = comm(n - 1, k) + comm(n - 1, k - 1)
```

Write and test a recursive Java program to compute $comm(n, k)$ for $n, k >= 1$.

3.2.4 Define a *generalized Fibonacci sequence* of $f0$ and $f1$ as the sequence $gfib(f0, f1, 0)$, $gfib(f0, f1, 1)$, $gfib(f0, f1, 2)$, ..., where

```
gfib(f0, f1, 0) = f0
gfib(f0, f1, 1) = f1
gfib(f0, f1, n) = gfib(f0, f1, n - 1) + gfib(f0, f1, n - 2) if n
> 1
```

Write a recursive Java method to compute $gfib(f0, f1, n)$. Find an iterative method for computing this function.

3.2.5 Write a recursive Java method to compute the number of sequences of n binary digits that do not contain two 1's in a row. (*Hint*: compute how many such sequences exist that start with 0, and how many exist that start with a 1.)

3.2.6 An *order n matrix* is an $n \times n$ array of numbers. For example,

(3)

is a 1×1 matrix,

$$\begin{array}{rr} 1 & 3 \\ -2 & 8 \end{array}$$

is a 2×2 matrix and

$$\begin{array}{rrrr} 1 & 3 & 4 & 6 \\ 2 & -5 & 0 & 8 \\ 3 & 7 & 6 & 4 \\ 2 & 0 & 9 & -1 \end{array}$$

is a 4×4 matrix. Define the *minor* of an element x in a matrix as the submatrix formed by deleting the row and column containing x. In the above example of a 4×4 matrix, the minor of the element 7 is the 3×3 matrix

$$\begin{array}{rrr} 1 & 4 & 6 \\ 2 & 0 & 8 \\ 2 & 9 & -1 \end{array}$$

Clearly, the order of a minor of any element is 1 less than the order of the original matrix. Denote the minor of an element $a[i, j]$ by $minor(a[i, j])$.

Define the *determinant* of a matrix a (written $det(a)$) recursively as follows:

1. If a is a 1×1 matrix (x), then $det(a) = x$.
2. If a is of an order greater than 1, compute the determinant of a as follows:

   a. Choose any row or column. For each element $a[i, j]$ in this row or column, form the product:

   ```
   power(-1,i + j) * a[i, j] * det(minor(a[i, j]))
   ```

   where i and j are the row and column positions of the element chosen, $a[i, j]$ is the element chosen, $det(minor(a[I, j]))$ is the determinant of the minor of $a[i, j]$, and $power(m, n)$ is the value of m raised to the nth power.

b. *det*(*a*) = sum of all these products.
(More concisely, if *n* is the order of *a*,

```
det(a) = Σᵢ power(-1, i + j) * a[i, j] * det(minor(a[i,
j])), for any j
```

or

```
det(a) = Σⱼ power(-1, i + j) * a[i, j] * det(minor(a[i,
j])), for any i).
```

Write a Java program that reads *a*, prints *a* in matrix form, and prints the value of *det*(*a*), where *det* is a method that computes the determinant of a matrix.

3.2.7 Write a recursive Java program to sort an array *a* as follows:

1. Let *k* be the index of the middle element of the array.
2. Sort the elements up to and including *a*[*k*].
3. Sort the elements past *a*[*k*].
4. Merge the two subarrays into a single sorted array.

This method is called a ***merge sort***.

3.2.8 Show how to transform the following iterative method into a recursive method. *f*(*i*) is a method returning a Boolean value based on the value of *i*, and *g*(*i*) is a method that returns a value with the same attributes as *i*.

```
public void iter(int n) {
    int i;

    i = n;
    while(f(i)) {
        // any group of Java statements that
        // does not change the value of i
        i = g(i);
    } // end while
} // end iter
```

3.3 WRITING RECURSIVE PROGRAMS

In the last section we saw how to transform a recursive definition or algorithm into a Java program. It is much more difficult to develop a recursive Java solution to a problem specification whose algorithm is not supplied. It is not only the program but also the original definitions and algorithms that must be developed. There is generally no reason to look for a recursive solution when faced with the task of writing a program to solve a problem. Most problems can be solved in a straightforward manner using nonrecursive methods. However, some problems can be solved logically and most elegantly by recursion. In this section we shall identify the kinds of problems that can be solved recursively, develop a technique for finding recursive solutions, and present some examples.

Let us reexamine the factorial function. Since the iterative solution is so direct and simple, factorial is a prime example of a problem that should not be solved recursively. However, let us examine the elements that make the recursive solution work. First of all, we can recognize a large number of distinct cases to solve. That is, we want to write a program to compute 0!, 1!, 2!, etc. We can also identify a "trivial" case for which a nonrecursive solution is directly obtainable. This is the case of 0!, which is defined as 1. The next step is to find a method of solving a "complex" case in terms of a "simpler" case. This allows the reduction of a complex problem to a simpler problem. The transformation of the complex case to the simpler case should eventually result in the trivial case. This would mean that the complex case is ultimately defined in terms of the trivial case.

Let us examine what this means when applied to the factorial function. 4! is a more "complex" case than 3!. The transformation that is applied to the number 4 to obtain the number 3 is simply the subtraction of 1. Repeatedly subtracting 1 from 4 eventually results in 0, which is a "trivial" case. Thus, if we are able to define 4! in terms of 3!, and in general $n!$ in terms of $(n - 1)!$, we will be able to compute 4! by first working our way down to 0! and then working our way back up to 4! using the definition of $n!$ in terms of $(n - 1)!$. In the case of the factorial function, we have such a definition, since

```
n! = n * (n - 1)!
```

Thus $4! = 4 * 3! = 4 * 3 * 2! = 4 * 3 * 2 * 1! = 4 * 3 * 2 * 1 * 0! = 4 * 3 * 2 * 1 * 1 = 24$.

These are the essential ingredients of a recursive routine—being able to define a "complex" case in terms of a "simpler" case and having a directly solvable (nonrecursive) "trivial" case. Once this has been done, one can develop a solution using the assumption that the simpler case has already been solved. The Java version of the factorial function assumes that $(n - 1)!$ is defined and uses that quantity in computing $n!$.

Let us see how these ideas apply to other examples from the previous sections. In defining $a * b$, the case of $b = 1$ is trivial, since in that case $a * b$ is defined as a. In general, $a * b$ may be defined in terms of $a * (b - 1)$ by the definition $a * b = a * (b - 1) + a$. Again the complex case is transformed into a simpler case by subtracting 1, eventually leading to the trivial case of $b = 1$. Here the recursion is based solely on the second parameter, b.

In the case of the Fibonacci function, two trivial cases were defined: $fib(0) = 0$ and $fib(1) = 1$. A complex case, $fib(n)$, is then reduced to two simpler cases: $fib(n - 1)$ and $fib(n - 2)$. It is because of the definition of $fib(n)$ as $fib(n - 1) + fib(n - 2)$ that two trivial cases directly defined are necessary. $fib(1)$ cannot be defined as $fib(0) + fib(-1)$, because the Fibonacci function is not defined for negative numbers.

The binary search method is an interesting case of recursion. The recursion is based on the number of elements in the array that must be searched. Each time the routine is called recursively, the number of elements to be searched is halved (approximately). The trivial case is the one in which there are either no elements to be searched or the element being searched for is at the middle of the array. If $low > high$, then the first of these two conditions holds and -1 is returned. If $x = a[mid]$, the second condition holds, and mid is returned as the answer. In the more complex case of $high - low + 1$ elements to be searched, the search is reduced to taking place in one of two subregions,

1. The lower half of the array from low to $mid - 1$
2. The upper half of the array from $mid + 1$ to $high$

Thus a complex case (a large area to be searched) is reduced to a simpler case (an area to be searched that is approximately half the size of the original area). This eventually reduces to a comparison with a single element (*a*[*mid*]) or a search within an array of no elements.

The Towers of Hanoi Problem

Thus far we have been looking at recursive definitions and examining how they fit the pattern we have established. Let us now look at a problem that is not specified in terms of recursion and see how we can use recursive techniques to produce a logical and elegant solution. The problem is the Towers of Hanoi problem. The initial setup is shown in Figure 3.3.1. There are three pegs, *A*, *B*, and *C*. Five disks of differing diameters are placed on peg *A* so that a larger disk is always below a smaller disk. The object is to move the five disks to peg *C* using peg *B* as auxiliary. Only the top disk on any peg may be moved to any other peg, and a larger disk may never rest on a smaller one. See if you can produce a solution. Indeed, it is not even apparent that a solution is possible.

Let us see if we can develop a solution. Instead of focusing our attention on a solution for five disks, let us consider the general case of *n* disks. Suppose we had a solution for *n* − 1 disks and could state a solution for *n* disks in terms of the solution for *n* − 1 disks. Then the problem would be solved. This is true because the solution is simple in the trivial case of one disk (continually subtracting 1 from *n* will eventually produce 1): merely move the single disk from peg *A* to peg *C*. Therefore, we will have developed a recursive solution if we can state a solution for *n* disks in terms of *n* − 1. See if you can find such a relationship. In particular, for the case of five disks, suppose we knew how to move the top four disks from peg *A* to another peg according to the rules. How could we then complete the job of moving all five? Recall that there are three pegs available.

Suppose we could move four disks from peg *A* to peg *C*. Then we could move them just as easily to *B*, using *C* as auxiliary. This would result in the situation depicted in Figure 3.3.2a. We could then move the largest disk from *A* to *C* (Figure 3.3.2b) and finally again apply the solution for four disks to move the four disks from *B* to *C*, using the now empty peg *A* as an auxiliary (Figure 3.3.2c). Thus we may state a recursive solution to the Towers of Hanoi problem as follows:

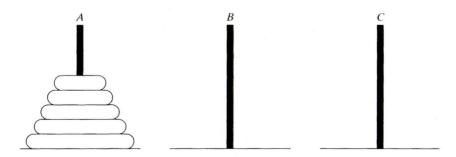

FIGURE 3.3.1   Initial setup of the Towers of Hanoi.

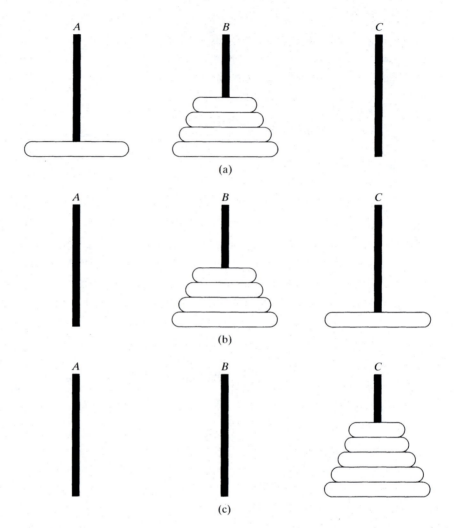

FIGURE 3.3.2   Recursive solution to the Towers of Hanoi.

To move *n* disks from *A* to *C*, using *B* as auxiliary:

1. If $n == 1$, then move the single disk from *A* to *C* and stop.
2. Move the top $n - 1$ disks from *A* to *B*, using *C* as auxiliary.
3. Move the remaining disk from *A* to *C*.
4. Move the $n - 1$ disks from *B* to *C*, using *A* as auxiliary.

We are sure that this algorithm will produce a correct solution for any value of *n*. If $n == 1$, step 1 will result in the correct solution. If $n == 2$, we know that we already have a solution for $n - 1 == 1$, so that steps 2 and 4 will perform correctly. Similarly, when $n == 3$, we have already produced a solution for $n - 1 == 2$, so that steps 2 and 4 can be performed. In this fashion, we can show that the solution works for

$n == 1, 2, 3, 4, 5, \ldots$ up to any value for which we desire a solution. Note that we developed the solution by identifying a trivial case ($n == 1$) and a solution for a general complex case (n) in terms of a simpler case ($n - 1$).

How can this solution be converted into a Java applet? We are no longer dealing with a mathematical function such as factorial, but with concrete actions such as "move a disk." How are we to represent such actions in the computer? The problem is not completely specified. What are the inputs to the program? What are its outputs to be? Whenever you are told to write a program, you must receive specific instructions as to exactly what the program is expected to do. A problem statement such as "Solve the Towers of Hanoi problem" is quite insufficient. Specifying a problem of this kind usually entails that the inputs and outputs as well as the program must be so designed as to reasonably correspond to the problem description. The design of inputs and outputs is an important phase of a solution and should be given as much attention as the rest of the program. There are two reasons for this. First, the user (who must ultimately evaluate and pass judgment on your work) will not see the elegant method you incorporated in your program but will struggle mightily to decipher the output or to adapt the input data to your input conventions. Failures to agree early on input and output details have been the cause of much grief to programmers and users. Second, a slight change in the input or output format may make the program much simpler to design. Thus the programmer can make the job much easier by designing an input or output format compatible with the algorithm. Of course these two considerations, convenience to the user and convenience to the programmer, often conflict sharply, and some happy medium must be found. However, the user must be a full participant with the programmer in the decisions on input and output formats.

Let us, then, proceed to design the inputs and outputs for this program. The only input needed is the value of n, the number of disks. At least that may be the programmer's view. The user may want the names of the disks (e.g., "red", "blue", "green") and perhaps the names of the pegs (e.g., "left", "right", "middle") as well. The programmer can probably convince the user that naming the disks $1, 2, 3, \ldots, n$ and the pegs A, B, C is just as convenient. If the user is adamant, the programmer can write a small function to convert the user's names to his own, and vice versa.

A reasonable form for the output would be a list of statements, such as:

```
move disk nnn from peg yyy to peg zzz
```

where *nnn* is the number of the disk to be moved, and *yyy* and *zzz* are the names of the pegs involved. The action to be taken for a solution would be to perform each of the output statements in the order that they appear in the output. (We use the *append* method of the *TextArea* object in order to place the multiline output on the applet. Objects of type *TextArea* contain scrollbars that allow the user to move forward and backward through the output produced by our applet.)

The programmer then decides to write a method *towers* to print the above output (but is purposely vague about the parameters at this point). The *action* method of the applet would then invoke the *towers* method by

```
n = Integer.parseInt(input1.getText());   // get the number of disks
towers(parameters);
```

Let us assume that the user will be satisfied to name the disks $1, 2, 3, \ldots, n$ and the pegs *A, B,* and *C.* What should the parameters to *towers* be? Clearly, they should include n, the number of disks to be moved. This includes information about how many disks there are and what their names are. The programmer then notices that in the recursive algorithm, it will be necessary to move $n - 1$ disks using a recursive call to *towers.* Thus, on the recursive call, the first parameter to *towers* will be $n - 1$. But this implies that the top $n - 1$ disks are numbered $1, 2, 3, \ldots, n - 1$, and that the smallest disk is numbered 1. This is a good example of programming convenience determining problem representation. There is no a priori reason for labeling the smallest disk 1; logically the largest disk could have been labeled 1 and the smallest disk n. However, since it leads to a simpler and more direct program, we choose to label the disks so that the smallest disk has the smallest number.

What are the other parameters to *towers*? At first glance, it might appear that no additional parameters are necessary since the pegs are named *A, B,* and *C* by default. However, a closer look at the recursive solution leads us to the realization that on the recursive calls disks will not be moved from *A* to *C* using *B* as auxiliary but from *A* to *B* using *C* (step 2) or from *B* to *C* using *A* (step 4). We therefore include three more parameters in *towers.* The first, *fromPeg*, represents the peg from which we are removing disks; the second, *toPeg*, represents the peg to which we will take the disks; and the third, *auxPeg*, represents the auxiliary peg. This situation is one which is quite typical of recursive methods; additional parameters are necessary to handle the recursive call situation. We already saw one example of this in the binary search applet, where the parameters *low* and *high* were necessary.

The complete applet to solve the Towers of Hanoi problem, closely following the recursive solution, may be written as follows:

```java
// An Applet to solve the Towers of Hanoi problem
import java.awt.*;
import java.applet.Applet;
public class TowersOfHanoi extends Applet {
  Label prompt1, prompt2;       // labels the input and output values
  TextField input1;             // input the value
  TextArea output1;             // output the solution
  int n;

  // setup applet gui
  public void init() {

        prompt1 = new Label("Enter the number of disks");
        input1 = new TextField(5);
        prompt2 = new Label("The solution is");
        output1 = new TextArea(10,35);
        output1.setEditable(false);

        add(prompt1);                        // place i/o fields on applet
        add(input1);
        add(prompt2);
        add(output1);
  } // end init
```

```
            // process the user's input
            public boolean action(Event e, Object o) {
              n = Integer.parseInt(input1.getText());   // get the number of disks
              showStatus("Calculating...");              // display result

              towers(n, 'A', 'C', 'B');

              output1.append("\n\n");
              showStatus("Done.");
              return true;
            } // end action

            void towers(int n, char fromPeg, char toPeg, char auxPeg) {
                  // If only one disk, make the move and return
                  if (n == 1) {
                        output1.append("\nmove disk 1 from peg " + fromPeg +
                                                    " to peg " + toPeg);
                        return;
                  } // end if
                  // Move top n - 1 disks from A to B, using C as auxiliary
                  towers(n - 1, fromPeg, auxPeg, toPeg);
                  output1.append("\nmove disk " + n + " from peg " + fromPeg +
                                                    " to peg " + toPeg);
                  // Move n - 1 disk from B to C using A as auxiliary
                  towers(n - 1, auxPeg, toPeg, fromPeg);
            } // end towers

        } // end class TowersOfHanoi
```

Trace the actions of the above program when it reads the value 4 for *n*. Be careful to keep track of the changing values of the parameters *fromPeg*, *auxPeg*, and *toPeg*. Verify that it produces the following output:

```
move disk 1 from peg A to peg B
move disk 2 from peg A to peg C
move disk 1 from peg B to peg C
move disk 3 from peg A to peg B
move disk 1 from peg C to peg A
move disk 2 from peg C to peg B
move disk 1 from peg A to peg B
move disk 4 from peg A to peg C
move disk 1 from peg B to peg C
move disk 2 from peg B to peg A
move disk 1 from peg C to peg A
move disk 3 from peg B to peg C
move disk 1 from peg A to peg B
move disk 2 from peg A to peg C
move disk 1 from peg B to peg C
```

Verify that the above solution actually works and does not violate any of the rules.

Translation from Prefix to Postfix Using Recursion

Let us examine another problem for which recursion offers the most direct and elegant solution. This is the problem of converting a prefix expression to a postfix. Prefix and postfix notations were discussed in the last chapter. Briefly, prefix and postfix notations are methods of writing mathematical expressions without parentheses. In prefix notation each operator immediately precedes its operands. In postfix notation each operator immediately follows its operands. To refresh your memory, here are a few conventional (infix) mathematical expressions with their prefix and postfix equivalents:

infix	prefix	postfix
$A + B$	$+AB$	$AB +$
$A + B * C$	$+A * BC$	$ABC * +$
$A * (B + C)$	$* A + BC$	$ABC + *$
$A * B + C$	$+ * ABC$	$AB * C+$
$A + B * C + D - E * F$	$-++A * BCD * EF$	$ABC * + D + EF * -$
$(A + B) * (C + D - E) * F$	$** + AB - + CDEF$	$AB + CD + E - * F *$

The most convenient way to define postfix and prefix is by using recursion. Assuming no constants and using only single letters as variables, a prefix expression is a single letter or an operator followed by two prefix expressions. A postfix expression may be similarly defined as a single letter or as an operator preceded by two postfix expressions. The above definitions assume that all operations are binary—that is, each requires two operands. Examples of such operations are addition, subtraction, multiplication, division, and exponentiation. It is easy to extend the above definitions of prefix and postfix to include unary operations, such as negation or factorial, but in the interest of simplicity we will not do so here. Verify that each of the above prefix and postfix expressions is valid by showing that they satisfy the definitions, and make sure that you can identify the two operands of each operator.

We will put these recursive definitions to use in a moment, but first let us return to our problem. Given a prefix expression, how can we convert it into a postfix expression? We can immediately identify a trivial case: a prefix expression that consists of only a single variable is its own postfix equivalent. That is, an expression such as A is valid as both a prefix and a postfix expression.

Now consider a longer prefix string. If we knew how to convert any shorter prefix string to postfix, could we convert a longer prefix string? The answer is yes, with one proviso. Every prefix string longer than a single variable contains an operator, a first operand, and a second operand (remember, we are assuming binary operators only). Assume we are able to identify the first and second operands, which are necessarily shorter than the original string. We can then convert the long prefix string to postfix by first converting the first operand to postfix, then converting the second operand to postfix and appending it to the end of the first converted operand, and finally appending the initial operator to the end of the resultant string. Thus we have developed a recursive algorithm for converting a prefix string to postfix with the single provision that we must specify a method for identifying the operands in a prefix expression. We can summarize our algorithm as follows:

1. If the prefix string is a single variable, it is its own postfix equivalent.
2. Let *op* be the first operator of the prefix string.
3. Find the first operand *opnd*1 of the string. Convert it to postfix and call it *post*1.
4. Find the second operand *opnd*2 of the string. Convert it to postfix and call it *post*2.
5. Concatenate *post*1, *post*2, and *op*.

One operation that will be required by this program is concatenation. For example, if two strings represented by *a* and *b* represent the strings "abcde" and "xyy" respectively, the statement

```
a = a + b;
```

places into *a* the string "abcdexyz" (i.e., the string consisting of all the elements of *a* followed by all the elements of *b*). Alternatively, we could have used the *string.concat*(*String str*) method, which returns a string that represents the concatenation of *string*'s characters followed by the *str*'s characters.

We also make use of the *length* method. *str.length*() returns the length of the string *str*.

This application will also require the *substring* method. *string.substring*(*int beginIndex, int endIndex*) returns a new string that is a substring of this string. The substring begins at the specified *beginIndex* and extends to the character at index *endIndex* - 1. Thus the *s2* = *s1.substring*(*i, j*) statement sets the string *s2* to the substring of *s*1 starting at position *i* containing *j* − *i* characters. For example, after executing *s* = "abcd".*substr*(1, 3), *s* equals "bc". The methods *concat, length,* and *substring* are defined as part of the *String* class.

Before transforming the conversion algorithm into a Java application, let us examine its inputs and outputs. We wish to write a method *convert* that accepts a character string. This string represents a prefix expression in which all variables are single letters and the allowable operators are '+', '−', '*', and '/'. The method produces a string that is the postfix equivalent of the prefix parameter.

Assume the existence of a function *find* which accepts a string and returns an integer that is the length of the longest prefix expression contained within the input string that starts at the beginning of that string. For example, *find*("*A* + *CD*") returns 1, because "*A*" is the longest prefix string starting at the beginning of "*A* + *CD*". *find*("+ * *ABCD* + *GH*") returns 5 because "+ * *ABC*" is the longest prefix string starting at the beginning of "+ * *ABCD* + *GH*". If no such prefix string exists within the input string starting at the beginning of the input string, *find* returns 0. (For example, *find*("* + *AB*") returns 0.) This function is used to identify the first and second operands of a prefix operator. *convert* also calls the *Character* method *isLetter*, which determines whether its parameter is a letter. Thus the statement

```
if (Character.isLetter(prefix.charAt(0)))
```

determines whether the character at the head of the *prefix* string is a letter.

We now turn our attention to the method *find*, which accepts a character string and a starting position and returns the length of the longest prefix string which is contained in that input string starting at that position. The word "longest" in this definition is superfluous, since there is at most only one substring starting at a given position of a given string that is a valid prefix expression.

We first show that there is at most one valid prefix expression starting at the beginning of a string. To see this, note that it is trivially true in a string of length 1. Assume it is true for a short string. Then a long string that contains a prefix expression as an initial substring must begin with either a variable, in which case the variable is the desired substring, or with an operator. Deleting the initial operator, the remaining string is shorter than the original string and can therefore have at most a single initial prefix expression. This expression is the first operand of the initial operator. Similarly, the remaining substring (after the first operand is deleted) can only have a single initial substring that is a prefix expression. This expression must be the second operand. Therefore, we have uniquely identified the operator and operands of the prefix expression starting at the first character of an arbitrary string, if such an expression exists. Since there is at most one valid prefix string starting at the beginning of any string, there is at most one such string starting at any position of an arbitrary string. This is obvious when we consider the substring of the given string starting at the given position. Note that this proof has given us a recursive method for finding a prefix expression in a string.

We now present a class *Expression* that implements the conversion from prefix to postfix:

```java
import java.io.IOException;  // To delay ending of program

public class Expression {

  public final static int MAXCOLS = 80;

  public static void main(String[] args) throws IOException{
        String inString;
        String outString = new String();

        System.out.println("Enter a prefix string: ");
        inString = readString();
        System.out.println("The original prefix expression is " +
        inString);
        outString = convert(inString);
        System.out.println("In postfix it is " + outString);
  } // end main

  public static String readString() throws IOException {
        char[] charArray = new char[MAXCOLS];
        int position = 0;
        char c;

        while ((c = (char) System.in.read()) != '\n')
                charArray[position++] = c;
```

```java
      return  String.copyValueOf(charArray,0,position-1);
} // end readString

public static String convert(String prefix) {
      String opnd1, opnd2;
      String post1, post2;
      String temp;
      char op;
      int m, n, length;

      if ((length = prefix.length()) == 1) {
            if (Character.isLetter(prefix.charAt(0))) {
                  // The prefix string is a single letter
            return new String(prefix);
            } // end if
            System.out.println("Illegal prefix string");
            System.exit(1);
      } // end if

      // The prefix string is longer than a single character.
      // Extract the operator and the two operand lengths.
      op = prefix.charAt(0);

      temp = new String(prefix.substring(1, length));
      m = find(temp);
      temp = new String(prefix.substring(m+1, length));
      n = find(temp);

      if ((op != '+' && op != '-' && op != '*' && op != '/')
               || (m == 0) || (n == 0) || (m+n+1 != length)) {
            System.out.println("Illegal prefix string");
            System.exit(1);
      } // end if
      opnd1 = new String(prefix.substring(1, m+1));
      opnd2 = new String(prefix.substring(m+1, length));
      post1 = new String();
      post2 = new String();
      post1 = convert(opnd1);
      post2 = convert(opnd2);
      post1 = post1 + post2;
      post1 = post1 + op;
      return (post1.toString()).substring(0, length);
} // end convert

public static int find(String str) {
      String temp;
      int m, n, length;

      if ((length = str.length()) == 0)
            return 0;
      if (Character.isLetter(str.charAt(0)))
            // First character is a letter.
```

```
                                // That letter is the initial substring.
                                return 1;
                if (str.length() < 2)
                                return 0;
                // otherwise find the first operand
                temp = str.substring(1, length);
                m = find(temp);
                if (m == 0 || str.length() == m)
                                // no valid prefix operand or no second operand
                                return 0;
                temp = str.substring(m+1, length);
                n = find(temp);
                if (n == 0)
                                return 0;
                return m+n+1;
        } // end find

    } // end class Expression
```

Note that several checks have been incorporated into *convert* to ensure that the parameter is a valid prefix string. One of the most difficult classes of errors to detect are
those resulting from invalid inputs and the programmer's neglect to check for validity.

Make sure that you understand how these methods work by tracing their actions
on both valid and invalid prefix expressions. More important, make sure that you understand how they were developed and how logical analysis led to a natural recursive
solution that was directly translatable into a Java application.

EXERCISES

3.3.1   Suppose that another provision were added to the Towers of Hanoi problem: that
        one disk may not rest on another disk that is more than one size larger (e.g., disk 1
        may only rest on disk 2 or on the ground, disk 2 may only rest on disk 3 or on the
        ground). Why does the solution in the text fail to work? What is faulty about the
        logic that led to it under the new rules?

3.3.2   Prove that the number of moves performed by *towers* in moving n disks equals
        $2^n - 1$. Can you find a method of solving the Towers of Hanoi problem in fewer
        moves? Either find such a method for some n or prove that none exists.

3.3.3   Define a postfix and prefix expression to include the possibility of unary operators.
        Write a program to convert a prefix expression possibly containing the unary nega-
        tion operator (represented by the symbol '@') to postfix.

3.3.4   Rewrite the method *find* in the text so that it is nonrecursive and computes the
        length of a prefix string by counting the number of operators and single-letter
        operands.

3.3.5   Write a recursive method that accepts a prefix expression consisting of binary op-
        erators and single-digit integer operands and returns the value of the expression.

3.3.6   Consider the method *convert*, for converting a prefix expression to postfix, defined
        for the *Expression* class given below.

```
public class Expression {
  private String prefix;

  public Expression(String str) {
      prefix = str;
  }

  public Expression() {
      prefix = new String();
  }

  public String convert() {
      String first = prefix.substring(0, 1);
      String postfix = new String();

      prefix = prefix.substring(1);
      char ch = first.charAt(0);
      if (ch == '+' || ch == '*' || ch == '-' || ch == '/') {
          String t1 = convert();
          String t2 = convert();
          t1 = t1 + t2;
          t1 = t1 + first;
          postfix = t1;
          return postfix;
      } // end if
      postfix = first;
      return postfix;
  } // end convert
} // end Expression
```

The method *convert* would be invoked by:

```
Expression preString = new Expression(inString);
postString = preString.convert();
```

Explain how the method works. Is it better or worse than the method in the text? What happens if the method is called with an invalid prefix string as input? Can you incorporate a check for such an invalid string in *convert*? Can you design such a check for the calling application after *convert* has returned?

3.3.7 Develop a recursive method (and program it) to compute the number of different ways in which an integer k can be written as a sum each of whose operands is less than n.

3.3.8 Consider an array a containing positive and negative integers. Define *contigsum*(i, j) as the sum of the contiguous elements $a[i]$ through $a[j]$ for all array indexes $i <= j$. Develop a recursive method that determines i and j such that *contigsum*(i, j) is maximized. The recursion should consider the two halves of the array a.

3.3.9 Write a recursive Java application to find the kth smallest element of an array a of numbers by choosing any element $a[i]$ of a and partitioning a into those elements smaller than, equal to, and greater than $a[i]$.

3.3.10 In the Eight Queens Problem, one has to place eight queens on a chessboard positioned so that no queen is attacking any other queen. The following is a recursive program to solve the problem. *board* is an 8×8 array that represents a chessboard.

board[i][j]==true if there is a queen at position *[i][j]*, and *false* otherwise. *good*() is a method that returns *true* if no two queens on the chessboard are attacking each other and *false* otherwise. At the end of the program, the method *drawboard*() displays a solution to the problem

```
// An Applet to solve the Eight Queens Problem
import java.awt.*;
import java.applet.Applet;

public class EightQueens extends Applet {
  private static boolean[][] board = new boolean [8][8];
  private static int xPosition, yPosition;

  public void init() {
      for (int i = 0; i < 8; i++)
          for (int j = 0; j < 8; j++)
              board[i][j] = false;

      xPosition = 20;
      yPosition = 20;
  } // end init

  // Paint the applet
  public void paint(Graphics g) {
      if(trial(0))
              drawboard(g);
  } // end paint

  public static boolean trial(int n) {
      for (int i = 0; i < 8; i++) {
          board[n][i] = true;
          if (n == 7 && good())
              return true;
          if (n < 7 && good() && trial(n+1))
              return true;
          board[n][i] = false;
      } // end for
      return false;
  } // end trial

      ...

} // end class EightQueens
```

The recursive method *trial* returns *true* if it is possible, given the *board* at the time it is called, to add queens in rows *n* through 7 to achieve a solution. *trial* returns *false* if there is no solution that has queens at the positions in *board* that already contain *true*. If *true* is returned, the function also adds queens in rows *n* through 7 to produce a solution.

Write the methods *good* and *drawboard* used above, and verify that the program produces a solution. The idea behind the solution is as follows: *board* represents the global situation during an attempt to find a solution. The next step toward finding a solution is chosen arbitrarily (place a queen in the next untried position in row *n*) and recursively test whether it is possible to produce a solution which includes that step. If it is, then return. If it is not, then backtrack from the attempted next step (*board*[*n*][*i*] = *false*) and try another possibility. This method is called ***backtracking***.

3.3.11 A 10 × 10 array *maze* of 0s and 1s represents a maze in which a traveler must find a path from *maze*[0][0] to *maze*[9][9]. The traveler may move from a square into any adjacent square in the same row or column, but may not skip over any squares or move diagonally. In addition, the traveler may not move into any square that contains a 1. *maze*[0][0] and *maze*[9][9] contain 0s. Write a method that accepts such a *maze* and prints either a message that no path through the maze exists or a list of positions representing a path from [0][0] to [9][9].

3.4 SIMULATING RECURSION

In this section we examine more closely some of the mechanisms used to implement recursion so that we can simulate them using nonrecursive techniques. This activity is important for several reasons. First of all, older programming languages (e.g., FORTRAN, COBOL, and many machine languages) do not allow recursive programs. Problems like the Towers of Hanoi and prefix to postfix conversion, whose solutions can be derived and stated quite simply using recursive techniques, can be programmed in these languages by simulating the recursive solution using more elementary operations. If we know that the recursive solution is correct (and it is often fairly easy to prove such a solution correct), and we have established techniques for converting a recursive solution to a nonrecursive one, then we can create a correct solution in a nonrecursive language. Programmers are often able to state recursive solutions to problems. The ability to generate nonrecursive solutions from recursive algorithms is indispensable when using a compiler that does not support recursion.

Another reason for examining the implementation of recursion is that it will allow us to understand the implications of recursion and some of its hidden pitfalls. While these pitfalls do not occur in mathematical definitions that employ recursion, they seem to be an inevitable accompaniment of implementations in a real language on a real machine.

Finally, even in a language like Java that supports recursion, a recursive solution to a problem is often more expensive than a nonrecursive solution, in terms of both time and space. Frequently, this expense is a small price to pay for the logical simplicity and self-documentation of the recursive solution. However, in a production program (e.g., a compiler) that may be run thousands of times, the recurrent expense is a heavy burden on the system's limited resources. Thus a program may be designed to incorporate a recursive solution in order to reduce the expense of design and certification, and then carefully converted to a nonrecursive version to be put into actual day-to-day use. As we shall see, in performing such a conversion it is often possible to identify parts of the implementation of recursion that are superfluous in a particular application and thereby to significantly reduce the amount of work the program must perform.

Before examining the actions of a recursive routine, let us take a step back and examine the action of a nonrecursive routine. We will then be able to see what mechanisms

must be added to support recursion. Before proceeding we adopt the following convention. Suppose we have the statement:

```
rout(x);
```

where *rout* is defined as a method by the header:

```
void rout(a)
```

we refer to *x* as an **argument** (of the calling function) and to *a* as a **parameter** (of the
called method).

What happens when a method is called? The action of invoking a method may be
divided into three parts:

1. Passing arguments
2. Allocating and initializing local variables
3. Transferring control to the method.

Let us examine each of these three steps in turn.

1. *Passing Arguments.* For a parameter in Java, local storage is allocated for the
   parameter, and the value of the argument is copied into the parameter. Any
   changes to the parameter within the method are made to the local copy. The
   effect of this scheme is that the original input argument cannot be altered. In this
   method, storage for the argument is allocated in the data area of the method.
2. *Allocating and Initializing Local Variables.* After arguments have been passed,
   the local variables of the method are allocated. These include all the local
   variables declared directly in the method and any temporaries that must be
   created during the course of execution. For example, in evaluating the expression

   ```
   x + y + z
   ```

   a storage location must be set aside to hold the value of $x + y$ so that z can be
   added to it. Another storage location must be set aside to hold the value of the
   entire expression after it has been evaluated. Such locations are called
   temporaries because they are needed only temporarily during the course of execution. Similarly, in a statement such as

   ```
   x = fact(n);
   ```

   a temporary must be set aside to hold the value of *fact(n)* before it can be assigned to *x*.
3. *Transferring Control to the Method.* At this point control may still not be passed
   to the method because provision has not yet been made for saving the **return
   address**. If a method is given control, it must eventually restore control to the
   calling routine by means of a branch. However, it cannot execute the branch
   unless it knows the location to which it must return. Since this location is within
   the calling routine and not within the method, the only way the method can know
   this address is to have it passed as an argument. This is exactly what happens.

Aside from the explicit arguments specified by the programmer, there are also a set of implicit arguments that contain information necessary for the method to execute and return correctly. Chief among these implicit arguments is the return address. The method stores this address in its own data area. When it is ready to return control to the calling program, the method retrieves the return address and branches to that location.

Once the arguments and the return address have been passed, control may be transferred to the method, since everything required has been done to ensure that the method can operate on the appropriate data and then safely return to the calling routine.

Return from a Method

When a method returns, three actions are performed. First, the return address is retrieved and stored in a safe location. Second, the method's data area is freed. This data area contains all the local variables (including local copies of arguments), the temporaries, and the return address. Finally, a branch is taken to the return address that was previously saved. This restores control to the calling routine at the point immediately following the instruction that initiated the call. In addition, if the method returns a value, it is placed in a secure location from which the calling program may retrieve it. Usually this location is a hardware register set aside for this purpose.

Suppose an application has called a method b, which has called c, which has, in turn, called d. This is illustrated in Figure 3.4.1a, where we indicate that control currently

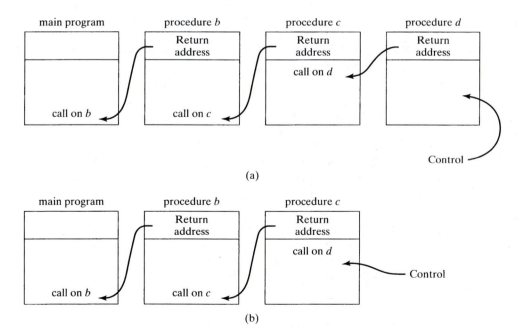

FIGURE 3.4.1   Series of procedures calling one another.

resides somewhere within *d*. A location in each function is set aside for the return address. Thus the return address area of *d* contains the address of the instruction in *c* immediately following the call to *d*. Figure 3.4.1b shows the situation immediately following *d*'s return to *c*. The return address within *d* has been retrieved and control transferred to that address.

You may have noticed that the string of return addresses forms a stack; that is, the return address most recently added to the chain is the first to be removed. At any point, we can only access the return address from within the method that is currently executing which represents the top of the stack. When the stack is popped (i.e., when the method returns), a new top is revealed within the calling routine. Invoking a method has the effect of pushing an element onto the stack, and returning pops the stack.

Implementing Recursive Methods

What must be added to this description in the case of a recursive method? The answer is, surprisingly little. Each time a recursive method calls itself, an entirely new data area must be allocated for that particular call. As before, this data area contains all the parameters, local variables, and temporaries, and a return address. The point to remember is that in recursion a data area is associated not with a method alone, but with a particular call to that method. Each call causes a new data area to be allocated, and each reference to an item in the method's data area is to the data area of the most recent call. Similarly, with each return, the current data area is freed, and the data area allocated immediately prior to it becomes current. This behavior, of course, suggests the use of a stack.

In Section 3.1.2, where we described the action of the recursive factorial method, we used a set of stacks to represent the successive allocations of each of the local variables and parameters. These stacks may be thought of as separate stacks, one for each local variable. Alternatively, and closer to reality, we may think of all of these stacks as a single large stack. Each element of this large stack is an entire data area containing subparts representing the individual local variables or parameters.

Each time the recursive routine is called, a new data area is allocated. The parameters in this data area are initialized to refer to the values of their corresponding arguments. The return address in the data area is initialized to the address following the call instruction. Any reference to local variables or parameters is via the current data area.

When the recursive routine returns, the returned value (if any) and the return address are saved, the data area is freed, and a branch to the return address is executed. The calling method retrieves the returned value (if any), resumes execution, and refers to its own data area, which is now on top of the stack.

Let us now examine how we can simulate the actions of a recursive function. We will need a stack of data areas defined by

```
Stack dataStack = new Stack();
```

dataArea is a stack containing objects representing a class containing the various items that exist in a data area. This class, which we call *DataArea*, must be defined as a class that consists of the fields required for the particular method being simulated. (We use the Java convention of starting class names with a capital letter and objects of a class with a lowercase letter.)

Simulation of Factorial

Let us look at a specific example, the factorial method. We present the code for that method, including temporary variables explicitly and omitting the test for negative input:

```
public long fact(int n) {
    int x;
    long y;

    if (n == 0)
        return 1;
    x = n - 1;
    y = fact(x);
    return n * y;
} // end fact
```

We wish to develop an algorithm for the simulation of this method using stacks. Once an algorithm has been developed, it will be a simple matter to turn it into a method that calculates the factorial of a number without the use of explicit recursion.

How are we to define the data area for this function? It must contain the parameter n and the local variables x and y. As we shall see, no temporaries are needed. The data area must also contain a return address. In this case, there are two possible points to which we might want to return: the assignment of $fact(x)$ to y, and the main applet that called $fact$.

For the purpose of our algorithm, let us assume a new statement of the form **goto** *label*; that unconditionally transfers control to a statement whose label is *label*. (Note that a statement label is different from a label appearing on an applet. It identifies a particular statement in a program.) Although in general the uncontrolled use of a **goto** statement is frowned upon and is not in keeping with the tenets of structured programming, the concept will be useful in the initial development of algorithms for the simulation of recursion. (The Java language reserves the **goto** keyword, but does not implement it.)

Suppose we have two labels. Let the label *label2* be the label of a section of code:

```
label2: y = result;
```

in the simulating method. Let the label *label1* be the label of a statement

```
label1: return result;
```

This reflects a convention that the variable *result* contains the value to be returned by an invocation of the *fact* method. *label2* represents a return from a recursive call, and *label1* represents a return from a nonrecursive call. The return address will be stored as an integer i (equal to either 1 or 2).

To effect a return from a recursive call, our algorithm executes the statement:

```
switch (i) {
  case 1:        goto label1;
  case 2:        goto label2;
}
```

Thus if $i==1$, a return is executed to the applet that called *fact*, and if $i==2$, a return is simulated to the assignment of the returned value to the variable y in the previous execution of *fact*.

We define a class *DataArea* that contains the parameter, n, the local variables x and y, and the return address, i.

```
public class DataArea {
  int param, x, retAddr;
  long y;
  public DataArea(int n, int x, long y, int i) {
        this.param = n;
        this.x = x;
        this.y = y;
        this.retAddr = i;
  }
} // end DataArea class
```

Using the Java container class, *Stack*, the stack of *DataArea* objects for this example can be defined as follows:

```
import java.util.*;
  …
Stack dataStack = new Stack();
```

The field in the data area that contains the simulated parameter is called *param* rather than n, to avoid confusion with the parameter n passed to the simulating function. Each time a new *DataArea* object is created, the class constructor intitalizes it with the appropriate parameters.

We also declare a current data area to hold the values of the variables in the simulated "current" call on the recursive function. The declaration is:

```
DataArea currArea = new DataArea(n, x, y, i);
```

In addition, we declare a single variable *result* by:

```
long result;
```

This variable is used to communicate the returned value of *fact* from one recursive call of *fact* to its caller, and from *fact* to the outside calling method.

In our algorithm, a return from *fact* is simulated by the code:

```
result = value to be returned;
i = currArea.retaddr;
currArea = (DataArea) dataStack.pop();
```

```
switch(i) {
  case 1:       goto label1;
  case 2:       goto label2;
}
```

A recursive call on *fact* is simulated by pushing the current data area on the stack, reinitializing the members of the *currArea* class, *currArea.param* and *currArea.retAddr*, respectively, to the parameter and return address of this call, and then transfering control to the start of the simulated routine. Recall that *currArea.x* holds the value of $n - 1$, which is to be the new parameter. Recall also that on a recursive call we wish to eventually return to *label2*. The code to accomplish this is:

```
dataArea.push(currArea);
DataArea currArea = new DataArea(x, 0, 0, 2);
goto start;             // start is the label of start of the simulated
                        // routine
```

When the simulation first begins, the current area must be initialized so that *currArea.param* equals *n* and *currArea.retAddr* equals 1 (indicating a return to the calling routine). A dummy data area must be pushed onto the stack so that an underflow does not occur when the *pop* method is executed in returning to the calling applet. This dummy data area must also be initialized so as not to cause an error in the *push* method. Thus the simulated algorithm of the recursive *fact* method is as follows:

```
import java.util.*;

public long simFact(long n) {
        Stack dataStack = new Stack();
        int i;
        long result;
        // initialize a dummy data area
        DataArea currArea = new DataArea(0, 0, 0, 0);
        dataStack.push(currArea);

        // set the parameter and the return address of the
        // current data area to their proper values
        DataArea currArea = new DataArea(n, 0, 0, 1);
start:  // this is the beginning of the simulated factorial method
        if (currArea.param == 0) {
                // simulation of return 1;
                result = 1;
                i = currArea.retAddr;
                currArea = (DataArea) dataStack.pop();
                switch(i) {
                        case 1:      goto label1;
                        case 2:      goto label2;
                }
        } // end if
        DataArea currArea = new DataArea
                (currArea.param, currArea.param - 1,0, i);
        dataStack.push(currArea);
```

```
            currArea.param = currArea.x;
            currArea.retAddr = 2;
            goto start;
   label2: // This is the point to which we return from the recursive call.
            // Set currArea.y to the returned value.
            CurrArea.y = result;
            // simulation of return(n * y);
            result = currArea.param * currArea.y;
            i = currArea.retAddr;
            currArea = (DataArea) dataStack.pop();
            switch(i) {
                   case 1:        goto label1;
                   case 2:        goto label2;
            }
   label1: // At this point we return to the calling applet
            return result;
} // end simFact
```

Trace through the execution of this program for $n = 5$ and be sure that you understand what the program does and how it does it.

Note that no space was reserved in the data area for temporaries, since they need not be saved for later use. The temporary location that holds the value of $n * y$ in the original recursive routine is simulated by the temporary for *currArea.param * currArea.y* in the simulating routine. This is generally not the case. For example, if a recursive method *funct* contained a statement such as:

```
x = a * funct(b) + c * funct(d);
```

the temporary for $a * funct(b)$ must be saved during the recursive call on *funct(d)*. However, stacking the temporary is not required in the example of the factorial function.

Improving the Simulated Routine

The foregoing discussion leads naturally to the question of whether all the local variables really need to be stacked. A variable must be saved on the stack only if its value at the point of initiation of a recursive call must be reused after return from that call. Let us examine whether the variables n, x, and y meet this requirement. Clearly n does have to be stacked. In the statement:

```
y = n * fact(x);
```

the old value of n must be used in the multiplication after return from the recursive call on *fact*. However, this is not the case for x and y. In fact, the value of y is not even defined at the point of the recursive call, so clearly it need not be stacked. Similarly, although x is defined at the point of call, it is never used again after returning, so why bother saving it?

This point is illustrated even more sharply by the realization that the routine would work just as well if x and y were not declared within the recursive method *fact*, but were declared as instance variables of the class containing the *fact* method (global variables). Thus the automatic stacking and unstacking action performed by recursion for the local variables x and y is unnecessary.

Another interesting question to consider is whether the return address is really needed on the stack. Since there is only one textual recursive call to *fact*, there is only one return address within *fact*. The other return address is to the main applet that originally called *fact*. But suppose a dummy data area had not been stacked upon initialization of the simulation. Then a data area is placed on the stack only in simulating a recursive call. When the stack is popped in returning from a recursive call, that area is removed from the stack. However, when an attempt is made to pop the stack in simulating a return to the main procedure, an underflow will occur. We can test for this underflow by catching the *EmptyStackException*, and when it is caught we can return directly to the outside calling routine rather than through a local label. This means that one of the return addresses can be eliminated. Since this leaves only a single possible return address, it need not be placed on the stack. Thus the data area has been reduced to contain the parameter alone, and the current data area is reduced to a single variable declared by

```
int currParam;
```

The algorithm is now quite compact and comprehensible.

```
import java.util.*;

public long simFact(int n) {
        Stack paramStack = new Stack();
        int currParam, x;
        long result = 1, y;
        boolean underFlow = false;
        currParam = n;
start:  // This is the beginning of the simulated factorial method.
        if (currParam == 0) {
                // simulation of return 1;
                result = 1;
                try {
                        currParam = ((Integer)
                        paramStack.pop()).intValue();
                        underFlow = false;
                }
                catch (EmptyStackException ese) {
                        underFlow = true;
                }
                if (underFlow)
                        goto label1;
                else
                        goto label2;
        }
        } // end if
        // currParam != 0
        x = currParam - 1;
        // Simulation of recursive call to fact.
        paramStack.push(new Integer(currParam));
        currParam = x;
        goto start;
```

```
    label2: // This is the point to which we return from the recursive call.
            // Set y to the returned value.
            y = result;
            // simulation of return n * y;
            result = currParam * y;
            try {
                    currParam = ((Integer)
                    paramStack.pop()).intValue();
                    underFlow = false;
            }
            catch (EmptyStackException ese) {
                                underFlow = true;
            }
            if (underFlow)
                    goto label1;
            else
                    goto label2;
            }
    label1:    // At this point we return to the main applet.
            return result;
    } // end simFact
```

Eliminating *gotos*

The Java language does not support the *goto* statement. Furthermore, if you were to look at the program without having seen its derivation, you probably would not be able to identify it as computing the factorial function. The algorithmic statements

```
    goto start;
```

and

```
    goto label2;
```

are especially irritating because they interrupt the flow of thought at a time when one might otherwise come to an understanding of what is happening. Let us see if we can transform this program into a still more readable version.

The use of a ***flowchart*** is often helpful in untangling the complexities of an algorithm. Figure 3.4.2 diagrammatically represents our simplified algorithm. We repeat the algorithm indicating the statements that correspond to the flowchart.

```
    import java.util.*;

    public long simFact(int n) {
```

```
        Stack paramStack= new Stack();
        int currParam, x;
        long result = 1, y;
        boolean underFlow = false;

        currParam = n;
```
Initializations

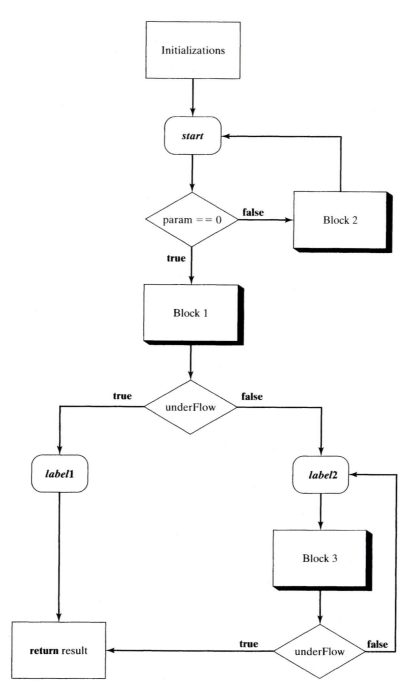

FIGURE 3.4.2   Flowchart for the factorial simulation.

```
start: // This is the beginning of the simulated factorial
       // method.
       if (currParam == 0) {
```

```
                    // simulation of return 1;
                    result = 1;
                    try {
                         currParam = ((Integer)
                                        paramStack.pop()).intValue();   Block 1
                         underFlow = false;
                    }
                    catch (EmptyStackException ese) {
                              underFlow = true;
                    }
```

```
            if (underFlow)
                    goto label1;
            else
                    goto label2;
       } // end if
```

```
            // currParam != 0
            x = currParam - 1;
            // simulation of recursive call to fact
            paramStack.push(new Integer(currParam));          Block 2
            currParam = x;
```

```
       goto start;
label2: // This is the point to which we return from
       // the recursive call. Set y to the returned value.
```

```
            y = result;
            // simulation of return n * y;
            result = currParam * y;
            try {
                    currParam = ((Integer)
                                   paramStack.pop()).intValue();   Block 3
                    underFlow = false;
            }
            catch (EmptyStackException ese) {
                              underFlow = true;
            }
```

```
       if (underFlow)
              goto label1;
       else
              goto label2;
```

```
    label1:       // At this point we return to the main applet.
                  return result;
} // end simFact
```

Close examination of the flowchart reveals that the loop containing block 2 can be replaced by the following *while* loop:

```
while (currParam != 0) {
```

```
// currParam != 0
x = currParam - 1;
// simulation of recursive call to fact
paramStack.push(new Integer(currParam));
currParam = x;
```
Block 2

```
} // end while
```

Similarly, the loop containing block 3 can be replaced by the following *while* loop:

```
while (!underFlow) {
```

```
y = result;
// simulation of return n * y;
result = currParam * y;
try {
      currParam = ((Integer)
      paramStack.pop()).intValue();
      underFlow = false;
}
catch (EmptyStackException ese) {
      underFlow = true;
}
```
Block 3

```
} // end while
```

Substituting the revised block2 and block 3 in the algorithm obviates the need for the *goto* statements. Thus our *simFact* algorithm may be implemented by the following Java method:

```
import java.util.*;

public int simFact(long n) {
```

```
Stack paramStack = new Stack();
int currParam, x;
long result = 1, y;
boolean underFlow = false;

currParam = n;
```
Initializations

```
         start:  // This is the beginning of the simulated factorial method.
```

```
              while (currParam != 0) {
                     // currParam != 0
                     x = currParam - 1;
                     // Simulation of recursive call to fact.       Block 2
                     paramStack.push(new Integer (currParam));
                     currParam = x;
              } // end while
```

```
         if (currParam == 0) {
```

```
                     // simulation of return 1;
                     result = 1;
                     try {
                           currParam = ((Integer)
                                        paramStack.pop()).intValue();
                           underFlow = false;                       Block 1
                     }
                     catch (EmptyStackException ese) {
                           underFlow = true;
                     }
```

```
         } // end if
         if (underFlow) {
                     // At this point we return to the main applet.
                     return result;
         }
```

```
              while (!underFlow) {
                     y = result;
                     // simulation of return n * y;
                     result = currParam * y;
                     try {
                           currParam = ((Integer)
                                        paramStack.pop()).intValue();
                           underFlow = false;                       Block 3
                     }
                     catch (EmptyStackException ese) {
                           underFlow = true;
                     }
              } // end while
```

```
         label1: // At this point we return to the main applet.
         return result;
     } // end simFact
```

Let us examine these two loops more closely. In block 1, x starts off at the value of the input parameter n and is reduced by 1 each time the subtraction loop is repeated. Each time x is set to a new value, the old value of x is saved on the stack. This continues until x is 0. Thus, after the first loop has been executed, the stack contains, from top to bottom, the integers 1 to n.

The multiplication loop merely removes each of these values from the stack and sets *y* to the product of the popped value and the old value of *y*. Since we know what the stack contains at the start of the multiplication loop, why bother popping the stack? We can use those values directly. We can eliminate the stack and the first loop entirely and replace the multiplication loop with a loop that multiplies *y* by each of the integers from 1 to *n* in turn. The resulting method is:

```
public long simFact(int n) {
   int x;
   long  y;

   for (y=x=1; x <= n; x++)
        y *= x;
   return y;
} // end simfact
```

But this program is a direct Java implementation of the iterative version of the factorial method as presented in Section 3.1. The only change is that *x* varies from 1 to *n* rather than from *n* to 1.

Simulating the Towers of Hanoi

We have shown that successive transformations of a nonrecursive simulation of a recursive routine may lead to a simpler program for solving a problem. Let us now look at a more complex example of recursion, the Towers of Hanoi problem presented in Section 3.3. We will simulate its recursion and attempt to simplify the simulation to produce a nonrecursive solution. We present again the recursive method from Section 3.3.

```
void towers(int n, char fromPeg, char toPeg, char auxPeg) {
   // If only one disk, make the move and return
   if (n == 1) {
     output1.append("\nmove disk 1 from peg " + fromPeg +
                                      " to peg " + toPeg);
     return;
   } // end if
   // Move top n - 1 disks from A to B, using C as auxiliary
   towers(n - 1, fromPeg, auxPeg, toPeg);
   output1.append("\nmove disk " + n + " from peg " + fromPeg +
                                      " to peg " + toPeg);
   // Move n - 1 disk from B to C using A as auxiliary
   towers(n - 1, auxPeg, toPeg, fromPeg);
} // end towers
```

Make sure that you understand the problem and the recursive solution before proceeding. If you do not, reread Section 3.3.

Earlier in this section, we developed a technique for simulating recursion using a stack. Our method involves the following steps:

1. Define a stack, *dataStack* of objects, of the *DataArea* class, representing the parameters, local variables, and return address of the recursive call. Use the class constructor to initialize an object prior to pushing it on the stack.

2. Construct an algorithm that

   a. pushes the current *DataArea* onto the stack each time a recursive call is initiated, and

   b. pops the stack, branching to the current return address, each time a recursive return is to be simulated.

3. Use a flowchart to analyze the algorithm.

4. Construct a Java method, using the techniques of structured programming in order to eliminate the ***goto*** statements.

There are four parameters in the *towers* method, each of which is subject to change in a recursive call. Therefore, the data area must contain elements representing all four. There are no local variables. There is a single temporary that is needed to hold the value of $n - 1$, but this can be represented by a similar temporary in the simulating program and does not have to be stacked. There are three possible points to which the function returns on various calls: the calling applet and the two points following the recursive calls. Therefore, four labels are necessary:

```
start:
label1:
label2:
label3: .
```

The return address is encoded as an integer (either 1, 2, or 3) in each data area.

   We define a class *DataArea* which contains the parameters, *n*, representing the number of pegs; *fromPeg*, *toPeg*, and *auxPeg*, respectively representing the peg from which we are removing disks, the peg to which we will take the disks, and the auxiliary peg; and the return address, *retAddr*.

```java
public class DataArea {
  int nParam;
  char fromParam, toParam, auxParam;
  int retAddr;

  public DataArea(int n, char fromPeg, char toPeg,  char auxPeg,
  int retAddr) {
      this.nParam = n;
      this.fromParam = fromPeg;
      this.toParam = toPeg;
      this.auxParam = auxPeg;
      this.retAddr = retAddr;
  }

  public DataArea(DataArea dataArea) {
      this.nParam = dataArea.nParam;
      this.fromParam = dataArea.fromParam;
      this.toParam = dataArea.toParam;
      this.auxParam = dataArea.auxParam;
```

```
          this.retAddr = dataArea.retAddr;
   }

} // end DataArea class
```

The first constructor allows for the initialization of an object of the *DataArea* class by individually specifying each of the parameters. For example:

```
CurrArea = new DataArea(n, fromPeg, toPeg, AuxPeg, retAddr);
```

It is also convenient to have a constructor that allows us to instantiate a new object from an existing object of the same class (without having to specify each member individually). For example, assuming a ***stack dataStack***, it is easier to write

```
dataStack.push(new DataArea(currArea));
```

than to write

```
dataStack.push(new DataArea(currArea.nParam, currArea.fromParam,
                            currArea.toParam, currArea.auxParam,
                            currArea.retAddr);
```

Consider the following nonrecursive algorithm for the simulation of *towers*: (The highlighted sections refer to the flowchart in Figure 3.4.3.)

```
import java.util.*;

public void simTowers(int n, char fromPeg, char toPeg, char
auxPeg) {
          Stack dataStack = new Stack();
          DataArea currArea;
          char temp;
          int i;
```

```
          // Initialize a dummy data area.
          currArea = new DataArea(0, ' ', ' ', ' ', 0);
          // Push dummy data area onto stack.
          dataStack.push(new DataArea(currArea));

          // Set the parameters and the return addresses of the
          // current data area to their proper values.
          currArea = new DataArea(n, fromPeg, toPeg,
          auxPeg, 1);
```
Initializations

```
start:    // This is the start of the simulated routine.

          if (currArea.nParam == 1) {
```

```
                    output1.append("\nmove disk 1 from peg " +
                          currArea.fromParam + " to peg " +
                          currArea.toParam);
                    i = currArea.retAddr;
                    currArea = (DataArea) dataStack.pop();
```
Block 0

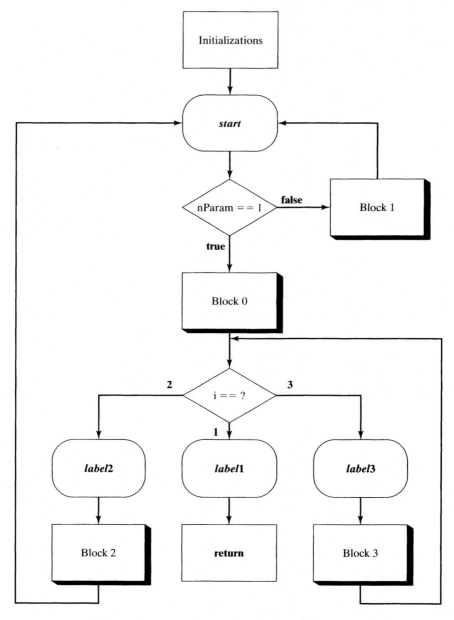

FIGURE 3.4.3 Flowchart for Towers of Hanoi simulation.

```
switch (i) {
        case 1:    goto label1;
        case 2:    goto label2;
        case 3:    goto label3;
    }
} // end if
```

```
                    // This is the first recursive call.
                    dataStack.push(new DataArea(currArea));
                    --currArea.nParam;                           Block 1
                    temp = currArea.auxParam;
                    currArea.auxParam = currArea.toParam;
                    currArea.toParam = temp;
                    currArea.retAddr = 2;
```

goto start;

label2: // We return to this point from the first recursive call.

```
                    output1.append("\nmove disk " + currArea.nParam +
                            " from peg " + currArea.fromParam +
                            " to peg " + currArea.toParam);
                    // This is the second recursive call.
                    dataStack.push(currArea);
                    --currArea.nParam;                           Block 2
                    temp = currArea.fromParam;
                    currArea.fromParam = currArea.auxparam;
                    currArea.auparam = temp;
                    currArea.retAddr = 3;
```

goto start;

label3:   // Return to this point from the second recursive call.

```
                    i = currArea.retAddr;                        Block 3
                    currArea = (DataArea) dataArea.pop();
```

```
        switch (i) {
            case 1:    goto label1;
            case 2:    goto label2;
            case 3:    goto label3;
        }
label1:    return;
} // end simTowers
```

Close examination of the flowchart in Figure 3.4.3 reveals that the algorithm may be rewritten in outline form as:

```
    initializations;
    while (true) {
      while (nParam != 1)
            Block 1;
      Block 0;
      if (i == 1)
            return;
      while (i == 3)
            Block 3;
```

```
    if (i == 1)
            return;
    Block 2;
} // end while
```

where initializations, block 0 through block 3 correspond to the lines highlighted in the original algorithm. Thus our *simTowers* algorithm may be implemented by the following Java method:

```
import java.util.*

public void simTowers(int n, char fromPeg, char toPeg, char auxPeg) {
    Stack dataStack = new Stack();
    DataArea currArea;
    char temp;
    int i;
```

```
        // Initialize a dummy data area.
        currArea = new DataArea(0, ' ', ' ', ' ', 0);
        // Push dummy data area onto stack.
        dataStack.push(currArea);
        // Set the parameters and the return addresses of the    | Initializations
        // current data area to their proper values.
        currArea = new DataArea(n, fromPeg, toPeg, auxPeg, 1);
```

```
    while (true) {

        while (currArea.nParam != 1) {
```

```
            // This is the first recursive call.
            dataStack.push(new DataArea(currArea));
            --currArea.nParam;
            temp = currArea.auxParam;                              | Block 1
            currArea.auxParam = currArea.toParam;
            currArea.toParam = temp;
            currArea.retAddr = 2;
```

```
        } // end while
```

```
            // This is the start of the simulated routine.
            output1.append("\nmove disk 1 from peg " +
            currArea.fromParam + " to peg " + currArea.toParam);   | Block 0
            i = currArea.retAddr;
            currArea = (DataArea) dataArea.pop();
```

```
        if (i == 1)
                return;
        while (i == 3) {
```

```
            // Return to this point from the second recursive
            call.                                                  | Block 3
            i = currArea.retAddr;
            currArea = (DataArea) dataStack.pop();
```

```
} // end while
if (i == 1)
        return;
```

```
        // We return to this point from the first recursive
        // call.
        output1.append("\nmove disk " + currArea.nParam +
                    " from peg " + currArea.fromParam +
                    " to peg " + currArea.toParam);
        // This is the second recursive call.
        dataStack.push(new DataArea(currArea));                    Block 2
        --currArea.nParam;
        temp = currArea.fromParam;
        currArea.fromParam = currArea.auxParam;
        currArea.auxParam = temp;
        currArea.retAddr = 3;
```

```
    } // end while
} // end simTowers
```

Trace through the actions of this program and see how it reflects the actions of the original recursive version.

EXERCISES

3.4.1 Write a nonrecursive simulation of the functions *convert* and *find* presented in Section 3.3.

3.4.2 Write a nonrecursive simulation of the recursive binary search procedure, and transform it into an iterative procedure.

3.4.3 Write a nonrecursive simulation of *fib*. Can you transform it into an iterative method?

3.4.4 Write nonrecursive simulations of the recursive routines in Sections 3.2 and 3.3 and the exercises in those sections.

3.4.5 Show that any solution to the Towers of Hanoi problem that uses a minimum number of moves must satisfy the conditions listed below. Use these facts to develop a direct iterative algorithm for the Towers of Hanoi. Implement the algorithm as a Java applet.

1. The first move involves moving the smallest disk.

2. A minimum-move solution consists of alternately moving the smallest disk and a disk that is not the smallest.

3. At any point, there is only one possible move involving a disk that is not the smallest.

4. Define the cyclic direction from *fromPeg* to *toPeg* to *auxPeg* to *fromPeg* as clockwise, and the opposite direction (from *fromPeg* to *auxPeg* to *toPeg* to *fromPeg*) as counterclockwise. Assume that a minimum-move solution to move a k-disk tower from *fromPeg* to *toPeg* always moves the smallest disk in one direction. Show that a minimum-move solution to move a $(k + 1)$-disk tower from *fromPeg* to *toPeg* would then always move the smallest disk in the other direction. Since the solution for one disk moves the smallest disk clockwise (the single move from *fromPeg* to *toPeg*), this means that for an odd

number of disks, the smallest disk always moves clockwise, and for an even number of disks, the smallest disk always moves counterclockwise.

5. The solution is completed as soon as all the disks are on a single peg.

3.4.6   Convert the following recursive program scheme into an iterative version that does not use a stack. *f(n)* is a method that returns *true* or *false* based on the value of *n*, and *g(n)* is a function that returns a value of the same type as *n* (without modifying *n*).

```
int rec(int n) {
        if (!f(n)) {
                // any group of Java statements that
                // do not change the value of n
                rec(g(n));
        } // end if
} // end rec
```

Generalize your result to the case in which *rec* returns a value.

3.4.7   Let *f(n)* be a method and *g(n)* and *h(n)* be methods that return a value of the same type as *n* without modifying *n*. Let *(stmts)* represent any group of Java statements that do not modify the value of *n*. Show that the recursive program scheme *rec* is equivalent to the iterative scheme *iter*:

```
void rec(int n) {
        if (!f(n)) {
                (stmts)
                rec(g(n));
                rec(h(n));
        } // end if
} // end rec

void iter(int n) {
    Stack s = new Stack();
    s.push(n);
    while (!s.empty()) {
            n = s.pop();
            if (!f(n)) {
                    (stmts)
                    s.push(h(n));
                    s.push(g(n));
            } // end if
    } // end while
} // end iter
```

Show that the *if* statements in *iter* can be replaced by the loop:

```
while(!f(n)) {
        (stmts)
        s.push(h(n));
        n = g(n);
} // end while
```

3.5   EFFICIENCY OF RECURSION

In general, a nonrecursive version of a program will execute more efficiently in terms of time and space than a recursive version. This is because the overhead involved in entering and exiting a block is avoided in the nonrecursive version. As we have seen, it is often possible to identify a good number of local variables and temporaries that do not have to be saved and restored through the use of a stack. A nonrecursive program can eliminate this needless stacking activity. However, since the compiler in a recursive procedure is usually unable to identify such variables, they are stacked and unstacked to ensure that no problems arise.

We have also seen that a recursive solution is sometimes the most natural and logical way of solving a problem. It is doubtful whether a programmer could have developed the nonrecursive solution to the Towers of Hanoi problem directly from the problem statement. Much the same may be said about the problem of converting prefix to postfix, where the recursive solution flows directly from the definitions. A nonrecursive solution involving stacks is more difficult to develop and more prone to error.

Thus there is a conflict between machine efficiency and programmer efficiency. With the cost of programming increasing steadily, and the cost of computation decreasing, we have reached the point where in most cases it is not worth a programmer's time to laboriously construct a nonrecursive solution to a problem that is most naturally solved recursively. Of course an incompetent overly clever programmer may come up with a complicated recursive solution to a simple problem that can be solved directly by nonrecursive methods. (An example of this is the factorial function or even the binary search.) However, if a competent programmer identifies a recursive solution as the simplest and most straightforward method for solving a particular problem, it is probably not worth the time and effort to discover a more efficient method.

This is not always the case, though. If a program is to be run very frequently (often, entire computers are dedicated to continually running the same program), so that increased efficiency in execution speed significantly increases throughput, then the extra investment in programming time is worthwhile. Even in such cases, it is probably better to create a nonrecursive version by simulating and transforming the recursive solution than by attempting to create a nonrecursive solution from the problem statement.

To do this most efficiently, what is required is to first write the recursive routine and then its simulated version, including all the stacks and temporaries. Next, eliminate any superfluous stacks and variables. The final version is a refinement of the original program, and is certainly more efficient. The elimination of superfluous and redundant operations improves the efficiency of the resulting program. Nonetheless, every transformation applied to a program is another opening through which an unanticipated error may creep in.

When a stack cannot be eliminated from the nonrecursive version of a program and the recursive version does not contain any extra parameters or local variables, the recursive version can be as fast or faster than the nonrecursive version under a good compiler. The Towers of Hanoi is an example of such a recursive program. Factorial, whose nonrecursive version does not need a stack, and calculation of Fibonacci numbers, which contains an unnecessary second recursive call (and does not need a stack either), are examples of cases where recursion should be avoided in a practical implementation. We examine another example of efficient recursion (inorder tree traversal) in Section 5.2.

Another point to remember is that explicit calls to *pop*, *push*, and *empty*, as well as tests for underflow and overflow, are quite expensive. In fact, they can often outweigh the expense of the overhead of recursion. Thus, to maximize the actual runtime efficiency of a nonrecursive translation, these calls should be replaced by inline code and the overflow/underflow tests eliminated when it is known that we are operating within the array bounds.

The ideas and transformations that we have put forward in presenting the factorial function and the Towers of Hanoi can be applied to more complex problems whose nonrecursive solutions are not readily apparent. The extent to which a recursive solution (actual or simulated) can be transformed into a direct solution depends on the specifics of the problem and the ingenuity of the programmer.

EXERCISES

3.5.1   Run the recursive and nonrecursive versions of the factorial method in Sections 3.2 and 3.4, and examine how much space and time each requires as *n* becomes larger.

3.5.2   Do the same as Exercise 3.5.1 above for the Towers of Hanoi problem.

C H A P T E R 4

Queues and Lists

This chapter introduces the queue and the priority queue, two important data structures often used to simulate real-world situations. The concepts of the stack and queue are then extended to a new structure, the list. Various forms of lists and their associated operations are examined, and several applications are presented.

4.1 THE QUEUE AND ITS SEQUENTIAL REPRESENTATION

A *queue* is an ordered collection of items from which items may be deleted at one end (called the *front* of the queue) and into which items may be inserted at the other end (called the *rear* of the queue).

Figure 4.1.1a illustrates a queue containing three elements: *A, B*, and *C. A* is at the front of the queue, and *C* is at the rear. In Figure 4.1.1b, an element has been deleted from the queue. Since elements may be deleted only from the front of the queue, *A* is removed and *B* is now at the front. In Figure 4.1.1c, when items *D* and *E* are inserted, they must be inserted at the rear of the queue.

Since *D* was inserted into the queue before *E*, it will be removed earlier. The first element inserted into a queue is the first element to be removed. For this reason, a queue is sometimes called a *fifo* (first-in, first-out) list, as opposed to a stack, which is a *lifo* (last-in, first-out) list. Examples of queues abound in the real world. A line at a bank or at a bus stop, and a group of cars waiting at a toll booth are all familiar examples of queues.

Three primitive operations can be applied to a queue. The operation *q.insert(x)* inserts item *x* at the rear of the queue *q*. The operation *x = q.remove()* deletes the front element from the queue *q* and sets *x* to its contents. The third operation, *q.empty()*, returns *false* or *true* depending on whether or not the queue contains any elements. The queue in Figure 4.1.1 can be obtained by the following sequence of operations. We assume that the queue is initially empty.

```
q.insert(A);
q.insert(B);
q.insert(C);                (Figure 4.1.1a)
x = q.remove();             (Figure 4.1.1b;  x is set to A)
q.insert(D);
q.insert(E);                (Figure 4.1.1c)
```

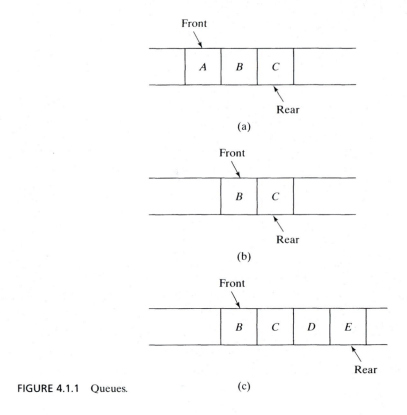

FIGURE 4.1.1 Queues.

The *insert* operation can always be performed because there is no limit to the number of elements a queue may contain. The *remove* operation, however, can be applied only if the queue is not empty; there is no way to remove an element from a queue containing no elements. The result of an illegal attempt to remove an element from an empty queue is called **underflow**. The *empty* operation is, of course, always applicable.

The Queue as an Abstract Data Type

The representation of a queue as an abstract data type is straightforward. We use *eltype* to denote the type of the queue element and parameterize the queue type with *eltype*.

```
abstract class <<eltype> QUEUE(eltype) {
      abstract QUEUE(eltype) q.empty()
      postcondition     empty == (q.length() == 0);

      abstract eltype QUEUE(eltype) q.remove()
      precondition      q.empty() == FALSE;
      postcondition     remove == q'.first();
                        q == q'.sub(1, q'.length() - 1);
```

```
      abstract QUEUE(eltype) q.insert(eltype elt)
      postcondition    q == q' + <elt>;
}
```

Java Implementation of Queues

How is a queue represented in Java? One idea is to define a class containing an array to hold the elements of the queue and to use two variables, *front* and *rear*, to hold the positions within the array of the first and last elements of the queue. Although we could define a separate class for queues of integers, queues of chars, queues of strings, and so on, we might as well declare a queue of type *Object* which can be used to store an object of any type:

```
public class ArrayObjectQueue {
    private final int MAXQUEUE = 100;
    private Object[] items;
    private int front, rear;

    // queue methods go here

} // end class ArrayObjectQueue
```

Once this has been done, an actual queue object *q* may be declared by:

```
Queue q = new Queue();
```

Of course, using an array to hold a queue introduces the possibility of **overflow** if the queue should grow larger than the size of the array. Ignoring the possibility of underflow and overflow for the moment, the method *q.insert(x)* could be implemented by the statement:

```
items [++rear] = x;
```

and the method *x = q.remove*() could be implemented by:

```
x = items [front++];
```

Initially, *rear* is set to -1 and *front* is set to 0. The queue is empty whenever *rear* < *front*. The number of elements in the queue at any time is equal to the value of *rear* − *front* + 1.

Let us examine what might happen under this representation. Figure 4.1.2 illustrates an array of five elements used to represent a queue (i.e., *MAXQUEUE* equals 5). Initially (Figure 4.1.2a), the queue is empty. In Figure 4.1.2b, items *A, B,* and *C* have been inserted. In Figure 4.1.2c, two items have been deleted, and in Figure 4.1.2d, two new items, *D* and *E*, have been inserted. The value of *front* is 2 and the value of *rear* is 4, so that there are only 4 − 2 + 1 = 3 elements in the queue. Since the array contains five elements, there should be room for the queue to expand without the worry of overflow.

However, to insert *F* into the queue, *rear* must be increased by 1 to 5, and *items*[5] must be set to the value *F*. But *items* is an array of only five elements, so the insertion cannot be made. It is possible to reach the absurd situation where the queue is empty, but no new element can be inserted (see if you can come up with a sequence of insertions and deletions to reach this situation). Clearly, the array representation outlined above is unacceptable.

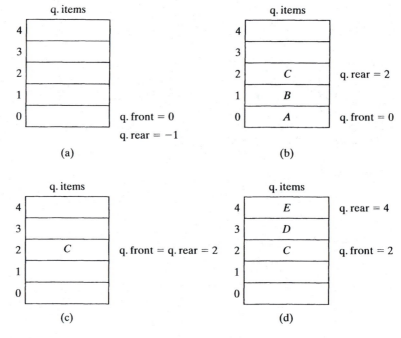

FIGURE 4.1.2

One solution is to modify the *remove* method so that when an item is deleted, the entire queue is shifted to the beginning of the array. The operation $x = q.remove()$ would then be modified (again, ignoring the possibility of underflow) to:

```
x = items[0];
for (i = 0; i < rear; i++)
    items[i] = items[i+1];
rear--;
```

The queue need no longer contain a *front* field, since the element at position 0 of the array is always at the front of the queue. The empty queue is represented by the queue in which *rear* equals −1.

This method, however, is too inefficient. Each deletion involves moving every remaining element of the queue. If a queue contains five hundred or a thousand elements, this is too high a price to pay. Further, the operation of removing an element from a queue logically involves manipulation of only one element—the one currently at the front of the queue. The implementation of the operation should reflect this and should not involve a host of extraneous operations (see Exercise 4.1.3 for a more efficient alternative).

Of course, we can implement a queue in a vector rather than in an array, so that additional elements can always be added in the rear. As items are removed from the vector, using the vector method *remove*, the items remaining shift to the front of the vector. Thus *front* can always equal zero. We leave to the reader the implementation of a queue using a vector. However, insertions and removals from a vector are very inefficient and are not recommended when many insertions and removals are expected.

Another solution is to view an array that holds a queue as a circle rather than as a straight line. That is, we imagine the first element of the array (i.e., the element at position 0) as immediately following its last element. This implies that even if the last element is occupied, a new value can be inserted behind it in the first element of the array as long as the first element is empty.

Let us look at an example. Assume that a queue contains three items in positions 2, 3, and 4 of a five-element array. This is the situation in Figure 4.1.2d, reproduced as Figure 4.1.3a. Although the array is not full, its last element is occupied. If item *F* is now inserted into the queue, it can be placed in position 0 of the array, as shown in Figure 4.1.3b. The first item of the queue is in *items*[2], which is followed in the queue by *items* [3], *items*[4], and *items*[0]. Figures 4.1.3c, d, and e show the status of the queue as two items, *C* and *D*, are deleted, then *G* is inserted, and finally *E* is deleted.

Unfortunately, it is difficult under this representation to determine when the queue is empty. The condition *rear* < *front* is no longer valid as a test for an empty queue, since Figures 4.1.3b, c, and d all illustrate situations in which the condition is true yet the queue is not empty.

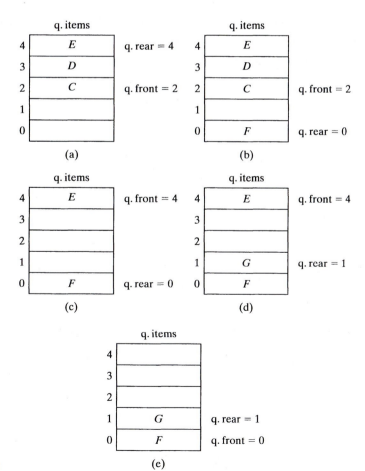

FIGURE 4.1.3

One way of solving this problem is to establish the convention that the value of *front* is the array index immediately preceding the first element of the queue rather than the index of the first element itself. Thus, since *rear* is the index of the last element of the queue, the condition *front==rear* implies that the queue is empty.

The class constructor for the a queue of Objects using the array implementation may then be written as:

```
public ArrayObjectQueue() {
  items = new Object[MAXQUEUE];
  front = items.length - 1;
  rear = items.length - 1;
} // end constructor
```

Note that *front* and *rear* are initialized to the last index of the array, rather than −1 or 0, because the last element of the array immediately precedes the first one in the queue under this representation. Since *rear* equals *front*, the queue is initially empty.

The *empty* method may be coded as:

```
public boolean empty() {
  if (front == rear)
        return true;
  else
        return false;
} // end empty
```

Once this function exists, a test for the empty queue is implemented by the statement

```
if (q.empty())
    // queue is empty
else
    // queue is not empty
```

The method *remove* may be coded as:

```
public Object remove(){
  if (empty()) {
        System.out.println("Queue Underflow.");
        System.exit(1);
  }
  if (front == items.length - 1)
        front = 0;
  else
        front++;
  return items[front];
} // end remove
```

Note that *front* must be updated before an element is extracted.

Of course, an underflow condition is often meaningful and serves as a signal for a new phase of processing. We may wish to use the method *removeAndTest* which returns an object of the utility class *RemoveAndTestResult*. *RemoveAndTestResult* may be defined by

```
class RemoveAndTestResult {
    public boolean underflow;
    public Object value;

    RemoveAndTestResult(boolean u) {
        underflow = u;
    } // end constructor

    RemoveAndTestResult(boolean u, Object v) {
        underflow = u;
        value = v;
    } // end constructor
} // end class RemoveAndTestResult
```

The header for the *removeAndTest* method is

```
public RemoveAndTestResult removeAndTest()
```

If the queue is nonempty, this method sets *underflow* to *false* and *value* to the object removed from the queue. If the queue is empty, so that underflow occurs, the routine sets *underflow* to *true*. The coding of the routine is left to the reader.

Insert Operation

The *insert* operation involves testing for overflow, which occurs when the entire array is occupied by items of the queue and an attempt is made to insert yet another element into the queue. For example, consider the queue in Figure 4.1.4a. There are three

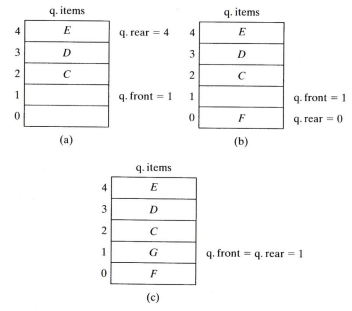

FIGURE 4.1.4

elements in the queue: *C, D*, and *E* in *items*[2], *items*[3], and *items*[4], respectively. Since the last item of the queue occupies *items*[4], *rear* equals 4. Since the first element of the queue is in *items*[2], *front* equals 1. In Figure 4.1.4b and c, items *F* and *G* are inserted into the queue. At that point, the array is full and an attempt to perform any more insertions causes an overflow. But this is indicated by the fact that *front* equals *rear*, which is precisely the indication for underflow. There is no way to distinguish between an empty queue and a full queue under this implementation. Such a situation is clearly unsatisfactory.

One solution is to sacrifice one element of the array and to allow a queue to grow only as large as one less than the size of the array. Thus, if an array of one hundred elements is declared as a queue, the queue may contain up to ninety-nine elements. An attempt to insert a hundredth element into the queue causes an overflow. The *insert* routine may then be written as follows:

```java
public void insert(Object x) {
    // make room for new element
    if (rear == items.length - 1)
        rear = 0;
    else
        rear++;
    // check for overflow
    if (rear == front) {
        System.out.println("Queue Overflow.");
        System.exit(1);
    }
    items[rear] = x;
} // end insert
```

The test for overflow in *insert* occurs after *rear* has been adjusted, while the test for underflow in *remove* occurs immediately upon entering the routine, before *front* is updated.

Priority Queue

The stack and the queue are data structures whose elements are ordered based on the sequence in which they are inserted. The *pop* operation retrieves the last element inserted, and the *remove* operation retrieves the first element inserted. If there is an intrinsic order among the elements (e.g., numeric order or alphabetic order), it is ignored in the stack or queue operations.

A ***priority queue*** is a data structure in which the intrinsic ordering of the elements does determine the results of its basic operations. There are two types of priority queues: ascending priority queues and descending priority queues. An ***ascending priority queue*** is a collection of items into which items can be inserted arbitrarily and from which only the smallest item can be removed. If *apq* is an ascending priority queue, the operation *apq.pqInsert(x)* inserts element *x* into *apq*, and *apq.pqMinDelete*() removes the minimum element from *apq* and returns its value.

A ***descending priority queue*** is similar but allows deletion of only the *largest* item. The operations applicable to a descending priority queue, *dpq*, are *dpq.pqInsert(x)* and *dpq.pqMaxDelete(). dpq.pqInsert(x)* inserts element *x* into *dpq* and is logically identical to *pqInsert* for an ascending priority queue. *dpq.pqMaxDelete()* removes the maximum element from *dpq* and returns its value.

The operation *pq.empty()* applies to both types of priority queue and determines whether a priority queue is empty. *pqMinDelete* or *pqMaxDelete* can only be applied to a nonempty priority queue [i.e., if *pq.empty()* is *false*].

Once *pqMinDelete* has been applied to retrieve the smallest element of an ascending priority queue, it can be applied again to retrieve the next smallest, and so on. Thus the operation successively retrieves elements of a priority queue in ascending order. (However, if a small element is inserted after several deletions, the next retrieval will return that small element, which may be smaller than a previously retrieved element.) Similarly, *pqMaxDelete* retrieves elements of a descending priority queue in descending order. This explains the designation of a priority queue as either ascending or descending.

The elements of a priority queue need not be numbers or characters that can be compared directly. They may be complex objects that are ordered on one or several fields. For example, telephone book listings consist of last names, first names, addresses, and phone numbers, and are ordered by last name.

Sometimes, the field on which the elements of a priority queue is ordered is not even part of the elements themselves; it may be a special, external value used specifically for the purpose of ordering the priority queue. For example, a stack may be viewed as a descending priority queue whose elements are ordered by time of insertion. The element that was inserted last has the greatest insertion-time value and is the only item that can be retrieved. A queue may similarly be viewed as an ascending priority queue whose elements are ordered by time of insertion. In both cases, the time of insertion is not part of the elements themselves but is used to order the priority queue.

We leave as an exercise for the reader the development of an ADT specification for a priority queue. We now look at implementation considerations.

Array Implementation of a Priority Queue

As we have seen, stacks and queues can be implemented in an array such that each insertion or deletion involves accessing only a single element of the array (ignoring the possibilities of overflow). Unfortunately, this is not possible for a priority queue.

Suppose the *n* elements of a priority queue *pq* are maintained in positions 0 to *n* − 1 of an array *items* of size MAXPQ, and suppose *rear* equals the first empty array position, *n*. Then *pq.pqInsert(x)* would seem to be a fairly straightforward operation:

```
if (rear >= MAXPQ) {
    System.out.println("priority queue overflow");
    System.exit(1);
} // end if
items[rear] = x;
rear++;
```

Note that under this insertion method, the elements of the priority queue are not kept ordered in the array.

As long as only insertions take place, this implementation works well. Suppose, however, that we attempt the operation *pq.pqMinDelete*() on an ascending priority queue. This raises two issues. First, in order to locate the smallest element, every element of the array from *items*[0] through *items*[*rear* − 1] must be examined. Therefore, a deletion requires accessing every element of the priority queue.

Second, how can an element in the middle of the array be deleted? Stack and queue deletions involve removal of an item from one of the two ends and do not require searching. Priority queue deletion under this implementation requires both searching for the element to be deleted and removal of an element in the middle of an array.

There are several solutions to this problem, none of them entirely satisfactory.

1. A special "empty" indicator can be placed in a deleted position. This indicator can be a value that is invalid as an element (e.g., −1 in a priority queue of nonnegative numbers), or a separate field can be contained in each array element to indicate whether it is empty. Insertion proceeds as before, but when *rear* reaches MAXPQ, the array elements are compacted into the front of the array and *rear* is reset to one more than the number of elements. There are several disadvantages to this approach. First, the search process to locate the maximum or minimum element must examine all the deleted array positions in addition to the actual priority queue elements. If many items have been deleted but compaction has not yet taken place, the deletion operation accesses many more array elements than exist in the priority queue. Second, once in a while insertion requires accessing every single position of the array as it runs out of room and begins compaction.

2. The deletion operation labels a position empty, as in the previous solution, but insertion is modified to insert a new item in the first "empty" position. Insertion then involves accessing every array element up to the first one that has been deleted. The decreased efficiency of insertion is a major drawback to this solution.

3. Each deletion can compact the array by shifting all elements past the deleted element by one position, and then decrementing *rear* by one. Insertion remains unchanged. On average, half of all priority queue elements are shifted for each deletion, so that deletion becomes quite inefficient. A slightly better alternative is to shift either all preceding elements forward or all succeeding elements backward, depending on which group is smaller. This would require maintaining both *front* and *rear* indicators and treating the array as a circular structure, as we did for the queue.

4. Instead of maintaining the priority queue as an unordered array, maintain it as an ordered, circular array, as follows:

```
private final int MAXQUEUE = 100;
private Object items[];
private int front, rear;
```

front is the position of the smallest element, *rear* is one greater than the position of the largest. Deletion involves merely increasing *front* (for the ascending queue) or decreasing *rear* (for a descending queue). However, insertion requires locating the proper position of the new element and shifting the preceding or succeeding elements (again, the technique of shifting whichever group is smaller is helpful). This method moves the work of searching and shifting from the deletion operation to the insertion operation. However, since the array is ordered, the search for the position of the new element in an ordered array is only half as expensive, on average, as finding the maximum or minimum of the unordered array, and a binary search might be used to reduce the cost even more. Other techniques that involve leaving gaps in the array between elements of the priority queue to allow for subsequent insertions are also possible.

We leave the Java implementations of *pqInsert*, *pqMinDelete*, and *pqMaxDelete* for the array representation of a priority queue as exercises for the reader. Searching ordered and unordered arrays is discussed further in Section 7.1. In general, using an array is not an efficient method for implementing a priority queue. More efficient implementations are examined in the next section and in Sections 6.3 and 7.3.

EXERCISES

4.1.1   Write the method *pq.remvAndTest(RemoveAndTestResult result)*, which sets *result.underflow* to *false* and *result.value* to the item removed from a nonempty queue *pq*, and sets *result.underflow* to *true* if the queue is empty.

4.1.2   What set of conditions is necessary and sufficient for a sequence of *insert* and *remove* operations on a single empty queue to leave the queue empty without causing underflow? What set of conditions is necessary and sufficient for such a sequence to leave a nonempty queue unchanged?

4.1.3   If an array holding a queue is not considered circular, the text suggests that each *remove* operation must shift down every remaining element of a queue. An alternative method is to postpone shifting until *rear* equals the last index of the array. When that situation occurs and an attempt is made to insert an element into the queue, the entire queue is shifted down so that its first element is in position 0 of the array. What are the advantages of this method over performing a shift at each *remove* operation? What are the disadvantages? Rewrite the routines *remove, insert*, and *empty* using this method.

4.1.4   Show how a sequence of insertions and removals from a queue represented by a linear array can cause overflow to occur upon an attempt to insert an element into an empty queue.

4.1.5   Write a class to implement a queue as a vector.

4.1.6   We can avoid sacrificing one element of a queue if a field *qEmpty* is added to the queue representation. Show how this can be done, and rewrite the queue manipulation routines under that representation.

4.1.7   How would you implement a queue of stacks? a stack of queues? a queue of queues? Write routines to implement the appropriate operations for each of these data structures.

4.1.8   Show how to implement a queue of objects in Java by using an array *queue*[100], where *queue*[0] is used to indicate the front of the queue, *queue*[1] is used to indicate its rear, and *queue*[2] through *queue*[99] are used to contain the queue elements.

Show how to initialize such an array to represent the empty queue, and write methods *remove, insert,* and *empty* for such an implementation.

4.1.9 Show how to implement a queue in Java in which each item consists of a variable number of integers.

4.1.10 A *deque* is an ordered set of items from which items may be deleted at either end and into which items may be inserted at either end. Call the two ends of a deque *left* and *right*. How can a deque be represented as a Java array? Write four Java methods:

> `remvLeft, remvRight, insrtLeft, insrtRight`

to remove and insert elements at the left and right ends of a deque. Make sure that the routines work properly for the empty deque and that they detect overflow and underflow.

4.1.11 Define an ***input-restricted deque*** as a deque (see the previous exercise) for which only the operations *remvLeft, remvRight,* and *insrtLeft* are valid, and an ***output-restricted deque*** as a deque for which only the operations *remvLeft, insrtLeft,* and *insrtRight* are valid. Show how each of these can be used to represent both a stack and a queue.

4.1.12 The Scratchemup Parking Garage contains a single lane that holds up to ten cars. Cars arrive at the south end of the garage and leave from the north end. If a customer arrives to pick up a car which is not the northernmost, all the cars to the north of his car are moved out, his car is driven out, and the other cars are restored in the same order that they were in originally. Whenever a car leaves, all the cars to the south are moved forward so that at all times all the empty spaces are in the south part of the garage. Write an applet that reads a group of input lines. Each line contains an 'A' for arrival or a 'D' for departure, and a license plate number. Cars are assumed to arrive and depart in the order specified by the input. The program should print a message each time a car arrives or departs. When a car arrives, the message should specify whether or not there is room for it in the garage. If there is no room, the car waits until there is room or until a departure line is read for the car. When room becomes available, another message should be printed. When a car departs, the message should include the number of times the car was moved within the garage, including the departure itself but not the arrival. This number is 0 if the car departs from the waiting line.

4.1.13 Develop an ADT specification for a priority queue.

4.1.14 Write classes to implement an ascending priority queue and its operations, *pqInsert, pqMinDelete,* and *empty,* using each of the four methods presented in the text.

4.1.15 Show how to sort a set of input numbers using a priority queue and the operations *pqInsert, pqMinDelete,* and *empty.*

4.2 LINKED LISTS

What are the drawbacks of using sequential storage to represent stacks and queues? One major drawback is that a fixed amount of storage remains allocated to the stack or queue even when the structure is actually using a smaller amount or possibly no storage at all. Further, no more than that fixed amount of storage may be allocated, thus introducing the possibility of overflow.

Assume that a program uses two stacks implemented in two separate arrays, *items*1 and *items*2. Further, assume that each of these arrays has one hundred elements. Then, despite the fact that two hundred elements are available for the two stacks, neither can grow beyond one hundred items. Even if the first stack contains only twenty-five items, the second cannot contain more than one hundred.

One solution to this problem is to allocate a single array *items* of two hundred elements. The first stack occupies *items*[0], *items*[1], ..., *items*[*top*1], while the second stack is allocated from the other end of the array, occupying *items*[199], *items*[198], ..., *items*[*top*2]. Thus, when one stack is not occupying storage, the other stack can use that storage. Of course, two distinct sets of *pop, push*, and *empty* methods are necessary for the two stacks, since one grows by incrementing *top*1, and the other grows by decrementing *top*2.

Unfortunately, while this scheme allows two stacks to share a common area, there is no simple solution for three or more stacks or even for two queues. Instead, one must keep track of the tops and bottoms (or fronts and rears) of all the structures sharing a single large array. Each time the growth of one structure is about to impinge on the storage currently being used by another, neighboring structures must be shifted within the single array to allow for the growth.

Of course, if two or more stacks or queues are kept in a vector rather than in arrays, the Java system will reclaim any unused space in the vectors and no space will be wasted. However, as we have already mentioned, inserting and removing from vectors is inefficient in terms of time.

In a sequential representation, the items in a stack or queue are implicitly ordered by the sequential order of storage. Thus, if *items*[*x*] represents an element of a queue, the next element will be *items*[*x* + 1] (or if *x* equals MAXQUEUE-1, *items*[0]). Suppose that the items of a stack or a queue were explicitly ordered; that is, each item contained within itself the address of the next item. Such an explicit ordering gives rise to the data structure pictured in Figure 4.2.1, which is known as a ***linear linked list***. Each item in the list is called a ***node*** and contains two fields, an ***information*** field and a ***next address*** field. The information field holds the actual element in the list. The next address field contains the address of the next node in the list. The address used to access a particular node is known as a ***pointer***. The entire linked list is accessed from an external pointer *list* that points to (contains the address of) the first node in the list. (By an "external" pointer, we mean one that is not included in a node. Its value can be accessed directly by referencing a variable.) The next address field of the last node in the list contains a special value, known as *null*, which is not a valid address. This ***null pointer*** is used to signal the end of a list.

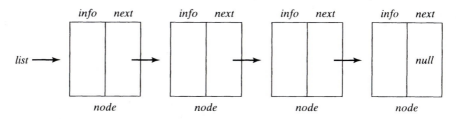

FIGURE 4.2.1 Linear linked list.

A list with no nodes on it is called an *empty list* or *null list*. The value of the external pointer *list* to such a list is the null pointer. A list can be initialized to an empty list by the operation *list = null*.

We now introduce some notation for use in algorithms (but not in Java programs). If p is a pointer to a node, *node(p)* refers to the node pointed to by p, *info(p)* refers to the information portion of that node, and *next(p)* refers to the next address portion and is therefore a pointer. Thus, if *next(p)* is not *null*, *info(next(p))* refers to the information portion of the node that follows *node(p)* in the list.

Before proceeding with further discussion of linked lists, we should mention that we are presenting them primarily as a data structure (i.e., an implementation method) rather than as a data type (i.e., a logical structure with precisely defined primitive operations). We therefore do not present an ADT specification for linked lists here. In Section 9.1, we discuss lists as abstract structures and present some primitive operations for them.

In this section, we present the concept of a linked list and show how it is used. In the next section, we show how linked lists can be implemented in Java.

Inserting and Removing Nodes from a List

A list is a dynamic data structure. The number of nodes on a list may vary dramatically as elements are inserted and removed. The dynamic nature of a list may be contrasted with the static nature of an array, whose size remains constant.

For example, suppose we are given a list of integers, as illustrated in Figure 4.2.2a, and we desire to add the integer 6 to the front of the list. That is, we wish to change the list so that it appears as in Figure 4.2.2f. The first step is to obtain a node in which to house the additional integer. If a list is to grow and shrink, there must be some mechanism for obtaining empty nodes to be added onto the list. Note that a list, unlike an array, does not come with a presupplied set of storage locations into which elements can be placed.

Let us assume the existence of a mechanism for obtaining empty nodes. The operation

```
p = getnode();
```

obtains an empty node and sets the contents of a variable named p to its address. The value of p is then a pointer to the newly allocated node. Figure 4.2.2b illustrates the list and the new node after performing the *getnode* operation. The details of how this operation works will be explained shortly.

The next step is to insert the integer 6 into the *info* portion of the newly allocated node. This is done by the operation

```
info(p) = 6;
```

The result of this operation is illustrated in Figure 4.2.2c.

After setting the *info* portion of *node(p)*, it is necessary to set the *next* portion of the node. Since *node(p)* is to be inserted at the front of the list, the node that follows should be the current first node on the list. Since the variable *list* contains the address of the first node, *node(p)* can be added to the list by performing the operation

```
next(p) = list;
```

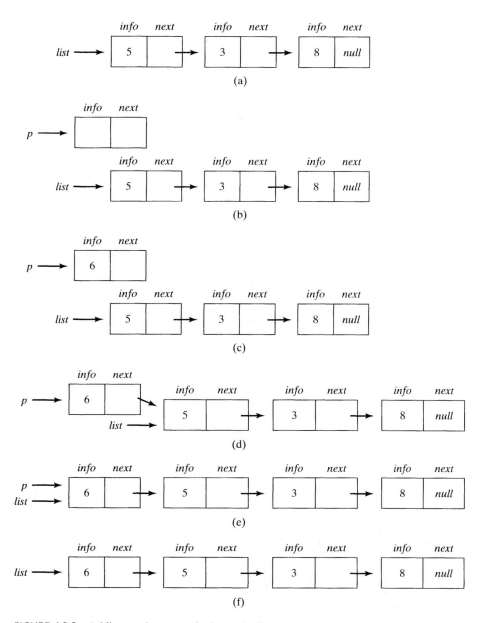

FIGURE 4.2.2 Adding an element to the front of a list.

This operation places the value of *list* (which is the address of the first node on the list) into the *next* field of *node(p)*. Figure 4.2.2d illustrates the result of this operation.

At this point, *p* points to the list with the additional item included. However, since *list* is the external pointer to the desired list, its value must be modified to the address of the new first node of the list. This can be done by performing the operation

```
list = p;
```

which changes the value of *list* to the value of *p*. Figure 4.2.2e illustrates the result of this operation. Note that Figures 4.2.2e and f are identical except that the value of *p* is not shown in Figure 4.2.2f. This is because *p* is used as an auxiliary variable during the process of modifying the list but its value is irrelevant to the status of the list before and after the process. Once the above operations have been performed, the value of *p* may be changed without affecting the list.

Putting all the steps together, we have an algorithm for adding the integer 6 to the front of the list *list*:

```
p = getnode();
info(p) = 6;
next(p) = list;
list = p;
```

The algorithm can obviously be generalized so that it adds any object *x* to the front of a list *list* by replacing the operation $info(p) = 6$ with $info(p) = x$. Convince yourself that the algorithm works correctly even if the list is initially empty (*list == null*).

Figure 4.2.3 illustrates the process of removing the first node of a nonempty list and storing the value of its *info* field into a variable *x*. The initial configuration is shown in Figure 4.2.3a, and the final configuration is shown in Figure 4.2.3f. The process itself is almost the exact opposite of the process to add a node to the front of a list. To obtain Figure 4.2.3d from Figure 4.2.3a, the following operations (whose actions should be clear) are performed:

```
p = list;            (Figure 4.2.3b)
list = next(p);      (Figure 4.2.3c)
x = info(p);         (Figure 4.2.3d)
```

At this point, the algorithm has accomplished what it was supposed to do: the first node has been removed from *list*, and *x* has been set to the desired value. However, the algorithm is not yet complete. In Figure 4.2.3d, *p* still points to the node that was formerly first on the list. However, that node is currently useless because it is no longer on the list and its information has been stored in *x*. (The node is not considered to be on the list, despite the fact that *next(p)* points to a node on the list, because there is no way to reach *node(p)* from the external pointer *list*.)

The variable *p* is used as an auxiliary variable during the process of removing the first node from the list. The starting and ending configurations of the list make no reference to *p*. It is therefore reasonable to expect that *p* will be used for some other purpose soon after this operation has been performed. But once the value of *p* is changed, there is no way to access the node at all, since neither an external pointer nor a *next* field contains its address. Therefore, the node is currently useless and cannot be reused, yet it is taking up valuable storage.

It would be desirable to have some mechanism for making *node(p)* available for reuse even if the value of the pointer *p* is changed. The operation that does this is

```
freenode(p);         (Figure 4.2.3e)
```

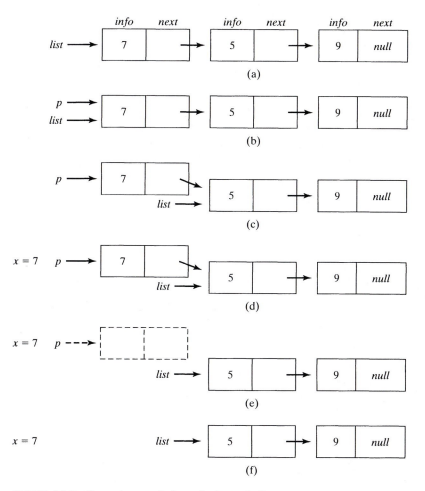

FIGURE 4.2.3   Removing a node from the front of a list.

Once this operation has been performed, it becomes illegal to reference *node(p)* because the node is no longer allocated. Since the value of *p* is a pointer to a node that has been freed, any reference to that value is also illegal.

However, the node might be reallocated and a pointer to it reassigned to *p* by the operation *p = getnode()*. Note that we say that the node "might be" reallocated, since the *getnode* operation returns a pointer to some newly allocated node. There is no guarantee that this new node is the same as the one that has just been freed.

Another way of thinking of *getnode* and *freenode* is that *getnode* creates a new node, whereas *freenode* destroys a node. Under this view, nodes are not used and reused but are created and destroyed. We shall say more below about the two operations *getnode* and *freenode* and about the concepts they represent, but first we make the following interesting observation.

Linked Implementation of Stacks

The operation of adding an element to the front of a linked list is quite similar to that of pushing an element onto a stack. In both cases, a new item is added as the only immediately accessible item in a collection. A stack can be accessed only through its top element, and a list can be accessed only from the pointer to its first element. Similarly, the operation of removing the first element from a linked list is analogous to popping a stack. In both cases, the only immediately accessible item of a collection is removed from it, and the next item becomes immediately accessible.

Thus we have discovered another way of implementing a stack. A stack may be represented by a linear linked list. The first node of the list is the top of the stack. If an external pointer *s* points to such a linked list, the method *s.push(x)* may be implemented by:

```
p = getnode();
info(p) = x;
next(p) = s;
s = p;
```

The operation *s.empty()* is merely a test as to whether *s* equals *null*. The operation *x = pop(s)* removes the first node from a nonempty list and signals underflow if the list is empty:

```
if (s.empty()) {
    System.out.println("stack underflow");
    System.out.exit(1);
}
else {
    p = s;
    s = next(p);
    x = info(p);
    freenode(p);
} // end if
```

Figure 4.2.4a illustrates a stack implemented as a linked list, and Figure 4.2.4b illustrates the same stack after another element has been pushed onto it.

The advantage of the list implementation of stacks is that all the stacks being used by a program can share the same available list. When any stack needs a node, it can obtain it from the single available list. When any stack no longer needs a node, it returns it to the same available list. As long as the total amount of space needed by all the stacks at any one time is less than the amount of space initially available to them, each stack is able to grow and shrink to any size. No space has been preallocated to any single stack, and no stack is using space that it does not need. Furthermore, other data structures, such as queues, may share the same set of nodes.

getnode and *freenode* Operations

We now return to a discussion of the *getnode* and *freenode* operations. In an abstract, idealized world, it is possible to postulate an infinite number of unused nodes available for use by abstract algorithms. The *getnode* operation finds one such node and makes it

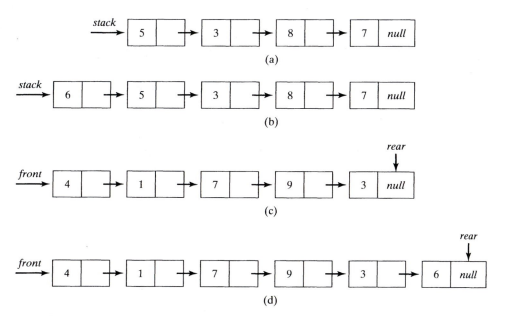

FIGURE 4.2.4   Stack and queue as linked lists.

available to the algorithm. Alternatively, the *getnode* operation may be regarded as a machine that manufactures nodes and never breaks down. Thus, each time that *getnode* is invoked, it presents its caller with a brand-new node, different from all the nodes previously in use.

In an ideal world, the *freenode* operation would be unnecessary to make a node available for reuse. Why use an old, second-hand node when a simple call to *getnode* can produce a new, never-before-used node? The only harm an unused node can do is to reduce the number of nodes that can possibly be used, but if an infinite supply of nodes is available, then such a reduction is meaningless. Therefore, there is no reason to reuse a node.

Unfortunately, we live in the real world. Computers do not have an infinite amount of storage and cannot manufacture more storage for immediate utilization (at least not yet). Therefore, the number of available nodes is finite, and it is impossible to use more than that number at any given instant. In order to use more than that number over a given period of time, some nodes must be reused. The function of *freenode* is to make a node that is no longer being used in its current context available for reuse in a different context.

We might think of a finite pool of empty nodes existing initially. The pool cannot be accessed by the programmer except through the *getnode* and *freenode* operations. *getnode* removes a node from the pool, and *freenode* returns a node to the pool. Since any unused node is as good as any other, it makes no difference which node is retrieved by *getnode* or where in the pool a node is placed by *freenode*.

The most natural form for the pool to take is that of a linked list acting as a stack. The list is linked together by the *next* field in each node. The *getnode* operation removes the first node from the list and makes it available for use. The *freenode* operation adds a node to the front of the list, making it available for reallocation by the next *getnode*. The list of available nodes is called the ***available list***.

What happens when the available list is empty? This means that all the nodes are currently in use and it is impossible to allocate any more. If a program calls on *getnode* when the available list is empty, the amount of storage assigned for the program's data structures will be too small. Therefore, overflow occurs. This is similar to the situation of a stack implemented in an array overflowing the array bounds.

As long as data structures are abstract, theoretical concepts in a world of infinite space, there is no possibility of overflow. It is only when they are implemented as real objects in a finite area that the possibility of overflow arises.

Assume that an external pointer *avail* points to a list of available nodes. Then the operation

```
p = getnode();
```

is implemented as follows:

```
if (avail == null) {
    System.out.println("overflow");
    System.out.exit(1);
}
p = avail;
avail = next(avail);
```

Since the possibility of overflow is accounted for in the *getnode* operation, it need not be mentioned in the list implementation of *push*. If a stack is about to overflow all the available nodes, the statement *p = getnode()*; in the *push* operation results in an overflow.

The implementation of *freenode(p)* is straightforward:

```
next(p) = avail;
avail = p;
```

Linked Implementation of Queues

Let us now examine how to represent a queue as a linked list. Recall that items are deleted from the front of a queue and inserted at the rear. Let a pointer to the first element of a list represent the front of the queue. Another pointer to the last element of the list represents the rear of the queue, as shown in Figure 4.2.4c. Figure 4.2.4d illustrates the same queue after a new item has been inserted.

Under the list representation, a queue *q* consists of a list and two pointers, *front* and *rear*. The methods *q.empty()* and *x = q.remove()* are completely analogous to *s.empty()* and *x = s.pop()*, with the pointer *front* replacing *s*. However, special attention is required when the last element is removed from a queue. In this case, *rear* must also be set to *null*, because in an empty queue, both *front* and *rear* must be *null*. The algorithm for *x = q.remove()* is therefore as follows:

```
if (q.empty()) {
    System.out.println("queue underflow");
    System.out.exit(1);
}
```

```
p = front;
x = info(p);
front = next(p);
if (front == null)
      rear = null;
freenode(p);
return x;
```

The method *q.insert*(*x*) is implemented by:

```
p = getnode;
info(p) = x;
next(p) = null;
if (rear == null)
      front = p;
else
    next(rear) = p;
rear = p;
```

What are the disadvantages of representing a stack or queue by a linked list? A node in a linked list occupies more storage than a corresponding element in an array, since two pieces of information per element are necessary in a list node (*info* and *next*), whereas only one piece of information is needed in the array implementation. However, the space used for a list node is usually not twice the space used by an array element, since the elements in such a list usually consist of objects with many members (*instance variables*). For example, if each element on a stack were an object occupying ten words, the addition of an eleventh word to contain a pointer increases the space requirement by only 10 percent. Further, it is sometimes possible (although not in Java) to compress information and a pointer into a single word, so that there is no space degradation.

Another disadvantage is the additional time spent in managing the available list. Each addition and deletion of an element from a stack or a queue involves a corresponding deletion or addition to the available list.

The advantage of using linked lists is that all the stacks and queues of a program have access to the same free list of nodes. Nodes not used by one stack may be used by another, as long as the total number of nodes in use at any one time is not greater than the total number of nodes available.

The Linked List as a Data Structure

Linked lists are important not only as a means of implementing stacks and queues, but as data structures in their own right. An item is accessed in a linked list by traversing the list from its beginning. An array implementation allows access to the *n*th item in a group using a single operation, while a list implementation requires *n* operations. It is necessary to pass through each of the first $n - 1$ elements before reaching the *n*th element because there is no relation between the memory location occupied by an element of a list and its position in the list.

The advantage of a list over an array occurs when it is necessary to insert or delete an element in the middle of a group of other elements. For example, suppose we wished to insert an element x between the third and fourth elements in an array of size 10 that currently contains seven items ($x[0]$ through $x[6]$). Items 6 through 3 must first be moved one slot and the new element inserted in the newly available position 3. This process is illustrated by Figure 4.2.5a. In this case, insertion of one item involves moving four items in addition to the insertion. If the array contained five hundred or a thousand elements, a correspondingly larger number of elements would have to be moved. Similarly, to delete an element from an array without leaving a gap, all the elements beyond the deleted element must be moved one position.

On the other hand, suppose the items are stored as a list. If p points to an element of the list, inserting a new element after $node(p)$ involves allocating a node, inserting the information, and adjusting two pointers. The amount of work required is independent of the size of the list. This is illustrated in Figure 4.2.5b.

Let *insAfter* (p, x) denote the operation of inserting an item x into a list after a node pointed to by p. This operation is implemented as follows:

```
q = getnode();
info(q) = x;
next(q) = next(p);
next(p) = q;
```

An item can be inserted only after a given node, not before it. This is because there is no way to proceed from a given node to its predecessor in a linear list without traversing the list from its beginning. To insert an item before $node(p)$, the *next* field of its

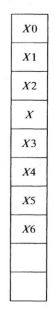

X0	X0	X0
X1	X1	X1
X2	X2	X2
X3		X
X4	X3	X3
X5	X4	X4
X6	X5	X5
	X6	X6

FIGURE 4.2.5a   Inserting an element into an array.

(a)

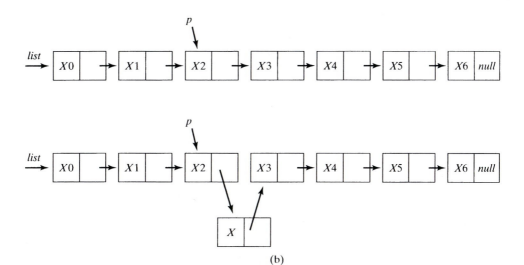

FIGURE 4.2.5b   Inserting an element into a list.

predecessor must be changed to point to a newly allocated node. But, given p, there is no way to find the predecessor. (However, it is possible to achieve the effect of inserting an element before $node(p)$ by inserting the element immediately after $node(p)$ and then interchanging $info(p)$ with the $info$ field of the newly created successor. We leave the details for the reader.)

Similarly, to delete a node from a linear list it is insufficient to be given a pointer to the node. This is because the $next$ field of the node's predecessor must be changed to point to the node's successor, and there is no direct way of reaching the predecessor of a given node. The best that can be done is to delete a node following a given node. (However, it is possible to save the contents of the following node, delete the following node, and then replace the contents of the given node with the saved information. This achieves the effect of deleting a given node.)

Let $delAfter(p, x)$ denote the operation of deleting the node following $node(p)$ and assigning its contents to the variable x. This operation may be implemented as follows:

```
q = next (p) ;
x = info (q) ;
next (p) = next (q) ;
freenode (q) ;
```

The freed node is placed onto the available list for reuse in the future.

Examples of List Operations

We illustrate these two operations, as well as the *push* and *pop* operations for lists, with some simple examples. In the first example, all occurrences of the number 4 are deleted from a list *list*. The list is traversed in a search for nodes that contain 4 in their *info* fields. Each such node must be deleted from the list. But in order to delete a node from a list, its predecessor must be known. For this reason, two pointers, *p* and *q*, are used. *p* is used to traverse the list, and *q* always points to the predecessor of *p*. The algorithm makes use of the *pop* operation to remove nodes from the beginning of the list, and the *delAfter* operation to remove nodes from the middle of the list.

```
q = null;
p = list;
while (p != null) {
    if (info(p) == 4)
            if (q == null) {
                    // remove first node of the list
                    x = pop(list);
                    p = list;
            }
            else {
                    // delete the node after q and move up p
                    p = next(p);
                    delAfter(q, x);
            } // end if
    else {
            // continue traversing the list
            q = p;
            p = next(p);
    } // end else
} // end while
```

The practice of using two pointers, one following the other, is very common in working with lists. This technique is used in the next example as well. Assume that a list *list* is ordered so that smaller items precede larger ones. Such a list is called an **ordered list**. It is desired to insert an item *x* into this list in its proper place. The algorithm to do so makes use of the *push* operation to add a node to the front of the list and the *insAfter* operation to add a node in the middle of the list.

```
q = null;
for (p = list; p != null && x > info(p); p = next(p))
        q = p;
// at this point, a node containing x must be inserted
if (q == null)
        // insert x at the head of the list
        push(list, x);
else
        insAfter(q, x);
```

This is a very common operation and will be denoted by *place*(*list*, *x*).

Let us examine the efficiency of the *place* operation. How many nodes are accessed, on average, in inserting a new element into an ordered list? Let us assume that the list contains *n* nodes. Then *x* can be placed in one of $n + 1$ positions; that is, it can be found to be less than the first element of the list, between the first and the second, ..., between the $(n - 1)$st and the *n*th, and greater than the *n*th. If *x* is less than the first, then *place* accesses only the first node of the list (aside from the new node containing *x*); that is, it immediately determines that $x < info\,(list)$ and inserts a node containing *x* using *push*. If *x* is between the *k*th and $(k + 1)$st element, then *place* accesses the first *k* nodes; only after finding *x* to be less than the contents of the $(k + 1)$st node is *x* inserted using *insAfter*. If *x* is greater than the *n*th element, then all *n* nodes are accessed.

Now suppose that it is equally likely that *x* is inserted into any one of the $n + 1$ possible positions. (If this is true, we say that the insertion is **random**.) Then the probability of inserting at any particular position is $1/(n + 1)$. If the element is inserted between the *k*th and the $(k + 1)$st position, then the number of accesses is $k + 1$. If the element is inserted after the *n*th element, the number of accesses is *n*. The average number of nodes accessed, *A*, equals the sum, over all possible insertion positions, of the products of the probability of inserting at a particular position and the number of accesses required to insert an element at that position. Thus

$$A = \left(\frac{1}{n+1}\right) \times 1 + \left(\frac{1}{n+1}\right) \times 2 + \cdots + \left(\frac{1}{n+1}\right) \times (n-1)$$
$$+ \left(\frac{1}{n+1}\right) \times n + \left(\frac{1}{n+1}\right) \times n$$

or

$$A = \left(\frac{1}{n+1}\right) \times (1 + 2 + \cdots + n) + \frac{n}{n+1}$$

Now $1 + 2 + \cdots + n = n \times \dfrac{n+1}{2}$. (This can be proved easily by mathematical induction.) Therefore,

$$A = \left(\frac{1}{n+1}\right) \times \left(n \times \frac{n+1}{2}\right) + \frac{n}{n+1} = \frac{n}{2} + \frac{n}{n+1}$$

When *n* is large, $n/(n + 1)$ is very close to 1, so *A* is approximately $n/2 + 1$ or $(n + 2)/2$. For a large *n*, *A* is close enough to $n/2$ for us to say that the operation of randomly inserting an element into an ordered list requires approximately $n/2$ node accesses on average.

List Implementation of Priority Queues

An ordered list can be used to represent a priority queue. For an ascending priority queue, insertion (*pqInsert*) is implemented by the *place* operation, which keeps the list ordered, and deletion of the minimum element (*pqMinDelete*) is implemented by the *pop* operation, which removes the first element from the list. A descending priority queue can be implemented by keeping the list in descending, rather than ascending, order or by using *remove* to implement *pqMaxDelete*. A priority queue implemented as an ordered linked list requires examining an average of approximately $n/2$ nodes for insertion, but only one node for deletion.

An unordered list may also be used as a priority queue. Such a list requires examining only one node for insertion (by implementing *pqInsert* using *push* or *insert*) but always requires examining *n* elements for deletion (traverse the entire list to find the minimum or maximum and then delete that node). Thus an ordered list is somewhat more efficient than an unordered list in implementing a priority queue.

The advantage of a list over an array for implementing a priority queue is that no shifting of elements or gaps is necessary in a list. An item can be inserted into a list without moving any other items, but this is impossible for an array unless extra space is left empty. We examine other, more efficient implementations of the priority queue in Sections 6.3 and 7.3.

Header Nodes

Sometimes it is desirable to keep an extra node at the front of a list. Such a node does not represent an item in the list and is called a ***header node*** or a ***list header***. The *info* portion of a header node may be unused, as illustrated in Figure 4.2.6a. More often, the *info* portion of such a node is used to keep global information about the entire list. For example, Figure 4.2.6b illustrates a list in which the *info* portion of the header node contains the number of nodes (not including the header) in the list. In such a data structure, more work is needed to add or delete an item from the list, since the count in the header node must be adjusted. However, the number of items in the list may be obtained directly from the header node without traversing the entire list.

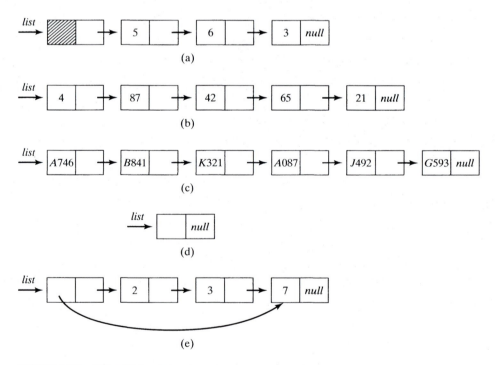

FIGURE 4.2.6 Lists with header nodes.

Another example of the use of header nodes is the following. Suppose a factory assembles machinery out of smaller units. A particular machine (inventory number *A*746) might be composed of a number of different parts (numbers *B*841, *K*321, *A*087, *J*492, *G*593). This assembly could be represented by a list like the one illustrated in Figure 4.2.6c, where each item on the list represents a component and the header node represents the entire assembly. The empty list would no longer be represented by the null pointer, but rather by a list with a single header node, as in Figure 4.2.6d.

Of course, the algorithms for operations such as *empty*, *push*, *pop*, *insert*, and *remove* must be rewritten to account for the presence of a header node. Most of the routines become a bit more complex, but some, like *insert*, become simpler, since an external list pointer is never null. We leave the rewriting of the routines as an exercise for the reader. The routines *insAfter* and *delAfter* need not be changed at all. In fact, when a header node is used, *insAfter* and *delAfter* can be used instead of *push* and *pop*, since the first item in such a list appears in the node that follows the header node, rather than in the first node on the list.

If the *info* portion of a node can contain a pointer, then additional possibilities for the use of a header node present themselves. For example, the *info* portion of a list header might contain a pointer to the last node in the list, as in Figure 4.2.6e. Such an implementation simplifies the representation of a queue. Until now, two external pointers, *front* and *rear*, were necessary for a list to represent a queue. Now, however, only a single external pointer q to the header node of the list is necessary. $next(q)$ points to the front of the queue, and $info(q)$ to its rear.

Another possibility for the use of the *info* portion of a list header is as a pointer to a "current" node in the list during a traversal process. This would eliminate the need for an external pointer during traversal.

EXERCISES

4.2.1   Write a set of routines for implementing several stacks and queues within a single array.

4.2.2   What are the advantages and disadvantages of representing a group of items as an array versus a linear linked list?

4.2.3   Write an algorithm to perform each of the following operations:

    a.   Append an element to the end of a list.

    b.   Concatenate two lists.

    c.   Free all the nodes in a list.

    d.   Reverse a list, so that the last element becomes the first, and so on.

    e.   Delete the last element from a list.

    f.   Delete the *n*th element from a list.

    g.   Combine two ordered lists into a single ordered list.

    h.   Form a list containing the union of the elements of two lists.

    i.   Form a list containing the intersection of the elements of two lists.

    j.   Insert an element after the *n*th element of a list.

    k.   Delete every second element from a list.

    l.   Place the elements of a list in increasing order.

      m. Return the sum of the integers in a list.

      n. Return the number of elements in a list.

      o. Move *node(p)* forward *n* positions in a list.

      p. Make a second copy of a list.

4.2.4   Write algorithms to perform each of the operations in the previous exercise on a group of elements in contiguous positions of an array.

4.2.5   What is the average number of nodes accessed in searching for a particular element in an unordered list? In an ordered list? In an unordered array? In an ordered array?

4.2.6   Write algorithms for *pqInsert* and *pqMinDelete* for an ascending priority queue implemented as an unordered list and as an ordered list.

4.2.7   Write algorithms to perform each of the operations in Exercise 4.2.3 assuming that each list contains a header node containing the number of elements in the list.

4.2.8   Write an algorithm that returns a pointer to a node containing element *x* in a list with a header node. The *info* field of the header should contain the pointer that traverses the list.

4.3   LISTS IN JAVA

Array Implementation of Lists

How can linear lists be represented in Java? Since a list is simply a collection of nodes, an array of node objects immediately suggests itself. We first define a class *Node* containing an information item *info* which may contain any item of type *Object*. However, the nodes cannot be ordered by the array ordering; each must contain within itself a pointer to its successor. In this scheme, a pointer to a node is represented by an array index. A node, therefore, must also include an integer *next* which represents the array position of the next node. The null pointer is represented by the integer -1.

```
class Node {
    public Object info;
    public int next;

    Node(Object x, int n) {
        info = x;
        next = n;
    }

} // end Node class
```

Each time a node is created, the class constructor will allow us to set the *info* and *next* fields.

    Once a *node* object has been defined, a pool of five hundred nodes can be declared as an array *nodePool*, as follows:

```
public class NodePool {
  static final int NUMNODES = 500;
```

```
static Node nodePool[] = new Node[NUMNODES];
static int avail;
    ...
```

In the array implementation of a list, a pointer is an integer between 0 and $NUMNODES - 1$ that identifies a particular element of the array *nodePool*. Under this implementation, the Java expression *nodePool*[*p*] is used to reference *node*(*p*), *info*(*p*) is referenced by *nodePool*[*p*].*info*, and *next*(*p*) is referenced by *nodePool*[*p*].*next*. *null* is represented by -1. We will explain the data member *avail* shortly.

For example, suppose the variable *list* represents a pointer to a list. If *list* has the value 7, then *nodePool*[7] is the first node on the list, and *nodePool*[7].*info* is the first data item on the list. The second node of the list is given by *nodePool*[7].*next*. Suppose *nodePool*[7].*next* equals 385. Then *nodePool*[385].*info* is the second data item on the list, and *nodePool*[385].*next* points to the third node.

The nodes of a list may be scattered throughout the array *nodePool* in any arbitrary order. Each node carries within itself the location of its successor until the last node in the list, whose *next* field contains -1, which is the null pointer. There is no relation between the contents of a node and the pointer to it. The pointer *p* to a node merely specifies which element of the array *nodePool* is being referenced; it is *nodePool*[*p*].*info* that represents the information contained within the node.

Figure 4.3.1 illustrates a portion of an array *nodePool* that contains four linked lists. The list *list*1 starts at *nodePool*[16] and contains the integers 3, 7, 14, 6, 5, 37, 12. The nodes that contain these integers in their *info* fields are scattered throughout the array. The *next* field of each node contains the index within the array of the node containing the next element of the list. The last node on the list is *nodePool*[23], which contains the integer 12 in its *info* field and the null pointer (-1) in its *next* field to indicate that it is last on the list.

Similarly, *list*2 begins at *nodePool*[4] and contains the integers 17 and 26, *list*3 begins at *nodePool*[11] and contains the integers 31, 19, and 32, and *list*4 begins at *nodePool*[3] and contains the integers 1, 18, 13, 11, 4, and 15. The variables *list*1, *list*2, *list*3, and *list*4 are integers representing external pointers to the four lists. Thus the fact that the variable *list*2 has the value 4 represents the fact that the list to which it points begins at *nodePool*[4].

Initially, all nodes are unused, since no lists have yet been formed. Therefore, they must all be placed on an available list, which contains nodes that are not currently used in other lists. The data member *avail* is used to point to the available list. The class constructor *NodePool*() initially organizes the available list as follows:

```
private NodePool() { }

static {              // static initializer
    avail = 0;
        for (int i = 0; i < NUMNODES - 1; i++)
                nodePool[i] = new Node(null, i + 1);
                nodePool[NUMNODES - 1] = new Node(null, -1);
} // end constructor
```

		info	next
	0	26	−1
	1	11	9
	2	5	15
list4 =	3	1	24
list2 =	4	17	0
	5	13	1
	6		
	7	19	18
	8	14	12
	9	4	21
	10		
list3 =	11	31	7
	12	6	2
	13		
	14		
	15	37	23
list1 =	16	3	20
	17		
	18	32	−1
	19		
	20	7	8
	21	15	−1
	22		
	23	12	−1
	24	18	5
	25		
	26		

FIGURE 4.3.1 Array of nodes containing four linked lists.

Each *node* is created with a *null Object* in its *info* field, and the five hundred nodes are initially linked in their natural order, so that *node[i]* points to *node[i + 1]*. *node[0]* is the first node on the available list, *node[1]* is the second, and so on. *node[499]* is the last node on the list because *node[499].next* equals −1. There is no reason other than convenience for initially ordering the nodes in this fashion. We could just as well have set *node[0].next* to 499, *node[499].next* to 1, *node[1].next* to 498, and so forth, until *node[249].next* is set to 250 and *node[250].next* to −1. The important point is that the ordering is explicit within the nodes and is not implied by some other underlying structure.

You will note that the constructor body of *NodePool()* is empty. Instead we make use of the Java language feature known as a ***static initializer***. Static initializers are used whenever it is desired to perform some initial action only the first time the class is instantiated. Since all the data members of *NodePool* are **static** and the constructor uses a static initializer, only one copy of *NodePool* can exist and it is initialized only once.

We assume a method of *NodePool* named *isEmpty*, as follows:

```
static boolean isEmpty() {
    return avail == -1;
}
```

After you have seen the code for *getNode* below, think about how it is possible for *avail* to equal −1.

When a node is needed for use in a particular list, it is obtained from the available list. Similarly, when a node is no longer necessary, it is returned to the available list. The Java methods *getNode* and *freeNode* of the *NodePool* class implement these two operations. *getNode* is a method that removes a node from the available list and returns a pointer to it.

```
static int getNode() {
  if (isEmpty()) {
        System.out.println("Node Pool Overflow");
        System.exit(1);
  }
  int p = avail;
  avail = nodePool[avail].next;
  return p;
} // end getNode
```

If *avail* equals −1 when this method is invoked, there are no nodes available. This means that the list structures of a particular program have overflowed the available space because *getNode* has been called enough times to exhaust all the nodes of the available list. Note that the member *next* of the last node of the available list contains −1, so if *getNode* returns that node, *getNode* sets *avail* to −1.

The method *freeNode* accepts a pointer to a node and returns the node to the available list:

```
static void freeNode(int p) {
  nodePool[p].next = avail;
  avail = p;
} // end freeNode
```

Under the array implementation, a new list is instantiated by declaring an object of the *ArrayList* class.

```
public class ArrayList{
  private int list;
  public ArrayList() {
      list = -1;
  }
      ...
}
```

The *ArrayList* constructor initializes its list pointer to −1, indicating that the list currently does not contain any items.

Whenever we want to determine whether an *ArrayList* is empty, we use the following method of the *ArrayList* class:

```
public boolean isEmpty() {
  return list == -1;
}
```

The primitive operations for lists are straightforward Java versions of the corresponding algorithms. The method *insAfter* of the class *ArrayList* accepts a pointer *p* to a node and an item *x* as parameters. It first ensures that *p* is not null and then inserts *x* into a node following the node pointed to by *p*.

```java
public void insertAfter(int p, Object x) {
  if (p == -1) {
        System.out.println("void insertion");
        System.exit(1);
  }
  int q = NodePool.getNode();
  NodePool.nodePool[q].info = x;
  NodePool.nodePool[q].next = NodePool.nodePool[p].next;
  NodePool.nodePool[p].next = q;
} // end insertAfter
```

The method *delAfter* of the class *ArrayList* deletes the node following *node(p)* and returns its contents. *delAfter* would be invoked by a statement *alist.delAfter(p)*, where *alist* is an object of type *ArrayList*.

```java
public Object deleteAfter(int p) {
  if ((p == -1) || NodePool.nodePool[p].next == -1) {
        System.out.println("void deletion");
        System.exit(1);
  }
  int q = NodePool.nodePool[p].next;
  Object temp = NodePool.nodePool[q].info;
  NodePool.nodePool[p].next = NodePool.nodePool[q].next;
  NodePool.freeNode(q);
  return temp;
} // end deleteAfter
```

Before invoking *insAfter* we must be sure that *p* is not null. Before calling *delAfter* we must be sure that neither *p* nor *node[p].next* is null.

The addition and deletion of the first element of a list must be treated as a special case, since we must ensure that the pointer to the head of the list is appropriately modified. Before performing their tasks, the methods *insertFirst* and *deleteFirst*, of the class *ArrayList*, examine the list pointer in order to determine whether or not the list is currently empty.

```java
public void insertFirst(Object x) {
  int q = NodePool.getNode();

  NodePool.nodePool[q].info = x;
  If (isEmpty())
        NodePool.nodePool[q].next = -1;
  else
        NodePool.nodePool[q].next = list;
  list = q;
} // end insertFirst
```

Note that the entire *if* statement could be replaced by *NodePool.nodePool[q].next = list*;

```
public Object deleteFirst() {
  if (isEmpty()) {
        System.out.println("void deletion");
        System.exit(1);
  }
  Object temp = NodePool.nodePool[list].info;

  if (NodePool.nodePool[list].next == -1) { // if the list has 1
                                            // element
        NodePool.freeNode(list);
        list = -1;
  }
  else {
        int q = list;
        list = NodePool.nodePool[list].next;
        NodePool.freeNode(q);
  }
  return temp;
} // end deleteFirst
```

Limitations of the Array Implementation

As we have seen in Section 4.2, the notion of a pointer allows us to build and manipulate linked lists of various types. The concept of a pointer introduces the possibility of assembling a collection of building blocks, called nodes, into flexible structures. By altering the values of pointers, nodes can be attached, detached, and reassembled in patterns that grow and shrink as the execution of a program proceeds.

Under the array implementation, a fixed set of nodes represented by an array is established at the start of execution. A pointer to a node is represented by the relative position of the node within the array. The disadvantage of this approach is twofold. First, the number of nodes that are needed often cannot be predicted when a program is written. The data with which the program is executed usually determine the number of nodes necessary. Thus, no matter how many elements the array of nodes contains, it is always possible that the program will be executed with input that requires a larger number.

The second disadvantage of the array approach is that whatever number of nodes is declared must remain allocated to the program throughout its execution. For example, if five hundred nodes of a given type are declared, the amount of storage required for them is reserved for that purpose. If the program actually uses only hundred nodes in its execution, or even ten, the additional nodes are still reserved and their storage cannot be used for any other purpose.

The solution to this problem is to allow nodes that are *dynamic* rather than static. That is, when a node is needed, storage is reserved for it, and when it is no longer needed, the storage can be released. Thus the storage for nodes that are no longer in use is available for another purpose. Also, no predefined limit on the number of nodes is established. As long as sufficient storage is available to the job as a whole, part of the storage can be reserved for use as a node.

Linked Lists Using Dynamic Variables

The allocation and release of storage for a variable is an important function of the operating system and is controlled by the designers of the programming language. The Java language automatically allocates storage for an object each time the programmer invokes the **new** keyword. Each time a new object is instantiated, the ***default constructor*** for that object allocates storage for its members and methods. Of course, a programmer may specify that a method's constructor may perform any number of actions at the time the object is created.

The release of storage, known as ***storage deallocation***, is of equal importance. If storage could not be released, programs would soon run out of memory space. This error, known as a ***memory leak***, frequently occurs in languages like C and C++, where the responsibility for freeing of storage explicitly allocated by the programmer lies with the programmer. In an important language-design decision by the designers of the Java language, Java uses ***garbage collection***, in which reclamation of unneeded storage is performed automatically. As a result, the programmer can create new objects without worrying about releasing the storage allocated for them when it is no longer needed. (Although Java automatically performs garbage collection, the programmer can invoke the *System.gc()* method to force the reclamation of unused storage by calling the garbage collection method. Java also allows you to define a method named *finalize()* in which you can perform any cleanup actions on an object before Java reclaims its storage through garbage collection. When garbage collection is ready to free an object's storage, the *finalize* method of the object's class is automatically invoked.)

Now that we have the capability of dynamically allocating and freeing a variable, let us see how dynamic variables can be used to implement linked lists. Recall that a linked list consists of a set of nodes, each of which has two fields: an information field and a pointer to the next node in the list. Thus we define the *DynamicNode* class by:

```java
public class DynamicNode {
  private Object info;
  private DynamicNode next;

  public DynamicNode(Object x, DynamicNode n) {
      info = x;
      next = n;
  }

  public Object getInfo() {
      return info;
  }

  public DynamicNode getNext() {
      return next;
  }

  public void setInfo(Object x) {
      info = x;
  }
}
```

```
    public void setNext(DynamicNode n) {
        next = n;
    }

} // end DynamicNode class
```

A node of this type is identical to the nodes of the array implementation except that the *next* field is declared to be of the same type as the node itself (i.e., *DynamicNode*) rather than an integer (containing the index within an array where the next node in the list is kept). Such classes are known as ***self-referential*** because they are defined in terms of themselves. The *next* field, being of type *DynamicNode*, can thus refer to the next node on our list. Each time an object of type *DynamicNode* is instantiated, the class constructor places the object being stored in the node into the *info* field and "points" the *next* field to the next node in the list.

The remaining methods in the class allow us to perform the basic node operations. *setInfo*() inserts and *getInfo*() extracts the object stored in the node. *SetNext*() sets the *next* field to the next node in the list, and *getNext*() "points" us to the node following the current node.

Let us employ the dynamic allocation features to implement linked lists. Instead of declaring an array to represent an aggregate collection of nodes, nodes are allocated (by the programmer) and freed (by the Java Virtual Machine) as necessary. The need for a declared collection of nodes is eliminated.

The declaration

```
DynamicNode q = new DynamicNode(x, null);
```

creates a new node "pointed" to by *q*, assigns *x* to its *info* field, and places a ***null*** value into the node's *next* field.

Both *getnode* and *freenode* are no longer needed. The programmer need not be concerned with managing available storage, since the system governs the allocating and freeing of nodes, and keeps track of the first available node. Note also that there is no test to determine whether overflow has occurred. This is because such a condition will be detected during the execution of the program and is system-dependent. An "overflow" represents running out of system memory and should be trapped by the operating system.

We now present the *DynamicList* class, which allows an application to make use of this data structure. The *DynamicList* constructor instantiates a new list and initializes its *list* pointer to ***null***.

```
    public class DynamicList {
      private DynamicNode list;
      public DynamicList() {
          list = null;
      }

      public boolean isEmpty() {
          return list == null;
      }

      public void insertFirst(Object x) {
          DynamicNode q = new DynamicNode(x, null);
```

```
            if (!isEmpty())
                  q.setNext(list);
            list = q;
      } // end insertFirst

      public void insertAfter(DynamicNode p, Object x) {
            if (p == null) {
               System.out.println("void insertion");
               System.exit(1);
            }
            DynamicNode q = new DynamicNode(x, p.getNext());
            p.setNext(q);
      } // end insertAfter

      public Object deleteFirst() {
            if (isEmpty()) {
                  System.out.println("void deletion");
                  System.exit(1);
            }
            Object temp = list.getInfo();
            if (list.getNext() = null)
                  list = null;
            else
                  list = list.getNext();
            return temp;
      } // end deleteFirst

      public Object deleteAfter(DynamicNode p) {
            if (p == null || p.getNext() == null) {
                  System.out.println("void deletion");
                  System.exit(1);
            }
            DynamicNode q = p.getNext();
            Object temp = q.getInfo();
            p.setNext(q.getNext());
            return temp;
       } // end deleteAfter

            ...                                    // other list methods

   } // end DynamicList class
```

Note the striking similarity between the above routines and those of the array implementation earlier in this section. Both are implementations of the algorithms in Section 4.2. In fact, the only difference between the two versions is in the manner in which nodes are referenced.

Queues as Lists in Java

As a further illustration of how the Java list implementations are used, we present Java methods for manipulating a queue represented as a linear list. We leave the methods for manipulating a stack and a priority queue as exercises for the reader. For comparison purposes, we show both the array and dynamic implementation. We assume that the *Node* and *DynamicNode* classes have been declared as above.

Array Implementation

```
public class ArrayListQueue {
    private int front, rear;
    public ArrayListQueue() {
        front = -1;
        rear = -1;
    }
        ...



}
```

Dynamic Implementation

```
public class DynamicQueue {
    private DynamicNode front, rear;



    public DynamicQueue() {
        front = null;
        rear = null;
    }


        ...

}
```

front and *rear* are pointers to the first and last nodes of a queue represented as a list. The empty queue is represented by *front* and *rear*, both equaling the null pointer. The method *empty* need check only one of these pointers, because neither *front* nor *rear* will be **null** in a nonempty queue.

```
public boolean empty() {
    return front == -1;
} // end empty
```

```
public boolean empty() {
    return (front == null);
} // end empty
```

The routine to insert an element into a queue may be written as follows:

```
public void insert(Object x) {
    int p = NodePool.getNode();

    NodePool.nodePool[p].info = x;
    NodePool.nodePool[p].next = -1;
    if (empty())
        front = p;
    else
        NodePool.nodePool[rear].next = p;
    rear = p;
} // end insert
```

```
public void insert(Object x) {
    DynamicNode p =
            new DynamicNode(x, null);

    if (empty())
        front = p;
    else
        rear.setNext(p);

    rear = p;
} // end insert
```

The *remove* method deletes the first element from a queue and returns its value:

```
public Object remove() {
    if (empty()) {
        System.out.println
            ("Queue underflow");
        System.exit(1);
    }
```

```
public Object remove(){
    if (empty()) {
        System.out.println
            ("Queue underflow");
        System.exit(1);
    }
```

```
int p = front;                          DynamicNode p = front;
Object x =                              Object temp = p.getInfo();
    NodePool.nodePool[p].info;          front = p.getNext();
front = NodePool.nodePool[p].next;      if (front == null)
if (empty())                                rear = null;
    rear = -1;                          return temp;
NodePool.freeNode(p);               } // end remove
return x;
} // end remove
```

Examples of List Operations in Java

Let us look at several somewhat more complex list operations implemented in Java. We have seen that the dynamic implementation is superior to the array implementation. For that reason, the majority of Java programmers use the dynamic implementation to implement lists. From this point on we restrict ourselves to the dynamic implementation of linked lists, although we may refer to the array implementation when appropriate.

We have previously defined the operation *place(list, x)*, where *list* points to a sorted linear list and *x* is an element to be inserted into its proper position on the list. Recall that this operation is used to implement the operation *pqInsert* to insert into a priority queue. We assume that we have already implemented the methods *insertFirst* and *insertAfter*. The code to implement the *place* method of the class *DynamicList* follows. We assume that the objects on the list are of type *Sortable* which can be placed in some linear order (i.e., any object of the type is either less than, greater than, or equal to any other object of the type). A method *compareTo* of the class *Sortable* returns a positive number if and only if the object that invokes *compareTo* is greater than the parameter of *compareTo* in their linear order.

```
public void place(Sortable x) {
DynamicNode p, q = null;

    for (p = list; p != null && x.compareTo(p.getInfo()) > 0; p = p.getNext())
        q = p;

    if (q == null)                    // insert x at the head of the list
        insertFirst(x);
    else
        insertAfter(q, x);

} // end place
```

The above method would be invoked by the statement *list.place(x);*.

In order to place an object in its proper position, it is necessary to have some method *compareTo* by which one can compare the object, *x*, with the items already on the list. Unfortunately, Java does not provide a general method for comparing *Objects*. It is therefore necessary for us to provide an appropriate *compareTo* method. In Java, an **interface** is used when it is desired to specify a class of objects while deferring the actual implementation of its methods. In our *place* method we wish to provide a nonspecific method for "ordering" the members of the list. We therefore define a *Sortable* class to serve as an *interface* between our various linked-list classes and the actual object that is being inserted on the list. This may be accomplished by declaring:

```
public interface Sortable {

  public int compareTo(Object b);

} // end interface Sortable
```

An interface is prefaced by the keyword ***interface***, and provides the method headers for any class that wishes to inherit its methods. Before an object of the interface class may be used, it is necessary to ***implement*** all of its methods. This is accomplished by declaring a class that is said to implement the methods of the interface. For example, suppose we wish to place objects of type *Integer* into the list. We would then define a class *IntData* by:

```
public class IntData implements Sortable {
  private int data;

  public IntData(int x) {
        data = x;
    }

    public int compareTo(Object b) {
        IntData temp = (IntData) b;

        return (data - temp.getData());
    }

    public int getData() {
        return data;
    }

} // end class IntData
```

IntData implements the *compareTo* method, which can then be invoked by any object that is declared to be of the *Sortable* class.

If we want to place objects of type *String* into the list, we would define another class *StringData* that also implements *Sortable*, as follows:

```
public class StringData implements Sortable {
  private String data;
    public StringData(String x) {
        data = x;
    }

    public int compareTo(Object b) {
        StringData temp = (StringData) b;

        return (temp.getData()).compareTo(data);
    }
```

```
   public String getData() {
     return data;
   }
} // end StringData class
```

Throughout this book we assume the existence of an appropriate implementation class of the *Sortable* interface.

As a second example, we write a method *insertLast* of class *DynamicList* to insert the element *x* at the end of a list.

```
public void insertLast(Object x) {
    DynamicNode p = new DynamicNode(x, null);
    DynamicNode q = null;

    if (isEmpty())
        list = p;
    else {
        // search for the last node
        for (q = list; q.getNext() != null; q = q.getNext())
            ;
        q.setNext(p);

    }
} // end insertLast
```

We now present a method *search* of class *DynamicList* that returns the node containing the first occurrence of *x* in the list and the *null* pointer if *x* does not occur in the list. The method *equals* determines whether its invoking object has a value equal to its parameter object's value.

```
public DynamicNode search(Object x) {
  DynamicNode p;

  for (p = list; p != null; p = p.getNext())
        if (p.getInfo().equals(x))
                return p;
  // x is not on the list
  return null;
} // end search
```

The next method of class *DynamicList* deletes all nodes whose *info* field contains the value *x*.

```
public void removeX(Object x) {
  DynamicNode p = list, q = null;

  while (p != null) {
        if (p.getInfo().equals(x)) {
                p = p.getNext();
                if (q == null)
                        deleteFirst(); // remove first node of the list
                else
                        deleteAfter(q);

        }
```

```
        else {
                // advance to next node of list
                q = p;
                p = p.getNext();
        }
    } // end while
} // end removeX
```

Comparing the Dynamic and Array Implementations of Lists

It is instructive to examine the advantages and disadvantages of the dynamic and array implementations of linked lists. The major disadvantage of the dynamic implementation is that it may be more time-consuming to call upon the system to allocate and free storage than to manipulate a programmer-managed available list. Its major advantage is that a set of nodes is not reserved in advance for use by a particular group of lists.

Another advantage of the dynamic implementation is that a reference to node p does not involve the address computation that is necessary in computing the address of *node*[p]. To compute the address of *node*[p], the contents of p must be added to the base address of the array *node*, whereas in the case of dynamic nodes, the address of p is given by the contents of p directly.

Implementing Header Nodes

At the end of Section 4.2, we introduced the concept of header nodes, which can contain global information about a list, such as its length, or a pointer to the current or last node on the list. When the data type of the header contents is identical to the type of the list node contents, then the header can be implemented simply as just another node at the beginning of the list.

It is also possible for header nodes to be declared as variables separate from the set of list nodes. This is especially useful when the header contains information of different type than the data in list nodes. For example, consider the case where it is desirable to know the number of nodes currently in a given list.

```
public class List {
  private DynamicNode list;
  private int size;

  public List() {
        list = null;
        size = 0;
  }
```

The variable *size* acts as a header for the list. The *List* constructor initializes the *list* "pointer" to *null* and the header information *size* to zero. Of course, the various methods of the class must be rewritten to modify *size*. As an exercise, you may wish to implement these methods.

EXERCISES

4.3.1   Implement the methods *empty, push, pop*, and *popAndTest* using the array and the dynamic storage implementations of a linked stack.

4.3.2   Implement the methods *empty, insert*, and *remove* using a dynamic storage implementation of a linked queue.

4.3.3   Implement the methods *empty, pqInsert*, and *pqMinDelete* using a dynamic storage implementation of a linked priority queue.

4.3.4   Write Java methods using both the array and dynamic variable implementations of a linked list to implement the operations in Exercise 4.2.3.

4.3.5   Write a Java method to interchange the *m*th and *n*th elements of a list.

4.3.6   Write a routine *l1.insSub*($i1, l2, i2, len$) to insert the elements of list *l2* beginning at the *i2*th element and continuing for *len* elements into the list *l1* beginning at position *i1*. No elements of the list *l1* are to be removed or replaced. If $i1 > l1.length() + 1$ (where $l1.length()$ denotes the number of nodes in the list *i1*), or if $i2 + len - 1 > l2.length()$, or if $i1 < 1$, or if $i2 < 1$, print an error message. The list *l2* should remain unchanged.

4.3.7   Write a Java method *l.search*(x) that searches a list of integers for an integer x and returns the node containing x, if it exists, and the null otherwise. Write another method *l.srchInsrt*(x) that adds x to *l* if it is not found and always returns the node containing x.

4.3.8   Write a Java application to read a group of input lines, each containing one word. Print each word that appears in the input and the number of times that it appears.

4.3.9   Suppose a character string is represented by a list of single characters. Write a set of methods as shown below to manipulate such a list (in the following, *l1, l2*, and *list* lists represent a character string, *str* is an array of characters, and *i1* and *i2* are integers):

a.   *list.strCnvCL*(str) to convert the character string *str* to a list. This method returns a list.

b.   *str.strCnvLC*($list$) to convert a list into a character string.

c.   *l1.strPosL*($l2$) to perform the *strPos* method from Section 1.2 on two character strings represented by lists. This method returns an integer.

d.   *l1.strVrfyL*($l2$) to determine the first position of the string represented by *l1* that is not contained in the string represented by *l2*. This method returns an integer.

e.   *l1.strSubStr*($i1, i2$) to perform the *subStr* method from Section 1.2 on a character string represented by list *l1* and integers *i1* and *i2*. This method returns a list representing a character string that is the desired substring. The list *l1* remains unchanged.

f.   *l1.strPsbl*($i1, i2, l2$) to perform a pseudo-*subStr* assignment to list *l1*. The elements of list *l2* should replace the *i2* elements of *l1* beginning at position i1. The list *l2* should remain unchanged.

g.   *l1.strCmpL*($l2$) to compare two character strings represented by lists. This method returns -1 if the character string represented by *l1* is less than the string represented by *l2*, 0 if they are equal, and 1 if the string represented by *l1* is greater.

4.3.10   Write a method *binSrch*, which accepts two parameters, an array of references to a group of sorted objects, and a single object. The method should use a binary search (see Section 3.1) to return the position of the single object if it is in the group. If the object is not present in the group, the value -1 is returned.

4.3.11 Assume that we wish to form N lists, where N is a constant. Define a class *ArrayOfLists* by

```
public class ArrayofLists {
    static final int N = ... ;

    static List arrayOfLists[] = new List[N];
```

Read two numbers from each input line, the first number being the index of the list into which the second number is to be placed in ascending order. When there are no more input lines, print all the lists.

4.3.12 Write a class *OrderedList* to implement a sorted list into which elements can only be inserted in their proper places.

4.3.13 Add a method *insertafter2*(**int** *oldvalue*, **int** *n*, **int** *newvalue*) to the *DynamicList* class that inserts a node with value *newvalue* after the *n*th occurrence of *oldvalue*.

4.4   AN EXAMPLE: SIMULATION USING LINKED LISTS

Simulation is one of the most useful applications of queues, priority queues, and linked lists. A simulation program attempts to model a real-world situation in order to learn something about it. Every object and action in the real situation has its counterpart in the program. If the simulation is accurate—that is, if the program successfully mirrors the real world—the result of the program should mirror the result of the actions being simulated. Thus it is possible to understand what occurs in the real-world situation without actually observing its occurrence.

Let us look at an example. Suppose there is a bank with four tellers. A customer enters the bank at a specific time ($t1$), desiring to conduct a transaction with any teller. The transaction may be expected to take a certain amount of time ($t2$) before it is completed. If a teller is free, the customer's transaction is transacted immediately, and the customer leaves the bank as soon as it is completed, at time $t1 + t2$. The total time spent in the bank by the customer is exactly equal to the duration of the transaction ($t2$).

However, perhaps none of the tellers are free; they are all servicing customers who arrived previously. In that case, there is a line waiting at each teller's window. The line for a teller may consist of only a single person—the one currently transacting business with the teller—or it may be a very long. The customer proceeds to the end of the shortest line and waits until all the other customers on the line have completed their transactions and left the bank. At that time, the customer may transact his or her business. The customer leaves the bank at $t2$ time units after reaching the front of a teller's line. In this case the time spent in the bank is $t2$ plus the time spent waiting on line.

Given this system, we would like to compute the average time a customer spends in the bank. One way of doing so is to stand in the bank doorway, ask departing customers the time of their arrival and record the time of their departure, subtract the first from the second for each customer, and take the average over all customers. However, this would not be very practical. It would be difficult to ensure that no customer is overlooked when leaving the bank. Furthermore, it is doubtful that most customers would remember the exact time of arrival.

Instead, we write a program to simulate the customer actions. Each part of the real-world situation has its analog in the program. The real-world action of a customer arriving is modeled by input of data. As each customer arrives, two facts are known: the time of arrival and the duration of the transaction (since, presumably, the customers know what they wish to do at the bank). Thus the input data for each customer consists of a pair of numbers: the time (in minutes since the bank opened) of the customer's arrival, and the amount of time (again in minutes) necessary for the transaction. The data pairs are ordered by increasing arrival time. We assume at least one input line.

The four lines in the bank are represented by four queues. Each node of the queues represents a customer waiting on a line, and the node at the front of a queue represents the customer currently being serviced by a teller.

Suppose that at a given instant of time the four lines each contain a specific number of customers. What can happen to alter the status of the lines? Either a new customer enters the bank, in which case one of the lines will have an additional customer, or the first customer on one of the four lines completes a transaction, in which case that line will have one customer less. Thus there are a total of five actions (a customer entering plus four cases of a customer leaving) that can change the status of the lines. Each of these five actions is called an *event*.

Simulation Process

The simulation proceeds by finding the next event to occur and effecting the change in the queues that mirrors the change in the lines at the bank due to that event. In order to keep track of events, the program uses an ascending priority queue, called the *event list*. This list contains at most five nodes, each representing the next occurrence of one of the five types of event. Thus the event list contains one node representing the next customer arriving and four nodes representing each of the four customers at the head of a line completing a transaction and leaving the bank. Of course, it is possible that one or more of the lines in the bank are empty, or that the doors of the bank have been closed for the day so that no more customers are arriving. In such cases, the event list contains fewer than five nodes.

An event node representing a customer's arrival is called an *arrival node*, and a node representing a departure is called a *departure node*. At each point in the simulation, it is necessary to know the next event to occur. For this reason, the event list is ordered by increasing time of event occurrence, so that the first event node on the list represents the next event to occur. Thus the event list is an ascending priority queue represented by an ordered linked list.

The first event to occur is the arrival of the first customer. The event list is therefore initialized by reading the first input line and placing an arrival node representing the first customer's arrival on the event list. Initially, of course, all four teller queues are empty. The simulation then proceeds as follows: The first node on the event list is removed and the changes the event causes are made to the queues. As we shall soon see, these changes may also cause additional events to be placed on the event list. The process of removing the first node from the event list and effecting the changes that it causes is repeated until the event list is empty.

When an arrival node is removed from the event list, a node representing the arriving customer is placed on the shortest of the four teller queues. If that customer is the only one on a queue, a node representing departure is also placed on the event list, since the customer is at the front of the queue. At the same time, the next input line is read and an arrival node representing the next customer to arrive is placed on the event list. There will always be exactly one arrival node on the event list (as long as the input is not exhausted, at which point no more customers arrive), since as soon as one arrival node is removed from the event list, another is added to it.

When a departure node is removed from the event list, the node representing the departing customer is removed from the front of one of the four queues. At that point, the amount of time the departing customer has spent in the bank is computed and added to a total. At the end of the simulation, this total will be divided by the number of customers to yield the average time spent by a customer. After a customer node has been deleted from the front of its queue, the next customer on the queue (if any) becomes the one being serviced by that teller, and a departure node for that next customer is added to the event list.

This process continues until the event list is empty, at which point the average time is computed and printed. Note that the event list itself does not mirror any part of the real-world situation. It is used as part of the program to control the entire process. A simulation of this kind, which proceeds by changing the simulated situation in response to the occurrence of one of several events, is called an ***event-driven simulation***.

Data Structures

We now examine the data structures necessary for this program. Since customers are served in a first-in first-out fashion, each teller at the bank is naturally represented by a queue. The nodes on the queues represent customers and therefore must contain fields representing the customer's id, arrival time and transaction duration, the total amount of time spent in the bank, and the number of the customer's teller.

The nodes on the event list represent events and therefore must contain the time the event occurs, the type of the event, and any other information associated with the event.

Our simulation must therefore deal with two separate node classes (*Customer* and *Event*) as well as two different data structures (*DynamicQueue* and *PriorityQueue*). The *Customer* class is used to represent a customer. Information about a particular customer is kept here as well as information about all the customers (static data members). The *Event* class is used to represent an event. Since events are ordered in time, an ascending priority queue, *PriorityQueue*, is used to hold the *Event* nodes. An event may represent a customer's arrival or a departure from one of the four teller lines in the bank. Thus an *Event* object contains data members to represent the time of occurrence, a link to additional information, and an event type. *Event* objects are inserted in the event list in order so the *Event* class must implement the *Sortable* interface.

DynamicQueue and *PriorityQueue* have been described in Section 4.2. A more efficient representation of a priority queue (as will be presented in Sections 6.3 and 7.3) would allow the program to operate somewhat more efficiently. We leave their implementation to the reader. We now present the *Customer* and *Event* classes.

```
public class Customer {
    private int arrivalTime;   // the time of customer's arrival in
                               // the bank
```

```
        private int duration;     // the length of the customer's
                                  // transaction
        private int waitingTime;  // the total time spent in the bank
        private int teller;       // the number of the customer's teller
        private int id;           // the customer's id

        private static double aveWaitingTime = 0;
                                  // the current average waiting
                                  // time for all departed customers

        private static int totalWaitingTime = 0;
                                  // the total waiting time for
                                  // all departed customers

        private static int totalCustomers = 0;
                                  // the number of customers
                                  // that have departed so far

        private static int idCounter = 0;
                                  // the number of customers
                                  // at the bank

        public Customer(int arrivalTime, int duration) {
            this.arrivalTime = arrivalTime;
            this.duration = duration;
            waitingTime = 0;
            teller = -1;
            id = idCounter;
            idCounter++;
        } // end Customer

        // customerDeparts updates the simulation totals when a
        // customer departs
        public void customerDeparts(int departureTime){

            totalCustomers++;
            waitingTime = departureTime - arrivalTime;
            totalWaitingTime += waitingTime;
            aveWaitingTime = totalWaitingTime / totalCustomers;
        } // end customerDeparts

        // accessor and mutator methods for the Customer class
        public int getArrivalTime() {
            return arrivalTime;
        }

        public int getDuration() {
            return duration;
        }

        public int getWaitingTime() {
            return waitingTime;
        }
```

```java
    public static double getAveWaitingTime() {
         return aveWaitingTime;
    }

    public static int getTotalCustomers() {
         return totalCustomers;
    }

    public static int getTotalWaitingTime() {
         return totalWaitingTime;
    }

    public int getTeller() {
         return teller;
    }

    public int getId() {
         return id;
    }

    public void setTeller(int i) {
         teller = i;
    }
} // end Customer class
public class Event implements Sortable {
  private int eventTime;     // the time at which the event occurs
  private Object link;       // an object that contains more
                             // information about the event
  private String eventType;  // the type of the event

  public Event(int eventTime, Object link, String eventType) {
         this.eventTime = eventTime;
         this.link = link;
         this.eventType = eventType;
  } // end event

  public int compareTo(Object b) {
         Event temp = (Event) b;
         return (this.eventTime - temp.eventTime);
  }

  // accessor and mutator methods for the Customer class
  public int getEventTime() {
         return eventTime;
  }

  public Object getLink() {
         return link;
  }

  public void setLink(Object x) {
         link = x;
  }
```

```
    public String getEventType() {
        return eventType;
    }

} // end Event class
```

Simulation Program

The *Main* class instantiates the *BankSimulation* object with an input file and runs the simulation. We assume an input file consisting of a header representing the number of customers and a series of lines each consisting of a customer's arrival time followed by the duration of the customer's transaction.

```java
import java.io.*;

public class Main {
    public static void main(String args[]) throws IOException {
        File f = new File("input.dat");

        BankSimulation b = new BankSimulation(f);
        System.out.println("\nAverage Waiting Time: " + b.run());

    }
} // end Main class
```

The actual simulation is run by the *BankSimulation* class. Upon being instantiated by the *main* method of the *Main* application, the *BankSimulation* constructor is invoked in order to perform initializations, and then the *run* method (called by the *main* method) is invoked. The methods *arrive* and *depart* are members of this class. The class *PriorityQueue* is assumed to implement an ascending priority queue.

```java
import java.io.*;
import java.util.*;

public class BankSimulation {
    private final int NUMTELLERS = 4;
    private DynamicQueue queues[];
    private PriorityQueue eventList;
    private RandomAccessFile infile;
    private int inputData[][];
    private int inputDataIndex;
    private int currentTime;

    public BankSimulation(File f) throws IOException{
        queues = new DynamicQueue[NUMTELLERS];

        for (int i = 0; i < queues.length; i++)
            queues[i] = new DynamicQueue();
        eventList = new PriorityQueue();
        currentTime = 0;
        infile = new RandomAccessFile(f, "r");
        String temp = infile.readLine();    // get the header
        temp = temp.trim();
```

```
        int header = Integer.parseInt(temp);
        inputData = new int[header][2];
        inputDataIndex = 0;

        for (int i = 0; i < header; i++) {
            temp = infile.readLine();
            if (temp == null)
                break;

            StringTokenizer st = new StringTokenizer(temp);
            inputData[i][0] =
            Integer.parseInt((String)st.nextToken()); // arrival
            inputData[i][1] =
            Integer.parseInt((String)st.nextToken()); // duration
        }
    } // end BankSimulation constructor

    // runs the bank simulation and returns the average waiting time
    public double run() {
        // initialize the event list with the first arrival
        Customer firstCustomer = new Customer(inputData[0][0],
        inputData[0][1]);
        inputDataIndex++;
        currentTime = inputData[0][0];
        Event firstEvent = new Event(currentTime, firstCustomer,
                                        "Customer Arrival");
        eventList.insert(firstEvent);

        // process the remaining events
        while (!eventList.isEmpty()) {
            // get the next event
            Event nextEvent = (Event)eventList.remove();
            Customer cust = (Customer)nextEvent.getLink();
            currentTime = nextEvent.getEventTime();

            // check if the next event is an arrival or a
            // departure
            if (nextEvent.getEventType().equals("Customer Arrival"))
                arrive(cust);
            else {
                cust.customerDeparts(currentTime);
                depart(cust.getTeller());
            }
        }
        return Customer.getAveWaitingTime();
    } // end run
    private void arrive(Customer newCust) {
        // find the shortest queue
        int smallest = 0;
        for (int i = 1; i < NUMTELLERS; i++)
            if (queues[i].getSize() < queues[smallest].getSize())
                smallest = i;
```

```
        // queue smallest is the shortest, insert the new customer
        queues[smallest].insert(newCust);
        newCust.setTeller(smallest);

        // Check if this is the only node on the queue.  If it is, the
        // customer's departure node must be placed on the event list
        if (queues[smallest].getSize() == 1) {
                Event newEvent = new Event(currentTime +
                        newCust.getDuration(), newCust,
                        "Customer Departure");
                eventList.insert(newEvent);
        }

        // If any input remains, read the next data pair and place
        // an arrival on the event list
        if (inputDataIndex < inputData.length) {
                int arrivalTime = inputData[inputDataIndex][0];
                int duration = inputData[inputDataIndex][1];
                inputDataIndex++;
                Customer c = new Customer(arrivalTime, duration);
                Event e = new Event(arrivalTime, c, "Customer Arrival");
                eventList.insert(e);
        }
} // end arrive

private void depart(int q) {
        // remove the first customer from the given queue
        Customer firstCust = (Customer)queues[q].remove();

        // if there are any more customers on the queue, place
        // the departure of the next customer onto the event
        // list after computing its departure time
        if (queues[q].getSize() > 0) {
                Customer nextCust = (Customer)queues[q].peek();
                Event e = new Event(currentTime + nextCust.getDuration(),
                                nextCust, "Customer Departure");
                eventList.insert(e);
} // end depart
} // end BankSimulation class
```

The *BankSimulation* constructor initializes the *Event, PriorityQueue*, and *Customer* queues, and reads the header, and the first customer's arrival and departure times. The *nextToken* method of the *StringTokenizer* class is used in order to break the input string into tokens that can be inserted into the *inputData* array for processing.

The *run* method repeatedly removes the next event node from the event list to drive the simulation until the event list is empty. The event list is ordered by increasing value of the *eventTime* field. If the item at the head of the event list represents a customer's arrival, it invokes the *arrive* method to insert the customer into the shortest teller queue. The method uses *eventList.insert(newEvent)* to insert an event node in its proper place in the event list. Then, the next data pair (if any) is read and an arrival node is placed on the event list to replace the arrival that has just been processed. If there is no more input, the function returns without adding a new arrival node and the program processes the remaining (departure) nodes on the event list.

If the item at the head of the list represents a customer's departure, the *run* method calls upon the *customerDeparts* method of the *Customer* class to add the customer's *totalWaitingTime* to the simulation's totals and then invokes the *depart* method. After computing its departure time, the *depart* method removes the event node from the event list, and places the departure of the next customer onto the event list.

Simulation programs are rich in their use of list structures. The reader is urged to explore the use of Java for simulation and the use of special-purpose simulation languages.

EXERCISES

4.4.1   In the bank-simulation application in the text, a departure node on the event list represents the same customer as the first node on a customer queue. Is it possible to use a single node for a customer currently being serviced? Rewrite the application in the text so that only a single node is used. Is there any advantage to using two nodes?

4.4.2   The application in the text uses the same type of node for both customer and event nodes. Rewrite the application using two different types of nodes for these two purposes. Does this save space?

4.4.3   Revise the bank-simulation application to determine the average length of the four lines.

4.4.4   Modify the bank-simulation application to compute the standard deviation of the time spent by a customer in the bank. Write another application which simulates a single line for all four tellers, with the customer at the head of the single line going to the next available teller. Compare the means and standard deviations of the two methods.

4.4.5   Modify the bank-simulation application so that whenever the length of one line exceeds the length of another by more than two, the last customer on the longer line moves to the end of the shorter.

4.4.6   Write a Java application to simulate a simple multiuser computer system as follows: Each user has a unique ID and wishes to perform a number of transactions on the computer. However, only one transaction may be processed by the computer at any given moment. Each input line represents a single user and contains the user's ID followed by a starting time and a series of integers representing the duration of each of his or her transactions. The input is sorted by increasing starting time, and all times and durations are in seconds. Assume that a user does not request time for a transaction until the previous transaction is complete, and that the computer accepts transactions on a first-come, first-served basis. The application should simulate the system and print a message containing the user ID and the time whenever a transaction begins and ends. At the end of the simulation, it should print the average waiting time for a transaction. (The waiting time is the amount of time between the time the transaction was requested and the time it was started.)

4.4.7   What parts of the bank-simulation application would have to be modified if the priority queue of events were implemented as an array or as an unordered list? How would they be modified?

4.4.8   Many simulations do not simulate events given by input data, but instead generate events according to a probability distribution. The following exercises explain how. Most computer installations have a random number generating function *rand(x)*. (The name and parameters of the function vary from system to system. *rand* is used only as an example.) *x* is initialized to a value called a ***seed***. The statement $x = rand(x)$ resets the value of the variable x to a uniform random real number between 0 and 1. By this we mean that if the statement is executed a sufficient number of times, and any two equal-length intervals between 0 and 1 are chosen, approximately as many of the successive values of x fall into one interval as into the other. Thus the probability of a value of x falling in an interval of length $l \leq 1$ equals l. Find out the name of the random number generating function on your system and verify that the above is true. Given a random number generator *rand*, consider the following statements:

```
x = rand(x);
y = (b - a) * x + a;
```

a. Show that, given any two equal-length intervals within the interval from a to b, if the statements are repeated sufficiently often, an approximately equal number of successive values of y fall into each of the two intervals. Show that if a and b are integers, the successive values of y truncated to an integer equal each integer between a and $b - 1$ an approximately equal number of times. The variable y is said to be a ***uniformly distributed random variable***. What is the average of the values of y in terms of a and b?

b. Rewrite the bank simulation assuming that the transaction duration is uniformly distributed between 1 and 15. Each data pair represents an arriving customer and contains only the time of arrival. Upon reading an input line, generate a transaction duration for that customer by computing the next value according to the method outlined above.

4.4.9   The successive values of y generated by the following statements are called ***normally distributed***. (Actually, they are approximately normally distributed, but the approximation is close enough.)

```
long x[] = new long[15];
double m, s, sum, y;
// statements initializing the values of s, m and the array x
// go here
while ( /* a terminating condition goes here */ ) {
        sum = 0;
        for (int i = 0; i < 15; i++) {
                Random rnd = new Random(x[i]);
                x[i] = rnd.nextLong();
                sum = sum + (long) x[i];
        }
        y = s * (sum - 7.5) / Math.sqrt(1.25) + m;
        // statements that use the value of y go here
}
```

a. Verify that the average of the values of y (the mean of the distribution) equals m, and that the standard deviation equals s.

b. A certain factory produces items according to the following process: an item must be assembled and polished. Assembly time is uniformly distributed between one hundred and three hundred seconds, and polishing time is normally distributed, with a mean of twenty seconds and a standard deviation of seven seconds (but values below five are discarded). Each item must be polished after it is assembled, and a worker cannot begin assembling a new item until the item just assembled has been polished. There are ten workers but only one polishing machine. If the machine is not available, workers who have finished assembling items must wait for it. Compute the average waiting time per item by means of a simulation. Do the same under the assumption of two and three polishing machines.

4.5   OTHER LIST STRUCTURES

Linked linear lists are a useful data structure, but they have several shortcomings. In this section we present other methods of organizing lists and show how they can be used to overcome these shortcomings.

Circular Lists

Given a pointer p to a node in a linear list, we cannot reach any of the nodes that precede $node(p)$. If a list is traversed, the external pointer to the list must be preserved in order to be able to reference the list again.

Suppose a small change is made to the structure of a linear list so that the *next* field in the last node contains a pointer back to the first node rather than the null pointer. Such a list is called a ***circular list*** and is illustrated in Figure 4.5.1. From any point in such a list it is possible to reach any other point in the list. If we begin at a given node and traverse the entire list, we ultimately end up at the starting point.

Note that a circular list does not have a natural "first" or "last" node. We must, therefore, establish a first and last node by convention. One useful convention is to let the external pointer to the circular list point to the last node, and to allow the following node to be the first node, as illustrated in Figure 4.5.2. If p is an external pointer to a circular list, this convention allows access to the last node of the list by referencing

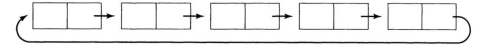

FIGURE 4.5.1   Circular list.

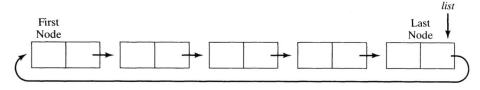

FIGURE 4.5.2   First and last nodes of a circular list.

node(p) and to the first node of the list by referencing *node(next(p))*. This convention provides the advantage of being able to add or remove an element conveniently from either the front or the rear of a list. We also establish the convention that a null pointer represents an empty circular list.

Stack as a Circular List

A circular list can be used to represent a stack or a queue. Let *s* be a stack represented by a circular list with data member *list* being a "pointer" to the last node of a circular list. Let us adopt the convention that the first node of the circular list is the top of the stack and that an empty stack is represented by a null list. The class definition follows:

```java
public class DynamicCircularStack {
   private DynamicNode list;

   public DynamicCircularStack() {
        list = null;
   } // end constructor

   public boolean empty() {
        return list == null;
   } // end empty

   public void push(Object x) {
        DynamicNode p = new DynamicNode(x, null);

        if (empty())
             list = p;
        else
             p.setNext(list.getNext());
        list.setNext(p);
    } // end push

   public Object pop() {
        if (empty()) {
             System.out.println("stack underflow.");
             System.exit(1);
        }

        DynamicNode p = list.getNext();
        Object temp = p.getInfo();
        if (p == list)
             // only one node on the stack
             list = null;
        else
             list.setNext(p.getNext());

        return temp;
    } // end pop
} // end DynamicCircularStack class
```

A stack *s* is created by

```java
DynamicCircularStack s = new DynamicCircularStack();
```

Queue as a Circular List

It is easier to represent a queue as a circular list than as a linear list. As a linear list, two pointers specify a queue, one to the front of the list and the other to its rear. However by using a circular list, a queue may be specified by a single pointer to the last node in the list.

We may define the class *DynamicCircularQueue* as follows:

```
public class DynamicCircularQueue {
    private DynamicNode queue;

    public DynamicCircularQueue() {
        queue = null;
    } // end constructor

    public boolean empty() {
        return queue == null;
    } // end empty

    public void insert(Object x) {
        DynamicNode p = new DynamicNode(x, null);
        if (empty())
            queue = p;
        else
            p.setNext(queue.getNext());
        queue.setNext(p);
        queue = p;
    } // end insert

    public Object remove() {
        if (empty()) {
            System.out.println("queue underflow.");
            System.exit(1);
        }

        DynamicNode p = queue.getNext();
        Object temp = p.getInfo();
        if (p == queue)
            // only one node on the stack
            queue = null;
        else
            queue.setNext(p.getNext());
        return temp;
    } // end remove
} // end DynamicCircularQueue class
```

Note that the method *empty* is the same as for stacks and the method *remove()* called by *q*.remove() is identical to *pop*. Also note that to insert an element into the rear of a circular queue, the element is inserted into the front of the queue and the circular list pointer is then advanced one element, so that the new element becomes the rear.

Primitive Operations on Circular Lists

We can define a class *DynamicCircularList* that implements a circular list using *DynamicNode*. *DynamicCircularList* contains the data member *list* that is a reference to the last node of the circular list. It also contains the methods *insertAfter*, *deleteAfter*, *insertFirst*, *insertLast*, *deleteFirst*, and *deleteLast*. We leave the methods *insertFirst*, *insertLast*, *deleteFirst*, and *deleteLast* to the reader, noting that these are very similar to the *push*, *pop*, *insert*, and *remove* methods presented for stacks and queues implemented by circular lists. If *lst* is an object of the class *DynamicCircularList*, then the method *lst.insertAfter(p, x)*, which inserts a node containing *x* after *node(p)* in the list *lst*, is similar to the corresponding routine for linear lists as presented in Section 4.3.

```
public void insertAfter(DynamicNode p, Object x) {
    if (p == null) {
            System.out.println("void insertion");
            System.exit(1);
    }

    // if we are not inserting after the last node
    if (p != list) {
            DynamicNode q = new DynamicNode(x, p.getNext());
            p.setNext(q);
    }
    else {
            // inserting after the last node
            DynamicNode q = new DynamicNode(x, list.getNext());
            list.setNext(q);
            list = q;
    }
} // end insertAfter
```

However, the method *lst.deleteAfter(p, x)* must be modified slightly. Looking at the corresponding routine for linear lists as presented in Section 4.3, we note one additional consideration in the case of a circular list. Suppose *p* points to the only node in the list. In a linear list, *next(p)* is null in that case, making the deletion invalid. In the case of a circular list, however, *next(p)* points to *node(p)* so that *node(p)* follows itself. The question is whether or not it is desirable to delete *node(p)* from the list in this case. It is unlikely that we would want to do so, since the method *deleteAfter* is usually invoked when pointers to each of two nodes are given, one immediately following another, and it is desired to delete the second. *deleteAfter* for circular lists using the dynamic node implementation is implemented as follows:

```
public Object deleteAfter(DynamicNode p) {
    if (p == null || p == p.getNext()) {
            System.out.println("Void deletion.");
            return null;
    }

    Object temp = null;

    // if the last node is not after p
    if (p.getNext() != list) {
            DynamicNode q = p.getNext();
            temp = q.getInfo();
            p.setNext(q.getNext());
    }
```

```
else {
        // delete the last node
        temp = list.getInfo();
        p.setNext(list.getNext());
        list = p;
}
return temp;
} // end deleteAfter
```

Note that *insertAfter* can be used to insert a node following the last node in a circular list and *deleteAfter* can be used to delete the last node of a circular list. In both cases, the external pointer to the list must be modified to point to the new last node. These methods, which are modified from those presented in Section 4.3, determine whether or not we are dealing with the last node of the circular list and change the *list* "pointer" when necessary.

If we are managing our own available list of nodes (as, for example, under the array implementation), it is also easier to free an entire circular list than to free a linear list. In the case of a linear list, the entire list must be traversed, as one node at a time is returned to the available list. For a circular list, we can write a method *freeList* that effectively frees an entire list by simply rearranging pointers. This is left as an exercise for the reader.

Similarly, we may write a method *CircularList.concat(list1, list2)* that concatenates two lists; that is, it appends the circular list pointed to by *list2* to the end of the circular list pointed to by *list1*. Using circular lists, this can be done without traversing either list.

```
public static void concat(CircularList list1, CircularList list2) {
    // list1 or list2 does not point at a circular list. There is
    // nothing to do.
    If (list1 == null || list2 == null)
            return;
    if (list2.isEmpty())
            return;
    if (list1.isEmpty()) {
            list1.list = list2.list;
            return;
    }

    DynamicNode p = list1.list.getNext();
    list1.list.setNext(list2.list.getNext());
    list2.list.setNext(p);
    list1.list = list2.list;
} // end concat
```

The Josephus Problem

Let us consider a problem that can be solved in a straightforward manner by using a circular list. The problem is known as the Josephus Problem and postulates a group of soldiers surrounded by an overwhelming enemy force. There is no hope for victory without reinforcements but there is only a single horse available for escape. The soldiers agree to a pact to determine which of them is to escape and summon help. They form a circle and a number *n* is picked from a hat. One of their names is also picked from a hat. Beginning with the soldier whose name is picked, they begin to count clockwise around the circle. When the count reaches *n*, that soldier is removed from the circle, and the count begins again with the next soldier. The process continues, so with another soldier removed from the circle each time the count reaches *n*. Any soldier removed from the circle is no longer counted. The last soldier remaining is to take the horse and escape. The problem is: given a number *n*, the ordering of the soldiers in the circle, and the soldier from whom the count begins, determine the order in which soldiers are eliminated from the circle and which soldier escapes.

The input to the application is the number *n* and a list of names that is the clockwise ordering of the circle, beginning with the soldier from whom the count is to start. The last input line contains the string "*end*" indicating the end of the input. The application should print the names in the order that they are eliminated and the name of the soldier who escapes.

For example, suppose *n* = 3 and there are five soldiers named *A, B, C, D*, and *E*. We count three soldiers starting at *A*, so that *C* is eliminated first. We then begin at *D* and count *D, E*, and back to *A*, so that *A* is eliminated next. Then we count *B, D*, and *E* (*C* has already been eliminated), and finally *B, D*, and *B*, so that *D* is the one who escapes.

Clearly a circular list in which each node represents one soldier is a natural data structure to use in solving this problem. It is possible to reach any node from any other by counting around the circle. The removal of a soldier from the circle is represented by deleting a node from the circular list. Finally, when only one node remains on the list, the result is determined.

An outline of the program might be the following:

```
read(n);
read(name);
while (name != END) {
  insert name at the end of the circular list;
  read(name);
}
// start from the first node on the list
while (there is more than one node on the list) {
  count through n - 1 nodes on the list;
  print the name in the nth node;
  delete the nth node;
}
print the name of the only node on the list;
```

In order to read the input from the keyboard, we define a *readLine* method as part of a *Console* class. The *readLine* method constructs a string, one character at a time, from those typed by the user. We assume at least one name in the input.

```
import java.io.*;

public class Console {
  public static String readLine() {
```

```
                String str = new String();
                int ch = 0;

                while(true) {
                        try {
                                ch = System.in.read();
                        }
                        catch(IOException e) {
                                break;
                        }
                        if (ch < 0 || (char) ch == '\n')
                                break;
                        else if ((char) ch != '\r')
                                str += (char) ch;
                }
                return str;
        } // end readLine
} // end Console class
```

We also assume that a *DynamicNode* class has been declared as before. In order to keep track of the number of nodes currently in the circular list, a *size* member has been added to the *DynamicCircularList*. *size* is initialized to zero in the class constructor and is modified each time a node is added to or deleted from the list. A *getSize* method is added to the class to return the current size of the circular list. In order to add a node at the end of the circular list, we also define a method *insertLast*. We leave these modifications to the reader.

It is often desirable to step though each of the elements of a data structure one at a time. The *java.util* package contains an *Enumeration* interface that, when implemented, generates a series of elements and allows them to be retrieved sequentially. The *Enumeration* interface defines two methods: *hasMoreElements*(), which tests whether the enumeration contains more elements, and *nextElement*(), which returns the next element of the enumeration.

Recall from our discussion of the *Sortable* interface in Section 4.3 that an interface cannot be used until it is implemented. There are two approaches that may be used when implementing the *Enumeration* interface for a circular linked list. Suppose we wish to traverse a circular list. This can be done by repeatedly executing $p = p.getNext(p)$; where p is initially a pointer to the beginning of the list. However, since the list is circular, we will not know when the entire list has been traversed unless another pointer *first* points to the first node and a test is made for the condition $p == first$.

(An alternative method is to place a header node as the first node of a circular list. This list header may be recognized by a special value in its *info* field that cannot be the valid contents of a list node in the context of the problem, or it may contain a flag marking it as a header. The list can then be traversed using a single pointer, with the traversal halting when the header node is reached. The external pointer to the list is to its header node, as illustrated in Figure 4.5.3. This means that a node cannot easily be added onto the rear of such a circular list, as could be done when the external pointer was to the last node of the list. Of course, it is possible to keep a pointer to the last node of a circular list even when a header node is being used.

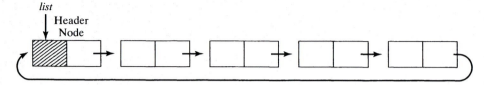

FIGURE 4.5.3   Circular list with a header node.

If a stationary external pointer to a circular list is used in addition to the pointer used for traversal, then the header node need not contain a special code but can be used in much the same way as a header node of a linear list to contain global information about the list. The end of a traversal would be signaled by the equality of the traversing pointer and the external stationary pointer.)

Using the first approach, we define a *CircularListEnumerator* class that implements the *Enumeration* class for a circular list.

```
import java.util.*;

class CircularListEnumerator implements Enumeration {
   private DynamicNode p;
   private DynamicNode first;
   private boolean flag;

   public CircularListEnumerator(DynamicNode nd) {
        p = nd.getNext();
        first = p;
        flag = false;        // whether or not we have gone through
                             // the entire list yet
   } // end constructor

   public boolean hasMoreElements() {
        return !(p == first && flag);
   } // end hasMoreElements

   public Object nextElement() {
        flag = true;
        Object temp = p.getInfo();
        p = p.getNext();
        return temp;
   } // end nextElement
} // end CircularListEnumerator class
```

The *DynamicCircularList* class contains a method, *elements*, that returns an object of type *Enumerator* by invoking the *CircularListEnumerator* constructor. The method *elements* may be written as:

```
public Enumeration elements() {
  return new CircularListEnumerator(list);
}
```

Using these methods, we can now implement the Josephus algorithm.

```java
import java.util.*;
import java.io.*;

public class JosephusProblem {

  public static void main(String args[]) throws IOException {
        josephus();
  } // end main

  public static void josephus() throws IOException {
        System.out.print("Enter n: ");
        String str = Console.readLine().trim();
        int n = Integer.parseInt(str);

        System.out.println("Enter names");
        String name = Console.readLine().trim();
        DynamicCircularList clist = new DynamicCircularList();
        while(!name.equals("end"))
                if (name.length() != 0) {
                        clist.insertLast(name);
                        name = Console.readLine();
                }
        System.out.println("The order in which the soldiers are
        eliminated is:");
        Enumeration enum = clist.elements();
        while (clist.getSize() > 1) {
                String temp = null;
                // count through n - 1 nodes on the list
                for (int i = 0; i < n; i++)
                        temp = (String) enum.nextElement();
                // delete the nth node
                clist.removeX(temp);
        }
        System.out.print("\nThe soldier who escapes is: " +
        clist.deleteFirst());
  } // end josephus

} // end JosephusProblem class
```

The *removeX* method of the *DynamicCircularList* class removes the element specified by its parameter from the list and is left for the reader.

While the *Enumeration* interface is useful for simple traversals of data structures, it is limited in that it does not provide any methods for directly interacting with the underlying data. For example, in the *Josephus* method above, the *Enumerator nextElement* method is used to traverse the list, but once we find the element to be deleted, we must use the *removeX* method to search the list for that element in order to perform the actual deletion. Not only is this extremely inefficient, since it requires the list to be traversed twice (once by the enumerator and once by the *removeX* method), but should there be two identical items on the list, the *removeX* method may remove the wrong one!

The Java 2 API includes an interface known as an *Iterator* used to interact with a generalized group of objects known as a *Collection*. Although the Java API does not actually implement the generalized *Collection* interface, it provides several subinterfaces for lists and sets. The *Iterator* interface improves on the *Enumeration* interface by allowing interaction with the underlying list, through the *hasNext*, *next*, and *remove* methods. Furthermore, a subinterface of the *Iterator* interface known as *ListIterator* provides many additional methods for the processing of lists.

As with any interface, the *Iterator* interface must be implemented before it can be used. Although the Java SDK provides a comprehensive *ListIterator* interface, only a few of its methods are necessary for our application. We therefore choose to implement our own *ListIterator* interface as an implementation of the *Iterator* interface. The implementation of the *ListIterator* interface for a *DynamicCircularList* is straightforward:

```java
import java.util.*;
class ListIterator implements Iterator {
    private DynamicNode list;

    public ListIterator(DynamicNode nd) {
        list = nd;
    } // end ListIterator constructor

    public Object getInfo() {
        return list.getInfo();
    } // end getInfo

    public DynamicNode getNext() {
        return list.getNext();
    } // end getNext

    public boolean hasNext() {
        return (list.getNext() != list);
    } // end hasNext

    public Object next() {
        list = list.getNext();
        Object temp = list.getInfo();
        return temp;
    } // end next

    public void remove() {
        DynamicNode q;
        q = list.getNext();
        list.setNext(q.getNext());
    } // end remove
} // end ListIterator class
```

Using the *ListIterator* methods, we can now revise our *Josephus* application to traverse a circular linked list and delete nodes directly.

```java
import java.util.*;
import java.io.*;
```

```
public class Josephus2 {
  public static void main(String args[]) throws IOException {
      josephus();
   } // end main

  public static void josephus() throws IOException {
      System.out.print("Enter n: ");
      String str = Console.readLine().trim();
      int n = Integer.parseInt(str);

      System.out.println("Enter names");
      DynamicCircularList clist = new DynamicCircularList();

      String name = Console.readLine();
      while (!name.equals("end"))
              if (name.length() != 0) {
                      clist.insertLast(name);
                      name = Console.readLine();
              }

      ListIterator liter = new ListIterator(clist.getRear());
      int i;
      System.out.print("The order in which the soldiers are
      eliminated is: ");
      while (liter.hasNext()) {
              Object temp = null;

              for (i = 1; i < n; i++)
                      temp = liter.next();

              temp = liter.getNext().getInfo();
              liter.remove();
              System.out.print(temp + ", ");
      }
      System.out.println("\nThe soldier who escapes is: " +
      liter.getInfo());
   } // end josephus
} // end Josephus2 class
```

Addition of Long Positive Integers Using Circular Lists

We now present a second application of circular lists. The hardware of most computers and most language-system software allow integers of only a specific maximum length. Suppose we wish to represent positive integers of arbitrary length and to write a method that returns the sum of two such integers.

To add two long integers, their digits are traversed from right to left, and corresponding digits and a possible carry from the sum of the previous digits are added. This suggests that long integers can be represented by storing their digits from right to left in a list so that the first node on the list contains the least significant digit (rightmost) and the last node contains the most significant (leftmost). However, in order to save space, we keep nine digits in each node. (Although the maximum size of an integer in Java is defined by the language, this is not the case for many other languages. The maximum size of an integer is language-implementation-dependent, so you may have to modify the routines to hold smaller numbers in each node.)

The *main* application prompts the user for two numbers and, using the *Console.readLine*() method, developed earlier, constructs the two input strings. After instantiating two objects of the *LongInteger* class (to be described below), it invokes the *LongInteger.addInt* method to compute and display the sum.

```
public class LongIntegerTest {
  public static void main(String args[]) {
      while (true) {
          System.out.print("Enter the first number: ");
          String str1 = Console.readLine();
          System.out.print("Enter the second number: ");
          String str2 = Console.readLine();
          if (str1.equalsIgnoreCase("end") ||
          str2.equalsIgnoreCase("end"))
              break;

          LongInteger li1 = new LongInteger(str1);
          LongInteger li2 = new LongInteger(str2);

          System.out.println("You entered: " + li1 + " " + " " + li2);
          System.out.println("The answer: " + li1.addInt(li2));
      }
  } // end main
} // end LongIntegerTest class
```

The *LongInteger* class represents a long integer by using a circular list. We assume that the classes *DynamicNode*, *CircularList*, and the *Sortable* interface have been defined. Since we wish to traverse the lists during the addition, we also implement the *CircularListEnumerator* class.

```
import java.util.*;

public class LongInteger {
  private CircularList list;
  private static final int NUMDIGITS = 9;    // the number of
                                             // digits per node
  private static final int divisor = (int) Math.pow(10.0,
                                         (double) NUMDIGITS);

  // Constructs a LongInteger from a string
  public LongInteger(String s) {
      s = s.trim();
      list = new CircularList();

      // remove leading zeros
      int index = 0;
      while (s.charAt(index) == '0' && index < s.length() - 1)
          index++;
      s = s.substring(index);
```

```
        int endIndex = s.length();       // start from the end
        int beginIndex;
        if (s.length() < NUMDIGITS)
                beginIndex = 0;
        else
                beginIndex = endIndex - NUMDIGITS;

        while (true) {
                // get a group of NUMDIGITS digits or less
                String group = s.substring(beginIndex, endIndex);
                // insert the group of digits on the list as a string
                list.insertLast(group);

                if (beginIndex == 0)                // no more groups
                        break;

                // select the next group
                endIndex = beginIndex;
                if (beginIndex - NUMDIGITS < 0)
                        beginIndex = 0;
                else
                        beginIndex -= NUMDIGITS;
        }
} // end LongInteger constructor

public LongInteger addInt(LongInteger li) {
        Enumeration enum1 = list.elements();
        Enumeration enum2 = li.list.elements();
        StringBuffer totalSum = new StringBuffer();
        totalSum.setLength(NUMDIGITS);

        int carry = 0;                    // initially there is no carry
        int total = 0, number = 0;

        while (enum1.hasMoreElements() && enum2.hasMoreElements()) {
                // get the two digit groups
                String s1 = (String) enum1.nextElement();
                String s2 = (String) enum2.nextElement();
                int int1 = Integer.parseInt(s1);
                int int2 = Integer.parseInt(s2);

                // add the two digit groups and previous carry
                total = int1 + int2 + carry;

                // determine the low order NUMDIGITS digits of the sum
                number = total % divisor;

                // insert number in totalSum and pad with zeros if
                // necessary
                String str = String.valueOf(number);
                int maxLen = Math.max(s1.length(), s2.length());
                totalSum.insert(0, str);
                if (str.length() < maxLen) {
                        StringBuffer sb = new StringBuffer(maxLen);
```

```
                                for (int i = str.length(); i < maxLen; i++)
                                        sb.append("0");
                                totalSum.insert(0, sb.toString());

                        }

                        // determine whether there is a carry
                        carry = total / divisor;
                } // end while

                // at this point, there may be nodes left in one of the
                // two input lists
                while (enum1.hasMoreElements()) {
                        int i = Integer.parseInt((String)enum1.nextElement());
                        total = i + carry;
                        number = total % divisor;
                        carry = total / divisor;

                        // pad with zeros if necessary
                        String str = String.valueOf(number);
                        if (str.length() < NUMDIGITS)
                                str = pad(str);
                        totalSum.insert(0, str);
                } // end while

                while (enum2.hasMoreElements()) {
                        int i = Integer.parseInt((String)enum2.nextElement());
                        total = i + carry;
                        number = total % divisor;
                        carry = total / divisor;

                        // pad with zeros if necessary
                        String str = String.valueOf(number);
                        if (str.length() < NUMDIGITS)
                                str = pad(str);
                        totalSum.insert(0, str);
                } // end while

                // check if there is an extra carry from the first digit group
                if (carry == 1)
                        totalSum.insert(0, String.valueOf(carry));

                return new LongInteger(totalSum.toString());
        } // end addInt
        // returns a string representation of this object
        public String toString() {
                Enumeration enum = list.elements();
                StringBuffer str = new StringBuffer();
                Stack stack = new Stack();

                while (enum.hasMoreElements())
                        stack.push(enum.nextElement());
                while (!stack.isEmpty())
                        str.append((String) stack.pop());
```

```
        return str.toString();
    } // end toString

    // pads the string with zeros
    private static String pad(String str) {
        StringBuffer sb = new StringBuffer(str);
        for (int j = 0; j < NUMDIGITS - str.length(); j++)
                sb.insert(0, "0");
        return sb.toString();
    } // end pad
} // end LongInteger class
```

The *LongInteger* constructor accepts a string consisting of the digits of a long integer and constructs a circular-list representation of that long integer having *NUMDIGITS* digits per node. The constructor is invoked each time the *main* method of the *LongIntegerTest* class instantiates a *LongInteger* object.

The *addInt* method returns a circular list representing the addition of the integer represented by the parameter and the integer represented by the class object. Both lists are traversed in parallel (using an *Enumeration* object), and nine digits are added at a time. If the sum of two nine-digit numbers is x, the low-order nine digits of x can be extracted by using the expression x % 1000000000, which yields the remainder of x on division by 1000000000. The carry can be computed by the integer division x/1000000000. When the end of one list is reached, the carry is propagated to the remaining digits of the other list.

Once the *totalSum* circular list is created, the *toString* method is invoked in order to convert the circular list back to a string. Using the *Enumerator* class and Java's own *Stack* class, the circular list is traversed and the string result is recreated.

Doubly Linked Lists

Although a circularly linked list has advantages over a linear list, it still has several drawbacks. One cannot traverse such a list backwards, nor can a node be deleted from a circularly linked list given only a pointer to that node. In cases where these facilities are required, the appropriate data structure is a ***doubly linked list***. Each node in such a list contains two pointers, one to its predecessor and the other to its successor. In fact, in the context of doubly linked lists, the terms "predecessor" and "successor" are meaningless, since the list is entirely symmetric. Doubly linked lists may be either linear or circular and may or may not contain a header node, as illustrated in Figure 4.5.4.

We may consider the nodes on a doubly linked list to consist of three fields: an *info* field that contains the information stored in the node, and *left* and *right* fields that contain pointers to the nodes on either side. Using the dynamic implementation, a *DoublyLinkedNode* class may be declared by:

```
public class DoublyLinkedNode {
  private Object info;
  private DoublyLinkedNode left, right;

  public DoublyLinkedNode(Object info, DoublyLinkedNode right,
                                        DoublyLinkedNode left) {
```

```
        this.info = info;
        this.right = right;
        this.left = left;
    } // end DoublyLinkedNode constructor
    // accessor and mutator methods for the DoublyLinkedNode class
    public Object getInfo() {
        return info;
    }

    public void setInfo(Object info) {
        this.info = info;
    }

    public DoublyLinkedNode getRight() {
        return right;
    }

    public void setRight(DoublyLinkedNode right) {
        this.right = right;
    }

    public DoublyLinkedNode getLeft() {
        return left;
    }

    public void setLeft(DoublyLinkedNode left) {
        this.left = left;
    }

} // end DoublyLinkedNode class
```

The array representation of a doubly linked list is left as an exercise for the reader.

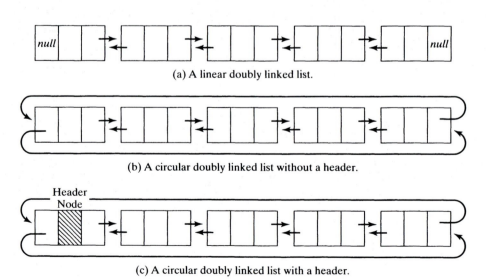

(a) A linear doubly linked list.

(b) A circular doubly linked list without a header.

(c) A circular doubly linked list with a header.

FIGURE 4.5.4 Doubly linked lists.

We now present the *DoublyLinkedList* methods to operate on doubly linked circular lists. A convenient property of such lists is that if *p* is a reference to any node, then letting *left(p)* be an abbreviation for *p.getLeft()*, and *right(p)* an abbreviation for *p.getRight()*, we have

```
left(right(p)) = p = right(left(p))
```

Deleting a given node is an operation that can be performed on doubly linked lists but not on ordinary linked lists. The following Java method deletes the node pointed to by *p* from a doubly linked list, *list*, and stores its contents in *x*, using the dynamic node implementation. It is called by *x = list.delete(p)*.

```java
public Object delete(DoublyLinkedNode p) {
    if (p == null) {
        System.out.println("void deletion");
        return null;
    }
    Object temp = p.getInfo();
    if (p.getRight() == null)
        p.getLeft().setRight(null);
    else if (p.getLeft() == null) {
        list = p.getRight();
        p.getRight().setLeft(null);
    }
    else {
        DoublyLinkedNode l = p.getLeft();
        DoublyLinkedNode r = p.getRight();
        l.setRight(p.getRight());
        r.setLeft(p.getLeft());
    }
    size--;
    return temp;
} // end delete
```

The method *insertRight* inserts a node with information field *x* to the right of *node(p)* in a doubly linked list.

```java
public void insertRight(DoublyLinkedNode p, Object x) {
    if (p == null) {
        System.out.println("void deletion");
        return;
    }
    DoublyLinkedNode q = null;
    if (p.getRight() != null) {
        q = new DoublyLinkedNode(x, p.getRight(), p);
        p.getRight().setLeft(q);
    }
    else
        q = new DoublyLinkedNode(x, null, p);
```

```
        p.setRight(q);
        size++;
    } // end insertRight
```

The routine *insertLeft* to insert a node with information field *x* to the left of *node(p)* in a doubly linked list is similar and is left as an exercise for the reader.

When space efficiency is a consideration, a program may not be able to afford the overhead of two pointers for each element of a list. There are several techniques for compressing the left and right pointers of a node into a single field. For example, a single pointer field *ptr* in each node can contain the sum of the pointers to its left and right neighbors. (We are assuming here that pointers are represented in such a way that arithmetic can readily be performed on them. For example, pointers represented by array indexes can be added and subtracted. Although Java does not support the direct use of pointers, many compilers will allow pointer arithmetic.) Given two external pointers, *p* and *q*, to two adjacent nodes such that $p == left(q)$, $right(q)$ can be computed as $ptr(q) - p$, and $left(p)$ can be computed as $ptr(p) - q$. Given *p* and *q*, it is possible to delete either node and reset its pointer to the preceding or succeeding node. It is also possible to insert a node to the left of *node(p)* or to the right of *node(q)* or to insert a node between *node(p)* and *node(q)* and reset either *p* or *q* to the newly inserted node. In using such a scheme, it is crucial always to maintain two external pointers to two adjacent nodes in the list.

Addition of Long Integers Using Doubly Linked Lists

As an illustration of the use of doubly linked lists, let us consider extending the list implementation of long integers to include negative as well as positive integers. The header node of a circular list representing a long integer contains an indication of whether the integer is positive or negative.

In order to add a positive and a negative integer, the smaller absolute value must be subtracted from the larger absolute value, and the result must be given the sign of the integer with the larger absolute value. Thus some method is needed for testing which of two integers represented as circular lists has the larger absolute value.

The first criterion that may be used to identify the integer with the larger absolute value is the length of the integers (assuming that they do not contain leading zeros). The list with more nodes represents the integer with the larger absolute value. However, actually counting the number of nodes involves an extra traversal of the list. Instead of counting the number of nodes, the count could be kept as part of the list and referenced as needed.

However, if both lists have the same number of nodes, then the integer whose first node value is larger has the greater absolute value. If the leading digits of both integers are equal, then it is necessary to traverse the lists from the most significant digit to the least significant to determine which number is larger. Note that this traversal is in the opposite direction of the traversal used in actually adding or subtracting two integers. Since we must be able to traverse the lists in both directions, doubly linked lists are used to represent such integers. Using the *Enumeration* interface then allows us to define the *backwardEnumerator* and *fowardEnumerator* classes:

```
class ForwardEnumerator implements Enumeration {
    private DoublyLinkedListNode next;
    private DoublyLinkedListNode list;
    private boolean flag = false;

    public ForwardEnumerator(DoublyLinkedListNode list) {
        next = list;
        this.list = list;
    }

    public boolean hasMoreElements() {
        return !(next == list && flag);
    }

    public Object nextElement() {
        flag = true;
        Object temp = next.getInfo();
        next = next.getRight();
        return temp;
    }
} // end ForwardEnumerator class

class BackwardEnumerator implements Enumeration {
    public BackwardEnumerator(DoublyLinkedListNode list) {
        next = list.getLeft();
        this.list = list;
    }

    public boolean hasMoreElements() {
        return !(next == list.getLeft() && flag);
    }

    public Object nextElement() {
        flag = true;
        Object temp = next.getInfo();
        next = next.getLeft();
        return temp;
    }
} // end BackwardEnumerator class
```

Consider the format of a long integer represented as a doubly linked list. In addition to the list itself (i.e., a right and left pointer, the length of the list, and the digits of the integer), we must also maintain an indication of whether the number is positive or negative. We therefore define a **boolean** field *positive*, which is ***true*** if the linked list represents a positive integer, and *false* otherwise. We also assume that a circular doubly linked list is represented by a class *CircularDoublyLinkedList* whose data members are defined in terms of a *DoublyLinkedListNode* class. We now present partial definitions of the *DoublyLinkedListNode* and *CircularDoublyLinkedList* classes and leave the complete definition for the reader.

```
public class DoublyLinkedListNode {
    private Object info;
```

```
    private DoublyLinkedListNode left, right;

    public DoublyLinkedListNode(Object info, DoublyLinkedListNode
                             right, DoublyLinkedListNode left) {
        this.info = info;
        this.right = right;
        this.left = left;
    } // end DoublyLinkedListNode constructor

      // DoublyLinkedListNode methods getInfo, setInfo, getRight,
      // setRight, getLeft, and setLeft are left for the reader

} // end DoublyLinkedListNode class

public class CircularDoublyLinkedList {
  private DoublyLinkedListNode list;
  private int size;

  public CircularDoublyLinkedList() {
        list = null;
        size = 0;
  } // end CircularDoublyLinkedList constructor

      // CircularDoublyLinkedList methods delete, insertRight,
      // insertLeft, insertFirst, insertLast, deleteFirst,
      // deleteLast, isEmpty, fowardEnumeration, and
      // backwardEnumeration are left for the reader

} // end CircularDoublyLinkedList class
```

Figure 4.5.5 indicates a sample node and the representation of three integers as doubly linked lists. Note that the least significant digits are to the right of the list.

Using the above representation, we may now define the *LongInteger2* class:

```
import java.util.*;

public class LongInteger2 {
  private CircularDoublyLinkedList cdl;
  private static final int NUMDIGITS = 9;    // the # of digits per
                                             // node
  private static final int divisor =
                           (int) Math.pow(10.0, (double) NUMDIGITS);

  private boolean positive;
  // true if the number is positive, false if negative

  // Constructs a LongInteger from a string
  public LongInteger2(String s) {
        s = s.trim();
        cdl = new CircularDoublyLinkedList();
```

```
// check if the number is less than or greater than zero
if (s.startsWith("-")) {
        positive = false;
        s = s.substring(1);
}
else
        positive = true;

// remove leading zeros
int index = 0;
while (s.charAt(index) == '0' && index < s.length() - 1)
        index++;
s = s.substring(index);

int endIndex = s.length();                    // start from the end
```

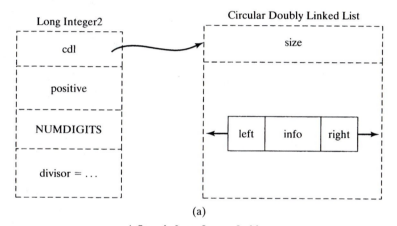

(a)

A Sample Long Integer2 object

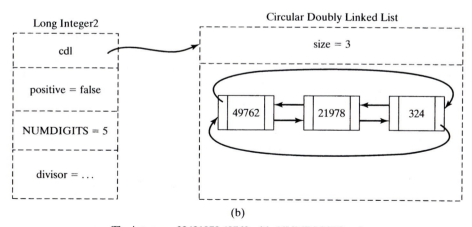

(b)

The integer −32421978 49762 with NUMDIGITS = 5

FIGURE 4.5.5   Representing long integers.

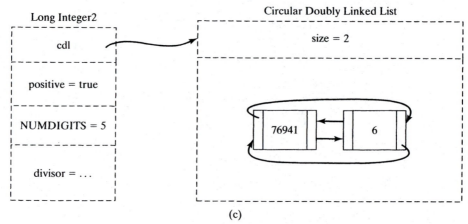

(c)

The Integer 676941
with NUMDIGITS = 5

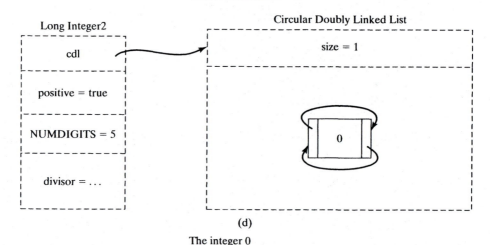

(d)

The integer 0
with NUMDIGITS = 5

FIGURE 4.5.5 (*Continued*)

```java
int beginIndex;
if (s.length() < NUMDIGITS)
        beginIndex = 0;
else
        beginIndex = endIndex - NUMDIGITS;

while (true) {
// get a group of NUMDIGITS digits or less
String group = s.substring(beginIndex, endIndex);

// insert the group of digits on the list as a string
cdl.insertLast(group);
```

```
        // check if done
        if (beginIndex == 0)
                break;
        // select the next group
        endIndex = beginIndex;
        if (beginIndex - NUMDIGITS < 0)
                beginIndex = 0;
        else
                beginIndex -= NUMDIGITS;
    } // end while
  } // end LongInteger constructor

  ...

} // end LongInteger2 class
```

The method *compAbs* compares the absolute values of two integers represented as doubly linked lists. It returns 1 if the long integer represented by the class object has a greater absolute value than the long integer represented by its parameter, −1 if the long integer represented by its parameter has the greater absolute value, and 0 if the absolute values of the two integers are equal.

```
public int compAbs(LongInteger2 li) {

    // compare the lengths
    if (cdl.getSize() > li.cdl.getSize())
            return 1;
    if (cdl.getSize() < li.cdl.getSize())
            return -1;

    // the lengths are equal, traverse the lists from the most
    // significant digits
    Enumeration e1 = cdl.backwardEnumeration();
    Enumeration e2 = li.cdl.backwardEnumeration();

    while (e1.hasMoreElements()) {
            String s1 = (String) e1.nextElement();
            String s2 = (String) e2.nextElement();
            int i1 = Integer.parseInt(s1);
            int i2 = Integer.parseInt(s2);

            if (i1 > i2)
                    return 1;
            if (i1 < i2)
                    return -1;
    } // end while

    // the absolute values are equal
    return 0;
} // end compAbs
```

We now present the method *addDiff*, which returns a reference to a circularly doubly linked list representing the addition of the class object and the parameter where the long integers are of different signs and where the absolute value of the class object is not less than that of the parameter. In this method, the class object represents the number with the larger absolute value, and *li* represents the number with the smaller absolute value. The values represented by these lists do not change. The sum is formed in the *StringBuffer result*, which upon return is used to construct a long integer represented as a doubly linked list.

```java
public LongInteger2 addDiff(LongInteger2 li) {
  Enumeration enum1 = cdl.forwardEnumeration();
  Enumeration enum2 = li.cdl.forwardEnumeration();
  StringBuffer result = new StringBuffer();
  int borrow = 0, diff = 0;
  // traverse the lists
  while (enum1.hasMoreElements() && enum2.hasMoreElements()) {
        // get the two digit groups
        String s1 = (String) enum1.nextElement();
        String s2 = (String) enum2.nextElement();
        int int1 = Integer.parseInt(s1);
        int int2 = Integer.parseInt(s2);

        diff = int1 - borrow - int2;
        if (diff >= 0)
                borrow = 0;
        else {
                diff += divisor;
                borrow = 1;
        }

        // insert the number into result and pad with zeros if
        // necessary
        String str = String.valueOf(diff);
        int maxLen = Math.max(s1.length(), s2.length());
        result.insert(0, str);
        if (str.length() < maxLen) {
                StringBuffer sb = new StringBuffer(maxLen);
                for (int i = str.length(); i < maxLen; i++)
                    sb.append("0");
                result.insert(0, sb.toString());
        } // end if
  } // end while

  // at this point, there may be nodes left on enum1
  while (enum1.hasMoreElements()) {
        String str = (String) enum1.nextElement();
        int num = Integer.parseInt(str);
        diff = num - borrow;
        if (diff >= 0)
                borrow = 0;
        else {
                diff += divisor;
                borrow = 1;
        }
```

```
                str = String.valueOf(diff);
                if (str.length() < NUMDIGITS)
                        str = pad(str);
                result.insert(0, str);
        } // end while

        // determine the sign of the result
        if (!isPositive() && compAbs(li) != 0)
                result.insert(0, "-");

        return new LongInteger2(result.toString());
    } // end addDiff
```

The methods *toString* and *pad* are identical to those used in the previous implementation of *addInt*.

We can also write a method *addSame* to add two numbers with like signs. This is very similar to the method *addInt* in the previous implementation except that it deals with a doubly linked list and must keep track of the number of nodes in the sum.

Using these methods we can write a new version of *addInt* that adds two integers represented by doubly linked lists.

```
    public LongInteger2 addInt(LongInteger2 li) {
        // check if the integers are of like sign
        if ((isPositive() && li.isPositive()) || (!isPositive() &&
                                        !li.isPositive()))
                return addSame(li);

        // check which has a larger absolute value
        LongInteger2 li1 = this;
        LongInteger2 li2 = li;
        if (compAbs(li) > 0)
                return li1.addDiff(li2);
        else
                return li2.addDiff(li1);
    } // end addInt
```

EXERCISES

4.5.1   Write an algorithm and a Java method to perform each of the operations in Exercise 4.2.3 for circular lists. Which are more efficient on circular lists than on linear lists? Which are less efficient?

4.5.2   Rewrite the method *place* in Section 4.3 to insert a new item in an ordered circular list.

4.5.3   Write a program to solve the Josephus problem by using an array rather than a circular list. Why is a circular list more efficient?

4.5.4   Consider the following variation of the Josephus problem. A group of people stand in a circle and each chooses a positive integer. One of their names and a positive integer n are chosen. Starting with the person whose name is chosen, they count around the circle clockwise and eliminate the nth person. The positive integer which that person chose is then used to continue the count. Each time that a person is eliminated, the number he or she chose is used to determine the next person eliminated. For example, suppose the five people are *A, B, C, D,* and *E* and they choose integers 3, 4, 6, 2, and 7, respectively, and the integer 2 is initially chosen. Then if we start from *A,* the order in which people are eliminated from the circle is *B, A, E, C,* leaving *D* as the last one in the circle.

4.5.5   Write an application that reads a group of input lines. Each input line except the first and last contains a name and a positive integer chosen by that person. The order of the names in the data is the clockwise ordering of the people in the circle, and the count is to start with the first name in the input. The first input line contains the number of people in the circle. The last input line contains only a single positive integer representing the initial count. The program prints the order in which people are eliminated from the circle.

4.5.6   Write a Java method *multInt(p, q)* to multiply two long positive integers represented by singly linked circular lists.

4.5.7   Write an applet to print the hundredth Fibonacci number.

4.5.8   Write an algorithm and a Java method to perform each of the operations in Exercise 4.2.3 for doubly linked circular lists. Which are more efficient on doubly linked than on singly linked lists? Which are less efficient?

4.5.9   Use an array representation to implement a doubly linked list. Note that the available list for such a set of nodes in the array implementation need not be doubly linked, since it is not traversed bidirectionally. The available list may be linked together by using either the *left* or *right* pointer. Of course, appropriate *getNode* and *freeNode* routines must be written.

4.5.10   Assume that a single pointer field in each node of a doubly linked list contains the sum of pointers to the node's predecessor and successor, as described in the text. Given pointers *p* and *q* to two adjacent nodes in such a list, write Java methods to insert a node to the right of *node(q)*, to the left of *node(p)*, and between *node(p)* and *node(q)*, modifying *p* to point to the newly inserted node. Write an additional method to delete *node(q)*, resetting *q* to the node's successor.

4.5.11   Assume that *first* and *last* are external pointers to the first and last nodes of a doubly linked list represented as in Exercise 4.5.9. Write Java methods to implement the operations in Exercise 4.2.3. for such a list.

4.5.12   Write a method *addSame* to add two long integers of the same sign represented by doubly linked lists.

4.5.13   Write a Java method *multInt(p, q)* to multiply two long integers represented by doubly linked circular lists.

4.5.14   How can a polynomial in three variables (*x, y,* and *z*) be represented by a circular list? Each node should represent a term and should contain the powers of *x, y,* and *z* as well as the coefficient of the term. Write Java methods to do the following:

   a.   Add two such polynomials.
   b.   Multiply two such polynomials.
   c.   Take the partial derivative of such a polynomial with respect to any of its variables.
   d.   Evaluate such a polynomial for given values of *x, y,* and *z.*
   e.   Divide one such polynomial by another, creating a quotient and a remainder polynomial.

f. Integrate such a polynomial with respect to any of its variables.

g. Print the representation of such a polynomial.

h. Given four such polynomials, $f(x,y,z)$, $g(x,y,z)$, $h(x,y,z)$, and $i(x,y,z)$, compute the polynomial $f(g(x,y,z), h(x,y,z), i(x,y,z))$.

4.5.15 Write a class *OrderedList* to implement a sorted doubly linked list into which elements can only be inserted in their proper place.

4.5.16 Add a method *insertafter2*(**int** *oldvalue*, **int** *n*, **int** *newvalue*) to the *DoublyLinked-List* class that inserts a node with value *newvalue* after the *n*th occurrence of *oldvalue*.

CHAPTER 5

Trees

In this chapter, we consider a data structure that is useful in many applications: the tree. We define several different forms of this data structure and show how they can be represented in Java and how they can be applied to solving a wide variety of problems. As with lists, we treat trees primarily as data structures rather than as data types. That is, we are primarily concerned with implementation, rather than mathematical definition.

5.1 BINARY TREES

A *binary tree* is a finite set of elements that is either empty or partitioned into three disjoint subsets. The first subset contains a single element called the *root* of the tree. The other two subsets are themselves binary trees, called the *left* and *right subtrees* of the original tree. A left or right subtree can be empty. Each element of a binary tree is called a *node* of the tree.

A conventional method of picturing a binary tree is shown in Figure 5.1.1. This tree consists of nine nodes with *A* as its root. Its left subtree is rooted at *B*, and its right subtree is rooted at *C*. This is indicated by the two branches emanating from *A*; to *B* on the left, and to *C* on the right. The absence of a branch indicates an empty subtree. For example, the left subtree of the binary tree rooted at *C* and the right subtree of the binary tree rooted at *E* are both empty. The binary trees rooted at *D*, *G*, *H*, and *I* have empty right and left subtrees.

Figure 5.1.2 illustrates some structures that are not binary trees. Be sure that you understand why each of them is not a binary tree as defined above.

If *A* is the root of a binary tree, and *B* is the root of its left or right subtree, then *A* is said to be the *father* of *B*, and *B* is said to be the *left* or *right son* of *A*. A node that has no sons (e.g., *D*, *G*, *H*, or *I* in Figure 5.1.1) is called a *leaf*. Node *n1* is an *ancestor* of node *n2* (and *n2* is a *descendant* of *n1*) if *n1* is either the father of *n2* or the father of some ancestor of *n2*. For example, in the tree in Figure 5.1.1, *A* is an ancestor of *G*, and *H* is a descendant of *C*, but *E* is neither an ancestor nor a descendant of *C*. Node *n2* is a *left descendant* of node *n1* if *n2* is either the left son of *n1* or a descendant of the left

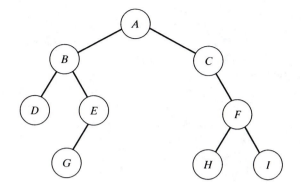

FIGURE 5.1.1 Binary tree.

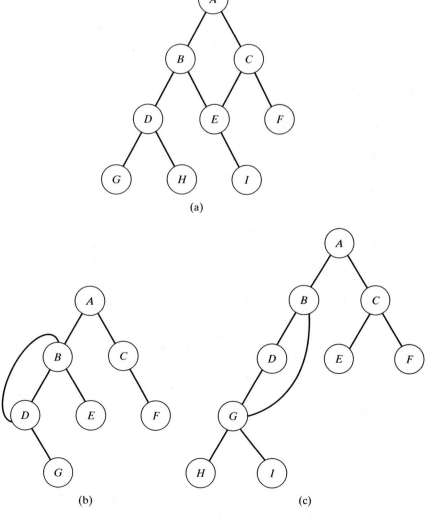

(a)

(b)   (c)

FIGURE 5.1.2 Structures that are not binary trees.

son of $n1$. A ***right descendant*** may be similarly defined. Two nodes are ***brothers*** if they are left and right sons of the same father.

Although natural trees grow with their roots in the ground and their leafs in the air, computer scientists almost universally portray tree data structures with the root at the top and leafs at the bottom. The direction from the root to the leafs is "down," and the opposite direction is "up." Going from the leafs to the root is called "climbing" the tree, while going from the root to the leafs is called "descending" the tree.

If every nonleaf node in a binary tree has nonempty left and right subtrees, the tree is termed a ***strictly binary tree***. Thus the tree in Figure 5.1.3 is strictly binary, whereas the one in Figure 5.1.1 is not (because nodes C and E have one son each). A strictly binary tree with n leafs always contains $2n - 1$ nodes. The proof of this fact is left as an exercise for the reader.

The ***level*** of a node in a binary tree is defined as follows: The root of the tree has level 0, and the level of any other node in the tree is one more than the level of its father. For example, in the binary tree in Figure 5.1.1, node E is at level 2, and node H is at level 3. The ***depth*** of a binary tree is the maximum level of any leaf in the tree. This equals the length of the longest path from the root to any leaf. Thus, the depth of the tree in Figure 5.1.1 is 3. A ***complete binary tree*** of depth d is a strictly binary tree all of whose leafs are at level d. Figure 5.1.4 illustrates a complete binary tree of depth 3.

If a binary tree contains m nodes at level l, then it contains at most $2m$ nodes at level $l + 1$. Since a binary tree can contain at most one node at level 0 (the root), it can contain at most 2^l nodes at level l. A complete binary tree of depth d is the binary tree of depth d that contains exactly 2^l nodes at each level l between 0 and d. (This is equivalent to saying that it is the binary tree of depth d that contains exactly 2^d nodes at level d.) The total number of nodes in a complete binary tree of depth d, tn, equals the sum of the number of nodes at each level between 0 and d. Thus

$$tn = 2^0 + 2^1 + 2^2 + \cdots + 2^d = \sum_{j=0}^{d} 2^j$$

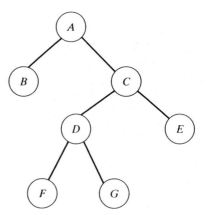

FIGURE 5.1.3   Strictly binary tree.

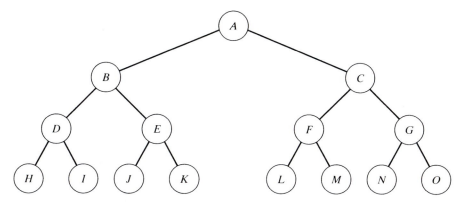

FIGURE 5.1.4   Complete binary tree of depth 3.

By induction, it can be shown that this sum equals $2^{d+1} - 1$. Since all the leafs in such a tree are at level d, the tree contains 2^d leafs and, therefore, $2^d - 1$ nonleaf nodes.

Similarly, if the number of nodes, tn, in a complete binary tree is known, we can compute its depth d from the equation $tn = 2^{d+1} - 1$. d equals one less than the number of times 2 must be multiplied by itself to reach $tn + 1$. In mathematics, $\log_b x$ is defined as the number of times b must be multiplied by itself to reach x. Thus we may say that, in a complete binary tree, d equals $\log_2(tn + 1) - 1$. For example, the complete binary tree in Figure 5.1.4 contains fifteen nodes and is of depth 3. Note that 15 equals $2^{3+1} - 1$, and 3 equals $\log_2(15 + 1) - 1$. $\log_2 x$ is much smaller than x (for example, $\log_2 1024$ equals 10, and $\log_2 1000000$ is less than 20). The significance of a complete binary tree is that it is the binary tree with the maximum number of nodes for a given depth. Put another way, although a complete binary tree contains many nodes, the distance from the root to any leaf (the tree's depth) is relatively small.

A binary tree of depth d is an ***almost complete binary tree*** if:

1. Any node nd at a level less than $d - 1$ has two sons.
2. For any node nd in the tree with a right descendant at level d, nd must have a left son, and every left descendant of nd is either a leaf at level d or has two sons.

The strictly binary tree in Figure 5.1.5a is not almost complete because it contains leafs at levels 1, 2, and 3, thereby violating condition 1. The strictly binary tree in Figure 5.1.5b satisfies condition 1 because every leaf is either at level 2 or level 3. However, condition 2 is violated because A has a right descendant at level 3 (J) but also has a left descendant that is a leaf at level 2 (E). The strictly binary tree in Figure 5.1.5c satisfies both condition 1 and condition 2, and is therefore an almost complete binary tree. The binary tree in Figure 5.1.5d is also an almost complete binary tree but is not strictly binary because node E has a left son but not a right son. (Many texts refer to such a tree as a "complete binary tree" rather than an "almost complete binary tree." Still other texts use the term "complete" or "fully binary" to refer to the concept that we call "strictly binary." We use the terms "strictly binary," "complete," and "almost complete" as we have defined them here.)

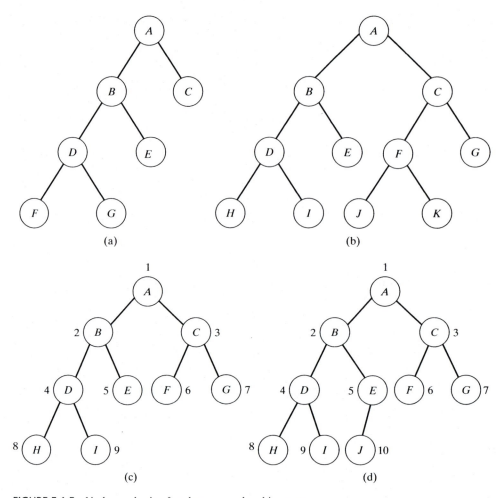

FIGURE 5.1.5 Node numbering for almost complete binary trees.

The nodes of an almost complete binary tree can be numbered so that the root is assigned the number 1, a left son is assigned twice the number assigned its father, and a right son is assigned one more than twice the number assigned its father. Figures 5.1.5c and d illustrate this numbering technique. Each node in an almost complete binary tree is assigned a unique number that defines its position in the tree.

An almost complete strictly binary tree with n leafs has $2n - 1$ nodes, as does any other strictly binary tree with n leafs. An almost complete binary tree with n leafs that is not strictly binary has $2n$ nodes. There are two distinct almost complete binary trees with n leafs, one of which is strictly binary and one of which is not. For example, the trees in Figures 5.1.5c and d are both almost complete and have five leafs; however, the tree in Figure 5.1.5c is strictly binary, while that in Figure 5.1.5d is not.

There is only a single almost complete binary tree with n nodes. This tree is strictly binary if and only if n is odd. Thus the tree in Figure 5.1.5c is the only almost complete binary tree with nine nodes and is strictly binary because 9 is odd, while the tree in Figure 5.1.5d is the only almost complete binary tree with ten nodes and is not strict-ly binary because 10 is even.

An almost complete binary tree of depth d is intermediate between the complete binary tree of depth $d - 1$, which contains $2^d - 1$ nodes, and the complete binary tree of depth d, which contains $2^{d+1} - 1$ nodes. If tn is the total number of nodes in an al-most complete binary tree, then its depth is the largest integer less than or equal to $\log_2 tn$. For example, the almost complete binary trees with four, five, six, and seven nodes have depth 2, and the almost complete binary trees with eight, nine, ten, eleven, twelve, thirteen, fourteen, and fifteen nodes have depth 3.

Operations on Binary Trees

There are a number of primitive operations that can be applied to a binary tree. If p is a pointer to a node nd of a binary tree, then the method $info(p)$ returns the contents of nd. The methods $left(p)$, $right(p)$, $father(p)$, and $brother(p)$ return pointers to the left son of nd, the right son of nd, the father of nd, and the brother of nd, respectively. These methods return the *null* pointer if nd has no left son, right son, father, or brother. Fi-nally, the logical methods $isLeft(p)$ and $isRight(p)$ return the value *true* if nd is a left or right son, respectively, of some other node in the tree, and *false* otherwise.

Note that the methods $isLeft(p)$, $isRight(p)$, and $brother(p)$ can be implemented using the methods $left(p)$, $right(p)$, and $father(p)$. For example, $isLeft$ may be imple-mented as follows:

```
q = father(p);
if (q == null)
    return false;    // p points to the root
if (left(q) == p)
    return true;
return false;
```

or, even simpler, as $father(p)! = null$ && $p == left(father(p))$. $isRight$ may be imple-mented in a similar manner or by calling $isLeft$. $brother(p)$ may be implemented using $isLeft$ or $isRight$, as follows:

```
if (father(p) == null)
    return null;            // p points to the root
if (isLeft(p))
    return right(father(p));
return left(father(p));
```

In constructing a binary tree, the operations *makeTree*, *setLeft*, and *setRight* are useful. *makeTree(x)* creates a new binary tree consisting of a single node with information field x and returns a pointer to that node. *setLeft(p, x)* accepts a pointer p to a binary tree node with no left son. It creates a new left son of $node(p)$ with information field x. *setRight(p, x)* is analogous to *setLeft* except that it creates a right son of $node(p)$.

Applications of Binary Trees

A binary tree is a useful data structure when two-way decisions must be made at each point in a process. For example, suppose we wanted to find all the duplicates in a list of numbers. One way of doing this is to compare each number with all those that precede it. However, this involves a large number of comparisons.

Using a binary tree can reduce the number of comparisons. The first number in the list is placed in a node that is established as the root of a binary tree with empty left and right subtrees. Each successive number in the list is then compared to the number in the root. If it matches, we have a duplicate. If it is smaller, we examine the left subtree; if it is larger, we examine the right subtree. If the subtree is empty, the number is not a duplicate and is placed into a new node at that position in the tree. If the subtree is nonempty, we compare the number to the contents of the root of the subtree and repeat the entire process with the subtree. An algorithm for doing this follows.

```
// read the first number and insert it
// into a single-node binary tree
number=System.in.readint();
tree = makeTree(number);
while (there are numbers left in the input) {
  number = System.in.readint();
  p = q = tree;
  while (number != info(p) && q != null) {
        p = q;
        if (number < info(p))
                q = left(p);
        else
                q = right(p);
  } // end while
  if (number == info(p))
        System.out.println("Duplicate: " + number);
  // insert number to the right or left of p
  else if (number < info(p))
        setLeft(p, number);
  else
        setRight(p, number);
} // end while
```

Figure 5.1.6 illustrates a tree constructed from the input 14, 15, 4, 9, 7, 18, 3, 5, 16, 4, 20, 17, 9, 14, 5.

Another common operation is to *traverse* a binary tree; that is, to pass through the tree, enumerating each of its nodes once. We may simply wish to print the contents of each node as we enumerate it, or we may wish to process it in some other fashion. In either case, we speak of *visiting* each node as it is enumerated.

The order in which the nodes of a linear list are visited in a traversal is clearly from first to last. However, there is no such "natural" linear order for the nodes of a tree. Thus different orderings are used for traversal in different cases. We shall define three of these traversal methods. In each of these methods, nothing need be done to traverse an empty binary tree. The methods are all defined recursively so that traversing a binary tree involves visiting the root and traversing its left and right subtrees. The only difference among the methods is the order in which these three operations are performed.

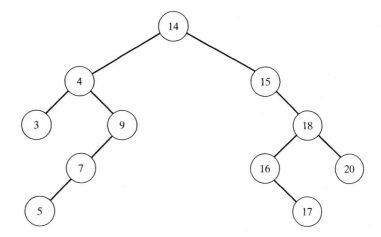

FIGURE 5.1.6 Binary tree
constructed for finding duplicates.

To traverse a nonempty binary tree in **preorder** (also known as **depth-first order**), we perform the following three operations:

1. Visit the root.
2. Traverse the left subtree in preorder.
3. Traverse the right subtree in preorder.

To traverse a nonempty binary tree in **inorder** (or **symmetric order**):

1. Traverse the left subtree in inorder.
2. Visit the root.
3. Traverse the right subtree in inorder.

To traverse a nonempty binary tree in **postorder**:

1. Traverse the left subtree in postorder.
2. Traverse the right subtree in postorder.
3. Visit the root.

Figure 5.1.7 illustrates two binary trees and their traversals in preorder, inorder, and postorder.

Many algorithms that use binary trees proceed in two phases. The first phase builds a binary tree, and the second traverses the tree. As an example of such an algorithm, consider the following sorting method. Given a list of numbers in an input file, we wish to print them in ascending order. As we read the numbers, they can be inserted into a binary tree like the one in Figure 5.1.6. However, unlike the previous algorithm used to find duplicates, duplicate values are also placed in the tree. When a number is compared to the contents of a node in the tree, a left branch is taken if the

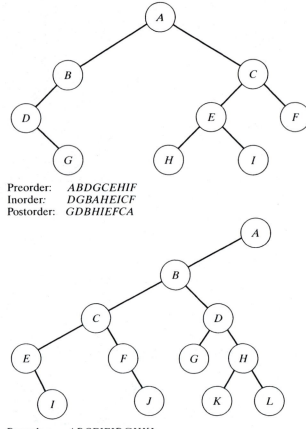

Preorder: *ABDGCEHIF*
Inorder: *DGBAHEICF*
Postorder: *GDBHIEFCA*

Preorder: *ABCEIFJDGHKL*
Inorder: *EICFJBGDKHLA*
Postorder: *IEJFCGKLHDBA*

FIGURE 5.1.7 Binary trees and their transversals.

number is smaller than the contents of the node, and a right branch if it is greater than or equal to the contents of the node. Thus, if the input list is

$$14 \quad 15 \quad 4 \quad 9 \quad 7 \quad 18 \quad 3 \quad 5 \quad 16 \quad 4 \quad 20 \quad 17 \quad 9 \quad 14 \quad 5$$

the binary tree in Figure 5.1.8 is produced.

This binary tree has the property that all the elements in the left subtree of a node n are less than the contents of n, and all the elements in the right subtree of n are greater than or equal to the contents of n. A binary tree that has this property is called a ***binary search tree***. If a binary search tree is traversed in inorder (left, root, right), and the contents of each node are printed as the node is visited, the numbers are printed in ascending order. Convince yourself that this is the case for the binary search tree in Figure 5.1.8. Binary search trees and their use in sorting and searching are discussed further in Sections 6.3 and 7.2.

As another application of binary trees, consider the following method of representing an expression containing operands and binary operators by a strictly binary

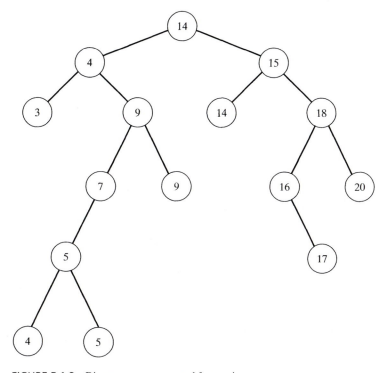

FIGURE 5.1.8   Binary tree constructed for sorting.

tree. The root of the strictly binary tree contains an operator that is to be applied to the results of evaluating the expressions represented by the left and right subtrees. A node representing an operator is a nonleaf, while a node representing an operand is a leaf. Figure 5.1.9 illustrates some expressions and their tree representations. (The character "$" is again used to represent exponentiation.)

Let us see what happens when these binary expression trees are traversed. Traversing such a tree in preorder means that the operator (the root) precedes its two operands (the subtrees). Thus a preorder traversal yields the prefix form of the expression. (For definitions of the prefix and postfix forms of an arithmetic expression, see Sections 2.3 and 3.3.) Traversing the binary trees in Figure 5.1.9 yields the prefix forms

$$+A * BC \qquad\qquad \text{(Figure 5.1.9a)}$$
$$* + ABC \qquad\qquad \text{(Figure 5.1.9b)}$$
$$+A * - BC \$ D * EF \qquad\qquad \text{(Figure 5.1.9c)}$$
$$\$ + A * BC * + ABC \qquad\qquad \text{(Figure 5.1.9d)}$$

Similarly, traversing a binary expression tree in postorder places an operator after its two operands, so that a postorder traversal produces the postfix form of the expression. The postorder traversals of the binary trees in Figure 5.1.9 yield the postfix forms

$$ABC * + \qquad\qquad \text{(Figure 5.1.9a)}$$
$$AB + C * \qquad\qquad \text{(Figure 5.1.9b)}$$

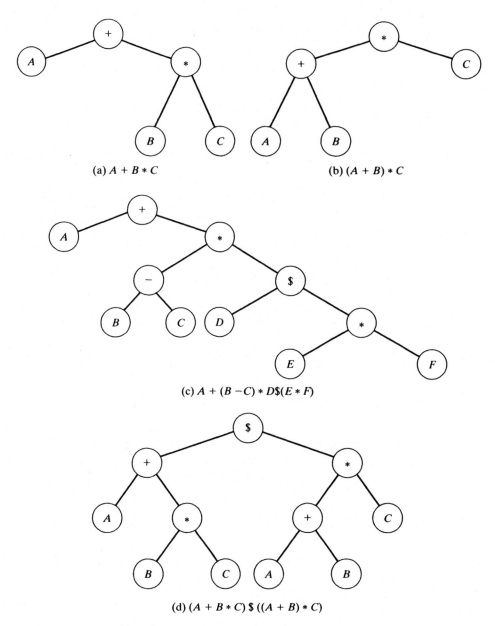

FIGURE 5.1.9 Expressions and their binary tree representations.

$$ABC - DEF * \$ * + \qquad \text{(Figure 5.1.9c)}$$
$$ABC * + AB + C * \$ \qquad \text{(Figure 5.1.9d)}$$

What happens when a binary expression tree is traversed in inorder? Since the root (operator) is visited after the nodes of the left subtree and before the nodes of the right subtree (the two operands), we might expect an inorder traversal to yield the infix form of the expression. Indeed if the binary tree in Figure 5.1.9a is traversed, the infix expression $A + B * C$ is obtained. However, a binary expression tree does not contain parentheses, because the ordering of the operations is implied by the structure of the tree. Thus an expression whose infix form requires parentheses to explicitly override the conventional precedence rules cannot be retrieved by a simple inorder traversal. The inorder traversals of the trees in Figure 5.1.9 yield the expressions

$$A + B * C \qquad \text{(Figure 5.1.9a)}$$
$$A + B * C \qquad \text{(Figure 5.1.9b)}$$
$$A + B - C * D \$ E * F \qquad \text{(Figure 5.1.9c)}$$
$$A + B * C \$ A + B * C \qquad \text{(Figure 5.1.9d)}$$

which are correct except for parentheses.

EXERCISES

5.1.1 Prove that the root of a binary tree is an ancestor of every node in the tree except itself.

5.1.2 Prove that a node of a binary tree has at most one father.

5.1.3 How many ancestors does a node at level n in a binary tree have? Prove your answer.

5.1.4 Write recursive and nonrecursive algorithms to determine:

   a. The number of nodes in a binary tree.

   b. The sum of the contents of all the nodes in a binary tree.

   c. The depth of a binary tree.

5.1.5 Write an algorithm to determine whether a binary tree is:

   a. Strictly binary

   b. Complete

   c. Almost complete

5.1.6 Prove that a strictly binary tree with n leafs contains $2n - 1$ nodes.

5.1.7 Given a strictly binary tree with n leafs, let $level(i)$ for i between 1 and n equal the level of the ith leaf. Prove that

$$\sum_{i=1}^{n} \frac{1}{2^{level(i)}} = 1$$

5.1.8 Prove that the nodes of an almost complete strictly binary tree with n leafs can be numbered from 1 to $2n - 1$ in such a way that the number assigned to the left son of the node numbered i is $2i$ and the number assigned to the right son of the node numbered i is $2i + 1$.

5.1.9 Two binary trees are **similar** if they are both empty or if they are both nonempty, their left subtrees are similar, and their right subtrees are similar. Write an algorithm to determine whether two binary trees are similar.

5.1.10   Two binary trees are ***mirror similar*** if they are both empty or if they are both nonempty and the left subtree of each is mirror similar to the right subtree of the other. Write an algorithm to determine whether two binary trees are mirror similar.

5.1.11   Write algorithms to determine whether or not one binary tree is similar or mirror similar to some subtree of another (see the previous exercises).

5.1.12   Develop an algorithm to find duplicates in a list of numbers without using a binary tree. If there are *n* distinct numbers in the list, how many times must two numbers be compared for equality in your algorithm? What if all *n* numbers are equal?

5.1.13   (a) Write an algorithm that accepts a pointer to a binary search tree and deletes the smallest element from the tree. (b) Show how to implement an ascending priority queue (see Section 4.1) as a binary search tree. Present algorithms for the operations *pqInsert* and *pqMinDelete* on a binary search tree.

5.1.14   Write an algorithm that accepts a binary tree representing an expression and returns the infix version of the expression that contains only those parentheses that are necessary.

5.2   BINARY TREE REPRESENTATIONS

In this section we examine various methods of implementing binary trees in Java and present routines that build and traverse binary trees. We also present some additional applications of binary trees.

Node Representation of Binary Trees

As is the case with list nodes, tree nodes may be implemented as array elements or as allocations of a dynamic variable. Each node contains *info*, *left*, *right*, and *father* fields. The *left*, *right*, and *father* fields of a node point, respectively, to the node's left son, right son, and father. Using the array implementation, we may declare

```
public class ArrayNode {
   final int NULL = -1;
   protected Object info;
   protected int left, right, father;
   protected boolean isleft;

   public ArrayNode (Object x, int l, int r, int f) {
         info = x;
         left = l;
         right = r;
         father = f;
         isleft = false;
   }

      ...
```

A pool of *ArrayNodes* may then be defined (similar to the array implementation of a linear linked list) by

```
public class ArrayNodePool {
   static final int NULL = -1;
   static final int NUMNODES=500;
```

```
static int avail;
static public ArrayNode arrayNode[] = new ArrayNode[NUMNODES];

public ArrayNodePool() { }

static {                      // static initializer
        avail = 0;
        for (int i = 0; i < NUMNODES - 1; i++)
                arrayNode[i] = new ArrayNode(null, i + 1, NULL,
                NULL);
        arrayNode[NUMNODES - 1] = new ArrayNode(null, NULL, NULL,
        NULL);
}
        ...
```

Under this representation, the operations *info(p)*, *left(p)*, *right(p)*, and *father(p)* are implemented, respectively, by references to *ArrayNodePool.arrayNode[p].info*, *ArrayNodePool.arrayNode[p].left*, *ArrayNodePool.arrayNode[p].right*, and *ArrayNodePool.arrayNode[p].father*. The operations *isLeft(p)*, *isRight(p)*, and *brother(p)* can be implemented in terms of the operations *left(p)*, *right(p)*, and *father(p)*, as described in the preceding section, without the need to reference the *isleft* data member.

To implement *isLeft* and *isRight* more efficiently, we include within each node an additional flag *isleft*. The value of this flag is *true* if the node is a left son and *false* otherwise. The root is uniquely identified by a *null* value in its *father* field. The external pointer to a tree usually points to its root.

Alternatively, the sign of the *father* field could be negative if the node is a left son or positive if it is a right son. The pointer to a node's father is then given by the absolute value of the *father* field. The *isLeft* or *isRight* methods would then only need to examine the sign of the *father* field.

To implement *brother(p)* more efficiently, we can also include an additional *brother* field in each node.

The static initializer for the *ArrayNodePool* class links the individual nodes creating the available list. Note that the available list is not a binary tree but a linear list whose nodes are linked together by the *left* field. Each node in a tree is taken from the available pool when needed and returned to the available pool when no longer in use. The methods *getnode* and *freenode* are straightforward and are left as exercises. This implementation is called the ***linked array representation*** of a binary tree.

Alternatively, a node may be defined by:

```
public class TreeNode {
  public Object info;
  public TreeNode left, right, father;
  boolean isleft;

        ...
```

The operations *info(p)*, *left(p)*, *right(p)*, and *father(p)* would be implemented, respectively, by references to *p.info*, *p.left*, *p.right*, and *p.father*. Under this implementation, an explicit available list is not needed. As with the dynamic node implementation of linear linked lists, the routines *getnode* and *freenode* are not necessary. Each time ***new*** *TreeNode()* is invoked, storage is automatically allocated by the Java Virtual Machine.

Whenever the Java Virtual Machine detects that a node is no longer being used, the node's storage is deallocated and garbage collection is performed. This implementation is called the ***dynamic node representation*** of a binary tree.

Both the linked array representation and the dynamic node representation are implementations of an abstract ***linked representation*** (also called the ***node representation***) in which explicit pointers link together the nodes of a binary tree.

We now present Java implementations of the binary tree operations under the dynamic node representation and leave the linked array implementations as simple exercises for the reader. Each time a new *TreeNode* object is created, the *TreeNode* constructor allocates a node and optionally sets its various fields with the arguments passed to it at the time it is called. The constructors for the *TreeNode* class may be written as follows:

```java
public TreeNode () {
        info = null;
        left = null;
        right = null;
        father = null;
        isleft = false;
}

public TreeNode (Object x) {
        info = x;
        left = null;
        right = null;
        father = null;
        isleft = false;
}

public TreeNode (Object x, TreeNode l, TreeNode r, TreeNode f) {
        info = x;
        left = l;
        right = r;
        father = f;
        isleft = false;
}
```

Note that the second constructor above implements our algorithmic operation *makeTree(x)*.

A binary tree is represented by an object of the *Tree* class that consists of a "pointer" to the root of the tree. The *Tree* class contains two constructors: the first simply sets its root "pointer" to null—representing a tree with no nodes, the second allocates an object of the *TreeNode* class and sets it as the root of a single-node binary tree.

```java
public class Tree {
   TreeNode root;

   public Tree() {
        root = null;
   }
```

```
public Tree(Object x) {
      root = new TreeNode(x);
}
      ...
```

A method *getRoot* should be defined in the class *Tree* to return the value of the member *root*.

The method *setLeft* of the class *TreeNode*, called by *nd.setLeft*(*x*), sets a newly allocated node with *info* field *x* as the left son of *node*(*nd*), assuming that *node*(*nd*) does not already have a left son.

```
public void setLeft(Object x) {
   if (this == null)
          throw new NullPointerException();

   else if (this.left!=null) {
          System.out.println("void insertion"); // or you can throw a
                                                 // new exception
          return;
      }
      else {
          TreeNode p = new TreeNode(x);
          this.left = p;
          p.father = this;
          p.isleft = true;
      }
} // end setLeft
```

The method *setRight*(*x*) to create a right son of a node is similar and is left as an exercise for the reader. We also assume the methods *getInfo*, *getLeft*, and *getRight*.

It is not always necessary to use *father*, *left*, and *right* fields. If a tree is always traversed in downward fashion (from the root to the leaves), the *father* method is never used; in that case, a *father* field is unnecessary. For example, preorder, inorder, and postorder traversal do not use the *father* field. Similarly, if a tree is always traversed in upward fashion (from the leaves to the root), *left* and *right* fields are not needed. The *isLeft* and *isRight* operations could be implemented even without *left* and *right* fields by using a signed pointer in the *father* field under the linked array representation, as discussed earlier: a right son contains a positive *father* value, and a left son a negative *father* field. Of course, the constructors for the *Tree* class and the methods *setLeft* and *setRight* must then be suitably modified for these representations. Under the dynamic node representation, an *isleft* logical field is required in addition to *father* if *left* and *right* fields are not present and it is desired to implement the *isLeft* or *isRight* operation.

The following application uses a binary search tree to find duplicate positive numbers in an input list in which each number is on a separate input line. It closely follows the algorithm in Section 5.1. Only top-down links are used, so no *father* field is needed.

```
import java.io.IOException;
import trees.*;
```

```java
public class DynamicTreesTest {
  public final static int MAXCOLS = 80;

  public static void main(String args[]) throws IOException {
        TreeNode p, q;
        TreeNode tree;
        int number;

        // place the first number into a single node binary tree
        number = readInt();
        Tree t=new Tree(new Integer(number));
        while ((number = readInt()) >= 0) {
                p = q = t.getRoot();
                while(number != (((Integer) p.getInfo()).intValue())
                               && q != null) {
                  p = q;
                  if (number < (((Integer) p.getInfo()).intValue()))
                     q = p.getLeft();
                  else
                     q = p.getRight();
                } // end while

            if (number ==(((Integer) p.getInfo()).intValue()))
               System.out.println("" + number + " is a duplicate\n");
               else if (number < (((Integer) p.getInfo()).intValue()))
                  p.setLeft(new Integer(number));
               else
                  p.setRight(new Integer(number));
        }// end while;
  } // end main

  public static int readInt() throws IOException {
    char[] charArray = new char[MAXCOLS];
    int position = 0;
    char c;

    System.out.println("\nEnter a Positive Integer (Negative to stop)");
    while ((c = (char) System.in.read()) != '\n')
      charArray[position++] = c;
    return  (Integer.parseInt
                    (String.copyValueOf(charArray,0,position-1)));
  } // end readInt

} // end DynamicTreesTest class
```

The method *readInt* prompts the user for an integer, constructs a string from the characters that are read, and subsequently uses the *parseInt* method of the *Integer* class to convert the string into an integer.

Internal and External Nodes

By definition, leaf nodes have no sons. Thus, in the linked representation of binary trees, left and right pointers are only needed in nonleaf nodes. Sometimes, two separate sets of nodes are used for nonleafs and leafs. Nonleaf nodes contain *info*, *left*, and *right* fields (often, no information is associated with nonleafs, so that an *info* field is unnecessary) and are allocated as dynamic records or as an array of records managed using an available list. Leaf nodes do not contain a *left* or *right* field and are kept as a single info array that is allocated sequentially as needed. (This assumes that leafs are never freed, which is often the case.) Alternatively, they can be allocated as dynamic objects containing only an *info* value. This saves a great deal of space, since leafs often represent a majority of the nodes in a binary tree. Each (leaf or nonleaf) node can also contain a *father* field, if necessary.

When this distinction is made between nonleaf and leaf nodes, nonleafs are called **internal nodes** and leafs are called **external nodes**. The terminology is also often used even when only a single type of node is defined. Of course, a son pointer within an internal node must be identified as pointing to an internal or an external node. This can be done in Java by declaring two different node classes where one node class (depending on whether the node is an internal or external node), does or does not contain left and right pointer fields. We will see an example of the latter technique at the end of this section.

Implicit Array Representation of Binary Trees

Recall from Section 5.1 that the n nodes of an almost complete binary tree can be numbered from 1 to n so that the number assigned a left son is twice the number assigned its father, and the number assigned a right son is one more than twice the number assigned its father. We can represent an almost complete binary tree without *father*, *left*, or *right* links. Instead, the nodes can be kept in an array *info* of size n. We refer to the node at position p simply as "node p." *info*[p] holds the contents of node p.

In Java, arrays start at position 0, so instead of numbering the tree nodes from 1 to n, we number them from 0 to $n - 1$. Because of the one-position shift, the two sons of a node numbered p are in positions $2p + 1$ and $2p + 2$ rather than $2p$ and $2p + 1$.

The root of the tree is at position 0, so that *tree*, the external pointer to the tree root, always equals 0. The node in position p (i.e., node p) is the implicit father of nodes $2p + 1$ and $2p + 2$. The left son of node p is node $2p + 1$, and its right son is node $2p + 2$. Thus the operation *left*(p) is implemented by $2p + 1$, and *right*(p) by $2p + 2$. Given a left son at position p, its right brother is at $p + 1$, and given a right son at position p, its left brother is at $p - 1$. *father*(p) is implemented by $(p - 1)/2$. p points to a left son if and only if p is odd. Thus the test for whether node p is a left son (the *isLeft* operation) is to check whether p % 2 is not equal to 0. Figure 5.2.1 illustrates arrays that represent the almost complete binary trees in Figures 5.1.5c and d.

We can extend this **implicit array representation** of almost complete binary trees to an implicit array representation of binary trees generally. We do this by identifying an almost complete binary tree that contains the binary tree being represented. Figure 5.2.2a illustrates two (non-almost-complete) binary trees, and Figure 5.2.2b illustrates the smallest almost complete binary trees that contain them. Finally, Figure 5.2.2c illustrates the implicit array representations of these almost complete binary trees, and, by extension, of the original binary trees. The implicit array representation is also called the **sequential representation**, as contrasted with the linked representation presented earlier, because it allows a tree to be implemented in a contiguous block of memory (an array) rather than via pointers connecting widely separated nodes.

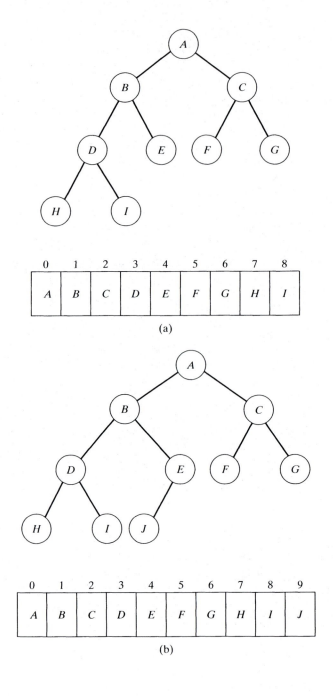

FIGURE 5.2.1

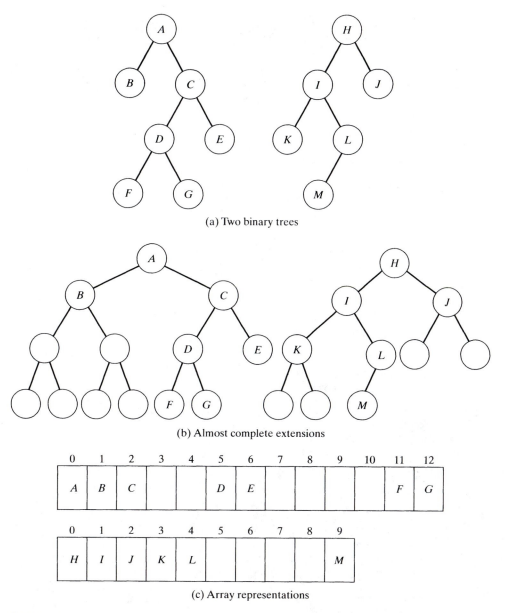

(a) Two binary trees

(b) Almost complete extensions

(c) Array representations

FIGURE 5.2.2

Under the sequential representation, an array element is allocated whether or not it serves to contain a node of a tree. We must, therefore, flag unused array elements as nonexistent, or ***null***, tree nodes. This may be accomplished by one of two methods. One method is to set *info*[*p*] to a special value if node *p* is null. This special value should be invalid as the information content of a legitimate tree node. For example, in a tree containing positive numbers, a null node may be indicated by a negative *info* value. Alternatively, we may add a logical flag field, *used*, to each node. Each node then contains two fields: *info* and *used*. The entire structure is contained in an array *node*. *used*(*p*), implemented as *node*[*p*].*used*, is ***true*** if node *p* is not a null node and ***false*** if it is a null node. *info*(*p*) is implemented by *node*[*p*].*info*. We use this latter method in implementing the sequential representation.

We now present an implementation of the sequential representation of binary trees. The class *ImplicitArrayNode* represents a node of the tree, and the class *ImplicitArrayTree* represents the entire tree.

```
public class ImplicitArrayNode {
  private Object info;
  private boolean used;

  public ImplicitArrayNode() {
        used = false;
  } // end constructor

  public ImplicitArrayNode(Object x) {
        info = x;
        used = true;
  } // end constructor

  public boolean getUsed() {
        return used;
  }

  public void setUsed() {
        used = true;
  }

  public setUnused() {
        used = false;
  }

  public void setInfo(Object x) {
        info = x;
  }

  public Object getInfo() {
        return info;
  }
}  // end ImplicitArrayNode class

public class ImplicitArrayTree {
  public static int NUMNODES = 2500;
  public final int NULL = -1;
  private ImplicitArrayNode[] implicitTree;     // the tree is
                                                // contained in the
                                                // array implicitTree

  public ImplicitArrayTree() {
        // creates an empty tree
        implicitTree = new ImplicitArrayNode[NUMNODES];
  } // end constructor
```

```
public void ImplicitArrayTree (Object x) {
    // creates a tree with a single node
    implicitTree = new ImplicitArrayNode[NUMNODES];
    implicitTree[0] = new ImplicitArrayNode(x);
} // end makeTree

public int getLeftPlace(int p) {
    // gets the position of the left son
    int i = p * 2 + 1;

    if (isUsed(i))
        return i;
    else
        return NULL;
} // end getLeftPlace

public int getRightPlace(int p) {

    // left to the reader

public Object getInfo(int p) {
    return implicitTree[p].getInfo();
} // end getInfo

public boolean isUsed(int p) {
        if ( p >= NUMNODES || implicitTree[p] == null)
            return false;
        return implicitTree[p].getUsed();
} // end isUsed

public void setLeft(int p, Object x) {
        int i = 2 * p + 1;

        if (i >= NUMNODES)
            System.out.println("array overflow");
        else if (isUsed(i))
            System.out.println("invalid insertion");
        else
            implicitTree[i] = new ImplicitArrayNode(x);
} // end setLeft

public void setRight(int p, Object x) {

    // left to reader

} // end ImplicitArrayTree class
```

The methods *getLeftPlace* and *getRightPlace* return the index of a node's left and right son, respectively. *setLeft*(*int p*, *Object x*) and *setRight*(*int p*, *Object x*) insert a node containing an info field of *x* as the left or right son of *p*, respectively. We leave the methods *getRightPlace* and *setRight* to the reader.

Note that under this implementation, the constructor *ImplicitArrayTree*, which implements the *makeTree* operation, initializes the fields *info* and *used* to represent a tree with a single node. It is no longer necessary for *makeTree* to return a value, since under this representation, the single binary tree represented by the *info* and *used* fields is always rooted at node 0. That is why *p* is initialized to 0 in the main method below before we move down the tree. Note also that under this representation it is always required to check that the range (*NUMNODES*) has not been exceeded whenever we move down the tree.

Using the sequential representation of a binary tree presented above, we now present an application to find duplicate positive numbers in an input list.

```java
import java.io.*;

public class ImplicitArrayMain {
  public static final int MAXCOLS = 80;
  public static final int NULL = -1;

  public static void main(String args[]) throws IOException {
        int p, q;
        int number = readInt();
        ImplicitArrayTree t = new ImplicitArrayTree
                                        (new Integer(number));
        while ((number = readInt()) >= 0) {
            p = q = 0;              // start at the root of the tree
            while(q != NULL  &&
                number != (((Integer) t.getInfo(p)).intValue())) {
                p = q;
                if (number <
                        (((Integer) t.getInfo(p)).intValue()))
                    q = t.getLeftPlace(p);
                else
                    q = t.getRightPlace(p);
            }

            if (number == (((Integer) t.getInfo(p)).intValue()))
                System.out.println(number + " is a duplicate\n");
            else if (number < (((Integer) t.getInfo(p)).intValue()))
                t.setLeft(p, new Integer(number));
            else
                t.setRight(p, new Integer(number));
        } // end while
  } // end main

  public static int readInt() throws IOException {

    ...

  } // end readInt

} // end ImplicitArrayMain class
```

Note that since the duplicate finding program does not involve the deletion of nodes, the ***while*** loop does not have to test a node to determine whether or not it is used.

Choosing a Binary Tree Representation

Which representation of binary trees is preferable? There is no general answer to this question. The sequential representation is somewhat simpler, although it is necessary to ensure that all the pointers are within the array bounds. The sequential representation clearly saves storage space for trees known to be almost complete, since it eliminates the need for the fields *left*, *right*, and *father*, and does not even require a *used* field. It is also space-efficient for trees that are only a few nodes short of being almost complete, or when nodes are successively eliminated from a tree that originates as almost complete, although a *used* field might then be required. However, the sequential representation can only be used in a context in which only a single tree is required, or where the number of trees needed and the maximum size of each are fixed in advance.

By contrast, the linked representation requires *left*, *right*, and *father* fields (although we have seen that one or two of these may be eliminated in specific situations) but allows much more flexible use of the collection of nodes. In the linked representation, a particular node may be placed at any location in any tree, whereas in the sequential representation a node can be utilized only if it is needed at a specific location in a specific tree. In addition, under the dynamic node representation, the total number of trees and nodes is limited only by the amount of available memory. Thus, the linked representation is preferable in the general, dynamic situation of many trees of unpredictable shape.

The duplicate-finding application is a good illustration of the tradeoffs involved. The first application presented utilizes the linked representation of binary trees. It requires *left* and *right* fields in addition to *info*. (The *father* field was not necessary in that program.) The second duplicate-finding program, which utilizes the sequential representation, requires only an additional field *used* (and this too can be eliminated if only positive numbers are allowed in the input so that a *null* tree node can be represented by a specific negative *info* value.) The sequential representation can be used for this example because only a single tree is required.

However, the second program might not work for as many input cases as the first. For example, suppose the input is in ascending order. Then the tree formed by either program has all *null* left subtrees (you are invited to verify that this is the case by simulating the programs for such input). In that case, the only elements of *info* that are occupied under the sequential representation are 0, 2, 6, 14, etc. (each position is two more than twice the previous one). If the value of *NUMNODES* is kept at 500, a maximum of only sixteen distinct ascending numbers can be accommodated (the last one will be at position 254). This can be contrasted with the program using the linked representation, in which up to five hundred distinct numbers in ascending order can be accommodated before it runs out of space. In the remainder of the text, except as noted otherwise, we assume the linked representation of a binary tree.

Binary Tree Traversals in Java

We may implement the traversal of binary trees in Java by recursive methods that mirror the traversal definitions. The three Java methods *preTrav*, *inTrav*, and *postTrav* print the contents of a binary tree in preorder, inorder, and postorder, respectively.

Each public method, when applied to a tree, invokes the tree's private method with a parameter representing a "pointer" to the root node of the binary tree. Assuming a binary tree declared by:

```
Tree t = new Tree( );
```

the *preTrav* traversal method may be invoked by specifying:

```
t.preTrav();
```

We use the dynamic node representation of a binary tree:

```java
public void preTrav() {
  preTrav(root);
}

private void preTrav(TreeNode tree) {
  if (tree != null) {
     System.out.println(tree.info);   // visit the root
     preTrav(tree.left);              // traverse the left subtree
     preTrav(tree.right);             // traverse the right subtree
  }
} // end preTrav

public void inTrav() {
  inTrav(root);
}

private void inTrav(TreeNode tree) {
  if (tree != null) {
     inTrav(tree.left);               // traverse the left subtree
     System.out.println(tree.info);   // visit the root
     inTrav(tree.right);              // traverse the right subtree
  }
} // end inTrav

public void postTrav() {
  postTrav(root);
}

private void postTrav(TreeNode tree) {
  if (tree != null) {
     postTrav(tree.left);             // traverse the left subtree
     postTrav(tree.right);            // traverse the right subtree
     System.out.println(tree.info);   // visit the root
  }
} // end postTrav
```

The reader is invited to simulate the actions of these routines on the trees in Figures 5.1.7 and 5.1.8.

Of course, the methods could be written nonrecursively to perform the necessary stacking and unstacking explicitly. For example, the following is a nonrecursive routine to traverse a binary tree in inorder:

```
public void inTrav2() {
    inTrav2(root);
}

private void inTrav2(TreeNode tree) {
    Stack s = new Stack();
    TreeNode p;

    p = tree;
    do {
        // travel down left branches as far as possible
        // saving pointers to nodes passed
        while (p != null) {
            s.push(p);
            p = p.left;
        }
        // check if finished
        if (!s.empty()) {
            // at this point the left subtree is empty
            p = (TreeNode) s.pop();
            System.out.println(p.info);     // visit the root
            p = p.right;                     // traverse right subtree
        }
    } while (!s.empty() || p != null);
} // end inTrav2
```

Nonrecursive routines to traverse a binary tree in postorder and preorder as well as nonrecursive traversals of binary trees using the sequential representation are left as exercises for the reader.

inTrav and *inTrav2* represent an excellent contrast between a recursive method and its nonrecursive counterpart. If both methods are executed, the recursive *inTrav* generally executes much more quickly than the nonrecursive *inTrav2*. This goes against the accepted "folk wisdom" that recursion is slower than iteration. The inefficiency of *inTrav2* as written is primarily caused by the calls to *push*, *pop*, and *empty*. Even when the code for these methods is inserted in-line into *inTrav2*, *inTrav2* is still slower than *inTrav* because of the often superfluous tests for overflow and underflow included in that code.

Nonetheless, even when the underflow/overflow tests are removed, *inTrav* is faster than *inTrav2* under a compiler that implements recursion efficiently! The efficiency of the recursive process in this case is due to a number of factors:

1. There is no "extra" recursion, as there is in computing the Fibonacci numbers, where $f(n - 2)$ and $f(n - 1)$ are both recomputed separately even though the value of $f(n - 2)$ is used in computing $f(n - 1)$.

2. The recursion stack cannot be entirely eliminated, as it can be in computing the factorial method. Thus the automatic stacking and unstacking of built-in recursion is more efficient than the programmed version. (In many systems, stacking can be accomplished by incrementing the value of a register that points to the stack top and moving all parameters into a new data area in a single block move. Program-controlled stacking, as we have implemented it, requires individual assignments and increments.)

3. There are no extraneous parameters and local variables, as there are, for example, in some versions of binary search. The automatic stacking of recursion does not stack any more variables than are necessary.

In cases of recursion that do not involve this excess baggage, such as inorder traversal, the programmer is well advised to use recursion directly.

The traversal methods that we have presented are derived directly from the definitions of the traversal methods. These definitions are in terms of the left and right sons of a node and do not reference a node's father. For this reason, the recursive and non-recursive routines do not require a *father* field and do not take advantage of such a field even if it is present. As we shall soon see, the presence of a *father* field allows us to develop nonrecursive traversal algorithms without using a stack. However, we first examine a technique for eliminating the stack in a nonrecursive traversal even if a *father* field is not available.

Threaded Binary Trees

Traversing a binary tree is a common operation, and it would be helpful to find a more efficient method for implementing the traversal. Let us examine the function *inTrav2* to discover the reason that a stack is needed. The stack is popped when *p* equals **null**. This happens in one of two cases. In one case, the **while** loop is exited after having been executed one or more times. This implies that the program has traveled down left branches until it reached a **null** pointer, stacking a pointer to each node as it was passed. Thus the top element of the stack is the value of *p* before it became **null**. If an auxiliary pointer *q* is kept one step behind *p*, the value of *q* can be used directly and need not be popped.

The other case in which *p* is **null** is when the **while** loop is skipped entirely. This occurs after reaching a node with an empty right subtree, executing the statement *p* = *p.right*, and returning to repeat the body of the **do while** loop. At this point, we would have lost our way were it not for the stack whose top points to the node whose left subtree was just traversed. Suppose, however, that instead of containing a **null** pointer in its *right* field, a node with an empty right subtree contained in its *right* field a pointer to the node that would be on top of the stack at that point in the algorithm (i.e., a pointer to its inorder successor). Then there would no longer be a need for the stack, since the last node visited during a traversal of a left subtree points directly to its inorder successor. Such a pointer is called a *thread* and must be differentiable from a tree pointer that is used to link a node to its left or right subtree.

Figure 5.2.3 shows the binary trees from Figure 5.1.7 with threads replacing **null** pointers in nodes with empty right subtrees. The threads are drawn with dotted lines to differentiate them from tree pointers. Note that the rightmost node in each tree still

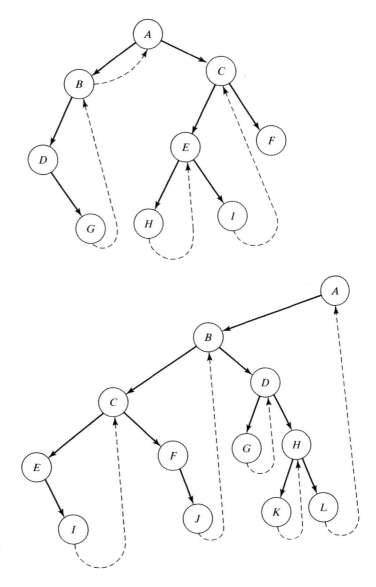

FIGURE 5.2.3   Right in-threaded
binary trees.

has a **null** right pointer because it has no inorder successor. Such trees are called **right
in-threaded** binary trees.

   To implement a right in-threaded binary tree under the dynamic node implementation of a binary tree, an extra logical field, *rthread*, is included within each node
to indicate whether or not its right pointer is a thread. For consistency, the *rthread*
field of the rightmost node of a tree (i.e., the last node in the tree's inorder traversal)
is also set to **true**, although its *right* field remains **null**. Thus a *ThreadedTreeNode* class
and its constructors are defined as follows (recall that we are assuming that no *father*
field exists):

```
public class ThreadedTreeNode {
  public Object info;
  public ThreadedTreeNode left, right;
  public boolean rthread;

public ThreadedTreeNode(Object x) {
    info = x;
    rthread = true;
    left = null;
    right = null;
}

    ...
```

In a right in-threaded binary tree, the inorder successor of any node can be found efficiently. Such a tree can also be constructed in a straightforward manner. The methods *setLeft* and *setRight* of the *ThreadedTreeNode* class are shown below. We assume *info*, *left*, *right*, and *rthread* instance variables in each node.

```
public void setLeft(Object x) {
  ThreadedTreeNode q;

  if (this == null)
        throw new NullPointerException();
  else if (left != null)
        System.out.println("invalid insertion left");
  else {
        q = new ThreadedTreeNode(x);
        left = q;
        q.left = null;
        q.right = this;
        q.rthread = true;
  }
} // end setLeft

public void setRight(Object x) {
  ThreadedTreeNode q, r;

  if (this == null)
        throw new NullPointerException();
  else if (!rthread)
        System.out.println("invalid insertion right");
  else {
        q = new ThreadedTreeNode(x);
        r = right;
        q.right = r;
        right = q;
        rthread = false;
        q.rthread = true;
  }
} // end setRight
```

The class *ThreadedTree* and its constructors may then be defined as:

```
public class ThreadedTree {
  ThreadedTreeNode root;

  public ThreadedTree() {
      root = null;
  } // end constructor

  public ThreadedTree(Object x) {
      root = new ThreadedTreeNode(x);
  } // end construcot

  ...
```

We present a method of the class *ThreadedTree* to implement inorder traversal of a right-inthreaded binary tree.

```
public void inTrav3() {
  ThreadedTreeNode p, q;

  p = root;
  do {
      q = null;
      while (p != null) {
          q = p;
          p = p.getLeft();
      }
      if (q != null) {
          System.out.println(q.getInfo());
          p = q.right;
          while (q.getRthread() && p != null) {
              System.out.println(p.getInfo());
              q = p;
              p = p.getRight();
          }
      }
  } while (q != null);
} // end inTrav3
```

In the linked array implementation, a thread can be represented by a negative value of *nodeArray[p].right*. The absolute value of *nodeArray[p].right* is the index in the array node of the inorder successor of *nodeArray[p]*. The sign of *nodeArray[p].right* indicates whether its absolute value represents a thread (minus) or a pointer to a nonempty subtree (plus). Under this implementation, the following routine traverses a right in-threaded binary tree in inorder. We leave *setLeft* and *setRight* for the linked array representation as exercises for the reader.

```
public void inTrav4() {
  int p, q;

  p = 0;
  do {
      // travel down left links keeping q behind p
      q = 0;
```

```
        while (nodeArray[p] != null) {
            q = p;
            p = nodeArray[p].getLeft();
        }
        if (nodeArray[q] != null) {
            System.out.println(nodeArray[q].getInfo());
            p = nodeArray[q].getRight();
            while (p >= 0 || p < 0) {
                if (p<0)
                        q = -p;
                else
                        q = p;
                if (nodeArray[q] != null) {
                        System.out.println(nodeArray[q].getInfo());
                        p = nodeArray[q].getRight();
                }
                else
                        return;
            } // end while
        } // end if
    } while (q != 0);
} // end inTrav4
```

Un der the sequential representation of binary trees, the *used* field indicates threads by means of negative or positive values. If i represents a node with a right son, $node[i].used$ equals 1 and its right son is at $2 * i + 2$. However, if i represents a node with no right son, $node[i].used$ contains the negative of the index of its inorder successor. (Note that use of negative numbers allows us to distinguish a node with a right son from a node whose inorder successor is the root of the tree.) If i is the rightmost node of the tree, so that it has no inorder successor, $node[i].used$ can contain the special value $+2$. If i does not represent a node, then $node[i].used$ is 0. We leave the implementation of traversal algorithms for this representation as an exercise for the reader.

A *left in-threaded* binary tree may be defined similarly as one in which each *null* left pointer is altered to contain a thread to that node's inorder predecessor. An *in-threaded* binary tree may then be defined as a binary tree that is both left in-threaded and right in-threaded. However, left in-threading does not yield the advantages of right in-threading.

We may also define right and left *pre-threaded* binary trees in which *null* right and left pointers of nodes are replaced, respectively, by their preorder successors and predecessors. A right prethreaded binary tree may be traversed efficiently in preorder without the use of a stack. A right in-threaded binary tree may also be traversed in preorder without the use of a stack. The traversal algorithms are left as exercises for the reader.

Traversal Using a *father* Field

If each tree node contains a *father* field, neither a stack nor threads are necessary for nonrecursive traversal. Instead, when the traversal process reaches a leaf node, the *father* field can be used to climb back up the tree. When $node(p)$ is reached from a left son, its right subtree must still be traversed, so the algorithm proceeds to *right*(*p*). When *node*(*p*) is reached from its right son, then both its subtrees have been traversed and the algorithm backs up further to *father*(*p*). The following method implements this process for inorder traversal.

```
public void inTrav5() {
   inTrav5(root);
}
private void inTrav5(TreeNode tree) {
   TreeNode p, q;
   q = null;
   p = tree;
   do {
        while (p != null) {
               q = p;
               p = p.getLeft();
        }
        if (q != null) {
               System.out.println(q.getInfo());
               p = q.getRight();
        }
        while (q != null && p == null) {
               do {
                      // node(q) has no right son. Back up until a
                      // left son or the tree root is encountered
                      p = q;
                      q = p.getFather();
               } while (!p.isLeft() && q != null);
               if (q != null) {
                      System.out.println(q.getInfo());
                      p = q.getRight();
               }
        }
   } while (q != null);
} // end inTrav5
```

Note that the *isLeft*() method does not require an *isLeft* field to determine whether *node*(*p*) is a left or a right son; we can simply check whether the node is its father's left son.

In this inorder traversal, a node is visited [*System.out.println(q.info());*] when its left son is recognized as **null** or when it is reached after backing up from its left son. Preorder and postorder traversal are similar except that, in preorder, a node is visited only when it is reached on the way down the tree, and in postorder, a node is visited only when its right son is recognized as **null** or when it is reached after backing up from its right son. We leave the details as an exercise for the reader.

Traversal using *father* pointers for backing up is less time-efficient than traversal of a threaded tree. A thread points directly to a node's successor, but a whole series of *father* pointers may have to be followed to reach the successor in an unthreaded tree. It is difficult to compare the time-efficiencies of stack-based traversal and father-based traversal because the former includes the overhead of stacking and unstacking.

This backup traversal algorithm also suggests a stackless nonrecursive traversal technique for unthreaded trees even if no *father* field exists. The technique is simple: simply reverse the *son* pointer on the way down the tree so that it can be used to find a way back up. On the way back up, the pointer is restored to its original value.

For example, in *inTrav5* above, a variable *f* can be introduced to hold a pointer to the father of *node(q)*. The statements

```
q = p;
p = p.getLeft();
```

in the first ***while*** loop can be replaced by

```
f = q;
q = p;
p = p.getLeft();
if (p != null)
    q.getLeft() = f;
```

This modifies the left pointer of *node(q)* to point to the father of *node(q)* when going left on the way down [note that *p* points to the left son of *node(q)* so that we have not lost our way]. The statement

```
p = q.getRight();
```

in both of its occurrences can be replaced by

```
p = q.getRight();
if (p != null)
    q.getRight() = f;
```

to similarly modify the right pointer of *node(q)* to point to its father when going right on the way down. Finally, the statements

```
p = q;
q = p.getFather();
```

in the inner ***do-while*** loop can be replaced by

```
p = q;
q = f;
if (q != null && p.isleft()) {
    f = left(q);
    left(q) = p;
}
else {
    f = right(q);
    right(q) = p;
}
```

to follow a modified pointer back up the tree and restore the pointer's value to point to its left or right son as appropriate.

However, now an *isleft* field is required, since the *isLeft* method cannot be implemented using a nonexistent *father* field. Also, this algorithm cannot be used in a multiuser environment if several users require access to the tree simultaneously. If one user is traversing the tree and temporarily modifying pointers, another user will be unable to use the tree as a coherent structure. Some sort of lockout mechanism is required to ensure that no one else uses the tree while pointers are reversed.

Heterogeneous Binary Trees

Different nodes of a binary tree often do not contain information of the same type. For example, in representing a binary expression with constant numerical operands, we may wish to use a binary tree whose leafs contain numbers but whose nonleaf nodes contain characters representing operators. Figure 5.2.4 illustrates such a binary tree.

To represent such a tree in Java, we may add a member *uType* to the tree node to indicate the type of object that its *info* field contains.

```java
public class ExpressionTreeNode {
   final static int OPERATOR = 0;
   final static int OPERAND = 1;
   public int uType;
   public Object info;
   public ExpressionTreeNode left, right, father;
   boolean isleft;

   ...
```

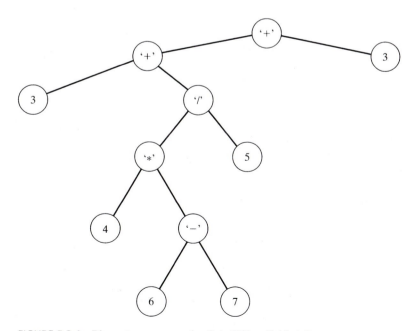

FIGURE 5.2.4   Binary tree representing $3 + 4*(6 - 7)/5 + 3$.

Let us also assume a class *ExpressionTree* defined by

```
public class ExpressionTree {
   ExpressionTreeNode tree;

            ...
```

and this class represents an expression tree.

Let us write a Java method *evalBinTree* of the class *ExpressionTree* that accepts a reference to such a tree node and returns the value of the expression represented by the tree rooted at that node. The method recursively evaluates the left and right subtrees and then applies the operator of the root to the two results. We use the auxiliary method *oper(symb,opnd1,opnd2)* of the class *ExpressionTree* introduced in Section 2.3. The first parameter of *oper* is a character representing an operator, and the last two parameters are real numbers that are the two operands. The method *oper* returns the result of applying the operator to the two operands.

```
public float evalBinTree (ExpressionTreeNode tree) {
   float opnd1, opnd2;
   char symb;

   if (tree.uType == OPERAND)
                     // expression is a single operand
       return ((Integer) tree.info()).intValue();
   // tree.utype == OPERATOR
   // evaluate the left subtree
   opnd1 = evalBinTree(tree.getLeft());
   // evaluate the right subtree
   opnd2 = evalBinTree(tree.getRight());
   symb = ((Character) tree.getInfo()).charValue();    // extract the
                                                        //operator

   // apply the operator and return the result
   return oper(symb, opnd1, opnd2);
} // end evalBinTree
```

Section 9.1 discusses additional methods of implementing linked structures that contain heterogeneous elements. Note also that in this example, all the operand nodes are leafs and all the operator nodes are nonleafs.

Another possibility is to use the reflexive capabilities of Java to determine the subtype of the object, as we did in Section 2.4. We leave this as an exercise for the reader.

EXERCISES

5.2.1 Write a Java method that accepts a reference to a node and returns *true* if the node is the root of a valid binary tree and *false* otherwise.

5.2.2 Write a Java method that accepts a reference to a binary tree and a reference to a node of the tree and returns the level of the node in the tree.

5.2.3   Write a Java method that accepts a reference to a binary tree and returns a reference to a new binary tree that is the mirror image of the first (i.e., all left subtrees are now right subtrees, and vice versa).

5.2.4   Write Java methods that convert a binary tree implemented using the linked array representation with only a *father* field (in which the left son's *father* field contains the negative of the pointer to its father, and the right son's *father* field contains a pointer to its father) to its representation using *left* and *right* fields, and vice versa.

5.2.5   Write a Java application to perform the following experiment: Generate one-hundred random numbers. As each number is generated, insert it into an initially empty binary search tree. When all one-hundred numbers have been inserted, print the levels of the leaf with the largest level and the leaf with the smallest level. Repeat this process fifty times. Print out a table with a count of how many of the fifty runs resulted in a difference between the maximum and minimum leaf levels of 0, 1, 2, 3, and so on.

5.2.6   Write Java methods to traverse a binary tree in preorder and postorder.

5.2.7   Implement inorder traversal, *makeTree*, *setLeft*, and *setRight* for right-inthreaded binary trees under the sequential representation.

5.2.8   Write Java methods to create a binary tree given:

a.   The preorder and inorder traversals of the tree.

b.   The preorder and postorder traversals of the tree.

Each function should accept two character strings as parameters. The tree created should contain a single character in each node.

5.2.9   The solution to the Towers of Hanoi problem for n disks (see Sections 3.3 and 3.4) can be represented by a complete binary tree of level $n - 1$, as follows:

a.   Let the root of the tree represent a move of the top disk on peg *fromPeg* to peg *topeg*. (We ignore the identification of the disks being moved, as there is only a single disk [the top one] that can be moved from any peg to any other peg.) If nd is a leaf node (at a level less than $n - 1$) representing the movement of the top disk from peg x to peg y, let z be the third peg that is neither the source nor the target of node nd. Then *left(nd)* represents a move of the top disk from peg x to peg z, and *right(nd)* represents a move of the top disk from peg z to peg y. Draw sample solution trees as described above for $n = 1, 2, 3, 4$, and show that an inorder traversal of such a tree produces the solution to the Towers of Hanoi problem.

b.   Write a recursive Java method that accepts a value for n and generates and traverses the tree, as discussed above.

c.   Because the tree is complete, it can be stored in an array of size $2^n - 1$. Show that the nodes of the tree can be stored in the array so that a sequential traversal of the array produces the inorder traversal of the tree, as follows: The root of the tree is in position $2^{n-1} - 1$; for any level j, the first node at that level is in position $2^{n-1-j} - 1$, and each successive node at level j is 2^{n-j} elements beyond the previous element at that level.

d.   Write a nonrecursive Java application to create the array as described in part (c) and show that a sequential pass through the array does indeed produce the desired solution.

e. How could the programs above be extended to include within each node the number of the disk being moved?

5.2.10   In Section 4.5, we introduced a method of representing a doubly-linked list with only a single pointer field in each node by maintaining its value as the exclusive *or* of pointers to the node's predecessor and successor. A binary tree can be maintained similarly in the linked array representation by keeping one field in each node set to the exclusive *or* of pointers to the node's *father* and *left* son [call this field *fLeft(p)*] and another field in the node set to the exclusive *or* of pointers to the node's *father* and *right* son [call this field *fRight(p)*].

a. Given *father(p)* and *fLeft(p)*, show how to compute *left(p)*. Given *father(p)* and *fRight(p)*, show how to compute *right(p)*.

b. Given *fLeft(p)* and *left(p)*, show how to compute *father(p)*. Given *fRight(p)* and *right(p)*, show how to compute *father(p)*.

c. Assume that a node contains only *info*, *fLeft*, *fRight*, and *isLeft* fields. Write algorithms for preorder, inorder, and postorder traversal of a binary tree, given an external pointer to the tree root, without using a stack or modifying any fields.

d. Can the *isLeft* field be eliminated?

5.2.11   The index of a textbook consists of major terms ordered alphabetically. Each major term is accompanied by a set of page numbers and a set of subterms. The subterms are printed on successive lines following the major term and are arranged alphabetically within the major term. Each subterm is accompanied by a set of page numbers.

Design a data structure to represent such an index and write a Java application to print an index from the data as follows: Each input line begins with an *m* (major term) or an *s* (subterm). An *m* line contains an *m* followed by a major term followed by an integer *n* (possibly zero) followed by *n* page numbers where the major term appears. An *s* line is similar except that it contains a subterm rather than a major term. The input lines appear in no particular order except that each subterm is considered to be a subterm of the major term which last precedes it. There may be many input lines for a single major term or subterm (all the page numbers appearing on any line for a given term should be printed with that term).

The index should be printed with one term on a line followed by all the pages on which the term appears in ascending order. Major terms should be printed in alphabetical order. Subterms should appear in alphabetical order immediately following their major term. Subterms should be indented five columns from the major terms.

The set of major terms should be organized as a binary tree. Each node in the tree contains (in addition to left and right pointers and the major term itself) pointers to two other binary trees. One of these represents the set of page numbers in which the major term occurs, and the other represents the set of subterms of the major term. Each node on a subterm binary tree contains (in addition to left and right pointers and the subterm itself) a pointer to a binary tree representing the set of page numbers in which the subterm occurs.

5.2.12   Write a Java method to implement the sorting method in Section 5.1 that uses a binary search tree.

5.2.13 a. Implement an ascending priority queue using a binary search tree by writing Java implementations of the algorithms *pqInsert* and *pqMindelete*, as in Exercise 5.1.13. Modify the routines to count the number of tree nodes accessed.

b. Use a random number generator to test the efficiency of the priority queue implementation as follows: First, create a priority queue with hundred elements by inserting hundred random numbers in an initially empty binary search tree. Then call *pqMinDelete* and print the number of tree nodes accessed in finding the minimum element, generate a new random number, and call *pqInsert* to insert the new random number and print the number of tree nodes accessed in the insertion. Note that after calling *pqInsert*, the tree still contains hundred elements. Repeat the delete/print/generate/insert/print process thousand times. Note that the number of nodes accessed in the deletion tends to decrease, while the number of nodes accessed in the insertion tends to increase. Explain this behavior.

5.2.14 Rewrite the method *evalBinTree* at the end of this section assuming that no data member *uType* is present, using different subtypes for operands and operators, and using the reflexive properties of Java classes, as in Section 2.4.

5.3   AN EXAMPLE: THE HUFFMAN ALGORITHM

Suppose we have an alphabet of n symbols and a long message consisting of symbols from this alphabet. We wish to encode the message as a long bit string (a bit is either 0 or 1) by assigning a bit string code to each symbol of the alphabet and concatenating the individual codes of the symbols making up the message to produce an encoding for the message. For example, suppose the alphabet consists of the four symbols $A, B, C,$ and D, and that codes are assigned to these symbols as follows:

Symbol	Code
A	010
B	100
C	000
D	111

The message *ABACCDA* would then be encoded as 010100010000000111010. Such an encoding is inefficient, since three bits are used for each symbol, so that twentyone bits are needed to encode the entire message. Suppose a two-bit code is assigned to each symbol, as follows:

Symbol	Code
A	00
B	01
C	10
D	11

Then the code for the message would be 00010010101100, which requires only fourteen bits. We wish to find a code that minimizes the length of the encoded message.

Let us reexamine the example. The letters B and D each appear only once in the message, while the letter A appears three times. If a code is chosen that assigns the letter A a shorter bit string than the letters B and D, then the length of the encoded message would be small. This is because the short code (representing the letter A) would appear more frequently than the long code. Indeed, codes can be assigned as follows:

Symbol	Code
A	0
B	110
C	10
D	111

Using this code, the message $ABACCDA$ is encoded as 0110010101110, which requires only thirteen bits. In very long messages containing symbols that appear very infrequently, the savings are substantial. Ordinarily, codes are not constructed on the basis of the frequency of characters in only a single message, but on the basis of their frequency in a whole set of messages. The same code set is then used for each message. For example, if messages consist of English words, the known relative frequency of occurrence of the letters of the alphabet in the English language might be used, although the relative frequency of the letters in any single message is not necessarily the same.

If variable-length codes are used, the code for one symbol may not be a prefix of the code for another. To see why, assume that the code for a symbol x, $c(x)$, is a prefix of the code of another symbol y, $c(y)$. Then, when $c(x)$ is encountered in a left-to-right scan, it is unclear whether $c(x)$ represents the symbol x or is the first part of $c(y)$.

In our example, decoding proceeds by scanning a bit string from left to right. If a 0 is encountered as the first bit, the symbol is an A; otherwise it is a B, C, or D, and the next bit is examined. If the second bit is a 0, then the symbol is a C; otherwise it must be a B or a D, and the third bit must be examined. If the third bit is a 0, the symbol is a B; if it is a 1, the symbol is a D. As soon as the first symbol has been identified, the process is repeated, starting at the next bit, to find the second symbol.

This suggests a method for developing an optimal encoding scheme, given the frequency of occurrence of each symbol in a message. Find the two symbols that appear least frequently. In our example, these are B and D. The last bits of their codes differentiate them: 0 for B, and 1 for D. Combine these two symbols into the single symbol BD, whose code represents the knowledge that a symbol is either a B or a D. The frequency of occurrence of this new symbol is the sum of the frequencies of its two constituent symbols. Thus the frequency of BD is 2. There are now three symbols: A (frequency 3), C (frequency 2), and BD (frequency 2). Again choose the two symbols with the smallest frequency: C and BD. The last bits of their codes differentiate them: 0 for C, and 1 for BD. The two symbols are then combined into the single symbol CBD, with frequency 4. There are now only two symbols remaining: A and CBD. These are combined into the single symbol $ACBD$. The last bits of the codes for A and CBD differentiate them: 0 for A, and 1 for CBD.

The symbol $ACBD$ contains the entire alphabet; it is assigned the *null* bit string of length 0 as its code. At the start of the decoding, before any bits have been examined, it is certain that any symbol is contained in $ACBD$. The two symbols that comprise $ACBD$ (A and CBD) are assigned the codes 0 and 1 respectively. If a 0 is encountered, the encoded symbol is an A; if a 1 is encountered, it is a C, B, or D. Similarly, the two symbols that constitute CBD (C and BD) are assigned the codes 10 and 11 respectively.

The first bit indicates that the symbol is one of the constituents of CBD, and the second bit indicates whether it is a C or a BD. The symbols that comprise BD (B and D) are then assigned the codes 110 and 111. By this process, symbols that appear frequently in the message are assigned shorter codes than symbols that appear infrequently.

The action of combining two symbols into one suggests the use of a binary tree. Each node of the tree represents a symbol, and each leaf represents a symbol of the original alphabet. Figure 5.3.1a shows the binary tree constructed using the previous example.

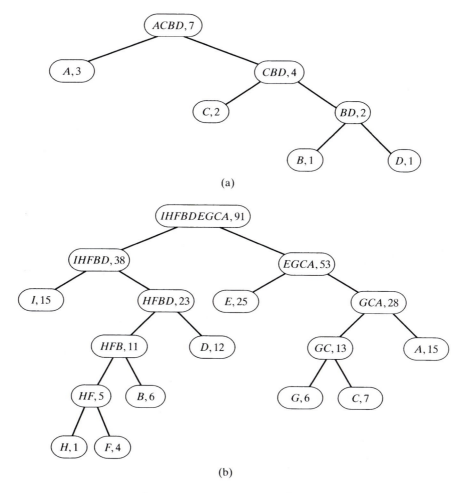

(a)

(b)

Symbol	Frequency	Code	Symbol	Frequency	Code	Symbol	Frequency	Code
A	15	111	D	12	011	G	6	1100
B	6	0101	E	25	10	H	1	01000
C	7	1101	F	4	01001	I	15	00

(c)

FIGURE 5.3.1   Huffman trees.

Each node in the illustration contains a symbol and its frequency. Figure 5.3.1b shows the binary tree constructed by this method for the alphabet and frequency table of Figure 5.3.1c. Such trees are called ***Huffman trees*** after the discoverer of this encoding method.

Once a Huffman tree is constructed, the code of any symbol in the alphabet can be constructed by starting at the leaf representing the symbol and climbing up to the root. The code is initialized to *null*. Each time that a left branch is climbed, 0 is appended to the beginning of the code; each time that a right branch is climbed, 1 is appended to the beginning of the code.

The Huffman Algorithm

The inputs to the Huffman algorithm are n, the number of symbols in the original alphabet, and *frequency*, an array of size at least n such that *frequency*[i] is the relative frequency of the ith symbol. The algorithm assigns values to an array *code* of size at least n so that *code*[i] contains the code assigned to the ith symbol. The algorithm also constructs an array *position* of size at least n such that *position*[i] points to the node representing the ith symbol. This array is necessary to identify the point in the tree from which to start in constructing the code for a particular symbol in the alphabet. Once the tree has been constructed, the *isLeft* operation introduced earlier can be used to determine whether 0 or 1 should be placed at the front of the code as we climb the tree. The *info* portion of a tree node contains the frequency of occurrence of the symbol represented by the node.

A set *rootNodes* is used to keep pointers to the roots of partial binary trees that are not yet left or right subtrees. Since this set is modified by removing elements with minimum frequency, combining them and then reinserting the combined element into the set, it is implemented as an ascending priority queue of pointers, ordered by the value of the *info* field of the pointers' target nodes. We use the operations *pqInsert* to insert a pointer to a node into the priority queue, and *pqMinDelete* to remove the pointer to the node with the smallest *info* value from the priority queue.

We may outline Huffman's algorithm as follows:

```
// initialize the set of root nodes
rootNodes = the empty ascending priority queue;

// construct a node for each symbol
for (i = 0; i < n; i++) {
    p = makeTree(frequency[i]);
    position[i] = p;            // a pointer to the leaf containing the
                                // ith symbol
    rootNodes.pqInsert(p);
} //* end for
while (rootNodes contains more than one item) {
    p1 = rootNodes.pqMinDelete();
    p2 = rootNodes.pqMinDelete();
    // combine p1 and p2 as branches of a single tree
    p = makeTree(p1.getInfo() + p2.getInfo());
    p.setLeft(p1);
```

```
        p.setRight(p2);
        rootNodes.pqInsert(p);
} // end while

// the tree is now constructed; use it to find codes
root = rootNodes.pqMinDelete();
for (i = 0; i < n; i++) {
    p = position[i];
    code[i] = the null bit string;
    while (p != root) {
            // travel up the tree
            if (isLeft(p))
                    code[i] = 0 followed by code[i];
            else
                    code[i] = 1 followed by code[i];
            p = father(p);
    } // end while
} // end for
```

Java Application

Note that the Huffman tree is strictly binary. Thus if there are n symbols in the alphabet, the Huffman tree (which has n leafs) can be represented by an array of nodes of size $2n - 1$. Since the amount of storage needed for the tree is known, it may be allocated in advance in an array *node*.

In constructing the tree and obtaining the codes, it is only necessary to keep a link from each node to its father and an indication of whether each node is a left or right son; left and right fields are unnecessary. Thus each node contains three fields: *father*, *isleft*, and *freq*. *father* is a pointer to the node's father. If the node is the root, then its *father* field is **null**. The value of *isleft* is **true** if the node is a left son and **false** otherwise. *freq* (which corresponds to the *info* field of the algorithm) is the frequency of occurrence of the symbol represented by that node. The class which implements these nodes is called *NodeType* and is implemented as follows:

```
package types;

public class NodeType {
  private int freq;
  private int father;          // if node[p] is not a root node, father
                               // points to the node's father; if it is,
                               // father points to the next root node
                               // in the priority queue
  private boolean isleft;

  public NodeType() {
  }

  public void isLeft(boolean b) {
        isleft = b;
  }
```

```
        public boolean isLeft() {
               return isleft;
        }

        public void setFreq(int fr) {
               freq = fr;
        }

        public int getFreq() {
               return freq;
        }

        public void setFather(int fa) {
               father = fa;
        }

        public int getFather() {
               return father;
        }
}     // end NodeType class
```

We allocate the array *node*, of *NodeType* objects, based on the maximum number of possible symbols (a constant *MAXSYMBS*) rather than on the actual number of symbols, n. Thus the array *node*, which should be of size $2n - 1$, must be declared as being of size $2 * MAXSYMBS - 1$. This means that some space is wasted. Of course, n itself could be made a constant rather than a variable, but then the application must be modified every time the number of symbols differs. The nodes can also be represented by dynamic variables without wasting space. However, we present a linked array implementation. (We could also input the value of n and allocate arrays of the proper size during execution. Then, no space would be wasted using the array implementation.)

In using the linked array implementation, *node*[0] through *node*[$n - 1$] can be reserved for the leafs representing the original n symbols of the alphabet, and *node*[n] through *node*[$2 * n - 2$] for the $n - 1$ nonleaf nodes required by the strictly binary tree. This means that the array *position* is not required as a guide to the leaf nodes representing the n symbols, since the node containing the ith input symbol (where i goes from 0 to $n - 1$) is known to be *node*[i]. If the dynamic node representation were used, the array *position* would be required.

The following application encodes a message using Huffman's algorithm. The input consists of a number n, which is the number of symbols in the alphabet, followed by a set of n pairs, each of which consists of a symbol and its relative frequency. The program first constructs a string *alph* consisting of all the symbols in the alphabet and an array code such that *code*[i] is the code assigned to the ith symbol in *alph*. The application then prints each character, its relative frequency, and its code.

Since the code is constructed from right to left, we define an object *CodeType* (in addition to the usual *NodeType*) as follows:

```
package types;

public class CodeType {
     final static int MAXBITS=50;
     final static int MAXSYMBS=50;
```

```
final static int MAXNODES=99;        // MAXNODES equals 2*MAXSYMBS-1

public int bits[] = new int[MAXBITS];
private int startPos;

public CodeType() { }

public void setStart(int s) {
   startPos = s;
}

public int getStart() {
   return startPos;
}

public String toString() {
   String s = "";
   for (int i = 0; i < MAXBITS; i++)
       s = s + bits[i];
   return s;
}
} // end CodeType class
```

MAXBITS is the maximum number of bits allowed in a code. If a code *cd* is **null**, then *startPos* is one more than *MAXBITS*. When a bit *b* is added to *cd* at the left, *startPos* is decremented by 1, and *cd.bits*[*cd.getStart*()] is set to *b*. When the code *cd* is completed, the bits of the code are in positions *cd.startPos* through $cd.bits[MAXBITS - 1]$ inclusive.

How to organize the priority queue of root nodes is an important issue. In the algorithm, this data structure was represented as a priority queue of node pointers. Implementing the priority queue by a linked list, as in Section 4.2, would require a new set of nodes, each holding a pointer to a root node and a *next* field. Fortunately, the *father* field of a root node is unused, so that it can be used to link all the root nodes into a list. The pointer *rootNodes* could point to the first root node on the list. The list itself can be ordered or unordered, depending on the implementation of *pqInsert* and *pqMinDelete*.

Each node on the priority queue contains the index to the array *node* and the frequency of the symbol represented by that node of the tree. Since the elements in a priority queue are ordered by their frequency, it is necessary to implement the *Sortable* class. The *Sortable* class may then be implemented as follows:

```
package list;
public class SmallNode implements Sortable {
    private int frequency;
    private int index;

    public SmallNode(int i, int f) {
        index = i;
        frequency = f;
    }

    public int compareTo(Object o) {
        SmallNode temp=(SmallNode) o;
        return (frequency - temp.freq());
    }
}
```

```
        public int freq() {
            return frequency;
        }

        public int ind() {
            return index;
        }

} // end SmallNode class
package list;

public interface Sortable {
    public int compareTo(Object b);

} // end Sortable interface
```

We make use of this technique in the following application, which implements the algorithm just presented.

```
import java.io.*;
import types.*;
import list.*;

public class Huffman {
    final static int MAXBITS=50;
    final static int MAXSYMBS=50;
    final static int MAXNODES=99;        // MAXNODES equals 2*MAXSYMBS-1

    public static void main (String[] args) {
        CodeType cd = new CodeType(), code[] = new CodeType[MAXSYMBS];
        NodeType node[] = new NodeType[MAXNODES];
        int i, k, n, p, p1, p2, root, freq;
        DynamicList rootNodes = new DynamicList();
        char symb, alph[] = new char[MAXSYMBS];

        for (i = 0; i < MAXSYMBS; i++)
            alph[i]=' ';
        // input the alphabet and frequencies
        System.out.print("Enter number of symbols> ");
        n = readInt();
        for (i = 0;  i < n; i++) {
            System.out.print("Symbol> ");
            symb = readString().charAt(0);
            System.out.print("Frequency> ");
            node[i] = new NodeType();
            freq = readInt();
            node[i].setFreq(freq);
            rootNodes.pqInsert(new SmallNode(i, freq));
            alph[i] = symb;
        }

        // we now build the trees
        for (p = n; p < 2*n-1; p++){
            // p points to the next available node.  Obtain the
```

```
            // root nodes p1 and p2 with smallest frequencies
            p1 = ((SmallNode)rootNodes.pqMinDelete()).ind();
            p2 = ((SmallNode)rootNodes.pqMinDelete()).ind();

            node[p1].setFather(p);
            node[p1].isLeft(true);
            node[p2].setFather(p);
            node[p2].isLeft(false);

            node[p]=new NodeType();
            freq = node[p1].getFreq() + node[p2].getFreq();
            node[p].setFreq(freq);
            rootNodes.pqInsert(new SmallNode(p, freq));
        }
        // there is now only one node left with a null father field
        root = ((SmallNode)rootNodes.pqMinDelete()).ind();

        // extract the codes from the tree
        for (i = 0; i< n; i++) {
            cd.setStart(MAXBITS);              // initialize code[i]
            p = i;                             // travel up the tree
            while (p != root){
                cd.setStart(cd.getStart()-1);
                if (node[p].isLeft())
                    cd.bits[cd.getStart()] = 0;
                else
                    cd.bits[cd.getStart()] = 1;
                p = node[p].getFather();
            }
            System.out.print(alph[i] + " is ");
            for (k = cd.getStart(); k < MAXBITS; k++) {
                code[i]=new CodeType();
                code[i].bits[k] = cd.bits[k];
                System.out.print(code[i].bits[k]);
            }
            System.out.println();
        }
    } // end main

    public static String readString() {
        int ch;
        String r = "";
        boolean done = false;

        while (!done) {
            try {
                ch = System.in.read();
                if (ch < 0 || (char) ch == '\n')
                    done = true;
                else if ((char) ch != '\r')
                    r = r + (char) ch;
            }
```

```
            catch(IOException e) {
                done = true;
            }
        }
        return r;
    } // end readString

    public static int readInt() {
        while (true) {
            try {
                return Integer.valueOf(readString().trim()).
                intValue();
            }
            catch (NumberFormatException e) {
                System.out.println("Not an integer");
            }
        }
    } // end readInt
} // end Huffman class
```

We leave to the reader the coding of the method *encode(alph, code, msge)*. This method accepts the string *alph*, the array *code* constructed in the above program, and a message *msge*, and returns the bit string encoding of the message.

Given the encoding of a message and the Huffman tree used in constructing the code, the original message can be recovered as follows: Begin at the root of the tree. Each time a 0 is encountered, move down a left branch, and each time a 1 is encountered, move down a right branch. Repeat this process until a leaf is encountered. The next character in the original message is the symbol that corresponds to that leaf. See if you can decode 1110100010111011 using the Huffman tree in Figure 5.3.1b.

To decode, it is necessary to travel from the root of the tree down to its leafs. This means that instead of *father* and *isleft* fields, two fields, *left* and *right*, are needed to hold the left and right sons of a particular node. The fields *left* and *right* can be computed straightforwardly from the fields *father* and *isleft*. Alternatively, the values *left* and *right* can be constructed directly from the frequency information for the symbols of the alphabet, using an approach similar to the one used in assigning the value of *father*. (Of course, if the trees are to be identical, the symbol/frequency pairs must be presented in the same order under both methods.) We leave these algorithms, as well as the decoding algorithm, as exercises for the reader.

EXERCISES

5.3.1 Write a Java method *encode(alph, code, msge)*. The method accepts the string *alph*, the array *code* produced by the application given in the text, and a message *msge*. The method returns the Huffman encoding of the message.

5.3.2 Write a Java method *decode(alph, left, right, bitCode)*, where *alph* is the string produced by the application given in the text, *left* and *right* are arrays used to represent a Huffman tree, and *bitCode* is a bit string. The method returns the Huffman decoding of *bitCode*.

5.3.3   Implement the priority queue *rootNodes* as an ordered list. Write appropriate *pqInsert* and *pqMinDelete* routines.

5.3.4   Is it possible to have two different Huffman trees for a set of symbols with given frequencies? Either give an example where two such trees exist or prove that there is only a single such tree.

5.3.5   Define a **Fibonacci binary tree of order n** as follows: If $n = 0$ or $n = 1$, then the tree consists of a single node. If $n > 1$, then the tree consists of a root, with the Fibonacci tree of order $n - 1$ as the left subtree and the Fibonacci tree of order $n - 2$ as the right subtree.

a.   Write a Java method that returns a pointer to the Fibonacci binary tree of order n.

b.   Is such a tree strictly binary?

c.   What is the number of leaves in the Fibonacci tree of order n?

d.   What is the depth of the Fibonacci tree of order n?

5.3.6   Given a binary tree t, its **extension** is defined as the binary tree $e(t)$ formed from t by adding a new leaf node at each **null** left and right pointer in t. The new leafs are called **external** nodes, and the original nodes (which are now all nonleaves) are called **internal** nodes. $e(t)$ is called an **extended binary tree**.

a.   Prove that an extended binary tree is strictly binary.

b.   If t has n nodes, how many nodes does $e(t)$ have?

c.   Prove that all the leaves in an extended binary tree are newly added nodes.

d.   Write a Java method that extends a binary tree t.

e.   Prove that any strictly binary tree with more than one node is an extension of one and only one binary tree.

f.   Write a Java method that accepts a pointer to a strictly binary tree $t1$ containing more than one node and deletes nodes from $t1$, creating a binary tree $t2$ such that $t1 = e(t2)$.

g.   Show that the complete binary tree of order n is the nth extension of the binary tree consisting of a single node.

5.3.7   Given a strictly binary tree t in which the n leaves are labeled as nodes 1 through n, let *level(i)* be the level of node i, and let *freq(i)* be an integer assigned to node i. Define the **weighted path length** of t as the sum of $freq(i) * level(i)$ over all leafs of t.

a.   Write a Java method to compute the weighted path length given fields *freq* and *father*.

b.   Show that the Huffman tree is a strictly binary tree with minimum weighted path length.

5.4   REPRESENTING LISTS AS BINARY TREES

Several operations can be performed on a list of elements. Among these are adding a new element to the front or rear of the list, deleting the first or last element of the list, retrieving the kth element or the last element of the list, inserting an element following or preceding a given element, deleting a given element, and deleting the predecessor or successor of a given element. Building a list with given elements is an additional operation that is frequently required.

Which of these operations are possible, and with what degree of efficiency, depends on the representation chosen for a list. For example, a list may be represented by successive elements in an array or as nodes in a linked structure. Inserting an element following a given element is relatively efficient in a linked list (involving modifications to a few pointers aside from the actual insertion) but relatively inefficient in an array (involving moving all subsequent elements in the array one position). However, finding the kth element of a list is far more efficient in an array (involving only the computation of an offset) than in a linked structure (which requires passing through the first $k - 1$ elements). Similarly, it is not possible to delete a specific element in a singly-linked linear list given only a pointer to that element, and it is only possible to do so inefficiently in a singly-linked circular list (by traversing the entire list to reach the previous element, and then performing the deletion). The same operation, however, is quite efficient in a doubly-linked (linear or circular) list.

In this section, we introduce a tree representation of a linear list in which the operations of finding the kth element of a list and deleting a specific element are relatively efficient. It is also possible to build a list with given elements using this representation. We also consider briefly the operation of inserting a single new element.

A list may be represented by a binary tree, as illustrated in Figure 5.4.1. Figure 5.4.1a shows a list in the usual linked format, while Figures 5.4.1b and c show two binary tree representations of the list. Elements of the original list are represented by leafs of the tree (shown as squares in the figure), while nonleaf nodes of the tree (shown as circles in the figure) are present as part of the internal tree structure. Associated with each leaf node are the contents of the corresponding list element. Associated with each nonleaf node is a count representing the number of leafs in the node's left subtree. (Although this count can be computed from the tree structure, it is maintained as a data element to avoid recomputing its value each time it is needed.) The elements of the list in their original sequence are assigned to the leafs of the tree in the inorder sequence of the leaves. Note from Figure 5.4.1 that several binary trees can represent the same list.

Finding the kth Element

To justify using so many extra tree nodes to represent a list, we present an algorithm to find the kth element of a list represented by a tree. Let *tree* point to the root of the tree, and let *lCount*(p) represent the count associated with the nonleaf node pointed to by p [*lCount*(p) is the number of leafs in the tree rooted at *node(left(p))*]. The following algorithm sets the variable *find* to point to the leaf containing the kth element of the list.

The algorithm maintains a variable r containing the number of list elements remaining to be counted. At the beginning of the algorithm, r is initialized to k. At each nonleaf *node(p)*, the algorithm determines from the values of r and *lCount*(p) whether the kth element is located in the left or right subtree. The algorithm proceeds directly to the left subtree if that is where the leaf is. It proceeds to the right subtree if that is where the desired leaf is, but first reduces the value of r by the value of *lCount*(p). k is assumed to be less than or equal to the number of elements in the list.

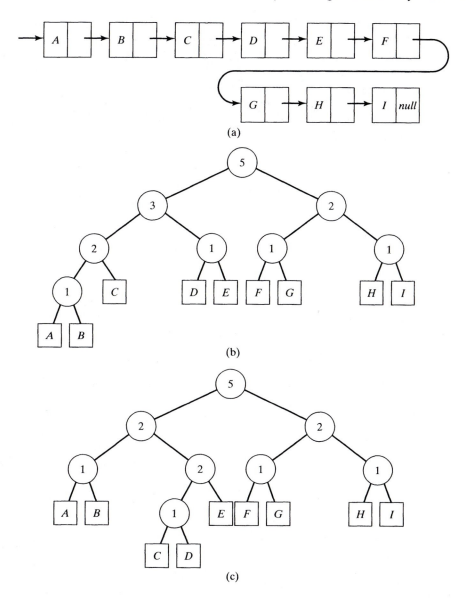

FIGURE 5.4.1   List and two corresponding binary trees.

```
r = k;
p = tree;
while (p is not a leaf node)
   if (r <= lCount(p))
          p = left(p);
   else {
          r -= lCount(p);
          p = right(p);
   }
find = p;
```

Figure 5.4.2a illustrates finding the fifth element of a list in the tree in Figure 5.4.1b, and Figure 5.4.2b illustrates finding the eighth element in the tree in Figure 5.4.1c. The dashed line represents the path taken by the algorithm down the tree to the appropriate leaf. We indicate the value of r (the remaining number of elements to be counted) next to each node encountered by the algorithm.

The number of tree nodes examined in finding the kth list element is less than or equal to one more than the depth of the tree (the longest path in the tree from the root to a leaf). Thus, four nodes are examined in Figure 5.4.2a in finding the fifth element in the list, and also in Figure 5.4.2b in finding the eighth element. If a list is represented as a linked structure, four nodes are accessed in finding the fifth element in a list [i.e., the operation $p = next(p)$ is performed four times], and seven nodes are accessed in finding the eighth element.

Although this is not a very impressive saving, consider a list with thousand elements. A binary tree of depth 10 is sufficient to represent such a list, since $\log_2 1000$ is

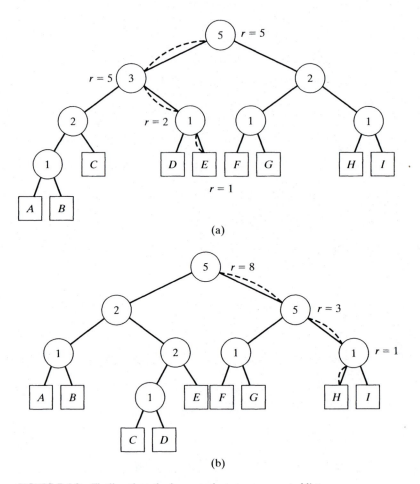

(a)

(b)

FIGURE 5.4.2 Finding the nth element of a tree-represented list.

less than 10. Thus, finding the *k*th element (regardless of whether *k* was 3, 253, 708, or 999) using such a binary tree would require examining no more than eleven nodes. Since the number of leafs of a binary tree increases as 2^d, where *d* is the depth of the tree, such a tree represents a relatively efficient data structure for finding the *k*th element of a list. If an almost complete tree is used, the *k*th element of an *n*-element list can be found in at most $\log_2 n + 1$ node accesses, whereas *k* accesses would be required if a linear linked list were used.

Deleting an Element

How can an element be deleted from a list represented by a tree? The deletion itself is relatively easy. It only involves resetting a left or right pointer in the father of the deleted leaf *dl* to **null**. However, in order to enable subsequent accesses, the counts in all the ancestors of *dl* may have to be modified. The modification consists of reducing *lCount* by one in each node *nd* of which *dl* was a left descendant, since the number of leafs in the left subtree of *nd* is one fewer. At the same time, if the brother of *dl* is a leaf, it can be moved up the tree to take the place of its father. We can then move that node up even further if it has no brother in its new position. This may reduce the depth of the resulting tree, making subsequent accesses slightly more efficient.

We may therefore present as shown below an algorithm to delete a leaf pointed to by *p* from a tree, and thus an element from a list (the line numbers at the left are for future reference).

```
1  if (p == tree) {
2       tree = null;
3       free node(p);
4  }
5  else {
6       f = father(p);
7       // remove node(p) and set b to point to its brother
8       if (p == left(f)) {
9         left(f) = null;
10        b = right(f);
11        --lCount(f);
12       }
13      else {
14        right(f) = null;
15        b = left(f);
16       } // end if
17      if (node(b) is a leaf) {
18        // move the contents of node(b) up to its
19        // father and free node(b)
20        info(f) = info(b);
21        left(f) = null;
22        right(f) = null;
23        lCount(f) = 0;
24        free node(b);
25       } // end if
26      free node(p);
```

```
27      // climb up the tree
28      q = f;
29      while (q != tree) {
30          f = father(q);
31          if (q == left(f)) {
32              // the deleted leaf was a left descendant of node(f)
33              --lCount(f);
34              b = right(f);
35          }
36          else
37              b = left(f);
38          // node(b) is the brother of node(q)
39          if (b == null && node(q) is a leaf) {
40              // move up the contents of node(q)
41              // to its father and free node(q)
42              info(f) = info(q);
43              left(f) = null;
44              right(f) = null;
45              lCount(f) = 0;
46              free node(q);
47          } // end if
48          q = f;
49      } // end while
50  }// end else
```

Figure 5.4.3 illustrates the results of this algorithm for a tree in which the nodes C, D, and B are deleted in that order. Make sure that you follow the actions of the algorithm on these examples. Note that the algorithm maintains a zero count in leaf nodes for consistency, although the count is not required for such nodes. Note also that the algorithm never moves up a nonleaf node even if this could be done. (For example, the father of A and B in Figure 5.4.3b has not been moved up.) We can easily modify the algorithm to do this (the modification is left to the reader), but have not done so for reasons that will become apparent shortly.

This deletion algorithm involves inspection of up to two nodes at each level (the ancestor of the node being deleted and the ancestor's brother). Thus, the operation of deleting the kth element of a list represented by a tree (which involves finding the element and then deleting it) requires a number of node accesses approximately equal to three times the tree depth. While deletion from a linked list requires accesses to only three nodes (the node preceding and following the deleted node as well as the deleted node), deleting the kth element requires a total of $k + 2$ accesses ($k - 1$ of which are to locate the node preceding the kth). For large lists, therefore, the tree representation is more efficient.

Similarly we can compare favorably the efficiency of tree-represented lists with array-represented lists. If an n-element list is maintained in the first n elements of an array, finding the kth element involves only a single array access, but deleting it requires shifting the $n - k$ elements that followed the deleted element. If gaps are allowed

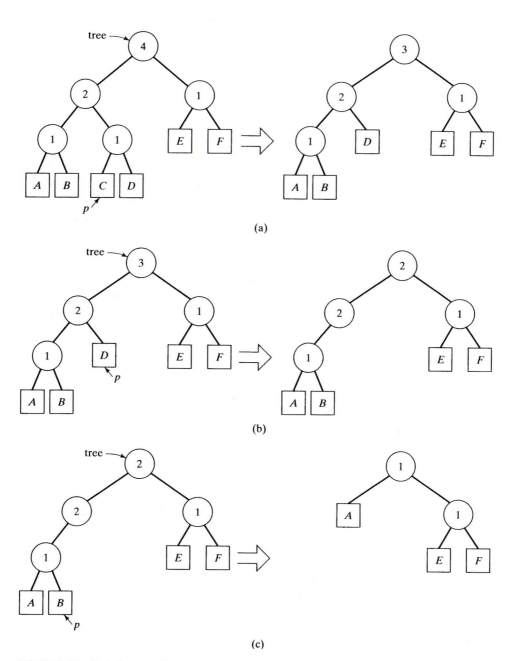

FIGURE 5.4.3   Deletion algorithm.

in the array, so that deletion can be implemented efficiently (by setting a flag in the array position of the deleted element without shifting any subsequent elements), then finding the kth element requires at least k array accesses. The reason is that it is no longer possible to know the array position of the kth element in the list because there may be gaps among the elements in the array. [Note, however, that if the order of the elements in the list is irrelevant, the kth element in an array can be deleted efficiently by overwriting it with the element in position n (the last element) and adjusting the count to $n - 1$. However, it is unlikely that we would want to delete the kth element from a list in which the order is irrelevant, since the kth element would then have no significance over any of the others.]

Inserting a new kth element into a tree-represented list [between the $(k - 1)$st and the previous kth] is also a relatively efficient operation. The insertion consists of locating the kth element, replacing it with a new nonleaf that has a leaf containing the new element as its left son and a leaf containing the old kth element as its right son, and adjusting appropriate counts among its ancestors. We leave the details to the reader. (However, repeatedly adding a new kth element by this method causes the tree to become highly unbalanced, because the branch containing the kth element becomes disproportionately long compared to the other branches. This means that the efficiency of finding the kth element is not as great as it would be in a balanced tree in which all paths are approximately the same length. The reader is encouraged to find a "balancing" strategy to alleviate this problem. Despite this problem, if insertions into the tree are made randomly, so that it is equally likely for an element to be inserted at any given position, the resulting tree remains fairly balanced, and finding the kth element remains efficient.)

Implementing Tree-Represented Lists in Java

The Java implementations of the search and deletion algorithms are straightforward using the linked representation of binary trees. However, such a representation requires *info*, *lCount*, *father*, *left*, and *right* fields for each tree node, while a list node requires only *info* and *next* fields. Coupled with the fact that the tree representation requires approximately twice as many nodes as a linked list, this space requirement may make the tree representation impractical. We could, of course, utilize external nodes containing only an *info* field (and perhaps a *father* field) for the leafs, and internal nodes containing *lCount*, *father*, *left*, and *right* fields for the nonleafs. We will not pursue that possibility here.

The space requirements are not nearly so great under the sequential representation of a binary tree. If we assume that no insertions are required once the tree is constructed and that the initial list size is known, we can set aside an array to hold an almost complete strictly binary tree representation of the list. Under this representation, *father*, *left*, and *right* fields are unnecessary. As we shall soon show, it is always possible to construct an almost complete binary tree representation of a list.

Once the tree has been constructed, the only fields required are *info*, *lcount*, and a field *used* to indicate whether or not an array element represents an existing or a deleted tree node. Also, as we have already noted, *lcount* is only required for nonleaf nodes of the tree, so that a class could be defined with either the *lcount* field or the *info* field, depending on whether or not the node is a leaf. We leave this possibility as a exercise for the reader. It is also possible to eliminate the need for the *used* field, at some expense to time efficiency (see Exercises 5.4.4 and 5.4.5). The following class defines each node of the list:

```
public class TreeListNode{
   private String info;
   private int lcount;
   private boolean used;

   // accessor and mutator methods: getInfo, setInfo, getLeftCount,
   // setLeftCount, getUsed, and setUsed

   // Methods incLeftCount, decLeftCount, and zeroLeftCount
   // increment, decrement, and zero lcount respectively

} // end TreeListNode class
```

We may now define a tree-represented list as a *TreeList* class (assume hundred elements in the list):

```
public class TreeList {
   public static final int MAXELTS = 100;   // maximum number of list
                                            // elements
   public static final int NUMNODES = 2*MAXELTS - 1;
   public static final String BLANKS = "                    ";   // 20 blanks
   private TreeListNode node[] = new TreeListNode[MAXELTS];

   public TreeList() {
       for (int i = 0; i < MAXELTS; i++)
             node[i]=new TreeListNode();
   }
   public TreeListNode getTreeListNode(int n) {
       return node[n];
   }
          ...
```

A nonleaf node can be recognized by an *info* value equal to *BLANKS*. *father*(p), *left*(p), and *right*(p) can be implemented in the usual way as $(p - 1)/2, 2 * p + 1$, and $2 * p + 2$, respectively.

A Java method of *TreeList* to find the *k*th element follows.

```
public int findElement(int k) {
   int p, r;

   r = k;
   p = 0;
   while (node[p].getInfo().equals(BLANKS)) {
           if (r <= node[p].getLeftCount())
               p = p*2 + 1;
```

```
          else {
                r -= node[p].getLeftCount();
                p = p*2 + 2;
          }
       }
     return p;
  } // end findElement
```

The Java method of *TreeList* to delete the leaf referenced by *p* using the sequential representation is somewhat simpler than the corresponding algorithm given above. Since pointers are not used, we can ignore all assignments of *null* (lines 2, 9, 14, 21, 22, 43, and 44). We can also ignore the assignments of zero to an *lcount* field (lines 23 and 45), because such an assignment is part of the conversion of a nonleaf to a leaf, and the *lcount* field in leaf nodes is unused in our Java representation. A node can be recognized as a leaf (lines 17 and 39) by a nonblank *info* value, and the pointer *b* as *null* (line 39) by a *false* value for *node[b].used*. Freeing a node (lines 3, 26, and 46) is accomplished by setting its *used* field to *false*.

```
    public void delete(int p) {
      int b, f, q;

      if (p == 0)
            node[p].setUsed(false);                  // Algorithm lines 1-4
      else {
            f = (p-1) / 2;                            // Algorithm line 6
            if (p % 2 != 0) {                         // Algorithm line 8
               b = 2*f + 2;
               node[f].decLeftCount();
            }
            else
               b = 2*f + 1;
            if (!((node[b].getInfo()).equals(BLANKS))) {
                                                      // Algorithm lines 17-25
               node[f].setInfo(new String(node[b].getInfo()));
               node[b].setUsed(false);
            }
            node[p].setUsed(false);                   // Algorithm line 26
            q = f;                                    // Algorithm line 28
            while (q != 0) {
               f = (q-1) / 2;                         // Algorithm line 30
               if (q % 2 != 0) {                      // Algorithm line 31
                     node[f].decLeftCount();
                     b = 2*f + 2;
               }
               else
                     b = 2*f + 1;
               if (!node[b].getUsed() &&
                  !node[q].getInfo().equals(BLANKS)) {
```

```
                                          // Algorithm lines 39-47
            node[f].setInfo(new String(node[q].getInfo()));
            node[q].setUsed(false);
      }
      q = f;
   } // end while
 } // end if
} // end delete
```

Our use of the sequential representation explains the reason for not moving a nonleaf without a brother further up in a tree during deletion. Under the sequential representation, such a moving-up process would involve copying the contents of all the nodes in the subtree within the array, whereas it involves modifying only a single pointer if the linked representation is used.

Constructing a Tree-Represented List

We now return to the claim that, given a list of n elements, it is possible to construct an almost complete strictly binary tree representing the list. We have already seen in Section 5.1 that it is possible to construct an almost complete strictly binary tree with n leafs and $2 * n - 1$ nodes. The leafs of such a tree occupy nodes numbered $n - 1$ through $2 * n - 2$. If d is the smallest integer such that 2^d is greater or equal to n (i.e., if d equals the smallest integer greater than or equal to $\log_2 n$), then d equals the depth of the tree. $2^d - 1$ is the number assigned to the first node on the bottom level of the tree. The first elements of the list are assigned to nodes numbered $2^d - 1$ through $2 * n - 2$, and the remainder (if any) to nodes numbered $n - 1$ through $2^d - 2$. In constructing a tree representing a list with n elements, we can assign elements to the *info* fields of tree leafs in this sequence and assign a blank string to the *info* fields of the nonleaf nodes, numbered 0 through $n - 2$. It is also a simple matter to initialize the *used* field to *true* in all nodes numbered 0 to $2 * n - 2$.

Initializing the values of the *lcount* array is more difficult. Two methods can be used: one involving more time, and the other involving more space. In the first method, all *lcount* fields are initialized to zero. Then the tree is climbed from each leaf to the tree root in turn. Each time a node is reached from its left son, 1 is added to its *lcount* field. All *lcount* values are properly assigned when this process has been performed for each leaf. The following method uses this technique to construct a tree from a list of input data:

```
public void buildTree(int n) {
   int d, f, i, p, power, size;

   // compute the tree depth d and the value of 2^d
   d = 0;
   power = 1;
   while (power < n){
        d++;
        power *= 2;
   }
   // assign the elements of the list, initialize the used flags,
   // and initialize the lcount field to 0 in all nonleafs
   size = 2*n - 1;
```

```
for (i = power-1; i < size; i++) {
        node[i].setInfo(readString());
        node[i].setUsed(true);
}
for (i = n-1; i < power-1; i++) {
        node[i].setInfo(readString());
        node[i].setUsed(true);
}
for (i=0; i < n-1; i++) {
        node[i].setUsed(true);
        node[i].zeroLeftCount();
        node[i].setInfo(new String(BLANKS));
}
for (i = n-1; i < size; i++) {
        // follow the path from each leaf to the root
        p = i;
        while (p != 0) {
                f = (p-1) / 2;
                if (p % 2 != 0)
                        node[f].incLeftCount();
                p = f;
        }
} // end for
} // end buildTree
```

The second method uses an additional field *rcount* in each node to hold the number of leafs in the right subtree of each nonleaf node. This field as well as the *lcount* field is set to 1 in each nonleaf that is the father of two leafs. If n is odd, so that there is a node (numbered $(n - 3)/2$) that is the father of a leaf and a nonleaf, *lcount* in that node is set to 2 and *rcount* to 1.

The algorithm then goes through the remaining array elements in reverse order, setting *lcount* in each node to the sum of *lcount* and *rcount* in the node's left son, and *rcount* to the sum of *lcount* and *rcount* in the node's right son. We leave to the reader the Java implementation of this technique. Note that the values of *rcount* are unused once the tree is built, and thus it can be implemented as a local array in *buildTree* rather than as a field in every node.

This second method has the advantage that it visits each nonleaf once to directly calculate its *lcount* (and *rcount*) value. The first method visits each nonleaf once for each of its leaf descendants, adding one to *lcount* each time that the leaf is found to be a left descendant. To counterbalance this advantage, the second method requires an extra *rcount* field, while the first methods needs no extra fields.

The Josephus Problem Revisited

The Josephus problem in Section 4.5 is a perfect example of the utility of the binary tree representation of a list. In that problem, it was necessary to repeatedly find the *m*th next element of a list and then delete it. These are operations that can be performed efficiently in a tree-represented list.

If *size* equals the number of elements currently in a list, the position of the *m*th node following the node in position k that has just been deleted is given by $1 + (k - 2 + m)\% \ size$.

(Here we assume that the first node in the list is considered to be in position 1, not in position 0.) For example, if a list has five elements and the third element is deleted, and we wish to find the fourth element following the deleted element, then $size = 4, k = 3$, and $m = 4$. Then $k - 2 + m$ equals 5, and $(k - 2 + m)\% size$ is 1, so that the fourth element following the deleted element is in position 2. (After deleting element 3, we count elements 4, 5, 1, and 2.) We can therefore write a Java method *follower* to find the *m*th node following a node in position *k* that has just been deleted and reset *k* to its position. *follower* calls the routine *findElement* presented earlier and uses an auxiliary *private* class *FollowerResult* in order to modify both *m* and *k*. *FollowerResult* and *TreeList* are initialized by the Josephus constructor.

The following Java application implements the Josephus algorithm using a tree-represented list. The application inputs the number of people in a circle (*n*), an integer count (*m*), and the names of the people in the circle in order, beginning with the person from whom the count starts. The people in the circle are counted in order, and the person at whom the input count is reached leaves the circle. The count then begins again from 1, starting at the next person. The program prints the order in which people leave the circle. Section 4.5 presented a program to do this using a circular list in which $(n - 1) * m$ nodes are accessed once the initial list is constructed. The following algorithm accesses fewer than $(n - 1) * \log_2 n$ nodes once the tree is built.

```
public class Josephus {
  private static TreeList tl;
  private static FollowerResult followerResult;

  public Josephus() {
      followerResult = new FollowerResult();
      tl = new TreeList();
  } // end constructor

  public static void follower (int size, int m) {
      int j;

      j = followerResult.k - 2 + m;
      followerResult.k = (j % size) + 1;
      followerResult.p = tl.findElement(followerResult.k);
  } // end follower

  public static void main(String[] args) {
      int m, n, size;
      new Josephus();

      System.out.print("Enter # of people in circle> ");
      n = TreeList.readInt();
      System.out.print("Enter count> ");
      m = TreeList.readInt();
      tl.buildTree(n);
      followerResult.k = n+1;  // initially we have "deleted" the
                               // (n+1)st person
      for (size = n; size > 1; size--){
          // repeat until one person is left
          follower(size, m);
```

```
                    System.out.println((tl. getTreeListNode
                    (followerResult.p)).getInfo() + " is out");
                    tl.delete(followerResult.p);
            }
            System.out.println((tl. getTreeListNode (0)).getInfo() +
                                                " is the last left");
        } // end main
    } // end Josephus class

    // Used by the follower method to reference a node and its successor
    class FollowerResult {
        int p;
        int k;
    } // end FollowerResult class
```

EXERCISES

5.4.1 Prove that the leftmost node at level n in an almost complete strictly binary tree is assigned the number 2^n.

5.4.2 Prove that the extension of an almost complete binary tree (see Exercise 5.3.5) is almost complete.

5.4.3 For what values of n and m is the solution to the Josephus problem given in this section faster than the solution given in Section 4.5? Why is this so?

5.4.4 Explain how we can eliminate the need for a *used* field if we elect not to move up a newly created leaf with no brother during deletion.

5.4.5 Explain how we can eliminate the need for a *used* field if we set *lcount* to −1 in a nonleaf that is converted to a leaf node and reset *info* to blanks in a deleted node.

5.4.6 Write a Java method *buildTree* in which each node is visited only once by using an *rcount* array as described in the text.

5.4.7 Show how to represent a linked list as an almost complete binary tree in which each list element is represented by one tree node. Write a Java method to return a reference to the kth element of such a list.

5.5 TREES AND THEIR APPLICATIONS

In this section, we consider general trees and their representations. We also investigate some of their uses in problem solving.

A ***tree*** is a finite nonempty set of elements in which one element is called the ***root*** and the remaining elements are partitioned into $m >= 0$ disjoint subsets, each of which is itself a tree. Each element in a tree is called a ***node*** of the tree.

Figure 5.5.1 illustrates some trees. Each node may be the root of a tree with zero or more subtrees. A node with no subtrees is a ***leaf***. We use the terms ***father***, ***son***, ***brother***, ***ancestor***, ***descendant***, ***level***, and ***depth*** in the same sense that we used them for binary trees. We also define the ***degree*** of a node in a tree as the number of its sons. Thus in Figure 5.5.1a, node C has degree 0 (and is therefore a leaf), node D has degree 1, node B has degree 2, and node A has degree 3. There is no upper limit on the degree of a node.

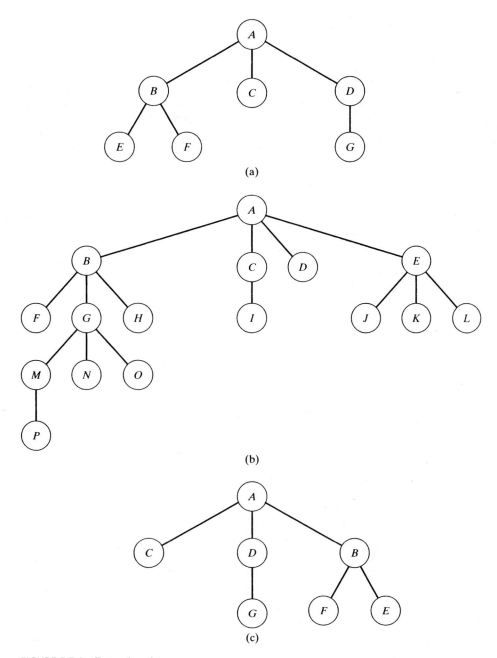

FIGURE 5.5.1   Examples of trees.

Let us compare the trees in Figures 5.5.1a and c. They are equivalent as trees. Each has A as its root and three subtrees. One of those subtrees has root C with no subtrees, another has root D with a single subtree rooted at G, and the third has root B with two subtrees rooted at E and F. The only difference between the two illustrations is the order in which the subtrees are arranged. The definition of a tree makes no distinction among subtrees of a general tree, unlike a binary tree, where a distinction is made between the left and right subtrees.

An ***ordered tree*** is defined as a tree in which the subtrees of each node form an ordered set. In an ordered tree, we may speak of the first, second, or last son of a particular node. The first son of a node in an ordered tree is often called the ***oldest*** son of that node, and the last son is called the ***youngest***. Although the trees in Figures 5.5.1a and c are equivalent as unordered trees, they are different as ordered trees. In the remainder of this chapter we use the word "tree" to refer to "ordered tree." A ***forest*** is an ordered set of ordered trees.

The question arises as to whether a binary tree is a tree. Every binary tree except for the empty binary tree is indeed a tree. However, not every tree is binary. A tree node may have more than two sons, but a binary tree node may not. Even a tree whose nodes have at most two sons is not necessarily a binary tree. This is because an only son in a general tree is not designated as a "left" or "right" son, whereas every son in a binary tree must be either a "left" son or a "right" son. In fact, although a nonempty binary tree is a tree, the designations of left and right have no meaning in the context of a tree (except perhaps to order the two subtrees of nodes with two sons). A nonempty binary tree is a tree each of whose nodes has a maximum of two subtrees which have the added designation of "left" or "right."

Java Representations of Trees

How can an ordered tree be represented in Java? Two alternatives immediately come to mind: an array of tree nodes may be declared, or a dynamic variable may be allocated for each node created. However, what should the structure of each individual node be? In the representation of a binary tree, each node contains an information field and two pointers to its two sons. But how many pointers should a tree node contain? The number of sons of a node is variable and may be as large or as small as desired. If we arbitrarily declare (using the dynamic implementation)

```
class TreeNode {
    public static int MAXSONS = 20;
    public Object info;
    public TreeNode father;
    public TreeNode [] sons;

    public TreeNode(){
        sons = new TreeNode[MAXSONS];
    } // end constructor
}
```

then we are restricting the number of sons a node may have to a maximum of twenty. Although in most cases this will be sufficient, it is sometimes necessary to create dynamically a node with twenty-one or one-hundred sons. Far worse than this remote possibility is the fact that twenty units of storage are reserved for each node in the tree even though a node may actually have only one or two (or even zero) sons. This is a tremendous waste of space.

One alternative is to link all the sons of a node together in a linear list. Thus the set of available nodes (using the array implementation) might be declared as follows:

```
public static int MAXNODES = 500;
class TreeNode {
        public Object info;
        public int father;
        public int son;
        public int next;
}
TreeNode Node[] = new TreeNode[MAXNODES];
```

TreeNode[p].son points to the oldest son of *TreeNode[p]*, and *TreeNode[p].next* points to the next-younger brother of *TreeNode[p]*.

Alternatively, a node may be declared as a dynamic variable:

```
class TreeNode {
        public Object info;
        public TreeNode father;
        public TreeNode son;
        public TreeNode next;
}
```

If all traversals are from a node to its sons, the *father* field may be omitted. Figure 5.5.2 illustrates the representations of the trees in Figure 5.5.1 under these methods if no *father* field is needed.

Even if it is necessary to access the father of a node, the *father* field can be omitted by placing a reference to the father in the *next* field of the youngest son instead of leaving it **null**. An additional logical field could then be used to indicate whether the *next* field points to a "real" next son or to the father. Alternatively (in the array of nodes implementation), the contents of the *next* field can contain negative as well as positive indices. A negative value would indicate that the *next* field points to the node's father rather than to its brother, and the absolute value of the *next* field yields the actual pointer. This is similar to the representation of threads in binary trees. Of course, in either of these two methods, accessing the father of an arbitrary node would require a traversal of the list of its younger brothers.

If we think of *son* as corresponding to the *left* pointer of a binary tree node, and *next* as corresponding to its *right* pointer, then this method actually represents a general ordered tree by a binary tree. We may picture this binary tree as the original tree tilted 45 degrees, with all father-son links removed except for those between a node and its oldest son, and with links added between each node and its next-younger brother. Figure 5.5.3 illustrates the binary trees corresponding to the trees in Figure 5.5.1.

In fact, a binary tree may be used to represent an entire forest, since the *next* pointer in the root of a tree can be used to point to the next tree in the forest. Figure 5.5.4 illustrates a forest and its corresponding binary tree.

son info next

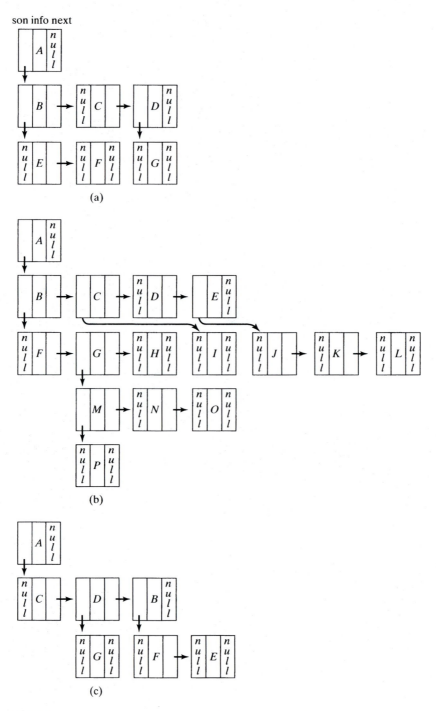

(a)

(b)

(c)

FIGURE 5.5.2 Tree representations. (See reference on page 321.)

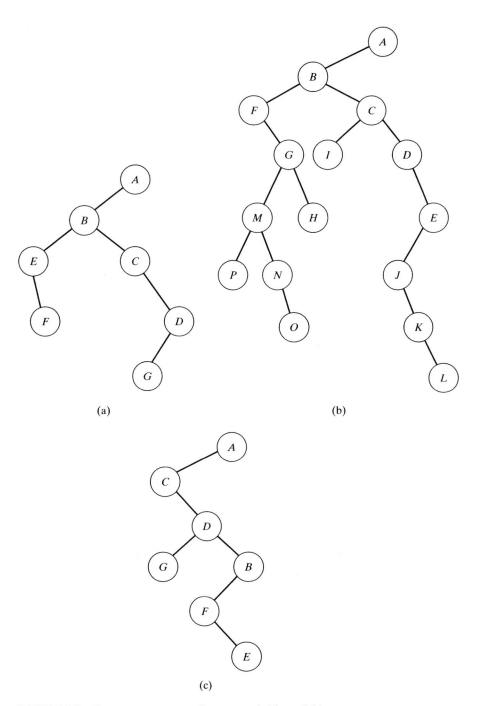

(a)

(b)

(c)

FIGURE 5.5.3   Binary trees corresponding to trees in Figure 5.5.1

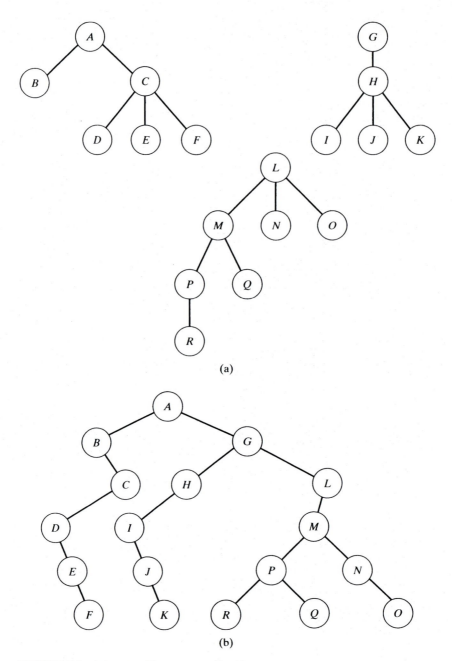

(a)

(b)

FIGURE 5.5.4 A forest and its corresponding binary tree.

Tree Traversals

The traversal methods for binary trees induce traversal methods for forests. The pre-order, inorder, or postorder traversals of a forest may be defined as the preorder, in-order, or postorder traversals of its corresponding binary tree. If a forest is represented as a set of dynamic variable nodes with *son* and *next* references as above, a Java method to print the contents of its nodes in inorder may be written as follows:

```
public void inTrav(TreeNode p) {
    if (p != null) {
        inTrav(p.son);
        System.out.println(p.info);
        inTrav(p.next);
    } // end if
} // end inTrav
```

The routines for preorder and postorder traversals are similar.

These traversals of a forest may also be defined directly, as follows:

PREORDER

1. Visit the root of the first tree in the forest.
2. Traverse in preorder the forest formed by the subtrees of the first tree, if any.
3. Traverse in preorder the forest formed by the remaining trees in the forest, if any.

INORDER

1. Traverse in inorder the forest formed by the subtrees of the first tree in the forest, if any.
2. Visit the root of the first tree.
3. Traverse in inorder the forest formed by the remaining trees in the forest, if any.

POSTORDER

1. Traverse in postorder the forest formed by the subtrees of the first tree in the for-est, if any.
2. Traverse in postorder the forest formed by the remaining trees in the forest, if any.
3. Visit the root of the first tree in the forest.

The nodes of the forest in Figure 5.5.4a may be listed in preorder as *ABCDEFGHIJKLMPRQNO*, in inorder as *BDEFCAIJKHGRPQMNOL*, and in postorder as *FEDCBKJIHRQPONMLGA*. Let us call a traversal of a binary tree a **binary traversal**, and a traversal of an ordered general tree a **general traversal**.

General Expressions as Trees

An ordered tree may be used to represent a general expression in much the same way that a binary tree may be used to represent a binary expression. Since a node may have

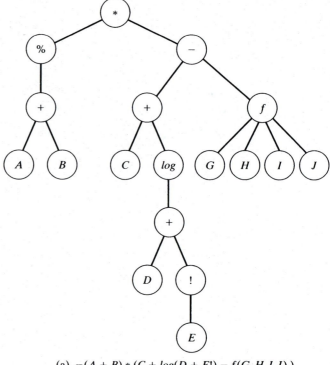

(a) $-(A + B) * (C + log(D + E!) - f(G, H, I, J))$

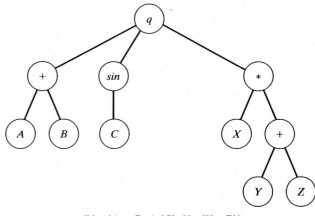

FIGURE 5.5.5 Tree representation of
arithmetic expressions.

(b) $q(A + B, sin(C), X * (Y + Z))$

any number of sons, nonleaf nodes need not represent only binary operators but can
represent operators with any number of operands. Figure 5.5.5 illustrates two expressions and their tree representations. The symbol "%" is used to represent unary negation, to avoid confusion with binary subtraction, which is represented by a minus sign.
A function reference such as $f(g,h,i,j)$ is viewed as the operator f applied to the
operands g,h,i, and j.

A general traversal of the trees in Figure 5.5.5 in preorder results in the strings $*\% + AB - + C \log + D!EFGHIJ$ and $q + AB \sin C * X + YZ$ respectively. These are the prefix versions of the two expressions. Thus we see that preorder general traversal of an expression tree produces its prefix expression. Inorder general traversal yields the strings $AB + \%CDE! + \log + GHIJF - *$ and $AB + C \sin XYZ + * q$, which are the postfix versions of the two expressions.

The fact that an inorder general traversal yields a postfix expression may seem surprising at first glance. However, the reason becomes clear upon examination of the transformation that takes place when a general ordered tree is represented by a binary tree. Consider an ordered tree in which each node has zero or two sons. Such a tree is shown in Figure 5.5.6a, and its binary tree equivalent is shown in Figure 5.5.6b. Traversing the binary tree in Figure 5.5.6b is the same as traversing the ordered tree in Figure 5.5.6a. However, a tree such as the one in Figure 5.5.6a may be considered as a binary tree in its own right rather than as an ordered tree. Thus it is possible to perform a binary traversal (rather than a general traversal) directly on the tree in Figure 5.5.6a. Beneath that figure are the binary traversals of the tree, while beneath Figure 5.5.6b are the binary traversals of the tree in that figure, which are the same as the traversals of the tree in Figure 5.5.6a if it were considered an ordered tree.

Note that the preorder traversals of the two binary trees are the same. Thus if a preorder traversal on a binary tree representing a binary expression yields the prefix of

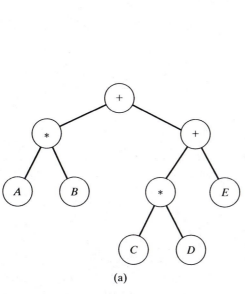

(a)

Preorder: $+ * AB + * CDE$
Inorder: $A * B + C * D + E$
Postorder: $AB * CD * E + +$

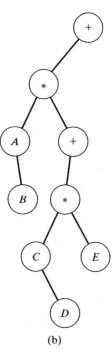

(b)

Preorder: $+ * AB + * CDE$
Inorder: $AB * CD * E + +$
Postorder: $BADCE * + * +$

FIGURE 5.5.6

the expression, then that traversal on an ordered tree representing a general expression which happens to have only binary operators yields the prefix as well. However, the postorder traversals of the two binary trees are not the same. Instead, the inorder binary traversal of the second (which is the same as the inorder general traversal of the first, if it is considered as an ordered tree) is the same as the postorder binary traversal of the first. Thus, the inorder general traversal of an ordered tree representing a binary expression is equivalent to the postorder binary traversal of the binary tree representing that expression, which yields the postfix.

Evaluating an Expression Tree

Suppose that it is desired to evaluate an expression whose operands are all numerical constants. Such an expression can be represented in Java by a tree each of whose nodes is declared by:

```java
public class ExpressionTreeNode {
    public final static int OPERATOR = 0;
    public final static int OPERAND = 1;
    private int uType;                 // OPERATOR or OPERAND
    private Object info;
    private ExpressionTreeNode son;
    private ExpressionTreeNode next;

    public ExpressionTreeNode() {}

    public ExpressionTreeNode(Object o, int t) {
        info = o;
        uType = t;
    } // end ExpressionTreeNode constructor

    ...

} // end ExpressionTreeNode class
```

The *son* and *next* fields are used to link together the nodes of a tree, as previously illustrated. Since a node may contain information that is either a number (operand) or a character string (operator), the information portion of the node is implemented as an *Object*.

We also assume a class *ExpressionTree* defined by

```java
public class ExpressionTree {
  public final static  int MAXCOLS = 80 ;
  private ExpressionTreeNode tree;

  public void ExpressionTree() {}

  public ExpressionTreeNode getTree() {
      return tree;
  } // end getTree

    ...
```

with additional methods as described below.

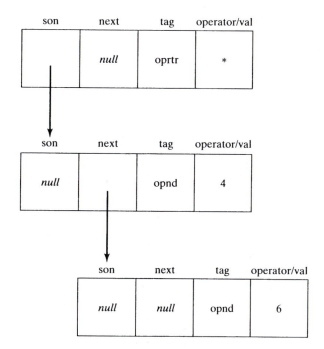

son	next	tag	operator/val
	null	oprtr	*

son	next	tag	operator/val
null		opnd	4

son	next	tag	operator/val
null	*null*	opnd	6

FIGURE 5.5.7 Expression tree.

We wish to write a Java method *evalTree(p)* of the *ExpressionTree* class that accepts a reference to an *ExpressionTree* node and returns the value of the expression represented by the subtree rooted at that node. The method *evalBinTree* presented in Section 5.2 performs a similar function for binary expressions. *evalBinTree* utilizes a method *oper* which accepts an operator symbol and two numerical operands and returns the numerical result of applying the operator to the operands. However, in the case of a general expression, we cannot use such a method, because the number of operands (and hence the number of arguments) varies with the operator. We therefore introduce a new method, *apply(p)* of the *ExpressionTree* class, that accepts a reference to an *ExpressionTreeNode* that is the root of a subtree that contains a single operator and its numerical operands, and returns the result of applying the operator to its operands. For example, the result of calling the method *apply* with parameter *p* pointing to the tree in Figure 5.5.7 is 24. If the node that is passed to *evalTree* represents an operator, each of the subtrees represented by its sons is replaced by a tree node representing the numerical result of its evaluation so that the method *apply* may be called. As the expression is evaluated, the tree nodes representing operands are freed, and operator nodes are converted to operand nodes.

We present a recursive method, *replace* of the *ExpressionTree* class, that accepts a reference to an *ExpressionTreeNode* and replaces the subtree rooted at that node with a tree node containing the numerical result of the expression's evaluation.

```
private void replace(ExpressionTreeNode p) {
    double value;
    ExpressionTreeNode q;
```

```
        if (p.getType() == ExpressionTreeNode.OPERATOR) {
                // the tree has an operator as its root
                q = p.getSon();
                while (q != null) {
                        // replace each of its subtrees by operands
                        replace(q);
                        q = q.getNext();
                }
                // apply the operator in the root to the operands in the
                // subtrees
                value = apply(p);
                // replace the operator by the result
                p.setType(ExpressionTreeNode.OPERAND);
                p.setValue(new Double(value));
                p.SetSon(null);
        } // end if
} // end replace
```

The method *evalTree* may now be written as follows:

```
public double evalTree(ExpressionTreeNode p) {
    replace(p);
    return ((Double)p.getValue()).doubleValue();
} // end evalTree
```

After invoking *evalTree*(*p*) the tree is no longer necessary. Java's automatic system of garbage collection ensures that the storage used by the nodes of the original tree may be reclaimed. However, not all languages provide automatic garbage collection. In languages that allow the programmer to use pointers directly (e.g., C), the value of *p* would be meaningless once the tree is destroyed. This is a case of a ***dangling pointer***, in which a pointer variable contains the address of a variable that has been freed. C programmers who use dynamic variables should be careful to recognize such pointers and not use them subsequently.

Constructing a Tree

A number of operations are frequently used in constructing a tree. We now present some of these operations and their Java implementations. In the Java representation, since we assume that father pointers are not needed, the *father* field is not used, and the *next* pointer in the youngest node is ***null***. The routines would be slightly more complex and less efficient if this were not the case.

The first method that we examine is *setSons*. This method operates on a reference to a tree node with no sons and a linear list of nodes linked together through the *next* field. *setSons* establishes the nodes in the list as the sons of the node in the tree. The Java method to implement this operation is straightforward (we use the dynamic storage implementation).

```
public void setSons(TreeNode p, TreeNode list) {
        // p refers to a tree node, list is a list of nodes
        // linked together through their next fields
```

```
    if (p == null) {
            System.out.println( "invalid insertion");
            System.exit(1);
    } // end if
    if (p.son != null) {
            System.out.println("invalid insertion");
            System.exit(1);
    } // end if
    p.son = list;
} // end setSons
```

Another common method is *addSon*(*p, x*), where *p* refers to a node in a tree and it is desired to add a node containing *x* as the youngest son of *node*(*p*). The Java routine to implement *addSon* is as follows:

```
public void addSon(TreeNode p, Object x) {
    TreeNode q, r;

    if (p == null) {
            System.out.println("void insertion");
            System.exit(1);
    } // end if
    // the pointer q traverses the list of sons
    // of p.  r is one node behind q
    r = null;
    q = p.son;
    while (q != null) {
            r = q;
            q = q.next;
    } // end while
    // At this point, r points to the youngest
    // son of p, or is null if p has no sons
    q = new TreeNode( );
    q.info = x;
    q.next = null;
    if (r == null)
            p.son = q;
    else
            r.next = q;
} // end addSon
```

Note that the list of existing sons must be traversed in order to add a new son to a node. Since adding a son is a common operation, a representation is often used which makes this operation more efficient. Under this alternative representation, the list of sons is ordered from youngest to oldest rather than vice versa. Thus *son*(*p*) points to the youngest son of *node*(*p*), and *next*(*p*) points to its next older brother. Under this representation the method *addSon* may be written as follows:

```
public void addSon(TreeNode p, Object x) {
    TreeNode q;
```

```
if (p == null) {
        System.out.println("void insertion");
        System.exit(1);
} // end if
q = new TreeNode( );
q.info = x;
q.next = p;
} // end addSon
```

EXERCISES

5.5.1 How many trees exist with *n* nodes?

5.5.2 How many trees exist with *n* nodes and maximum level *m*?

5.5.3 Prove that if *m* pointer fields are set aside in each node of a general tree to point to a maximum of *m* sons, and if the number of nodes in the tree is *n*, then the number of **null** son pointer fields is $n * (m - 1) + 1$.

5.5.4 If a forest is represented by a binary tree, as in the text, show that the number of **null** right links is 1 greater than the number of nonleafs of the forest.

5.5.5 Define the **breadth-first** *order* of the nodes of a general tree as the root followed by all the nodes on level 1, followed by all the nodes on level 2, and so on. The nodes on each level should be ordered so that children of the same father appear in the same order as they appear in the tree, and if *n1* and *n2* have different fathers, *n1* appears before *n2* if the father of *n1* appears before the father of *n2*. Extend the definition to a forest. Write a Java application to traverse a forest represented as a binary tree in breadth-first order.

5.5.6 Consider the following method of transforming a general tree *gt* into a strictly binary tree *bt*. Each node of *gt* is represented by a leaf of *bt*. If *gt* consists of a single node, then *bt* consists of a single node. Otherwise, *bt* consists of a new root node, a left subtree *lt*, and a right subtree *rt*. *lt* is the strictly binary tree formed recursively from the oldest subtree of *gt*, and *rt* is the strictly binary tree formed recursively from *gt* without its oldest subtree. Write a Java method to convert a general tree into a strictly binary tree.

5.5.7 Write a Java method *compute* that accepts a pointer to a tree representing an expression with constant operands and returns the result of evaluating the expression without destroying the tree.

5.5.8 Write a Java method to convert an infix expression into an expression tree. Assume that all nonbinary operators precede their operands. Let the input expression be represented as follows: an operand is represented by the character 'N' followed by a number, an operator by the character 'T' followed by a character representing the operator, and a function by the character 'F' followed by the name of the function.

5.5.9 Consider the definitions of expression, term, and factor given at the end of Section 3.2. Given a string of letters, signs, asterisks, and parentheses that forms a valid expression, a **parse tree** can be formed for the string. Such a tree is illustrated in Figure 5.5.8 for the string "(A + B) * (C + D)". Each node in the tree represents a substring and contains a letter (*E* for expression, *T* for term, *F* for factor, or *S* for symbol) and two integers. The first is the position in the input string where the substring represented by that node begins, and the second is the length of the substring. (The substring represented by each node is shown below that node in the figure.) The leaves are all *S* nodes and represent single symbols of the original

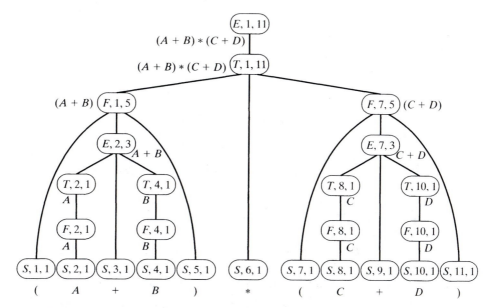

FIGURE 5.5.8 Parse tree for the string (A + B)*(C + D).

input. The root of the tree must be an *E* node. The sons of any non-*S* node *N* represent the substrings that make up the grammatical object represented by *N*. Write a Java method that accepts such a string and constructs a parse tree for it.

5.6 EXAMPLE: GAME TREES

One application of trees is to game playing by computer. We illustrate this application by writing a Java application to determine the best move in tic-tac-toe from a given board position.

Assume that there is a method *evaluate* that accepts a board position and an indication of a player (X or O) and returns a numerical value that represents how good the position seems to be for that player (the larger the value returned by *evaluate*, the better the position). A winning position yields the largest possible value, and a losing position yields the smallest. An example of such an evaluation function for tic-tac-toe is the number of rows, columns, and diagonals remaining open for one player minus the number remaining open for the opponent (except that the value 9 would be returned for a position that wins, and −9 for a position that loses). This function does not "look ahead" to consider any possible board positions that might result from the current position; it merely evaluates a static board position.

Given a board position, the best next move could be determined by considering all the possible moves and resulting positions. The move selected should be the one that results in the board position with the highest evaluation. Such an analysis however, does not necessarily yield the best move. Figure 5.6.1 illustrates a position and the five possible moves that X can make from it. Applying the evaluation function described above to the five resulting positions yields the values shown. Four moves yield

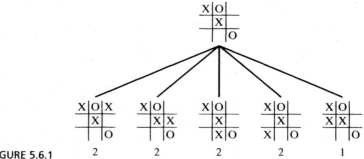

FIGURE 5.6.1

the same maximum evaluation, although three of them are distinctly inferior to the fourth. (The fourth position yields a certain victory for X, while the other three can be drawn by O.) In fact, the move that yields the smallest evaluation is as good as or better than the moves that yield a higher evaluation. The static evaluation function, therefore, is not good enough to predict the outcome of the game. While a better evaluation function could easily be produced for the game of tic-tac-toe (even if it were by the brute force method of listing all the positions and the appropriate responses), most games are too complex for static evaluators to determine the best response.

Suppose it were possible to look ahead several moves. Then the choice of a move could be improved considerably. Define the **look ahead level** as the number of future moves to be considered. Starting at any position, it is possible to construct a tree of the possible board positions that may result from each move. Such a tree is called a **game tree**. The game tree for the opening tic-tac-toe position with a look ahead level of 2 is illustrated in Figure 5.6.2. (Other positions exist, but because of symmetry considerations, they are effectively the same as the positions shown.) Note that the maximum level (called the **depth**) of the nodes in such a tree is equal to the look ahead level.

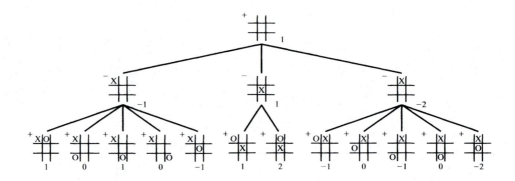

FIGURE 5.6.2   Game tree for tic-tac-toe.

Let us designate the player who must move at the root's game position as ***plus***, and the opponent as ***minus***. We attempt to find the best move for *plus* from the root's game position. The remaining nodes of the tree may be designated as ***plus nodes*** or ***minus nodes***, depending upon which player must move from the node's position. Each node in Figure 5.6.2 is marked as a *plus* or *minus* node.

Suppose the game positions of all the sons of a *plus* node have been evaluated for player *plus*. Clearly, *plus* should choose the move that yields the maximum evaluation. Thus, the value of a *plus* node to player *plus* is the maximum of the values of its sons. On the other hand, once *plus* has moved, *minus* will select the move that yields the minimum evaluation for player *plus*. Thus the value of a *minus* node to player *plus* is the minimum of the values of its sons.

Therefore, in order to decide the best move for player *plus* from the root, the positions in the leafs must be evaluated for player *plus* using a static evaluation function. These values are then moved up the game tree by assigning to each *plus* node the maximum of its sons' values, and to each *minus* node the minimum of its sons' values, on the assumption that *minus* will select the move that is worst for *plus*. The value assigned to each node in Figure 5.6.2 by this process is indicated in the figure immediately below the node.

The move that *plus* should select, given the board position in the root node, is the one that maximizes its value. Thus the opening move for X should be the middle square, as illustrated in Figure 5.6.2. Figure 5.6.3 illustrates the determination of O's best reply. Note that the designation of "*plus*" and "*minus*" depends on whose move is being calculated. Thus, X is designated as *plus* in Figure 5.6.2, and O is designated as *plus* in Figure 5.6.3. In applying the static evaluation function to a board position, the value of the position to whichever player is designated as *plus* is computed. This method

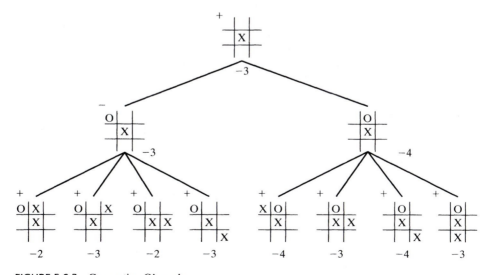

FIGURE 5.6.3   Computing O's reply.

is called the ***minimax*** method, since the maximum and minimum functions are applied alternately as the tree is climbed.

The best move for a player from a given position may be determined by first constructing the game tree and applying a static evaluation function to the leafs. These values are then moved up the tree by applying the minimum and maximum at the *minus* and *plus* nodes respectively. Each node of the game tree must include a representation of the board and an indication of whether the node is a *plus* node or a *minus* node. Nodes may therefore be defined by:

```java
public class Node {
  char board[][];
  int turn;
  Node son;
  Node next;

  public Node() {
        board = new char[3][3];
        son = null;
        next = null;
  } // end constructor
} // end Node class
```

p.board[*i*][*j*] has the value 'X', 'O', or ' ' depending on whether the square in row *i* and column *j* of the node is occupied by either of the players or is unoccupied. *p.turn* has the value +1 or −1 depending on whether the node is a plus or minus node. The remaining two fields of a node are used to position the node within the tree. *p.son* points to the oldest son of the node, while *p.next* points to its next-younger brother.

The Java method *nextMove(brd, looklevel, player)* computes the best next move. *brd* is a 3 × 3 array representing the current board position, *player* is 'X' or 'O' depending on whose move is being computed (note that in tic-tac-toe the value of *player* could be computed from *brd*, so this parameter is not strictly necessary), and *looklevel* is the look-ahead level used in constructing the tree. The *nextMove* method creates a new board, *best*, that represents the best board position that can be achieved by *player* from position *brd*.

nextMove uses two auxiliary methods, *buildTree* and *bestBranch*. The method *buildTree* builds the game tree and returns a reference to its root. The method *bestBranch* computes the value of *best*, which is a reference to the tree node representing the best move, and an array *value*, whose single element is the evaluation of that move using the minimax technique.

```java
public void nextMove(char player) {
  int[] value = new int[1];

  Node tree = buildTree();
  Node best = bestBranch(tree,player,value);
  copyBoard(playing_board, best.board);
} // end nextMove
```

The method *buildTree* returns a reference to the root of a game tree. It uses the auxiliary method *copyBoard* that copies the *brd* to *tree*. It also uses the method *expand(p, level, depth)* in which *p* is a reference to a node in a game tree, *level* is its level, and *depth* is the depth of the game tree that is to be constructed. *expand* produces the subtree rooted at *p* to the proper depth.

```
public Node buildTree() {
   Node root = new Node();
   // create the root of the tree and initialize it
   copyBoard(root.board, playing_board);
   root.turn = 1;
   expand(root, 0);
   return(root);
} // end buildTree
```

expand may be implemented by generating all the board positions that may be obtained from the board position pointed to by *p* and establishing them as the sons of *p* in the game tree. *expand* then calls itself recursively, using these sons as parameters, until the desired depth is reached. *expand* uses an auxiliary method *generate*, which accepts a board position *brd* and returns a reference to a list of nodes containing the board positions that can be obtained from *brd*. This list is linked together by the *next* field. We leave the coding of *generate* as an exercise for the reader.

```
public void expand(Node p, int level) {
   Node q = null;

   if (level < lookLevel) {
     // p is not at the maximum level
     q = generate(p.board);
     p.son = q;
     while (q != null) {
           // traverse the list of nodes
           if (p.turn == 1)
                 q.turn = -1;
           else
                 q.turn = 1;
           q.son = null;
           expand(q, level+1);
           q = q.next;
     } // end while
   } // end if
} // end expand
```

Once the game tree has been created, *bestBranch* evaluates the nodes of the tree. When a pointer to a leaf is passed to *bestBranch*, it calls a function, *evaluate*, that statically evaluates the board position of the leaf for the player whose move we are determining. The coding of *evaluate* is left as an exercise. When a pointer to a nonleaf is passed to *bestBranch*, the routine calls itself recursively on each of its sons, and then assigns the maximum of its sons' values to the nonleaf if it is a *plus* node, and the minimum if it is a *minus* node. *bestBranch* also keeps track of which son yielded this minimum or maximum value.

If *p.turn* is -1, then the node pointed to by *p* is a minus node and is to be assigned the minimum of the values assigned to its sons. If, however, *p.turn* is $+1$, the node pointed to by *p* is a *plus* node and its value should be the maximum of the values assigned to the sons of the node. If *min(x,y)* is the minimum of *x* and *y*, and *max(x,y)* is their maximum, then $min(x, y) = -max(-x, -y)$ (you are invited to prove this as a trivial exercise). Thus, the correct maximum or minimum can be found as follows: in the case of a *plus* node, compute the maximum; in the case of a *minus* node, compute the maximum of the negatives of the values, and then reverse the sign of the result. These ideas are incorporated into *bestBranch*. The results *best* and *value*[0] are, respectively, a reference to the son of the tree's root that maximizes its value and the value of the son that has now been assigned to the root.

```java
public Node bestBranch(Node tree, char player, int[] value) {
    Node best, p=null, best2=null;
    int[] val = new int[1];

    if (tree.son == null) {
        // p is a leaf
        value[0] = evaluate(tree.board, player);
        best = tree;
    }
    else {
        // the node is not a leaf, traverse the list of sons
        p = tree.son;
        best = bestBranch(p,player,value);
        best = p;
        if (tree.turn == -1)
            value[0] = -value[0];
        p = p.next;
        while (p!= null) {
            best2 = bestBranch(p,player,val);
            if (tree.turn == -1)
                val[0] = -val[0];
            if (val[0] > value[0]) {
                value[0] = val[0];
                best = p;
            } // end if
            p = p.next;
        } // end while
        if (tree.turn == -1)
            value[0] = -value[0];
    } // end else
    return best;
} // end bestBranch
```

EXERCISES

5.6.1 Examine the methods in this section and determine whether all the parameters are actually necessary. How would you revise the parameter lists?

5.6.2 Write the Java methods *generate* and *evaluate* as described in the text.

5.6.3 Rewrite the applications in this and the preceding section under the implementation in which each tree node includes a member *father* containing a reference to its father. Under which implementation are they more efficient?

5.6.4 Write nonrecursive versions of the methods *expand* and *bestBranch* given in the text.

5.6.5 Modify the method *bestBranch* in the text so that the nodes of the tree are freed after they are no longer needed.

5.6.6 Combine the processes of building the game tree and evaluating its nodes into a single process so that the entire game tree need not exist at any one time and nodes are freed when no longer necessary.

5.6.7 Modify the application in the previous exercise so that, if the evaluation of a *minus* node is greater than the minimum of the values of its father's older brothers, the program does not expand that *minus* node's younger brothers, and if the evaluation of a *plus* node is less than the maximum of the values of its father's older brothers, then the program does not to expand that *plus* node's younger brothers. This method is called the **alpha-beta minimax** method. Explain why it is correct.

5.6.8 The game of **kalah** is played as follows: Two players have seven holes each, six of which are called **pits** and the seventh a **kalah**. These are arranged according to the following diagram:

Player 1
K P P P P P P
 P P P P P P K
Player 2

Initially there are six stones in each pit and no stones in either kalah, so that the opening position looks like this:

0 6 6 6 6 6 6
 6 6 6 6 6 6 0

The players alternate turns, each turn consisting of one or more moves. To make a move, a player chooses one of his nonempty pits, removes the stones from it, and distributes them counterclockwise into the pits and into his own kalah (the opponent's kalah is skipped), one stone per hole, until there are no stones remaining. For example, if player 1 moves first, a possible opening move might result in the following board position:

1 7 7 7 7 7 0
 6 6 6 6 6 6 0

A player whose last stone lands in his own kalah gets another move. If the last stone lands in one of his own pits which is empty, that stone and the stones in the opponent's pit directly opposite are removed and placed in the player's kalah. The game ends when these are no more stones in either player's pits. At this point, all of the stones in the opponent's pits are placed in the opponent's kalah and the game ends. The player with the most stones in his kalah is the winner.

Write an applet that accepts a kalah board position and an indication of whose turn it is and produces that player's best move.

5.6.9   How would you modify the ideas in the tic-tac-toe program to compute the best move in a game that contains an element of chance, such as backgammon?

5.6.10   Why have computers been programmed to play perfect tic-tac-toe but not perfect chess or checkers?

5.6.11   The game of *nim* is played as follows: A number of sticks are placed in a pile. Two players alternate in removing one or two sticks at a time from the pile. The player who removes the last stick is the loser. Write a Java method to determine the best move in nim.

C H A P T E R 6

Sorting

Sorting and searching are among the most typical functions of programming systems. In the first section of this chapter we discuss some of the considerations involved in sorting. In the remainder of the chapter we discuss some of the more common sorting techniques and the advantages or disadvantages of one technique over another. In the next chapter we discuss searching and some applications.

6.1   GENERAL BACKGROUND

The concept of an ordered set of elements has a major impact on our daily lives. Consider, for example, the process of finding a telephone number in a telephone directory. This process, called a *search*, is greatly simplified by the fact that the names in the directory are listed in alphabetical order. Imagine how much trouble you would have in locating a telephone number if the names were listed in the order in which the customers obtained their phone service from the telephone company. In such a case, the names might just as well be entered in random order. Sorting the entries in alphabetical rather than chronological order simplifies the process of searching. Or, imagine the case of someone searching for a book in a library. Since the books are shelved in a specific order (Library of Congress, Dewey System, etc.), each book is assigned a specific position relative to the others and can be retrieved in a reasonable amount of time (if it is there). Or, consider a set of numbers sorted sequentially in a computer's memory. As we shall see in the next chapter, it is usually easier to find an element of a set if the numbers are maintained in sorted order. In general, a set of items is kept sorted in order to either produce a report (i.e., to simplify manual retrieval of information, as in a telephone book or a library shelf) or to make machine access to data more efficient.

We now present some basic terminology. A *file* of size n is a sequence of n items $r[0], r[1], \ldots, r[n-1]$. Each item in the file is called a *record*. A key, $k[i]$, is associated with each record $r[i]$. The key is usually (but not always) a subfield of the entire record. The file is said to be *sorted on the key* if $i < j$ implies that $k[i]$ precedes $k[j]$ in some ordering on the keys. In the example of the telephone book, the file consists of all the entries in the book. Each entry is a record. The key upon which the file is sorted is the name field of the record. Each record also contains fields for an address and a telephone number. A *sort* is a process that rearranges the records in a file into a sequence that is sorted on some key.

A sort can be classified as *internal* if the records it is sorting are in main memory and as *external* if some of the records it is sorting are in auxiliary storage. We restrict our attention to internal sorts.

It is possible for two records in a file to have the same key. A sorting technique is called *stable* if for all records i and j such that $k[i]$ equals $k[j]$, if $r[i]$ precedes $r[j]$ in the original file, then $r[i]$ precedes $r[j]$ in the sorted file.

A sort takes place either on the records themselves or on an auxiliary table of pointers. For example, a file of five records is shown in Figure 6.1.1a. If the file is sorted in increasing order on the numeric key shown, then the resulting file is as shown in Figure 6.1.1b. In this case the actual records themselves have been sorted.

Suppose, however, that the amount of data stored in each of the records in the file in Figure 6.1.1a is so large that the overhead involved in moving the actual data is prohibitive. In this case, an auxiliary table of pointers may be used, so that the pointers are moved instead of the actual data, as shown in Figure 6.1.2. (This is called *sorting by*

	Key	Other fields
Record 1	4	*DDD*
Record 2	2	*BBB*
Record 3	1	*AAA*
Record 4	5	*EEE*
Record 5	3	*CCC*

File
(a) Original file.

1	*AAA*
2	*BBB*
3	*CCC*
4	*DDD*
5	*EEE*

File
(b) Sorted file.

FIGURE 6.1.1   Sorting actual records.

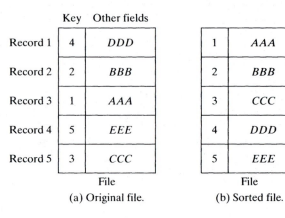

FIGURE 6.1.2   Sorting by using an auxiliary table of pointers.

address.) The table in the center is the file, and the table at the left is the initial table of pointers. The entry in position *j* in the table of pointers points to record *j*. The entries in the pointer table are adjusted during the sorting process so that the final table is as shown at the right. Originally, the first pointer was to the first entry in the file; upon completion, it is to the fourth entry in the table. Note that none of the original file entries are moved. In most of the programs in this chapter, we illustrate techniques for sorting actual records. The extension of these techniques to sorting by address is straightforward and will be left as an exercise for the reader. (Actually, for the sake of simplicity, we sort only the keys in the examples presented in this chapter; we leave it to the reader to modify the programs to sort full records.)

Because of the relationship between sorting and searching, the first question to ask in any application is whether or not a file should be sorted. Sometimes, there is less work involved in searching a set of elements for a file than in first sorting the entire set and then extracting the desired element. On the other hand, if frequent use of the file is required for the purpose of retrieving specific elements, then it might be more efficient to sort the file. This is because the overhead of successive searches may far exceed the overhead involved in sorting the file once and subsequently retrieving elements from the sorted file. Thus it cannot be said that it is more efficient either to sort or not to sort. The programmer must make a decision based on individual circumstances. Once a decision to sort has been made, other decisions must be made, including what is to be sorted and what methods are to be used. There is no one sorting method that is universally superior to all others. The programmer must carefully examine the problem and the desired results before deciding these very important questions.

Efficiency Considerations

As we shall see in this chapter, there are a great number of methods which can be used to sort a file. The programmer must be aware of several interrelated and often conflicting efficiency considerations to make an intelligent choice as to which sorting method is most appropriate to a particular problem. Three of the most important of these considerations are: the length of time the programmer must spend in coding a particular sorting program, the amount of machine time necessary for running the program, and the amount of space necessary for the program.

If a file is small, sophisticated sorting techniques designed to minimize space and time requirements are usually worse or only marginally better in achieving efficiencies than simpler, generally less efficient methods. Similarly, if a particular sorting program is to be run only once, and there is sufficient machine time and space in which to run it, it would be ludicrous for a programmer to spend days investigating the best methods of obtaining the last ounce of efficiency. In such cases, the amount of time which must be spent by the programmer is properly the overriding consideration in determining which sorting method to use. However, a strong word of caution must be inserted. Programming time is never a valid excuse for using an incorrect program. A sort that is run only once may be able to afford the luxury of an inefficient technique, but it cannot afford an incorrect one. The presumably sorted data may be used in an application in which the assumption of ordered data is crucial.

However, a programmer must be able to recognize the fact that a particular sort is inefficient and be able to justify its use in a particular situation. Too often, programmers take the easy way out and code an inefficient sort which is then incorporated into a larger system in which the sort is a key component. The designers and planners of the system are then surprised at the inadequacy of their creation. In order to maximize their own efficiency, programmers must be familiar with a wide range of sorting techniques and be cognizant of the advantages and disadvantages of each, so that when the need for a sort arises they can supply the one that is most appropriate for the situation.

This brings us to the other two efficiency considerations: time and space. As in most other computer applications, the programmer must often optimize one of these at the expense of the other. In considering the time necessary to sort a file of size n, we do not concern ourselves with actual time units, because these will vary from one machine to another, from one program to another, and from one set of data to another. Rather, we are interested in the corresponding change in the amount of time required to sort a file induced by a change in the file size n. Let us see if we can make this concept more precise. We say that y is ***proportional*** to x if the relation between y and x is such that multiplying x by a constant multiplies y by the same constant. Thus if y is proportional to x, doubling x will double y, and multiplying x by 10 will multiply y by 10. Similarly, if y is proportional to x^2, then doubling x will multiply y by 4, and multiplying x by 10 will multiply y by 100.

Often we do not measure the time efficiency of a sort by the number of time units required but by the number of critical operations performed. Examples of such critical operations are key comparisons (i.e., comparisons of the keys of two records in the file to determine which is greater), movements of records or pointers to records, and interchanges of two records. The critical operations chosen are those that take the most time. For example, a key comparison may be a complex operation, especially if the keys are long or the ordering among them is nontrivial. Thus a key comparison requires much more time than, say, a simple increment of an index variable in a *for* loop. Also, the number of simple operations required is usually proportional to the number of key comparisons. For this reason, the number of key comparisons is a useful measure of a sort's time efficiency.

There are two ways to determine the time requirements of a sort, neither of which yields results that are applicable to all cases. One method is to go through a sometimes intricate and involved mathematical analysis of various cases (e.g., best case, worst case, average case). The result of this analysis is often a formula giving the average time (or number of operations) required for a particular sort as a method of the file size n. (Actually, the time requirements of a sort depend on factors other than file size, but we are concerned here only with dependence on file size.) Suppose that such a mathematical analysis on a particular sorting program results in the conclusion that the program takes $0.01n^2 + 10n$ time units to execute. The first and fourth columns in Figure 6.1.3 show the time needed by the sort for various values of n. You will notice that for small values of n, the quantity $10n$ (third column in Figure 6.1.3) overwhelms the quantity $0.01n^2$ (second column). This is because the difference between n^2 and n is small for small values of n and is more than compensated for by the difference between 10 and 0.01. Thus, for small values of n, an increase in n by a factor of 2 (e.g., from 50 to 100) increases the time needed for sorting by approximately that

n	$a = 0.01\,n^2$	$b = 10n$	$a + b$	$(a + b)\dfrac{(a + b)}{n^2}$
10	1	100	101	1.01
50	25	500	525	0.21
100	100	1,000	1,100	0.11
500	2,500	5,000	7,500	0.03
1,000	10,000	10,000	20,000	0.02
5,000	250,000	50,000	300,000	0.01
10,000	1,000,000	100,000	1,100,000	0.01
50,000	25,000,000	500,000	25,500,000	0.01
100,000	100,000,000	1,000,000	101,000,000	0.01
500,000	2,500,000,000	5,000,000	2,505,000,000	0.01

FIGURE 6.1.3

same factor of 2 (from 525 to 1100). Similarly, an increase in n by a factor of 5 (e.g., from 10 to 50) increases the sorting time by approximately 5 (from 101 to 525).

However, as n becomes larger, the difference between n^2 and n increases so quickly that it eventually more than compensates for the difference between 10 and 0.01. Thus, when n equals 1000, the two terms contribute equally to the amount of time needed by the program. As n becomes even larger, the term $0.01n^2$ overwhelms the term $10n$, and the contribution of the term $10n$ becomes almost insignificant. Thus, for large values of n, an increase in n by a factor of 2 (e.g., from 50,000 to 100,000) results in an increase in sorting time of approximately 4 (from 25.5 million to 101 million), and an increase in n by a factor of 5 (e.g., from 10,000 to 50,000) increases the sorting time by approximately a factor of 25 (from 1.1 million to 25.5 million). Indeed, as n becomes larger and larger, the sorting time becomes more closely proportional to n^2, as is clearly illustrated by the last column in Figure 6.1.3. Thus, for large n the time required by the sort is almost proportional to n^2. Of course, for small values of n, the sort may exhibit drastically different behavior (as in Figure 6.1.3), a situation which must be taken into account in analyzing its efficiency.

O Notation

To capture the concept of one function becoming proportional to another as it grows, we introduce some terminology and a new notation. In the previous example, the function $0.01n^2 + 10n$ is said to be "on the order of" the function n^2 because, as n becomes large, it becomes more nearly proportional to n^2.

To be precise, given two functions $f(n)$ and $g(n)$, we say that $f(n)$ is **on the order of** $g(n)$ or that $f(n)$ is $O(g(n))$ if there exist positive integers a and b such that $f(n) \leq a * g(n)$ for all $n \geq b$). For example, if $f(n) = n^2 + 100n$, and $g(n) = n^2$, $f(n)$ is $O(g(n))$, since $n^2 + 100n$ is less than or equal to $2n^2$ for all n greater than or equal to 100. In this case, a equals 2 and b equals 100. This same $f(n)$ is also $O(n^3)$, since $n^2 + 100n$ is less than or equal to $2n^3$ for all n greater than or equal to 8. Given a function $f(n)$, there may be many functions $g(n)$ such that $f(n)$ is $O(g(n))$.

If $f(n)$ is $O(g(n))$, then "eventually" (i.e., for $n \geq b$) $f(n)$ becomes permanently smaller or equal to some multiple of $g(n)$. In a sense, we are saying that $f(n)$ is bounded by $g(n)$ from above, or that $f(n)$ is a "smaller" function than $g(n)$. Another formal way of saying this is that $f(n)$ is **asymptotically bounded** by $g(n)$. Yet another interpretation is that $f(n)$ grows more slowly than $g(n)$, since, proportionately (i.e., up to a factor of a), $g(n)$ eventually becomes larger.

It is easy to show that if $f(n)$ is $O(g(n))$ and $g(n)$ is $O(h(n))$, then $f(n)$ is $O(h(n))$. For example, $n^2 + 100n$ is $O(n^2)$ and n^2 is $O(n^3)$ (to see this, set a and b both equal to 1); consequently $n^2 + 100n$ is $O(n^3)$. This is called the **transitive property**.

Note that if $f(n)$ is a constant function [i.e., $f(n) = c$ for all n], then $f(n)$ is $O(1)$, since, setting a to c and b to 1, we have $c \leq c * 1$ for all $n \geq 1$. (In fact, the value of b or n is irrelevant, since a constant function's value is independent of n.)

It is also easy to show that the function $c * n$ is $O(n^k)$ for any constants c and k. To see this, simply note that $c * n$ is less than or equal to $c * n^k$ for any $n \geq 1$ (i.e., set $a = c$ and $b = 1$). It is also obvious that n^k is $O(n^{k+j})$ for any $j \geq 0$ (use $a = 1$, $b = 1$). We can also show that if $f(n)$ and $g(n)$ are both $O(h(n))$, then the new function $f(n) + g(n)$ is also $O(h(n))$. All of these facts together can be used to show that if $f(n)$ is any polynomial whose leading power is k [i.e., $f(n) = c_1 * n^k + c_2 * n^{k-1} + \ldots +c_k * n + c_{k+1}]$, $f(n)$ is $O(n^k)$. Indeed, $f(n)$ is $O(n^{k+j})$ for any $j \geq 0$.

Although a function may be asymptotically bounded by many other functions [e.g., $10n^2 + 37n + 153$ is $O(n^2)$, $O(10n^2)$, $O(37n^2 + 10n)$, and $O(0.05n^3)$], we usually look for an asymptotic bound that is a single term with a leading coefficient of 1 and is as "close a fit" as possible. Thus we would say that $10n^2 + 37n + 153$ is $O(n^2)$, although it is also asymptotically bounded by many other functions. Ideally, we would like to find a function $g(n)$ such that $f(n)$ is $O(g(n))$ and $g(n)$ is $O(f(n))$. If $f(n)$ is a constant or a polynomial, this can always be done by using its highest term with a coefficient of 1. For more complex functions, however, it is not always possible to find such a tight fit.

An important function in the study of algorithm efficiency is the logarithm function. Recall that $log_m n$ is the value x such that m^x equals n. m is called the **base** of the logarithm. Consider the functions $log_m n$ and $log_k n$. Let xm be $log_m n$ and xk be $log_k n$. Then

$$m^{xm} = n \text{ and } k^{xk} = n$$

so that

$$m^{xm} = k^{xk}$$

Taking log_m of both sides,

$$xm = \log_m(k^{xk})$$

Now it can easily be shown than $log_z(x^y)$ equals $y * log_z x$ for any x, y, and z, so that the last equation can be rewritten as (recall that $xm = log_m n$)

$$\log_m n = xk * \log_m k$$

or as (recall that $xk = log_k n$)

$$\log_m n = (\log_m k) * \log_k n$$

Thus $log_m n$ and $log_k n$ are constant multiples of each other.

It is easy to show that if $f(n) = c * g(n)$, where c is a constant, then $f(n)$ is $O(g(n))$ [indeed, we have already shown that this is true for the method $f(n) = n^k$].

Thus $\log_m n$ is $O(\log_k n)$ and $\log_k n$ is $O(\log_k$ n) for any m and k. Since each logarithm function is on the order of any other, we usually omit the base when speaking of methods of logarithmic order and say that all such methods are $O(\log n)$.

The following facts establish an order hierarchy of methods:

c is $O(1)$ for any constant c.

c is $O(\log n)$, but $\log n$ is not $O(1)$.

$c * \log_k n$ is $O(\log n)$ for any constants c, k.

$c * \log_k n$ is $O(n)$, but n is not $O(\log n)$.

$c * n^k$ is $O(n^k)$ for any constants c, k.

$c * n^k$ is $O(n^{k+j})$, but n^{k+j} is not $O(n^k)$.

$c * n * \log_k n$ is $O(n \log n)$ for any constants c, k.

$c * n * \log_k n$ is $O(n^2)$, but n^2 is not $O(n \log n)$.

$c * n^j * \log_k n$ is $O(n^j \log n)$ for any constants c, j, k.

$c * n^j * \log_k n$ is $O(n^{j+1})$, but n^{j+1} is not $O(n^j \log n)$.

$c * n^j * (\log_k n)^l$ is $O(n^j (\log_k n)^l)$ for any constants c, j, k, l.

$c * n^j * (\log_k n)^l$ is $O(n^{j+1})$, but n^{j+1} is not $(n^j (\log n)^l)$.

$c * n^j * (\log_k n)^l$ is $O(n^j (\log n)^{l+1})$, but $n^j (\log_k n)^{j+1}$ is not $O(n^j (\log n)^l)$.

$c * n^k$ is $O(d^n)$, but d^n is not $O(n^k)$ for any constants c and k, and $d > 1$.

The hierarchy of functions established by these facts, with each method of lower order than the next, is $c, \log n, (\log n)^k, n, n(\log n)^k, n^k, n^k(\log n)^l, n^{k+1}, d^n$.

Functions that are $O(n^k)$ for some k are said to be of **polynomial** order, while functions that are $O(d^n)$ for some $d > 1$ but not $O(n^k)$ for any k are said to be of **exponential order**.

The distinction between polynomial-order functions and exponential-order functions is extremely important. Even a small exponential-order function, such as 2^n, grows far larger than any polynomial-order function, such as n^k regardless of the size of k. As an illustration of the rapidity with which exponential-order functions grow, consider that 2^{10} equals 1024 but 2^{100} (i.e., 1024^{10}) is greater than the number formed by a 1 followed by thirty zeros. The smallest k for which 10^k exceeds 2^{10} is 4, but the smallest k for which 100^k exceeds 2^{100} is 16. As n becomes larger, larger values of k are needed for n to keep up with 2^n. For any single k, 2^n eventually becomes permanently larger than n^k.

Because of the incredible rate of growth of exponential-order functions, problems that require exponential-time algorithms for solution are considered to be **intractable** on current computing equipment. That is, such problems cannot be practically solved except in the simplest cases.

Efficiency of Sorting

Using the concept of the order of a sort, we can compare various sorting techniques and classify them, in general terms, as "good" or "bad". One might hope to discover the "optimal" sort which is $O(n)$ regardless of the contents or order of the input. Unfortunately, however, it can be shown that no such generally useful sort exists. Most of the classical sorts we shall consider have time requirements that range from $O(n \log n)$ to

n	$n \log_{10} n$	n^2
1×10^1	1.0×10^1	1.0×10^2
5×10^1	8.5×10^1	2.5×10^3
1×10^2	2.0×10^2	1.0×10^4
5×10^2	1.3×10^3	2.5×10^5
1×10^3	3.0×10^3	1.0×10^6
5×10^3	1.8×10^4	2.5×10^7
1×10^4	4.0×10^4	1.0×10^8
5×10^4	2.3×10^5	2.5×10^9
1×10^5	5.0×10^5	1.0×10^{10}
5×10^5	2.8×10^6	2.5×10^{11}
1×10^6	6.0×10^6	1.0×10^{12}
5×10^6	3.3×10^7	2.5×10^{13}
1×10^7	7.0×10^7	1.0×10^{14}

FIGURE 6.1.4   Comparison of $n \log n$ and n^2 for various values of n.

$O(n^2)$. In the former, multiplying the file size by 100 will multiply the sorting time by less than 200; in the latter, multiplying the file size by 100 multiplies the sorting time by a factor of 10,000. Figure 6.1.4 shows the comparison of $n \log n$ with n^2 for a range of values of n. It can be seen from the figure that for large n, as n increases, n^2 increases at a much more rapid rate than $n \log n$. However, a sort should not be selected simply because it is $O(n \log n)$. The relation of the file size n and the other terms comprising the actual sorting time must be known. Terms that play an insignificant role for large values of n may play a very dominant role for small values of n. All of these issues must be considered before an intelligent sort selection can be made.

A second method of determining the time requirements of a sorting technique is to actually run the program and measure its efficiency (either by measuring absolute time units or by the number of operations performed). In order for such results to be used in measuring the efficiency of a sort, the test must be run on "many" sample files. Even when such statistics have been gathered, the application of the sort to a specific file may not yield results that follow the general pattern. Peculiar attributes of the file in question may make the sorting speed deviate significantly. In the sorts in the subsequent sections, we shall give an intuitive explanation as to why a particular sort is classified as $O(n^2)$ or $O(n \log n)$; we leave mathematical analysis and sophisticated testing of empirical data as exercises for the ambitious reader.

In most cases, the time needed by a sort depends upon the original sequence of the data. For some sorts, input data that is almost in sorted order can be completely sorted in time $O(n)$, while input data that is in reverse order needs time which is $O(n^2)$. For other sorts, the time required is $O(n \log n)$ regardless of the original order of the data. Thus if we have some knowledge about the original sequence of the data, we can make a more intelligent decision as to which sorting method to select. On the other hand, if we have no such knowledge, we may wish to select a sort based either on the worst possible case or on the "average" case. In any event, the only general comment that can be made about sorting techniques is that there is no "best" general sorting technique. The choice of a sort must, of necessity, depend on the specific circumstances.

Once a sorting technique has been selected, the programmer should make the program as efficient as possible. In many programming applications it is necessary to sacrifice efficiency for the sake of clarity. With sorting, the situation is usually the opposite. Once a sorting program has been written and tested, the programmer's chief goal is to improve its speed, even if it becomes less readable. The reason for this is that a sort may account for the major part of a program's efficiency, so that any improvement in sorting time significantly affects overall efficiency. Another reason is that a sort is often used quite frequently, so that a small improvement in its execution speed saves a great deal of computer time. It is usually a good idea to remove method calls, especially from inner loops, and replace them with the code of the method in line, since the call-return mechanism of a language can be prohibitively expensive in terms of time. Also, a method call may involve the assignment of storage to local variables, an activity that sometimes requires a call to the operating system. In many programs we do not do this so as not to obfuscate the intent of the program with huge blocks of code.

Space constraints are usually less important than time considerations. One reason is that the amount of space needed for most sorting programs is closer to $O(n)$ than to $O(n^2)$. A second reason is that if more space is required, it can almost always be found in auxiliary storage. An ideal sort is an ***in-place sort*** whose additional space requirements are $O(1)$. That is, an in-place sort manipulates the elements to be sorted within the array or list space that contained the original unsorted input. The additional space that is required is in the form of a constant number of locations (e.g., declared individual program variables) regardless of the size of the set to be sorted.

The expected relationship between time and space usually holds for sorting algorithms: programs that require less time usually require more space, and vice versa. However, there are clever algorithms that utilize both minimum time and minimum space; that is, they are $O(n \log n)$ in-place sorts. These may, however, require more programmer time to develop and verify. They also have higher constants of proportionality than many sorts that use more space or have higher time-orders and so require more time to sort small sets.

In the remaining sections we investigate some of the more popular sorting techniques and indicate some of their advantages and disadvantages.

EXERCISES

6.1.1   Choose any sorting technique with which you are familiar.
   a. Write a program for the sort.
   b. Is the sort stable?
   c. Determine the time requirements of the sort as a method of the file size, both mathematically and empirically.
   d. What is the order of the sort?
   e. At what file size does the most dominant term begin to overshadow the others?

6.1.2   Show that the method $(\log_m n)^k$ is $O(n)$ for all m and k, but that n is not $O((\log n)^k)$ for any k.

6.1.3   Suppose a time requirement is given by the formula $a * n^2 + b * n * \log_2 n$, where a and b are constants. Answer the following questions by both proving your results mathematically and writing a program to validate the results empirically.

    a. For what values of n (expressed in terms of a and b) does the first term dominate the second?

    b. For what value of n (expressed in terms of a and b) are the two terms equal?

    c. For what values of n (expressed in terms of a and b) does the second term dominate the first?

6.1.4   Show that any process that sorts a file can be extended to find all the duplicates in the file.

6.1.5   A ***sort decision tree*** is a binary tree that represents a sorting method based on comparisons. Figure 6.1.5 illustrates such a decision tree for a file of three elements. Each nonleaf of such a tree represents a comparison between two elements. Each leaf represents a completely sorted file. A left branch from a nonleaf indicates that the first key was smaller than the second; a right branch indicates that it was larger. (We assume that all the elements in the file have distinct keys.) For example, the tree in Figure 6.1.5 represents a sort on three elements $x[0], x[1], x[2]$ that proceeds as follows:

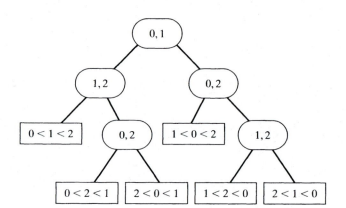

FIGURE 6.1.5   Decision tree for a file of three elements.

Compare $x[0]$ to $x[1]$. If $x[0] < x[1]$, then compare $x[1]$ with $x[2]$, and if $x[1] < x[2]$, then the sorted order of the file is $x[0], x[1], x[2]$; otherwise if $x[0] < x[2]$, the sorted order is $x[0], x[2], x[1]$, and if $x[0] > x[2]$, then the sorted order is $x[2], x[0], x[1]$. If $x[0] > x[1]$, then proceed in a similar fashion down the right subtree.

    a. Show that a sort decision tree that never makes a redundant comparison (i.e., never compares $x[i]$ and $x[j]$ if the relationship between $x[i]$ and $x[j]$ is known) has $n!$ leafs.

    b. Show that the depth of such a decision tree is at least $\log_2(n!)$.

    c. Show that $n! \geq (n/2)^{n/2}$ so that the depth of such a tree is $O(n \log n)$.

    d. Explain why this proves that any sorting method that uses comparisons on a file of size n must make at least $O(n \log n)$ comparisons.

6.1.6   Given a sort decision tree for a file, as in the previous exercise, show that if the file contains some equal elements, the result of applying the tree to the file (where either a left or right branch is taken whenever two elements are equal) is a sorted file.

6.1.7   Extend the concept of the binary decision tree in the previous exercises to a ternary tree that includes the possibility of equality. How many comparisons are necessary to determine which elements of the file are equal, in addition to the order of the distinct elements of the file?

6.1.8   If k is the smallest integer greater than or equal to $n + \log_2 n - 2$, show that k comparisons are necessary and sufficient to find the largest and second-largest elements of a set of n distinct elements.

6.1.9   How many comparisons are necessary to find the largest and smallest of a set of n distinct elements?

6.1.10   Show that the function $f(n)$ defined by

$$f(1) = 1$$
$$f(n) = f(n - 1) + 1/n \text{ for } n > 1$$

is $O(\log n)$.

6.2   EXCHANGE SORTS

Bubble Sort

The first sort we present is probably the most widely known among beginning students of programming: the ***bubble sort***. One of the characteristics of this sort is that it is easy to understand and program. Yet, of all the sorts we shall consider, it is probably the least efficient.

In each of the subsequent examples, x is an array of integers of which the first n are to be sorted so that $x[i] \le x[j]$ for $0 \le i < j < n$. This simple format can be straightforwardly extended to one which is used in sorting n records, each with a subfield key k.

The basic idea underlying the bubble sort is to pass through the file sequentially several times. Each pass consists of comparing each element in the file with its successor ($x[i]$ with $x[i + 1]$) and interchanging the two elements if they are not in proper order. Consider the following file:

$$25 \quad 57 \quad 48 \quad 37 \quad 12 \quad 92 \quad 86 \quad 33$$

The following comparisons are made on the first pass:

$x[0]$ with $x[1]$ (25 with 57) No interchange
$x[1]$ with $x[2]$ (57 with 48) Interchange
$x[2]$ with $x[3]$ (57 with 37) Interchange
$x[3]$ with $x[4]$ (57 with 12) Interchange
$x[4]$ with $x[5]$ (57 with 92) No interchange
$x[5]$ with $x[6]$ (92 with 86) Interchange
$x[6]$ with $x[7]$ (92 with 33) Interchange

Thus, after the first pass, the file is in the order

$$25 \quad 48 \quad 37 \quad 12 \quad 57 \quad 86 \quad 33 \quad 92$$

Note that after this first pass, the largest element (in this case 92) is in its proper position within the array. In general, $x[n - i]$ will be in its proper position after iteration i. The method is called the bubble sort because each number slowly "bubbles" up to its proper position. After the second pass the file is

$$25 \quad 37 \quad 12 \quad 48 \quad 57 \quad 33 \quad 86 \quad 92$$

Note that 86 has now found its way to the second-highest position. Since each iteration places a new element into its proper position, a file of n elements requires no more than $n - 1$ iterations.

The complete set of iterations is the following:

Iteration 0 (original file)	25 57 48 37 12 92 86 33
Iteration 1	25 48 37 12 57 86 33 92
Iteration 2	25 37 12 48 57 33 86 92
Iteration 3	25 12 37 48 33 57 86 92
Iteration 4	12 25 37 33 48 57 86 92
Iteration 5	12 25 33 37 48 57 86 92
Iteration 6	12 25 33 37 48 57 86 92
Iteration 7	12 25 33 37 48 57 86 92

On the basis of the above discussion we could proceed to code the bubble sort. However, there are some obvious improvements to the method. First, since all the elements in positions greater than or equal to $n - i$ are already in proper position after iteration i, they need not be considered in succeeding iterations. Thus, on the first pass $n - 1$ comparisons are made, on the second pass $n - 2$ comparisons, and on the $(n - 1)^{\text{th}}$ pass only one comparison is made (between $x[0]$ and $x[1]$). Therefore, the process speeds up as it proceeds through successive passes.

We have shown that $n - 1$ passes are sufficient to sort a file of size n. However, in the above sample file of eight elements, the file was sorted after five iterations, making the last two iterations unnecessary. In order to eliminate unnecessary passes, we must be able to detect the fact that the file is already sorted. But this is a simple task, since in a sorted file, no interchanges are made on any pass. By keeping a record of whether or not any interchanges are made in a given pass, it can be determined whether any further passes are necessary. Under this method, if the file can be sorted in fewer than $n - 1$ passes, then the final pass makes no interchanges.

Using these improvements, we present a method *bubble* that accepts a variable x, which is the array of numbers to be sorted. (Often it is desirable to sort only the first n elements of an array. In that case, n, which is an integer representing the number of elements to be sorted, is also passed to the method. In the sorting methods given below, *x.length* must then be replaced by n.)

```
public static void bubble(int x[ ]) {
    int j, pass, hold;
    boolean switched = true;
    for (pass = 0; pass < x.length-1 && switched == true; pass++) {
        switched = false;
        for (j=0; j < x.length-pass-1; j++)
```

```
            if (x[j] > x[j+1]) {
                    switched = true;
                    hold = x[j];
                    x[j] = x[j+1];
                    x[j+1] = hold;
            }
    }
} // end bubble
```

What can be said about the efficiency of the bubble sort? In the case of a sort that does not include the two improvements outlined above, the analysis is simple. There are $n - 1$ passes and $n - 1$ comparisons on each pass. Thus the total number of comparisons is $(n - 1) * (n - 1) = n^2 - 2n + 1$, which is $O(n^2)$. Of course, the number of interchanges depends on the original order of the file. However, the number of interchanges cannot be greater than the number of comparisons. It is likely that it is the number of interchanges rather than the number of comparisons that takes up the most time in the program's execution.

Let us see how the improvements that we introduced affect the speed of the bubble sort. The number of comparisons on iteration i is $n - i$. Thus, if there are k iterations, the total number of comparisons is $(n - 1) + (n - 2) + (n - 3) + \ldots + (n - k)$, which equals $(2kn - k^2 - k)/2$. It can be shown that the average number of iterations, k, is $O(n)$, so that the entire formula is still $O(n^2)$, although the constant multiplier is smaller than before. However, there is additional overhead involved in testing and initializing the variable *switched* (once per pass) and setting it to **true** (once for every interchange).

The only redeeming features of the bubble sort are that it requires little additional space (one additional record to hold the temporary value for interchanging and several simple integer variables) and that it is $O(n)$ in the case that the file is completely sorted (or almost completely sorted). This follows from the observation that only one pass of $n - 1$ comparisons (and no interchanges) is necessary to establish that a sorted file is sorted.

There are some other ways to improve the bubble sort. One of these is to observe that the number of passes necessary to sort the file is the largest distance by which a number must move "down" in the array. In our example, for instance, 33, which starts at position 7 in the array, ultimately finds its way to position 2 after five iterations. The bubble sort can be speeded up by having successive passes go in opposite directions, so that the small elements move quickly to the front of the file in the same way that the large ones move to the rear. This reduces the required number of passes. This version is left as an exercise.

Quicksort

The next sort we consider is the **partition exchange sort** (or **quicksort**). Let x be an array, and n the number of elements in the array to be sorted. Choose an element a from a specific position within the array (e.g. a can be chosen as the first element, so that $a = x[0]$). Suppose the elements of x are partitioned so that a is placed in position j and the following conditions hold:

1. Each of the elements in positions 0 through $j - 1$ is less than or equal to a.
2. Each of the elements in positions $j + 1$ through $n - 1$ is greater than or equal to a.

Note that if these two conditions hold for a particular a and j, then a is the jth smallest element of x, so that a remains in position j when the array is completely sorted. (You are asked to prove this fact as an exercise.) If the above process is repeated with the subarrays $x[0]$ through $x[j-1]$ and $x[j+1]$ through $x[n-1]$ and any subarrays created by the process in successive iterations, the final result is a sorted file.

Let us illustrate the quicksort with an example. If an initial array is given as

$$25 \quad 57 \quad 48 \quad 37 \quad 12 \quad 92 \quad 86 \quad 33$$

and the first element (25) is placed in its proper position, then the resulting array is

$$12 \quad 25 \quad 57 \quad 48 \quad 37 \quad 92 \quad 86 \quad 33$$

At this point, 25 is in its proper position in the array ($x[1]$), each element below that position (12) is less than or equal to 25, and each element above that position (57, 48, 37, 92, 86, and 33) is greater than or equal to 25. Since 25 is in its final position, the original problem has been decomposed into the problem of sorting the two subarrays

$$(12) \quad \text{and} \quad (57 \quad 48 \quad 37 \quad 92 \quad 86 \quad 33)$$

Nothing need be done to sort the first of these subarrays; a file of one element is already sorted. To sort the second subarray, the process is repeated and the subarray is further subdivided. The entire array may now be viewed as:

$$12 \quad 25 \quad (57 \quad 48 \quad 37 \quad 92 \quad 86 \quad 33)$$

where parentheses enclose the subarrays that are yet to be be sorted. Repeating the process on the subarray $x[2]$ through $x[7]$ yields

$$12 \quad 25 \quad (48 \quad 37 \quad 33) \quad 57 \quad (92 \quad 86)$$

and further repetitions yield

$$12 \quad 25 \quad (37 \quad 33) \quad 48 \quad 57 \quad (92 \quad 86)$$
$$12 \quad 25 \quad (33) \quad 37 \quad 48 \quad 57 \quad (92 \quad 86)$$
$$12 \quad 25 \quad 33 \quad 37 \quad 48 \quad 57 \quad (92 \quad 86)$$
$$12 \quad 25 \quad 33 \quad 37 \quad 48 \quad 57 \quad (86) \quad 92$$
$$12 \quad 25 \quad 33 \quad 37 \quad 48 \quad 57 \quad 86 \quad 92$$

Note that the final array is sorted.

By this time you should have noticed that the quicksort may be defined most conveniently as a recursive method. We may outline an algorithm, $quick(lb,ub)$, to sort all the elements in an array x between positions lb and ub (lb is the lower bound, ub the upper bound) as follows:

```
if (lb >= ub)
        return;                 // no elements to be sorted
j = partition(x, lb, ub);       // partition the elements of the
                                // subarray such that one of the
                                // elements (possibly x[lb]) is now
                                // at x[j] and:
```

```
                                 //     1.  x[i]  ≤ x[j] for lb ≤ i < j
                                 //     2.  x[i]  ≥ x[j] for j < i ≤ ub
                                 // x[j] is now at its final position

quick(x, lb, j - 1);             // recursively sort the subarray
                                 // between positions lb and j - 1

quick(x, j + 1, ub);             // recursively sort the subarray
                                 // between positions j + 1 and ub
```

There are now two problems. We must produce a mechanism to implement *partition* and a method to implement the entire process nonrecursively.

The object of *partition* is to allow a specific element to find its proper position with respect to the others in the subarray. Note that the manner in which this partition is performed is irrelevant to the sorting method. All that is required by the sort is that the elements be partitioned properly. In the above example, the elements in each of the two subfiles remain in the same relative order as they appear in the original file. However, such a partition method is relatively inefficient to implement.

One way to effect a partition efficiently is the following: Let $a = x[lb]$ be the element whose final position is sought. (No appreciable efficiency is gained by selecting the first element of the subarray as the one that is inserted into its proper position; it merely makes some of the programs easier to code.) The pointers *up* and *down* are initialized, respectively, to the upper and lower bounds of the subarray. At any point during execution, each element in a position above *up* is greater than or equal to *a*, and each element in a position below *down* is less than or equal to *a*. The two pointers *up* and *down* are moved toward each other in the following fashion:

Step 1: Repeatedly increase the pointer *down* by one position until $x[down] > a$.
Step 2: Repeatedly decrease the pointer *up* by one position until $x[up] \leq a$.
Step 3: If $up > down$, interchange $x[down]$ with $x[up]$.

The process is repeated until the condition in step 3 fails ($up \leq down$), at which point $x[up]$ is interchanged with $x[lb]$ (which equals *a*), whose final position was sought, and *j* is set to *up*.

We illustrate this process on the sample file, showing the positions of *up* and *down* as they are adjusted. The direction of the scan is indicated by an arrow at the pointer being moved. Three asterisks on a line indicates that an interchange is being made.

$a = x[lb] = 25$

down →							*up*
25	57	48	37	12	92	86	33

	down						*up*
25	57	48	37	12	92	86	33

	down						←*up*
25	57	48	37	12	92	86	33

	down					←*up*	
25	57	48	37	12	92	86	33

	down				←*up*		
25	57	48	37	12	92	86	33

	down			*up*			
25	57	48	37	12	92	86	33

	down			*up*			
25	12	48	37	57	92	86	33	***

	down →			*up*			
25	12	48	37	57	92	86	33

		down		*up*			
25	12	48	37	57	92	86	33

		down		←*up*			
25	12	48	37	57	92	86	33

		down ←*up*					
25	12	48	37	57	92	86	33

	←*up, down*						
25	12	48	37	57	92	86	33

	up	*down*					
25	12	48	37	57	92	86	33

	up	*down*					
12	25	48	37	57	92	86	33	***

At this point 25 is in its proper position (position 1), every element to its left is less than or equal to 25, and every element to its right is greater than or equal to 25. We could now proceed to sort the two subarrays (12) and (48 37 57 92 86 33) by applying the same method.

This algorithm can be implemented by the following method.

```
public static int partition (int x[ ], int lb, int ub) {
    int down, up, a, temp;

    a = x[lb];                          // a is the element whose final
                                        // position is sought
    up = ub;
    down = lb;
    while (down < up) {
        while (x[down] <= a && down < ub)
            down++; // move up the array
        while (x[up] > a)
            up--;    //  move down the array
        if (down < up) {
            // interchange x[down] and x[up]
            temp = x[down];
            x[down] = x[up];
            x[up] = temp;
        }
    }
    x[lb] = x[up];
    x[up] = a;
    return up;
} // end partition
```

Note that if k equals $ub - lb + 1$, so that we are rearranging a subarray of size k, the routine uses k key comparisons (of $x[down]$ with a and $x[up]$ with a) to perform the partition.

The routine can be made slightly more efficient by eliminating some of the redundant tests. You are asked to do this as an exercise.

While the recursive quicksort algorithm is relatively clear in terms of what it accomplishes and how, it is desirable to avoid the overhead of routine calls in sorts and other programs in which execution efficiency is a significant consideration. The recursive calls to *quick* can easily be eliminated by using a stack, as in Section 3.4. Once *partition* has been executed, the current parameters to *quick* are no longer needed, except in computing the arguments to the two subsequent recursive calls. Thus, instead of stacking the current parameters upon each recursive call, we can compute and stack the new parameters for each of the two recursive calls. Under this approach, the stack at any point contains the lower and upper bounds of all the subarrays that must still be sorted. Furthermore, since the second recursive call immediately precedes the return to the calling program (as in the Towers of Hanoi problem), it may be eliminated entirely and replaced with a branch. Finally, since the order in which the two recursive calls are made does not affect the correctness of the algorithm, we elect in each case to stack the larger subarray and process the smaller subarray immediately. As we will explain shortly, this technique keeps the size of the stack to a minimum.

We may now code a method to implement the quicksort. As in the case of *bubble*, the parameter is the array *x* to be sorted. (Should it be desired to sort only the first *n* elements of the array, we may send *n* as an additional paramerter and replace *x.length*() with *n*.) The method *push* pushes an object of type *BoundType* (containing members *lb* and *ub*) onto the stack, *pop* pops them from the stack, and *empty* determines whether the stack is empty.

```
class BoundType {
    public int lb;
    public int ub;
}

public static void quicksort(int x[ ]) {
    int i, j;
    Stack bounds = new Stack();
    BoundType newbounds = new BoundType();
    newbounds.lb = 0;
    newbounds.ub = x.length - 1;
    bounds.push(newbounds);
    while (!bounds.empty()) {
            newbounds = (BoundType) bounds.pop();
            while (newbounds.ub > newbounds.lb) {
                    j = partition(x, newbounds.lb, newbounds.ub);
                    if (j - newbounds.lb > newbounds.ub - j) {
                            BoundType bnd1 = new BoundType();
                            bnd1.ub = j - 1;
                            bnd1.lb = newbounds.lb;
                            bounds.push(bnd1);
                            newbounds.lb = j + 1;
                    }
                    else {
                            BoundType bnd2 = new BoundType();
                            bnd2.ub = newbounds.ub;
                            bnd2.lb = j + 1;
                            bounds.push(bnd2);
                            newbounds.ub = j - 1;
                    }
            }
    }
} // end quicksort
```

The methods *partition*, *empty*, *pop*, and *push* should be inserted in line for maximum efficiency. Trace the action of *quicksort* on the sample file.

Note that we have chosen to use *x*[*lb*] as the element around which to partition each subfile because of programming convenience in the method *partition*, but any other element could have been chosen as well. The element around which a file is partitioned is called a *pivot*. It is not even necessary that the pivot be an element of the subfile; *partition* can be written with the header

```
j = partition(x, newbounds.lb, newbounds.ub, pivot);
```

to partition $x[lb]$ through $x[ub]$, so that all the elements between $x[lb]$ and $x[j - 1]$ are less than *pivot*, and all the elements between $x[j]$ and $x[ub]$ are greater than or equal to *pivot*. In that case, the element $x[j]$ is itself included in the second subfile (since it is not necessarily in its proper position), so the second recursive call to *quick* is $quick(x, j, ub)$ rather than $quick(x, j + 1, ub)$.

Several choices for the pivot value have been found to improve the efficiency of quicksort by guaranteeing more nearly balanced subfiles. The first technique uses the median of the first, last, and middle elements of the subfile to be sorted (i.e., the median of $x[lb]$, $x[ub]$, and $x[(lb + ub)/2]$) as the pivot value. This median-of-three value is closer to the median of the subfile being partitioned than $x[lb]$, and thus the two partitions of the subfile are more nearly equal in size. In this method, the pivot value is an element of the file, so that $quick(x, j + 1, ub)$ can be used as the second recursive call.

A second method, called **meansort**, utilizes $x[lb]$ or the median-of-three as pivot when partitioning the original file but adds code in *partition* to compute the means (averages) of the two subfiles being created. In subsequent partitions, the mean of each subfile, calculated when the subfile was created, is used as a pivot value. Again, this mean is closer to the median of the subfile than $x[lb]$ and results in more nearly balanced files. Since the mean is not necessarily an element of the file, $quick(x, j, ub)$ must be used as the second recursive call. The code to find the mean does not require any additional key comparisons but does add some extra overhead.

Another technique, called **Bsort**, uses the middle element of a subfile as the pivot. During partition, whenever the pointer *up* is decreased, $x[up]$ is interchanged with $x[up + 1]$ if $x[up] > x[up + 1]$. Whenever the pointer *down* is increased, $x[down]$ is interchanged with $x[down - 1]$ if $x[down] < x[down - 1]$. Whenever $x[up]$ and $x[down]$ are interchanged, $x[up]$ is interchanged with $x[up + 1]$ if $x[up] > x[up + 1]$, and $x[down]$ is interchanged with $x[down - 1]$ if $x[down] < x[down - 1]$. This guarantees that $x[up]$ is always the smallest element in the right subfile (from $x[up]$ to $x[ub]$), and that $x[down]$ is always the largest element in the left subfile (from $x[lb]$ to $x[down]$).

This allows two optimizations: If no interchanges between $x[up]$ and $x[up + 1]$ were required during the partition, then the right subfile is known to be sorted and need not be stacked, and if no interchanges between $x[down]$ and $x[down - 1]$ were required, then the left subfile is known to be sorted and need not be stacked. This is similar to the technique of keeping a flag in bubblesort that detects that no interchanges have taken place during an entire pass, so that no additional passes are necessary. Second, a subfile of size 2 is known to be sorted and need not be stacked. A subfile of size 3 can be directly sorted with just a single comparison and possible interchange (between the first two elements in a left subfile and between the last two in a right subfile). Both optimizations in Bsort reduce the number of subfiles that must be processed.

Efficiency of Quicksort

How efficient is quicksort? Assume that the file size n is a power of 2, say $n = 2^m$, so that $m = \log_2 n$. Assume also that the proper position for the pivot always turns out to be the exact middle of the subarray. In that case there will be approximately n comparisons (actually $n - 1$) on the first pass, after which the file is split into two subfiles each of size $n/2$ approximately. For each of these two files there are approximately $n/2$ comparisons, and a total of four files each of size $n/4$ are formed. Each of these files requires

$n/4$ comparisons, yielding a total of $n/8$ subfiles. After halving the subfiles m times, there are n files of size 1. Thus the total number of comparisons for the entire sort is approximately

$$n + 2 * (n/2) + 4 * (n/4) + 8 * (n/8) + \ldots + n * (n/n)$$

or

$$n + n + n + n + \ldots + n(m \text{ terms})$$

comparisons. There are m terms because the file is subdivided m times. Thus the total number of comparisons is $O(n * m)$ or $O(n \log n)$ (recall that $m = \log_2 n$). Thus, if the above properties describe the file, then the quicksort is $O(n \log n)$, which is relatively efficient.

For the unmodified quicksort in which $x[lb]$ is used as the pivot value, this analysis assumes that the original array and all the resulting subarrays are unsorted, so that the pivot value $x[lb]$ always finds its proper position at the middle of the subarray. Suppose the above conditions do not hold and the original array is sorted (or almost sorted). If, for example, $x[lb]$ is in its correct position, then the original file is split into subfiles of sizes 0 and $n - 1$. If this process continues, then a total of $n - 1$ subfiles are sorted, the first of size n, the second of size $n - 1$, the third of size $n - 2$, and so on. Assuming k comparisons to rearrange a file of size k, the total number of comparisons to sort the entire file is

$$n + (n - 1) + (n - 2) + \ldots + 2$$

which is $O(n^2)$. Similarly, if the original file is sorted in descending order, the final position of $x[lb]$ is ub, and the file is again split into two subfiles which are heavily unbalanced (sizes $n - 1$ and 0). Thus the unmodified quicksort has the seemingly absurd property that it works best for files which are "completely unsorted" and worst for files which are completely sorted. The situation is precisely the opposite for the bubble sort, which works best for sorted files and worst for unsorted files.

It is possible to speed up quicksort for sorted files by choosing a ***random*** element of each subfile as the pivot value. If a file is known to be nearly sorted, this might be a good strategy (although choosing the middle element as a pivot would be even better). However, if nothing is known about the file, such a strategy does not improve the worst case behavior, since it is possible (although improbable) that the random element chosen each time might consistently be the smallest element of each subfile. As a practical matter, sorted files are more common than a good random number generator happening to repeatedly choose the smallest element.

The analysis for the case where the file size is not an integral power of 2 is similar but slightly more complex; the results, however, remain the same. It can be shown, though, that on average (over all files of size n), the quicksort makes approximately $1.386n \log_2 n$ comparisons even in its unmodified version. In practical situations, quicksort is often the fastest available because of its low overhead and its average $O(n \log n)$ behavior.

If the median-of-three technique is used, quicksort can be $O(n \log n)$ even if the file is sorted (assuming that *partition* leaves the subfiles sorted). However, there are pathological files in which the first, last and middle elements of each subfile are always the three smallest or largest elements. In such cases, quicksort remains $O(n^2)$. Fortunately, these are rare.

Meansort is $O(n \log n)$ as long as the elements of the file are uniformly distributed between the largest and the smallest. Again, some rare distributions may make it $O(n^2)$, but this is less likely than the worst case of the other methods. For random files, meansort does not offer any significant reductions in comparisons or interchanges over standard quicksort. Its significant overhead for computing the mean requires far more CPU time than standard quicksort. For a file known to be almost sorted, meansort does provide significant reduction in comparisons and interchanges. However, the mean-finding overhead makes it slower than quicksort unless the file is very close to being completely sorted.

Bsort requires far less time than quicksort or meansort on sorted or nearly sorted input, although it does require more comparisons and interchanges than meansort for nearly sorted input (but meansort has significant overhead in finding the mean). It requires fewer comparisons but more interchanges than meansort and more of both than quicksort for randomly sorted input. However, its CPU requirements are far lower than meansort's, although somewhat greater than quicksort's for random input.

Thus Bsort can be recommended if the input is known to be nearly sorted or if we are willing to forgo moderate increases in average sorting time to avoid very large increases in worst-case sorting time. Meansort can be recommended only for input known to be very nearly sorted, and standard quicksort for input likely to be random or if average sorting time must be as fast as possible. In Section 6.5, we present a technique that is faster than either Bsort or meansort on nearly sorted files.

The space requirements for quicksort depend upon the number of nested recursive calls or on the size of the stack. Clearly the stack can never grow larger than the number of elements in the original file. How much smaller than n the stack grows depends upon the number and sizes of the subfiles generated. The size of the stack is somewhat contained by always stacking the larger of the two subarrays and applying the routine to the smaller. This guarantees that all smaller subarrays are subdivided before larger subarrays, giving the net effect of having fewer elements on the stack at any given time. The reason for this is that a smaller subarray will be divided fewer times than a larger subarray. Of course, the larger subarray will ultimately be processed and subdivided, but this will occur after the smaller subarrays have already been sorted and therefore removed from the stack.

Another advantage of quicksort is locality of reference. That is, over a short time all array accesses are to one or two relatively small portions of the array (a subfile or portion thereof). This ensures efficiency in a virtual memory environment where pages of data are constantly being swapped back and forth between external and internal storage. Thanks to locality of reference, fewer page swaps are required for any particular program. A simulation study has shown that in such an environment, quicksort uses less space-time resources than any other sort considered.

EXERCISES

6.2.1 Prove that the number of passes necessary in the bubble sort in the text before the file is in sorted order (not including the last pass, which detects the fact that the file is sorted) equals the largest distance by which an element must move from a larger index to a smaller index.

6.2.2 Rewrite the routine *bubble* so that successive passes go in opposite directions.

6.2.3 Prove that, in the sort in the previous exercise, if two elements are not interchanged during two consecutive passes in opposite directions, they are in their final position.

6.2.4 A sort by **counting** is performed as follows. Declare an array *count*, and set *count*[i] to the number of elements that are less than $x[i]$. Then place $x[i]$ in position *count*[i] of an output array. (However, beware of the possibility of equal elements.) Write a routine to sort an array x of size n using this method.

6.2.5 Assume that a file contains integers between a and b, with many numbers repeated several times. A **distribution sort** proceeds as follows. Declare an array *number* of size $b - a + 1$, and set *number*[$i - a$] to the number of times that integer i appears in the file, and then reset the values in the file appropriately. Write a routine to sort an array x of size n containing integers between a and b by this method.

6.2.6 The **odd-even transposition sort** proceeds as follows. Pass through the file several times. On the first pass, compare $x[i]$ with $x[i + 1]$ for all odd i. On the second pass, compare $x[i]$ with $x[i + 1]$ for all even i. Each time that $x[i] > x[i + 1]$, interchange the two. Continue alternating in this fashion until the file is sorted.

    a. What is the condition for the termination of the sort?

    b. Write a Java routine to implement the sort.

    c. On the average, what is the efficiency of this sort?

6.2.7 Rewrite the program for the quicksort by starting with the recursive algorithm and applying the methods from Chapter 3 to produce a nonrecursive version.

6.2.8 Modify the quicksort program in the text so that the bubble sort is used if a subarray is small. Determine, by actual computer runs, how small the subarray has to be for this mixed strategy to be more efficient than an ordinary quicksort.

6.2.9 Modify *partition* so that the middle value of $x[lb]$, $x[ub]$, and $x[ind]$ (where $ind = (ub + lb)/2$) is used to partition the array. In what cases is the quicksort using this method more efficient than the version in the text? In what cases is it less efficient?

6.2.10 Implement the meansort technique. *partition* should use the mean of the subfile being partitioned, computed when the subfile was created, as the pivot value, and should compute the means of each of the two subfiles that it creates. When the upper and lower bounds of a subfile are stacked, their means should be stacked as well.

6.2.11 Implement the Bsort technique. The middle element of each file should be used as the pivot, the last element of the left subfile being created should be maintained as the largest in the left subfile, and the first element of the right subfile should be maintained as the smallest in the right subfile. Two **boolean** variables should be used to keep track of whether the two subfiles are sorted at the end of the partition.

A sorted subfile need not be processed further. If a subfile has three or fewer elements, sort it directly by a single interchange, at most.

6.2.12 a. Rewrite the routines for the bubble sort and the quicksort as presented in the text and the sorts in the exercises so that a record is kept of the actual number of comparisons and the actual number of interchanges made.

b. Write a random-number generator (or use the appropriate methods from either the *java.lang.Math* or *java.util.Random* classes) that generates integers between 0 and 999.

c. Using the generator in part (b), generate several files of size 10, size 100, and size 1000. Apply the sorting routines in part (a) to measure the time requirements for each of the sorts on each of the files.

d. Measure the results in part (c) against the theoretical values presented in this section. Do they agree? If not, explain. Rearrange the files so that they are completely sorted and in reverse order, and see how the sorts behave with these inputs.

6.3 SELECTION AND TREE SORTING

A *selection sort* is one in which successive elements are selected in order and placed in their proper sorted positions. The elements of the input may have to be preprocessed to make the ordered selection possible. Any selection sort can be conceptualized as the general algorithm, shown below, that uses a descending priority queue (recall that *pqInsert* inserts into a priority queue, and *pqMaxDelete* retrieves the largest element of a priority queue).

```
set dpq to the empty descending priority queue;
// preprocess the elements of the input array
// by inserting them into the priority queue
for (i = 0; i < n; i++)
        pqInsert(dpq, x[i]);
// select each successive element in order
for (i = n-1; i >= 0; i--)
    x[i] = pqMaxDelete(dpq);
```

This algorithm is called the *general selection sort*.

We now examine several different selection sorts. Two features distinguish specific selection sorts. One feature is the data structure used to implement the priority queue. The second is the method used to implement the general algorithm. A data structure may allow significant optimization of the general selection sort algorithm.

Note that the general algorithm can be modified to use an ascending priority queue *apq* rather than *dpq*. The second loop that implements the selection phase would be modified to

```
for (i = 0; i < n; i++)
    x[i] = pqMinDelete(apq);
```

Straight Selection Sort

The *straight selection sort*, or *push-down sort*, implements the descending priority queue as an unordered array. The input array x is used to hold the priority queue, thus eliminating the need for additional space. The straight selection sort is, therefore, an in-place sort. Moreover, because the input array x is itself the unordered array that will represent the descending priority queue, the input is already in appropriate format and the preprocessing phase is unnecessary.

Therefore, the straight selection sort consists entirely of a selection phase in which the largest of the remaining elements, *large*, is repeatedly placed in its proper position, i, at the end of the array. To do so, *large* is interchanged with the element $x[i]$. The initial n-element priority queue is reduced by one element after each selection. After $n - 1$ selections, the entire array is sorted. Thus the selection process need be done only from n down to 1 rather than down to 0. The following Java method implements straight selection:

```java
public static void selectsort(int x[ ]) {
    int i, index, j, large;

    for (i = x.length-1; i > 0; i--) {
            // place the largest number of x[0] through x[i]
            // into large and its index into index
            large = x[0];
            index = 0;
        for (j = 1; j <= i; j++) {
                if (x[j] > large) {
                            large = x[j];
                            index = j;
                }
        }
        x[index] = x[i];
        x[i] = large;
    }
} //end selectsort
```

Analysis of the straight selection sort is straightforward. The first pass makes $n - 1$ comparisons, the second pass makes $n - 2$, and so on. Therefore, there is a total of

$$(n - 1) + (n - 2) + (n - 3) + \ldots + 1 = n * (n - 1)/2$$

comparisons, which is $O(n^2)$. The number of interchanges is always $n - 1$ (unless a test is added to prevent the interchanging of an element with itself). Little additional storage is required (except to hold a few temporary variables). The sort may, therefore, be categorized as $O(n^2)$, although it is faster than the bubble sort. Since the testing proceeds to completion without regard to the makeup of the file, there is no improvement if the input file is completely sorted or unsorted. Despite the fact that it is simple to code, the straight selection sort would probably not be used on any files except those for which n is small.

It is also possible to implement a sort by representing the descending priority queue by an ordered array. Interestingly, this leads to a sort consisting of a preprocessing phase that forms a sorted array of n elements. The selection phase is, therefore, superfluous. This sort is presented in Section 6.4 as the *simple insertion sort*; it is not a selection sort because no selection is required.

Binary Tree Sorts

In the remainder of this section we illustrate several selection sorts that represent priority queues by binary trees. The first method is the *binary tree sort*, which uses a binary search tree. The reader is advised to review the discussion of this sort in Section 5.1 before proceeding.

The method involves scanning each element of the input file and placing it in its proper position in a binary tree. To find the proper position for an element, y, a left or right branch is taken at each node depending upon whether y is less than the element in the node or greater than or equal to it. Once each input element is in its proper position in the tree, the sorted file can be retrieved by an inorder traversal of the tree. We present the algorithm for this sort, modifying it to accommodate the input as a preexisting array. Translating the algorithm to a Java method is straightforward.

```
// establish the first element as root
tree = maketree(x[0]);
// repeat for each successive element
for (i = 1; i < x.length; i++) {
y = x[i];
q = tree;
p = q;
// travel down the tree until a leaf is reached
while (p != null) {
    q = p;
    if (y < p.info());
        p= p.left();
    else
        p = p.right();
}
if (y < q.info())
    q.setLeft(y);
else
    q.setRight(y);
}
// the tree is built, traverse it in inorder
tree.inTrav();
```

In order to convert the algorithm into a routine to sort an array, it is necessary to revise *inTrav* so that visiting a node involves placing the contents of the node into the next position of the original array.

Actually, the binary search tree represents an ascending priority queue, as described in Exercises 5.1.13 and 5.2.13. Constructing the tree represents the preprocessing phase of the general selection sort algorithm, and the traversal represents the selection phase.

Ordinarily, extracting the minimum element (*pqMinDelete*) of a priority queue represented by a binary search tree involves traveling down the left side of the tree from the root. Indeed, that is the first step of the inorder traversal process. However,

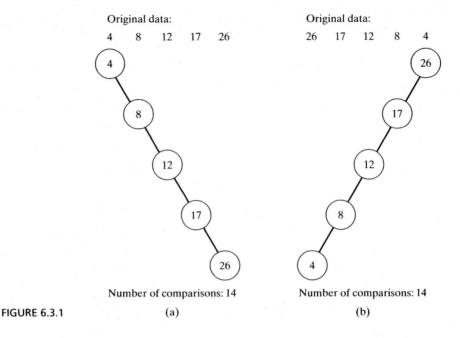

FIGURE 6.3.1   (a)   (b)

since no new elements are inserted into the tree once it is constructed, and the minimum element does not actually have to be deleted, the inorder traversal efficiently implements the successive selection process.

The relative efficiency of this method depends on the original order of the data. If the original array is completely sorted (or sorted in reverse order), then the resulting tree appears as a sequence of only right (or left) links, as in Figure 6.3.1. In this case the insertion of the first node requires no comparisons, the second node requires two comparisons, the third node three comparisons, and so on. Thus the total number of comparisons is

$$2 + 3 + \ \ldots\ + n = n * (n + 1)/2 - 1$$

which is $O(n^2)$.

On the other hand, if the data in the original array is organized so that approximately half the numbers following any given number a in the array are less than a and half are greater than a, then balanced trees like those in Figure 6.3.2 result. In such a case, the depth of the resulting binary tree is the smallest integer d greater than or equal to $\log_2 (n + 1) - 1$. The number of nodes at any level l (except possibly for the last) is 2^l, and the number of comparisons necessary to place a node at level l (except when $l = 0$) is $l + 1$. Thus, the total number of comparisons is between

$$d + \sum_{l=1}^{d-1} 2^l \times (l + 1) \text{ and } \sum_{l=1}^{d} 2^l \times (l + 1)$$

It can be shown that the resulting sums are $O(n \log n)$. (Mathematically inclined readers might be interested in proving this fact as an exercise.)

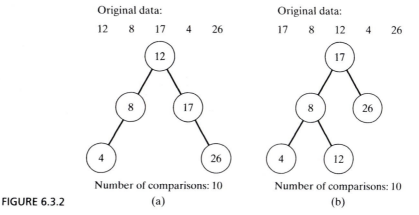

FIGURE 6.3.2

Original data:

12   8   17   4   26

Number of comparisons: 10

(a)

Original data:

17   8   12   4   26

Number of comparisons: 10

(b)

Fortunately, if every possible ordering of the input is considered equally likely, balanced trees result more often than not. The average sorting time for a binary tree sort is therefore $O(n \log n)$, although the constant of proportionality is larger on the average than in the best case. However, in the worst case (sorted input), the binary tree sort is $O(n^2)$. Of course, once the tree is has been created, time is expended in traversing it. If the tree is threaded as it is created, the traversal time is reduced and the need for a stack (implicit in the recursion or explicit in a nonrecursion inorder traversal) is eliminated.

This sort requires that one tree node be reserved for each array element. Depending on the method used to implement the tree, space may be required for tree pointers and threads, if any. This additional space requirement, together with the poor $O(n^2)$ time efficiency for sorted or reverse-order input, represents the primary drawback of the binary tree sort.

Heapsort

The drawbacks of the binary tree sort are remedied by the **heapsort**, an in-place sort that requires only $O(n \log n)$ operations regardless of the order of the input. Define a **descending heap** (also called a **max heap** or a **descending partially ordered tree**) of size n as an almost complete binary tree of n nodes such that the content of each node is less than or equal to the content of its father. If the sequential representation of an almost complete binary tree is used, this condition reduces to the inequality

$$info[j] \le info[(j - 1)/2] \text{ for } 0 \le ((j - 1)/2) < j \le n - 1$$

It is clear from this definition of a descending heap that the root of the tree (or the first element of the array) contains the largest element in the heap. Note, too, that any path from the root to a leaf (or indeed, any path in the tree that includes no more than one node at any level) is an ordered list in descending order. An **ascending heap** (or a **min heap**) can be defined as an almost complete binary tree such that the content of each node is greater than or equal to the content of its father. In an ascending heap, the root contains the smallest element of the heap, and any path from the root to a leaf is an ascending ordered list.

A heap allows a very efficient implementation of a priority queue. Recall from Section 4.2 that an ordered list containing n elements allows priority queue insertion (*pqInsert*) to be implemented using an average of approximately $n/2$ node accesses, and deletion of the minimum or maximum (*pqMinDelete* or *pqMaxDelete*) using only one node access. Thus a sequence of n insertions and n deletions from an ordered list, as is required by a selection sort, could require $O(n^2)$ operations. Although priority queue insertion using a binary search tree might require only as few as $\log_2 n$ node accesses, it could require as many as n node accesses if the tree is unbalanced. Thus a selection sort using a binary search tree could also require $O(n^2)$ operations, although on average only $O(n \log n)$ are needed.

As we shall see, a heap allows both insertion and deletion to be implemented in $O(\log n)$ operations. Thus, even in the worst case, a selection sort consisting of n insertions and n deletions can be implemented using a heap in $O(n \log n)$ operations. An additional bonus is that the heap itself can be implemented within the input array x using the sequential implementation of an almost complete binary tree. The only additional space required is for program variables. The heapsort is, therefore, an $O(n \log n)$ in-place sort.

Heap as a Priority Queue

Let us now implement a descending priority queue using a descending heap. Suppose that *dpq* is an array that implicitly represents a descending heap of size k. Because the priority queue is contained in array elements 0 to $k - 1$, we add k as a parameter of the insertion and deletion operations. Then the operation *dpq.pqInsert(k, elt)* can be implemented by simply inserting *elt* into its proper position in the descending list formed by the path from the root of the heap (*dpq[0]*) to the leaf *dpq[k]*. Once *dpq.pqInsert(k, elt)* has been executed, *dpq* becomes a heap of size $k + 1$.

The insertion is done by traversing the path from the empty position k to position 0 (the root), seeking the first element greater than or equal to *elt*. When that element is found, *elt* is inserted immediately preceding it in the path (i.e., *elt* is inserted as its son). As each element less than *elt* is passed during the traversal, it is shifted down one level in the tree to make room for *elt*. (This shifting is necessary because we are using the sequential representation rather than a linked representation of the tree. A new element cannot be inserted between two existing elements without shifting some existing elements.)

This heap insertion operation is also called the *siftUp* operation because *elt* sifts its way up the tree. The following algorithm implements *dpq.pqInsert(k, elt)*:

```
s = k;
f = (s - 1)/2;
// f is the father of s
while (s > 0 && dpq[f] < elt) {
        dpq[s] = dpq[f];
        s = f;
        // advance up the tree
        f = (s - 1)/2;
}
dpq[s] = elt;
```

Insertion is clearly $O(\log n)$, since an almost complete binary tree with n nodes has $\log_2 n + 1$ levels, and at most one node per level is accessed.

We now examine how to implement *dpq.pqMaxDelete(k)* for a descending heap of size k. First we define *subTree(p, m)*, where m is greater than p, as the subtree (of the descending heap) rooted at position p within the elements *dpq[p]* through *dpq[m]*. For example *subTree(3,10)* consists of the root *dpq[3]*, and its two children *dpq[7]* and *dpq[8]*. *subTree(3,17)* consists of *dpq[3]*, *dpq[7]*, *dpq[8]*, *dpq[15]*, *dpq[16]*, and *dpq[17]*. If *dpq[i]* is included in *subTree(p, m)*, *dpq[2 * i + 1]* is included if and only if $2 * i + 1 \le m$, and *dpq[2 * i + 2]* is included if and only if $2 * i + 2 \le m$. If m is less than p, *subTree(p, m)* is defined as the empty tree.

In order to implement *dpq.pqMaxDelete(k)*, we note that the maximum element is always at the root of a k-element descending heap. When that element is deleted, the remaining $k - 1$ elements in positions 1 through $k - 1$ must be redistributed into positions 0 through $k - 2$, so that the resulting array segment from *dpq[0]* through *dpq[k − 2]* remains a descending heap. Let *adjustHeap(root, k)* be the operation of rearranging the elements *dpq[root + 1]* through *dpq[k]* into *dpq[root]* through *dpq[k − 1]*, so that *subTree(root, k − 1)* forms a descending heap. Then *pqMaxDelete(dpq, k)* for a k-element descending heap can be implemented by

```
p = dpq[0];
adjustHeap(0, k −1);
return p;
```

In a descending heap, not only is the root element the largest element in the tree, but an element in *any* position p must be the largest element in *subTree(p, k)*. Now, *subTree(p, k)* consists of three groups of elements: its root, *dpq[p]*; its left subtree, *subTree(2*p + 1, k)*; and its right subtree, *subTree(2*p + 2, k)*. *dpq[2*p + 1]*, the left son of the root, is the largest element of the left subtree, and *dpq[2*p + 2]*, the right son of the root, is the largest element of the right subtree. When the root *dpq[p]* is deleted, the larger of these two sons must move up to take its place as the new largest element of *subTree(p, k)*. Then the subtree rooted at the position of the larger element moved up must be readjusted in turn.

Let us define *largeSon(p, m)* as the larger son of *dpq[p]* within *subTree(p, m)*. It may be implemented as

```
s = 2 * p + 1;
if (s + 1 ≤ m  &&  x[s] < x[s + 1])
      s = s + 1;
// check if out of bounds
if (s > m)
      return -1;
else
      return s;
```

Then *adjustHeap(root, k)* may be implemented recursively by

```
f  = root;
s  = largeSon(f, k - 1);
```

```
if (s ≥ 0 && dpq[k] < dpq[s]) {
    dpq[f] = dpq[s];
    adjustHeap(s, k);
}
else
    dpq[f] = dpq[k];
```

The following is an iterative version of *adjustHeap*. The algorithm uses a temporary variable *kValue* to hold the value of *dpq*[*k*]:

```
f = root;
kValue = dpq[k];
s = largeSon(f, k-1);
while (s ≥ 0 && kValue < dpq[s]) {
    dpq[f] = dpq[s];
    f = s;
    s = largeSon(f, k - 1);
}
dpq[f] = kValue;
```

Note that we traverse a path of the tree from the root toward a leaf, shifting up by one position all the elements in the path greater than *dpq*[*k*], and inserting *dpq*[*k*] in its proper position in the path. Again, the shifting is necessary because we are using the sequential representation rather than a linked implementation of the tree. The adjustment method is often called the *siftDown* operation because *dpq*[*k*] sifts its way from the root down the tree.

This heap deletion algorithm is also $O(\log n)$, since there are $\log n + 1$ levels in the tree, and at most two nodes are accessed at each level. However, the overhead of shifting and computing *largeSon* is significant.

Sorting Using a Heap

Heapsort is an implementation of the general selection sort using the input array *x* as a heap representing a descending priority queue. The preprocessing phase creates a heap of size *n* using the siftup operation, and the selection phase redistributes the elements of the heap in order as it deletes elements from the priority queue using the siftdown operation. In both phases, the loops need not include the case where *i* equals 0, since *x*[0] is already a one-element priority queue, and the array is sorted once *x*[1] through *x*[*n* − 1] are in proper position.

A note about notation: Although we normally follow the usual Java notation, and denote a method *m* of an object *o* by *o.m*(), in the following algorithm we use the notation *pqInsert*(*x*, *i*, *x*[*i*]) and *pqMaxDelete*(*x*, *i*) in referring to the descending priority queue routines. This is because the descending priority queue is contained within the array *x*. Thus *x* serves as both input and output parameter.

```
// Create the priority queue; before each loop iteration
// the priority queue consists of elements x[0] through
// x[i - 1]. Each iteration adds x[i] to the queue.
for (i = 1; i < n; i++)
    pqInsert(x, i, x[i]);
// select each successive element in order
```

```
for (i = n - 1; i > 0; i--)
    x[i] = pqMaxDelete(x, i + 1);
```

Figure 6.3.3 illustrates the creation of a heap of size 8 from the original file

$$25 \quad 57 \quad 48 \quad 37 \quad 12 \quad 92 \quad 86 \quad 33$$

The dotted lines in the figure indicate an element being shifted down the tree.

Figure 6.3.4 illustrates the adjustment of the heap as $x[0]$ is repeatedly selected and placed in its proper position in the array and the heap is readjusted, until all the

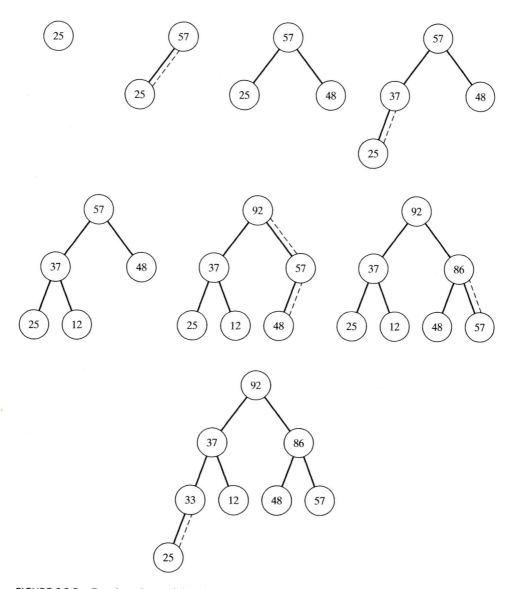

FIGURE 6.3.3   Creating a heap of size 8.

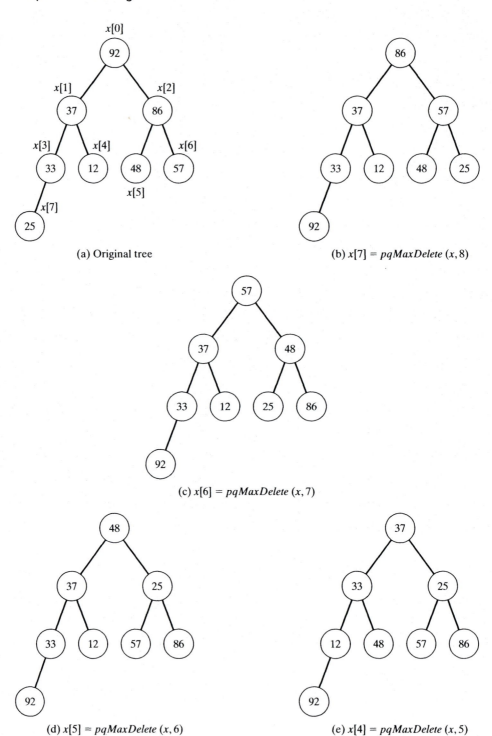

(a) Original tree

(b) $x[7] = pqMaxDelete\,(x, 8)$

(c) $x[6] = pqMaxDelete\,(x, 7)$

(d) $x[5] = pqMaxDelete\,(x, 6)$

(e) $x[4] = pqMaxDelete\,(x, 5)$

FIGURE 6.3.4 Adjusting a heap.

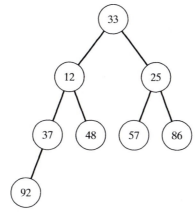

(f) $x[4] = pqMaxDelete\,(x,4)$

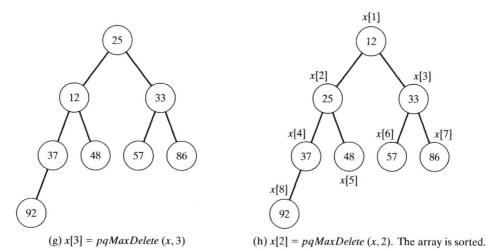

(g) $x[3] = pqMaxDelete\,(x,3)$ 　　　　(h) $x[2] = pqMaxDelete\,(x,2)$. The array is sorted.

FIGURE 6.3.4   (*Continued*)

heap elements are processed. Note that after an element has been "deleted" from the heap, it remains in the array but is ignored in subsequent processing.

Heapsort Method

We now present a heapsort method with all the submethods (*pqInsert, pqMaxDelete, adjustHeap*, and *largeSon*) expanded in-line and integrated for maximal efficiency.

```
public static void heapsort(int[ ] x) {
    int i, f, s;

    if (x.length == 0)
            return;
    // preprocessing phase; create initial heap
    for (i = 1; i < x.length; i++) {
            int elt = x[i];
            // pqInsert(x, i, elt)
```

```
                s = i;
                f = (s - 1)/2;
                while (s > 0 && x[f] < elt) {
                        x[s] = x[f];
                        s = f;
                        f = (s - 1)/2;
                }
                x[s] = elt;
        }
        // selection phase; repeatedly remove x[0], insert it
        // in its proper position, and adjust the heap
        for (i = x.length - 1; i > 0; i--) {
                // pqMaxDelete(x, i + 1)
                int iValue = x[i];
                x[i] = x[0];
                f = 0;
                // s = largeSon(0, i - 1)
                if (i == 1)
                        s = -1;
                else
                        s = 1;
                if (i > 2 && x[2] > x[1])
                        s = 2;
                while (s >= 0 && iValue < x[s]) {
                        x[f] = x[s];
                        f = s;
                        // s = largeSon(f, I - 1)
                        s = 2*f + 1;
                        if (s + 1 <= i - 1 && x[s] < x[s+1])
                                s = s + 1;
                        if (s > i - 1)
                                s = -1;
                }
                x[f] = iValue;
        }
} // end heapsort
```

To analyze the heapsort, note that a complete binary tree with n nodes (where n is one less than a power of two) has $\log_2 (n + 1)$ levels. Thus if each element in the array were a leaf, which would require that it be filtered through the entire tree while the heap is created and also while it is adjusted, the sort would still be $O(n \log n)$.

In the average case, the heapsort is not as efficient as the quicksort. Experiments indicate that heapsort requires twice as much time as quicksort for randomly sorted input. However, heapsort is far superior to quicksort in the worst case. In fact, heapsort remains $O(n \log n)$ in the worst case. Heapsort is also not very efficient for small n because of the overhead of initial heap creation and computation of the location of fathers and sons.

The space requirement for the heapsort (aside from array indices) is only one additional record to hold the temporary for switching, provided the array implementation of an almost complete binary tree is used.

EXERCISES

6.3.1   Explain why the straight selection sort is more efficient than the bubble sort.

6.3.2   Consider the following **quadratic selection sort**: Divide the n elements of the file into $sqrt(n)$ groups of $sqrt(n)$ elements each. Find the largest element of each group and insert it into an auxiliary array. Find the largest of the elements in the auxiliary array. This is the largest element of the file. Then replace this element in the array by the next-largest element of the group from which it came. Again find the largest element of the auxiliary array. This is the second-largest element of the file. Repeat the process until the file has been sorted. Write a Java method to implement a quadratic selection sort as efficiently as possible.

6.3.3   A **tournament** is an almost complete strictly binary tree in which each nonleaf contains the larger of the two elements in its two sons. Thus the contents of a tournament's leafs completely determine the contents of all its nodes. A tournament with n leafs represents a set of n elements.

    a.   Develop an algorithm $pqInsert(t,n,elt)$ to add a new element elt to a tournament containing n leafs represented implicitly by an array t.

    b.   Develop an algorithm $pqMaxDelete(t,n)$ to delete the maximum element from a tournament with n elements by replacing the leaf containing the maximum element with a dummy value smaller than any possible element (e.g., -1 in a tournament of nonnegative integers) and then readjusting all the values in the path from that leaf to the root.

    c.   Show how to simplify $pqMaxDelete$ by maintaining a pointer to a leaf in each nonleaf *info* field, rather than an actual element value.

    d.   Write a Java program to implement a selection sort using a tournament. The pre-processing phase builds the initial tournament from the array x, and the selection phase repeatedly applies $pqMaxDelete$. Such a sort is called a **tournament sort**.

    e.   How does the efficiency of the tournament sort compare with that of the heapsort?

    f.   Prove that the tournament sort is $O(n \log n)$ for all input.

6.3.4   Define an **almost complete ternary tree** as a tree in which every node has at most three sons and the nodes can be numbered from 0 to $n - 1$ so that the sons of $node[i]$ are $node[3 * i + 1]$, $node[3 * i + 2]$, and $node[3 * i + 3]$. Define a **ternary heap** as an almost complete ternary tree in which the content of each node is greater than or equal to the contents of all its descendants. Write a sorting method similar to the heapsort using a ternary heap.

6.3.5   Write a method $combine(x)$ that accepts an array x in which the subtrees rooted at $x[1]$ and $x[2]$ are heaps and which modifies the array x so that it represents a single heap.

6.3.6   Rewrite the application in Section 5.3 that implements the Huffman algorithm so that the set of root nodes forms a priority queue implemented by an ascending heap.

6.3.7   Write a Java application that uses an ascending heap to merge n input files, each sorted in ascending order, into a single output file. Each node of the heap contains a file number and a value. The value serves as the key by which the heap is organized. Initially, one value is read from each file and the n values are formed into an ascending heap, with the file number from which each value came kept together with that value in a node. The smallest value is then in the root of the heap and is the output, and the next value of its associated file input takes its place. This value, together with its associated file number, is sifted down to find its proper place in the heap, and the new root value is output. The process of output/input/siftdown is repeated until no input remains.

6.3.8   Develop an algorithm using a heap of k elements to find the largest k numbers in a large, unsorted file of n numbers.

6.4   INSERTION SORTS

Simple Insertion

An ***insertion sort*** is one that sorts a set of records by inserting records into an existing sorted file. The following method is an example of a simple insertion sort:

```
public static void insertionsort(int x[ ]) {
    int i, k, y;

    // Initially x[0] may be thought of as a sorted file of one
    // element. After each repetition of the following loop, the
    // elements x[0] through x[k] are in order.
    for (k = 1; k < x.length; k++) {
        // Insert x[k] into the sorted file
        y = x[k];
        // Move down 1 position all elements greater than y
        for (i = k - 1; i >= 0 && y < x[i]; i--)
                x[i+1] =x [i];
        // Insert y at its proper position
        x[i+1] = y;
    }
} // end insertionsort
```

As we noted at the beginning of Section 6.3, a simple insertion sort may be viewed as a general selection sort in which the priority queue is implemented as an ordered array. Only the preprocessing phase of inserting the elements into the priority queue is necessary; once the elements have been inserted, they are already sorted so that no selection is necessary.

If the initial file is sorted, only one comparison is made on each pass, so that the sort is $O(n)$. If the file is initially sorted in the reverse order, the sort is $O(n^2)$, since the total number of comparisons is

$$(n - 1) + (n - 2) + \ldots + 3 + 2 + 1 = (n - 1)* n/2$$

which is $O(n^2)$. However, a simple insertion sort is still usually better than a bubble sort. The closer the file is to sorted order, the more efficient the simple insertion sort becomes. The average number of comparisons in a simple insertion sort (by considering all possible permutations of the input array) is also $O(n^2)$. The space requirements for the sort consist of only one temporary variable, y.

The speed of the sort can be improved somewhat by using a binary search (see Sections 3.1, 3.2, and 7.1) to find the proper position for $x[k]$ in the sorted file $x[0], \ldots, x[k - 1]$. This reduces the total number of comparisons from $O(n^2)$ to $O(n \log n)$.

However, even if the correct position i for $x[k]$ is found in $O(\log n)$ steps, each of the elements $x[i + 1], \ldots, x[k - 1]$ must be moved one position. This latter operation performed n times requires $O(n^2)$ replacements. Unfortunately, therefore, the binary search technique does not significantly improve the overall time requirements of the sort.

Another improvement to the simple insertion sort can be made by using *list insertion*. In this method there is an array *link* of pointers, one for each of the original array elements. Initially $link[i] = i + 1$ for $0 <= i < n - 1$, and $link[n - 1] = -1$. Thus the array may be thought of as a linear list pointed to by an external pointer *first* initialized to 0. To insert the kth element, the linked list is traversed until the proper position for $x[k]$ is found, or until the end of the list is reached. At that point, $x[k]$ can be inserted into the list by merely adjusting the list pointers without shifting any elements in the array. This reduces the time required for insertion but not the time required for searching for the proper position. The space requirements are also increased because of the extra *link* array. The number of comparisons is still $O(n^2)$, although the number of replacements in the *link* array is $O(n)$. The list insertion sort may be viewed as a general selection sort in which the priority queue is represented by an ordered list. Again, no selection is needed because the elements are sorted as soon as the preprocessing, insertion phase is complete. You are asked to code both the binary insertion sort and the list insertion sort as exercises.

Both the straight selection sort and the simple insertion sort are more efficient than the bubble sort. A selection sort requires fewer assignments than an insertion sort but more comparisons. Thus selection sort is recommended for small files when records are large, so that assignment is inexpensive, but keys are simple, so that comparison is cheap. If the reverse situation holds, then the insertion sort is recommended. If the input is initially in a linked list, then list insertion is recommended even if the records are large, since no data movement (as opposed to pointer modification) is required.

Of course, heapsort and quicksort are both more efficient than insertion or selection for large n. The break-even point is approximately 20–30 for quicksort; for fewer than thirty elements, use insertion sort; for more than thirty, use quicksort. A useful speedup of quicksort uses insertion sort on any subfile of size less than 20. For heapsort, the break-even point with insertion sort is approximately 60–70.

Shell Sort

A more significant improvement on the simple insertion sort, as compared to binary or list insertion, can be achieved by using the *Shell sort* (or *diminishing increment sort*), named after its discoverer. This method sorts separate subfiles of the original file. These subfiles contain every kth element of the original file. The value of k is called an *increment*. For example, if k is 5, the subfile consisting of $x[0], x[5], x[10], \ldots$ is first sorted. Five subfiles, each containing one-fifth of the elements of the original file, are sorted in this manner. These are (reading across):

subfile 1	$\rightarrow$	$x[0]$	$x[5]$	$x[10]$	$\ldots$
subfile 2	$\rightarrow$	$x[1]$	$x[6]$	$x[11]$	$\ldots$
subfile 3	$\rightarrow$	$x[2]$	$x[7]$	$x[12]$	$\ldots$
subfile 4	$\rightarrow$	$x[3]$	$x[8]$	$x[13]$	$\ldots$
subfile 5	$\rightarrow$	$x[4]$	$x[9]$	$x[14]$	$\ldots$

The ith element of the jth subfile is $x[(i - 1) * 5 + j - 1]$. If a different increment k is chosen, the k subfiles are divided so that the ith element of the jth subfile is $x[(i - 1) * k + j - 1]$.

After the first k subfiles are sorted (usually by simple insertion), a new smaller value of k is chosen, and the file is again partitioned into a new set of subfiles. Each of these larger subfiles is sorted, and the process is repeated yet again with an even smaller value of k. Eventually, the value of k is set to 1, so that the subfile consisting of the entire file is sorted. A decreasing sequence of increments is fixed at the start of the entire process. The last value in this sequence must be 1.

For example, if the original file is

$$25 \quad 57 \quad 48 \quad 37 \quad 12 \quad 92 \quad 86 \quad 33$$

and the sequence (5, 3, 1) is chosen, then the following subfiles are sorted on each iteration.

First iteration (increment = 5)

$$(x[0], x[5])$$
$$(x[1], x[6])$$
$$(x[2], x[7])$$
$$(x[3])$$
$$(x[4])$$

Second iteration (increment = 3)

$$(x[0], x[3], x[6])$$
$$(x[1], x[4], x[7])$$
$$(x[2], x[5])$$

Third iteration (increment = 1)

$$(x[0], \quad x[1], \quad x[2], \quad x[3], \quad x[4], \quad x[5], \quad x[6], \quad x[7])$$

Figure 6.4.1 illustrates the Shell sort on this sample file. The lines underneath each array join individual elements of the separate subfiles. Each of the subfiles is sorted using the simple insertion sort.

We present below a routine to implement the Shell sort. In addition to the standard parameters x, it requires an array *incrmnts* containing the diminishing increments of the sort.

```
public static void shellsort(int x[ ], int incrmnts[ ]) {
    int incr, j, k, span, y;
```

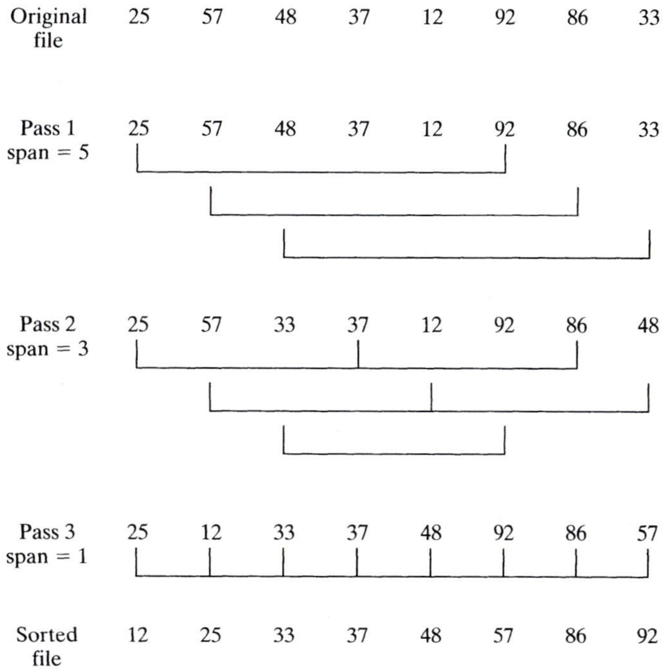

Original file	25	57	48	37	12	92	86	33

Pass 1 span = 5	25	57	48	37	12	92	86	33

Pass 2 span = 3	25	57	33	37	12	92	86	48

Pass 3 span = 1	25	12	33	37	48	92	86	57

Sorted file	12	25	33	37	48	57	86	92

FIGURE 6.4.1

```
for (incr = 0; incr < incrmnts.length; incr++) {
        // span is the size of the increment
        span = incrmnts[incr];
        for (j = span; j < x.length; j++) {
                // Insert element x[j] into its proper position
                within its subfile
                y = x[j];
                for (k = j - span; k >= 0 && y < x[k]; k -= span)
                        x[k + span] = x[k];
                x[k + span] = y;
        }
}
} // end shellsort
```

Be sure that you can trace the actions of this program on the sample file in Figure 6.4.1. Note that on the last iteration, where *span* equals 1, the sort reduces to a simple insertion.

The idea behind the Shell sort is a simple one. We have already noted that the simple insertion sort is highly efficient on a file that is in almost sorted order. It is also important to realize that when the file size n is small, an $O(n^2)$ sort is often more efficient than an $O(n \log n)$ sort. The reason for this is that $O(n^2)$ sorts are generally quite simple to program and involve very few actions other than comparisons and replacements on each pass. Because of this low overhead, the constant of proportionality is rather small. An $O(n \log n)$ sort is generally quite complex and employs a large number of extra operations on

each pass in order to reduce the work of subsequent passes. Thus its constant of proportionality is larger. When n is large, n^2 overwhelms $n * \log(n)$, so that the constants of
proportionality do not play a major role in determining the faster sort. However, when n
is small, n^2 is not much larger than $n * \log(n)$, so that a large difference in the constants
often causes an $O(n^2)$ sort to be faster.

Since the first increment used by the Shell sort is large, the individual subfiles are
quite small, and thus the simple insertion sorts on these subfiles are fairly fast. Each
sort of a subfile causes the entire file to be more nearly sorted. Thus, although successive passes of the Shell sort use smaller increments and therefore deal with larger subfiles, the subfiles are almost sorted due to the actions of previous passes. As a result, the
insertion sorts on the subfiles are also quite efficient. In this connection, it is worth noting that a file partially sorted using an increment k, and subsequently partially sorted
using an increment j, remains partially sorted on the increment k. That is, subsequent
partial sorts do not disturb earlier ones.

The efficiency analysis of the Shell sort is mathematically involved and beyond
the scope of this book. The actual time requirements for a specific sort depend upon
the number of elements in the array *incrmnts* and their actual values. One requirement
that is intuitively clear is that the elements of *incrmnts* should be relatively prime (i.e.,
have no common divisors other than 1). This guarantees that successive iterations in-
termingle subfiles so that the entire file is indeed almost sorted when *span* equals 1 on
the last iteration.

It has been shown that the order of the Shell sort can be approximated by
$O(n(\log n)^2)$ if an appropriate sequence of increments is used. For other series of increments, the running time can be proven to be $O(n^{1.5})$. Empirical data indicate that the
running time is of the form $a * n^b$, where a is between 1.1 and 1.7, and b is approximately 1.26, or of the form $c * n * (ln(n))^2 - d * n * ln(n)$, where c is approximately
0.3, and d is between 1.2 and 1.75. In general, the Shell sort is recommended for moderately sized files of several hundred elements.

Knuth recommends choosing increments as follows: define a method h recursively so that $h(1) = 1$ and $h(i + 1) = 3 * h(i) + 1$. Let x be the smallest integer such that
$h(x) \geq n$, and set *numinc*, the number of increments, to $x - 2$, and *incrmnts*[i] to
$h(numinc - i + 1)$ for i from 1 to *numinc*.

A technique similar to the Shell sort can also be used to improve the bubble sort.
In practice, a major source of the bubble sort's inefficiency is not the number of comparisons but the number of interchanges. If a series of increments are used to define
subfiles to be bubble sorted individually, as in the case of the Shell sort, then the initial
bubble sorts are on small files, and the later ones are on more nearly sorted files in
which few interchanges are necessary. This modified bubble sort, which requires very
little overhead, works well in practical situations.

Address Calculation Sort

As a final example of sorting by insertion, consider the following technique, called sorting by **address calculation** (sometimes called sorting by **hashing**). In this method, a
function f is applied to each key. The result of this function determines which of several
subfiles the record is to be placed in. The function f should have the property that if

$x \le y$, then $f(x) \le f(y)$. Such a function is called ***order-preserving***. Thus all of the records in one subfile will have keys that are less than or equal to the keys of the records in another subfile. An item is placed in a subfile in correct sequence by using any sorting method; simple insertion is often used. After all of the items in the original file have been placed in subfiles, the subfiles may be concatenated to produce the sorted result.

For example, consider again the sample file:

$$25 \quad 57 \quad 48 \quad 37 \quad 12 \quad 92 \quad 86 \quad 33$$

Let us create ten subfiles, one for each of the ten possible first digits. Initially, each of these subfiles is empty. An array of pointers $f[10]$ is declared, where $f[i]$ points to the first element in the file whose first digit is i. After scanning the first element (25), it is placed in the file headed by $f[2]$. Each of the subfiles is maintained as a sorted linked list of the original array elements. After each of the elements in the original file is processed, the subfiles appear as in Figure 6.4.2.

We present a method to implement the address calculation sort. The routine assumes an array of two-digit numbers and uses the first digit of each number to assign that number to a subfile.

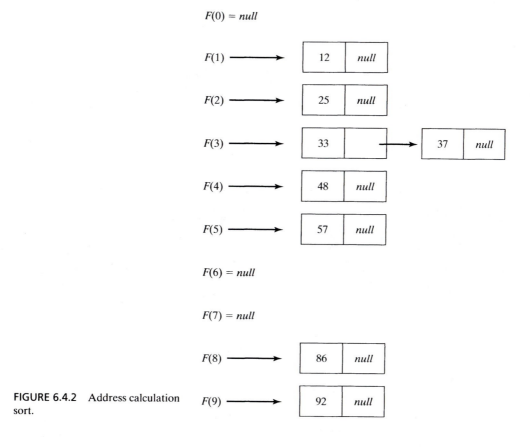

FIGURE 6.4.2 Address calculation sort.

```
private static final int NUMELTS = …;

class Node {
  public int info;
  public int next;
}

public static void addrsort(int x[ ]) {
  int f[ ], i, j, p, y, first, s;

  f = new int[10];
  Node n[ ] = new Node[NUMELTS];

  // Initialize available linked list
  int avail = 0;
  for (i = 0; i < x.length - 1; i++) {
          n[i] = new Node();
          n[i].next = i + 1;
  }
  n[x.length - 1] = new Node();
  n[x.length - 1].next = -1;

  // Initialize "pointers"
  for (i = 0; i < 10; i++)
          f[i] = -1;

  for (i = 0; i < x.length; i++) {
          // We insert each element into its respective subfile
          // using list insertion
          y = x[i];
          first = y/10;                      // Find the first digit of a
                                             // two-digit number
          // Search the linked list
          if (avail == -1)
                  System.exit(1);
          s = avail;
          avail = n[s].next;
          n[s].info = y;

          int p1 = f[first], p2 = -1;

          // Place the node on the list
          while (p1 != -1 && n[s].info > n[p1].info) {
                  p2 = p1;
                  p1 = n[p1].next;
          }

          if (p2 == -1) {                    // insert at front
                  n[s].next = p1;
                  f[first] = s;
          }
          else {
                  int hold = n[p2].next;
                  n[p2].next = s;
```

```
                        n[s].next = hold;
            }
    } // end for

    // Copy numbers back into the array x
    i = 0;
    for (j = 0; j < 10; j++) {
            p = f[j];
            while (p != -1) {
                    x[i++] = n[p].info;
                    p = n[p].next;
            }
    }
} // end addrsort
```

The space requirements of the address calculation sort are approximately $2 * n$ (used by the array *node*) plus some header nodes and temporary variables. Note that if the original data are given in the form of a linked list rather than as a sequential array, it is not necessary to maintain both the array x and the linked structure *node*.

To evaluate the time requirements for the sort, note the following: If the n original elements are approximately uniformly distributed over the m subfiles, and the value of n/m is approximately 1, the time of the sort is nearly $O(n)$, since the method assigns each element to its proper file and little extra work is required to place the element in the subfile itself. On the other hand, if n/m is much larger than 1, or if the original file is not uniformly distributed over the m subfiles, then significant work is required to insert an element into its proper subfile and the time is therefore closer to $O(n^2)$.

EXERCISES

6.4.1 The *two-way insertion sort* is a modification of the simple insertion sort as follows: A separate output array of size n is set aside. This output array acts as a circular structure, as in Section 4.1. $x[0]$ is placed in the middle element of the array. Once a contiguous group of elements are in the array, room for a new element is made by shifting all the smaller elements one step to the left or all the larger elements one step to the right. The choice of which shift to perform depends on which would cause the smallest amount of shifting. Write a Java method to implement this technique.

6.4.2 The *merge insertion sort* proceeds as follows:

Step 1: For all odd i between 0 and $n - 2$, compare $x[i]$ with $x[i + 1]$. Place the larger in the next position of an array *large*, and the smaller in the next position of an array *small*. If n is odd, place $x[n - 1]$ in the last position of the array *small*. (*large* is of size *ind* where $ind = (n - 1)/2$; *small* is of size *ind* or $ind + 1$ depending on whether n is even or odd.)

Step 2: Sort the array *large* using merge insertion recursively. Whenever an element *large*[j] is moved to *large*[k], *small*[j] is also moved to *small*[k]. (At the end of this step, $large[i] \leq large[i + 1]$ for all i less than *ind*, and $small[i] \leq large[i]$ for all i less than or equal to *ind*.)

Step 3: Copy *small*[0] and all the elements of *large* into $x[0]$ through $x[ind]$.

Step 4: Define the integer $num[i]$ as $(2^{i+1} + (-1)^i)/3$. Beginning with $i = 0$, and proceeding by 1 while $num[i] \leq (n/2) + 1$, insert the elements $small[num[i + 1]]$ down to $small[num[i] + 1]$ into x in turn, using binary insertion. (For example, if $n = 20$, then the successive values of num are: $num[0] = 1$, $num[1] = 1$, $num[2] = 3$, $num[3] = 5$, $num[4] = 11$, which equals $(n/2) + 1$. Thus the elements of $small$ are inserted in the following order: $small[2], small[1]$; then $small[4], small[3]$; then $small[9], small[8], small[7], small[6], small[5]$. In this example, there is no $small[10]$.)

Write a Java method to implement this technique.

6.4.3 Modify the quicksort in Section 6.2 so that it uses a simple insertion sort when a subfile is below some size s. Determine by experiments what value of s should be used for maximum efficiency.

6.4.4 Prove that if a file is partially sorted using an increment j in the Shell sort, it remains partially sorted on that increment even after it is partially sorted on another increment, k.

6.4.5 Explain why it is desirable to choose increments for the Shell sort that are relatively prime.

6.4.6 What is the number of comparisons and interchanges (in terms of file size n) performed by each of the sorting methods (a-j) for the following files:

1. A sorted file.
2. A file that is sorted in reverse order (i.e., from largest to smallest).
3. A file in which the elements $x[0], x[2], x[4], \ldots$ are the smallest elements and are in sorted order, and in which the elements $x[1], x[3], x[5], \ldots$ are the largest elements and are in reverse sorted order (i.e., $x[0]$ is the smallest, $x[1]$ is the largest, $x[2]$ is next to smallest, $x[3]$ is the next to the largest, etc.).
4. A file in which $x[0]$ through $x[ind]$ (where $ind = (n - 1)/2$) are the smallest elements and are sorted, and in which $x[ind + 1]$ through $x[n - 1]$ are the largest elements and are in reverse sorted order.
5. A file in which $x[0], x[2], x[4], \ldots$ are the smallest elements in sorted order, and in which $x[1], x[3], x[5], \ldots$ are the largest elements in sorted order.

   a. Simple insertion sort.
   b. Insertion sort using a binary search.
   c. List insertion sort.
   d. Two-way insertion sort of Exercise 1.
   e. Merge insertion sort of Exercise 2.
   f. Shell sort using increments 2 and 1.
   g. Shell sort using increments 3, 2 and 1.
   h. Shell sort using increments 8, 4, 2, and 1.
   i. Shell sort using increments 7, 5, 3, and 1.
   j. Address calculation sort presented in the text.

6.4.7 Under what circumstances would you recommend the use of each of the following sorts over the others?

   a. Shell sort in this section
   b. Heapsort in Section 6.3
   c. Quicksort in Section 6.2

6.4.8   Determine which of the following sorts is most efficient:

    a.   The simple insertion sort in this section

    b.   The straight selection sort in Section 6.3

    c.   The bubble sort in Section 6.2

6.5   MERGE AND RADIX SORTS

Merge Sorts

Merging is the process of combining two or more sorted files into a third sorted file. An example of a routine that accepts two sorted arrays, *a* and *b*, and merges them into a third array, *c*, is the following:

```
private static void mergeArrays(int a[ ], int b[ ], int c[ ]) {
   int apoint=0, bpoint=0, cpoint=0;
   int alimit, blimit, climit;
   // apoint and bpoint are indicators of how far we are in
   // arrays a and b respectively

   alimit = a.length - 1;
   blimit = b.length - 1;
   climit = c.length - 1;
   if (a.length + b.length != c.length) {
         System.out.println("array bounds incompatible\n");
         return;
   }
   for (cpoint = 0; apoint <= alimit && bpoint <= blimit; cpoint++)
         if (a[apoint] < b[bpoint])
               c[cpoint] = a[apoint++];
         else
               c[cpoint] = b[bpoint++];
   while (apoint <= alimit)
         c[cpoint++] = a[apoint++];
   while (bpoint <= blimit)
         c[cpoint++] = b[bpoint++];
} // end mergeArrays
```

We can use this technique to sort a file in the following way. Divide the file into *n* sub-files of size 1, and merge adjacent (disjoint) pairs of files. We then have approximately *n*/2 files of size 2. Repeat this process until there is only one file remaining of size *n*. Figure 6.5.1 illustrates how this process operates on a sample file. Each individual file is enclosed in brackets.

We present a method to implement the above description of a ***straight merge sort***. An auxiliary array *aux* of size *n* is required to hold the results of merging two sub-arrays of *x*. The variable *size* contains the size of the subarrays being merged. Since at any time the two files being merged are both subarrays of *x*, lower and upper bounds are required to indicate the subfiles of *x* being merged. *l*1 and *u*1 represent the lower and upper bounds of the first file, and *l*2 and *u*2 represent the lower and upper bounds

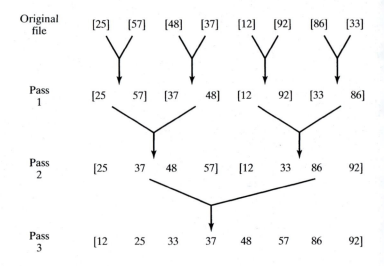

FIGURE 6.5.1 Successive passes of the merge sort.

of the second file. *i* and *j* are used to reference elements of the source files being merged, and *k* indexes the destination file *aux*. The method follows:

```
private static final int NUMELTS = …;

public static void mergesort (int x[ ]) {
    int i, j, k, l1, l2, , u1, u2, size = 1;
    int aux[ ] = new int[NUMELTS];

    while (size < x.length) {
        l1 = 0;
        k = 0;
        while (l1+size < x.length) {
            l2 = l1 + size;
            u1 = l2 - 1;
            u2 = (l2 + size-1 < x.length) ? l2 + size - 1 :
                x.length - 1;
            for (i = l1, j = l2; I <= u1 && j <= u2; k++)
                if (x[i] <= x[j])
                    aux[k] = x[i++];
                else
                    aux[k] = x[j++];
            for ( ; i <= u1; k++)
                aux[k] = x[i++];
            for ( ; j <= u2; k++)
                aux[k] = x[j++];
            l1 = u2 + 1;
        }
        for (i = l1; k < x.length; i++)
            aux[k++] = x[i];
        for (i = 0; I < x.length; i++)
            x[i] = aux[i];
```

```
        size *= 2;
    }
} // end mergesort
```

There is one deficiency in the above method, but it is easily remedied to make the program practical for sorting large arrays. Instead of merging each set of files into the auxiliary array *aux* and then recopying the array *aux* into *x*, alternate merges can be performed from *x* to *aux* and from *aux* to *x*. We leave this modification as an exercise for the reader.

There are obviously no more than $\log_2 n$ passes in mergesort, each involving *n* or fewer comparisons. Thus mergesort requires no more than $n * \log_2 n$ comparisons. In fact, it can be shown that mergesort requires fewer than $n * \log_2 n - n + 1$ comparisons, on the average, compared to $1.386 * n * \log_2 n$ average comparisons for quicksort. In addition, quicksort can require $O(n^2)$ comparisons in the worst case, whereas mergesort never requires more than $n * \log_2 n$. However, mergesort does require approximately twice as many assignments as quicksort on the average, even if alternating merges go from *x* to *aux* and *aux* to *x*.

Mergesort also requires $O(n)$ additional space for the auxiliary array, while quicksort requires only $O(\log n)$ additional space for the stack. An algorithm has been developed for an in-place merge of two sorted subarrays in $O(n)$ time. This algorithm would allow mergesort to become an in-place $O(n \log n)$ sort. However, the technique requires a great deal many more assignments and thus would not be as practical as finding the $O(n)$ extra space.

There are two modifications of the above method that can result in more efficient sorting. The first of these is the ***natural merge***. In the straight merge, the files are all the same size (except perhaps for the last file). We can, however, exploit any order that may already exist among the elements and let the subfiles be defined as the longest subarrays of increasing elements. You are asked to code such a method as an exercise.

The second modification uses linked allocation instead of sequential allocation. By adding a single pointer field to each record, the need for the second array *aux* can be eliminated. This can be done by explicitly linking together each input and output subfile. The modification can be applied to both the straight merge and the natural merge. You are asked to implement these in the exercises.

Note that using mergesort on a linked list eliminates both of its drawbacks relative to quicksort: It no longer requires significant additional space and does not require significant data element movement. Generally, data elements can be large and complex, so that the assignment of data elements requires more work than the reassignment of pointers that is still required by a list-based mergesort.

Mergesort can also be presented quite naturally as a recursive process in which the two halves of the array are first recursively sorted using mergesort and, once sorted, are joined by merging. For details, see Exercises 6.5.1 and 6.5.2. Both mergesort and quicksort are methods that involve splitting the file into two parts, sorting them separately, and then joining the two sorted halves together. In mergesort, the splitting is trivial (simply taking two halves) and the joining is hard (merging the two sorted files). In quicksort, the splitting is hard (partitioning) and the joining is trivial (the two halves and the pivot automatically form a sorted array).

Insertion sort may be considered a special case of mergesort in which the two halves consist of a single element and the remainder of the array; selection sort may be considered a special case of quicksort in which the file is partitioned into one half consisting of the largest element alone and a second half consisting of the remainder of the array.

The Cook-Kim Algorithm

Frequently, it is known that a file is almost sorted with only a few elements out of order. Or, it may be known that an input file is likely to be sorted. For small files that are very nearly sorted or for sorted files, simple insertion is the fastest sort (considering both comparisons and assignments) that we have encountered. For large files or files that are slightly less sorted, quicksort using the middle element as pivot is fastest. (If comparisons alone are considered, mergesort is fastest.) However, another hybrid algorithm discovered by Cook and Kim is faster than both insertion sort and middle-element quicksort for nearly sorted input.

The Cook-Kim algorithm operates as follows: The input is examined for unordered pairs of elements (e.g., $x[k] > x[k + 1]$). The two elements in an unordered pair are removed and added to the end of a new array. The next pair examined after an unordered pair is removed consists of the predecessor and successor of the removed pair. The original array, with the unordered pairs removed, is now in sorted order. The array of unordered pairs is then sorted, using middle-element quicksort if it contains more than thirty elements, and simple insertion otherwise. The two arrays are then merged.

The Cook-Kim algorithm takes more advantage of the sortedness of the input than any other sorts and is significantly better than middle-element quicksort, insertion sort, merge sort, or Bsort on nearly sorted input. However, for randomly ordered input, Cook-Kim is less efficient than Bsort (and certainly than quicksort or merge sort). Middle-element quicksort, merge sort, or Bsort is therefore preferable when large, sorted input files are likely but good random-input behavior is also required.

Radix Sort

The next sorting method we consider is called the ***radix sort***. This sort is based on the values of the actual digits in the positional representations of the numbers being sorted. For example, the number 235 in decimal notation is written with a 2 in the hundreds position, a 3 in the tens position, and a 5 in the units position. The larger of two such integers of equal length can be determined as follows: Start at the most significant digit, and advance through the least significant digits as long as the corresponding digits in the two numbers match. The number with the larger digit in the first position in which the digits of the two numbers do not match is the larger of the two numbers. Of course, if all the digits of both numbers match, then the numbers are equal.

We can write a sorting method based on the above algorithm. Using the decimal base, for example, the numbers can be partitioned into ten groups based on their most significant digits. (For simplicity, we assume that all the numbers have the same number of digits, by padding with leading zeros, if necessary.) Thus, every element in the "0" group is less than every element in the "1" group, all of whose elements are less than every element in the "2" group, and so on. We can then sort within the individual groups based on the next significant digit. We repeat this process until each subgroup has been subdivided so that the least significant digits are sorted. At this point the original file has been sorted. (Note that the division of a subfile into groups with the same digit in a given position is similar to the *partition* operation in the quicksort in which a subfile is divided into two groups based on comparison with a particular element.) This method is sometimes called the **radix-exchange sort**; its coding is left as an exercise for the reader.

Let us now consider an alternative to the method described above. It is apparent from the above discussion that considerable bookkeeping is involved in constantly subdividing files and distributing their contents into subfiles based on particular digits. It would certainly be easier if we could process the entire file as a whole rather than deal with many individual files.

Suppose we perform the following actions on the file for each digit, beginning with the least significant digit and ending with the most significant digit. Take each number in the order in which it appears in the file and place it in one of ten queues, depending on the value of the digit currently being processed. Then restore each queue to the original file, starting with the queue of numbers with a 0 digit, and ending with the queue of numbers with a 9 digit. When these actions have been performed for each digit, starting with the least significant and ending with the most significant, the file is sorted. This sorting method is called the **radix sort**.

Note that this scheme sorts on the less significant digits first. Thus, when all the numbers are sorted on a more significant digit, numbers that have the same digit in that position but different digits in a less significant position are already sorted on the less significant position. This allows processing of the entire file without subdividing the files and keeping track of where each subfile begins and ends. Figure 6.5.2 illustrates this sort on the sample file

25   57   48   37   12   92   86   33

Be sure that you can follow the actions depicted in the two passes in Figure 6.5.2.

We can therefore outline an algorithm to sort in the above fashion as follows:

```
for (k = least significant digit; k <= most significant digit; k++) {
    for (i = 0; i < n; i++) {
        y = x[i];
        j = kth digit of y;
        place y at rear of queue[j];
    }
    for (qu = 0; qu < 10; qu++)
        place elements of queue[qu] in next sequential positions
        of x;
}
```

We now present an application to implement the above sort on *m*-digit numbers. In order to save a considerable amount of work in processing the queues (especially in the step where we return the queue elements to the original file), we write the application using linked allocation. If the initial input to the routine is an array, then that input is first converted into a linear linked list; if the original input is already in linked format,

Original file

	25	57	48	37	12	92	86	33

Queues based on least significant digit.

	Front	Rear
queue [0]		
queue [1]		
queue [2]	12	92
queue [3]	33	
queue [4]		
queue [5]	25	
queue [6]	86	
queue [7]	57	37
queue [8]	48	
queue [9]		

After first pass:

	12	92	33	25	86	57	37	48

Queues based on most significant digit.

	Front	Rear
queue [0]		
queue [1]	12	
queue [2]	25	
queue [3]	33	37
queue [4]	48	
queue [5]	57	
queue [6]		
queue [7]		
queue [8]	86	
queue [9]	92	

FIGURE 6.5.2   Illustration of the radix sort.

Sorted file:

	12	25	33	37	48	57	86	92

then this step is not necessary and, in fact, space is saved. This is the same situation as in the *addr* method (address calculation sort) in Section 6.4. As in previous applications, we do not make any internal calls to methods but perform their actions in place.

```
private static final int NUMELTS = …;

class Node {
  public int info;
  public int next;
}

public static void radixsort(int x[ ]) {
  int front[ ], rear[ ];
  front = new int[10];
  rear = new int[10];
  Node n[ ] = new Node[NUMELTS];
  int exp, first, i, j, k, p = 0, q, y;

  // Initialize linked list
  for (i = 0; i < x.length - 1; i++) {
          n[i] = new Node();
```

```
               n[i].info = x[i];
               n[i].next = I + 1;
    }
    n[x.length - 1] = new Node();
    n[x.length - 1].info = x[x.length - 1];
    n[x.length - 1].next = -1;
    first = 0;         // first is the head of the linked list
    for (k = 1; k < 3; k++) {
               // Assume we have two-digit numbers
               for (i = 0; i < 10; i++) {
                        // Initialize queues
                        rear[i] = -1;
                        front[i] = -1;
               }
               // Process each element on the list
               while (first != -1) {
                        p = first;
                        first = n[first].next;
                        y = n[p].info;
                        // Extract the kth digit
                        // raise 10 to the (k - 1)th power
                        exp = (int)Math.pow(10,(double)(k-1));
                        j = (y/exp) % 10;
                        // Insert y into queue[j]
                        q = rear[j];
                        if (q == -1)
                                front[j] = p;
                        else
                                n[q].next = p;
                        rear[j] = p;
               } // end while
               // At this point each record is in its proper queue
               based on digit k
               // We now form a single list from all the queue
               elements.
               // Find the first element.
               for (j = 0; j < 10 && front[j] == -1; j++)
                        ;
               first = front[j];
               // Link up remaining queues
               while (j <= 9) {                 // Check if finished
                        // Find the next element
                        for (i = j + 1; i < 10 && front[i] == -1; i++)
                                 ;
                        if (i <= 9) {
                                p = i;
                                n[rear[j]].next = front[i];
                        }
                        j = i;
               }
```

```
            n[rear[p]].next =- 1;
    } // end for
    // Copy back to the original array
    for (i = 0; i < x.length; i++) {
            x[i] = n[first].info;
            first = n[first].next;

    }
} // end radixsort
```

The time requirements for the radix sorting method clearly depend on the number of digits (m) and the number of elements in the file (n). Since the outer loop *for* $(k = 1; k < = m; k + +)$ is traversed m times (once for each digit), and the inner loop n times (once for each element in the file), the sort is approximately $O(m * n)$. Thus the sort is reasonably efficient if the number of digits in the keys is not too large. It should be noted, however that many machines have the hardware facilities to order digits of a number (particularly if they are in binary) much more rapidly than they can execute a compare of two full keys. Therefore, it is not reasonable to compare the $O(m * n)$ estimate with some of the other results we arrived at in this chapter. Note also that if the keys are dense (i.e., if almost every number which can possibly be a key is actually a key), then m approximates $\log n$ so that $O(m * n)$ approximates $O(n \log n)$. The sort requires space to store pointers to the fronts and rears of the queues in addition to an extra field in each record to be used as a pointer in the linked lists. If the number of digits is large, it is sometimes more efficient to sort the file by first applying the radix sort to the most significant digits and then using straight insertion on the rearranged file. In cases where most of the records in the file have different most significant digits, this process eliminates wasteful passes on the least significant digits.

EXERCISES

6.5.1 Write an algorithm for a method $merge(x, lb1, ub1, ub2)$ that assumes that $x[lb1]$ through $x[ub1]$ and $x[ub1 + 1]$ through $x[ub2]$ are sorted and merges the two into $x[lb1]$ through $x[ub2]$.

6.5.2 Consider the following recursive version of the merge sort which uses the routine *merge* from the previous exercise. It is initially called by $msort2(x, 0, n - 1)$. Rewrite the routine by eliminating recursion and simplifying. How does the resulting routine differ from the one in the text?

```
public static void msort2(x, lb, ub) {
        if (lb != ub) {
                mid = (ub + lb)/2;
                msort2(x, lb, mid);
                msort2(x, mid + 1, ub);
                merge(x, lb, mid, ub);
        }
    }
```

6.5.3 Let $a(l1, l2)$ be the average number of comparisons necessary to merge two sorted arrays of length $l1$ and $l2$, where the elements of the arrays are chosen at random from among $l1 + l2$ elements.

a. What are the values of $a(l1, 0)$ and $a(0, l2)$?

b. Show that for $l1 > 0$ and $l2 > 0$, $a(l1, l2)$ is equal to $(l1/(1 + l2))$ $* (1 + a(l1 - 1, l2)) + (l2/(l1 + l2)) * (1 + a(l1, l2 - 1))$. (Hint: Express the average number of comparisons in terms of the average number of comparisons after the first comparison.)

c. Show that $a(l1, l2)$ equals $(l1 * l2 * (l1 + l2 + 2))/((l1 + 1) * (l2 + 1))$.

d. Verify the formula in part c for two arrays, one of size 2 and one of size 1.

6.5.4 Consider the following procedure for merging two arrays a and b into c: Perform a binary search for $b[0]$ in the array a. If $b[0]$ is between $a[i]$ and $a[i + 1]$, output $a[1]$ through $a[i]$ to the array c, then output $b[0]$ to the array c. Next, perform a binary search for $b[1]$ in the subarray $a[i + 1]$ to $a[la]$ (where la is the number of elements in the array a) and repeat the output process. Repeat this procedure for every element of the array b.

a. Write a Java method to implement this procedure.

b. In which cases is this method more efficient than the method in the text? In which cases is it less efficient?

6.5.5 Consider the following method (called **binary merging**) of merging two sorted arrays a and b into c: Let la and lb be the number of elements of a and b respectively, and assume that $la \geq lb$. Divide a into $lb + 1$ approximately equal subarrays. Compare $b[0]$ with the smallest element of the second subarray of a. If $b[0]$ is smaller, then find $a[i]$ such that $a[i] \leq b[0] \leq a[i + 1]$ by a binary search in the first subarray. Output all elements of the first subarray up to and including $a[i]$ into c, and then output $b[0]$ into c. Repeat this process with $b[1], b[2], \ldots, b[j]$, where $b[j]$ is found to be larger than the smallest element of the second subarray. Output all remaining elements of the first subarray and the first element of the second subarray into c. Then compare $b[j]$ to the smallest element of the third subarray of a, and so on.

a. Write an application to implement the binary merge.

b. Show that if $la = lb$, the binary merge acts like the merge described in the text.

c. Show that if $lb = 1$, the binary merge acts like the merge in the previous exercise.

6.5.6 Determine the number of comparisons (as a function of n and m) that are performed in merging two ordered files a and b of sizes n and m respectively by each of the following merge methods, on each of the following sets of ordered files:

Merge Methods:

a. the merge method presented in the text

b. the merge in Exercise 6.5.4

c. the binary merge in Exercise 6.5.5

Sets of Files:

a. $m = n$ and $a[i] < b[i] < a[i + 1]$ for all i

b. $m = n$ and $a[n] < b[1]$

c. $m = n$ and $a[n/2] < b[1] < b[m] < a[(n/2) + 1]$

d. $n = 2 * m$ and $a[i] < b[i] < a[i + 1]$ for all i between 1 and m

e. $n = 2 * m$ and $a[m + i] < b[i] < a[m + i + 1]$ for all i between 1 and m

f. $n = 2 * m$ and $a[2 * i] < b[i] < a[2 * i + 1]$ for all i between 1 and m

g. $m = 1$ and $b[1] = a[n/2]$

h. $m = 1$ and $b[1] < a[1]$

i. $m = 1$ and $a[n] < b[1]$

6.5.7 Generate two random sorted files of size 100 and merge them by each of the methods in the previous exercise, keeping track of the number of comparisons made. Do the same for two files of size 10 and two files of size 1000. Repeat the experiment ten times. What do the results indicate about the average efficiency of the merge methods?

6.5.8 Write a routine that sorts a file by first applying the radix sort to the most significant r digits (where r is a given constant) and then uses straight insertion to sort the entire file. This eliminates excessive passes on low-order digits that may not be necessary.

6.5.9 Write a program that prints all sets of six positive integers $a1, a2, a3, a4, a5$, and $a6$ such that:

$$a1 \leq a2 \leq a3 \leq 20$$
$$a1 < a4 \leq a5 \leq a6 \leq 20$$

and the sum of the squares of $a1, a2$, and $a3$ equals the sum of the squares of $a4, a5$, and $a6$. (*Hint:* Generate all possible sums of three squares, and use a sorting method to find duplicates.)

CHAPTER 7

Searching

In this chapter, we consider methods of searching large amounts of data to find one particular piece of information. As we shall see, certain methods of organizing data make the search process more efficient. Since searching is such a common task in computing, a knowledge of these methods goes a long way toward making a good programmer.

7.1 BASIC SEARCH TECHNIQUES

Before we consider specific search techniques, let us define some terms. A *table* or a *file* is a group of elements, each of which is called a *record*. Associated with each record is a *key*, which is used to differentiate the record from all other records. The association between a record and its key may be simple or complex. In the simplest form, the key is contained within the record at a specific offset from the start of the record. Such a key is called an *internal key* or an *embedded key*. In other cases, there is a separate table of keys that includes pointers to the records or some other method of identifying a record from a key. Such keys are called *external*.

For every file there is at least one set of keys (possibly more) that is unique (i.e., no two records have the same key value). Such a key is called a *primary key*. For example, if the file is stored as an array, then the index within the array of an element is a unique external key for that element. However, since any field of a record can serve as the key in a particular application, keys need not always be unique. For example, in a file of names and addresses, if the state is used as the key for a particular search, then it will probably not be unique, since there may be two records with the same state in the file. Such a key is called a *secondary key*. Some of the algorithms we present assume unique keys; others allow for duplicate keys. When adopting an algorithm for an application, the programmer should know whether the keys are unique and make sure that the algorithm selected is appropriate.

A *search algorithm* is an algorithm that accepts an argument a and tries to find a record whose key is a. The algorithm may return the entire record, but more commonly it returns a pointer to the record. Sometimes a search for an argument in a table will be unsuccessful; that is, there is no record in the table with that argument as its key. In such a case, the algorithm may return a special "null record" or a null pointer. If a search is unsuccessful, it is very often desirable to add a new record with the argument as its key. An algorithm that does this is called a ***search and insertion*** algorithm. A successful search is often called a ***retrieval***. A table of records in which a key is used for retrieval is often called a ***search table*** or a ***dictionary***.

In some cases it is desirable to insert a record with a primary key *key* into a file without first searching for another record with the same key. Such a situation could arise if it has already been determined that no such record already exists in the file. In subsequent discussions, we investigate and comment upon the relative efficiency of various algorithms. In such cases, the reader should note whether the comments refer to a search, an insertion, or a search and insertion.

We have said nothing so far about the manner in which the table or file is organized. It may be an array of records, a linked list, a tree, or even a graph. Because different search techniques may be suitable for different table organizations, a table is often designed with a specific search technique in mind. The table may be contained completely in memory, completely in auxiliary storage, or may be divided between the two. Different search techniques are necessary under these different assumptions. Searches in which the entire table is constantly in main memory are called ***internal searches***, whereas those in which most of the table is kept in auxiliary storage are called ***external searches***. As with sorting, we concentrate primarily on internal searching; however, we mention some techniques of external searching when they relate closely to the methods we are studying.

Dictionary as an Abstract Data Type

A search table, or ***dictionary***, can be presented as an abstract data type (ADT). See Chapter 1 for a discussion of ADTs. We first assume two type declarations of the key and record types and a function that extracts the key of a record from the record. We also define a null record to represent a failed search.

```
abstract class KEYTYPE  ...      // a type of key
abstract class RECTYPE  ...      // a type of record
RECTYPE nullRec =  ...           // a "null" record

public KEYTYPE keyFunct(RECTYPE r) {
  ...
};
```

We may then represent the abstract data type *Table* as simply a set of records. This is our first example of an ADT defined in terms of a set rather than a sequence. We use the notation [*eltype*] to denote a set of objects of the type *eltype*. The method *s.inSet*(*elt*) returns ***true*** if *elt* is in set *s* and ***false*** otherwise. The set operation $x - y$ denotes the set *x* with all the elements of set *y* removed. The function *keyFunct* (*r*) returns the key of record *r*.

```
abstract class [RECTYPE] TABLE (RECTYPE) {
  abstract TABLE(RECTYPE) tbl.member(KEYTYPE k)
  postcondition if (there exists an r in tbl such that keyFunct(r)
                 == k)
              member = true
```

```
                  else
                        member = false
    abstract RECTYPE TABLE(RECTYPE) tbl.search(KEYTYPE k)
    postcondition       ! tbl.member(k) && (search == nullRec)
                               || (tbl.member(k) &&
                               keyFunct(search) == k);

    abstract TABLE(RECTYPE) tbl.insert(RECTYPE r)
    precondition      tbl.member(keyFunct(r)) == false
    postcondition     tbl.inSet(r);
                      (tbl - [r]) == tbl';

    abstract TABLE(RECTYPE).tbl delete(KEYTYPE k)
    postcondition     tbl == (tbl' - [tbl.search(k)]);
}
```

Because no relation is presumed to exist among the records or their associated keys, the table that we have specified is called an ***unordered table***. Although such a table allows elements to be retrieved based on their key values, the elements cannot be retrieved in a specific order. There are times when, in addition to the facilities provided by an unordered table, it is also necessary to retrieve elements based on some ordering of their keys. Once an ordering among the records is established, it becomes possible to refer to the first element of a table, the last element of a table, and the successor of a given element. A table that supports these additional facilities is called an ***ordered table***. The ADT for an ordered table must be specified as a sequence to indicate the ordering of the records rather than as a set. We leave the ADT specification as an exercise for the reader.

Algorithmic Notation

Most of the techniques presented in this chapter are presented as algorithms rather than as Java applications. The reason for this is that a table may be represented in a wide variety of ways. For example, a table (keys plus records) organized as an array might be declared by:

```
private static final int TABLESIZE = 1000;
class KeyType { … }
class RecType { … }
class TableType {
   KeyType k;
   RecType r;
}

TableType table[] = new TableType[TABLESIZE];
```

or it might be declared as two separate arrays:

```
KeyType k[] = new KeyType[TABLESIZE];
RecType r[] = new RecType[TABLESIZE];
```

In the first case, the ith key would be referenced as *table*[i].*getKey*(), in the second case, as $k[i]$.

Similarly, for a table organized as a list, either the array representation of a list or the dynamic representation of a list could be used. In the former case, the key of the record referenced by *p* would be referenced as *node[p].k*; in the latter case, as *p.getKey()*.

However, the techniques for searching these tables are very similar. Thus, in order to free ourselves from the necessity of choosing a specific representation, we adopt the algorithmic convention of referencing the *i*th key as *k(i)* and the key of the record pointed to by *p* as *k(p)*. Similarly, we reference the corresponding record as *r(i)* or *r(p)*. In this way we can focus on details of technique rather than of implementation.

Sequential Searching

The simplest form of a search is the ***sequential search***. This search is applicable to tables organized either as arrays or as linked lists. Let us assume that *k* is an array of *n* keys, *k(0)* through *k(n − 1)*, and *r* an array of records, *r(0)* through *r(n − 1)*, such that *k(i)* is the key of *r(i)*. (Note that we are using the algorithmic notation, *k(i)* and *r(i)*, as described above.) Let us also assume that *key* is a search argument. We wish to return the smallest integer *i* such that *k(i)* equals *key* if such an *i* exists and −1 otherwise. The algorithm for doing this is as follows:

```
for (i = 0; i < n; i++)
    if (key == k(i))
        return i;
return -1;
```

The algorithm examines each key in turn; upon finding one that matches the search argument, its index (which acts as pointer to its record) is returned. If no match is found, −1 is returned.

This algorithm can be modified easily to add a record *rec* with key *key* to the table if *key* is not already there. The last statement is modified to read

```
k(n) = key;      // insert the new key and
r(n) = rec;      // record
n++;             // increase the table size
return n - 1;
```

Note that if insertions are made using the above revised algorithm only, then no two records can have the same key. When this algorithm is implemented in Java, we must ensure that incrementing *n* does not make its value go beyond the upper bound of the array. To use a sequential insertion search on an array, sufficient storage must have been previously allocated for the array.

An even more efficient search method involves inserting the argument key at the end of the array before beginning the search, thus guaranteeing that the key will be found.

```
k(n) = key;
for (i = 0; key != k(i); i++)
    ;
if (i < n)
    return i;
else
    return -1;
```

For a search and insertion, the entire *if* statement is replaced by

```
if (i == n)
    r(n++) = rec;
return i;
```

The extra key inserted at the end of the array is called a ***sentinel***.

Storing a table as a linked list has the advantage that the size of the table can be increased dynamically as needed. Let us assume that the table is organized as a linear linked list referenced by *table* and linked by a pointer field *next*. Then assuming k, r, key, and rec as before, the sequential insertion search for a linked list may be written as follows:

```
q = null;
for (p = table; p != null && k(p) != key; p = next(p))
    q = p;
if (p != null)                  // this means that k(p) == key
    return p;
// insert a new node
s = getnode();
k(s) = key;
r(s) = rec;
next(s) = null;
if (q == null)
    table = s;
else
    next(q) = s;
return s;
```

The efficiency of searching a list can be improved by the same technique just suggested for an array. A sentinel node containing the argument key can be added to the end of the list before beginning the search, so that the condition in the *for* loop is the simple condition $k(p) \;!= key$. The sentinel method, however, requires maintaining an additional external pointer to the last node in the list. We leave additional details (as, for example, what happens to the newly added node when the key is found within the list) to the reader.

Deleting a record from a table stored as an unordered array is implemented by replacing the record to be deleted with the last record in the array and reducing the table size by one. If the array is ordered in some way (even if the ordering is not by key), this method cannot be used, and half the elements in the array must be moved, on the average. (Why?) If the table is stored as a linked list, then it is quite efficient to delete an element regardless of the ordering.

Efficiency of Sequential Searching

How efficient is a sequential search? Let us examine the number of comparisons made by a sequential search in searching for a given key. We assume no insertions or deletions, so that we are searching through a table of constant size n. The number of comparisons depends on where the record with the argument key appears in the table. If the record is the first one in the table, only one comparison is performed; if the record is the last one in the table, n comparisons are necessary. If it is equally likely for the argument to appear at any given table position, then a successful search will take (on the average) $(n + 1)/2$ comparisons, and an unsuccessful search will take n comparisons. In any case, the number of comparisons is $O(n)$.

However, it is usually the case that some arguments are presented to the search algorithm more often than others. For example, in the files of a college registrar, the records of a senior who is applying for transcripts for graduate school, or of a freshman whose high school average is being updated, are more likely to be called for than those of the average sophomore and junior. Similarly, the records of scofflaws and tax cheats are more likely to be retrieved from the files of a motor vehicles bureau or the Internal Revenue Service than those of a law-abiding citizen. (As we shall see later in this chapter, these examples are unrealistic because it is unlikely that a sequential search would be used for such large files; but for the moment, let us assume that a sequential search is being used.) Then, if frequently accessed records are placed at the beginning of the file, the average number of comparisons is sharply reduced, since the most commonly accessed records take the least amount of time to retrieve.

Let $p(i)$ be the probability that record i is retrieved. ($p(i)$ is a number between 0 and 1 such that if m retrievals are made from the file, $m * p(i)$ of them will be from $r(i)$.) Let us also assume that $p(0) + p(1) + \ldots + p(n - 1) = 1$ so that there is no possibility that an argument key is missing from the table. Then the average number of comparisons in searching for a record is:

$$p(0) + 2 * p(1) + 3 * p(2) + \ldots + n * p(n - 1)$$

Clearly, this number is minimized if

$$p(0) \geq p(1) \geq p(2) \geq \ldots \geq p(n - 1)$$

(Why?). Thus, given a large stable file, reordering the file in order of decreasing probability of retrieval achieves a greater degree of efficiency each time the file is searched.

If many insertions and deletions are to be performed on a table, a list structure is preferable to an array. However, even in a list it would be better to maintain the relationship

$$p(0) \geq p(1) \geq \ldots \geq p(n - 1)$$

to provide for efficient sequential searching. This can be done most easily if a new item is inserted into the list at its proper place. If *prob* is the probability that a record with a given key is the search argument, then that record should be inserted between records $r(i)$ and $r(i + 1)$, where i is such that

$$p(i) \geq prob \geq p(i + 1)$$

Of course this method implies that an extra field p is kept with each record or that p can be computed based on some other information in each record.

Reordering a List for Maximum Search Efficiency

Unfortunately, the probabilities $p(i)$ are rarely known in advance. Although certain records are frequently retrieved more often than others, it is almost impossible to identify those records in advance. Also, the probability that a given record will be retrieved may change over time. To use the example of the college registrar given earlier, a student begins as a freshman (high probability of retrieval) and then becomes a sophomore and a junior (low probability) before becoming a senior (high probability). Thus it would be helpful to have an algorithm that continually reorders the table so that more frequently accessed records drift to the front while less frequently accessed records drift to the back.

There are two search methods that accomplish this. One of these, known as the **move-to-front** method, is efficient only for a table organized as a list. In this method, whenever a search is successful (i.e., when the argument is found to match the key of a given record), the retrieved record is removed from its current location in the list and placed at the head of the list.

In the other method, known as the **transposition** method, a successfully retrieved record is interchanged with the record that immediately precedes it. We present an algorithm to implement the transposition method on a table stored as a linked list. The algorithm returns a reference to the retrieved record, or **null** if the record is not found. As before, *key* is the search argument, *k* and *r* are the tables of keys and records. *table* is a reference to the first node of the list.

```
q = s = null;    // q is one step behind p;
                 // s is two steps behind p
for (p = table; p != null && k(p) != key; p = next(p)) {
    s = q;
    q = p;
}
if (p == null)
    return p;
// We have found the record at position p.
// Transpose the records pointed to by p and q.
if (q == null)
    // The key is in the first table position.
    // No transposition is necessary.
    return p;
// Transpose node(q) and node(p).
next(q) = next(p);
next(p) = q;
(s = null) ? table = p : next(s) = p;
return p;
```

Note that the two *if* statements in the algorithm can be combined, for conciseness, into the single statement *if* (*p* == **null** || *q* == **null**) **return** *p*. We leave the implementation of the transposition method for an array and the move-to-front method as exercises for the reader.

Both of these methods are based on the observed phenomenon that a record that has been retrieved is likely to be retrieved again. Advancing such records toward the front of the table makes subsequent retrievals more efficient. The rationale behind the move-to-front method is that, since the record is likely to be retrieved again, it should be placed at the position within the table at which such retrieval is most efficient. However, the counterargument for the transposition method is that a single retrieval does not imply that the record will be retrieved frequently; placing it at the front of the table reduces search efficiency for all the other records that formerly preceded it. By advancing a record only one position each time that it is retrieved, we ensure that it advances to the front of the list only if it is retrieved frequently.

It has been shown that the transposition method is more efficient over a large number of search requests with an unchanging probability distribution. However, the move-to-front method yields better results for a small to medium number of requests and responds more quickly to a change in probability distribution. It also has better worst-case behavior than transposition. For this reason, move-to-front is preferred in most practical situations involving sequential search.

If large numbers of searches with an unchanging probability distribution are required, then a mixed strategy may be best: use move-to-front for the first s searches to rapidly organize the list in good sequence and then switch to transposition to obtain even better behavior. The exact value of s to optimize overall efficiency depends on the length of the list and the exact access probability distribution.

One advantage of the transposition method over the move-to-front method is that it can be applied efficiently to tables stored in array form as well as to list structured tables. Transposing two elements in an array is a rather efficient operation, while moving an element from the middle of an array to its front involves (on the average) moving half the array. (However, in this case the average number of moves is not so large, since the element to be moved most often comes from the upper portion of the array.)

Searching an Ordered Table

If a table is stored in ascending or descending order of the record keys, then there are several techniques that can be used to improve the efficiency of searching. This is especially true if the table is of fixed size. One obvious advantage of sequentially searching a sorted file over searching an unsorted file occurs in situations where the argument key is absent from the file. In the case of an unsorted file, n comparisons are needed to detect this fact. In the case of a sorted file, assuming that the argument keys are uniformly distributed over the range of keys in the file, only $n/2$ comparisons (on the average) are needed. This is because we know that a given key is missing from a file sorted in ascending order of keys as soon as we encounter a key that is greater than the argument.

Suppose that it is possible to collect a large number of retrieval requests before any of them are processed. For example, in many applications a response to a request for information may be deferred to the next day. In such a case, all requests on a specific day may be collected and the actual searching may be done overnight, when no new requests are coming in. If both the table and the list of requests are sorted, then the sequential search can proceed through both concurrently. Thus, it is not necessary to search through the entire table for each retrieval request. In fact, if there are many such requests uniformly distributed over the entire table, then each request will require only a few lookups (if the number of requests is less than the number of table entries) or perhaps only a single comparison (if the number of requests is greater than the number of table entries). In such situations sequential searching is probably the best method to use.

Because of the simplicity and efficiency of sequential processing on sorted files, it may be worthwhile to sort a file before searching for keys in it. This is especially true in the situation described in the preceding paragraph, where we are dealing with a "master" file and a large "transaction" file of requests for searches.

Indexed Sequential Search

There is another technique that improves search efficiency for a sorted file, but it involves an increase in the amount of space required. This method is called the **indexed sequential** search method. An auxiliary table, called an **index**, is set aside in addition to the sorted file itself. Each element in the index consists of a key, *kindex*, and a pointer to the record in the file that corresponds to *kindex*. The elements in the index, as well as the elements in the file, must be sorted on the key. If the index is one-eighth the size of the file, then every eighth record in the file is represented in the index. This is illustrated by Figure 7.1.1.

   The algorithm used for searching an indexed sequential file is straightforward. Let *r, k*, and *key* be defined as before, let *kindex* be an array of the keys in the index, and let *pindex* be the array of pointers within the index to the actual records in the file. We assume that the file is stored as an array, that *n* is the size of the file, and that *indxSize* is the size of the index.

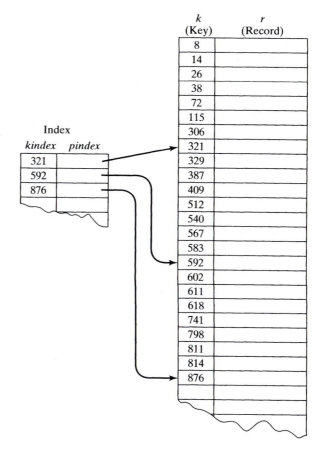

FIGURE 7.1.1 Indexed sequential file.

```
for (i = 0; i < indxSize && kindex(i) <= key; i++)
    ;
lowLim = (i == 0) ? 0 : pindex(i - 1);
hiLim = (i == indxSize) ? n - 1 : pindex(i) - 1;
for (j = lowLim; j <= hiLim && k(j) != key; j++)
    ;
return (j > hiLim) ? -1 : j;
```

Note that in the case of multiple records with the same key, the above algorithm does not necessarily return a pointer to the first such record in the table.

The real advantage of the indexed sequential method is that the items in the table can be examined sequentially if all the records in the file must be accessed, yet the search time for a particular item is sharply reduced. A sequential search is performed on the smaller index rather than on the larger table. Once the correct index position has been found, a second sequential search is performed on a small portion of the record table.

The use of an index is applicable to sorted tables stored as linked lists as well as to those stored as arrays. Use of a linked list implies a larger space overhead for pointers, although insertions and deletions can be performed much more readily.

If the table is so large that even the use of an index does not achieve sufficient efficiency (either because the index is large, in order to reduce sequential searching in the table, or because the index is small, so that adjacent keys in the index are far from each other in the table), then a secondary index can be used. The secondary index acts as an index to the primary index, which points to entries in the sequential table. This is illustrated in Figure 7.1.2.

Deletions from an indexed sequential table can be made most easily by flagging deleted entries. In sequential searching through the table, deleted entries are ignored. Note that if an element is deleted, then even if its key is in the index, nothing need be done to the index; only the original table entry is flagged.

Insertion into an indexed sequential table is more difficult, because there may not be room between two already existing table entries, thus necessitating a shift in a large number of table elements. However, if a nearby item has been flagged as deleted in the table, then only a few items need be shifted and the deleted item can be overwritten. This may in turn require alteration of the index if an item pointed to by an index element is shifted. An alternative method is to keep an overflow area at some other location and link together any inserted records. However, this would require an extra pointer field in each record of the original table. You are asked to explore these possibilities as an exercise.

Binary Search

The most efficient method of searching a sequential table without the use of auxiliary indices or tables is the binary search. You should be familiar with this search technique from Sections 3.1 and 3.2. Basically, the argument is compared with the key of the middle element of the table. If they are equal, then the search ends successfully; otherwise, either the upper or lower half of the table must be searched in a similar manner.

In Chapter 3, it was noted that the binary search can best be defined recursively. As a result, a recursive definition, a recursive algorithm, and a recursive program were

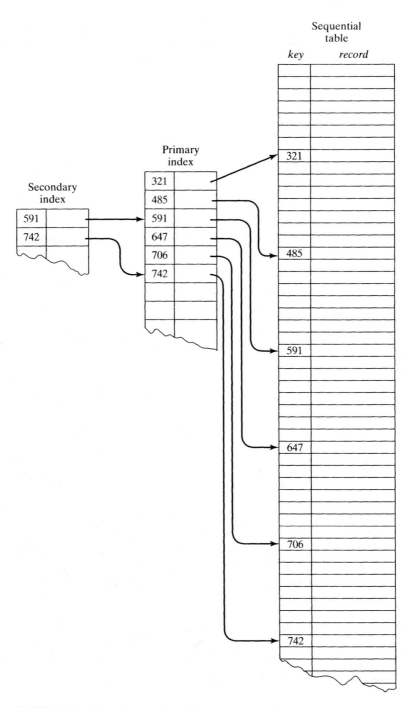

FIGURE 7.1.2   Use of a secondary index.

presented for the binary search. However, the overhead associated with recursion may make it inappropriate for use in practical situations in which efficiency is a prime consideration. We therefore present the following nonrecursive version of the binary search algorithm:

```
low = 0;
hi = n - 1;
while (low <= hi) {
    mid = (low + hi)/2;
    if (key == k(mid))
            return(mid);
    if (key < k(mid))
            hi = mid - 1;
    else
            low = mid + 1;
}
return -1;
```

Each comparison in a binary search reduces the number of possible candidates by a factor of 2. Thus, the maximum number of key comparisons is approximately $\log_2 n$. (Actually, it is $2 * \log_2 n$, since in Java, two key comparisons are made each time through the loop: $key == k(mid)$ and $key < k(mid)$. However, only one comparison is made in assembly language or in FORTRAN using an arithmetic IF statement. An optimizing compiler should be able to eliminate the extra comparison.) Thus, we may say that the binary search algorithm is $O(\log_2 n)$.

Note that the binary search may be used in conjunction with the indexed sequential table organization mentioned earlier. Binary search can be used instead of searching the index sequentially. It can also be used in searching the main table once two boundary records are identified. However, the size of this table segment is likely to be small enough that a binary search is not more advantageous than a sequential search.

Unfortunately, the binary search algorithm can only be used if the table is stored as an array. This is because it makes use of the fact that the indices of array elements are consecutive integers. For this reason, the binary search is practically useless in situations where there are so many insertions or deletions that an array structure is inappropriate.

One method for utilizing binary search in the presence of insertions and deletions if the maximum number of elements is known involves a data structure known as the **padded list**. The method uses two arrays: an element array and a parallel flag array. The element array contains the sorted keys in the table with "empty" slots initially evenly interspersed among the keys of the table to allow for growth. An empty slot is indicated by a 0 value in the corresponding flag array element, while a full slot is indicated by the value 1. Each empty slot in the element array contains a key value greater than or equal to the key value in the previous slot and less than the key value in the following full slot. Thus the entire element array is sorted, and a valid binary search can be performed on it.

To search for an element, perform a binary search on the element array. If the argument key is not found, the element does not exist in the table. If it is found and the corresponding flag value is 1, the element has been located. If the corresponding flag value is 0, check whether the previous full slot contains the argument key. If it does, the element has been located; if it doesn't, the element does not exist in the table.

To insert an element, first locate its position. If the position is empty, insert the element in the empty position, resetting its flag value to 1, and adjust the contents of all previous contiguous empty positions to equal the contents of the previous full element, and of all following contiguous empty positions to the inserted element, leaving their flags at 0. If the position is full, shift forward by one position all the following elements up to the first empty position (overwriting the first empty position and resetting its flag to 1) to make room for the new element. Deletion simply involves locating a key and changing its associated flag value to 0. Of course, the drawbacks of this method are the shifting that must be done at insertion and the limited room for growth. Periodically, it may be desirable to redistribute the empty spaces evenly through the array to improve insertion speed.

Interpolation Search

Another technique for searching an ordered array is called ***interpolation search***. If the keys are uniformly distributed between $k(0)$ and $k(n-1)$, then the method may be even more efficient than binary search.

Initially, as in binary search, *low* is set to 0 and *high* is set to $n-1$, and throughout the algorithm, the argument key *key* is known to be between $k(low)$ and $k(high)$. On the assumption that the keys are uniformly distributed between these two values, *key* would be expected to be at approximately position

```
mid = low + (high - low) * ((key - k(low)) / (k(high) - k(low)))
```

If *key* is lower than $k(mid)$, then reset *high* to $mid-1$; if higher, reset *low* to $mid+1$. Repeat the process until the key has been found or $low > high$.

Indeed, if the keys are uniformly distributed through the array, interpolation search requires an average of $\log_2(\log_2 n)$ comparisons and rarely requires much more, compared to binary search's $\log_2 n$ (again, considering the two comparisons for equality and inequality of *key* and $k(mid)$ as one). However, if the keys are not uniformly distributed, interpolation search can have very poor average behavior. In the worst case, the value of *mid* can consistently equal $low+1$ or $high-1$, in which case interpolation search degenerates into sequential search. By contrast, binary search's comparisons are never greater than approximately $\log_2 n$. In practical situations, keys often tend to cluster around certain values and are not uniformly distributed. For example, since more names begin with S than with Q, there are likely to be many Smiths and very few Quodnots. In such situations, binary search is far superior to interpolation search.

A variation of interpolation search, called ***robust interpolation search*** (or ***fast search***), attempts to remedy the poor practical behavior of interpolation search while extending its advantage over binary search to nonuniform key distributions. This is done by establishing a value *gap* so that $mid-low$ and $high-mid$ are always greater than *gap*. Initially, *gap* is set to $sqrt(high-low+1)$. *probe* is set to $low + (high-low)*((key-k(low))/(k(high)-k(low)))$, and *mid* is set equal to $min(high-gap, max(probe, low+gap))$ (where *min* and *max* return the minimum and maximum, respectively, of two values). That is, we guarantee that the next position used for comparison (*mid*) is at least *gap* positions from the ends of the interval, where *gap* is at least the square root of the interval. When the argument key is found to be restricted to the smaller of the two intervals, from *low* to *mid* and *mid* to *high*, *gap* is reset to the square root of the new interval size. However, if the argument key is found to lie in the larger of the two intervals, the value of *gap* is doubled, although it is never allowed to be greater than half the interval size. This guarantees escape from a large cluster of similar key values.

The expected number of comparisons for robust interpolation search for a random distribution of keys is $O(\log \log n)$. This is superior to binary search. On a list of approximately 40,000 names, binary search requires an average of approximately 16 key comparisons. Due to clustering of names in practical situations, interpolation search required 134 average comparisons in an actual experiment, while robust interpolation search required only 12.5. On a uniformly distributed list of approximately 40,000 elements— $\log_2 (\log_2 40{,}000)$ is approximately 3.9—robust interpolation search required 6.7 average comparisons. (It should be noted that the extra computation time required for robust interpolation search may be substantial but is ignored in these findings.) The worst case for robust interpolation search is $O((\log n)^2)$ comparisons, which is higher than that for binary search, but much better than the $O(n)$ worst case of regular interpolation search.

On most computers, the computation required by interpolation search are very slow, however, since they involve arithmetic on keys and complex multiplications and divisions. Binary search requires arithmetic only on integer indexes and division by two, which can be performed efficiently by shifting one bit to the right. Thus, the computational requirements of interpolation search often cause it to perform more slowly than binary search even when it requires fewer comparisons.

EXERCISES

7.1.1   Modify the search and insertion algorithms of this section so that they become update algorithms. If an algorithm finds an *i* such that *key* equals $k(i)$, then change the value of $r(i)$ to *rec*.

7.1.2   Implement the sequential search and the sequential search and insertion algorithms in Java for both arrays and linked lists.

7.1.3   Compare the efficiency of searching an ordered sequential table of size *n* and searching an unordered table of the same size for the key *key*:

   a.   If no record with key *key* is present.
   b.   If one record with key *key* is present and only one is sought.
   c.   If more than one record with key *key* is present and it is desired to find only the first one.
   d.   If more than one record with key *key* is present and it is desired to find them all.

7.1.4   Assume that an ordered table is stored as a circular list with two external pointers: *table* and *other*. *table* always points to the node containing the record with the smallest key. *other* is initially equal to *table*, but is reset each time a search is performed to point to the record that is retrieved. If a search is unsuccessful, *other* is reset to *table*. Write a Java method *table.search(other, key)* that implements this method and returns a reference to a retrieved record or a null reference if the search is unsuccessful. Explain how keeping a reference to *other* can reduce the average number of comparisons in a search.

7.1.5 Consider an ordered table implemented as an array or as a doubly-linked list so that the table can be searched sequentially either backwards or forwards. Assume that a single pointer p points to the last record successfully retrieved. The search always begins at the record pointed to by p but may proceed in either direction. Write a method *table.search*(p, *key*) for the case of an array and a doubly-linked list to retrieve a record with key *key* and to modify p accordingly. Prove that the number of key comparisons in the successful and unsuccessful cases is the same as in the method in the previous exercise, where the table may be scanned in only one direction but the scanning process may start at one of two points.

7.1.6 Consider a program written with the following code:

```
if (c₁)
    if (c₂)
        if (c₃)
            ...
            if (cₙ) {
                statement
            }
```

where c_i is a condition that is either true or false. Note that rearranging the conditions in a different order results in an equivalent program, since the { statement } is only executed if all the c_i are true. Assume that *time*(i) is the time needed to evaluate condition c_i, and that *prob*(i) is the probability that condition c_i is true. In what order should the conditions be arranged to make the program most efficient?

7.1.7 Modify the indexed sequential search so that it returns the first record in the table in the case of multiple records with the same key.

7.1.8 Consider the following Java implementation of an indexed sequential file:

```
private static final int INDXSIZE = 100;
private static final int TABLESIZE = 1000;

class IndxType {
    int kindex;
    int pindex;
}

class TableType {
    int k;
    int r;
    boolean flag
}

class IsFileKeyType {
    IndxType indx[ ] = new IndxType[INDXSIZE];
    TableType table[ ] = new TableType[TABLESIZE];
}

ISFileKeyType ISFile;
```

Write a Java method *create*() for the *IsFileKeyType* class that initializes such a file from input data. Each input line contains a key and a record. The input is sorted in ascending key order. Each index entry corresponds to ten table entries. *flag* is set to **true** in an occupied table entry and to **false** in an unoccupied entry. Two out of every ten table entries are left unoccupied to allow for future growth.

7.1.9 Given an indexed sequential file, as in the previous exercise, write a Java method *search(key)* for the *IsFileKeyType* class to print the record in the file with key *key* if it is present, and with an indication that the record is missing if no record with that key exists. (How can you ensure that an unsuccessful search is as efficient as possible?) Also, write methods *insert(key, rec)* to insert a record *rec* with key *key* and *delete(key)* to delete the record with key *key*.

7.1.10 Consider the following version of a binary search, which assumes that the keys are contained in $k(1)$ through $k(n)$, and that the special element $k(0)$ is smaller than every possible key:

```
mid = n/2;
len = (n - 1)/2;
while (key != k(mid)) {
        if (key < k(mid)) {
                mid -= len/2;
        else
                mid += len/2;
        if (len == 0)
                return -1;
        len /= 2;
}
return mid;
```

Prove that this algorithm is correct. What are the advantages and/or disadvantages of this method over the method presented in the text?

7.1.11 The following search algorithm on a sorted array is known as the **Fibonaccian search** because of its use of Fibonacci numbers. (For a definition of Fibonacci numbers and the *fib* function, see Section 3.1.)

```
for (j = 1; fib(j) < n; j++)
        ;
mid = n - fib(j - 2) + 1;
f1 = fib(j - 2);
f2 = fib(j - 3);
while (key != k(mid))
        if (mid < 0 || key > k(mid)) {
                if (f1 == 1)
                        return -1;
                mid += f2;
                f1 -= f2;
                f2 -= f1;
        }
        else {
                if (f2 == 0)
                        return -1;
                mid -= f2;
                t = f1 - f2;
                f1 = f2;
                f2 = t;
        }
return mid;
```

Explain how this algorithm works. Compare the number of key comparisons with the number used by the binary search. Modify the initial portion of this algorithm so that it computes the Fibonacci numbers efficiently, rather than looking them up in a table or computing each anew.

7.1.12   Modify the binary search in the text so that, in the case of an unsuccessful search, it returns the index i such that $k(i) < key < k(i + 1)$. If $key < k(0)$, then it returns -1, and if $key > k(n - 1)$, then it returns $n - 1$. Do the same for the searches in Exercises 7.1.10 and 7.1.11.

7.2   TREE SEARCHING

In Section 7.1 we discussed search operations on a file that is organized either as an array or as a list. In this section we consider several ways of organizing files as trees and some associated searching algorithms.

In Sections 5.1 and 6.3 we presented a method of using a binary tree to store a file in order to make sorting the file more efficient. In that method, all the left descendants of a node with key *key* have keys that are less than *key*, and all the right descendants have keys that are greater than or equal to *key*. The inorder traversal of such a binary tree yields the file in ascending key order.

Such a tree may also be used as a binary search tree. Using binary tree notation, the algorithm for searching for the key *key* in such a tree is as follows (we assume that each node contains four fields: *k*, which holds the record's key value, *r*, which holds the record itself, and *left* and *right*, which are pointers to the subtrees):

```
p = tree;
while (p != null && key != k(p))
    p = (key < k(p)) ? left(p) : right(p);
return p;
```

The efficiency of the search process can be improved by using a sentinel, as in sequential searching. A sentinel node, with a separate external pointer pointing to it, remains allocated with the tree. All *left* or *right* tree pointers that do not point to another tree node now point to the sentinel node instead of equaling **null**. When a search is performed, the argument key is first inserted into the sentinel node, thus guaranteeing that it will be located in the tree. This enables the header of the search loop to be written **while** $(key! = k(p))$ without the risk of an infinite loop. If p equals the external sentinel pointer after leaving the loop, the search is unsuccessful; otherwise, p points to the desired node. We leave the actual algorithm to the reader.

Note that the binary search in Section 7.1 actually uses a sorted array as an implicit binary search tree. The middle element of the array can be thought of as the root of the tree, the lower half of the array (all of whose elements are less than the middle element) can be considered the left subtree, and the upper half (all of whose elements are greater than the middle element) can be considered the right subtree.

A sorted array can be produced from a binary search tree by traversing the tree in inorder and inserting each element sequentially into the array as it is visited. On the other hand, there are many binary search trees that correspond to a given sorted array. Viewing the middle element of the array as the root of a tree and viewing the remaining elements recursively as left and right subtrees produces a relatively balanced binary search tree (Figure 7.2.1a). Viewing the first element of the array as the root of a tree and each successive element as the right son of its predecessor produces a very unbalanced binary tree (Figure 7.2.1b).

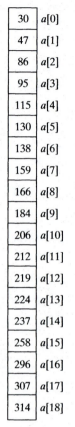

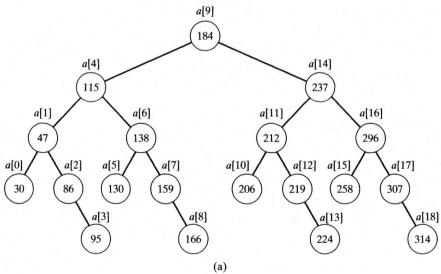

(a)

FIGURE 7.2.1 Sorted array and two of its binary tree representations.

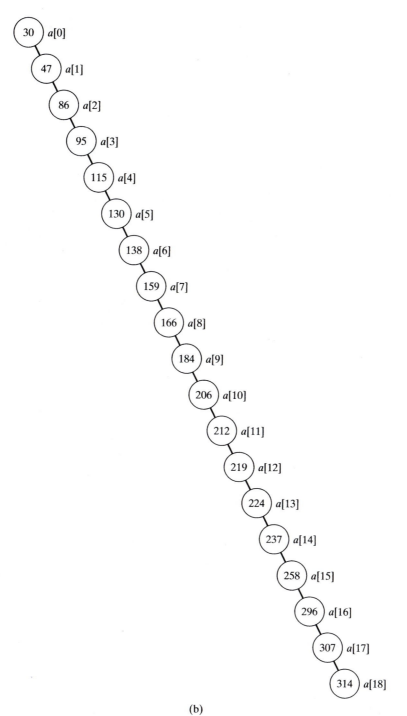

(b)

FIGURE 7.2.1   (*Continued*)

The advantage of using a binary search tree over an array is that a tree enables search, insertion, and deletion operations to be performed efficiently. If an array is used, then an insertion or deletion requires that approximately half of the elements of the array be moved. (Why?) Insertion or deletion in a search tree, on the other hand, requires that only a few pointers must be adjusted.

Inserting into a Binary Search Tree

The following algorithm searches a binary search tree and inserts a new record into it if the search is unsuccessful. (We assume the existence of a method *makeTree* that constructs a binary tree consisting of a single node whose information field is passed as an argument and returns a pointer to the tree. This method is described in Section 5.1. However, in our version, we assume that *makeTree* accepts two arguments, a record and a key.)

```
q = null;
p = tree;
while (p != null) {
    if (key == k(p))
            return p;
    q = p;
    if (key < k(p))
            p = left(p);
    else
            p = right(p);
}
v = makeTree(rec, key);
if (q == null)
    tree = v;
else
    if (key < k(q))
            left(q) = v;
    else
            right(q) = v;
return v;
```

Note that after a new record is inserted, the tree retains the property of being sorted in an inorder traversal.

Deleting from a Binary Search Tree

We now present an algorithm to delete a node with key *key* from a binary search tree. There are three cases to consider. If the node to be deleted has no sons, then it may be deleted without further adjustment to the tree. This is illustrated in Figure 7.2.2a. If the node to be deleted has only one subtree, then its only son can be moved up to take its place. This is illustrated in Figure 7.2.2b. If, however, the node *p* to be deleted has two subtrees, then its inorder successor *s* (or predecessor) must take its place. The inorder successor cannot have a left subtree (since a left descendant would be the inorder

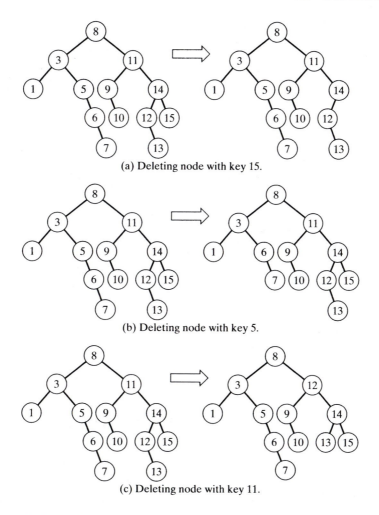

(a) Deleting node with key 15.

(b) Deleting node with key 5.

(c) Deleting node with key 11.

FIGURE 7.2.2   Deleting nodes from a binary search tree.

successor of p). Thus the right son of s can be moved up to take the place of s. This is illustrated in Figure 7.2.2c, where the node with key 12 replaces the node with key 11 and is replaced, in turn, by the node with key 13.

In the following algorithm, the tree is left unchanged if no node with key *key* exists in it.

```
p = tree;
q = null;
// search for the node with the key key, set p to point to
// the node and q to its father, if any.
while (p != null && k(p) != key) {
    q = p;
    p = (key < k(p)) ? left(p) : right(p);
}
```

```
if (p == null)
    // the key does not exist in the tree; leave the tree unchanged
    return;
// set the variable rp to the node that will replace node(p)
// first two cases: the node to be deleted has at most one son
if (left(p) == null)
    rp = right(p);
else
    if (right(p) == null)
        rp = left(p);
else {
    // third case: node(p) has two sons. Set rp to the
    // inorder successor of p and f to the father of rp
    f = p;
    rp = right(p);
    s = left(rp);
    // s is always the left son of rp
    while (s != null) {
        f = rp;
        rp = s;
        s = left(rp);
    }
    // at this point, rp is the inorder successor of p
    if (f != p) {
        // p is not the father of rp and rp == left(f)
        left(f) = right(rp);
        // remove node(rp) from its current position and
        // replace it with the right son of node(rp)
        // node(rp) takes the place of node(p)
        right(rp) = right(p);
    }
    // set the left son of node(rp) so that
    // node(rp) takes the place of node(p)
        left(rp) = left(p);
} // end if
// insert node(rp) into the position formerly occupied by node(p)
if (q == null)
    // node(p) was the root of the tree
    tree = rp;
else
    (p == left(q)) ? left(q) = rp : right(q) = rp;
freenode(p);
return;
```

Efficiency of Binary Search Tree Operations

As we have already seen in Section 6.3 (see Figures 6.3.1 and 6.3.2), the time required to search a binary search tree varies between $O(n)$ and $O(\log n)$ depending on the structure of the tree. If elements are inserted into the tree by the insertion algorithm presented above, the structure of the tree depends on the order in which the records are inserted. If the records are inserted in sorted (or reverse) order, the resulting tree contains all null left (or right) links, and the tree search reduces to a sequential search. If, however, the records are inserted so that half the records inserted after any given record r with key k have keys smaller than k, and half have keys greater than k, then a balanced tree is achieved in which approximately $\log n$ key comparisons are sufficient to retrieve an element. (Again, it should be noted that examining a node in our insertion algorithm requires two comparisons: one for equality and the other for less than. However, in machine language and in some compilers, these can be combined into a single comparison.)

If the records are presented in random order (i.e., any permutation of the n elements is equally likely), balanced trees result more often than not, so that, on the average, the search time remains $O(\log n)$. To see this, let us define the **internal path length**, i, of a binary tree as the sum of the levels of all the nodes in the tree (note that the level of a node equals the length of the path from the root to the node). In the initial tree in Figure 7.2.2, for example, i equals 30 (one node at level 0, two at level 1, four at level 2, four at level 3, and two at level 4: $1*0 + 2*1 + 4*2 + 4*3 + 2*4 = 30$). Since the number of comparisons required to access a node in a binary search tree is one greater than the node's level, the average number of comparisons required for a successful search in a binary search tree with n nodes equals $(i + n)/n$, assuming equal likelihood for accessing every node in the tree. Thus, for the initial tree in Figure 7.2.2, $(30 + 13)/13$, or approximately 3.31, comparisons are required for a successful search. Let s_n equal the average number of comparisons required for a successful search in a random binary search tree of n nodes in which the search argument is equally likely to be any of the n keys, and let i_n be the average internal path length of a random binary search tree of n nodes. Then s_n equals $(i_n + n)/n$.

Let u_n be the average number of comparisons required for an unsuccessful search of a random binary search tree of n nodes. There are $n + 1$ possible ways for an unsuccessful search for a key key to occur: key is less than $k(1)$, key is between $k(1)$ and $k(2)$, ..., key is between $k(n - 1)$ and $k(n)$, and key is greater than $k(n)$. These correspond to the $n + 1$ null subtree pointers in any n-node binary search. (It can be shown that any binary search tree with n nodes has $n + 1$ null pointers.)

Consider the **extension** of a binary tree formed by replacing each null left or right pointer with a pointer to a separate, new leaf node, called an **external node**. The extension of a binary tree of n nodes has $n + 1$ external nodes, each corresponding to one of the $n + 1$ key ranges for an unsuccessful search. For example, the initial tree in Figure 7.2.2 contains thirteen nodes. Its extension would add two external nodes as sons of each of the leafs containing one, seven, ten, thirteen, and fifteen and one external node as an additional son of each of the one-son nodes containing five, six, nine, and twelve, for a total of fourteen external nodes. Define the **external path length**, e, of a binary tree as the sum of the levels of all the external nodes of its extension. The extension of the initial tree in Figure 7.2.2 has four external nodes at level 3, six at level 4, and four at level 5, for an external path length of 56. Note that the level of an external node equals the number of comparisons in an unsuccessful search for a key in the range represented by that external node. Then, if e_n is the average external path length of a random binary search tree of n nodes, $u_n = e_n/(n + 1)$. (This assumes that each of the

$n + 1$ key ranges is equally likely in an unsuccessful search. In Figure 7.2.2, the average number of comparisons for an unsuccessful search is 56/14 or 4.0.) However, it can be shown that $e = i + 2n$ for any binary tree of n nodes (e.g., in Figure 7.2.2, $56 = 30 + 2*13$), so that $e_n = i_n + 2n$. Since $s_n = (i_n + n)/n$, and $u_n = e_n/(n + 1)$, this means that $s_n = ((n + 1)/n)u_n - 1$.

The number of comparisons required to access a key is one more than the number required when the node was inserted. But the number required to insert a key equals the number required in an unsuccessful search for that key before it was inserted. Thus $s_n = 1 + (u_0 + u_1 + \ldots + u_{n-1})/n$. (That is, the average number of comparisons in retrieving an item in an n-node tree equals the average number in accessing each of the first item through the nth, and the number for accessing the ith equals one more than the number for inserting the ith or $1 + u_{i-1}$.) Combining this with the equation $s_n = ((n + 1)/n)u_n - 1$ yields

$$(n + 1)u_n = 2n + u_0 + u_1 + \ldots + u_{n-1}$$

for any n. Replacing n by $n - 1$ yields

$$nu_{n-1} = 2(n - 1) + u_0 + u_1 + \ldots + u_{n-2}$$

and subtracting from the previous equation yields

$$(n + 1)u_n - nu_{n-1} = 2 + u_{n-1}$$

or

$$u_n = u_{n-1} + 2/(n + 1)$$

Since $u_1 = 1$, we have

$$u_n = 1 + 2/3 + 2/4 + \ldots + 2/(n + 1)$$

and, therefore, since $s_n = ((n + 1)/n)u_n - 1$,

$$s_n = 2((n + 1)/n)(1 + 1/2 + 1/3 + \ldots + 1/n) - 3$$

As n grows large, $(n + 1)/n$ is approximately 1, and it can be shown that $1 + 1/2 + \ldots + 1/n$ is approximately $\log(n)$, where $\log(n)$ is the natural logarithm of n. (This is implemented as the method $\log(n)$ in the Java *Math* class.) Thus s_n may be approximated (for large n) by $2*\log(n)$, which equals $1.386*\log_2 n$. This means that average search time in a random binary search tree is $O(\log n)$ and requires approximately only 39 percent more comparisons, on the average, than a balanced binary tree.

As already noted, insertion in a binary search tree requires the same number of comparisons as an unsuccessful search for the key. Deletion requires the same number of comparisons as a search for the key to be deleted, although it does involve additional work in finding the inorder successor or predecessor. It can be shown that the deletion algorithm that we have presented actually improves the subsequent average search cost of the tree. That is, a random n-key tree created by inserting $n + 1$ keys and then deleting a random key has lower internal path length (and therefore lower average search cost) than a random n-key tree created by inserting n keys. The process of deleting a one-son node by replacing it with its son, regardless of whether that son is a right or left son, yields a better than average tree; a similar deletion algorithm which only replaces a one-son node by its son if it is a left son (i.e., if its successor is not contained in its subtree), and otherwise replaces the node with its inorder successor, does produce a random tree, assuming no additional insertions. The latter algorithm is called the ***asymmetric deletion algorithm***.

Strangely enough, however, as additional insertions and deletions are made using the asymmetric deletion algorithm, the internal path length and search time initially decrease but then begin to rise rapidly again. For trees containing more than 128 keys, the internal path length eventually becomes worse than for a random tree, and for trees with more than 2048 keys, the internal path length eventually becomes more than 50 percent worse than for a random tree.

An alternative ***symmetric deletion algorithm***, which alternates between deleting the inorder predecessor and successor on alternate deletions (but still replaces a one-son node with its son only when the predecessor or successor is not contained in its subtree), does eventually produce better than random trees after additional mixed insertions and deletions. Empirical data indicate that path length is reduced after many alternating insertions and symmetric deletions to approximately 88 percent of its corresponding random value.

Efficiency of Nonuniform Binary Search Trees

All of the preceding assumes that it is equally likely for the search argument to equal any key in the table. However, in actual practice it is usually the case that some records are retrieved very often, some moderately often, and some are almost never retrieved. Suppose that records are inserted into the tree so that a more frequently accessed record precedes one that is not so frequently accessed. Then the most frequently retrieved records will be nearer the root of the tree, reducing the average successful search time. (Of course, this assumes that reordering the keys in order of reduced frequency of access does not seriously unbalance the binary tree, since if it did, then the reduced number of comparisons for the most frequently accessed records might be offset by the increased number of comparisons for the vast majority of records.)

If the elements to be retrieved form a constant set, with no insertions or deletions, then it may pay to set up a binary search tree that makes subsequent searches more efficient. For example, consider the binary search trees in Figure 7.2.3. The trees in Figures 7.2.3a and 7.2.3b both contain three elements, $k1$, $k2$, and $k3$, where $k1 < k2 < k3$, and are valid binary search trees for that set. However, a retrieval of $k3$ requires two comparisons in Figure 7.2.3a but only one comparison in Figure 7.2.3b. Of course, there are still other valid binary search trees for this set of keys.

The number of key comparisons necessary to retrieve a record equals the level of that record in the binary search tree plus one. Thus a retrieval of $k2$ requires one comparison in the tree in Figure 7.2.3a but three comparisons in the tree in Figure 7.2.3b. An unsuccessful search for an argument lying immediately between two keys a and b requires as many key comparisons as the maximum number of comparisons required by successful searches for either a or b. (Why?) This is equal to one plus the maximum of the levels of a or b. For example, a search for a key lying between $k2$ and $k3$ requires two key comparisons in Figure 7.2.3a and three comparisons in Figure 7.2.3b, whereas a search for a key greater than $k3$ requires two comparisons in Figure 7.2.3a, but only one comparison in Figure 7.2.3b.

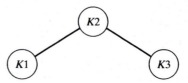

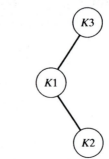

(a) Expected number of comparisons:
$2p1 + p2 + 2p3 + 2q0 + 2q1 + 2q2 + 2q3$

(b) Expected number of comparisons:
$2p1 + 3p2 + p3 + 2q0 + 3q1 + 3q2 + q3$

FIGURE 7.2.3   Two binary search trees.

Suppose $p1, p2$, and $p3$ are the probabilities that the search argument equals $k1$, $k2$, and $k3$, respectively. Suppose also that $q0$ is the probability that the search argument is less than $k1, q1$ is the probability that it is between $k1$ and $k2, q2$ is the probability that it is between $k2$ and $k3$, and $q3$ is the probability that it is greater than $k3$. Then $p1 + p2 + p3 + q0 + q1 + q2 + q3 = 1$. The ***expected number*** of comparisons in a search is the sum of the probabilities that the argument has a given value times the number of comparisons required to retrieve that value, where the sum is taken over all possible search argument values. For example, the expected number of comparisons in searching the tree in Figure 7.2.3a is

$$2p1 + p2 + 2p3 + 2q0 + 2q1 + 2q2 + 2q3$$

and the expected number of comparisons in searching the tree in Figure 7.2.3b is:

$$2p1 + 3p2 + p3 + 2q0 + 3q1 + 3q2 + q3$$

This expected number of comparisons can be used as a measure of how "good" a particular binary search tree is for a given set of keys and a given set of probabilities. Thus, for the probabilities listed below on the left, the tree in Figure 7.2.3a is more efficient; for the probabilities listed on the right, the tree in Figure 7.2.3b is more efficient.

$p1 = .1$	$p1 = .1$
$p2 = .3$	$p2 = .1$
$p3 = .1$	$p3 = .3$
$q0 = .1$	$q0 = .1$
$q1 = .2$	$q1 = .1$
$q2 = .1$	$q2 = .1$
$q3 = .1$	$q3 = .2$

Expected number for 7.2.3a = 1.7
Expected number for 7.2.3b = 2.4

Expected number for 7.2.3a = 1.9
Expected number for 7.2.3b = 1.8

Optimum Search Trees

A binary search tree that minimizes the expected number of comparisons for a given set of keys and probabilities is called **optimum**. The fastest-known algorithm to produce an optimum binary search tree is $O(n^2)$ in the general case. This is too expensive unless the tree is maintained unchanged over a very large number of searches. An $O(n)$ algorithm to create an optimum binary search tree does exist, however, in cases where all the $p(i)$ equal zero (i.e., all searches are "unsuccessful" because the keys act only to define range values with which data are associated).

Although an efficient algorithm to construct an optimum tree in the general case does not exist, there are several methods for constructing near-optimum trees in $O(n)$ time. Assume n keys, $k(1)$ through $k(n)$. Let $p(i)$ be the probability of searching for a key $k(I)$, and $q(i)$ the probability of an unsuccessful search between $k(i - 1)$ and $k(i)$ (with $q(0)$ the probability of an unsuccessful search for a key below $k(1)$, and $q(n)$ the probability of an unsuccessful search for a key above $k(n)$). Define $s(i, j)$ as $q(i) + p(i + 1) + \ldots + q(j)$.

One method, called the **balancing method**, attempts to find a value i that minimizes the absolute value of $s(0, i - 1) - s(i, n)$ and establishes $k(i)$ as the root of the binary search tree, with $k(1)$ through $k(i - 1)$ in its left subtree, and $k(i + 1)$ through $k(n)$ in its right subtree. The process is then applied recursively to build the left and right subtrees.

The value i at which $abs(s(0, i - 1) - s(i, n))$ is minimized can be located efficiently as follows. Set up an array $s0[n + 1]$ such that $s0[i]$ equals $s(0, i)$. This can be done by initializing $s0[0]$ to $q(0)$ and $s0[j]$ to $s0[j - 1] + p(j) + q(j)$ for j from 1 to n in turn. Once $s0$ has been initialized, $s(i, j)$ can be computed for any i and j as $s0[j] - s0[i - 1] - p(i)$ whenever necessary. We define $si(j)$ as $s(0, j - 1) - s(j, n)$. We wish to minimize $abs(si(i))$.

After $s0$ has been initialized, we begin the process of finding an i to minimize $abs(s(0, i - 1) - s(i, n))$, or $si(i)$. Note that si is a monotonically increasing function. Note also that $si(0) = q(0) - 1$, which is negative, and $si(n) = 1 - q(n + 1)$, which is positive. Check the values of $si(1), si(n), si(2), si(n - 1), si(4), si(n - 3), \ldots,$ $si(2^j), si(n + 1 - 2^j)$ in turn until discovering the first positive $si(2^j)$ or the first negative $si(n + 1 - 2^j)$. If a positive $si(2^j)$ is found first, then the desired i that minimizes $abs(si(i))$ lies within the interval $[2^{j-1}, 2^j]$; if a negative $si(n + 1 - 2^j)$ is found first, then the desired i lies within the interval $[n + 1 - 2^j, n + 1 - 2^{j-1}]$. In either case, i has been narrowed down to an interval of size 2^{j-1}. Within the interval, use a binary search to narrow down on i. The doubling effect in the interval size guarantees that the entire recursive process is $O(n)$, whereas if a binary search were used on the entire interval $[0, n]$ to start, the process would be $O(n \log n)$.

A second method used to construct near-optimum binary search trees is called the **greedy method**. Instead of building the tree from the top down, as in the balancing method, the greedy method builds the tree from the bottom up. The method uses a doubly-linked linear list in which each list element contains four pointers, one key value, and three probability values. The four pointers are left and right list pointers used to organize the doubly-linked list, and left and right subtree pointers used to keep track of binary search subtrees containing keys less than and greater than the key value in the node. The three probability values are the sum of the probabilities in the left subtree, called the *left probability*, the probability $p(i)$ of the node's key value $k(i)$, called the *key probability*, and the sum of the probabilities in the right subtree, called the *right probability*. The *total probability* of a node is defined as the sum of its left, key, and right probabilities. Initially, there are n nodes in the list. The key value in the ith node is $k(i)$, its left probability is $q(i - 1)$, its right probability is $q(i)$, its key probability is $p(i)$, and its left and right subtree pointers are *null*.

Each iteration of the algorithm finds the first node *nd* on the list whose total probability is less than or equal to its successor's (if no node qualifies, *nd* is set to the last node in the list). The key in *nd* becomes the root of a binary search subtree whose left and right subtrees are the left and right subtrees of *nd*. *nd* is then removed from the list. The left subtree pointer of its successor (if any) and the right subtree pointer of its predecessor (if any) are reset to point to the new subtree, and the left probability of its successor and the right probability of its predecessor are reset to the total probability of *nd*. This process is repeated until only one node remains on the list. (Note that it is not necessary to begin a full list traversal from the list beginning on each iteration; it is only necessary to begin from the second predecessor of the node removed on the previous iteration.) When only one node remains on the list, its key is placed in the root of the final binary search tree, with the left and right subtree pointers of the node as the left and right subtree pointers of the root.

Another technique for reducing average search time when search probabilities are known is a *split tree*. Such a tree contains two keys rather than one in each node. The first, called the *node key*, is tested for equality with the argument key. If they are equal, then the search ends successfully; if not, the argument key is compared to the second key in the node, called the *split key*, to determine whether the search should continue in the left or right subtree. A special type of split tree, called a *median split tree*, sets the node key in each node to the most frequent among the keys in the subtree rooted at that node, and sets the split key to the median of the keys in that subtree (i.e., the key k such that an equal number of keys in the subtree are less than and greater than k). This has the twin advantage of guaranteeing a balanced tree and ensuring that frequent keys are found near the root. Although median split trees require an extra key in each node, they can be constructed as almost complete binary trees implemented in an array, saving space for tree pointers. A median split tree from a given set of keys and frequencies can be built in time $O(n \log n)$, and a search in such a tree always requires fewer than $\log_2 n$ node visits, although each visit does require two separate comparisons.

Balanced Trees

As noted above, if the probability of searching for a key in a table is the same for all keys, a balanced binary tree yields the most efficient search. Unfortunately, the search and insertion algorithm presented above does not ensure that the tree remains balanced; the degree of balance is dependent on the order in which keys are inserted into the tree. We would like to have an efficient search and insertion algorithm that maintains the search tree as a balanced binary tree.

Let us first define more precisely the notion of a "balanced" tree. The **height** of a binary tree is the maximum level of its leafs (this is also sometimes known as the **depth** of the tree). For convenience, the height of a null tree is defined as -1. A **balanced binary tree** (sometimes called an **avl tree**) is a binary tree in which the heights of the two subtrees of every node never differ by more than one. The **balance** of a node in a binary tree is defined as the height of its left subtree minus the height of its right subtree. Figure 7.2.4a illustrates a balanced binary tree. Each node in a balanced binary tree has a balance of 1, -1, or 0, depending on whether the height of its left subtree is greater

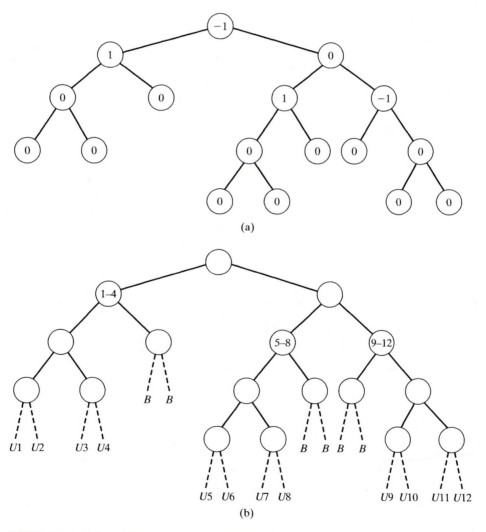

(a)

(b)

FIGURE 7.2.4 Balanced binary tree and possible additions.

than, less than, or equal to the height of its right subtree. The balance of each node is indicated in Figure 7.2.4a.

Suppose that we are given a balanced binary tree and use the search and insertion algorithm above to insert a new node p into it. Then the resulting tree may or may not remain balanced. Figure 7.2.4b illustrates all the possible insertions that may be made to the tree in Figure 7.2.4a. Each insertion that yields a balanced tree is indicated by a B. The unbalanced insertions are indicated by a U and are numbered from 1 to 12. It is easy to see that the tree becomes unbalanced only if the newly inserted node is a left descendant of a node that previously had a balance of 1 (this occurs in cases $U1$ through $U8$ in Figure 7.2.4b) or if it is a right descendant of a node that previously had a balance of -1 (cases $U9$ through $U12$). In Figure 7.2.4b, the youngest ancestor that becomes unbalanced in each insertion is indicated by the numbers contained in three of the nodes.

Let us examine further the subtree rooted at the youngest ancestor to become unbalanced as a result of an insertion. We illustrate the case where the balance of this subtree was previously 1, leaving the other case to the reader. Figure 7.2.5 illustrates this case. Let us call the unbalanced node A. Since A had a balance of 1, its left subtree was nonnull; we may therefore designate its left son as B. Since A is the youngest ancestor of the new node to become unbalanced, node B must have had a balance of 0. (You are asked to prove this fact as an exercise.) Thus, node B must have had (before the insertion) left and right subtrees of equal height n (where possibly $n = -1$). Since the balance of A was 1, the right subtree of A must also have been of height n.

There are now two cases to consider, illustrated by Figures 7.2.5a and b. In Figure 7.2.5a, the newly created node is inserted into the left subtree of B, changing the balance of B to 1, and the balance of A to 2. In Figure 7.2.5b, the newly created node is inserted into the right subtree of B, changing the balance of B to -1, and the balance of A to 2. In order to maintain a balanced tree, it is necessary to perform a transformation on the tree so that

1. The inorder traversal of the transformed tree is the same as for the original tree (i.e., the transformed tree remains a binary search tree).
2. The transformed tree is balanced.

Consider the trees in Figures 7.2.6a and b. The tree in Figure 7.2.6b is said to be a **_right rotation_** of the tree rooted at A in Figure 7.2.6a. Similarly, the tree in Figure 7.2.6c is said to be a **_left rotation_** of the tree rooted at A in Figure 7.2.6a.

An algorithm to implement a left rotation of a subtree rooted at P is as follows:

```
q = right(p);
hold = left(q);
left(q) = p;
right(p) = hold;
```

Let us call this operation *leftRotation(p)*. *rightRotation(p)* may be defined similarly. Of course, in any rotation the value of the pointer to the root of the subtree being rotated must be changed to point to the new root. (In the case of the above left rotation, this new root is q.) Note that the order of the nodes in an inorder traversal is preserved under both right and left rotations. It therefore follows that any number of rotations

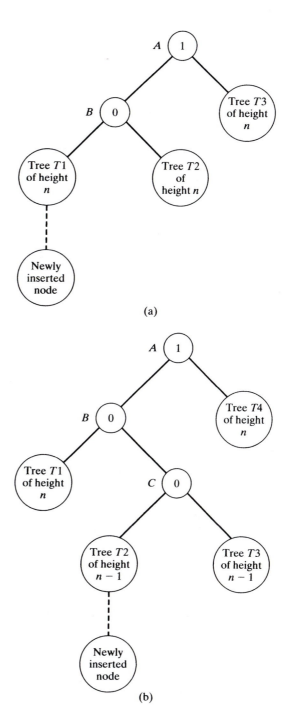

FIGURE 7.2.5   Initial insertion; all balances are prior to insertion.

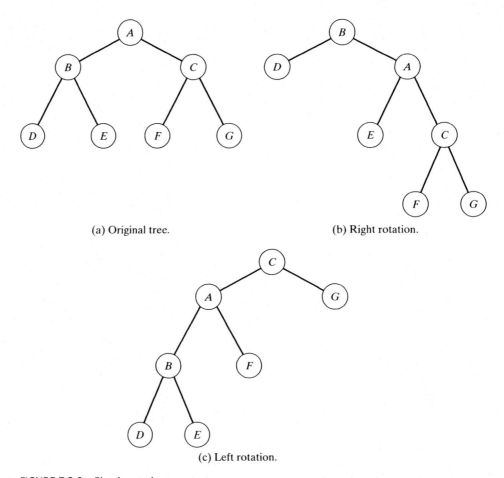

(a) Original tree.

(b) Right rotation.

(c) Left rotation.

FIGURE 7.2.6 Simple rotation on a tree.

(left or right) can be performed on an unbalanced tree in order to obtain a balanced tree, without disturbing the order of the nodes in an inorder traversal.

Let us now return to the trees in Figure 7.2.5. Suppose a right rotation is performed on the subtree rooted at A in Figure 7.2.5a. The resulting tree is shown in Figure 7.2.7a. Note that the tree in Figure 7.2.7a yields the same inorder traversal as the one in Figure 7.2.5a and is also balanced. Also, since the height of the subtree in Figure 7.2.5a was $n + 2$ before the insertion, and the height of the subtree in Figure 7.2.7a is $n + 2$ with the inserted node, the balance of each ancestor of node A remains undisturbed. Thus, replacing the subtree in Figure 7.2.5a with its right rotation in Figure 7.2.7a guarantees that a balanced binary search tree is maintained.

Let us now turn to the tree in Figure 7.2.5b, where the newly created node is inserted into the right subtree of B. Let C be the right son of B. (There are three cases: C may be the newly inserted node, in which case $n = -1$, or the newly inserted node may be in the left or right subtree of C. Figure 7.2.5b illustrates the case where it is in the left subtree; the analysis of the other cases is analogous.) Suppose a left rotation on the

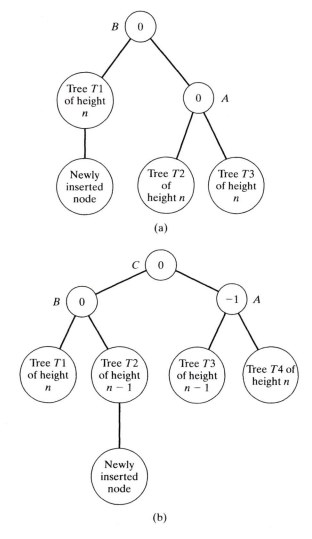

FIGURE 7.2.7 After rebalancing, all balances are after insertion.

(b)

subtree rooted at B is followed by a right rotation on the subtree rooted at A. Figure 7.2.7b illustrates the resulting tree. Verify that the inorder traversals of the two trees are the same, and that the tree of Figure 7.2.7b is balanced. The height of the tree in Figure 7.2.7b is $n + 2$, which is the same as the height of the tree in Figure 7.2.5b before the insertion, so that the balance in all the ancestors of a is unchanged. Therefore, replacing the tree in Figure 7.2.5b with the one in Figure 7.2.7b wherever it occurs after insertion maintains a balanced search tree.

Let us now present an algorithm to search and insert into a nonempty balanced binary tree. Each node of the tree contains five fields: k and r, which hold the key and record respectively, *left* and *right*, which are pointers to the left and right subtrees respectively, and *bal*, whose value is 1, -1, or 0 depending on the node's balance. In the first part of the algorithm, if the desired key is not found in the tree, a new node is inserted into the binary search tree without regard to balance. This first phase also keeps track of *ya*, the youngest ancestor that may become unbalanced upon insertion. The algorithm makes use of the method *makeTree* described above and the methods *rightRotation* and *leftRotation*, which accept a pointer to the root of a subtree and perform the desired rotation.

```
//* PART I: search and insert into the binary tree
fp = null;
p = tree;
fya = null;
ya = p;
// ya points to the youngest ancestor which may become unbalanced.
// fya points to the father of ya, and fp points to the father of p.
while (p != null) {
    if (key == k(p))
        return p;
        q = (key < k(p)) ? left(p) : right(p);
        if (q != null)
            if (bal(q) != 0) {
                fya = p;
                ya = q;
            }
        fp = p;
        p = q;
}
// insert new record
q = makeTree(rec, key);
bal(q) = 0;
(key < k(fp)) ? left(fp) = q : right(fp) = q;
// the balance on all nodes between node(ya) and node(q)
// must be changed from 0
p = (key < k(ya)) ? left(ya) : right(ya);
s = p;
while (p != q) {
    if (key < k(p)) {
        bal(p) = 1;
        p = left(p);
    }
    else {
        bal(p) = -1;
        p = right(p);
    }
}
// PART II: ascertain whether or not the tree is unbalanced. If it is,
// q is the newly inserted node, ya is its youngest unbalanced ancestor,
// fya is the father of ya and s is the son of ya in the direction
of the imbalance
imbal = (key < k(ya)) ? 1 : -1;
if (bal(ya) == 0) {
```

```
    // another level has been added to the tree
    // the tree remains balanced
    bal(ya) = imbal;
    return q;
}
if (bal(ya) != imbal) {
    // the added node has been placed in the opposite direction
    // of the imbalance the tree remains balanced
    bal(ya) = 0;
    return q;
}
// PART III: the additional node has unbalanced the tree
// rebalance it by performing the required rotations and
// then adjust the balances of the nodes involved
if (bal(s) == imbal) {
    // ya and s have been unbalanced in the same direction;
    // see Figure 7.2.5a where ya = a and s = b
    p = s;
    if (imbal == 1)
        rightRotation(ya);
    else
        leftRotation(ya);
    bal(ya) = 0;
    bal(s) = 0;
}
else {
    // ya and s are unbalanced in opposite directions;
    // see Figure 7.2.5b
    if (imbal == 1) {
        p = right(s);
        leftRotation(s);
        left(ya) = p;
        rightRotation(ya);
    }
    else {
        p = left(s);
        right(ya) = p;
        rightRotation(s);
        leftRotation(ya);
    }
    // adjust bal field for involved nodes
    if (bal(p) == 0) {
        // p was inserted node
        bal(ya) = 0;
        bal(s) = 0;
    }
    else
        if (bal(p) == imbal) {
            // see Figures 7.2.5b and 7.2.7b
            bal(ya) = -imbal;
```

```
            bal(s) = 0;
        }
        else {
            // see Figures 7.2.5b and 7.2.7b
            // but the new node was inserted into t3
            bal(ya) = 0;
            bal(s) = imbal;
        }
            bal(p) = 0;
    }
    // adjust the pointer to the rotated subtree
    if (fya == null)
        tree = p;
    else
        (ya == right(fya)) ? right(fya) = p : left(fya) = p;
    return q;
```

Since the maximum height of a balanced binary search tree is $1.44 \log_2 n$, a search in such a tree never requires more than 44 percent more comparisons than for a completely balanced tree. In actual practice, balanced binary search trees behave even better, yielding search times of $\log_2 n + 0.25$ for large n. On the average, a rotation is required in 46.5 percent of the insertions.

The algorithm to delete a node from a balanced binary search tree while maintaining its balance is even more complex. While insertion requires at most a double rotation, deletion may require one (single or double) rotation at each level of the tree, or $O(\log n)$ rotations. However, in practice, an average of only 0.214 (single or double) rotations has been found to be required per deletion.

The balanced binary search trees that we have looked at are called **height-balanced trees** because their height is used as the criterion for balancing. There are a number of other ways of defining balanced trees. In one method, the **weight** of a tree is defined as the number of external nodes in the tree (this equals the number of null pointers in the tree). If the ratio of the weight of the left subtree of every node to the weight of the subtree rooted at the node is between some fraction a and $1 - a$, then the tree is a **weight-balanced tree of ratio a** or is said to be in the class $wb[a]$. When an ordinary insertion or deletion on a tree in class $wb[a]$ would remove the tree from the class, rotations are used to restore the weight-balanced property.

Another type of tree, called a **balanced binary tree** by Tarjan, requires that for every node nd, the length of the longest path from nd to an external node is at most twice the length of the shortest path from nd to an external node. (Recall that external nodes are nodes added to the tree at every null pointer.) Again, rotations are used to maintain balance after insertion or deletion. Tarjan's balanced trees have the property that at most one double and one single rotation restore balance after either insertion or deletion, as opposed to a possible $O(\log n)$ rotations for deletion in a height-balanced tree.

Balanced trees may also be used for efficient implementation of priority queues (see Sections 4.1 and 6.3). Inserting a new element requires at most $O(\log n)$ steps to find its position, $O(1)$ steps to access the element (by following left pointers to the leftmost leaf), and $O(\log n)$ or $O(1)$ steps to delete that leaf. Thus, like a priority queue implemented using a heap (Section 6.3), a priority queue implemented using a balanced tree can perform any sequence of n insertions and minimum deletions in $O(n \log n)$ steps.

EXERCISES

7.2.1   Write an efficient insertion algorithm for a binary search tree to insert a new record whose key is known not to exist in the tree.

7.2.2   Show that it is possible to obtain a binary search tree in which only a single leaf exists even if the elements of the tree are not inserted in strictly ascending or descending order.

7.2.3   Verify by simulation that if records are presented to the binary tree search and insertion algorithm in random order, the number of key comparisons is $O(\log n)$.

7.2.4   Prove that every n-node binary search tree is not equally likely (assuming items are inserted in random order), and that balanced trees are more probable than straight-line trees.

7.2.5   Write an algorithm to delete a node from a binary tree that replaces the node with its inorder predecessor rather than its inorder successor.

7.2.6   Suppose that the data elements of a binary search tree node are defined as follows:

```
class NodeType {
    int k;
    int r;
    NodeType left;
    NodeType right;
}
```

Assume that the class *Tree* contains the element

```
NodeType root;
```

The k and r fields contain the key and record of the node; *left* and *right* are pointers to the node's sons. Write a Java method for the *Tree* class *sInsert(key, rec)* to search and insert a record *rec* with key *key* into a binary search tree.

7.2.7   Write a Java method *Delete(key)* to search and delete a record *record* with key *key* from a binary search tree implemented as in the previous exercise. If such a record is found, the function returns the value of its r field; if it is not found, the function returns 0.

7.2.8   Write a Java method *delete(key1, key2)* to delete all records with keys between *key1* and *key2* (inclusive) from a binary search tree whose nodes are declared as in the previous exercises.

7.2.9   Consider the search trees in Figure 7.2.8.

   a.   How many permutations of the integers 1 through 7 would produce the binary search trees in Figures 7.2.8a, b, and c, respectively?

   b.   How many permutations of the integers 1 through 7 produce binary search trees similar to the trees in Figures 7.2.8a, b, and c, respectively? (See Exercise 5.1.9.)

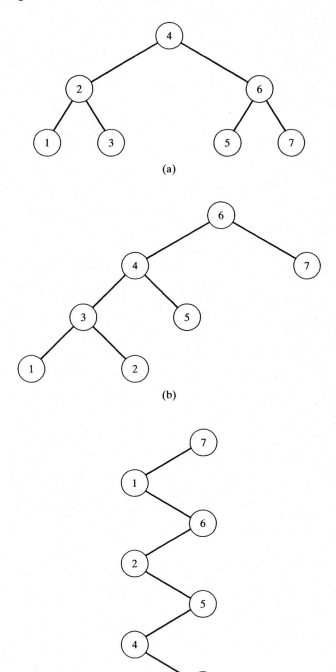

(a)

(b)

(c)

FIGURE 7.2.8

c. How many permutations of the integers 1 through 7 produce binary search trees with the same number of nodes at each level as the trees in Figure 7.2.8a, b, and c, respectively?

d. Find an assignment of probabilities to the first seven positive integers as search arguments that makes the trees in Figures 7.2.8a, b, and c optimum.

7.2.10 Show that the Fibonacci tree of order $h + 1$ (see Exercise 5.3.5) is a height-balanced tree of height h and has fewer nodes than any other height-balanced tree of height h.

7.3   GENERAL SEARCH TREES

General nonbinary trees are also used as search tables, particularly in external storage. There are two broad categories of such trees: multiway search trees and digital search trees. We examine each in turn.

Multiway Search Trees

In a binary search tree, each node *nd* contains a single key and points to two subtrees. One of these subtrees contains all the keys in the tree rooted at *nd* that are less than the key in *nd*, and the other subtree contains all the keys in the tree rooted at *nd* that are greater than (or equal to) the key in *nd*.

We may extend this concept to a general search tree in which each node contains one or more keys. A ***multiway search tree of order n*** is a general tree in which each node has n or fewer subtrees and contains one fewer key than it has subtrees. That is, if a node has four subtrees, it contains three keys. In addition, if $s_0, s_1, \ldots, s_{m-1}$ are the m subtrees of a node containing keys $k_0, k_1, \ldots, k_{m-2}$ in ascending order, then all the keys in subtree s_0 are less than or equal to k_0, all the keys in the subtree s_j (where j is between 1 and $m - 2$) are greater than k_{j-1} and less than or equal to k_j, and all the keys in the subtree s_{m-1} are greater than k_{m-2}. The subtree s_j is called the ***left subtree*** of key k_j and its root is called the ***left son*** of key k_j. Similarly, s_j is called the ***right subtree***, and its root the ***right son***, of key k_{j-1}. One or more of the subtrees of a node may be empty. (The term "multiway search tree" is sometimes used to refer to any nonbinary tree used for searching, including the digital trees that we introduce at the end of this section. However, we use the term strictly for trees that can contain complete keys in each node.)

Figure 7.3.1 illustrates a number of multiway search trees. Figure 7.3.1a is a multiway search tree of order 4. The eight nodes of the tree have been labeled *A* through *H*. Nodes *A*, *D*, *E*, and *G* contain the maximum number of subtrees, four, and the maximum number of keys, three. Such nodes are called ***full nodes***. However, some of the subtrees of nodes *D* and *E* and all of the subtrees of node *G* are empty, as indicated by arrows emanating from the appropriate positions in the nodes. Nodes *B*, *C*, *F*, and *H* are not full and also contain some empty subtrees. The first subtree of *A* contains the keys 6 and 10, both smaller than 12, which is the first key of *A*. The second subtree of *A* contains 25 and 37, both greater than 12 (the first key of *A*) and less than 50 (the second key). The third subtree contains 60, 70, 80, 62, 65, and 69, all of which are between 50 (the second key of *A*) and 85 (the third key). Finally, the last subtree of *A* contains

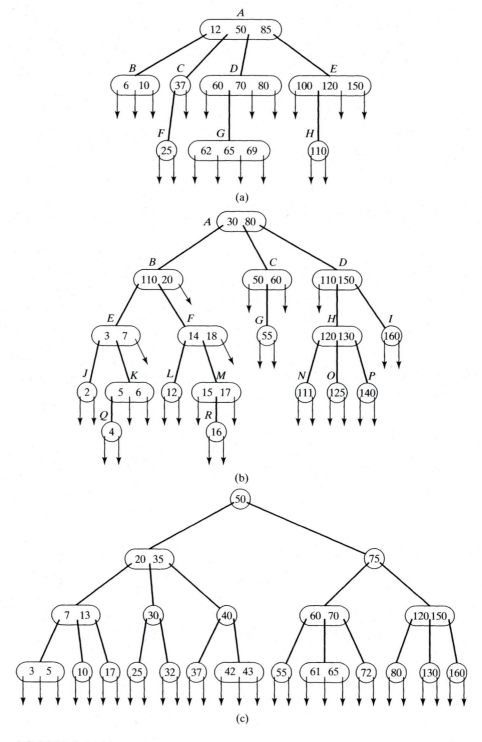

FIGURE 7.3.1 Multiway search trees.

100, 120, 150, and 110, all greater than 85, the last key in node *A*. Similarly, each subtree of any other node contains only keys between the appropriate two keys of that node and its ancestors.

Figure 7.3.1b illustrates a ***top-down multiway search tree***. Such a tree is characterized by the condition that any nonfull node is a leaf. Note that the tree in Figure 7.3.1a is not top-down, since node *C* is nonfull, yet contains a nonempty subtree. Define a ***semileaf*** as a node with at least one empty subtree. In Figure 7.3.1a, nodes *B* through *H* are all semileafs. In Figure 7.3.1b, nodes *B* through *G* and *I* through *R* are semileafs. In a top-down multiway tree, a semileaf must be either full or a leaf.

Figure 7.3.1c is yet another multiway search tree of order 3. It is not top-down, since there are four nodes with only one key and nonempty subtrees. However, it does have another special property in that it is ***balanced***. That is, all its semileafs are at the same level (3). This implies that all semileafs are leafs. Neither the trees in Figure 7.3.1a (which has leafs at levels 1 and 2) nor the ones in Figure 7.3.1b (leafs at levels 2, 3, and 4) are balanced multiway search trees. (Although a binary search tree is a multiway search tree of order 2, note that a balanced binary search tree, as defined at the end of Section 7.2, is not necessarily balanced as a multiway search tree, since it can have leafs at different levels.)

Searching a Multiway Tree

The algorithm to search a multiway search tree, regardless of whether it is top-down, balanced, or neither, is straightforward. Each node contains a single integer field, a variable number of pointer fields, and a variable number of key fields. If *node(p)* is a node, then the integer field *numTrees(p)* equals the number of subtrees of *node(p)*. *numTrees(p)* is always less than or equal to the order of the tree, *n*. The pointer fields *son(p, 0)* through *son(p, numTrees(p)* − 1) reference the subtrees of *node(p)*. The key fields *k(p, 0)* through *k(p, numTrees(p)* − 2) are the keys contained in *node(p)* in ascending order. The subtree to which *son(p, i)* points (for *i* between 1 and *numTrees(p)* − 2 inclusive) contains all the keys in the tree between *k(p, i* − 1) and *k(p, i)*. *son(p, 0)* points to a subtree containing only the keys less than *k(p, 0)* and *son(p, numTrees(p)* − 1) points to a subtree containing only the keys greater than *k(p, numTrees(p)* − 2).

We also assume a method *nodeSearch(p, key)* that returns the smallest integer *j* such that *key* <= *k(p, j)*, or *numTrees(p)* − 1 if *key* is greater than all the keys in *node(p)*. (We will discuss shortly how *nodeSearch* is implemented.) The following recursive algorithm is for a method *tree.search()* that returns a reference to the node containing *key* [or −1 (representing ***null***) if there is no such node in the tree] and sets the global variable *position* to the position of *key* in that node:

```
p = tree;
if (p == null) {
    position = -1;
    return -1;
}
i = nodeSearch(p, key);
if (i < numTrees(p) - 1 && key == k(p, i)) {
```

```
        position = i;
        return p;
    }
    return search(son(p, i));
```

Note that after setting i to *nodeSearch*(p, *key*), we insist on checking that $i <$ *numTrees*(p) $- 1$ before accessing $k(p, i)$. This is to avoid using the possibly nonexistent or erroneous $k(p,$ *numTrees*(p) $- 1)$, in case *key* is greater than all the keys in *node*(p). The following is a nonrecursive version of the above algorithm:

```
p = tree;
while (p != null) {
    // search the subtree rooted at node(p)
    i = nodeSearch(p, key);
    if (i < numTrees(p) -1 && key == k(p, i)) {
        position = i;
        return p;
    }
    p = son(p, i);
}
position = -1;
return -1;
```

The method *nodeSearch* is responsible for locating the smallest key in a node greater than or equal to the search argument. The simplest technique for doing this is a sequential search through the ordered set of keys in the node. If all the keys are of fixed equal length, a binary search can also be used to locate the appropriate key. The decision whether to use a sequential or binary search depends on the order of the tree, which determines how many keys must be searched. Another possibility is to organize the keys within the node as a binary search tree.

Implementing a Multiway Tree

Note that we have implemented a multiway search tree of order n using nodes with up to n sons rather than a binary tree with son and brother pointers, as outlined in Section 5.5 for general trees. The reason for this is that in multiway trees, there is a limit to the number of sons of a node, and we can expect most nodes to be as full as possible, whereas in a general tree, there is no such limit, and many nodes may contain only one or two items. Therefore, the flexibility of allowing as many or as few items in a node as necessary and the space saving when a node is nearly empty was worth the overhead of extra brother pointers.

Nevertheless, when nodes are not full, multiway search trees, as implemented here, do waste considerable storage. Despite the possible waste of storage, multiway trees are frequently used, especially to store data on an external direct-access device such as a disk. The reason is that accessing each new node during a search requires reading a block of storage from the external device. The read operation is relatively expensive in terms of time because of the mechanical work involved in positioning the device properly. However, once the device is positioned, the task of actually reading a large amount of sequential data is relatively fast. This means that the total time for reading a storage block (i.e., a "node") is only minimally affected by its size. Once a node has been read and is contained in internal computer memory, the cost of searching it at electronic internal speeds is minuscule compared to the cost of initially reading it into memory. In addition, since external storage is fairly inexpensive, a technique that improves time-efficiency at the expense of external storage space utilization is real-cost (i.e., dollars) effective. For this reason, external storage systems based on multiway search trees try to maximize the size of each node, and trees of order 200 or more are not uncommon.

The second factor to consider in implementing multiway search trees is storage of the data records. As in any storage system, the records may be stored with the keys or remotely from the keys. The first technique requires keeping entire records within the tree nodes, while the second requires keeping a pointer to the associated record with each key in a node. (Still another technique involves duplicating keys and keeping records only at the leafs. This mechanism is discussed later in more detail when we discuss B^+-trees.)

In general, we would like to keep as many keys as possible in each node. To see why this is so, consider two top-down trees with 4000 keys and minimum depth, one of order 5 and the other of order 11. The order-5 tree requires 1000 nodes (of 4 keys each) to hold the 4000 keys, while the order-11 tree requires only 400 nodes (of 10 keys each). The depth of the order-5 tree is at least 5 (level 0 contains 1 node, level 1 contains 5, level 2 contains 25, level 3 contains 125, level 4 contains 625, and level 5 contains the remaining 219), while the depth of the order-11 tree can be as low as 3 (level 0 contains 1 node, level 1 contains 11, level 2 contains 121, level 3 contains the remaining 267). Thus five or six nodes must be accessed in searching the order-5 tree for most of the keys, but only three or four nodes must be accessed for the order-11 tree. But as we noted above, accessing a node is the most expensive operation in searching external storage where multiway trees are most used. Thus a tree with a higher order leads to a more efficient search process. The actual storage required by both situations is approximately the same, since each node is larger, although fewer large nodes are required to hold a file of a given size when the order is high.

Since the size of a node is usually fixed by other external factors (e.g., the amount of storage physically read from disk in one operation), a higher-order tree is obtained by keeping the records outside the tree nodes. Even if this causes an extra external read to obtain a record after its key has been located, keeping records within a node typically reduces the order by a factor of between 5 and 40 (which is the typical range of the ratio of record size to key size), so the tradeoff is not worthwhile.

If a multiway search tree is maintained in external storage, a pointer to a node is an external storage address that specifies the starting point of a storage block. The block of storage that makes up a node must be read into internal storage before any of the fields *numTrees*, *k*, or *son* can be accessed. Assume that the method *block.directRead(p)* reads a node at external storage address *p* into an internal storage buffer *block*. Assume also that the *numTrees*, *k*, and *son* fields in the buffer are accessed by the Java-like notations *block.numTrees*, *block.k*, and *block.son*. Assume also that the method *nodeSearch* is modified to accept an (internal) storage block rather than a reference to a node [i.e., it is invoked by *block.nodeSearch(key)* rather than by *nodeSearch(p, key)*]. Then the following is a nonrecursive algorithm for searching an externally stored multiway search tree:

```
p = tree;
while (p != null) {
  block.directRead(p);
  i = block.nodeSearch(key);
  if (i < block.numtrees - 1 && key == block.k(i)) {
        position = i;
        return p;
  }
  p = block.son(i);
}
position = -1;
return -1;
```

The algorithm also sets *block* to the node at external address *p*. The record associated with *key* or a pointer to it may be found in *block*. Note that **null** as used in this algorithm references a null external storage address rather than the Java reference **null**.

Traversing a Multiway Tree

Traversal, a common operation on data structures, consists of accessing all the elements of the structure in a fixed sequence. The following is a recursive algorithm *traverse(tree)* to traverse a multiway tree and print its keys in ascending order:

```
if (tree != null) {
    nt = numTrees(tree);
    for (i = 0; i < nt - 0; i++) {
        traverse(son(tree, i));
        System.out.println(k(tree, i));
    }
    traverse(son(tree, nt));
}
```

In implementing the recursion, we must keep a stack of references to all the nodes in a path beginning with the root of the tree down to the node currently being visited.

If each node is a block of external storage, and *tree* is the root node's external storage address, then a node must be read into internal memory before its *son* or *k* fields can be accessed. Thus the algorithm becomes

```
if (tree != null) {
    block.directRead(tree);
    nt = block.numTrees();
    for (i = 0; i < nt - 1; i++) {
        traverse(block.son(i));
        System.out.println(block.k(i));
    }
    traverse(block.son(nt));
}
```

where *directRead* is a system routine that reads a block of storage at a particular external address (*tree*) into an internal memory buffer (*block*). This requires keeping a stack of buffers. If *d* is the depth of the tree, then $d + 1$ buffers must be kept in memory.

Alternatively, all but one of the buffers can be eliminated if each node contains two additional fields: a *father* field referencing its father, and an *index* field indicating which son of its father the node is. Then, when the last subtree of a node has been traversed, the algorithm uses the *father* field of the node to access its father, and its *index* field to determine which key in the father node to output and which subtree of the father to traverse next. However, this would require numerous reads for each node and is probably not worth the savings in buffer space, especially since a high-order tree with a very large number of keys requires very low depth. (As previously illustrated, a tree of order 11 with four thousand keys can be accommodated comfortably with depth 3. A tree of order 100 can accommodate over a million keys with a depth of only 2.)

Direct sequential access, another common operation, is closely related to traversal. This refers to accessing the next key following a key whose location in the tree is known. Let us assume that we have located a key $k1$ by searching the tree, and that it is located at position $k(n1, i1)$. Ordinarily, the successor of $k1$ can be found by executing the following method *next*$(n1, i1)$. (*NULLKEY* is a special value indicating that a proper key cannot be found.)

```
p = son(n1, i1 + 1);
q = null;              // q is one node behind p
while (p != null) {
   q = p;
   p = son(p, 0);
}
if (q != null)
   return k(q, 0);
if (i1 < n1.numTrees() - 2)
   return k(n1, i1 + 1);
return NULLKEY;
```

This algorithm relies on the fact that the successor of $k1$ is the first key in the subtree that follows $k1$ in *node*$(n1)$ or, if that subtree is empty [*son*$(n1, i1 + 1)$ equals ***null***] and if $k1$ is not the last key in its node ($i1 < numTrees(n1) - 2$), that the successor is the next key in *node*$(n1)$.

However, if $k1$ is the last key in its node and the subtree following it is empty, then its successor can only be found by backing up the tree. Assuming *father* and *index* fields in each node as outlined above, a complete algorithm *successor*$(n1, i1)$ to find the successor of the key in position $i1$ of the node referred to by $n1$ may be written as follows:

```
p = son(n1, i1 + 1);
if (p != null && i1 < numTrees(n1) - 2)
   // use the previous algorithm
   return next(n1, i1);
f = father(n1);
i = index(n1);
```

```
    while (f != null && i == numTrees(f) - 1) {
        i = index(f);
        f = father(f);
    }
    if (f == null)
        return NULLKEY;
    return k(f, i);
```

Of course, we would like to avoid backing up the tree whenever possible. Since a traversal beginning at a specific key is quite common, the initial search process is often modified to retain, in internal memory, all the nodes in the path from the tree root to the located key. Then, if the tree must be backed up, the path to the root is readily available. As noted above, the fields *father* and *index* are not needed if this is done.

Later in this section, we examine a specialized adaptation of a multiway search tree, called a B^+-tree, that does not require a stack for efficient sequential traversal.

Insertion in a Multiway Search Tree

Now that we have examined how to search and traverse multiway search trees, let us examine insertion techniques for these structures. We examine two insertion techniques for multiway search trees. The first is analogous to binary search tree insertion and results in a top-down multiway search tree. The second is a new insertion technique and produces a special kind of balanced multiway search tree. It is this second technique, or a slight variation thereof, that is most commonly used in direct-access external file storage systems.

For convenience, we assume that duplicate keys are not permitted in the tree, so that no insertion takes place if the argument *key* is found in the tree. We also assume that the tree is nonempty. The first step in both insertion procedures is to search for the argument *key*. If the argument *key* is found in the tree, then we return a pointer to the node containing the key, and set the variable *position* to its position within the node, just as in the search procedure presented above. However, if the argument *key* is not found, we return a pointer to the semileaf *node(s)* that would contain the key if it were present, and set *position* to the index of the smallest key in *node(s)* that is greater than the argument *key* (i.e., the position of the argument *key* if it were in the tree). If all the keys in *node(s)* are less than the argument *key*, *position* is set to *numTrees(s)* − 1. A variable, *found*, is set to **true** or **false** depending on whether the argument key is or is not found in the tree.

Figure 7.3.2 illustrates the result of this procedure for an order-4 top-down balanced multiway search tree and several search arguments. The algorithm for *find* is straightforward:

```
    q = null;
    p = tree;
    while (p != null) {
        i = nodeSearch(p, key);
        q = p;
        if (i < numTrees(p) - 1 && key == k(p, i)) {
            found = true;
            position = i;
            return p;        // the key is found in node(p)
        }
```

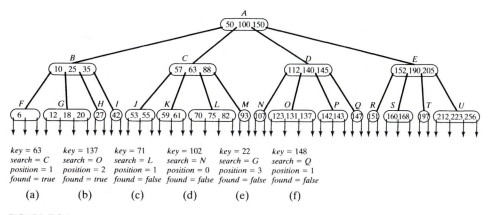

key = 63   key = 137   key = 71   key = 102   key = 22   key = 148
search = C   search = O   search = L   search = N   search = G   search = Q
position = 1   position = 2   position = 1   position = 0   position = 3   position = 1
found = true   found = true   found = false   found = false   found = false   found = false

(a)   (b)   (c)   (d)   (e)   (f)

FIGURE 7.3.2

```
        p = son(p, i);
    }
    found = false;
    position = i;
    return q;                    // p is null. q points to a semileaf
```

To implement this algorithm in Java, we would write a method *find* with the following header:

```
Node find(Node tree, Keytype key, int [ ] position, boolean [ ] found)
```

References to the variables *position* and *found* in the algorithm are replaced by references to a one-element array *position* and *found*, respectively, in the Java method. The declaration of these parameters as arrays allows the method to pass both the position of the desired node in the tree as well as a Boolean flag back to the method that invokes the *find* method.

Let us assume that *s* is a pointer to the node returned by *find*. The second step of the insertion procedure applies only if the key is not found (remember, no duplicate keys are permitted) and if *node(s)* is not full (i.e., if *numTrees(s)* < *n*, where *n* is the order of the tree). In Figure 7.3.2, this applies to cases d and f only. The second step consists of inserting the new key (and record) into *node(s)*. Note that if the tree is top-down or balanced, a nonfull semileaf discovered by *find* is always a leaf. Let *insRec(p, i, rec)* be a routine to insert the record *rec* in position *i* of *node(p)* as appropriate. Then the second step of the insertion process may be described as follows:

```
nt = numTrees(s);
numTrees(s) = nt + 1;
for (i = nt - 1; i > position; i--)
    k(s, i) = k(s, i - 1);
k(s, position) = key;
insRec(s, position, rec);
```

We call this method *insLeaf(s, position, key, rec)*.

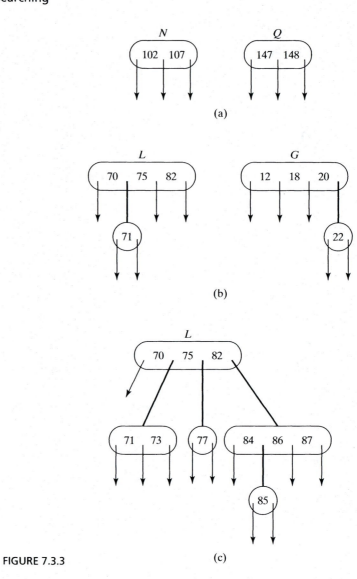

FIGURE 7.3.3

Figure 7.3.3a illustrates the nodes located by the find procedure in Figures 7.3.2d and f with the new keys inserted. Note that it is unnecessary to copy the son pointers associated with the keys being moved because the node is a leaf so that all pointers are *null*. We assume that they were initialized to *null* when the node was initially added to the tree.

If step 2 is appropriate (i.e., if a nonfull leaf node where the key can be inserted has been found), then both insertion routines terminate. The two techniques differ only in the third step, which is invoked when the find procedure locates a full semileaf.

The first insertion technique, which results in top-down multiway search trees, mimics the actions of the binary search tree insertion algorithm. That is, it allocates a new node, inserts the key and record into the new node, and places the new node as the appropriate son of *node(s)*. It uses the method *makeTree(key, rec)* to allocate a node, set the *n* pointers in it to **null**, its *numTrees* field to 2, and its first key field to *key. makeTree* then invokes *insRec* to insert the record as appropriate and finally returns a reference to the newly allocated node. Using *makeTree*, the method *insFull* to insert the key when the appropriate semileaf is full may be implemented trivially as:

```
p = makeTree(key, rec);
s.son(position) = p;
```

If *father* and *index* fields are maintained in each node, the operations

```
p.father() = s;
p.index() = position;
```

are required as well.

Figure 7.3.3b illustrates the result of inserting keys 71 and 22, respectively, into the nodes located by *find* in Figure 7.3.2c and e. Figure 7.3.3c illustrates subsequent insertions of keys 86, 77, 87, 84, 85, and 73 in that order. Note that the order in which keys are inserted very much affects where they are placed. For example, consider what would happen if the keys were inserted in the order 85, 77, 86, 87, 73, 84.

Note also that this insertion technique can transform a leaf into a nonleaf (although it remains a semileaf) and therefore unbalances the multiway tree. Thus it is possible for successive insertions to produce a tree that is heavily unbalanced and in which an inordinate number of nodes must be accessed to locate certain keys. In practical situations, however, multiway search trees created by this insertion technique, while not completely balanced, are not too greatly unbalanced, so that too many nodes are not accessed in searching for a key in a leaf. However, the technique does have one major drawback. Since leafs are created containing only one key, and other leafs may be created before previously created leafs are filled, multiway trees created by successive insertions in this manner waste much space with leaf nodes that are nearly empty.

Although this insertion method does not guarantee balanced trees, it does guarantee top-down trees. To see this, note that a new node is not created unless its father is full. Thus any nonfull node has no descendants and is therefore a leaf, which by definition implies that the tree is top-down. The advantage of a top-down tree is that the upper nodes are full so that as many keys as possible are found on short paths.

Before examining the second insertion technique, we put all the pieces of the first technique together to form a complete search and insertion algorithm for top-down multiway search trees.

```
if (tree == null) {
    tree = makeTree(key, rec);
    position = 0;
    return tree;
}
s = find(tree, key, position, found);
if (found == true)
    return s;
```

```
if (numTrees(s) < n) {
    insLeaf(s, position, key, rec);
    return s;
}
p = makeTree(key, rec);
son(s, position) = p;
position = 0;
return p;
```

B-Trees

The second insertion technique for multiway search trees is more complex. Compensating for this complexity, however, is the fact that it creates balanced trees, so that the maximum number of nodes accessed to find any particular key is kept small. In addition, the technique yields one further bonus, in that all the nodes (except the root) in a tree created by this technique are at least half full, so that very little storage space is wasted. This last advantage is the primary reason that the second insertion technique (or a variation thereof) is used so frequently in actual file systems.

A balanced order-*n* multiway search tree in which each nonroot node contains at least $(n - 1)/2$ keys is called a **B-tree of order n**. (Note that the slash denotes integer division, so that a B-tree of order 12 contains at least five keys in each nonroot node, as does a B-tree of order 11.) A B-tree of order *n* is also called an **n-(n − 1) tree** or an **(n − 1)-n tree**. (The dash outside the parentheses is a hyphen, and the dash inside the parentheses is a minus sign.) This reflects the fact that each node in the tree has a maximum of $n - 1$ keys and *n* sons. Thus, a 4–5 tree is a B-tree of order 5, as is a 5–4 tree. In particular, a 2–3 (or 3-2) tree is the most elementary nontrivial (i.e., nonbinary) B-tree, with one or two keys per node and two or three sons per node.

(At this point, we should say something about terminology. In discussing B-trees, the word "order" is used differently by different authors. The **order** of a B-tree is often defined to mean the minimum number of keys in a nonroot node [i.e., $(n - 1)/2$], and the **degree** of a B-tree to mean the maximum number of sons [i.e., *n*]. Still other authors use "order" to mean the maximum number of keys in a node [i.e., $n - 1$]. We use **order** consistently for all multiway search trees to mean the maximum number of sons.)

The first two steps of the insertion technique are identical for B-trees and for top-down trees. First, use *find* to locate the leaf into which the key should be inserted, and second, if the located leaf is not full, add the key using *insLeaf*. It is in the third step, when the located leaf is found to be full, that the methods differ. Instead of creating a new node with only one key, split the full leaf in two: a left leaf and a right leaf. For simplicity, assume that *n* is odd. The *n* keys consisting of the $n - 1$ keys in the full leaf and the new key to be inserted are divided into three groups: the lowest *n*/2 keys are placed into the left leaf, the highest *n*/2 keys are placed into the right leaf, and the middle key [there must be a middle key, since $2*(n/2)$ equals $n - 1$ if *n* is odd] is placed into the father node if possible (i.e., if the father node is not full). The two pointers on either side of the key inserted into the father are set to the newly created left and right leaves respectively.

Figure 7.3.4 illustrates this process on a B-tree of order 5. Figure 7.3.4a shows a subtree of a B-tree, and Figure 7.3.4b shows part of the same subtree as it is altered by

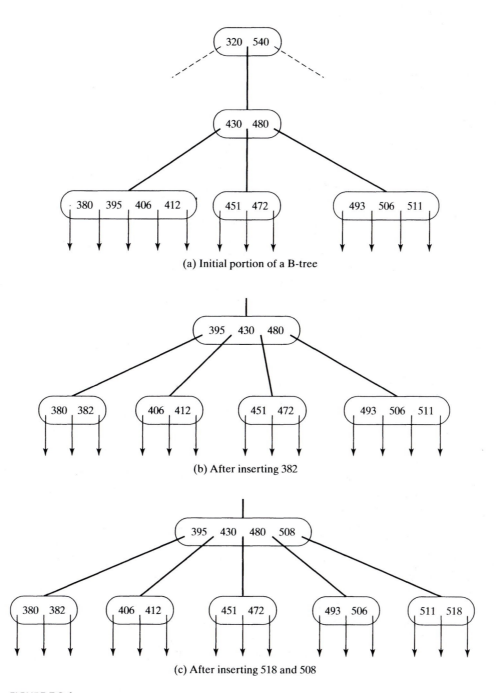

(a) Initial portion of a B-tree

(b) After inserting 382

(c) After inserting 518 and 508

FIGURE 7.3.4

the insertion of 382. Since the leftmost leaf was already full, the five keys 380, 382, 395, 406, and 412 are divided, with 380 and 382 placed in a new left leaf, 406 and 412 placed in a new right leaf, and the middle key, 395, advanced to the father node with pointers to the left and right leafs on either side. There is no problem placing 395 in the father node because it contained only two keys and has room for four.

Figure 7.3.4c shows the same subtree with first 518 and then 508 inserted. (The same result would be achieved if they were inserted in reverse order.) 518 can be inserted directly in the rightmost leaf, since there is room for one additional key. However, when 508 arrives, the leaf is already full. The five keys 493, 506, 508, 511, and 518 are divided, with the lower two (493 and 506) placed in a new left leaf, the higher two (511 and 518) in a new right leaf, and the middle key (508) advanced to the father, which still has room to accommodate it. Note that the key advanced to the father is always the middle key, regardless of whether it arrived before or after the other keys.

If the order of the B-tree is even, then the $n - 1$ keys, excluding the middle key, must be divided into two unequal-sized groups: one of size $n/2$, and the other of size $(n - 1)/2$. [The second group is always of size $(n - 1)/2$, regardless of whether n is odd or even, because when n is odd, $(n - 1)/2$ equals $n/2$.] For example, if n equals 10, then $10/2$ (or five) keys are in one group, $9/2$ (or four) keys are in the other group, and one key is advanced, for a total of ten keys. These may be divided, with the larger-sized group always in the left or right leaf, or divisions may be alternated so that the right leaf contains more keys on one split, and the left leaf contains more keys on the next split. In practice, it makes little difference which technique is used.

Figure 7.3.5 illustrates both left and right biases in a B-tree of order 4. Note that whether a left or right bias is chosen determines which key is to be advanced to the father.

One basis on which to decide whether to leave more keys in the left or right leaf is to examine the key ranges under both possibilities. In Figure 7.3.5b, utilizing a left bias, the key range of the left node is 87 to 102, or 15, and the key range of the right node is 102 to 140, or 38. In Figure 7.3.5c, utilizing a right bias, the key ranges are 13 (87 to 100) and 40 (100 to 140). Thus we would select a left bias in this case, since it more nearly equalizes the probability of a new key going into the left and right, assuming a uniform distribution of keys.

The discussion thus far has assumed that there is room in the father for the middle node to be inserted. What if the father node, too, is full? For example, what happens with the insertion in Figure 7.3.2c, where 71 must be inserted into the full node L, and C, the father of L, is full as well? The solution is quite simple. The father node is also split in the same way, and its middle node is advanced to its father. This process continues until a key is inserted in a node with room, or the root node, A, is itself split. When that happens, a new root node NR is created containing the key advanced from the splitting of A, and with the two halves of A as sons.

Figures 7.3.6 and 7.3.7 illustrate this process with the insertions from Figures 7.3.2c and e. In Figure 7.3.6a, node L is split. (We assume a left bias throughout this illustration.) The middle element (75) should be advanced to C, but C is full. Thus, in Figure 7.3.6b, we see C being split as well. The two halves of L are now made sons of the appropriate halves of C. 75, which was advanced to C, must now be advanced to root node A, which also has no room. Thus A itself must be split, as shown in Figure 7.3.6c. Finally,

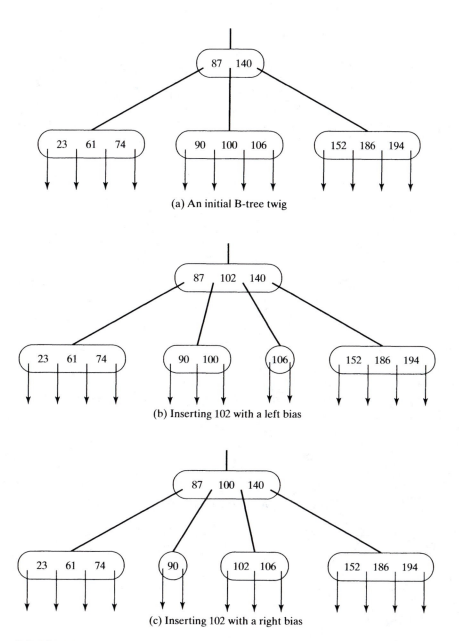

(a) An initial B-tree twig

(b) Inserting 102 with a left bias

(c) Inserting 102 with a right bias

FIGURE 7.3.5

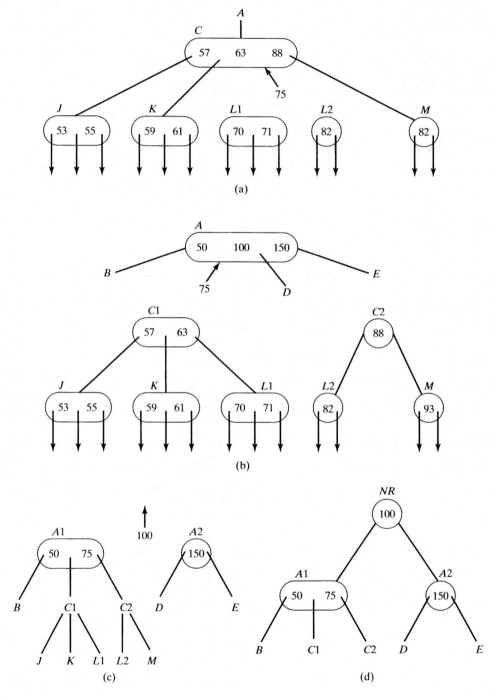

FIGURE 7.3.6

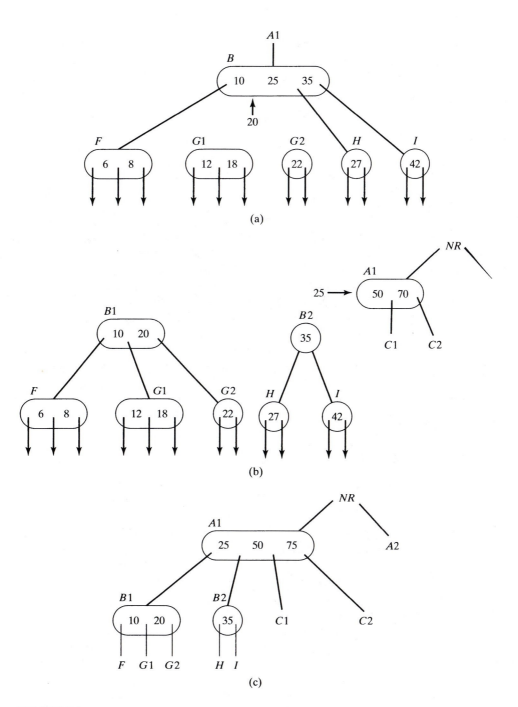

FIGURE 7.3.7

in Figure 7.3.6d a new root node, *NR*, is established, containing the key advanced from *A* and two pointers to the two halves of *A*.

Figure 7.3.7 illustrates the subsequent insertion of 22, as in Figure 7.3.2e. In that figure, 22 would have caused a split of nodes *G*, *B*, and *A*. But in the meantime, *A* has already been split by the insertion of 71, so the insertion of 22 proceeds as in Figure 7.3.7. First *G* is split and 20 is advanced to *B* (Figure 7.3.7a), which is split in turn (Figure 7.3.7b). 25 is then advanced to *A*1, which is the new father of *B*. But since *A*1 has room, no further splits are necessary. 25 is inserted into *A*1 and the insertion is complete (Figure 7.3.7c).

As a final illustration, Figure 7.3.8 shows the insertion of several keys into the order-5 B-tree from Figure 7.3.4c. It would be worthwhile for you to generate a list of keys and continually insert them into an order-5 B-tree to see how it develops.

Note that a B-tree grows in depth through the splitting of the root and the creation of a new root, and in width by the splitting of nodes. Thus B-tree insertion into a balanced tree keeps the tree balanced. However, a B-tree is rarely top-down, because when a full nonleaf node splits the two nonleafs created are not full. Thus, while the maximum number of accesses to find a key is low (since the tree is balanced), the average number of such accesses may be higher than in a top-down tree in which the upper levels are always full. In simulations, the average number of accesses is indeed slightly lower in searching a random top-down tree than in searching a random B-tree because random top-down trees are generally fairly balanced.

One other point to note in a B-tree is that older keys (those inserted first) tend to be closer to the root than younger keys, since they have had more opportunity to be advanced. However, it is possible for a key to remain in a leaf forever even if a large number of locally lower and higher keys are subsequently inserted. This is unlike a top-down tree, in which a key in an ancestor node must be older than any key in a descendant node.

Algorithms for B-Tree Insertion

As you might imagine, the algorithm for B-tree insertion is fairly involved. To simplify matters temporarily, let us assume that we can access a reference to the father of *node*(*nd*) by referring to *nd.father*() and the position of the pointer *nd* in *node*(*nd.father*()) by *nd.index*(), so that (*nd.father*()).*son*(*nd.index*()) equals *nd*. (This can be implemented most directly by adding *father* and *index* fields to each node, but there are complications to such an approach that we will discuss shortly.) We also assume that *p.r*(*i*) is a reference to the record associated with the key *p.k*(*i*). Recall that the method *find* returns a pointer to the leaf in which the key should be inserted and sets the variable *position* to the position in the leaf at which the key should be inserted. Recall also that *key* and *rec* are the argument key and record to be inserted.

The method *s.insert*(*key*, *rec*, *position*) inserts a record into a B-tree. It is called following a call to *find*, if the output parameter *found* of the routine is **false** (i.e., the key is not already in the tree), where *s* is a reference to the node returned by *find* (i.e., the node where *key* and *rec* should be inserted). The method uses two additional auxiliary methods that will be presented shortly. The first method, *split*, accepts four input parameters: *pos*, the position in *node*(*nd*) where a key and record are to be inserted; *newKey* and *newRec*, the key and record being inserted (these could be either the key

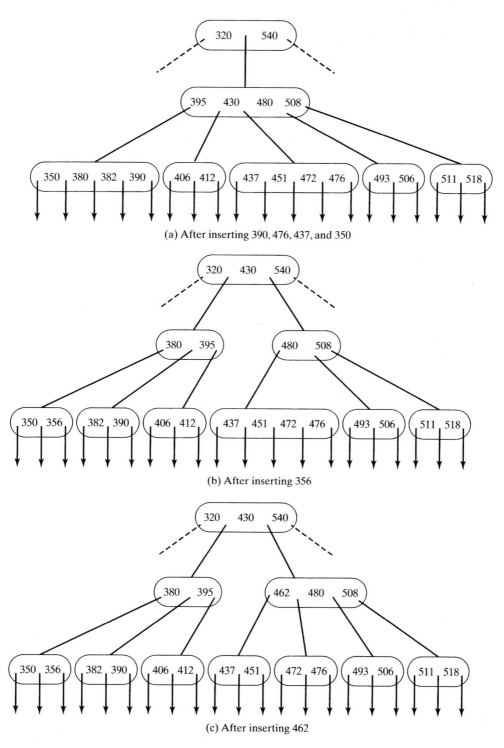

(a) After inserting 390, 476, 437, and 350

(b) After inserting 356

(c) After inserting 462

FIGURE 7.3.8

and record being advanced from a previously split node or the new key and record being inserted into the tree); and *newNode*, a reference to the subtree that contains the keys greater than *newKey* (i.e., a pointer to the right half of a node previously split), which must be inserted into the node currently being split. In order to maintain the proper number of sons within a node, a reference to a newly created son must be inserted into the node each time a new key and record are inserted. When a new key and record are inserted into a leaf, the reference to the son to be inserted is null. Because a key and record are inserted into one of the upper levels only when a node is split at a lower level, the reference to the new son that is being inserted (*newNode*) will be to the right half of the node that was split at the lower level. The left half remains intact within the previously allocated lower-level node. *split* arranges *newKey* and the keys of *node*(*nd*), so that the group of $n/2$ smallest keys remain in *node*(*nd*), the middle key and record are assigned to *midKey* and *midRec*, and the remaining keys are inserted into a new node, *node*(*nd2*).

The second method, *insNode*, inserts key *newKey*, record *newRec*, and the subtree referred to by *newNode* into *node*(*nd*) at position *pos* if there is room. Recall that the method *makeTree*(*key,rec*) creates a new node containing the single key *key*, record *rec*, and all references null. *makeTree* returns a reference to the newly created node. We present the algorithm for *insert* using the methods *split*, *insNode*, and *makeTree*.

```
nd = s;
pos = position;
newNode = null;        // reference to right half of split node
newRec = rec;          // the record to be inserted
newKey = key;          // the key to be inserted
f = nd.father();
while (f != null && nd.numTree() == n) {
    nd.split(pos, newKey, newRec, newNode, nd2, midKey, midRec);
    newNode = nd2;
    pos = nd.index();
    nd = f;
    f = nd.father();
    newKey = midKey;
    newRec = midRec;
}
if (numTrees(nd) < n) {
    nd.insNode(pos, newKey, newRec, newNode);
    return;
}
// f equals null and nd.numTrees() equals n so that nd is
// a full root; split it and create a new root
nd.split(pos, newKey, newRec, newNode, nd2, midKey, midRec);
tree = makeTree(midKey, midRec);
tree.son(0) = nd;
tree.son(1) = nd2;
```

The heart of this algorithm is the method *split*, which actually splits a node. *split* itself uses an auxiliary method, *nd1.copy*(*first, last, nd2*), which sets a local variable *numKeys* to

$last - first + 1$ and copies fields $nd1.k(first)$ through $nd1.k(last)$ into $nd2.k(0)$ through $nd2.k(numKeys)$, fields $nd1.r(first)$ through $nd1.r(last)$ (which contains pointers to the actual records) into $nd2.r(0)$ through $nd2.r(numKeys)$, and fields $nd1.son(first)$ through $nd1.son(last + 1)$ into $nd2.son(0)$ through $nd2.son(numKeys + 1)$. *copy* also sets $nd2.numTrees()$ to $numTrees + 1$. If $last < first$, *copy* sets $nd2.numTrees()$ to 1 but does not change any $k, r,$ or *son* fields. *split* also uses *getNode* to create a new node and *insNode* to insert a new key in a nonfull node.

The following is an algorithm for *split*. The n keys contained in $node(nd)$ and *newKey* must be distributed so that the smallest $n/2$ remain in $node(nd)$, the highest $(n - 1)/2$ (which equals $n/2$ if n is odd) are placed in a new node, $node(nd2)$, and the middle key is placed in *midKey*. In order to avoid recomputing $n/2$ on each occasion, assume that its value has been assigned to the public variable *ndiv2*. The input value *pos* is the position in $node(nd)$ in which *newKey* would be placed if there were room.

```
// create a new node for the right half; keep the first half in
node(nd)
nd2 = getNode();
if (pos > ndiv2) {    // newKey belongs to node(nd2)
    nd.copy(ndiv2 + 1, n - 2, nd2);
    nd2.insNode(pos - ndiv2 - 1, newKey, newRec, newNode);
    numTrees(nd) = ndiv2 + 1;
    midKey = nd.k(ndiv2);
    midRec = nd.r(ndiv2);
    return;
}
if (pos == ndiv2) {
    // newKey is the middle key
    nd.copy(ndiv2, n - 2, nd2);
    nd.numTrees() = ndiv2 + 1;
    nd2.son(0) = newNode;
    midKey = newKey;
    midRec = newRec;
    return;
}
if (pos < ndiv2) {
    // newKey belongs in node(nd)
    nd.copy(ndiv2, n - 2, nd2);
    nd.numTrees() = ndiv2;
    nd.insNode(pos, newKey, newRec, newNode);
    midKey = nd.k(ndiv2 - 1);
    midRec = nd.r(ndiv2 - 1);
    return;
}
```

The method $nd.insNode(pos, newKey, newRec, newNode)$ inserts a new record *newRec* with key *newKey* into position *pos* of a nonfull node, $node(nd)$. *newNode* is a reference to a subtree to be inserted to the right of the new record. The remaining keys and subtrees in positions *pos* or greater are moved up one position. The value of $nd.numTrees()$ is increased by one. An algorithm for *insNode* follows:

```
for (i = nd.numTrees() - 1; i >= pos + 1; i--) {
    nd.son(i + 1) = nd.son(i);
    nd.k(i) = nd.k(i - 1); nd.r(i) = nd.r(i - 1);
}
nd.son(pos + 1) = newNode;
nd.k(pos) = newKey;
nd.r(pos) = newRec;
nd.numTrees()++;
```

Computing *father* and *index*

Before examining the efficiency of the insertion procedure, we must clear up one out-standing issue: the matter of the *father* and *index* methods. Both functions are utilized in the *insert* method, and we suggested that they could be implemented most directly by adding *father* and *index* fields to each node, but as you may have noticed, these fields are not updated by the insertion algorithm. Let us examine how this update could be achieved and why we chose to omit that operation. We then examine alternative methods of implementing the two functions that do not require the update.

The *father* and *index* fields would have to be updated each time that *copy* or *insNode* was called. In the case of *copy*, both fields in each son whose pointer is copied must be modified. In the case of *insNode*, the *index* field of each son whose reference is moved must be modified, as well as both fields in the son being inserted. (In addition, the fields must be updated in the two halves of a root node being split in the *insert* method.) However, this would affect the efficiency of the insertion algorithm in an un-acceptable manner, especially when dealing with nodes in external storage. In the en-tire B-tree search and insertion process (excluding the update of *father* and *index* fields), at most two nodes at each level of the tree are accessed. In most cases, when a split does not occur on a level, only one node at the level is accessed. The *copy* and *insNode* operations, although they move nodes from one subtree to another, do so by moving pointers within one or two father nodes and thus do not actually require access to the son nodes being moved. Requiring an update to the *father* and *index* fields in those sons would require accessing and modifying all the son nodes. But reading and writing a node from and to external storage are the most expensive operations in the entire B-tree management process. In a practical information storage system, where a node can have several hundred sons, maintaining *father* and *index* fields could result in a hundred-fold decrease in system efficiency.

How then can we obtain the *father* and *index* data required for the insertion process without maintaining separate fields? First, recall that the method *p.nodeSearch(key)* returns the position of the smallest key in *node(p)* greater than or equal to *key*, so that *nd.index()* equals *(nd.father()).nodeSearch(key)*. Therefore, once *father* is available, *index* can be obtained without a separate field.

To understand how we can obtain *father*, let us look at a related problem. No B-tree insertion can take place without a prior search to locate the leaf where the new key must be inserted. This search proceeds from the root and accesses one node at each level until it reaches the appropriate leaf. That is, it proceeds along a single path from the root to a leaf. The insertion then backs up along the same path, splitting all the full nodes in the path from the leaf toward the root, until it reaches a nonfull node into which it can insert a key without splitting. Once that insertion is performed, the insertion process terminates.

The insertion process accesses the same nodes as the search process. Since we have seen that accessing a node from external storage is quite expensive, it would make sense for the search process to store the nodes on its path together with their external addresses in internal memory, where the insertion process can access them without an expensive second-read operation. But once all the nodes in a path are stored in internal memory, a node's father can be located by simply examining the previous node in the path. Thus there is no need to maintain and update a *father* field.

Let us then present modified versions of *find* and *insert* to locate and insert a key in a B-tree. Let *pathNode(i)* be a copy of the *i*th node in the path from the root to a leaf, let *location(i)* be its location (either a reference to a node if the tree is in internal memory, or an external storage address if it is in external storage), and let *index(i)* be the position of the node among the sons of its father (note that *index* can be determined during the search process and retained for use during insertion). We refer to *son(i, j)*, *k(i, j)*, and *r(i, j)* as the *j*th *son*, *key*, and *record* field respectively in *pathNode(i)*. Similarly, *numTrees(i)* is the *numTrees* field in *pathNode(i)*.

The following *find* algorithm utilizes the operation *access(i, loc)* to copy a node from location *loc* (either from internal or external memory) into *pathNode(i)* and *loc* itself into *location(i)*. If the tree is stored internally, this operation consists of

```
pathNode(i) = node(loc);
location(i) = loc;
```

If the tree is stored externally, the operation consists of

```
direcRread(loc, pathNode(i));
location(i) = loc;
```

where *directRead* reads a block of storage at a particular external address (*loc*) into an internal memory buffer (*pathNode(i)*). We also assume that *nodeSearch(i, key)* searches *pathNode(i)* rather than *node(i)*. We present the algorithm *find*:

```
q = null;
p = tree;
j = -1;
i = -1;
while (p != null) {
   index(++j) = i;
   access(j, p);
   i = nodeSearch(j, key);
   q = p;
   if (i < numTrees(j) - 1 && key == k(j, i))
           break;
   p = son(j, i);
}
position = i;
return j;                 // key is in pathNode(j) or belongs there
```

The insertion process is modified in several places. First, *insNode* and *copy* access *pathNode(nd)* rather than *node(nd)*. That is, *nd* is now an array index rather than a reference to a node, so that all references to $k, son, r,$ and $numTrees$ are to fields within an element of *pathNode*. The algorithms for *insNode* and *copy* do not have to be changed.

Second, *split* must be modified to write out the two halves of a split node. It assumes a method *replace(i)*, which replaces the node at *location(i)* with the contents of *pathNode(i)*. This method is the reverse of *access*. If the tree is stored internally, it may be implemented by

```
node(location(i)) = pathNode(i);
```

and if externally, by

```
directWrite(location(i), pathNode(i));
```

where *directWrite* writes a buffer in memory (*pathNode(i)*) into a block of external storage at a particular external address (*location(i)*). *split* also uses a method *makeNode(i)* that obtains a new block of storage at location *x*, places *pathNode(i)* in the block, and returns *x*. The following is a revised version of *split*:

```
if (pos > ndiv2) {
    copy(nd, ndiv2 + 1, n - 2, nd + 1);
    insNode(nd + 1, pos - ndiv2 - 1, newKey, newRec, newNode);
    numTrees(nd) = ndiv2 + 1;
    midKey = k(nd, ndiv2);
    midRec = r(nd, ndiv2);
    return;
}
if (pos == ndiv2) {
    copy(nd, ndiv2, n - 2, nd + 1);
    numTrees(nd) = ndiv2;
    son(nd + 1, 0) = newNode;
    midKey = newKey;
    midRec = newRec;
    return;
}
if (pos < ndiv2) {
    copy(nd, ndiv2, n - 2, nd + 1);
    numTrees(nd) = ndiv2;
    insNode(nd, pos, newKey, newRec, newNode);
    midKey = newKey;
    midRec = newRec;
}
replace(nd);
nd2 = makeNode(nd + 1);
```

Note that *nd* is now a position in *pathNode* rather than a reference to a node, and that *pathNode(nd + 1)* rather than *node(nd2)* is used to build the second half of the split node. This can be done because the node at level *nd + 1* (if any) of the path has already been updated by the time *split* is called on *nd*, so that *pathNode(nd + 1)* can be reused. *nd2* remains the actual location of the new node (allocated by *makeNode*). (It may be desirable to retain a path to the newly inserted key in *pathNode* if, for example, we wish to perform a sequential traversal or sequential insertions beginning at that point. In such cases, the algorithm must be suitably adjusted to place the appropriate left or right half of the split node at the appropriate position in *pathNode*. We would not be able to use *pathNode*(*i* + 1) to build the right half but would use an additional auxiliary internal memory node instead. We leave the details to the reader.)

The method *insert* itself is also modified in that it uses *nd* − 1 rather than *father*(*nd*). It also calls upon *replace* and *makeNode*. When the root must be split, *makeTtree* builds a new tree root node in internal storage. This node is placed in *pathNode*(*i*) (which is no longer needed because the old root node has been updated by *split*) and written out using *makeNode*. The following is the revised algorithm for *insert*:

```
nd = s;
pos = position;
newNode = null;
newRec = rec;
newKey = key;
while (nd != 0 && numTrees(nd) == n) {
    split(nd, pos, newKey, newRec, newNode, nd2, midKey, midRec);
    newNode = nd2;
    pos = index(nd);
    nd--;
    newKey = midKey;
    newRec = midRec;
}
if (numTrees(nd) < n) {
    insNode(nd, pos, newKey, newRec, newNode);
    replace(nd);
    return;
}
split(nd, pos, newKey, newRec, newNode, nd2, midKey, midRec);
pathNode(0) = makeTree(midKey, midRec);
son(0, 0) = nd;
son(0, 1) = nd2;
tree = makeNode(0);
```

Deletion in Multiway Search Trees

The simplest method for deleting a record from a multiway search tree is to retain the key in the tree but mark it in some way as representing a deleted record. This could be accomplished by setting the reference to the record corresponding to the key to **null** or by allocating an extra flag field for each key to indicate whether or not it has been deleted. The space occupied by the record itself can, of course, be reclaimed. In this way, the key remains in the tree as a guidepost to the subtrees but does not represent a record within the file.

The disadvantage of this approach is that the space occupied by the key is wasted, possibly leading to unnecessary nodes in the tree when a large number of records have been deleted. Extra "deleted" bits require still more space.

Of course, if a record with a deleted key is subsequently inserted, the space for the key can be recycled. In a nonleaf node, only the same key would be able to reuse the space because it is too difficult to determine dynamically that the newly inserted key is between the predecessor and successor of the deleted key. However, in a leaf node (or, in certain situations, in a semileaf), the deleted key's space can be reused by a neighboring key because it is relatively easy to determine proximity. Since a large portion of keys are in leaves or semileafs, if insertions and deletions occur with equal frequency (or if there are more insertions than deletions) and are uniformly distributed (i.e., the deletions are not bunched together to significantly reduce the total number of keys in the tree temporarily), the space penalty is tolerable in exchange for the advantage of ease of deletion. There is also a small time penalty in subsequent searches because some keys will require more nodes to be examined than if the deleted key had never been inserted in the first place.

If we are unwilling to pay the space/search-time penalty of simplified deletion, then there are more expensive deletion techniques that eliminate the penalty. In an unrestricted multiway search tree, a technique similar to deletion from a binary search tree can be employed:

1. If the key to be deleted has an empty left or right subtree, simply delete the key and compact the node. If it was the only key in the node, free the node.
2. If the key to be deleted has nonempty left and right subtrees, find its successor key (which must have an empty left subtree); let the successor key take its place and compact the node that contained the successor. If the successor was the only key in the node, free the node.

We leave the development of a detailed algorithm and application to the reader.

However, this procedure may result in a tree that does not satisfy the requirements for either a top-down tree or a B-tree, even if the initial tree did satisfy those requirements. In a top-down tree, if the key being deleted is from a semileaf that is not a leaf and the key has empty right and left subtrees, the semileaf will be left with fewer than $n - 1$ keys even though it is not a leaf. This violates the top-down requirement. In that case, it is necessary to choose a random nonempty subtree of the node and move the largest or smallest key from it into the semileaf from which the key was deleted. This process must be repeated until the semileaf from which a key is taken is a leaf. This leaf can then be compacted or freed. In the worst case, this might require rewriting one node at each level of the tree.

In a strict B-tree, we must preserve the requirement that each node contains at least $n/2$ keys. As noted above, if a key is being deleted from a nonleaf node, its successor (which must be in a leaf) is moved to the deleted position, and the deletion proceeds as if the successor were deleted from the leaf node. When a key (either the key to be deleted or its successor) is removed from a leaf node, and the number of keys in the node drops below $n/2$, remedial action must be taken. This situation is called an **underflow**. The simplest solution when an underflow occurs is to examine the leaf's younger or older brother. If the brother contains more than $n/2$ keys, then the key ks in the father node that separates the two brothers can be added to the underflow node, and the last or first key of the brother (last if the brother is older; first if younger) is added to the father in place of ks. Figure 7.3.9a illustrates this process on an order-5 B-tree. (Note that once a brother is being accessed, we could distribute the keys evenly

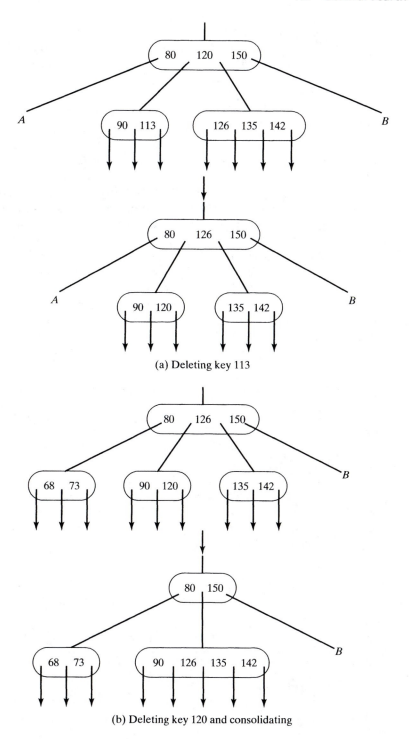

(a) Deleting key 113

(b) Deleting key 120 and consolidating

FIGURE 7.3.9

between the two brothers rather than simply shifting one key. For example, if the underflow node $n1$ contains 106 and 112, the separating key in the father f is 120, and the brother $n2$ contains 123, 128, 134, 139, 142, and 146 in an order-7 B-tree, we can rearrange them so that $n1$ contains 106, 112, 120, and 123, 128 moves up to f as the separator, and 134, 139, 142, and 146 remain in $n2$.)

If both brothers contain exactly $n/2$ keys, no keys can be shifted. In that case, the underflow node and one of its brothers are ***concatenated***, or ***consolidated***, into a single node which also contains the separator key from their father. This is illustrated in Figure 7.3.9b, where we combine the underflow node with its younger brother.

Of course, it is possible that the father contains only $n/2$ keys and thus has no extra key to spare. In that case, it can borrow from its father and brother, as in Figure 7.3.10a. In the worst case, when the father's brothers also have no spare keys, the father and its brother may also be consolidated and a key taken from the grandfather. This is illustrated in Figure 7.3.10b. Potentially, if all nonroot ancestors of a node and their brothers contain exactly $n/2$ keys, a key will be taken from the root, as consolidations take place at each level from the leafs to the level just below the root. If the root had more than one key, this ends the process, since the root of a B-tree need have only one key. If, however, the root contained only a single key, that key is used in the consolidation of the two nodes below the root, the root is freed, the consolidated node becomes the new root of the tree, and the depth of the B-tree is reduced. We leave to the reader the development of an actual algorithm for B-tree deletion from this description.

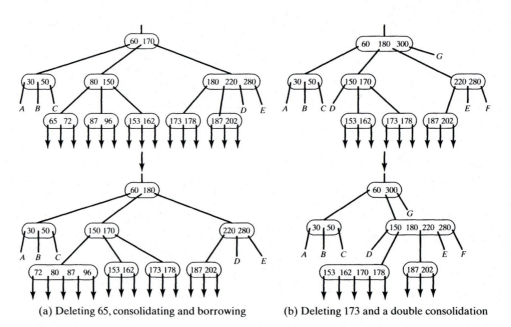

(a) Deleting 65, consolidating and borrowing   (b) Deleting 173 and a double consolidation

FIGURE 7.3.10

You should note, however, that it is foolish to form a consolidated node with $n - 1$ keys if a subsequent insertion will immediately split the node in two. In a B-tree of large order, it may make sense to leave an underflow node with fewer than $n/2$ keys (even though this violates the formal B-tree requirements) so that future insertions can take place without splitting. Typically a minimum number of keys, *min* less than $n/2$, is defined so that consolidation takes place only if fewer than *min* keys remain in a leaf node.

Efficiency of Multiway Search Trees

The primary considerations in evaluating the efficiency of multiway search trees, as for all data structures, are time and space. Time is measured by the number of nodes accessed or modified in an operation, rather than by the number of key comparisons. The reason for this, as mentioned earlier, is that accessing a node usually involves reading from external storage, and modifying a node involves writing to external storage. These operations are far more time-consuming than internal memory operations and therefore dominate the time required.

Similarly, space is measured by the number of nodes in the tree and their size rather than by the number of keys contained in the nodes, because the same space is allocated for a node regardless of the number of keys it contains. Of course, if the records are stored outside the tree nodes, the space requirement for them is determined by how the record storage is organized rather than by how the tree is organized. Since the storage requirements for the records generally overwhelm the requirements for the key tree, the actual tree space may not be significant.

First, let us examine top-down multiway search trees. Assuming an order-m tree and n records, there are two extreme possibilities. In the worst case for search time, the tree is totally unbalanced. Every node except one is a semileaf with one son and contains $m - 1$ keys. The single leaf node contains $((n - 1) \% (m - 1)) + 1$ keys. The tree contains $((n - 1)/(m - 1)) + 1$ nodes, one on each level. A search or an insertion accesses half that many nodes on the average and every node in the worst case. An insertion also requires writing one or two nodes (one if the key is inserted in the leaf, two if a new leaf must be created). A deletion always accesses every node and can modify as few as one node, but can potentially modify every node (unless a key can be simply marked as deleted).

In the best case for search time, the tree is almost balanced, each node except one contains $m - 1$ keys, and each nonleaf except one has m sons. There are still $((n - 1)/(m - 1)) + 1$ nodes, but there are fewer than $\log_m (n - 1) + 1$ levels. Thus the number of nodes accessed in a search, insertion, or deletion is less than this number. (In such a tree, more than half the keys are in a semileaf or leaf, so that the average search time is not much better than the maximum.) Fortunately, as is the case for binary trees, fairly balanced trees occur far more frequently than unbalanced trees, so that the average search time using multiway search trees is O($\log n$).

However, a general multiway tree and even a top-down multiway tree use an inordinate amount of storage. To see why this is so, see Figure 7.3.11, which illustrates a typical top-down multiway search tree of order 11 with one hundred keys. The tree is fairly balanced, and average search cost is approximately 2.19 [ten keys at level 0 require

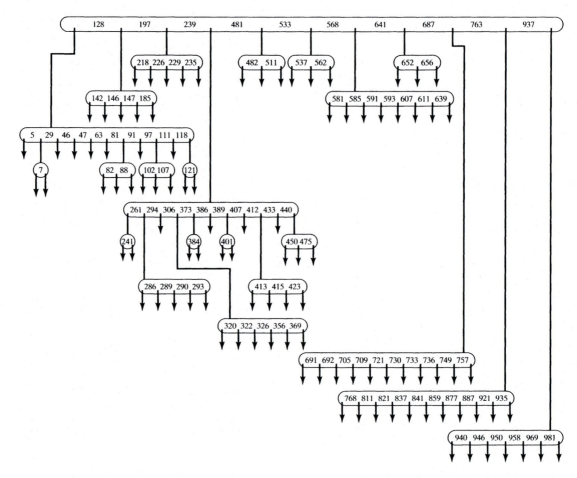

FIGURE 7.3.11

accessing one node, sixty-one at level 1 require accessing two nodes, and twenty-nine at level 2 require accessing three nodes: $(10*1 + 61*2 + 29*3)/100 = 2.19]$, which is reasonable. However, to accommodate the hundred keys, the tree uses twenty-three nodes, or 4.35 keys per node, representing a space utilization of only 43.5 percent. The reason for this is that many leafs contain only one or two keys, and the vast majority of the nodes are leafs. As the order and the number of keys increase, the utilization becomes worse, so that an order-11 tree with thousands of keys can expect 27 percent utilization, and an order-21 tree can expect only 17 percent utilization. As the order grows even larger, the utilization drops toward zero. Since high orders are required to produce reasonable search costs for large numbers of keys, top-down multiway trees are an unreasonable alternative for data storage.

Every B-tree is balanced, and each node contains at least $(m - 1)/2$ keys. Figure 7.3.12 illustrates the minimum and maximum number of nodes and keys at levels 0, 1, 2, and an arbitrary level i, as well as the minimum and maximum number

Level	Minimum		Maximum	
	Nodes	Keys	Nodes	Keys
0	1	1	1	$m - 1$
1	2	$2q$	m	$(m - 1)m$
2	$2(q + 1)$	$2q(q + 1)$	m^2	$(m - 1)m^2$
I	$2(q + 1)^{i - 1}$	$2q(q + 1)^{i - 1}$	m^i	$(m - 1)m^i$
Total	$1 + \dfrac{2(q + 1)^d - 1)}{q}$	$2(q + 1)^d$	$\dfrac{m^{d + 1} - 1}{m - 1}$	$m^{d + 1} - 1$

FIGURE 7.3.12

of total nodes and keys in a B-tree of order m and maximum level d. In the figure, q equals $(m - 1)/2$. Note that the maximum level is one less than the number of levels (since the root is at level 0), so that $d + 1$ equals the maximum number of node accesses needed to find an element. From the minimum total number of keys in Figure 7.3.12, we can deduce that the maximum number of node accesses for one of n keys in an order-m B-tree is $1 + \log_{q+1}(n/2)$. Thus, unlike top-down multiway trees, the maximum number of node accesses grows only logarithmically as the number of keys. Nevertheless, as we pointed out earlier, average search time is competitive between top-down multiway trees and B-trees because top-down trees are usually fairly balanced.

Insertion into a B-tree requires reading one node per level and writing one node at minimum plus two nodes for every split that occurs. If s splits occur, $2s + 1$ nodes are written (two halves of each split plus the father of the last node split). Deletion requires reading one node per level to find a leaf, writing one node if the deleted key is in a leaf and the deletion does not cause an underflow, and writing two nodes if the deleted key is in a nonleaf and removing the replacement key from a leaf does not cause that leaf to underflow. If an underflow does occur, one additional read (of the brother of each underflowed node) per underflow, one additional write for every consolidation except the last, and three additional writes for the final underflow if no consolidation is necessary (the underflow node, its brother, and its father) or two additional writes if a consolidation is necessary (the consolidated node and its father) are required. All of these operations are O(log N). As is the case with a heap (Section 6.3) and a balanced binary tree (Section 7.2), insertion and deletion of the minimum or maximum element are both 0(log N) in a B-tree, so the structure can be used to implement an (ascending or descending) priority queue efficiently. In fact a 3-2 tree (a B-tree of order 3) is probably the most efficient practical method for implementing a priority queue in internal memory.

Since each node in a B-tree (except the root) must be at least approximately half-full, the worst-case storage utilization approaches 50 percent. In practice, average storage utilization in a B-tree approaches 69 percent. For example, Figure 7.3.13 illustrates a B-tree of order 11 with the same hundred keys as the multiway tree in Figure 7.3.11. Average search time is 2.88 (one key requiring one node access, ten keys requiring two accesses, and eighty nine keys requiring two accesses), which is greater than the corresponding multiway tree. Indeed, a fairly balanced top-down multiway tree will have lower search cost than a B-tree, since all of its upper nodes are always completely full. However, the B-tree contains only fifteen nodes, yielding a storage utilization of 66.7 percent, far higher than the 43.5 percent utilization of the multiway tree.

Improving the B-Tree

There are a number of ways to improve the storage utilization of a B-tree. One method is to delay splitting a node when it overflows. Instead, the keys in the node and one of its adjacent brothers, as well as the key in the father that separates the two nodes, are redistributed evenly. This is illustrated in Figure 7.3.14 on a B-tree of order 7. When both a node and its brother are full, the two nodes are split into three. This guarantees a minimum storage utilization of almost 67 percent, and the storage utilization is higher in actual practice. Such a tree is called a B*-tree. This technique can be extended even further by redistributing keys among all the brothers and the father of a full node. Unfortunately, this method exacts its own price, since it requires expensive additional accesses upon overflow insertions, while the marginal additional space utilization achieved by considering each extra brother becomes smaller and smaller.

Another technique is to use a ***compact B-tree***. Such a B-tree has maximum storage utilization for a given order and number of keys. It can be shown that the maximum storage utilization for a B-tree of a given order and a given number of keys is attained when nodes toward the bottom of the tree contain as many keys as possible. Figure 7.3.15 illustrates a compact B-tree for the hundred keys in Figures 7.3.11 and 7.3.13. It can be shown that the average search cost for a compact B-tree is never more than one more than the minimum average search cost among all B-trees with the given order and number of keys. Thus, although a compact B-tree achieves a maximum storage utilization, it also achieves reasonable search cost. For example, the search cost for the tree in Figure 7.3.14 is only 1.91 (nine keys at level 0 requring one access, and ninety-one keys at level 1 requiring two accesses: $9*1 + 91*2 = 191/100 = 1.91$), which is very close to optimal. Yet the tree uses only eleven nodes, for a storage utilization of 90.9 percent. With more keys, storage utilization in compact B-trees reaches 98 percent or even 99 percent.

Unfortunately, there is no known efficient algorithm to insert a key into a compact B-tree and maintain compactness. Instead, insertion proceeds as in an ordinary B-tree, and compactness is not retained. Periodically (e.g., at night, when the file is not used), a compact B-tree can be constructed from a noncompact tree. However, a compact B-tree degrades so rapidly with insertions that, for high orders, storage utilization drops below that of a random B-tree after fewer than 2 percent additional keys have been inserted. Also, the number of splits required for an insertion is higher on the average than for a random B-tree. Thus a compact B-tree should only be used when the set of keys is highly stable.

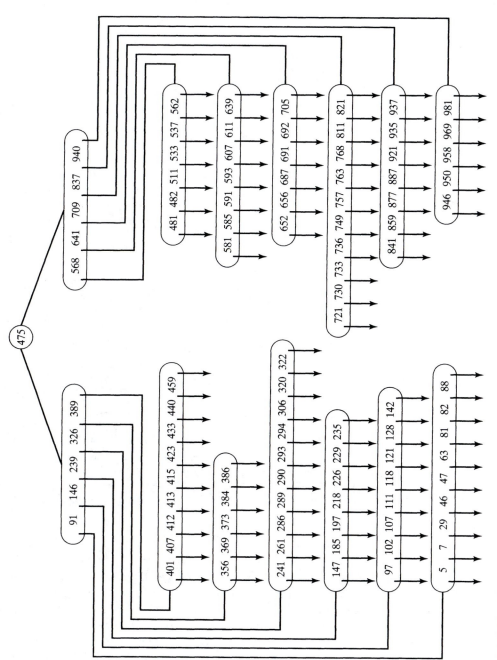

FIGURE 7.3.13

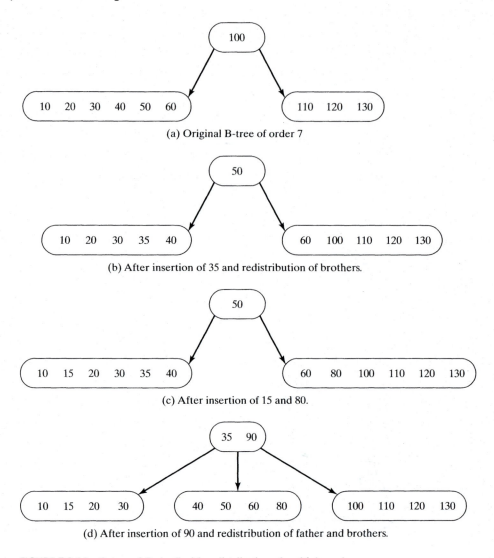

(a) Original B-tree of order 7

(b) After insertion of 35 and redistribution of brothers.

(c) After insertion of 15 and 80.

(d) After insertion of 90 and redistribution of father and brothers.

FIGURE 7.3.14 B-tree of Order 7 with redistribution of multiple nodes.

The use of various compression techniques on the keys is a popular approach for reducing space and time requirements in a B-tree. Since all the keys in a given node are fairly similar to each other, their initial bits are likely to be the same. Thus the initial bits can be stored once for the entire node (or can be determined as part of the search process from the root of the tree by noticing that if two adjacent keys in a node have the same prefix, then all the keys in the subtree between the two keys also have the same prefix). In addition, all the bits preceding the first bit that distinguishes a key from its preceding neighbor need not be retained (although an indication of its position must be). This is called *front compression*. A second technique, called *rear*

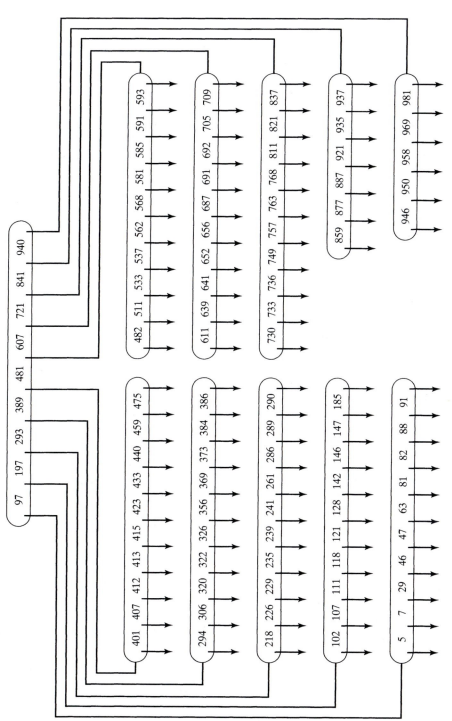

FIGURE 7.3.15

compression, maintains only enough of the rear of the key to distinguish a key from its successor.

For example, if three keys are *anchor, andrew*, and *antoin, andrew* can be encoded as *2d*, indicating that the first two characters are the same as its predecessor, and that the next character, *d*, distinguishes it from its predecessor and successor. If the successors of *andrew* in the node were *andule, antoin, append*, and *apples*, then *andrew* would be encoded as *2d, andule* as *3u, antoin* as simply 2, and *append* as *1ppe*.

If rear compression is used, it is necessary to access the record itself to determine whether a key is present in a file because the entire key cannot be reconstructed from the encoding. Also, under both methods, the key code that is retained is of variable length, and thus the maximum number of keys in a node is no longer fixed. Another disadvantage of variable-length key encoding is that binary search can no longer be used to locate a key in a node. In addition, the key code for some existing keys may have to be changed when a new key is inserted. The advantage of compression is that it enables more keys to be retained in a node so that the depth of the tree and the number of nodes required can be reduced.

B⁺-Trees

One of the major drawbacks of the B-tree is the difficulty of traversing the keys sequentially. A variation of the basic B-tree structure, the B⁺-tree, retains the rapid random access property of the B-tree but also allows rapid sequential access. In the B⁺-tree, all the keys are maintained in leafs, and keys are replicated in nonleaf nodes to define paths for locating individual records. The leafs are linked together to provide a sequential path for traversing the keys in the tree.

Figure 7.3.16 illustrates a B⁺-tree. To locate the record associated with key 53 (random access), the key is first compared with 98 (the first key in the root). Since it is less, proceed to node *B*. 53 is then compared with 36 and then 53 in node *B*. Since it is less than or equal to 53, proceed to node *E*.

Unlike the case in a B-tree, the search does not halt when the key is found. In a B-tree, a pointer to the record corresponding to a key is contained with each key in

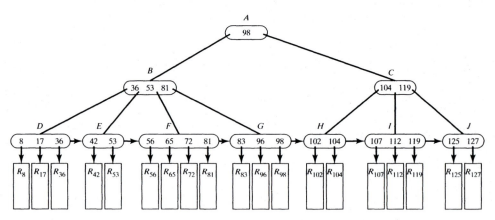

FIGURE 7.3.16

the tree, whether in a leaf or a nonleaf node. Thus, the record can be accessed once the key is found. In a B^+-tree, pointers to records are only associated with keys in leaf nodes, so the search is not complete until the key is located in a leaf. Therefore, when equality is obtained in a nonleaf, the search continues. In node E (a leaf), key 53 is located, and from it, the record associated with that key. If we now wish to traverse the keys in the tree sequentially beginning with key 53, we need only follow the pointers in the leaf nodes.

The linked list of leaf nodes is called a ***sequence set***. In actual implementations, the nodes of the sequence set frequently do not contain all the keys in the file. Rather, each sequence set node serves as an index to a large data area where a large number of records are kept. A search involves traversing a path in the B^+-tree, reading a block from the data area associated with the leaf node that is finally accessed, and then searching the block sequentially for the required record.

The B^+-tree may be considered to be a natural extension of the indexed sequential file in Section 7.1. Each level of the tree is an index to the succeeding level, and the lowest level, the sequence set, is an index to the file itself.

Insertion into a B^+-tree proceeds much like in a B-tree except that when a node is split, the middle key is retained in the left half-node as well as being promoted to the father. When a key is deleted from a leaf, it can be retained in the nonleafs because it is still a valid separator between the keys in the nodes below.

The B^+-tree retains the search and insertion efficiencies of the B-tree but increases the efficiency of finding the next record in the tree from $O(\log n)$ (in a B-tree where finding the successor involves climbing up or down the tree) to $O(1)$ (in a B^+-tree where it involves accessing one additional leaf at most). An additional advantage of the B^+-tree is that no record pointers need be kept in the nonleaf nodes, which increases the potential order of the tree.

Digital Search Trees

Another method of using trees to expedite searching is to form a general tree based on the symbols of which the keys are composed. For example, if the keys are integers, each digit position determines one of ten possible sons of a given node. A forest representing one such set of keys is illustrated in Figure 7.3.17. If the keys consist of alphabetic characters, each letter of the alphabet determines a branch in the tree. Note that every leaf node contains the special symbol *eok*, which represents the end of a key. Such a leaf node must also contain a pointer to the record that is being stored.

If a forest is represented by a binary tree, as in Section 5.5, each node of the binary tree contains three fields: *symbol*, which contains a symbol of the key; *son*, which is a pointer to the node's oldest son in the original tree; and *brother*, which is a pointer to the node's next-younger brother in the original tree. The first tree in the forest is pointed to by an external pointer *tree*, and the roots of the other trees in the forest are linked together in a linear list by the *brother* field. The *son* field of a leaf in the original forest points to a record; the concatenation of all the symbols in the original forest in the path of nodes from root to the leaf is the key of the record. We make two further stipulations that speed up the search and insertion process for such a tree. Each list of brothers is arranged in the binary tree in ascending order of the *symbol* field. The symbol *eok* is considered to be larger than any other.

Keys
180
185
1867
195
207
217
2174
21749
217493
226
27
274
278
279
2796
281
284
285
286
287
288
294
307
768

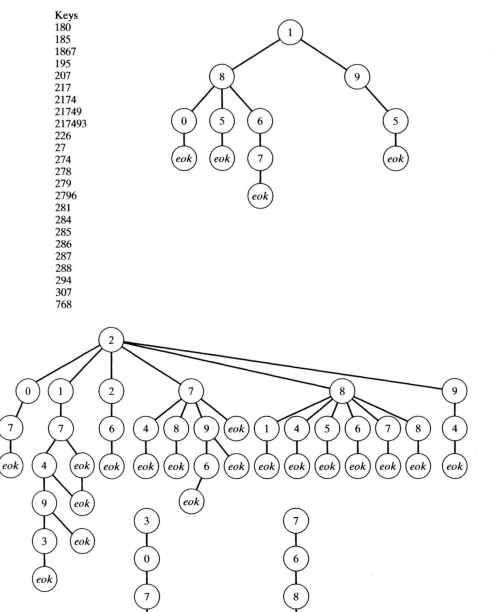

FIGURE 7.3.17   Forest representing a table of keys.

Using this binary tree representation, we may present an algorithm to search and insert into a nonempty ***digital tree***. As usual, *key* is the key for which we are searching, and *rec* is the record that we wish to insert if *key* is not found. We also let *key(i)* be the *i*th symbol of the key. If the key has *n* symbols, we assume that *key(n)* equals *eok*. The algorithm uses the *getNode* operation to allocate a new tree node when necessary. We assume that *recPtr* is a reference to the record *rec* to be inserted. The algorithm returns a reference to the record that is being sought and uses an auxiliary method *insert*, whose algorithm is also given.

```
p = tree;
father = null;   // father is the father of p
for (i = 0;  ; i++) {
    q = null;          // q points to the older brother of p
    while (p != null && symbol(p) < key(i)) {
        q = p;
        p = brother(p);
    }
    if (p == null || symbol(p) > key(i)) {
        insVal = insert(i, p, q);
        return insVal;
    }
    if (key(i) == eok)
        return son(p);
    else {
        father = p;
        p = son(p);
    }
}
```

The algorithm for *insert(i, p, q)* is as follows:

```
// insert the ith symbol of the key
s = getNode();
symbol(s) = key(i);
brother(s) = p;
if (tree == null)
    tree = s;
else if (q != null)
    brother(q) = s;
else
    (father == null) ? tree = s : son(father) = s;
// insert the remaining symbols of the key
for (j = i; key(j) != eok; j++) {
    father = s;
    s = getNode();
    symbol(s) = key(j + 1);
    son(father) = s;
    brother(s) = null;
}
son(s) = addr(rec);
return son(s);
```

By keeping the table of keys as a general tree, we need search only a small list of sons to find whether a given symbol appears at a given position within the keys of the table. However, it is possible to make the tree even smaller by eliminating those nodes from which only a single leaf can be reached. For example, in the keys in Figure 7.3.17, once the symbol '7' is recognized, the only key that can possibly match is 768. Similarly, upon recognizing the two symbols '1' and '9', the only matching key is 195. Thus the forest in Figure 7.3.17 can be abbreviated to the one in Figure 7.3.18. In that figure, a box indicates a key and a circle indicates a tree node. A dashed line is used to indicate a pointer from a tree node to a key.

There are some significant differences between the trees in Figures 7.3.17 and 7.3.18. In Figure 7.3.17, a path from a root to a leaf represents an entire key; thus there is no need to repeat the key. In Figure 7.3.18, however, a key may be recognized only by its first few symbols. In those cases where the search is made for a key that is known to be in the table, the record corresponding to the key can be accessed when the leaf is found. If, however, as is more likely, it is not known whether the key is present in the table, it must be confirmed that the key is indeed correct. Thus the entire key must be kept in the record as well. Furthermore, a leaf node in the tree in Figure 7.3.17 can be recognized because its contents are *eok*. Thus its *son* pointer can be used to point to the record which the leaf represents. However, a leaf node in Figure 7.3.18 may contain any symbol. Thus, to use the *son* pointer of a leaf to point to the record, an extra field is required in each node to indicate whether or not the node is a leaf. We leave the representation of the forest in Figure 7.3.18 and the implementation of a search-and-insert algorithm for it as an exercise for the reader.

The binary tree representation of a digital search tree is efficient when each node has relatively few sons. For example, in Figure 7.3.18 only one node has as many as six sons (out of a possible ten), whereas most nodes have only one, two, or three sons. Thus the process of searching through the list of sons to match the next symbol in the key is relatively efficient. However, if the set of keys is dense within the set of all possible keys (i.e., if almost any possible combination of symbols actually appears as a key), most nodes will have a large number of sons, and the cost of the search process becomes prohibitive.

Tries

A digital search tree need not be implemented as a binary tree. Instead, each node in the tree can contain m pointers, corresponding to the m possible symbols in each position of the key. Thus, if the keys were numeric, there would be ten pointers in a node, and if strictly alphabetic, there would be twenty-six. (There might also be an extra pointer corresponding to *eok*, or a flag with each pointer indicating that it pointed to a record rather than to a tree node.) A pointer in a node is associated with a particular symbol value based on its position in the node; that is, the first pointer corresponds to the lowest symbol value, the second pointer to the second-lowest, and so on. It is therefore unnecessary to keep the symbol values in the tree. The number of nodes that must be accessed to find a particular key is log mn. A digital search tree implemented in this way is called a **trie** (from the word re*trie*val).

A trie is useful when the set of keys is so dense that most of the pointers in each node are used. When the key set is sparse, a trie wastes a large amount of space with

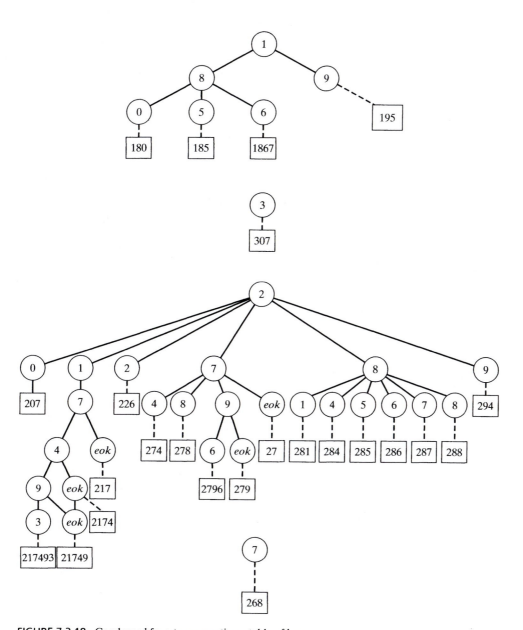

FIGURE 7.3.18 Condensed forest representing a table of keys.

large nodes that are mostly empty. If the set of keys in a trie is known in advance and does not change, there are a number of techniques for minimizing the space requirements. One technique is to establish a different order in which the symbols of a key are used for searching (so that, for example, the third symbol of the argument key might be used to access the appropriate pointer in the trie root, the first symbol in level 1 nodes, and so forth). Another technique is to allow trie nodes to overlap each other so that occupied pointers of one node overlay empty pointers of another.

EXERCISES

7.3.1 Show how a B-tree and a B^+-tree can be used to implement a priority queue (see Sections 4.1 and 6.3). Show that any sequence of n insertion and minimum-deletion operations can be performed in $O(n \log n)$ steps. Write Java methods to insert and delete from a priority queue implemented by a 2–3 tree.

7.3.2 Choose any large paragraph from a book. Insert each word of the paragraph, in order, into an initially empty top-down multiway search tree of order 5, omitting any duplicates. Do the same for a B-tree of order 5, a B^+-tree of order 5, and a digital search tree.

7.3.3 Write Java methods to implement the B-tree successor insertion operations if the B-tree is maintained

   a. In internal memory.

   b. In external direct access storage.

7.3.4 Write an algorithm and a Java method to delete a record from a top-down multiway search tree of order n.

7.3.5 Write an algorithm and a Java method to delete a record from a B-tree of order n.

7.3.6 Write an algorithm to create a compact B-tree from input in sorted order. Use the algorithm to write a Java method to produce a compact B-tree from an ordinary B-tree.

7.3.7 Write an algorithm and a Java method to search in a B-tree.

7.3.8 Write an algorithm and a Java method to

   a. Insert into a B^+-tree.

   b. Insert into a B^*-tree.

   c. Delete from a B^+-tree.

   d. Delete from a B^*-tree.

7.3.9 How many different 2–3 trees containing the integers 1 through 10 can you construct? How many permutations of these integers result in each tree if they are inserted into an initially empty tree in permutation order?

7.3.10 Develop algorithms to search and insert into a B-tree that uses front and rear compression.

7.3.11 Write a search-and-insert algorithm and a Java method for the digital search forest in Figure 7.3.18.

7.3.12 Show how to implement a trie in external storage. Write a Java search-and-insert method for a trie.

7.4   HASHING

In the preceding two sections we assumed that the record being sought is stored in a table, and that it is necessary to pass through some number of keys before finding the desired one. The organization of the file (sequential, indexed sequential, binary tree, and so forth) and the order in which the keys are inserted affect the number of keys that must be inspected before the desired one is obtained. Obviously, a search technique is efficient if it minimizes the number of comparisons. Optimally, we would like to have a table organization and search technique in which there are no unnecessary comparisons. Let us see if this is feasible.

If each key is to be retrieved in a single access, the location of the record in the table can depend only upon the key; it may not depend upon the locations of other keys, as in a tree. The most efficient way to organize such a table is as an array (i.e., each record is stored at a specific offset from the base address of the table). If the record keys are integers, the keys themselves can serve as indices to the array.

Let us consider an example of such a system. Suppose that a manufacturing company has an inventory file consisting of hundred parts, each part having a unique two-digit part number. The obvious way to store this file is to declare an array

```
PartType part[ ] = new PartType [100];
```

where *part*[*i*] represents the record whose part number is *i*. In this situation, the part numbers are keys that are used as indices to the array. Even if the company stocks fewer than one hundred parts, the same structure can be used to maintain the inventory file. Although many locations in *part* may correspond to nonexistent keys, this waste is offset by the advantage of direct access to each of the existent parts.

Unfortunately, however, such a system is not always practical. For example, suppose that the company has an inventory file of more than one hundred items and the key to each record is a seven-digit part number. To use direct indexing using the entire seven-digit key, an array of 10 million elements would be required. This clearly wastes an unacceptably large amount of space because it is extremely unlikely that a company will stock more than a few thousand parts.

What is necessary is some method of converting a key into an integer within a limited range. Ideally, no two keys should be converted into the same integer. Unfortunately, such an ideal method usually does not exist. Let us attempt to develop methods that come close to the ideal, and determine what action to take when the ideal is not achieved.

Let us reconsider the example of a company with an inventory file in which each record is keyed by a seven-digit part number. Suppose that the company has fewer than thousand parts and there is only a single record for each part. Then an array of one thousand elements is sufficient to contain the entire file. The array is indexed by an integer between 0 and 999 inclusive. The last three digits of the part number are used as the index for the part's record in the array. This is illustrated in Figure 7.4.1. Note that two keys that are relatively close to each other numerically, such as 4618396 and 4618996, may be farther from each other in the table than two keys that are widely separated numerically, such as 0000991 and 9846995. Only the last three digits of the key are used in determining the position of a record.

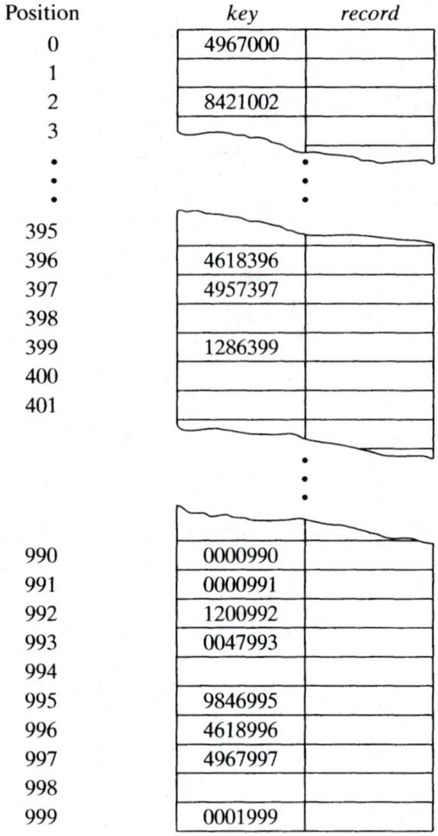

Position	key	record
0	4967000	
1		
2	8421002	
3		
.		
.		
.		
395		
396	4618396	
397	4957397	
398		
399	1286399	
400		
401		
.		
.		
.		
990	0000990	
991	0000991	
992	1200992	
993	0047993	
994		
995	9846995	
996	4618996	
997	4967997	
998		
999	0001999	

FIGURE 7.4.1

A function that transforms a key into a table index is called a ***hash function***. If h is a hash function and *key* is a key, then $h(key)$ is called the ***hash*** of *key* and is the index at which a record with key *key* should be placed. If r is a record whose key hashes into hr, then hr is called the ***hash key*** of r. The hash function in the example above is $h(k) = key\%1000$. The values that h produces should cover the entire set of indices in the table. For example, the function $x \% 1000$ can produce any integer between 0 and 999, depending upon the value of x. As we shall see shortly, it is a good idea for the table size to be somewhat larger than the number of records that are to be inserted. This is illustrated in Figure 7.4.1, where several positions in the table are unused.

The foregoing method has one flaw. Suppose that two keys, $k1$ and $k2$, are such that $h(k1)$ equals $h(k2)$. Then, when a record with key $k1$ is entered into the table, it is inserted at position $h(k1)$. But when $k2$ is hashed, because its hash key is the same as that of $k1$, an attempt may be made to insert the record into the same position where the record with key $k1$ is stored. Clearly, two records cannot occupy the same position. Such a situation is called a ***hash collision*** or a ***hash clash***. A hash clash occurs in the inventory example in Figure 7.4.1 if a record with key 0596397 is added to the table.

There are two basic methods of dealing with a hash clash. We explore both in detail in the remainder of this section. Briefly, the first technique, called ***rehashing***, involves using a secondary hash function on the hash key of the item. The rehash function is applied successively until an empty position is found where the item can be inserted. If the hash position of the item is found to be occupied during a search, the rehash function is again used to locate the item. The second technique, called **chaining**, builds a linked list of all items whose keys hash to the same values. During search, this short linked list is traversed sequentially for the desired key. This technique involves adding an extra link field to each table position.

However, it should be noted that a good hash function is one that minimizes collisions and spreads the records uniformly throughout the table. That is why it is desirable to have the array size larger than the number of actual records. The larger the range of the hash function, the less likely it is that two keys yield the same hash value. Of course, this involves a space/time trade-off. Leaving empty spaces in the array is inefficient in terms of space; but it reduces the necessity of resolving hash clashes and is therefore more efficient in terms of time.

Although hashing allows direct access to a table and is therefore preferable to other search techniques, the method has one serious flaw. Items in a hash table are not stored sequentially by key, nor is there any generally practical method for traversing the items in key sequence. **Order-preserving hash functions**, in which $h(key1) > h(key2)$ whenever $key1 > key2$, are usually nonuniform; that is, they do not minimize hash collisions and so do not serve the basic purpose of hashing: rapid access to any record directly from its key.

Resolving Hash Clashes by Open Addressing

Let us consider what would happen if it were desired to enter a new part number 0596397 into the table of Figure 7.4.1. Using the hash function $key \% 1000$, $h(0596397) = 397$ and so the record for that part belongs in position 397 of the array. However, position 397 is already occupied by the record with key 4957397. Therefore, the record with key 0596397 must be inserted elsewhere in the table.

The simplest method of resolving hash clashes is to place the record in the next available position in the array. In Figure 7.4.1, for example, since position 397 is already occupied, the record with key 0596397 is placed in location 398, which is still open. Once that record has been inserted, another record which hashes to either 397 (e.g., 8764397) or 398 (e.g., 2194398), is inserted at the next available position, which is 400.

This technique, called **linear probing**, is an example of a general method for resolving hash clashes called **rehashing** or **open addressing**. In general, a rehash function, rh, accepts one array index and produces another. If array location $h(key)$ is already occupied by a record with a different key, rh is applied to the value of $h(key)$ to find another location where the record may be placed. If position $rh(h(key))$ is also occupied, it, too, is rehashed to see if $rh(rh(h(key)))$ is available. This process continues until an empty location is found. Thus we may write a search-and-insertion method using hashing as follows. We assume the following declarations:

```
class KeyType {   ...
class RecType { ...
class Record {
    KeyType k;
    RecType r;
}
```

```
final static int TABLESIZE = … ;
static Record table[ ] = new Record[TABLESIZE];
```

We also assume a hash function $h(key)$ and a rehash function $rh(i)$. The special value *null* is used to indicate an empty record.

```
public int search(KeyType key, RecType rec) {
  int i;
  i = h(key);    // hash the key
  while (table[i] != null && table[i].k != null && table[i].k != key)
        i = rh(i);    // rehash

  if (table[i] == null) {
        table[i] = new Record();
        // insert the record into the empty position
        table[i].k = key;
        table[i].r = rec;
  }
  return i;
} // end search
```

In the example in Figure 7.4.1, $h(key)$ is the function $key \% 1000$, and $rh(i)$ is the function $(i + 1) \% 1000$ (i.e., the rehash of any index is the next sequential position in the array, except that the rehash of 999 is 0).

Let us examine the algorithm more closely to see if we can determine the properties of a "good" rehash function. In particular, we focus our attention on the loop, because the number of iterations determines the efficiency of the search. The loop can be exited in one of two ways: either i is set to a value such that $table[i].k$ equals key (in which case the record is found), or i is set to a value such that $table[i].k$ equals *null* (in which case an empty position is found and the record may be inserted).

It may happen, however, that the loop executes forever. There are two possible reasons for this. First, the table may be full, so that it is impossible to insert any new records. This situation can be detected by keeping a count of the number of records in the table. When the count equals the table size, no additional insertions are attempted.

However, it is possible for the algorithm to loop indefinitely even if there are some (or even many) empty positions. Suppose, for example, that the function $rh(i) + (i + 2) \% 1000$ is used as a rehash function. Then any key that hashes into an odd integer rehashes into successive odd integers, and any key that hashes into an even integer rehashes into successive even integers. Consider the situation in which all the odd positions of the table are occupied and all the even ones are empty. Despite the fact that half the positions of the array are empty, it is impossible to insert a new record whose key hashes into an odd integer. Of course, it is unlikely that all the odd positions will be occupied and none of the even positions. However, if the rehash function $rh(i) = (i + 200) \% 1000$ is used, each key can be placed in only one of five positions [since $x \% 1000 = (x + 1000) \% 1000$], and it is quite possible for these five places to be full while much of the table is empty.

One property of a good rehash function is that for any index i, the successive rehashes $rh(i), rh(rh(i)), \ldots$ cover as many of the integers between 0 and

$TABLESIZE - 1$ as possible (ideally, all of them). The rehash function $rh(i) = (i + 1) \% 1000$ has this property. In fact, any function $rh(i) = (i + c) \% TABLESIZE$ where c is a constant value such that c and $TABLESIZE$ are relatively prime (i.e., they cannot both be divided evenly by a single integer other than 1), produces successive values that cover the entire table. You are invited to confirm this fact by choosing some examples; the proof is left as an exercise. In general, however, there is no reason to choose a value of c other than 1. If the hash table is stored in external storage, it is desirable to have successive references as close to each other as possible (this minimizes seek delay on disks and may eliminate an *I/O* if the two references are on the same page).

There is another measure of the suitability of a rehash function. Consider the case of a linear rehash. Assuming that the hash function produces indices that are uniformly distributed over the interval 0 through $TABLESIZE - 1$ [i.e., it is equally likely that $h(key)$ is any particular integer in that range], then initially, when the entire array is empty, it is equally likely that a random record will be placed at any given (empty) position within the array. However, once entries have been inserted and several hash clashes have been resolved, this is no longer true. For example, in Figure 7.4.1 it is five times as likely for a record to be inserted at position 994 than at position 401. This is because any record whose key hashes into 990, 991, 992, 993, or 994 will be placed in 994, while only a record whose key hashes into 401 will be placed in that location. This phenomenon, where two keys that hash into different values compete with each other in successive rehashes, is called ***primary clustering***.

The same phenomenon occurs in   the case of the rehash function $rh(i) = (i + c) \% TABLESIZE$. For example, if $TABLESIZE = 1000$, $c = 21$, and positions 10, 31, 52, 73, and 94 are all occupied, any record whose key is any one of these five integers will be placed at location 115. In fact, any rehash function that depends solely upon the index to be rehashed causes primary clustering.

One way of eliminating primary clustering is to allow the rehash function to depend on the number of times the function is applied to a particular hash value. In this approach, the function rh is a function of two arguments. $rh(i, j)$ yields the rehash of the integer i if the key is being rehashed for the jth time. One example is $rh(i, j) = (i + j) \% TABLESIZE$. The first rehash yields $rh1 = rh(h(key), 1) = (h(key) + 1) \% TABLESIZE$, the second yields $rh2 = (rh1 + 2) \% TABLESIZE$, the third yields $rh3 = (rh2 + 3) \% TABLESIZE$, and so on.

Another approach is to use a random permutation of the numbers between 1 and t (where t equals $TABLESIZE - 1$, the largest index of the table), $p1, p2, \ldots, pt$, and to let the jth rehash of $h(key)$ be $(h(key) + pj) \% TABLESIZE$. This has the advantage of ensuring that no two rehashes of the same key conflict. Still a third approach is to let the jth rehash of $h(key)$ be $(h(key) + (j * j)) \% TABLESIZE$. This is called the ***quadratic rehash***. Yet another method of eliminating primary clustering is to allow the rehash to depend on the hash value, as in $rh(i, key) = (i + hkey) \% TABLESIZE$, where $hkey = 1 + h(key) \% t$. (We cannot use $hkey$ equal to $h(key)$, which might be 0, or to $h(key) + 1$, which might be $TABLESIZE$. Either of these cases would result in $rh(i, key)$ equaling i, which is unacceptable.) All of these methods allow keys that hash into different locations to follow separate rehash paths.

However, while these methods eliminate primary clustering, they do not eliminate another phenomenon, known as ***secondary clustering***, in which different keys that hash to the same value follow the same rehash path. One way to eliminate all clustering is *double hashing*, which involves the use of two hash functions, $h1(key)$ and $h2(key)$. $h1$, which is known as the *primary hash function*, is first used to determine the position at which the record should be placed. If that position is occupied, the rehash function $rh(i, key) = (i + h2(key)) \% TABLESIZE$ is used successively until an empty location is found. As long as $h2(key1)$ does not equal $h2(key2)$, records with keys $key1$ and $key2$ do not compete for the same set of locations. This is true despite the possibility that $h1(key1)$ may indeed equal $h1(key2)$. The rehash function depends not only on the index to be rehashed but also on the original key. Note that the value $h2(key)$ does not have to be recomputed for each rehash: it need be computed only once for each key that must be rehashed. Optimally, one should choose functions $h1$ and $h2$ that distribute the hashes and rehashes uniformly over the interval 0 to $TABLESIZE - 1$ and also minimize clustering. Such functions are not always easy to find.

Double hashing functions are exemplified by $h1(key) = key \% TABLESIZE$ and $h2(key) = 1 + key \% t$, where $TABLESIZE$ is a prime number and t equals $TABLESIZE - 1$. Another example is $h1(key)$ as above, and $h2(key) = 1 + (key/TABLESIZE) \% t$.

Deleting Items from a Hash Table

Unfortunately, it is difficult to delete items from a hash table that uses rehashing for search and insertion. For example, suppose that record $r1$ is at position p. To add a record $r2$ whose key $k2$ hashes into p, it must be inserted into the first free position from among $rh(p), rh(rh(p)), \ldots$. Suppose that $r1$ is then deleted, so that position p becomes empty. A subsequent search for record $r2$ begins at position $h(k2)$, which is p. But since that position is now empty, the search process may erroneously conclude that record $r2$ is absent from the table.

One possible solution to this problem is to mark a deleted record as "deleted" rather than "empty" and to continue searching whenever a "deleted" position is encountered in the course of a search. But this is possible only if there are a small number of deletions; otherwise, an unsuccessful search would require a search through the entire table because most positions will be marked "deleted" rather than "empty." Ideally, we would prefer a deletion mechanism in which retrieval time is the same whenever n records are in the table, regardless of whether the n records are a result of n insertions or w insertions and $w - n$ subsequent deletions. Later in this section, we examine alternatives to rehashing which allow us to accomplish this.

Efficiency of Rehashing Methods

The efficiency of a hashing method is usually measured by the average number of table positions that must by examined in searching for a particular item. This is called the number of *probes* required by the method. Note that in the algorithms we have presented, the number of key comparisons equals twice the number of probes, since the key at each probe position is compared to both the search argument and the *null* key. However, the comparison to the *null* key may be less expensive than the general key comparison. An extra key comparison can also be avoided by using an additional field in each table position to indicate whether it is empty.

Under rehashing, the average number of probes depends on both the hash function and the rehash method. The hash function is assumed to be uniform. That is, it is assumed that an arbitrary key is as likely as any other key to hash into any table index. Mathematical analysis of the average number of probes required to find an element in a hash table if the table was constructed using a specific hash and rehash method can be quite involved. Let n be the number of items currently in the hash table, and let *TABLESIZE* be the number of positions in the table. Then for large *TABLESIZE*, it has been proved that the average number of probes required for a successful retrieval in a table organized using linear rehashing is approximately

$$\frac{2*TABLESIZE - n + 1}{2*TABLESIZE - 2*n + 2}$$

If we set $x = (n - 1)/TABLESIZE$, this equals $(2 - x)/(2 - 2x)$. Define the **load factor** of a hash table, *lf*, as $n/TABLESIZE$, the fraction of the table that is occupied. Since *lf* is approximately equal to x for large *TABLESIZE*, we may approximate the number of probes for a successful search under linear rehashing by $(2 - lf)/(2 - 2*lf)$ or $0.5/(1 - lf) + 0.5$. When *lf* approximates 1 (i.e., when the table is almost full), this formula is not useful. Instead, it can be shown that the average number of key comparisons for a successful search in an almost full table may be approximated by $sqrt(\pi*TABLESIZE/8) + 0.33$.

For an unsuccessful search, the average number of probes in a table organized using linear rehashing is approximately equal to $0.5/(1 - lf)^2 + 0.5$ for large *TABLESIZE*. When the table is full (i.e., when $n = TABLESIZE - 1$, since one position must be left open to detect that the key is not present), the average number of probes for an unsuccessful comparison under linear rehashing is $(TABLESIZE + 1)/2$, which is the same as the average number of comparisons required to find a single empty slot among *TABLESIZE* slots by sequential search.

This performance is not unreasonable for tables with low load factors, but it can be improved considerably for high load factors. Eliminating primary clustering by setting $rh(i, key)$ to $(i + hkey)$ % *TABLESIZE* as defined above or by using quadratic rehashing sets the average number of probes to approximately $1 - \log(1 - lf) - lf/2$ for successful retrievals and $1/(1 - lf) - lf - \log(1 - lf)$ for unsuccessful searches. (Here log is the natural logarithm as defined in the *java.lang.Math* class library.) For full tables, successful search time approximates $\log(TABLESIZE + 1)$, and unsuccessful search time remains at $(TABLESIZE + 1)/2$.

Double hashing improves efficiency even further by eliminating both primary and secondary clustering. Uniform hashing is defined as any hashing scheme in which any newly inserted element is equally likely to be placed at any of the empty positions of the hash table. For such a theoretical scheme, it can be proved that successful search time is approximately $-\log(1 - lf)/lf$ for large *TABLESIZE*, and that unsuccessful searching requires $(TABLESIZE + 1)/(TABLESIZE + 1 - n)$, or approximately $1/(1 - lf)$, probes for large *TABLESIZE*. Experience with good double hashing functions shows that the average number of comparisons equals these theoretical values. For full tables, successful search time is approximately $\log(TABLESIZE + 1) - 0.5$, and unsuccessful search time is again $(TABLESIZE + 1)/2$.

The following table lists the approximate number of probes for each of the three methods for various load factors. Recall that these approximations are generally only valid for large table sizes.

Load factor	Successful			Unsuccessful		
%	Linear	$i + hkey$	Double	Linear	$i + hkey$	Double
25	1.17	1.16	1.15	1.39	1.37	1.33
50	1.50	1.44	1.39	2.50	2.19	2.00
75	2.50	2.01	1.85	7.50	4.64	4.00
90	5.50	2.85	2.56	50.50	11.40	10.00
95	10.50	3.52	3.15	200.50	22.04	20.00

For full tables (in the successful case, where n equals $TABLESIZE$; in the unsuccessful case, where n equals $TABLESIZE - 1$), the following are some approximations of the average number of probes. We have also included the value of $\log_2 (TABLESIZE)$ for comparison with binary search and tree searching.

Tablesize	Successful			Unsuccessful	Log_2 (tablesize)
	Linear	$i + hkey$	Double		
100	6.60	4.62	4.12	50.50	6.64
500	14.35	6.22	5.72	250.50	7.97
1,000	20.15	6.91	6.41	500.50	7.97
5,000	44.64	7.52	7.02	2,500.50	12.29
10,000	63.00	7.21	7.71	5,000.50	13.29

These data indicate that linear hashing should be strongly avoided for tables that become more than 75 percent full, especially if unsuccessful searches are common, since primary clustering does have a significant effect on search time for large load factors. The effects of secondary clustering, however, never add more than 0.5 probes to the average number required. Given the fact that double hashing requires an expensive additional computation to determine $h2(key)$, it may be preferable to accept the extra half probe and use $rh(i, key) = (i + hkey) \% TABLESIZE$.

One technique that can be used to improve the performance of linear rehashing is **split sequence linear rehashing**. Under this technique, when $h(key)$ is found to be occupied, we compare key with the key kh located in position $h(key)$. If $kh < h(key)$, then the rehash function $i + c1$ is used; if $kh > h(key)$, then another rehash function $i + c2$ is used. This splits the rehashes from a particular slot into two separate sequences and reduces clustering without requiring additional space or reordering the hash table. For tables with a load factor of 95 percent, the split sequence technique reduces the number of probes in a successful search by more than 50 percent, and the number of probes in an unsuccessful search by more than 80 percent. However, nonlinear rehash methods are still better. A similar technique yields some, but not significant, improvement for the linear rehash methods.

Another point to note regarding efficiency is that, in the context of rehashing, the modulus operation should not be obtained by using the system % operator, which involves division, but rather by a comparison and possibly a subtraction. Thus $rh(i, key) = (i + hkey) \% TABLESIZE$ should be computed as follows:

```
x = i + hkey;
rh = x < TABLESIZE ? x : x - TABLESIZE;
```

The foregoing tables also indicate the great expense of an unsuccessful search in a nearly full table. Insertion requires the same number of comparisons as unsuccessful search. When the table is nearly full, the insertion efficiency of hashing approaches that of sequential search and is far worse than tree insertion.

Hash Table Reordering

Many items in a nearly full hash table are not at the locations given by their hash keys, and thus numerous key comparisons must be made before some of them are found. If an item is not in the table, then an entire list of rehash positions must be examined before that fact is determined. There are several techniques for remedying this situation.

In the first technique, discovered by Amble and Knuth, the set of items that hash into the same location are maintained in descending order of the key. (We assume that the *null* key is less than any key possibly occupying the table.) When searching for an item, it is not necessary to rehash repeatedly until an empty slot is found; as soon as an item in the table whose key is less than the search key is found, we know that the search key is not in the table. When inserting a key *key*, if a rehash accesses a key smaller than *key*, *key* and its associated record replace the smaller key and record in the table and the insertion process continues with the displaced key. A hash table organized in this way is called an *ordered hash table*. The following is a search-and-insertion method for an ordered hash table. (Recall that the *null* key is less than any other key.)

```
public int search (KeyType key, RecType rec) {
  int i, j = 0;
  boolean first = true;
  Record newEntry, tempEntry;
  KeyType tk = null;
  i = h(key);
  newEntry = new Record();
  newEntry.k = key;
  newEntry.r = rec;
  while (table[i].k != null && table[i].compareTo(newEntry) <= 0) {
          i = rh(i);
  }
  if (table[i].k == null) {
          table[i] = newEntry;
          return i;
  }
  tk = table[i].k;
  while (tk != null && tk != newEntry.k) {
          // insert the new entry and displace the entry at
          // position i
          tempEntry = table[i];
          table[i] = newEntry;
```

```
                    newEntry = tempEntry;
                    i = rh(i);
                    if (table[i].k != null)
                         tk = table[i].k;
         }
         table[i] = newEntry;
         return i;
    } // end search
```

The ordered hash table method can be used with any rehashing technique in which a rehash depends only on the index and the key; it cannot be used with a rehash function that depends on the number of times the item is rehashed (unless that number is kept in the table).

Using an ordered hash table does not change the average number of key comparisons required to find a key that is in the table, but it reduces significantly the number of key comparisons necessary to determine that a key does not exist in the table. It can be shown that unsuccessful search in an ordered hash table requires the same average number of probes as successful search (in an ordered or unordered table). This is a significant improvement. Unfortunately, however, the average number of probes for insertion is not reduced in an ordered hash table and equals the number required for an unsuccessful search in an unordered table. Ordered hash table insertions also require a significant number of hash table modifications.

Brent's Method

A different reordering scheme, originated by Brent, can improve the average search time for successful retrievals when double hashing is used. The technique involves rehashing the search argument until an empty slot is found. Then each of the keys in the rehash path is itself rehashed to determine whether placing one of them in an empty slot would require fewer rehashes. (Recall that, under double hashing, the rehash paths for two keys that rehash to the same slot will diverge.) If this is the case, then the search argument replaces the existing key in the table, and the existing key is inserted in its empty rehash slot.

The following is a method to implement Brent's search-and-insertion algorithm. It uses the auxiliary methods *setEmpty*, which initializes a queue of table indexes to empty, *insert*, which inserts an index onto a queue, *remove*, which returns an index removed from a queue, and *freeQueue*, which frees all the nodes of a queue.

```
    int search (KeyType key, RecType rec) {
      Queue qq = new Queue();              // of table indices
      int i = 0, j = 0, jj = 0, minOldPos, minNewPos;
      int count = 0, minCount, rehashCount, displaceCount;
      KeyType displaceKey;
      // rehash repeatedly, placing each successive index in the queue
      // and keeping a count of the number of rehashes required
      i = h(key);
      for (count = 0; table[i] != null && table[i].k != null &&
        table[i].k != key; count++) {
            qq.insert(new Integer(i));
            i = rh(i);
      }
```

```
// minOldPos and minNewPos hold the initial and final indexes
// of the key on the rehash path of key that can be displaced
// with a minimum of rehashing. Initially, assume no
// displacement and set them both to i, the first empty index
// for key
minOldPos = i;
minNewPos = i;
// minCount is the minimum number of rehashes of key plus
// rehashes of the displaced key, displaceKey. rehashCount is the
// number of rehashes of key needed to reach the index of the
// key being displaced. Initially, assume no displacement
minCount = count;
rehashCount = 0;

// The following loop determines if displacement of the key at
// the next rehash of key will yield a lower total number of
// rehashes. If key was found in the table, then skip the loop
if (table[i] == null)
        while (!qq.isEmpty() && rehashCount+1 < minCount) {
            try {
                    j = ((Integer) qq.remove()).intValue();
            }
            catch (InterruptedException e) { }
            // the candidate key for displacement
            displaceKey = table[j].k;
            jj = rh(jj) % TABLESIZE;

            // displaceCount is the number of rehashes
            // required to displace displaceKey.
            for (displaceCount=1; table[jj] != null &&
                    table[jj].k != null; displaceCount++)
                jj = rh(jj) % TABLESIZE;
            if (rehashCount + displaceCount < minCount) {
                minCount = rehashCount + displaceCount;
                minOldPos = j;
                minNewPos = jj;
            }
            rehashCount++;
        }
// At this point, if no displacement is necessary minOldPos
// equals minNewPos. minOldPos is the position where key was
// found or should be inserted. minNewPos (if not equal to
// minOldPos) is the position where the key displaced from
// minOldPos should be placed.
if (minOldPos != minNewPos)
        table[minNewPos] = table[minOldPos];
if (minOldPos != minNewPos || table[minOldPos] == null) {
        table[minOldPos] = new Record();
        table[minOldPos].k = key;
        table[minOldPos].r = rec;
}
```

```
        return minOldPos;
    } // end search
```

Brent's method reduces the average number of comparisons for successful retrievals but has no effect on the number of comparisons for unsuccessful searches. Also, it substantially increases the effort required to insert a new item.

An extension of Brent's method that yields even greater improvements in retrieval times at the expense of correspondingly greater insertion time involves recursive insertion of items displaced in the table. That is, in determining the minimum number of rehashes required to displace an item on a rehash path, all the items on the item's subsequent rehash path are considered for displacement as well, and so on. However, the recursion cannot be allowed to proceed to its natural conclusion because the insertion time would then become so large as to become impractical even though insertion is infrequent. A maximum recursion depth of 4, plus an additional modification by which tentative rehash paths longer than 5 are penalized excessively, has been found to yield average retrievals very close to optimal with reasonable efficiency.

The following table shows the average number of probes required for retrieval and insertion under the unmodified Brent algorithm. The last column shows the number of retrievals per item required to make Brent's algorithm worthwhile (i.e., so the cumulative advantage on retrievals outweighs the disadvantage on insertion).

Load Factor %	Probes/ retrieval	Probes/ insertion	Breakeven numbers of Retrieval/item
20	1.10	1.15	2.85
60	1.37	1.92	2.48
80	1.60	2.97	2.32
90	1.80	4.27	2.26
95	1.97	5.84	2.26

As the table becomes full, approximately 2.5 probes per retrieval are required on the average, regardless of the table size. This compares very favorably with ordinary double hashing, in which retrieval from a full table requires $O(\log n)$ probes.

Binary Tree Hashing

Another method of improving Brent's algorithm, devised by Gonnet and Munro, is called **binary tree hashing**. Again, we assume the use of double hashing. Every time a key is to be inserted into the table, an almost complete binary tree is constructed. Figure 7.4.2 illustrates an example of such a tree, in which the nodes are numbered according to the array representation of an almost complete binary tree, as outlined in Section 5.2 (i.e., $node(0)$ is the root, and $node(2*i + 1)$ and $node(2*i + 2)$ are the left and right sons of $node(i)$). (The details of the figure will be explained shortly.) Each node of the tree contains an index into the hash table. For purposes of this discussion,

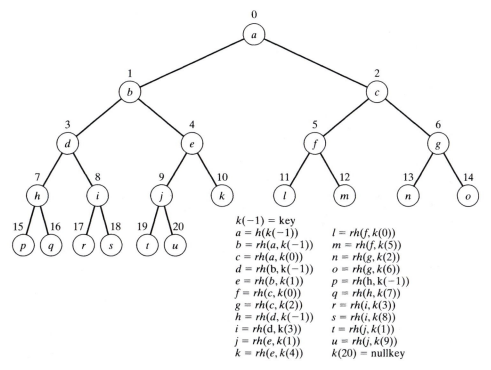

$$k(-1) = \text{key}$$

$a = h(k(-1))$	$l = rh(f, k(0))$
$b = rh(a, k(-1))$	$m = rh(f, k(5))$
$c = rh(a, k(0))$	$n = rh(g, k(2))$
$d = rh(b, k(-1))$	$o = rh(g, k(6))$
$e = rh(b, k(1))$	$p = rh(h, k(-1))$
$f = rh(c, k(0))$	$q = rh(h, k(7))$
$g = rh(c, k(2))$	$r = rh(i, k(3))$
$h = rh(d, k(-1))$	$s = rh(i, k(8))$
$i = rh(d, k(3))$	$t = rh(j, k(1))$
$j = rh(e, k(1))$	$u = rh(j, k(9))$
$k = rh(e, k(4))$	$k(20) = \text{nullkey}$

FIGURE 7.4.2

the hash table index contained in *node*(i) will be referred to as *index*(i), and the key at that position (i.e., *table*[*index*(i)].k) as $k(i)$. *key* is referred to as $k(-1)$.

To explain how the tree is constructed, we first define the ***youngest right ancestor*** of *node*[i], or *yra*(i), as the node number of the father of the youngest ancestor of *node*(i) that is a right son. For example, in Figure 7.4.2, *yra*(11) is 0, since *node*(11) (containing *l*) is a left son, and its father *node*(5) (containing *f*) is also a left son. Thus the youngest ancestor of *node*(11) that is a right son is *node*(2) (containing *c*), and its father is *node*(0). Similarly, *yra*(19) is 1, and *yra*(17) is 3. If *node*(i) is a right son, then *yra*(i) is defined as the node number of its father, (i-1)/2. Thus, *yra*(14) in Figure 7.4.2 is 6. If *node*(i) has no ancestor which is a right son (as, for example, nodes 0, 1, 3, 7, and 15 in Figure 7.4.2), then *yra*(i) is defined as minus one.

The binary tree is constructed in node number order. *index*(0) is set to *h*(key). *index*(i), for each subsequent i, is set to $rh(index((i - 1)/2), k(yra(i)))$. This process continues until $k(i)$ (i.e., *table*[*index*(i)].k) equals the ***null*** key and an empty position is found in the table.

For example, in Figure 7.4.2, *key* is hashed to obtain $a = h(key)$, which is established as the index in the root node. Its left son is $b = rh(a,key)$, and its right son is $c = rh(a,table(a).k) = rh(a,k(0))$. Similarly, the left son of *b* is $d = rh(b,key)$, the right son of *b* is $e = rh(b,table(b).k) = rh(b,k(1))$, the left son of *c* is $f = rh(c,table(a).k = rh(c,k(0))$, and the right son of *c* is $g = rh(c,table(c).k) = rh(c,k(2))$. This continues until $t = rh(j,table(b).k) = rh(j,k(1))$ is placed in *node*(19), and

$u = rh(j,table(j).k) = rh(j,k(9))$ is placed in $node(20)$. Since $table[u].k$ (which is $k(20)$) is the **null** key, an empty position in the hash table has been found, and the tree contruction is completed. Note that any path following a series of left pointers through the tree consists of successive rehashes of a particular key, and that a right pointer indicates that a new key is being rehashed.

Once the tree has been constructed, the keys along the path from the root to the last node are reordered in the hash table. Let i be initialized to the position of the last node of the tree. Then, if $yra(i)$ is nonzero, $k(yra(i))$ and its associated record are moved from $table[index(yra(i))]$ to $table[index(i)]$, and i is reset to $yra(i)$. This process is repeated until $yra(i)$ is minus one, at which point key and rec are inserted into $table[index(i)]$ and the insertion is complete. For example, in Figure 7.4.2, $yra(20) = 9$ and $index(9) = j$, so the key and record from position j of the hash table are moved to the previously empty position u. Then, since $yra(9) = 1$, and $index(1) = b$, the key and record from position b are moved to position j. Finally, since $yra(1) = -1$, key is inserted into position b.

When subsequently searching for key, two table positions are probed: a and b. When searching for the former $table[b].k$ (now at $table[j]$), two additional probes are required. When searching for the former $table[j].k$ (now at $table[u]$), one additional probe is required. Thus a total of five extra positions over the entire hash table contents must be probed as a result of the insertion of key, while at least six would have been required if key were inserted directly along its rehash path (consisting of $a, b, d, h,$ p and at least one more position). Similarly, under Brent's method, no path shorter than length 6 would have been found (considering paths $abejt$, $abdir$, $abdhg$, and $abdhp$, representing attempts to relocate $b, d, h,$ and p, the values on the initial rehash path of a. Each of these paths requires one more position before an empty table element is found).

Note also that if key had previously been inserted in the table using the Gonnet and Munro insertion algorithm, it would have been found along the leftmost path of the tree (in Figure 7.4.2, $abdhp$) before an empty table position was found at a different node. Thus the tree-building process can be initiated, in preparation for a possible insertion, as part of the search process. However, if insertions are infrequent, it may be desirable to construct the full left path of the tree until an empty position is found (i.e., to perform a straight search for key) before building the remainder of the tree.

Of course, the entire algorithm depends on the routine $yra(i)$. Fortunately, $yra(i)$ may be computed quite easily. $yra(i)$ can be derived directly from the following method: Find the binary representation of $i + 1$. Delete any trailing zero bits and the one bit preceding them. Subtract 1 from the resulting binary number to get $yra(i)$. For example, the binary representation of $11 + 1$ is 1100. Removing the trailing 100 yields 1, which is the binary representation of 1. Thus $yra(11) = 0$. Similarly, $17 + 1$ in binary is 10010, which yields 100 or 4, so that $yra(17) = 3$; $14 + 1$ in binary is 1111, which yields 111 or 7, so that $yra(14) = 6$, and $15 + 1$ in binary is 10000 (or 010000), which yields 0, so that $yra(15) = -1$. You may confirm this in Figure 7.4.2.

Gonnet and Munro's method yields results that are even closer to optimal than Brent's. However, they are not quite optimal, because the hash table can only be rearranged by moving elements to later positions in their hash sequence, never to earlier positions. At 90 percent loading, binary tree hashing requires 1.75 probes per retrieval (compared to Brent's 1.80), and at 95 percent, requires 1.88 (compared to 1.97). For a full table, 2.13 probes are required on average compared to Brent's 2.5. The maximum number of probes required to access an element under Brent's method is $O(sqrt(n))$, while under binary hashing it is $O(\log n)$. Note that the queue of Brent's method and the tree of Gonnet and Munro's can be reused for each insertion. If all insertions take place initially, and the table is subsequently required only for searches, the space for these data structures may be freed.

If the hash table is static, that is, if elements are initially inserted and the table remains unchanged for a long series of searches, then another reordering strategy is to perform all the insertions initially and then rearrange the elements of the table, so as to absolutely minimize the expected retrieval costs. Experiments show that the minimum expected retrieval cost is 1.4 probes per retrieval with a load factor of 0.5, 1.5 for a load factor of 0.8, 1.7 for a load factor of 0.95, and 1.83 for a full table. Unfortunately, the algorithms to optimally reorder a table to achieve this minimum are $O(n*TABLESIZE^2)$ and therefore impractical for large numbers of keys.

Improvements with Additional Memory

Thus far, we have assumed that no additional memory is available in each table element. If additional memory is available, we can maintain some information in each entry to reduce the number of probes required to find a record or to determine that the desired record is absent.

Before looking at specific techniques, we should make one observation. The most obvious use to which additional memory can be put is to expand the size of the hash table. This reduces the load factor and immediately improves efficiency. Therefore, in evaluating any efficiency improvements caused by adding more information to each table entry, one must consider whether the improvement outweighs utilizing the memory to expand the table.

On the other hand, the benefit of expanding each table entry by one or two bytes may indeed be worthwhile. Each table item (including space for the key and record) may require 10, 50, 100, or even 1000 bytes, so that utilizing the space to expand the table may not buy as much as utilizing the space for small increments in each table element. (In reality, long records would not be kept in a hash table, since empty table entries waste too much space. Instead, each table entry would contain the key and a pointer to the record. This could still require 30 or 40 bytes if the key were large, and 10 to 15 bytes for typical key sizes.) In addition, for technical reasons (e.g., word size), not all of the space in a table entry may actually be used, so there may be some extra space available that cannot be used for additional table entries. In that case, whatever use can be made of the storage is beneficial.

The first improvement that we consider reduces the time required for an unsuccessful search, but not that for a retrieval. It involves keeping with each table element a one-bit field whose value is initialized to 0 and is set to 1 whenever a key to be inserted hashes or rehashes to that position but the position is found occupied. When hashing or rehashing a key during a search, if we find the bit still set to 0, we immediately know that the key is not in the table, since if it were, it would either be found in that position or the bit would have been reset to 1 when it or some other key was inserted. Use of this technique together with the ordered hash table algorithm of Amble and Knuth reduces the average number of probes for an unsuccessful search in a table with a load factor of 95 percent from 10.5 to 10.3 using linear rehashing, and from 3.15 to 2.2 using double hashing. This method is called the ***pass-bit method*** because the additional bit indicates whether a table element has been passed over while inserting an item.

The next method can be used with both linear rehashing and quadratic rehashing. In both cases we can define a function $prb(j, key)$ that directly computes the position of the jth rehash of key, which is the position of the jth probe in searching for key. $prb(0, key)$ is defined as $h(key)$. For linear rehashing $[rh(i) = (i + c)\% TABLESIZE$ where c is a constant], $prb(j, key)$ is defined as $(h(key) + j*c)\% TABLESIZE$. For quadratic rehashing, $prb(j, key)$ is defined as $(h(key) + j*j)\% TABLESIZE$. Note that no such routine can be defined for double hashing, so the method is not applicable to that technique.

The method uses an additional integer field, called a ***predictor***, in each table position. Let $prd(i)$ be the predictor field in table position i. Initially, all predictor fields are zero. Under linear rehashing, the predictor field is reset as follows. Suppose key $k1$ is being inserted and j is the smallest integer such that $prb(j, k1)$ is a probe position whose predictor field $prd(prb(j, k1))$ is zero. Then, after $k1$ is rehashed several more times and is inserted in position $prb(p, k1)$, $prd(prb(j, k1))$ is reset from zero to $p - j$. Then, during a search, when position $prb(j, k1)$ is found not to contain $k1$, the next position examined is $prb(j + prd(prb(j, k1)), k1)$ or $prb(p, k1)$ rather than $prb(j + 1, k1)$. This eliminates $p - j - 1$ probes.

An advantage of this approach is that it can be adapted quite easily when only a few extra bits are available in each table position. Since the predictor field contains only the number of additional rehashes needed, in most cases this number is low and can fit in the available space. It would be very rare for a predictor value to be greater than the largest integer expressible in 4 or 5 bits. If only b bits are available for the prd field and the predictor field cannot fit, the field value can be set to $2^b - 1$ (the largest integer representable by b bits). Then we would skip at least $2^b - 2$ probes after reaching such a position.

Under linear rehashing, suppose two keys, $k1$ and $k2$, hash into different values, but the mth probe of one equals the nth probe of the other. (That is, $prb(n, k1) = prb(m, k2)$, where n and m are unequal.) Suppose $k1$ is inserted first into position $i = prb(m, k1)$. Then, when $k2$ is placed in position $prb(m + x, k2)$, $prd(i)$ is set to x. This presents no problem, since $prb(n + x, k1)$ and $prb(m + x, k2)$ both equal $(i + x*c)\% TABLESIZE$. Thus anything that hashes into either $h(k1)$ or $h(k2)$ and rehashes into i can be referred to $i + prd(i)$ for the next probe. This reflects the fact that linear rehashing involves primary clustering in which keys hashing into different locations follow the same rehash paths once those paths intersect.

Under quadratic rehashing, however, primary clustering is eliminated. Thus, the paths followed by $k1$ and $k2$ differ if $h(k1)$ does not equal $h(k2)$ even after those paths intersect. Thus $prb(n + x, k1)$, which equals $(h(k1) + (n + x)*(n + x))\% TABLESIZE$, does not equal $prb(m + x, k2)$, which equals $(h(k2) + (m + x)*(m + x))\% TABLESIZE$, even though $prb(n, k1)$ does happen to equal $prb(m, k2)$. Thus, if $prd(prb(i, k1))$ is set to x, and if we are searching for $k2$ at $prb(j, k2)$, which happens to equal $prb(i, k1)$, we cannot go directly to $prb(j + x, k2)$ unless $h(k1)$ equals $h(k2)$ (i.e., $k1$ and $k2$ are in the same secondary cluster) and i equals j. Therefore, under quadratic rehashing or any other rehashing method that involves only secondary clustering, we must ensure that $h(k(i))$ equals $h(key)$ before using or setting $prd(i)$ during a search or insertion of key. If the two hash values are unequal, then rehashing continues in the usual fashion until a location j is reached where $h(k(j))$ equals $h(key)$, where use of the prd field can be resumed.

Unfortunately, the predictor method cannot be used at all under double hashing. The reason for this is that even secondary clustering is eliminated, so there is no guarantee that $prb(n + x, k1)$ equals $prb(n + x, k2)$ even if $h(k1)$ equals $h(k2)$ and $prb(n, k1)$ equals $prb(n, k2)$.

An extension of the predictor method is the ***multiple predictor method***. Under this technique, np predictor fields are maintained in each table position. A predictor hash routine $ph(key)$ whose value is between 0 and $np - 1$ determines which predictor is used for a particular key. The jth predictor in table position i is referenced as $prd(i, j)$. When a key probes an occupied slot i which equals $prb(j, key)$ such that $ph(k(i))$ equals $ph(key)$, the next position probed is $prb(j + prd(i, ph(key)), key)$. Similarly, if $ph(k(i))$ equals $ph(key)$, and $prd(i, ph(key))$ is zero, then we know that key is not in the table. If key is inserted at $prb(i + x, key)$, then $prd(i, ph(key))$ is set to x.

The advantage of the multiple predictor method is similar to the advantages of double hashing; it eliminates the effects of secondary clustering by dividing the list of elements that hash or rehash into a particular location into np separate and shorter lists.

Simulation results for a slightly modified version of the predictor method using the quadratic rehash method are shown in the following table, which lists the average number of probes required for a successful search under various load factors, with various numbers of predictor fields and numbers of bits in each predictor. By comparison, recall that quadratic hashing without predictors required 1.44 average probes for a 50 percent load factor and 2.85 for 90 percent, and that double hashing required 1.39 and 2.56 probes, respectively.

Number of Predictors	Load Factor %	Bits in each predictor		
		3	4	5
1	50	1.25	1.25	1.25
	70	1.39	1.35	1.35
	90	1.83	1.55	1.46
2	50	1.24	1.23	1.23
	70	1.35	1.32	1.31
	90	1.79	1.50	1.41
4	50	1.23	1.23	1.23
	70	1.33	1.30	1.30
	90	1.74	1.47	1.38
8	50	1.22	1.22	1.22
	70	1.32	1.29	1.29
	50	1.72	1.46	1.37

As the number of bits in each predictor and the number of predictors grow very large, the average number of probes required for a successful search with a load factor lf becomes $2 - (1 - exp(-lf))/lf$. For a single full-integer predictor, the average number of probes is $1 + lf/2$. The predictor method also reduces the average number of probes for unsuccessful searches.

Coalesced Hashing

Perhaps the simplest use of additional memory to reduce retrieval time is to add a link field to each table entry. This field contains the next position of the table to examine in searching for an item. In fact, under this method, a rehash function is not required at all, so the technique is our first example of the second major method of collision resolution, called **chaining**. This method uses links rather than a rehash function to resolve hash clashes.

The simplest of the chaining methods is called **standard coalesced hashing**. A search and insertion algorithm for this method can be presented as follows. Assume that each table entry contains a key field k initialized to the **null** key and a *next* field initialized to -1. The algorithm uses an auxiliary method *getEmpty*, which returns the index of an empty table location.

```
i = h(key);
while (k(i) != key && next(i) >= 0)
    i = next(i);
if (k(i) == key)
    return i;
// set j to the position where the new record is to be inserted
if (k(i) == nullkey)
    // the hash position is empty
    j = i;
else {
    j = getEmpty();
    next(i) = j;
}
k(j) = key;
r(j) = rec;
return j;
```

The method *getEmpty* can use any technique to locate an empty position. The simplest method is to use a variable *avail* initialized to $TABLESIZE - 1$ and to execute

```
while (k(avail) != null)
    avail--;
return avail;
```

each time that *getEmpty* is invoked. When *getEmpty* is invoked, all the table positions between *avail* and $TABLESIZE - 1$ have already been allocated. *getEmpty* sequentially examines positions less than *avail* to locate the first empty position. *avail* is reset to that position, which is then allocated. Of course, it may be desirable to avoid the **null** key comparisons in *getEmpty*. This can be done in a number of ways. An additional one-bit *empty* field can be added to each table position, or the *next* fields can be initialized to -2 and modified to -1 when keys are inserted in the table. An alternative solution is to link the free positions together in a list that acts as a stack.

Figure 7.4.3 illustrates a table of ten elements that has been filled using standard coalesced hashing using the hash function $key \% 10$. The keys were inserted in the

	k	next
0	nullkey	−1
1	nullkey	−1
2	42	−1
3	38	−1
avail = 4	14	8
5	84	3
6	39	−1
7	28	5
8	34	7
9	29	6

FIGURE 7.4.3

order 14, 29, 34, 28, 42, 39, 84, and 38. Note that items hashing into both 4 and 8 have coalesced into a single list (in positions 4, 8, 7, 5, 3, containing items 14, 34, 28, 84, 38). This is how the method gets its name.

There are several advantages to standard coalesced hashing. First, it reduces the average number of probes to approximately $\exp(2*lf)/4 - lf/2 + 0.75$ for an unsuccessful search and approximately $\exp(2*lf) - 1)/(8*lf) + lf/4 + 0.75$ for a successful search. ($\exp(x)$, available in the *java.lang.Math* package, computes the value of e^x.) This compares favorably with all the previous methods other than the predictor method. A full table requires only an average of 1.8 probes to locate an item and 2.1 probes to determine that an item is not in the table. A fraction of approximately $1 - lf/2$ of items in the table can be found on the first probe.

Another major advantage of chaining methods is that they permit efficient deletion without penalizing the efficiency of subsequent retrievals. An item being deleted can be removed from its list, its position in the table freed, and *avail* reset to the following position (unless *avail* already points to a position later in the table). This may slow down the second subsequent insertion somewhat by forcing *avail* to be repeatedly decremented through a long series of occupied positions, but that is not very significant. If the free table positions are kept in a linked list, then this penalty also disappears.

A variation of standard coalesced hashing inserts a new element into its chain immediately following the item at its hash location rather than at the end of the chain. This technique, called *early insertion standard coalesced hashing*, or *EISCH*, requires the same average number of probes as ordinary standard coalesced hashing for an unsuccessful search, but fewer probes (approximately $(\exp(lf) - 1)/lf$) for a successful search. In a full table, EISCH requires approximately 5 percent fewer probes for a successful search.

A generalization of the standard coalesced hashing method, which we call *general coalesced hashing*, adds extra positions to the hash table that can be used for list nodes in the case of collisions, but not for initial hash locations. Thus the table would consist of t entries (numbered 0 to $t - 1$), but keys would hash only into one of $m < t$ values (0 to $m - 1$). The extra $t - m$ positions are called the *cellar* and are available for storing items whose hash positions are full.

Using a cellar results in less conflict between lists of items with different hash values and therefore reduces the lengths of the lists. However, a cellar that is too large could increase list lengths relative to what they might be if the cellar positions were permitted as hash locations. For full tables, the lowest average successful search time is achieved if the ratio m/t is 0.853 (i.e., approximately 15 percent of the table is used as a cellar). In that case, the average number of probes is only 1.69. The lowest average unsuccessful search time is attained if the ratio is 0.782, in which case only 1.79 probes are required for the average unsuccessful search. Higher values of m/t produce lowest successful and unsuccessful search times for lower load factors (when the table is not full).

Unlike the situation with standard coalesced hashing, the early insertion method yields worse retrieval times than if elements are added at the end of the chain in general coalesced hashing. A combination of the two techniques, called ***varied insertion coalesced hashing***, seems to yield the best results. Under this method, a colliding element is ordinarily inserted in the list immediately following its hash position, as in the early insertion method, unless the list emanating from that position contains a cellar element. When this occurs, the varied insertion method inserts the collider after the last cellar position in the chain. However, the extra overhead of varied insertion and early insertion often makes them less useful in practice.

Separate Chaining

Both rehashing and coalesced hashing assume fixed table sizes determined in advance. If the number of records grows beyond the number of table positions, it is impossible to insert them without allocating a larger table and recomputing the hash values of the keys of all the records already in the table using a new hash function. (In general coalesced hashing, the old table can be copied into the first half of the new table, and the remaining portion of the new table used to enlarge the cellar so items do not have to be rehashed.) To avoid the possibility of running out of room, too many locations may be initially allocated for a hash table, resulting in much wasted space.

Another method of resolving hash clashes, called ***separate chaining***, involves keeping a distinct linked list for all records whose keys hash into a particular value. Suppose that the hash routine produces values between 0 and $TABLESIZE - 1$. Then an array bucket of header nodes of size $TABLESIZE$ is declared. This array is called the ***hash table***. $bucket[i]$ points to the list of all records whose keys hash into i. In searching for a record, the list head $bucket[i]$ is accessed and the list that it initiates is traversed. If the record is not found, it is inserted at the end of the list. Figure 7.4.4 illustrates separate chaining. We assume a ten-element array and the hash routine *key* % 10. The keys in the figure are presented in the order

75   66   42   192   91   40   49   87   67   16   417   130   372   227

We may write a search-and-insertion method for separate chaining using a hash function h, an array *bucket*, and nodes that contain three fields: k for the key, r for the record, and *next* as a reference to the next node in the list. The requisite classes may now be defined as:

```
class KeyType {
    int k;
```

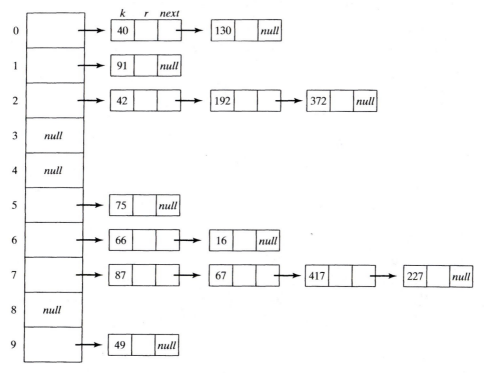

FIGURE 7.4.4

```
    KeyType(int i) {
         k = i;
    } // end constructor
} // end KeyType class
class RecType {
    ...              // define the members of the record here
} // end RecType class
class Record {
    KeyType k;
    RecType r;
    Record next;
    public Record() {
         k = null;
         r = null;
         next = null;
    } // end constructor
} // end Record class

public class Chaining {
    final static int TABLESIZE = 10;
    static Record table[];
    static Record bucket[];
```

```java
    public Chaining() {
        bucket = new Record[TABLESIZE];

        for (int i=0; i<TABLESIZE; i++)
            bucket[i] = new Record();
    } // end constructor

    public int h(KeyType k) {
        return (k.k) % 10;
    } // end h method

    public Record search(KeyType key, RecType rec) {
        Record p, q = null, s;
        int i;

        i = h(key);
        p = bucket[i];
        while (p != null && p.k != null && p.k.k != key.k) {
            q = p;
            p = p.next;
        }
        if (p != null && p.k != null && p.k.k == key.k) {
            System.out.println("Double of number " + key.k);
            return p;
        }
        // insert a new record
        s = new Record();
        s.k = key;
        s.r = rec;
        s.next = null;
        if (q == null)
            bucket[i] = s;
        else
            q.next = s;
        return s;
    } // end search method
} // end Chaining class
```

Note that the lists may be reordered dynamically for more efficient searching by the methods in Section 7.1. The time for unsuccessful searches can be reduced by keeping each of the lists ordered by *key*. Then only half the list, on the average, need be traversed to determine that an item is missing.

The primary disadvantage of chaining is the extra space required for the hash table and pointers. However, the initial array is usually smaller in schemes that use separate chaining than in those that use rehashing or coalesced hashing. This is because under separate chaining it is less catastrophic if the entire array becomes full; it is always possible to allocate more nodes and make them available to various lists. Of course, if the lists become very long, the whole purpose of hashing—direct addressing and resultant search efficiency—is defeated. One advantage of separate chaining is that the list items need not be in contiguous storage. Another advantage over all other hashing methods is that separate chaining allows traversal of the items in hash-key order, although not in sequential key order.

There is a technique that can be used to save some space in separate chaining. Consider the hash routine $h(key) = key \% TABLESIZE$. Then if we define $p(key) = key/TABLESIZE$, we can store $p(key)$ rather than key in the k field of each list node. When searching for key, we compute $h(key)$. Since key equals $p(key)*TABLESIZE + h(key)$, we can recompute the key value in each list node from the value of $p(key)$ stored in the k field. Since $p(key)$ requires less space than key, space is saved in each list node. The technique can be used for separate chaining, but not for any of the other hashing methods, because it is only in separate chaining that the value of $h(key)$ for the key stored in the position being probed is always known with certainty during the search process. However, this technique is not of much use for integer keys in a language like Java in which the size of an integer is fixed by the computer implementation.

Another space-efficiency decision that must be made is whether the hash table should be simply list headers (as we have presented it) or whether each list header should itself contain a key and a record (or record pointer). Space would be wasted for empty array items but gained for full ones.

The average number of probes required to locate an existing item under the separate chaining technique is approximately $1 + lf/2$. The average number required for an unsuccessful search is approximately $\exp(-lf) + lf$ if the lists are not kept ordered, and approximately $1 + lf/2 - (1 - \exp(-lf))/lf + \exp(-lf)$ if they are kept ordered. If there are $TABLESIZE$ keys and $TABLESIZE$ elements in the hash table (for a load factor of 1), this translates to 1.5 average probes per successful search, 1.27 probes for an unsuccessful search if unordered lists are used, and 1.05 probes for an unsuccessful search if ordered lists are used. Note that the average for an unsuccessful search is actually lower than for a successful search, because an unsuccessful search to an empty array element involves zero probes, while a successful search requires at least one probe. (This assumes that a key is not kept in each element, because an unsuccessful search to an empty element would then require a key comparison with ***null***.)

One technique that can be used to reduce the number of probes in separate chaining is to maintain the records that hash into the same value as a binary search tree emanating from the hash bucket rather than as a linked list. However, this requires that two pointers be kept with each record. Since chains are usually small (otherwise, the initial bucket table should be larger), the added space and programming complexity do not seem to be warranted.

Although the average number of probes for separate chaining appears to be quite low, the numbers are deceptive. The reason for this is that the ***load factor*** is defined as the number of keys in the table divided by the number of positions in the table. But in separate chaining, the number of positions in the hash table is not a valid measure of space utilization, since the keys are not stored in the hash table but in the list nodes. Indeed, the formulas for search time remain valid even if lf is greater than one. For example, if there are five times as many keys as buckets, $lf = 5$, and the average number of probes for a successful search is $1 + lf/2$, or 3.5. Thus the total space allocated to the hash table should be adjusted to include the list nodes. When this is done, coalesced hashing is quite competitive with separate chaining. Note also that rehashing with multiple predictors also performs better than separate chaining.

Hashing in External Storage

If a hash table is maintained in external storage on a disk or some other direct-access device, then time rather than space is the critical factor. Most systems have sufficient external storage to allow the luxury of unused allocated space for growth but cannot afford the time needed to perform an I/O operation for every element on a linked list. In such a situation, the table in external storage is divided into a number of blocks called **buckets**. Each bucket consists of a useful physical segment of external storage, such as a page or a disk track or track fraction. The buckets are usually contiguous and can be accessed by bucket offsets from 0 to $TABLESIZE - 1$ that serve as hash values, much like indexes of an array in internal storage.

Alternatively, one or more contiguous storage blocks can be used as a hash table containing pointers to buckets distributed noncontiguously. In this situation, the hash table is most likely read into memory as soon as the file is opened (or upon the first record read) and remains in memory until the file is closed. When a record is requested, its key is hashed, and the hash table (now in internal memory) is used to locate the external storage address of the appropriate bucket. Such a hash table is often called an **index** (not to be confused with the term "index" as used to refer to a particular table position).

Each external memory bucket contains room for a moderate number of records (in practical situations, from ten to one hundred). An entire bucket is read into memory at once, and sequentially searched for the appropriate record. (Of course, a binary search or some other appropriate search mechanism based on the internal organization of the records in the bucket can be used, but the number of records in a bucket is usually so small that no significant advantage is gained.)

We should note that, when dealing with external storage, the computational efficiency of a hash function is not as important as its success at avoiding hash clashes. It is more efficient to spend microseconds computing a complex hash function at internal CPU speeds than milliseconds or longer accessing additional buckets at I/O speeds when a bucket overflows. We also note that external storage space is usually inexpensive. Thus in deciding how many contiguous initial buckets to have, or how large a hash table, the choice should make it unlikely that any of the buckets will become full, even though this entails allocating unused space. Then, when a new record must be inserted, there will usually be room in the appropriate bucket and an additional expensive I/O is not required.

If a bucket is full and a record must be inserted, any of the rehash or chaining techniques discussed above can be used. Of course, additional I/O operations are required when searching for records that are not in the buckets directly corresponding to the hash value. The size of the hash table (which equals the number of buckets accessible in one I/O operation) is crucial. If a hash table is too large, most of the buckets will be empty, and a great deal of space is wasted. If a hash table is too small, the buckets will be full, and large numbers of I/O operations will be required to access many records. This simple hashing technique is inefficient in either space or time if a file is very volatile, growing and shrinking rapidly and unpredictably. We will see how to deal with this situation shortly.

The following table indicates the expected number of external storage accesses per successful search under linear rehashing, double rehashing, and separate chaining for various bucket sizes and load factors (the load factor is defined as the number of records in the file divided by the product of the number of buckets and the bucket size).

Bucket Size	Load Factor	Linear Rehashing	Double Hashing	Separate chaining
1	.5	1.500	1.386	1.250
	.8	3.000	2.012	1.400
	.95	10.5	3.153	1.5
5	.5	1.031	1.028	1.036
	.8	1.289	1.184	1.186
	.95	2.7	1.529	1.3
10	.5	1.005	1.005	1.007
	.8	1.110	1.079	1.115
	.95	1.8	1.292	1.3
15	.5	1.000	1.000	1.000
	.8	1.005	1.005	1.015
	.95	1.1	1.067	1.2

The table indicates that double hashing is the preferred method for moderate or large bucket sizes.

However, when dealing with external storage, such as a disk, the number of buckets that have to be read from external storage is not the only determinant of access efficiency. Another important factor is the dispersal of the buckets accessed; that is, how far apart the buckets accessed are from each other. A major factor in the time it takes to read a block from a disk is the ***seek time***. This is the time it takes for the disk head to move to the location of the desired data on the disk. If two buckets accessed one after the other are far apart, more time is required than if they are close together. Given this fact, it would seem that linear rehash is the most effective technique, because, although it may require accessing more buckets, the buckets it accesses are contiguous (assuming that $c = 1$ in the linear rehash, so that the next sequential bucket is checked if a record is not in a full bucket). Surprisingly, the table indicates that fewer buckets are accessed under linear rehashing than under separate chaining for large bucket sizes.

If separate chaining is used, it is desirable to reserve an overflow area in each cylinder of the file so that full buckets and overflow records in the same cylinder can link, thus minimizing seek time and essentially eliminating the dispersal penalty. The overflow area need not be organized into buckets and should be organized as individual records with links. Since few records overflow, there is only a small chance that enough will overflow from a single bucket to fill an additional complete bucket. Thus, by keeping individual overflow records, more buckets can overflow into the same cylinder. Since space is reserved in the file for overflow records, the load factor does not represent a true picture of storage utilization for this version of separate chaining. The number of accesses in separate chaining is therefore higher for a given amount of external storage than the numbers in the table above would indicate.

Although double hashing requires fewer accesses than linear rehashing, it disperses the buckets that must be accessed to a degree that may overwhelm this advantage. However, in systems where dispersal is not a factor, double hashing is preferred. This is true of modern large multiuser systems in which many users may be requesting access to a disk simultaneously, and the requests are scheduled by the operating system based on the way the data are arranged on the disk. In such situations, waiting time for disk access is required in any case, so dispersal is not a significant factor.

The major drawback in using hashing for external file storage is that sequential access (in ascending key order) is not possible because a good hash function disperses keys without regard to order. Access to records in key-sequential order is particularly important in external file systems.

Separator Method

One technique for reducing access time in external hash tables at the expense of increasing insertion time is due to Gonnet and Larson. We will call the technique the **separator method**. The method uses rehashing (either linear rehashing or double hashing) to resolve collisions but also uses an additional hash routine, s, called the **signature function**. Given a key key, let $h(key, i)$ be the ith rehash of key, and let $s(key, i)$ be the ith signature of key. If a record with key key is stored in bucket number $h(key, j)$, then the **current signature** of the record and the key, $sig(key)$, is defined as $s(key, j)$. That is, if a record is placed in a bucket corresponding to its key's jth rehash, then its current signature is its key's jth signature.

A separator table, sep, is maintained in internal memory. If b is a bucket number, then $sep(b)$ contains a signature value greater than the current signature of every record in $bucket(b)$. To access the record with key key, repeatedly hash key until a value j is obtained such that $sep(h(key, j)) > s(key, j)$. At that point, if the record is in the file, it must be in $bucket(h(key, j))$. This ensures the ability to access any record in the file with only a single external memory access.

If m is the number of bits allowed in each item of the separator table (so that it can hold values between 0 and $2^m - 1$), then the signature function, s, is restricted to producing values between 0 and $2^m - 2$. Initially, before any overflows have occurred in bucket b, the value of $sep(b)$ is set to $2^m - 1$, so that any record whose key hashes to b can be inserted directly into $bucket(b)$ regardless of its signature. Now, suppose $bucket(b)$ is full and a new record to be inserted hashes into b [i.e., $h(key, j)$ equals b, and j is the smallest integer such that $sep(h(key, j)) > s(key, j)$]. Then the records in b with the largest current signature lcs must be removed from $bucket(b)$ to make room for the new record. The new record is then inserted into $bucket(b)$, and the old records that had current signature lcs and were removed from bucket b are rehashed and relocated into new buckets (with new current signatures, of course). $sep(b)$ is then reset to lcs, since the current signatures of all the records in $bucket(b)$ are less than lcs. Future keys are directed to $bucket(b)$ only if their signatures are less than lcs. Note that more than one record may have to be removed from a bucket if they have equal maximal current signature values. This may leave a bucket with some remaining space after an insertion causes it to overflow.

Records that overflow from a bucket during an insertion may cause cascading overflows in other buckets when one attempts to relocate them. This means that an insertion may cause an indefinite number of additional external storage reads and writes. In practice, a limit is placed on the number of such cascading overflows beyond which the insertion fails. If the insertion does fail, it is necessary to restore the file to the status it was in before inserting the new record that caused the original overflow. This is usually done by delaying writing modified buckets to external storage, keeping the modified versions in internal memory until it is determined that the insertion can be completed successfully. If the insertion is aborted because the cascade limit is reached, then no writes are done, leaving the file in its original state.

With forty buckets per record, 4-bit signature values, and a load factor of 90 percent, an average of no more than two pages need be modified per insertion under this method. However, the number of modified pages per insertion rises rapidly as the load factor is increased, so that the technique is impractical with a load factor greater than 95 percent. Larger signature values and larger bucket sizes permit the method to be used with larger load factors.

Dynamic Hashing and Extendible Hashing

One of the most serious drawbacks of hashing for external storage is that it is insufficiently flexible. Unlike internal data structures, files and databases are semipermanent structures that are not usually created and destroyed within the lifetime of a single program. Further, the contents of an external storage structure tend to grow and shrink unpredictably. All the hash table structuring methods that we have examined have a sharp space/time tradeoff. Either the table uses a large amount of space for efficient access, resulting in much wasted space when the structure shrinks, or it uses a small amount of space and accommodates growth very poorly by sharply increasing the access time for overflow elements. We would like to develop a scheme that does not utilize too much extra space when a file is small but permits efficient access when it grows larger. Two such schemes are called ***dynamic hashing***, due to Larson, and ***extendible hashing***, due to Fagin, Nievergelt, Pippenger, and Strong.

The basic concept under both methods is the same. Initially, m buckets and a hash table (or index) of size m are allocated. Assume that m equals 2^b, and assume a hash routine h that produces hash values that are $w > b$ bits in length. Let $hb(key)$ be the integer between 0 and m represented by the first b bits of $h(key)$. Then, initially, hb is used as the hash routine, and records are inserted into the m buckets as in ordinary external storage hashing.

When a bucket overflows, it is split in two and its records are assigned to the two new buckets based on the $(b + 1)$st bit of $h(key)$. If the bit is zero, the record is assigned to the first (or left) new bucket; if the bit is 1, the record is assigned to the second (or right) bucket. (Of course, the original bucket can be reused as one of the two new buckets.) The records in each of the two new buckets now all have the same first $b + 1$ bits in their hash keys, $h(key)$. Similarly, when a bucket representing i bits overflows (where $b <= i <= w$), it is split, and the $(i + 1)$st bit of $h(key)$ for each record in the bucket is used to place the record in the left or right new bucket. Both new buckets then represent $i + 1$ bits of the hash key. We call the bucket whose keys have 0 in their $(i + 1)$st bit the **0-*bucket***, and the other bucket the **1-*bucket***.

Dynamic hashing and extendible hashing differ as to how the index is modified when a bucket splits. Under dynamic hashing, each of the m original index entries represents the root of a binary tree each of whose leaves contains a pointer to a bucket. Initially, each tree consists of only one node (a leaf node) that points to one of the m initially allocated buckets. When a bucket splits, two new leaf nodes are created to point to the two new buckets. The former leaf that pointed to the bucket being split is transformed into a nonleaf node whose left son is the leaf pointing to the 0-bucket and whose right son is the leaf pointing to the 1-bucket. Dynamic hashing with $b = 2$ ($m = 4$) is illustrated in Figure 7.4.5.

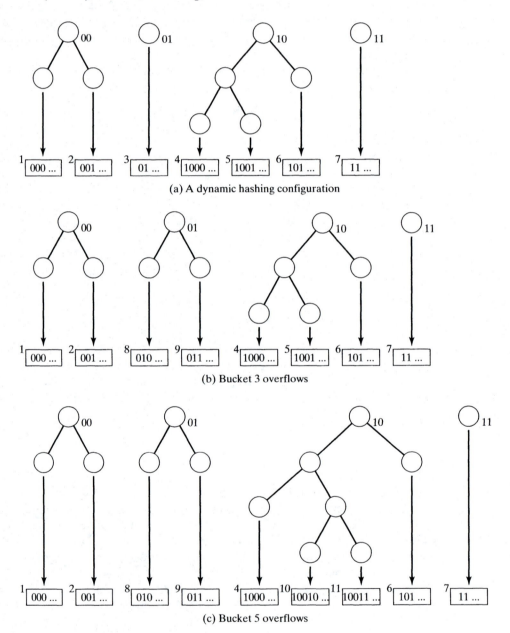

(a) A dynamic hashing configuration

(b) Bucket 3 overflows

(c) Bucket 5 overflows

FIGURE 7.4.5 Dynamic hashing with $b = 2$.

To locate a record under dynamic hashing, compute $h(key)$ and use the first b bits to locate a root node in the original index. Then, use each successive bit of $h(key)$ to move down the tree, going left if the bit is 0 and right if the bit is 1, until a leaf is reached. Then use the pointer in the leaf to locate the bucket that contains the desired record, if it exists.

In extendible hashing, each bucket contains an indication of the number of bits of $h(key)$ that determine which records are in the bucket. This number is called the ***bucket depth***. Initially, this number is b for all bucket entries; it is increased by 1 each time a bucket splits. Associated with the index is the ***index depth***, d, which is the maximum of all the bucket depths. The size of the index is always 2^d (initially, 2^b).

Suppose a bucket of depth i is to be split. Let $a1, a2, \ldots, ai$ (where each aj is either 0 or 1) be the first i bits of $h(key)$ for the records in the bucket being split. There are two cases to consider: $i < d$ and $i = d$. If $i < d$ (so that the bucket depth is being increased to $i + 1$, but the index depth remains at d), then all index positions with bit values $a1, a2, \ldots, ai00, \ldots, 0$ (up to a bit size of d) through $a1, a2, \ldots, ai01, \ldots, 1$ of the index (i.e., all positions starting with $a1, \ldots, ai0$) are reset to point to the 0-bucket, and index positions with bit values $a1, a2, \ldots, ai10, \ldots, 0$ through $a1, a2, \ldots, ai11, \ldots, 1$ (i.e., all positions starting with $a1, \ldots, ai1$) are reset to point to the 1-bucket. If $i = d$ (so that the bucket depth and the index depth are both being increased to $d + 1$), the index is doubled in size from 2^d to 2^{d+1}; the old contents of all index positions $x1, \ldots, xd$ are copied into the new positions $x1, \ldots, xd0$ and $x1, \ldots, xd1$; the contents of index position $a1, \ldots, ad0$ is set to point to the new 0-bucket, and the contents of index position $a1, \ldots, ad1$ to point to the new 1-bucket. Extendible hashing is illustrated in Figure 7.4.6. Figure 7.4.6a illustrates a configuration with index depth 4, Figure 7.4.6b illustrates an overflow that does not increase the index depth, and Figure 7.4.6c illustrates an overflow that does.

To locate a record under extendible hashing, compute $h(key)$ and use the first d bits (where d is the index depth) to obtain a position in the index. The contents of this position point to the bucket containing the desired record, if it exists.

Under both dynamic and extendible hashing, if the entire index is maintained in internal storage, only one I/O operation is required to locate a record regardless of how large the file grows. When a file shrinks, buckets can be combined and freed, and the index size can be reduced. Thus these methods achieve the twin goals of efficient space utilization and efficient access. Both schemes also allow effective sequential traversal of records in hash-key order.

However, neither method permits traversal in key order, and this often prevents the practical use of the techniques for file implementation. Of course, one could use the key itself as a hash value or some other order-preserving hash function, but such functions are usually nonuniform. The lack of uniformity is not as serious an obstacle under these methods as under static hashing methods, since any number of bits can be used. The more bits used, the less likely that two keys will clash. While too large a number of bits can result in too large an index for practical use, dynamic hashing, which does not use as large an index as extendible hashing, may indeed be practical with a nonuniform hash function.

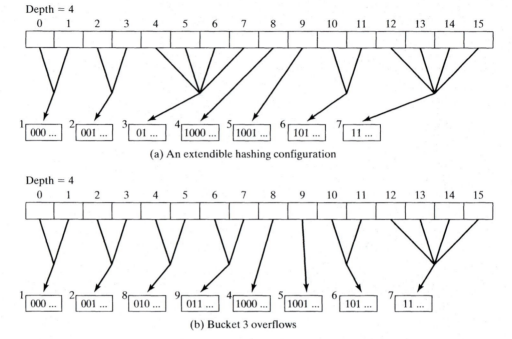

(a) An extendible hashing configuration

(b) Bucket 3 overflows

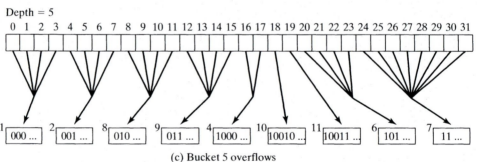

(c) Bucket 5 overflows

FIGURE 7.4.6   Extendible hashing.

A simple variation of extendible hashing uses the last bits of the hash key rather than the first to locate a bucket. This variation simplifies doubling the index because it allows merely copying the first half of the new index into the second and only modifying the two entries pointing to the two new buckets. However, such a scheme would not permit traversal even in hash-key sequence.

One suggestion for a hashing technique for use with these methods is to use a random number generator to produce an arbitrarily long sequence of 0s and 1s as needed, with the key or some function thereof as the seed. The same sequence would be produced for the same key every time, but there is no limit to the extendibility. This has the advantage of allowing the file to grow arbitrarily large, and in the case of dynamic hashing, of ensuring balanced trees.

In comparing dynamic and extendible hashing, we note that extendible hashing is more time-efficient, since a tree path need not be traversed as in dynamic hashing. However, if the entire index is kept in memory, the time spent in traversing the tree path does not involve any I/Os. Traversal time is therefore likely to be negligible compared to the time for accessing the bucket. The maximum number of tree nodes required in dynamic hashing is $2n - 1$, assuming n buckets, while there may be as many as 2^{n-1} index entries required under extendible hashing. However, usually fewer than twice as many extendible hashing index entries as dynamic hashing tree nodes are required, and the tree nodes require two pointer fields compared to one for each extendible hashing index entry. Thus the two methods are comparable in average internal space utilization.

It is also possible to compress very large extendible hashing indexes by keeping only one copy of each bucket pointer and maintaining from/to indicators. Another point to note is that extendible hashing performs the same way regardless of the value of m, the initial number of index entries, whereas dynamic hashing requires longer tree paths if m is smaller. In fact, there is no reason not to initialize m to 0 (i.e., $b = 0$) with a single empty bucket in extendible hashing, other than for contiguity of the buckets in external storage.

The external storage utilization of both dynamic and balanced hashing is approximately 69 percent, which is the same as with B-trees. However, the storage utilization of the hashing methods oscillates far more sharply and persists longer than for B-trees, so that there is a period of low utilization (approximately 50 percent) after buckets are split as they begin filling up. This is followed by a period of high utilization (approaching 90–100 percent) as new records are uniformly distributed into the buckets and they all become full more or less simultaneously. Finally, a short period of intensive splitting is observed, after which utilization is again low.

The reason for this oscillation is that the hash routine is expected to be uniform, so that all the buckets are filled at approximately the same time. It may be desirable to minimize this oscillation by purposely introducing some nonuniformity in the hash function. However, if this is done in extendible hashing, the nonuniformity could cause extremely large indexes. This problem can be solved by keeping a compressed version of the index, as noted.

Overflow buckets can be utilized to achieve storage utilization higher than 69 percent. When a bucket becomes full and an additional record is to be inserted, an overflow bucket is allocated and linked to the full bucket. When the overflow bucket also fills up, the contents of both buckets are redistributed into two nonoverflow buckets, with the overflow bucket linked to the new bucket with more than half of the records. This results in more than two full buckets of data distributed into three buckets (two regular, one overflow), yielding a minimum utilization of 67 percent, rather than 50 percent, once the initial buckets are filled. Of course, it is also possible to use overflow buckets that are smaller than the regular buckets (in which case not every split results in an overflow bucket remaining allocated), as well as to allow an overflow bucket to contain records that have overflowed from more than one bucket. The latter technique, however, complicates traversal in hash-key order.

Another method of increasing space utilization is to allow overflow records to be placed in a full bucket's brother (under extendible hashing, the brother of a 0 bucket is its corresponding 1 bucket, and vice versa). This method also complicates traversal in hash key order. Both the use of overflow buckets and the use of a brother bucket for overflow records increase the average number of accesses required for a search. However, if brother buckets are kept contiguous, this penalty may not be great.

Linear Hashing

One drawback of dynamic and extendible hashing is the need for an index. While the index may be kept in internal storage once the file is opened, this is not always possible if the index becomes very large. Also, the index requires external storage when the file is not in use. In addition, the external copy of the index may have to be constantly updated to guard against power failure or other interruptions that would prevent rewriting the index when the file is closed.

Another technique, *linear hashing* (not to be confused with linear rehashing), proposed by Litwin and modified by Larson, permits a hash table to expand and shrink dynamically without requiring an index. However, the basic technique requires the use of overflow buckets, unlike dynamic and extendible hashing. The version that we present is called *linear hashing with two partial expansions*, or *LH2P*.

Under LH2P, the initial file consists of m buckets, where m is even, numbered 0 to $m - 1$. The file is divided into ng groups of buckets, numbered 0 to $ng - 1$. Initially, there are $m/2$ groups of buckets ($ng = m/2$), each consisting of two buckets. Group i initially consists of buckets i and $i + ng$. For example, if m equals 6, the file initially contains six buckets, numbered 0 to 5. There are three groups: group 0 contains buckets 0 and 3, group 1 contains buckets 1 and 4, and group 2 contains buckets 2 and 5.

The file grows in two ways: overflow growth and regular growth. Unlike B-trees, dynamic hashing, or extendible hashing, a bucket is not split when it overflows. Instead, an overflow mechanism is used to contain the overflowing records from a bucket. This mechanism can utilize any of the techniques discussed earlier.

Regular growth takes place by expanding the size of the file by one bucket at a time. Expansion of the file by one bucket is called a *simple expansion*. A simple expansion takes place whenever the load factor (defined as the total number of records in the file divided by the number of records that fit into regular, nonoverflow buckets) exceeds a threshold percentage. When a simple expansion takes place, the number of regular buckets in the file, nb, increases by one. At any time, the file consists of buckets 0 through $nb - 1$ plus any overflow buckets or records. Initially, nb equals m.

Regular growth under LH2P takes place in a series of simple expansions, grouped into *partial expansions* and *full expansions*. Each full expansion doubles the number of regular buckets in the file and consists of two partial expansions. The first partial expansion increases the number of regular buckets by 50 percent, and the second increases the number by the same amount. Thus, after the first partial expansion, nb equals $3 * m/2$; after the first full expansion, nb equals $2 * m$; and after the second full expansion, nb equals $4 * m$.

Each simple expansion increases the size of a group of buckets by one bucket. The variable *nextGroup* always holds the number of the next group to be expanded (initially, *nextGroup* is 0). During the first partial expansion, two-bucket groups are expanded to three buckets by moving some records from buckets *nextGroup* and *nextGroup + ng* (and some of their associated overflow records) into bucket *nextGroup* + 2*ng. (Exactly which records are moved to the new bucket and which remain in place will be discussed shortly.) Note that the buckets are numbered from 0 to *nb* − 1, so that *nb* is always the number of the next bucket added to the file. During the first partial expansion, *nb* always equals *nextGroup* + 2*ng. (Initially, *nextGroup* = 0 and *ng* = *m*/2, so *nb* = *m*.) After a group has been expanded, *nextGroup* and *nb* are both increased by one, and the next group is ready for expansion.

After the first partial expansion, all *ng* groups have been expanded, and *nextGroup* is reset to zero. Each group now contains three regular buckets rather than two, and the file size (in number of buckets) has grown by 50 percent.

During the second expansion, *nb* always equals *nextGroup* + 3*ng. (At the start of a second partial expansion, *nextGroup* is 0 and *nb* equals 3*ng.) Three-bucket groups are expanded to four by moving some records from buckets *nextGroup*, *nextGroup* + *ng*, and *nextGroup* + 2*ng (and some of their associated overflow records) into bucket *nextGroup* + 3*ng (which equals *nb* during the second partial expansion). Any overflow records not moved to bucket *nb* during an expansion are moved back into their home bucket, if there is room.

After the second partial expansion, the file size has doubled and a full expansion has taken place. In preparation for the next full expansion, the number of groups (*ng*) is doubled, and the size of each group is halved, from four to two. That is, group *i*, consisting of buckets *i*, *i* + *j*, *i* + 2*j, and *i* + 3*j (where *j* is the old value of *ng*), is now viewed as two separate groups: group *i*, consisting of buckets *i* and *i* + 2*j, and group *i* + *j*, constisting of buckets *i* + *j* and *i* + 3*j. The first partial expansion of the next full expansion then begins.

Note that the group that is expanded is always the next sequential group and is independent of whether or not overflow has taken place in that group. Overflow is handled by a separate mechanism from expansion.

A key question is how a hash function is used to access a record directly. When the file contains *nb* buckets, the hash function must produce a value between 0 and *nb* − 1, but when the file size is increased by one bucket, it must produce a value between 0 and *nb*. Further, a record moved from bucket *i* to bucket *j* must have previously hashed into *i* and must henceforth hash into *j*. The hash function must also be used to determine whether or not a record should be moved during an expansion. The following method allows direct access to a record's bucket. Although it involves many CPU operations, it only requires one I/O operation to obtain the appropriate bucket from a nonoverflow record.

A function *h*1(*key*) that produces values in the range of 0 to *m* − 1 is used as a direct hashing function initially, before any expansions have taken place. The value *h*1(*key*) is called the **initial hash** of *key*. We also assume a function *h*2(*key*, *i*) for *i* > 0 that uniformly produces values in the range 1 to 4. The value of *h*2(*key*, *i*) determines whether the record with key *key* is moved during the *i*th full expansion, and, if so, whether it is moved to the first or the second expansion bucket of its group. If *h*2(*key*, *i*) is 1 or 2, then the record is not moved during the *i*th full expansion; if *h*2(*key*, *i*) is 3, then it is moved to the first expansion bucket of its group in the *i*th full expansion; if *h*2(*key*, *i*) is 4, then it is moved to the second expansion bucket. Thus a random record has a 50 percent chance of being moved during a full expansion and a 25 percent chance of being moved to either of the two expansion buckets.

During the first partial expansion of the ith full expansion, the hashing algorithm examines the values $h2(key, i)$, $h2(key, i + 1)$, $h2(key, i + 2)$, and so on, seeking the first value less than 4. If that value is 1 or 2, then the record is not moved; if it is 3, it is moved to the single expansion bucket. It will stay there after the second partial expansion if $h(key, i)$ is 3; it will be moved to the second partial expansion bucket by the second partial expansion if $h2(key, i)$ is 4. Thus a random record has a one-third chance of being moved to the third bucket of a group in a first partial expansion and a one-quarter chance of being moved to the fourth bucket in a second partial expansion. This guarantees that the records are distributed uniformly throughout the file.

Define the *level* of an LH2P file as the number of full expansions that have taken place, and let the variable *level* reference the level of the file. If *pe* is the number of the current partial expansion (either 1 or 2), then $pe + 1$ is the number of buckets in a group that has not yet been expanded in the current partial expansion, and $pe + 2$ is the number of buckets in a group that has been expanded. At all times,

$$ng = m * 2^{level-1}$$

and

$$nb = nextGroup + (pe + 1) * ng;$$

The values m, *level*, *nextGroup*, and *pe* therefore define the state of an LH2P file and must be kept with the file at all times.

To locate the address of a record, it is necessary to follow its relocations through the *level* full expansions, the $pe - 1$ completed partial expansions, and the *nextGroup* completed simple expansions of the current partial expansion. The hash of a key, $h(key)$, is therefore computed by the following algorithm:

```
h = h1(key);                    // initial hash
numGroups = m/2;                // initial number of groups
for (i = 1; i < level; i++) {
    // trace the movement of the record
    // through level full expansions
    bucketNum = h2(key, i);
    if (bucketNum > 2) {
        // record was moved in ith full expansion
        groupNum = h % numGroups;
        h = groupNum + (bucketNum - 1) * numGroups;
    }
    numGroups = 2 * numGroups;  // number of groups after i full
        expansions
}
// At this point h holds the key's hash after level full expansions
// and no partial expansions. Now, compute the record's current
// location after possible movement in the current full expansion.
```

```
groupNum = h % numGroups;        // current group number
i = level + 1;
bucketNum = h2(key, i);          // eventual bucket number at
                                 // end of current full expansion
/* compute the size of the current group
// pe holds the number of the current
// partial expansion
if (groupNum < nextGroup)
    groupSize = pe + 2;

else
    groupSize = pe + 1;
// if the eventual bucket number is larger than current group size,
// then continue hashing until the current bucket number is found
while (bucketNum > groupSize) {
    i++;
    bucketNum = h2(key, i);
}
if (bucketNum > 2)
        // the record was already moved
        // in the current full expansion
        h = groupNum + (bucketNum - 1) * numGroups;
```

The following example illustrates LH2P. Consider an LH2P file that initially contains six buckets, 0 through 5, consisting of three groups: $(0, 3)$, $(1, 4)$, and $(2, 5)$. In this case, m is 6, and nb is initially 6. Consider six records $r0$ through $r5$ with keys $k0$ through $k5$ that initially hash into 0 through 5, respectively (i.e., $h1(ki) = i$). Then $r0$ through $r5$ are initially placed in buckets 0 through 5.

Assume that the following are the values of $h2(key, i)$ for key equal to $k0$ through $k5$ and i from 1 to 4:

Key	$h2(key, 1)$	$h2(key, 2)$	$h2(key, 3)$	$h2(key, 4)$
$k0$	1	4	2	3
$k1$	4	2	1	2
$k2$	3	1	2	1
$k3$	4	4	3	1
$k4$	1	2	1	2
$k5$	2	4	4	3

The next table illustrates the rearrangement of records during expansion of this LH2P file. Each simple expansion is specified in the first column by a status triple consisting of the number of full expansions that have taken place (*level*), the number of the current partial expansion (*pe*), and the number of the group currently being expanded (*nextGroup*). Initially, there are three groups ($ng = 3$), six buckets ($nb = 6$), and two buckets per group. The second column shows the existing buckets of the current group in parentheses, followed by the bucket being added to the group in the current expansion step. We use the notation bi to indicate bucket i. Below the buckets of the group in each second-column entry are the records contained in that group. The third column indicates the results of the simple expansion. Of course, in order for the expansions to take place, additional records must be added so that the load factor exceeds the threshold. However, we do not illustrate these other records here but merely illustrate how existing records move into expansion buckets.

Status	Group and records	Result of expansion
$(0,1,0)$	$(b0,b3); b6$	$h2(k0,1) = 1$, so $r0$ remains in $b0$.
	$(r0,r3)$	$h2(k3,1) = 4; h2(r3,2) = 4; h2(k3,3) = 3$,
		so $r3$ moves to $b6$.
$(0,1,1)$	$(b1,b4); b7$	$h2(k1,1) = 4; h2(k1,2) = 2$ so $r1$ remains in $b1$.
		$h2(k4,1) = 1$, so $r4$ remains in $b4$.
$(0,1,2)$	$(b2,b5); b8$	$h2(k2,1) = 3$, so $r2$ moves to $b8$.
	$(r2,r5)$	$h2(k5,1) = 2$, so $r5$ remains in $b5$.

This ends the first partial expansion. There are still three groups, but each now contains three buckets, so $nb = 9$. The second partial expansion then begins:

Status	Group and records	Result of expansion
$(0,1,0)$	$(b0,b3,b6); b9$	$h2(k0,1) = 1$, so $r0$ remains in $b0$.
	$(r0,r3)$	$h2(k3,1) = 4$; so $r3$ moves to $b9$.
$(0,1,1)$	$(b1,b4,b7); b10$	$h2(k1,1) = 4$; so $r1$ moves to $b10$.
	$(r1,r4)$	$h2(k4,1) = 1$, so $r4$ remains in $b4$.
$(0,1,2)$	$(b2,b5,b8); b11$	$h2(k2,1) = 3$, so $r2$ remains in $b8$.
	$(r2,r5)$	$h2(k5,1) = 1$, so $r5$ remains in $b5$.

This ends the first full expansion. There are now three groups, and each contains four buckets, so $nb = 12$. To start the second full expansion, the number of groups is doubled ($ng = 6$), and the number of buckets in each is reset to 2. The second full expansion proceeds:

Status	Group and records	Result of expansion
$(1,1,0)$	$(b0,b6); b12$	$h2(k0,2) = 4; h2(k0,3) = 2$ so $r0$ remains in $b0$.
	$(r0)$	
$(1,1,1)$	$(b1,b7); b13$	No records in this group.
$(1,1,2)$	$(b2,b8); b14$	$h2(k2,2) = 4$, so $r2$ remains in $b8$.
	$(r2)$	
$(1,1,3)$	$(b4,b10); b15$	$h2(k3,2) = 4; h2(k3,3) = 3$ so $r3$ moves to $b15$.
	$(r3)$	
$(1,1,4)$	$(b4,b10); b16$	$h2(k1,2) = 2$; so $r1$ remains in $b10$.
	$(r1,r4)$	$h2(k4,2) = 2$, so $r4$ remains in $b4$.
$(1,1,5)$	$(b5,b11); b17$	$h2(k5,2) = 4; h2(k5,3) = 4; h2(k5,4) = 3$, so $r5$
		moves to $b5$.
	$(r5)$	

This ends the first partial expansion.

Status	Group and records	Result of expansion
$(1,2,0)$	$(b0,b6,b12); b18$	$h2(k0,2) = 4$; so $r0$ to $b18$.
	$(r0)$	
$(1,2,1)$	$(b1,b7,b13); b19$	No records in this group.

(1, 2, 2)	$(b2, b8, b14); b20$	$h2(k2, 2) = 1$, so $r1$ remains in $b8$.
	$(r2)$	
(1, 2, 3)	$(b3, b9, b15); b21$	$h2(k3, 2) = 4$; so $r3$ moves to $b21$.
	$(r3)$	
(1, 2, 4)	$(b4, b10, b16); b22$	$h2(k1, 2) = 2$; so $r1$ remains in $b10$.
	$(r1, r4)$	$h2(k4, 2) = 2$, so $r4$ remains in $b4$.
(1, 2, 5)	$(b5, b11, b17); b23$	$h2(k5, 2) = 4$; so $r5$ moves to $b23$.
	$(r5)$	

This ends the second full expansion.

The techniques of LH2P can be generalized to allow n partial expansions in each full expansion. Such a scheme is called LHnP. Each partial expansion increases the file size by the fraction $1/n$. While higher values of n reduce the average number of overflow records (since records hashing to a particular bucket are redistributed more frequently) and therefore the number of accesses for both search and insertion, more partial expansions require more frequent allocations of storage and more complex hash value computations. Thus, practical insertion costs and expansion costs are higher. The value $n = 2$, leading to the scheme LH2P, is a practical compromise.

Overflow can be handled by a variety of methods under linear hashing. Use of overflow buckets is the simplest technique but may require varying-sized buckets for efficiency. Such variation would complicate storage management. Ramamohanarao and Sacks-Davis suggest recursive linear hashing in which records that overflow the prime area are placed in a second linear hashing file, records that overflow that area are placed in a third, and so on. More than three areas are rarely needed.

There are several techniques that eliminate the need for separate, dedicated overflow areas. Mullin suggests using chaining in the linear hashing file, with the most recently expanded group used to contain overflow records (since it is most likely to have empty space). Larson suggests that every kth bucket in the primary area should be reserved for overflow records, with the hash function suitably modified to avoid the overflow buckets.

Larson also suggests the possibility of using linear rehashing to locate overflow records. When linear rehashing is used, it is more efficient to implement each partial expansion in several sweeps of step size $s > 1$ and go backward among the groups $ng - 1, ng - 1 - s, ng - 1 - 2*s$, and so on; the second step would expand groups $ng - 2, ng - 2 - s, ng - 2 - 2*s$, and so on. Linear rehashing can also be combined with the separator method of Gonnet and Larson to allow one-access retrieval and eliminate the overhead of overflow.

Choosing a Hash Function

Let us now turn to the question of how to choose a good hash function. Clearly, the function should produce as few hash clashes as possible; that is, it should spread the keys uniformly over the possible array indices. Of course, unless the keys are known in advance, it cannot be determined whether a particular hash function disperses them properly. However, although it is unusual to know the keys before one selects a hash function, it one may know some properties of the keys that affect their dispersal.

In general, a hash function should depend on every single bit of the key, so that two keys that differ in only one bit or one group of bits (regardless of whether the group is at the beginning, end, or middle of the key or strewn throughout the key) hash into different values. Thus a hash function that simply extracts a portion of a key is not suitable. Similarly, if two keys are simply digit or character permutations of each other (such as 139 and 319 or *meal* and *lame*), they should also hash into different values. The reason for this is that key sets frequently have clusters or permutations that might otherwise result in collisions.

For example, the most common hash function (which we have used in the examples in this section) uses the ***division*** method, in which an integer key is divided by the table size, and the remainder is taken as the hash value. This is the hash function $h(key) = key \% TABLESIZE$. Suppose, however, that *TABLESIZE* equals 1000, and that all the keys end in the same three digits (e.g., in a program being written for a plant, the last three digits of part numbers might represent the plant number). Then the remainder on dividing by 1000 yields the same value for all the keys, so that a hash clash occurs for each record except the first. Given such a collection of keys, a different hash function should be used.

It has been found that the best results with the division method are achieved when *TABLESIZE* is prime (i.e., is not divisible by any positive integer other than 1 and itself). However, even if *TABLESIZE* is prime, an additional restriction is called for. If r is the number of possible character codes on a particular computer (assuming an 8-bit byte, r is 256), then if *TABLESIZE* is a prime such that $r \% TABLESIZE$ equals 1, the hash function $key \% TABLESIZE$ is simply the sum of the binary representation of the characters in the key modulo *TABLESIZE*. For example, suppose r equals 256 and *TABLESIZE* equals 17, in which case $r \% TABLESIZE = 1$. Then the key 37956, which equals $148 * 256 + 68$ (so that the first byte of its representation is 148 and the second byte is 68), hashes into 37956 % 17, which equals 12, which equals $(148 + 68) \% 17$. Thus two keys that are simply character permutations (e.g., *steam* and *mates*) will hash into the same value. This may promote collisions and should be avoided. Similar problems occur if *TABLESIZE* is chosen so that $r^k \% TABLESIZE$ is very small or very close to *TABLESIZE* for some small value of k.

Another hash method is the ***multiplicative method***. In this method, a real number c between 0 and 1 is selected. $h(key)$ is defined as $floor(m * frac(c * key))$, where the method $floor(x)$, available in the *java.lang.Math* package, yields the integer part of the real number x, and $frac(x)$ yields the fractional part. (Note that $frac(x) = x - floor(x)$.) That is, multiply the key by a real number between 0 and 1, take the fractional part of the product yielding a random number between 0 and 1 dependent on every bit of the key, and multiply by m to yield an index between 0 and $m - 1$. If the word size of the computer is b bits, c should be chosen so that $2^b * c$ is an integer relatively prime to 2^b, and c should not be too close to either 0 or 1. Also if r, as before, is the number of possible character codes, avoid values of c such that $frac(r^k * c)$ is too close to 0 or 1 for some small value of k (these values yield similar hashes for keys with the same last k characters) and values of c of the form $i/(r - 1)$ or $i/(r^2 - 1)$ (these values yield similar hashes for keys that are character permutations). Values of c that yield good theoretical properties are .6180339887 [which equals $(sqrt(5) - 1)/2$] or .3819660113 [which equals $1 - (sqrt(5) - 1)/2$]. If m is chosen as a power of 2, such as 2^p, the computation of $h(key)$ can be done quite efficiently by multiplying the one-word integer key by the one-word integer $c * 2^b$ to yield a two-word product. The integer represented by the most significant p bits of the integer in the second word of this product is then used as the value of $h(key)$.

In another hash function, known as the ***midsquare method***, the key is multiplied by itself, and the middle few digits (the exact number depends on the number of digits allowed in the index) of the square are used as the index. If the square is considered as a decimal number, the table size must be a power of 10, whereas if it is considered as a binary number, the table size must be a power of 2. Alternatively, the number represented by the middle digits can be divided by the table size and the remainder used as the hash value. Unfortunately, the midsquare method does not yield uniform hash values and does not perform as well as the previous two techniques.

The ***folding method*** breaks up a key into several segments that are added or exclusive *or*ed together to form a hash value. For example, suppose that the internal bit string representation of a key is 010111001010110, and that five bits are allowed in the index. The three bit strings 01011, 10010, and 10110 are exclusive *or*ed to produce 01111, which is 15 as a binary integer. (The ***exclusive or*** of two bits is 1 if the two bits are different, and 0 if they are the same. It is the same as the binary sum of the bits, ignoring the carry.) The disadvantage of the folding method is that two keys that are k-bit permutations of each other (i.e., where both keys consist of the same groups of k bits in a different order) hash into the same k-bit value. Still another technique is to apply a multiplicative hash function to each segment individually before folding.

There are many other hash functions, each with its own advantages and disadvantages depending on the set of keys to be hashed. One consideration in choosing a hash function is efficiency of calculation; it does no good to be able to find an object on the first try if doing so takes longer than several tries in an alternative method.

If the keys are not integers, they must be converted into integers before applying one of the foregoing hash functions. There are several ways to do this. For example, for a character string, the internal bit representation of each character can be interpreted as a binary number. One disadvantage of this is that the bit representations of all the letters or digits tend to be very similar on most computers. If the keys consist of letters alone, the index of each letter in the alphabet can be used to create an integer. Thus the first letter of the alphabet (a) is represented by the digits 01, and the fourteenth (n) is represented by the digits 14. The key 'hello' is represented by the integer 0805121215. Once an integer representation of a character string exists, the folding method can be used to reduce it to manageable size. However, here too, every other digit is a 0, 1, or 2, which may result in nonuniform hashes. Another possibility is to view each letter as a digit in base-26 notation, so that 'hello' is viewed as the integer $8 * 26^4 + 5 * 26^3 + 12 * 26^2 + 12 * 26 + 15$.

One of the drawbacks of all these hash functions is that they are not order-preserving; that is, the hash values of the two keys are not necessarily in the same order as the keys themselves. It is therefore not possible to traverse the hash table in sequential order by key. An example of a hash function that is order-preserving is $h(key) = key/c$, where c is some constant chosen so that the highest-possible key divided by c equals $TABLESIZE - 1$. Unfortunately, order-preserving hash functions usually are severely nonuniform, leading to many hash clashes and a larger average number of probes to access an element. Note also that to enable sequential access to keys, the separate chaining method of resolving collisions must be used.

Perfect Hash Functions

Given a set of keys $k = \{k1, k2, \ldots, kn\}$, a ***perfect hash function*** is a hash function h such that $h(ki)!= h(kj)$ for all distinct i and j. That is, no hash clashes occur under a perfect hash function. In general, it is difficult to find a perfect hash function for a particular set of keys. Further, once a few more keys are added to the set for which a perfect hash function has been found, the hash function generally ceases to be perfect for the expanded set. Thus, although it is desirable to find a perfect hash function to ensure immediate retrieval, it is not practical to do so unless the set of keys is static and is frequently searched. The most obvious example of such a situation is a compiler in which the set of reserved words of the programming language being compiled does not change and must be accessed repeatedly. In such a situation, the effort required to find a perfect hashing function is worthwhile because, once the function is determined, it can save a great deal of time in repeated applications.

Of course, the larger the hash table, the easier it is to find a perfect hash function for a given set of keys. If ten keys must be placed in a table of hundred elements, 63 percent of the possible hash functions are perfect (although as soon as the number of keys reaches thirteen in a hundred-item table, the majority are no longer perfect). In the example given earlier, if the compiler symbol table is to contain all the symbols used in any program, so that a large table must be allocated to allow for a large number of user-declared identifiers, a perfect hash function can easily be found for the reserved symbols of the language. The table can be initialized with the reserved symbols already in the positions determined by that function, with the user-defined symbols inserted as they are encountered. While hash clashes may occur for user symbols, we are guaranteed immediate lookup for the reserved symbols.

In general, it is desirable to have a perfect hash function for a set of n keys in a table of only n positions. Such a perfect hash function is called ***minimal***. In practice, this is difficult to achieve. Sprugnoli has developed a number of perfect hash function determination algorithms. The algorithms are fairly complex and are not presented here. One technique finds perfect hash functions of the form $h(key) = (key + s)/d$ for some integers s and d. These are called ***quotient reduction perfect hash functions***, and, once found, are quite easy to compute.

For the key set 17, 138, 173, 294, 306, 472, 540, 551, 618, Sprugnoli's algorithm finds the quotient reduction hash function $(key + 25)/64$, which yields the hash values 0, 2, 3, 4, 5, 7, 8, 9, 10. The function is not minimal, since it distributes the nine keys to a table of eleven positions. Sprugnoli's algorithm does, however, find the quotient reduction perfect hash function with the smallest table size.

An improvement to the algorithm yields a minimal perfect hash function of the form

```
h(key) = (key + s)/d          if key <= t
h(key) = (key + s + r)/d      if key > t
```

where the values s, d, t, and r are determined by the algorithm. However, the algorithm to discover such a minimal perfect hash function is $O(n^3)$ with a large constant of proportionality, and thus it is not practical for even very small key sets. A slight modification yields a more efficient algorithm that produces near-minimal perfect hashing function of this form for small key sets. In the example above, such a function is

$$h(key) = (key - 7)/72 \quad \textbf{if } key <= 306$$
$$h(key) = (key - 42)/72 \quad \textbf{if } key > 306$$

which yields the hash values $0, 1, 2, 3, 4, 5, 6, 7, 8$ and happens to be minimal. A major advantage of quotient reduction hash functions and their variants is that they are order-preserving.

Sprugnoli also presents another group of hashing functions, called ***remainder reduction perfect hash functions***, which are of the form

$$h(key) = ((r + s * key) \% x)/d$$

and an algorithm to produce values $r, s, x,$ and d that yield such a perfect hash function for a given key set and a desired minimum load factor. If the minimum load factor is set to 1, a minimal perfect hash function results. However, the algorithm does not guarantee that a perfect reminder reduction hash function can be found in a reasonable time for high load factors. Nevertheless, the algorithm can often be used to find minimal perfect hash functions for small key sets in a reasonable time.

Unfortunately, Sprugnoli's algorithms are all at least $O(n^2)$ and therefore are only practical for small sets of keys (twelve or fewer). Given a larger set of keys, k, a perfect hash function can be developed by a technique called ***segmentation***. This technique involves dividing k into a number of small sets, $k_0, k_2, \ldots, k_p$, and finding a perfect hash function h_i for each small set k_i. Assume a grouping function *set* such that *key* is in the set $k_{set(key)}$. If m_i is the maximum value of h_i on k_i, and b_i is defined as $i + m_0 + m_1 + \ldots + m_{i-1}$, we can define the segmented hash function h as $h(key) = b_{set(key)} + h_{set(key)}(key)$. Of course, the function *set* that determines the grouping must be chosen with care to disperse the keys reasonably.

Jaeschke presents a method for generating minimal perfect hash functions using a technique called ***reciprocal hashing***. The reciprocal hash functions generated by Jaeschke's algorithm are of the form

$$h(key) = (c/(d * key + e)) \% TABLESIZE$$

for some constants $c, d,$ and e, and $TABLESIZE$ equal to the number of keys. Indeed, if the keys are all relatively prime integers, then a constant c can be found that yields a minimal perfect hash function of the form

$$(c/key) \% TABLESIZE$$

by the following algorithm. Assume that the keys are initially in a sorted array $k(0)$ through $k(n - 1)$, and that $f(c, key)$ is the function $(c/key) \% n$.

```
c = ((n - 2) * k(0) * k(n - 1))/(k(n - 1) - k(0));
while (true) {
    // check if c yields a perfect hash function
    bigi = -1;        // these will be set to the largest values
    bigj = -1;        // such that f(c, k(bigi)) = f(c, k(bigj))
    for (i = 0; i < n; i++)
            val(i) = f(c, k(i));
    for (i = n - 1; bigi < 0 && i >= 0; i--) {
```

```
                    vi = val(i);
                    j = i -1;
                    while (bigi < 0 && j >= 0)
                            if (vi == val(j)) {
                                    bigi = i;
                                    bigj = j;
                            }
                            else j--;
            }
            if (bigi < 0)
                    return;
            // increment c
            x = k(bigj) - (c % k(bigj));
            y = k(bigi) - (c % k(bigi));
            (x < y) ? c += x : c += y;
    }
```

Applying this algorithm to the key set 3, 5, 11, 14 yields $c = 11$ and the minimal perfect hash function $(11/key)$ % 4. For the key set 3, 5, 11, 13, 14, the algorithm produces $c = 66$. In practice, one would set an upper limit on the value of c to ensure that the algorithm does not go on indefinitely.

If the keys are not relatively prime, Jaeschke presents another algorithm to compute values d and e so that the values of $d * k(i) + e$ are relatively prime, and the algorithm can be used on them.

For low values of n, approximately 1.82^n values of c are examined by this algorithm, which is tolerable for $n <= 20$. For values of n up to 40, we can divide the keys into two sets $s1$ and $s2$ of size $n1$ and $n2$, where all the keys in $s1$ are smaller than those in $s2$. Then we can find values $c1, d1, e1$ and $c2, d2, e2$ for each of the sets individually, and use

```
    h(key) = (c1/(d1 * key + e1)) % n1
```

for keys in $s1$, and

```
    h(key) = n1 + (c2/(d2 * key + e2)) % n2
```

for keys in $s2$. For larger key sets, Sprugnoli's segmentation technique can be used.

Chang presents an order-preserving minimal perfect hash function that depends on the existence of a ***prime number function***, $p(key)$, for the set of keys. Such a function always produces a prime number corresponding to a given key and has the additional property that if $key1$ is less than $key2$, then $p(key1)$ is less than $p(key2)$. An example of such a prime number function is

```
    p(x) = x² - x + 41        for    1 <= x <= 40
```

If such a prime number function has been found, Chang presents an efficient algorithm to produce a value c such that the function $h(key) = c$ % $p(key)$ is an order-preserving minimal hash function. However, prime number functions are difficult to find, and the value c is too large to be practically useful.

Cichelli presents a very simple method that often produces a minimal or near-minimal perfect hash function for a set of character strings. The hash function produced is of the form

```
h(key) = val(key[0]) + val(key[length(key) - 1]) + length(key)
```

where $val(c)$ is an integer value associated with the character c, and $key[i]$ is the ith character of key. That is, add integer values associated with the first and last characters of the key to the length of the key. The integer values associated with particular characters are determined in two steps.

The first step is to order the keys so that the sums of the occurrence frequencies of the first and last characters of the keys are in decreasing order. Thus if e occurs ten times as a last or first character, g occurs six times, t occurs nine times, and o occurs four times, then the keys *gate*, *goat*, and *ego* have the occurrence frequencies $16(6 + 10)$, $15(6 + 9)$, and $14(10 + 4)$, respectively and are therefore ordered properly.

Once the keys have been ordered, attempt to assign integer values. Each key is examined in turn. If the key's first or last character has not been assigned values, attempt to assign one or two values between zero and some predetermined limit. If appropriate values can be assigned to produce a hash value that does not clash with the hash value of a previous key, then tentatively assign those values. If not, or if both characters have been assigned values that result in a conflicting hash value, then backtrack to modify tentative assignments made for a previous key. To find a minimal perfect hash function, the predetermined limit for each character is set to the number of distinct first- and last-character occurrences.

Cichelli perfect hash functions may not exist for some key sets. For example, if two keys of the same length have the same or reversed first and last characters, no such hash function can exist. In that case, different character positions may be used to develop the hash function. However, in other cases no such hash function can be found regardless of what character positions are used. In practice, it is often useful to attempt to find a Cichelli perfect hash function before trying other methods. If the predetermined limit is set high enough, so that minimality is not required, Cichelli's algorithm can be quite practical for up to fifty keys. Cook and Oldehoeft present several improvements on the basic Cichelli method.

Sager presents an important generalization and extension of Cichelli's method that efficiently finds perfect hash functions for as many as 512 keys. The method is fairly complex and is not presented here.

An additional technique for generating minimal perfect hash functions is due to Du, Hsieh, Jea, and Shieh. The technique uses a number of nonperfect random hash functions $h_1, \ldots, h_j$ and a separate ***hash indicator table*** (or ***hit***) of size n. The table is initialized as follows. First, set all its entries to zero. Next, apply h_1 to all the keys. For all values x between 0 and $n - 1$ such that only one key hashes to x using h_1, reset $hit[x]$ from 0 to 1. Remove all keys that hash to unique values using h_1 from the key set, and apply h_2 to the remaining keys. For all values x between 0 and $n - 1$ such that $hit[x] = 0$ and only one key hashes to x using h_2, reset $hit[x]$ from 0 to 2. This process continues until either the key set is empty (in which case *hit* has been initialized and any remaining unused hash functions are unnecessary) or until all the hash functions have been applied (in which case, if there are remaining keys, a perfect hash function cannot be found using this method and the given random hash functions).

Once *hit* has been fully initialized, the hashing algorithm is as follows:

```
for (i = 0; ; i++) {
    x = h_i(key);
    if (hit(x) == i)
            return x;
}
```

The probability that a perfect hash function will result rises very slowly as additional random hash functions are added. Therefore, a segmentation technique, with distinct *hit* tables, should be used for large sets of keys.

Universal Classes of Hash Functions

As we have seen, it is difficult to obtain a perfect hash function for a large set of keys. It is also not possible to guarantee that a specific hash function will minimize collisions without knowing the precise set of keys to be hashed. If a particular hash function is found not to work well in practice in a particular application, it is difficult to come up with another hash function that does better.

Carter and Wegman have introduced the concept of a **universal class of hash functions**. Such a class consists of a set of hash functions $hi(key)$. While an individual function in the class may work poorly on a particular input key set, enough of the functions work well for any random input set that if one function is chosen randomly from the class, it is likely to perform well on any input set that is actually presented.

Given a hash table of size m, and a set a of possible keys, a class of nh hash functions h is **universal$_2$** if there are no two keys in a on which more than nh/m of the functions in h result in collision. This means that no pair of distinct keys clash under more than $1/m$th of the functions. It can be shown that if k items have been inserted into a hash table of size m using a random member of a universal$_2$ class of hash functions with separate chaining, the expected number of probes for an unsuccessful search is less than $1 + k/m$ (the number for a successful search is even lower).

Carter and Wegman present several examples of such universal$_2$ classes. One example of such a class is for keys that can be represented as positive integers between 0 and $w - 1$ ($w - 1$ is usually the maximum value that fits into one computer word). Let p be a prime number larger than w, let s be an integer between 1 and $p - 1$, and let t be an integer between 0 and $p - 1$. Then define $H_{s,t}(key)$ as $((s * key + t) \% p) \% m$. The set of all such functions $H_{s,t}$ for given w and p is universal$_2$.

A second example is for keys consisting of i bits and a table size $m = 2^j$ for some j. Let a be an i-element array of table indexes (between 0 and $m - 1$). Then define $h_a(key)$ as the exclusive or of the indexes $a[k]$ such that the kth bit of key is 1. For example, if $m = 128$, $i = 16$, a is an array containing the values 47, 91, 35, 42, 16, 81, 113, 91, 12, 6, 47, 31, 106, 87, 95, and 11, and key is 15381 (which is 0011110000010101 as a 16-bit number), then $h_a(key)$ is the exclusive or of $a[3]$, $a[4]$, $a[5]$, $a[6]$, $a[12]$, $a[14]$, and $a[16]$ (these are 35, 42, 16, 47, 31, 87, and 11), which is 01110101, or 117. The set of functions h_a for all such array values a is universal$_2$.

If the hash table is maintained internally and is not required between program runs (as in a compiler, for example), then the hash function used may be generated by the program from a universal$_2$ class to guarantee reasonable average running time (although any particular run may be slow). In the examples above, a random number generator might be used to select s, t, and the elements of a. If the hash table remains between program runs, as in a file or database, then a random hash function from the universal$_2$ class might be selected initially, and if poor program behavior is observed (although this is unlikely), a new random function could be selected and the entire hash table reorganized at a convenient time.

Sarwate has introduced an even better category of hash functions classes, called **optimally universal$_2$ (OU$_2$)** classes. If there are nk possible keys and m table entries, a set H containing nh hash functions is OU$_2$ if any two keys collide under exactly $nh*(nk - m)/(m*(nk - 1))$ functions in OU$_2$, and if, for any function h in H, every key collides with exactly $nk/m - 1$ other keys. Sarwate provides several examples of such OU$_2$ classes. Unfortunately, hash functions in OU$_2$ classes are difficult to compute and may not be practically useful.

EXERCISES

7.4.1   Write a Java method *table.search(key)* which searches a hash table for a record with key *key*. The function accepts an integer key and a table declared by:

```
public final static int TABLESIZE = 100;
class Record {
        KeyType k;
        RecType r;
        int flag;
}
Record table[] = new table[TABLESIZE];
```

table[i].k and *table[i].r* are the *i*th key and record respectively. *table[i].flag* equals *false* if the *i*th table position is empty, and *true* if it is occupied. The method returns an integer in the range 0 to $TABLESIZE - 1$ if a record with key *key* is present in the table. If no such record exists, then the function returns -1. Assume the existence of a hashing routine, *h(key)*, and a rehashing routine, *rh(index)*, that both produce integers in the range 0 to $TABLESIZE - 1$.

7.4.2   Write a Java method *table.sInsert(key, rec)* to search and insert into a hash table, as in the previous exercise.

7.4.3   Develop a mechanism for detecting when all possible rehash positions of a given key have been searched. Incorporate this method into the Java methods *search* and *sInsert* from the previous exercises.

7.4.4   Consider a double hashing method using the primary hash function *h1(key)* and the rehash function $rh(i) = TABLESIZE \% (i + h2(key), TABLESIZE)$. Assume that *h2(key)* is relatively prime to *TABLESIZE*, for any key *key*. Develop a search algorithm and an algorithm to insert a record whose key is known not to exist in the table so that the keys at sucessive rehashes of a single key are in ascending order. The insertion algorithm may rearrange records previously inserted into the table. Can you extend these algorithms to a search-and-insertion algorithm?

7.4.5 Suppose a key is equally likely to be any integer between a and b. Suppose the midsquare hash method is used to produce an integer between 0 and 2^{k-1}. Is the result equally likely to be any integer within that range? Why?

7.4.6 Given a hash function $h(key)$, write a Java simulation program to determine each of the following quantities after $0.8 * TABLESIZE$ random keys have been generated. The keys should be random integers.

1. The percentage of integers between 0 and $TABLESIZE - 1$ that do not equal $h(key)$ for some generated key.
2. The percentage of integers between 0 and $TABLESIZE - 1$ that equal $h(key)$ for more than one generated key.
3. The maximum number of keys that hash into a single value between 0 and $TABLESIZE - 1$.
4. The average number of keys that hash into values between 0 and $TABLESIZE - 1$, not including those values into which no key hashes.

Run the program to test the uniformity of each of the following hash functions:

a. $h(key) = key \% TABLESIZE$ for $TABLESIZE$ a prime.
b. $h(key) = key \% TABLESIZE$ for $TABLESIZE$ a power of 2.
c. The folding method using *exclusive or* to produce five-bit indices, where $TABLESIZE = 32$.
d. The mid-square method using decimal arithmetic to produce four-digit indices, where $TABLESIZE = 10000$.

7.4.7 If a hash table contains $TABLESIZE$ positions, and n records currently occupy the table, then the **load factor** is defined as $n/TABLESIZE$. Show that if a hash function uniformly distributes keys over the $TABLESIZE$ positions of the table, and if lf is the load factor of the table, then $(n - 1) * lf/2$ of the n keys in the table collided upon insertion with a previously entered key.

7.4.8 Assume that n random positions of a $TABLESIZE$-element hash table are occupied, using hash and rehash functions that are equally likely to produce any index in the table. Show that the average number of comparisons needed to insert a new element is $(TABLESIZE + 1)/(TABLESIZE - n + 1)$. Explain why linear probing does not satisfy this condition.

C H A P T E R   8

Graphs and their Applications

In this chapter, we consider a new data structure: the graph. We define some of the terms associated with graphs and show how to implement them in Java. We also present several applications of graphs.

8.1 GRAPHS

A **graph** consists of a set of **nodes** (or **vertices**) and a set of **arcs** (or **edges**). Each arc in a graph is specified by a pair of nodes. Figure 8.1.1a illustrates a graph. The set of nodes is {*A,B,C,D,E,F,G,H*}, and the set of arcs is {(*A,B*),(*A,D*),(*A,C*),(*C,D*),(*C,F*),(*E,G*), (*A,A*)}. If the pairs of nodes that make up the arcs are ordered pairs, then the graph is said to be a **directed graph** (or **digraph**). Figures 8.1.1b, c, and d illustrate three digraphs. The arrows between nodes represent arcs. The head of each arrow represents the second node in the ordered pair of nodes making up an arc, and the tail of each arrow represents the first node in the pair. The set of arcs for the graph in Figure 8.1.1b is {<*A,B*>, <*A,C*>, <*A,D*>, <*C,D*>, <*F,C*>, <*E,G*>, <*A,A*>}. We use parentheses to indicate an unordered pair and angle brackets to indicate an ordered pair. In the first three sections of this chapter, we restrict our attention to digraphs. We consider undirected graphs again in Section 8.4.

Note that a graph need not be a tree (Figure 8.1.1a, b, d) but that a tree must be a graph (Figure 8.1.1c). Note also that a node need not have any arcs associated with it (node *H* in Figures 8.1.1a and b).

A node *n* is **incident** to an arc *x* if *n* is one of the two nodes in the ordered pair of nodes that comprise *x*. (We also say that *x* is incident to *n*.) The **degree** of a node is the number of arcs incident to it. The **indegree** of a node *n* is the number of arcs that have *n* as the head, and the **outdegree** of *n* is the number of arcs that have *n* as the tail. For example, node *A* in Figure 8.1.1d has indegree 1, outdegree 2, and degree 3. A node *n* is **adjacent** to a node *m* if there is an arc from *m* to *n*. If *n* is adjacent to *m*, then *n* is called a **successor** of *m*, and *m* a **predecessor** of *n*.

A **relation** *R* on a set *A* is a set of ordered pairs of elements of *A*. For example, if *A* = {3,5,6,8,10,17}, the set *R* = {<3,10>, <5,6>, <5,8>, <6,17>, <8,17>, <10,17>} is a relation. If <*x,y*> is a member of a relation *R*, then *x* is said to be **related** to *y* in *R*.

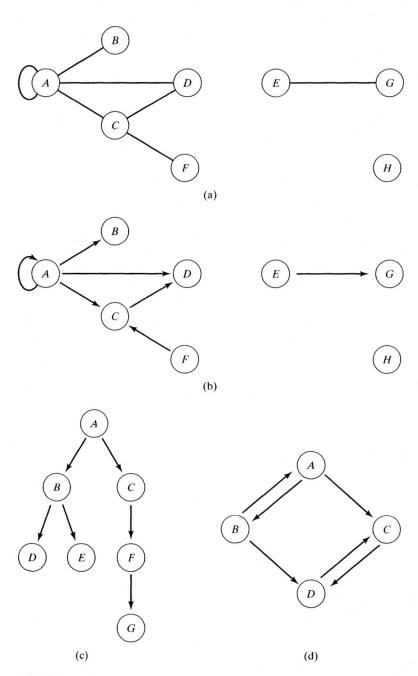

FIGURE 8.1.1   Examples of graphs.

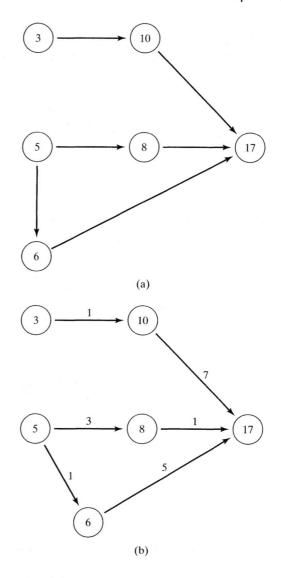

FIGURE 8.1.2 Relations and graphs.

(a)

(b)

The above relation R may be described by saying that x is related to y if x is less than y and the remainder obtained by dividing y by x is odd. $<8,17>$ is a member of this relation because 8 is smaller than 17 and the remainder on dividing 17 by 8 is 1, which is odd.

A relation may be represented by a graph in which the nodes represent the underlying set and the arcs represent the ordered pairs of the relation. Figure 8.1.2a illustrates a graph representing the above relation. A number may be associated with each arc of a graph, as in Figure 8.1.2b. In that figure, the number associated with each arc is the remainder obtained by dividing the integer at the head of the arc by the integer at the tail. Such a graph, in which a number is associated with each arc, is called a **weighted graph** or a **network**. The number associated with an arc is called its **weight**.

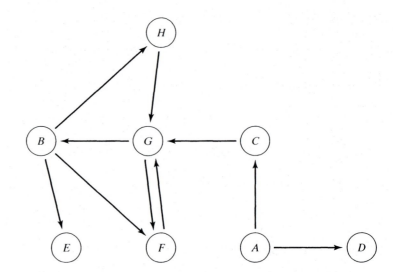

FIGURE 8.1.3

We identify several primitive operations that are useful in dealing with graphs. The operation *join(a,b)* adds an arc from node *a* to node *b* if one does not already exist. *joinWt(a,b,*x*)* adds an arc from *a* to *b* with weight *x* in a weighted graph. *remv(a,b)* and *remvWt(a,b,*x*)* remove an arc from *a* to *b* if one exists (*remvWt* also sets *x* to its weight). While we may also want to add or delete nodes from a graph, we postpone a discussion of these possibilities until a later section. The method *adjacent(a,b)* returns **true** if *b* is adjacent to *a*, and *false* otherwise.

A ***path of length k*** from node *a* to node *b* is defined as a sequence of $k + 1$ nodes $n_1, n_2, \ldots, n_{k+1}$ such that $n_1 = a$, $n_{k+1} = b$, and *adjacent*(n_i, n_{i+1}) is *true* for all *i* between 1 and *k*. If for some integer *k*, a path of length *k* exists between *a* and *b*, then there is a ***path*** from *a* to *b*. A path from a node to itself is called a ***cycle***. If a graph contains a cycle, it is ***cyclic***; otherwise it is ***acyclic***. A directed acyclic graph is called a ***dag*** from its acronym.

Consider the graph in Figure 8.1.3. There is a path of length 1 from *A* to *C*, two paths of length 2 from *B* to *G*, and a path of length 3 from *A* to *F*. There is no path from *B* to *C*. There are cycles from *B* to *B*, from *F* to *F*, and from *H* to *H*. Be sure that you can find all paths of length less than 9 and all cycles in the figure.

An Application of Graphs

We now consider an example. Assume one input line containing four integers followed by any number of input lines with two integers each. The first integer on the first line, *n*, represents a number of cities, which for simplicity are numbered from 0 to $n - 1$. The second and third integers on the line are between 0 and $n - 1$ and represent two cities. It is desired to travel from the first city to the second using exactly *nr* roads, where *nr* is the fourth integer on the first input line. Each subsequent input line contains two integers representing two cities, indicating that there is a road from the first city to the second. The problem is to determine whether there is a path of the required length by which one can travel from the first of the given cities to the second.

A plan for a solution follows: Create a graph with the cities as nodes and the roads as arcs. To find a path of length *nr* from node *A* to node *B*, look for a node *C* such that an arc exists from *A* to *C* and a path of length $nr - 1$ exists from *C* to *B*. If these conditions are satisfied for some node *C*, then the desired path exists. If the conditions are not satisfied for any node *C*, then the desired path does not exist. The algorithm uses an auxiliary recursive method *findPath(k,a,b)* whose algorithm we also present below. This method returns **true** if there is a path of length *k* from *A* to *B*, and **false** otherwise. The algorithms for the application and the method follow:

```
n = readInt();          // number of cities
create n nodes and label them from 0 to n - 1;
//seek path from a to b
a = readInt();
b = readInt();
nr = readInt();         // desired number of roads to take
while (there are more cities to process) {
    city1 = readInt();
    city2 = readInt();
    join(city1, city2);
}
if (findPath(nr, a, b))
      System.out.println("a path exists from" + a + "to" + b + "in" +
      nr + "steps");
else
    System.out.println("no path exists from" + a + "to" + b + "in" +
    nr + "steps");
```

The algorithm for the method *findPath(k, a, b)* follows:

```
if (k == 1)
    // search for a path of length 1
    return adjacent(a, b);
// determine if there is a path through c
for (c = 0; c < n; ++c)
    if (adjacent(a, c) && findPath(k-1, c, b))
            return true;
return false;           // assume no path exists
```

While the above algorithm is a solution to the problem, it has several deficiencies. Many paths are investigated several times during the recursive process. Also, while the algorithm must actually check each possible path, the final result merely ascertains whether a desired path exists, it does not produce the path itself. More likely than not, it is desirable to find the arcs of the path in addition to knowing whether or not a path exists. Finally, the algorithm does not test for the existence of a path regardless of length; it only tests for a path of specific length. We explore solutions to some of these problems later in this chapter and in the exercises.

Java Representation of Graphs

Let us now turn to the question of representing graphs in Java. Suppose that the number of nodes in the graph is constant; that is, arcs may be added or deleted, but nodes may not. A graph with fifty nodes could then be declared as follows:

```java
class Node {
    // information associated with each node
}

class Arc {
    private boolean adj;
    // information associated with each arc
}

class Graph {
    static final int MAXNODES = 50;    // package scope
    private Node nodes[ ];
    private Arc arc[ ][ ];
}
```

Each node of the graph is represented by an integer between 0 and MAXNODES-1, and the array *nodes* represents the appropriate information assigned to each node. The member *arcs* is a two-dimensional array representing every possible ordered pair of nodes. The value of *arc[i][j].adj* is either **true** or **false** depending upon whether or not node *j* is adjacent to node *i*. The two-dimensional array *adj* is called an **adjacency matrix**. In the case of a weighted graph, each arc can also be assigned information.

The nodes of a graph are often numbered from 0 to MAXNODES-1 and no information is assigned to them. Also, we may be interested in the existence of arcs but not in weights or any other information about them. In such cases the graph could be declared simply by:

```java
public class Graph {
    private static final int MAXNODES = 50;
    private boolean adj[][];    // the adjacency matrix

    public Graph() {
        adj = new boolean [MAXNODES][MAXNODES];

        // initially no nodes are adjacent to each other
        for (int i = 0; i < MAXNODES; i++)
          for (int j = 0; j < MAXNODES; j++)
                adj[i][j] = false;
    } // end Graph constructor

                    ...                    // other Graph methods
} // end Graph class
```

In effect, the graph is totally described by its adjacency matrix. We present the code for the primitive operations described above in the case where a graph is described by its adjacency matrix.

```
public void join(int node1, int node2) {
  // add an arc from node1 to node2
  adj[node1][node2] = true;
} // end join

public void remove(int node1, int node2) {
  // delete arc from node1 to node2 if one exists
  adj[node1][node2] = false;
} // end remove

boolean adjacent(int node1, int node2) {
  return ((adj[node1][node2] == true) ? true: false);
} // end adjacent
```

A weighted graph class, *Wgraph*, with a fixed number of nodes may be declared by first defining a class *Arc* which associates a weight with each.

```
public class Arc {
    private boolean adj;
    private int weight;

    // default constructor
    public Arc() {
            adj = false;
            weight = 0;
    } // end constructor

    public Arc(boolean adj, int weight) {
            this.adj = adj;
            this.weight = weight;
    } // end constructor

    public boolean getAdj(){
            return adj;
    } // end getAdj

    public void setAdj(boolean adj){
            this.adj = adj;
    } // end setAdj

    public int getWeight(){
            return weight;
    } // end getWeight

    public void setWeight(int weight){
            this.weight = weight;
    } // end setWeight
} // end Arc class

public class Wgraph {
  private static final int MAXNODES = 50;
  private Arc g[][];                // the adjacency matrix
```

```
public WGraph() {
    g = new Arc[MAXNODES][MAXNODES];
    for (int i = 0; i < MAXNODES; i++)
        for (int j = 0; j < MAXNODES; j++)
            g[i][j] = new Arc();
} // end Wgraph constructor

public void joinWt(int node1, int node2, int wt) {
    g[node1][node2].setAdj(true);
    g[node1][node2].setWeight(wt);
} // end join

public boolean adjacent(int node1, int node2) {
    return g[node1][node2].getAdj();
} // end adjacent

            ...                 // other WGraph methods
} // end WGraph class
```

The method *joinWt* adds an arc from *node*1 to *node*2 with a given weight *wt*, and the method *adjacent* determines whether *node*1 is adjacent to *node*2. The method *remvWt* is left to the reader as an exercise.

Transitive Closure

Let us assume that a graph is completely described by its adjacency matrix, *adj* (i.e., no data is associated with the nodes and the graph is not weighted). Consider the logical expression $adj[i][k]$ && $adj[k][j]$. Its value is *true* if and only if the values of both $adj[i][k]$ and $adj[k][j]$ are *true*, which implies that there is an arc from node i to node k and an arc from node k to node j. Thus $adj[i][k]$ && $adj[k][j]$ equals *true* if and only if there is a path of length 2 from i to j passing through k.

Now consider the expression

```
(adj[i][0]  &&  adj[0][j])  ||  (adj[i][1]  &&  adj[1][j])  || ... ||
            (adj[i][MAXNODES - 1]  &&  adj[MAXNODES - 1][j])
```

The value of this expression is *true* only if there is a path of length 2 from node i to node j either through node 0 or through node 1, ..., or through node $MAXNODES$ - 1. This is the same as saying that the expression evaluates to *true* if and only if there is some path of length 2 from node i to node j.

Consider an array adj_2 such that $adj_2[i][j]$ is the value of the above expression. adj_2 is called the **path matrix of length 2**. $adj_2[i][j]$ indicates whether or not there is a path of length 2 between i and j. (If you are familiar with matrix multiplication, you should realize that adj_2 is the product of *adj* with itself, with numerical multiplication replaced by conjunction (the && operation) and addition replaced by disjunction (the || operation).) adj_2 is said to be the **Boolean product** of *adj* with itself.

Figure 8.1.4 illustrates this process. Figure 8.1.4a depicts a graph and its adjacency matrix in which *true* is represented by 1 and *false* is represented by 0. Figure 8.1.4b is the Boolean product of the matrix with itself, and thus is the path matrix of length 2 for the graph. Convince yourself that a 1 appears in row i column j of the matrix in Figure 8.1.4b if and only if there is a path of length 2 from node i to node j in the graph.

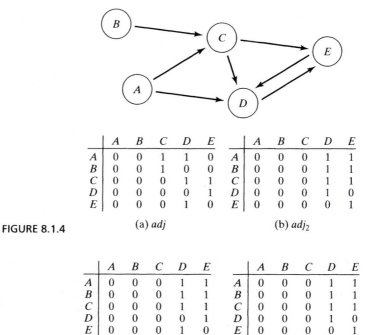

	A	B	C	D	E			A	B	C	D	E
A	0	0	1	1	0		A	0	0	0	1	1
B	0	0	1	0	0		B	0	0	0	1	1
C	0	0	0	1	1		C	0	0	0	1	1
D	0	0	0	0	1		D	0	0	0	1	0
E	0	0	0	1	0		E	0	0	0	0	1

FIGURE 8.1.4   (a) *adj*   (b) *adj$_2$*

	A	B	C	D	E			A	B	C	D	E
A	0	0	0	1	1		A	0	0	0	1	1
B	0	0	0	1	1		B	0	0	0	1	1
C	0	0	0	1	1		C	0	0	0	1	1
D	0	0	0	0	1		D	0	0	0	1	0
E	0	0	0	1	0		E	0	0	0	0	1

FIGURE 8.1.5   (a) *adj$_3$*   (b) *adj$_4$*

Similarly, define *adj$_3$*, the path matrix of length 3, as the Boolean product of *adj$_2$* with *adj*. *adj$_3$* [i][j] equals *true* if and only if there is a path of length 3 from *i* to *j*. In general, to compute the path matrix of length *l*, form the Boolean product of the path matrix of length *l* − 1 with the adjacency matrix. Figure 8.1.5 illustrates the matrices *adj$_3$* and *adj$_4$* of the graph in Figure 8.1.4a.

Assume we want to know whether a path of length 3 or less exists between two nodes of a graph. If such a path exists between nodes *i* and *j*, then it must be of length 1, 2, or 3. If there is a path of length 3 or less between nodes *i* and *j*, then the value of

```
adj[i][j]  ||  adj₂ [i][j]  ||  adj₃ [i][j]
```

must be *true*. Figure 8.1.6 shows the matrix formed by "or-ing" the matrices *adj, adj$_2$*, and *adj$_3$*. This matrix contains the value *true* (represented by the value 1 in the figure) in row *i* column *j* if and only if there is a path of length 3 or less from node *i* to node *j*.

Suppose we wish to construct a matrix *path* such that *path*[i][j] is *true* if and only if there is a path from node *i* to node *j* (of any length). Clearly,

```
path[i][j]  ==  adj[i][j]  ||  adj₂ [i][j]  ||  ...
```

	A	B	C	D	E
A	0	0	1	1	1
B	0	0	1	1	1
C	0	0	0	1	1
D	0	0	0	1	1
E	0	0	0	1	1

FIGURE 8.1.6

	A	B	C	D	E
A	0	0	1	1	1
B	0	0	1	1	1
C	0	0	0	1	1
D	0	0	0	1	1
E	0	0	0	1	1

FIGURE 8.1.7

path = adj or adj$_2$ or adj$_3$ or adj$_4$ or adj$_5$.

However, the above equation cannot be used in computing *path* because the process that it describes is an infinite one. However, if the graph has *n* nodes, it must true that

$$path[i][j] \ == \ adj[i][j] \ || \ adj_2 \ [i][j] \ || \ ... \ || \ adj_n[i][j].$$

This is because if there is a path of length $m > n$ from *i* to *j*, such as $i, i_2, i_3, \ldots, i_m, j$, then there must be another path from *i* to *j* of length less than or equal to *n*. To see this, note that since there are only *n* nodes in the graph, at least one node *k* must appear in the path twice. The path from *i* to *j* can be shortened by removing the cycle from *k* to *k*. This process is repeated until no two nodes in the path (except possibly *i* and *j*) are equal, and therefore the path is of length *n* or less. Figure 8.1.7 illustrates the matrix *path* for the graph in Figure 8.1.4a. The matrix *path* is often called the ***transitive closure*** of the matrix *adj*.

We may write a Java method that accepts an adjacency matrix *adj* and computes its transitive closure *path*. This method uses an auxiliary method *prod(a,b,c)*, which sets the array *c* equal to the Boolean product of *a* and *b*.

```java
public class TransitiveClosure {
    public static void transClose(boolean adj[][], boolean path[][],
                                                   int MAXNODES) {
        boolean newprod[][] = new boolean[MAXNODES][MAXNODES];
        boolean adjprod[][] = new boolean[MAXNODES][MAXNODES];

        for (int i = 0; i < MAXNODES; i++)
            for (int j = 0; j < MAXNODES; j++)
                adjprod[i][j] = path[i][j] = adj[i][j];
        for (int i = 1; i < MAXNODES; i++) {
            // i represents the number of times adj has been
            // multiplied by itself to obtain adjprod.  At this
            // point path represents all paths of length i or less.
            prod(adjprod, adj, newprod, MAXNODES);
            for (int j = 0; j < MAXNODES; j++)
                for (int k = 0; k < MAXNODES; k++)
                    path[j][k] = path[j][k] || newprod[j][k];
            for (int j = 0; j < MAXNODES; j++)
                for (int k = 0; k < MAXNODES; k++)
                    adjprod[j][k] = newprod[j][k];
        } // end for
    } // end transClose
    public static void prod(boolean a[][], boolean b[][],
    boolean c[][], int MAXNODES) {
```

```
            boolean val = false;

            for (int i = 0; i < MAXNODES; i++)          // pass through rows
                    for (int j = 0; j < MAXNODES; j++) {    // pass through columns
                        val = false;
                        for (int k = 0; k < MAXNODES; k++)
                                val = val || (a[i][k] && b[k][j]);
                        c[i][j] = val;
                } // end for j
        } // end prod
    } // end TransitiveClosure class
```

To analyze the efficiency (or inefficiency) of this routine, note that finding the Boolean product by the method we have presented is $O(n^3)$, where n is the number of graph nodes (i.e., *MAXNODES*). In *transclose*, this process (the call to *prod*) is embedded in a loop that is repeated $n - 1$ times, so the entire transitive closure routine is $O(n^4)$.

Warshall's Algorithm

The foregoing method is quite inefficient. Let us see if a more efficient method to compute *path* can be produced. Let us define the matrix $path_k$ such that $path_k[i][j]$ is **true** if and only if there is a path from node i to node j that does not pass through any nodes numbered higher than k (except, possibly, for i and j themselves). How can the value of $path_{k+1}[i][j]$ be obtained from $path_k$? Clearly, for any i and j such that $path_k[i][j] =$ **true**, $path_{k+1}[i][j]$ must be **true** (why?). The only situation in which $path_{k+1}[i][j]$ can be **true** while $path_k[i][j]$ equals **false** is if there is a path from i to j passing through node $k + 1$, but there is no path from i to j passing through only nodes 1 through k. But this means that there must be a path from i to $k + 1$ passing through only nodes 1 through k, and a similar path from $k + 1$ to j. Thus $path_{k+1}[i][j]$ equals **true** if and only if one of the following two conditions holds:

1. $path_k[i][j]$ == **true**
2. $path_k[i][k + 1]$ == **true** and $path_k[k + 1][j]$ == **true**.

This means that $path_{k+1}[i][j]$ equals $path_k[i][j] \,||\, (path_k[i][k + 1] \,\&\&\, path_k[k + 1][j])$. An algorithm to obtain the matrix $path_k$ from the matrix $path_{k-1}$ based on this observation follows:

```
    for (i = 0; i < MAXNODES; ++i)
        for (j = 0; j < MAXNODES; ++j)
            pathₖ[i][j] = pathₖ₋₁[i][j] || (pathₖ₋₁[i][k] && pathₖ₋₁[k][j]);
```

This may be logically simplified and made more efficient as follows:

```
    for (i = 0; i < MAXNODES; ++i)
        for (j = 0; j < MAXNODES; ++j)
```

$$path_k[i][j] = path_{k-1}[i][j];$$
```
for (i = 0; i < MAXNODES; ++i)
    if (path_{k-1}[i][k] == true)
        for (j = 0; j < MAXNODES; ++j)
            path_k[i][j] = path_{k-1}[i][j] || path_{k-1}[k][j];
```

Clearly, $path_0[i][j] = adj$, since the only way to go from node i to node j without passing through any other nodes is to go directly from i to j. Further, $path_{MAXNODES-1}[i][j] = path[i][j]$, since if a path may pass through any nodes numbered from 0 to $MAXNODES - 1$, then any path from node i to node j may be selected. The following Java method may therefore be used to compute the transitive closure:

```
public class Warshall {
    public static void transClose(boolean adj[ ][ ], boolean path[ ][ ],
                                  int MAXNODES) {
        for (int i = 0; i < MAXNODES; i++)
            for(int j = 0; j < MAXNODES; j++)
                path[i][j] = adj[i][j];            // path starts off
                                                   // as adj
        for (int k = 0; k < MAXNODES; k++)
            for (int i = 0; i < MAXNODES; i++)
                if (path[i][k])
                    for (int j = 0; j < MAXNODES; j++)
                        path[i][j] = path[i][j] || path[k][j];
    } // end transClose
}
```

This technique increases the efficiency of finding the transitive closure to $O(n^3)$. The method is often called ***Warshall's algorithm***, after its discoverer.

Shortest-Path Algorithm

In a weighted graph, or network, it is frequently desired to find the shortest path between two nodes, s and t. The shortest path is defined as a path from s to t such that the sum of the weights of the arcs on the path is minimized. To represent the network, we assume a weight function, such that $weight(i,j)$ is the weight of the arc from i to j. If there is no arc from i to j, then $weight(i,j)$ is set to an arbitrarily large value to indicate the infinite cost (i.e., the impossibility) of going directly from i to j.

If all the weights are positive, the following algorithm, due to Dijkstra, determines the shortest path from s to t. Let the variable *infinity* hold the largest possible integer. *distance*[i] keeps the cost of the shortest path known thus far from s to i. Initially, *distance*[s] = 0, and *distance*[i] = *infinity* for all $i! = s$. A set *perm* contains all the nodes whose minimal distance from s is known; that is, those nodes whose distance value is permanent and will not change. If a node i is a member of *perm*, then *distance*[i] is the minimal distance from s to i. Initially, the only member of *perm* is s. Once t becomes a member of *perm*, *distance*[t] is known to be the shortest distance from s to t, and the algorithm terminates.

The algorithm maintains a variable, *current*, which is the node added to *perm* most recently. Initially, *current* = *s*. Whenever a node *current* is added to *perm*, *distance* must be recomputed for all successors of *current*. For every successor *i* of *current*, if *distance*[*current*] + *weight*(*current*,*i*) is less than *distance*[*i*], the distance from *s* to *i* through *current* is smaller than any other distance from *s* to *i* found thus far. Thus *distance*[*i*] must be reset to this smaller value.

Once distance has been recomputed for every successor of *current*, then *distance*[*j*] (for any *j*) represents the shortest path from *s* to *j* that includes only members of *perm* (except for *j* itself). This means that for the node *k*, not in *perm*, for which *distance*[*k*] is smallest, there is no path from *s* to *k* whose length is shorter than *distance*[*k*]. (*distance*[*k*] is already the shortest distance to *k* that includes only nodes in *perm*, and any path to *k* that includes a node *nd* as its first node not in *perm* must be longer, since *distance*[*nd*] is greater than *distance*[*k*].) Thus *k* can be added to *perm*. *current* is then reset to *k*, and the process is repeated.

The following is a Java method to implement this algorithm. In addition to calculating distances, the program finds the shortest path itself by maintaining an array *precede* such that *precede*[*i*] is the node that precedes node *i* on the shortest path found thus far. An array *perm* is used to keep track of the corresponding set. *perm*[*i*] is 1 if *i* is a member of the set, and 0 if not. The routine accepts a weight matrix (with nonadjacent arcs having a weight of *infinity*) and two nodes, *s* and *t*, and calculates the minimum distance *d* from *s* to *t* as well as the array *precede* to define the path. The routine assumes the following definitions and declarations:

```java
public class ShortestPath {
    public static int shortPath(Arc weight[ ][ ], int numNodes, int s,
    int t, int precede[ ]) {
        final int INFINITY = Integer.MAX_VALUE;
        final int MAXNODES = numNodes;
        final boolean MEMBER = true;
        final boolean NONMEMBER = false;

        int distance[ ] = new int[MAXNODES];
        boolean perm[ ] = new boolean[MAXNODES];
        int current = 0, k = 0, dc = 0;
        int smallDist = 0, newDist = 0;

        // initialization
        for (int i = 0; i < MAXNODES; i++) {
            perm[i] = NONMEMBER;
            distance[i] = INFINITY;
        }
        perm[s] = MEMBER;
        distance[s] = 0;
        current = s;
        while (current != t) {
                smallDist = INFINITY;
                dc = distance[current];
```

```
for (int i = 0; i < MAXNODES; i++)
    if (perm[i] == NONMEMBER){
        // if either dc or weight[current][i] is
        // INFINITY, the result should also be INFINITY
        if (dc == Integer.MAX_VALUE ||
                weight[current][i].getWeight() ==
                Integer.MAX_VALUE)
            newDist = Integer.MAX_VALUE;
        else
            newDist = dc +
            weight[current][i].getWeight();
        // if newDist is negative, overflow must
        // have occurred
        if (newDist < 0)
            newDist = INFINITY;
        if (newDist < distance[i]) {
            // distance from s to i through current
            // is smaller than distance[i]
            distance[i] = newDist;
            precede[i] = current;
        }
        // determine the smallest distance
        if (distance[i] < smallDist) {
            smallDist = distance[i];
            k = i;
        }
    } // end for … if
    current = k;
    perm[current] = MEMBER;
} // end while
return distance[t];
} // end shortPath
} // end ShortestPath class
```

An alternative implementation that maintains the set of "permanent" nodes as a linked list instead of the array *perm* is left as an exercise for the reader.

Assuming that a method *all*(x) has been defined to return **true** if every element of array x is 1 and **false** otherwise, then Dijkstra's algorithm can be modified to find the shortest path from a node s to every other node in the graph by modifying the **while** header to

```
while (all(perm) == false)
```

To analyze the efficiency of this implementation of Dijkstra's algorithm, note that one node is added to *perm* in each iteration of the **while** loop, so that, potentially, the loop must be repeated n times (where $n = MAXNODES$, the number of nodes in the graph). Each iteration involves examining every node [**for** $(i = 0; I < MAXNODES; ++i)$], so the entire algorithm is $O(n^2)$. We examine a more efficient implementation of Dijkstra's algorithm in Section 8.3.

EXERCISES

8.1.1   For the graph in Figure 8.1.1b:

  a. Find its adjacency matrix.

  b. Find its path matrix using powers of the adjacency matrix.

  c. Find its path matrix using Warshall's algorithm.

8.1.2   Draw a digraph to correspond to each of the following relations on the integers from 1 to 12:

  a. x is related to y if $x - y$ is evenly divisible by 3.

  b. x is related to y if $x + 10*y < x*y$.

  c. x is related to y if the remainder on division of x by y is 2.

  Compute the adjacency and path matrices for each of these relations.

8.1.3   A node $n1$ is **reachable** from a node $n2$ in a graph if $n1$ equals $n2$ or there is a path from $n2$ to $n1$. Write a Java method $reach(adj,i,j)$ that accepts an adjacency matrix and two integers and determines whether the jth node in the digraph is reachable from the ith node.

8.1.4   Write Java methods which, given an adjacency matrix and two nodes of a graph, compute:

  a. The number of paths of a given length existing between them.

  b. The total number of paths existing between them.

8.1.5   A relation on a set S (and its corresponding digraph) is **symmetric** if for any two elements x and y in S such that x is related to y, y is also related to x.

  a. What must be true of a digraph if it represents a symmetric relation?

  b. Give an example of a symmetric relation and draw its digraph.

  c. What must be true of the adjacency matrix of a symmetric digraph?

  d. Write a Java method that accepts an adjacency matrix and determines whether the digraph it represents is symmetric.

8.1.6   A relation on a set S (and its corresponding digraph and adjacency matrix) is **transitive** if for any three elements x, y, and z in S, if x is related to y, and y is related to z, then x is related to z.

  a. What must be true of a digraph if it represents a transitive relation?

  b. Give an example of a transitive relation and draw its digraph.

  c. What must be true of the Boolean product of the adjacency matrix of a transitive digraph with itself?

  d. Write a Java method that accepts an adjacency matrix and determines whether the digraph it represents is transitive.

  e. Prove that the transitive closure of any digraph is transitive.

  f. Prove that the smallest transitive digraph that includes all the nodes and arcs of a given digraph is the transitive closure of that digraph.

8.1.7   Given a digraph, prove that it is possible to renumber its nodes so that the resultant adjacency matrix is lower triangular (see Exercise 1.2.8) if and only if the digraph is acyclic. Write a Java method $lowTri(adj,ltadj,perm)$ that accepts an adjacency matrix *adj* of an acyclic graph and creates a lower triangular adjacency matrix *ltadj* that represents the same graph. *perm* is a one-dimensional array such that *perm*[*i*] is set to the new number assigned to the node that was numbered *i* in the matrix *adj*.

8.1.8   Rewrite the method *shortPath* to implement the set of "permanent" nodes as a linked list. Show that the efficiency of the method remains $O(n^2)$.

8.2   FLOW PROBLEM

In this section we consider a real-world problem and illustrate a solution that uses a weighted graph. There are a number of formulations of this problem whose solutions carry over to a wide range of applications. We present one such formulation here and refer the reader to the literature for alternative versions.

Assume a water pipe system as in Figure 8.2.1a. Each arc represents a pipe, and the number above each arc represents the capacity of that pipe in gallons per minute. The nodes represent points at which pipes are joined and water is transferred from one pipe to another. Two nodes, *S* and *T*, are designated as a **source** of water and a **user** of water (or a **sink**) respectively. This means that water originating at *S* must be carried through the pipe system to *T*. Water may flow through a pipe in only one direction (pressure-sensitive valves may be used to prevent water from flowing backwards), and there are no pipes entering *S* or leaving *T*. Thus, a weighted directed graph, as in Figure 8.2.1a, is an ideal data structure to model the situation.

We would like to maximize the amount of water flowing from the source to the sink. Although the source may be able to produce water at a prodigious rate, and the sink may be able to consume water at a comparable rate, the pipe system may not have the capacity to carry it all from the source to the sink. Thus the limiting factor of the entire system is the pipe capacity. Many other real-world problems are similar in nature. The system could be an electrical network, a railway system, a communications network, or any other distribution system in which one wants to maximize the amount of an item being delivered from one point to another.

Define a **capacity function**, *c*(*a*,*b*), where *a* and *b* are nodes, as follows: If *adjacent*(*a*,*b*) is **true** (i.e., if there is a pipe from *a* to *b*), then *c*(*a*,*b*) is the capacity of the pipe from *a* to *b*. If there is no pipe from *a* to *b*, then *c*(*a*,*b*) = 0. At any point in the operation of the system, a given amount of water (possibly 0) flows through each pipe. Define a **flow function**, *f*(*a*,*b*), where *a* and *b* are nodes, as 0 if *b* is not adjacent to *a*, and as the amount of water flowing through the pipe from *a* to *b* otherwise. Clearly, $f(a,b) >= 0$ for all nodes *a* and *b*. Furthermore, $f(a,b) <= c(a,b)$ for all nodes *a* and *b*, since a pipe may not carry more water than its capacity. Let *v* be the amount of water that flows through the system from *S* to *T*. Then the amount of water leaving *S* through all pipes equals the amount of water entering *T* through all pipes, and both these amounts equal *v*. This can be stated by the equality:

$$\sum_{x \in nodes} f(S, x) = v = \sum_{x \in nodes} f(x, T)$$

No node other than *S* can produce water, and no node other than *T* can absorb water.

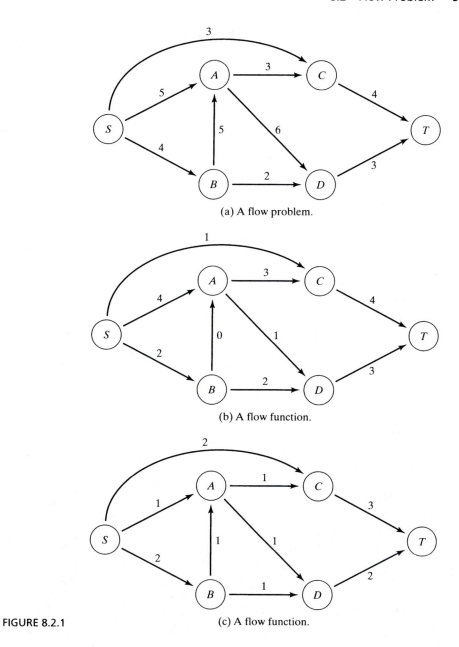

(a) A flow problem.

(b) A flow function.

FIGURE 8.2.1   (c) A flow function.

Thus the amount of water leaving any node other than S or T is equal to the amount of water entering that node. This can be stated by:

$$\sum_{y \in nodes} f(x, y) = \sum_{y \in nodes} f(y, x) \text{ for all nodes } x \mathrel{!=} S, T$$

Define the ***inflow*** of a node x as the total flow entering x, and the ***outflow*** as the total flow leaving x. The foregoing conditions may be rewritten as

$$outflow(S) = inflow(T) = v$$
$$inflow(x) = outflow(x) \text{ for all } x \mathrel{!=} S, T$$

Several flow functions may exist for a given graph and capacity function. Figures 8.2.1b and c illustrate two possible flow functions for the graph in Figure 8.2.1a. Make sure that you understand why both of them are valid flow functions, and why both satisfy the above equations and inequalities.

We wish to find a flow function that maximizes the value of v, the amount of water going from S to T. Such a flow function is called ***optimal***. Clearly, the flow function in Figure 8.2.1b is better than the one in Figure 8.2.1c, since v equals 7 in the former but only 5 in the latter. See if you can find a flow function which is better than the one in Figure 8.2.1b.

One valid flow function can be achieved by setting $f(a,b)$ to 0 for all nodes a and b. Of course this flow function is least optimal because no water flows from S to T. Given a flow function, it can be improved so that the flow from S to T is increased. However, the improved version must satisfy all the conditions for a valid flow function. In particular, if the flow entering any node (except for S or T) is increased or decreased, the flow leaving that node must be increased or decreased correspondingly. The strategy for producing an optimal flow function is to begin with the zero flow function and improve upon it successively until an optimal flow function is produced.

Improving a Flow Function

Given a flow function f, there are two ways to improve upon it. One way consists of finding a path $S = x_1, x_2, \ldots, x_n = T$ from S to T such that the flow along each arc in the path is strictly less than the capacity (i.e., $f(x_{k-1}, x_k) < c(x_{k-1}, x_k)$ for all k between 1 and $n - 1$). The flow can be increased on each arc in such a path by the minimum value of $c(x_{k-1}, x_k) - f(x_{k-1}, x_k)$ for all k between 1 and $n - 1$ (so that when the flow has been increased along the entire path, there is at least one arc $<x_{k-1}, x_k>$ in the path for which $f(x_{k-1}, x_k) = c(x_{k-1}, x_k)$ and through which the flow may not be increased).

This may be illustrated by the graph in Figure 8.2.2a, which gives the capacity and the current flow respectively for each arc. There are two paths from S to T with positive flow $((S,A,C,T)$ and $(S,B,D,T))$. However, each of these paths contains one arc $(<A,C>$ and $<B,D>)$ in which the flow equals the capacity. Thus the flow along these paths may not be improved. However, the path (S,A,D,T) is such that the capacity of each arc in the path is greater than its current flow. The maximum amount by which the flow can be increased along this path is 1, since the flow along arc $<D,T>$ cannot exceed 3. The resulting flow function is shown in Figure 8.2.2b. The total flow from S to T has been increased from 5 to 6. To see that the result is still a valid flow function, note that for each node (except T) whose inflow is increased, the outflow is increased by the same amount.

Are there any other paths whose flow can be improved? In this example, you should satisfy yourself that there are not. However, given the graph in Figure 8.2.2a, we

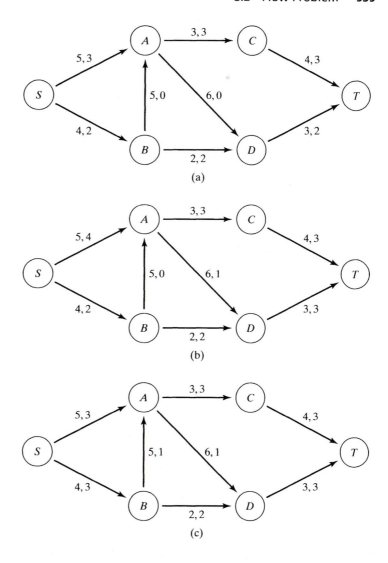

FIGURE 8.2.2 Increasing the flow
in a graph.

could have chosen to improve the path (S,B,A,D,T). The resulting flow function is
illustrated in Figure 8.2.2c. This function also provides for a net flow of 6 from S to
T and is therefore neither better nor worse than the flow function in Figure 8.2.2b.

Even if there is no path whose flow can be improved, there may be another
method of improving the net flow from the source to the sink. This is illustrated by
Figure 8.2.3. In Figure 8.2.3a there is no path from S to T whose flow may be improved.
But if the flow from X to Y is reduced, the flow from X to T can be increased. To com-
pensate for the decrease in the inflow of Y, the flow from S to Y could be increased,
thereby increasing the net flow from S to T. The flow from X to Y can be redirected to
T, as shown in Figure 8.2.3b, and the net flow from S to T can thereby be increased
from 4 to 7.

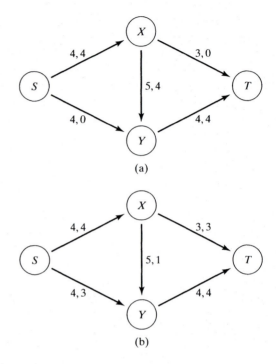

FIGURE 8.2.3 Increasing flow in a graph.

We may generalize this second method as follows. Suppose there is a path from S to some node Y, a path from some node X to T, and a path from X to Y with positive flow. Then the flow along the path from X to Y may be reduced, and the flows from X to T and from S to Y may be increased by the same amount. This amount is the minimum of the flow from X to Y and the differences between capacity and flow in the paths from S to Y and X to T.

These two methods may be combined by proceeding through the graph from S to T, as follows: The amount of water emanating from S toward T can be increased by any amount (since we have assumed no limit on the amount that can be produced by the source) only if the pipes from S to T can carry the increase. Suppose the pipe capacity from S to x allows the amount of water entering x to be increased by an amount a. If the pipe capacity to carry the increase from x to T exists, then the increase can be made. Then, if a node y is adjacent to x (i.e., there is an arc $<x,y>$), the amount of water emanating from y toward T can be increased by the minimum of a and the unused capacity of arc $<x,y>$. This is an application of the first method. Similarly, if node x is adjacent to some node y (i.e., there is an arc $<y,x>$), then the amount of water emanating from y toward T can be increased by the minimum of a and the existing flow from y to x. This can be done by reducing the flow from y to x, as in the second method. Proceeding in this fashion from S to T, the amount by which the flow to T may be increased can be determined.

Define a **semipath** from S to T as a sequence of nodes $S = x_1, x_2, \ldots, x_n = T$ such that, for all $0 < i < = n - 1$, either $<x_{i-1}, x_i>$ or $<x_i, x_{i-1}>$ is an arc. Using the above technique, we may describe an algorithm to discover a semipath from S to T

such that the flow to each node in the semipath may be increased. This is done by building upon already discovered partial semipaths from S. If the last node in a discovered partial semipath from S is a, the algorithm considers extending it to any node b such that either $<a,b>$ or $<b,a>$ is an arc. The partial semipath is extended to b only if the extension can be made in such a way that the inflow to b can be increased. Once a partial semipath has been extended to a node b, that node is removed from consideration as an extension of some other partial semipath. (This is because at this point we are trying to discover a single semipath from S to T.) The algorithm, of course, keeps track of the amount by which the inflow to b may be increased and whether its increase is due to consideration of the arc $<a,b>$ or $<b,a>$.

This process continues until some partial semipath from S has been completed by extending it to T. The algorithm then proceeds backwards along the semipath, adjusting all flows until S is reached. (This will be illustrated shortly with an example.) The entire process is then repeated in an attempt to discover yet another semipath from S to T. If no partial semipath may be successfully extended, then the flow cannot be increased and the existing flow is optimal. (You are asked to prove this as an exercise.)

Example

Let us illustrate this process with an example. Consider the arcs and capacities of the weighted graph in Figure 8.2.4. We begin by assuming a flow of 0 and attempt to discover an optimal flow. Figure 8.2.4a illustrates the initial situation. The two numbers above each arc represent the capacity and current flow respectively. We may extend a semipath from S to (S,X) and (S,Z) respectively. The flow from S to X may be increased by 4, and the flow from S to Z may be increased by 6. The semipath (S,X) may be extended to (S,X,W) and (S,X,Y) with corresponding increases of flow to W and Y of 3 and 4 respectively. The semipath (S,X,Y) may be extended to (S,X,Y,T) with an increase of flow to T of 4. (Note that at this point we could have chosen to extend (S,X,W) to (S,X,W,T). Similarly we could have extended (S,Z) to (S,Z,Y) rather than (S,X) to (S,X,W) and (S,X,Y). These decisions are arbitrary.)

Since we have reached T by the semipath (S,X,Y,T) with a net increase of 4, we increase the flow along each forward arc of the semipath by this amount. The results are depicted in Figure 8.2.4b.

We now repeat the above process with the flow in Figure 8.2.4b. (S) may only be extended to (S,Z) because the flow in arc $<S,X>$ is already at capacity. The net increase to Z through this semipath is 6. (S,Z) may be extended to (S,Z,Y), yielding a net increase of 4 to Y. (S,Z,Y) cannot be extended to (S,Z,Y,T) because the flow in arc $<Y,T>$ is at capacity. However, it can be extended to (S,Z,Y,X) with a net increase to node X of 4. Note that since this semipath includes a backwards arc $<Y,X>$, it implies a reduction in the flow from X to Y of 4. The semipath (S,Z,Y,X) may be extended to (S,Z,Y,X,W) with a net increase of 3 (the unused capacity of $<X,W>$) to W. This semipath may then be extended to (S,Z,Y,X,W,T) with a net increase of 3 in the flow to T. Since we have reached T with an increase of 3, we proceed backwards along this semipath. Since $<W,T>$ and $<X,W>$ are forward arcs, their flows may each be increased by 3. Since $<Y,X>$ is a backwards arc, the flow along $<X,Y>$ is reduced by 3. Since $<Z,Y>$ and $<S,Z>$ are forward arcs, their flows may be increased by 3. This results in the flow shown in Figure 8.2.4c.

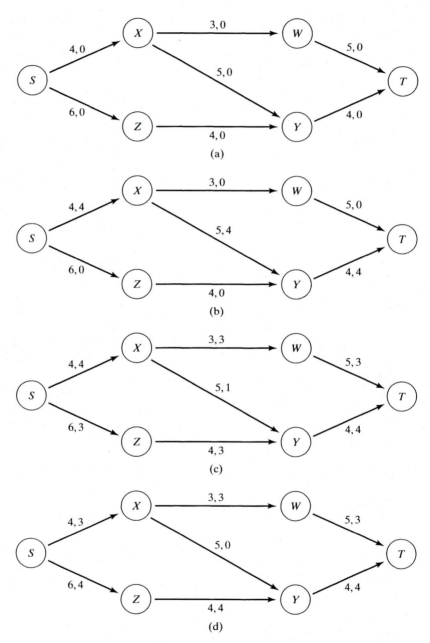

FIGURE 8.2.4 Producing an optimum flow.

We then attempt to repeat the process. (S) may be extended to (S,Z) with an increase of 3 to Z, (S,Z) may be extended to (S,Z,Y) with an increase of 1 to Y, and (S,Z,Y) may be extended to (S,Z,Y,X) with an increase of 1 to X. However, since arcs $<S,X>$, $<Y,T>$, and $<X,W>$ are at capacity, no semipath may be extended further and an optimum flow has been found. Note that this optimum flow need not be unique.

Figure 8.2.4d illustrates another optimum flow for the same graph which was obtained from Figure 8.2.4a by considering the semipaths (S,X,W,T) and (S,Z,Y,T).

Algorithm and Program

Given a weighted graph (an adjacency matrix and a capacity matrix) with a source S and a sink T, the algorithm to produce an optimum flow function for that graph may be outlined as follows:

```
1    initialize the flow function to 0 at each arc;
2    canimprove = true;
3    do {
4        attempt to find a semipath from S to T that increases the flow
         to T by x > 0;
5        if (a semipath cannot be found)
                canimprove = false;
6    else
                increase the flow to each node (except S) in the
                semipath by x;
7    } while (canimprove == true);
```

The heart of the algorithm lies in line 4. Once a node has been placed on a partial semipath, it can no longer be used to extend a different semipath. Thus the algorithm uses an array of flags, *onPath*, such that *onPath*[*node*] indicates whether or not *node* is on a semipath. It also needs an indication of which nodes are at the ends of partial semipaths so that the partial semipaths can be extended by adding adjacent nodes. *endPath*[*node*] indicates whether or not *node* is at the end of a partial semipath. For each node on a semipath, the algorithm must keep track of what node precedes it on the semipath and the direction of the arc. *precede*[*node*] points to the node that precedes *node* on its semipath, and *forward*[*node*] has the value *true* if and only if the arc is from *precede*[*node*] to *node*. *improve*[*node*] indicates the amount by which the flow to *node* may be increased along its semipath. The algorithm that attempts to find a semipath from S to T along which the flow may be increased may be written as follows (we assume that $c[a,b]$ is the capacity of the pipe from a to b, and that $f[a,b]$ is the current flow from a to b):

```
set endPath[node], onPath[node] to false for all nodes;
endPath[S] = true;
onPath[S] = true;
// compute maximum flow from S that pipes can carry
improve[S] = sum of c[S][node] over all nodes node;
while ((onPath[T] == false)
        && (there exists a node nd such that endPath[nd] == true)) {
    endPath[nd] = false;
    while (there exists a node i such that
            (onPath[i] == false) && (adjacent(nd,i) == true)
        && (f[nd][i] < c[nd][i])) {
        // the flow from nd to i may be increased place i on the semipath
```

```
                onPath[i] = true;
                endPath[i] = true;
                precede[i] = nd;
                forward[i] = true;
                x = c[nd][i] - f[nd][i];
                improve[i] = (improve[nd] < x) ? improve[nd] : x;
            } // end while there exists...
            while (there exists a node i such that (onPath[i] == false)
                     && (adjacent(i,nd) == true) && (f[i][nd] > 0)) {
                // the flow from i to nd may be decreased place i on the
                // semipath
                onPath[i] = true;
                endPath[i] = true;
                precede[i] = nd;
                forward[i] = false;
                improve[i] = (improve[nd] < f[i][nd]) ? improve[nd] :
                f[i][nd];
            } // end while there exists...
        } // end while (onPath[T] == false)
        if (onPath(T) == true)
            we have found a semipath from S to T;
        else
            the flow is already optimum;
```

Once a semipath from S to T has been found, the flow may be increased along that semipath (line 6 above) by the following algorithm:

```
x = improve[T];
nd = T;
while (nd != S) {
    pred = precede[nd];
    (forward[nd] == true) ? (f[pred, nd] += x) : (f[nd, pred] -= x);
    nd = pred;
} // end while
```

This method of solving the flow problem is known as the ***Ford-Fulkerson algorithm*** after its discoverers.

Let us now convert these algorithms into a Java method, *maxFlow(cap, s, t, flow, totFlow)*, where *cap* represents a capacity function defined on a weighted graph, *s* and *t represent* the source and sink, *flow* represents the maximum flow function, and *totFlow* is the amount of flow from *s* to *t* under the flow function *flow*.

The previous algorithms may easily be converted into Java applications. Five arrays are required: *endPath, forward, onPath, improve,* and *precede*. The question of whether *j* is adjacent to *i* can be answered by checking whether or not *cap[i][j]* == 0.

We present the method here as a straightforward implementation of the algorithms. *any* is a method that accepts an array of logical values and returns ***true*** if any element of the array is ***true***. If none of the elements of the array is ***true***, then *any* returns ***false***.

```java
public class FlowProblem {
    static final int INFINITY = Integer.MAX_VALUE;

    public static int maxFlow(int cap[ ][ ], int s, int t,
                                    int flow[ ][ ], int MAXNODES) {
        int numNodes = MAXNODES;
        int precede[ ] = new int[numNodes];
        int improve[ ] = new int[numNodes];
        boolean endPath[ ] = new boolean[numNodes];
        boolean forward[ ] = new boolean[numNodes];
        boolean onPath[ ] = new boolean[numNodes];
        int nd = 0, x = 0, totFlow = 0, pred = 0;

        for (nd = 0; nd < numNodes; nd++)
            for (int i = 0; i < numNodes; i++)
                flow[nd][i] = 0;
        do {
            // attemp to find a semipath from s to t
            for (nd = 0; nd < numNodes; nd++) {
                endPath[nd] = false;
                onPath[nd] = false;
            }
            endPath[s] = true;
            onPath[s] = true;
            improve[s] = INFINITY;
            // we assume that s can provide infinite flow
            while ((onPath[t] == false) && (any(endPath) == true)) {
                // attempt to extend an existing path
                for (nd = 0; endPath[nd] == false; nd++)
                    ;
                endPath[nd] = false;
                for (int i = 0; i < numNodes; i++) {
                    if (flow[nd][i] < cap[nd][i] && (onPath[i] ==
                    false)) {
                        onPath[i] = true;
                        endPath[i] = true;
                        precede[i]= nd;
                        forward[nd] = true;
                        x = cap[nd][i] - flow[nd][i];
                        improve[i] = (improve[nd] < x) ?
                        improve[nd] : x;
                    } // end if
                    if ((flow[i][nd] > 0) && (onPath[i] == false)) {
                        onPath[i] = true;
                        endPath[i] = true;
                        precede[i] = nd;
                        forward[nd] = false;
                        improve[i] = (improve[nd] < flow[i][nd]) ?
                                        improve[nd] : flow[i][nd];
```

```
                                } // end if
                        } // end for
                } // end while

        if (onPath[t] == true) {
                // flow on semipath to t can be increased
                x = improve[t];
                totFlow += x;
                nd = t;
                while (nd != s) {
                        // travel back along path
                        pred = precede[nd];
                        // increase or decrease flow from pred
                        (forward[pred] == true) ?
                                (flow[pred][nd] += x) : (flow[nd][pred] -= x);
                        nd = pred;
                } // end while
        } // end if
    } while(onPath[t] == true);          // end do
    return totFlow;
} // end maxFlow

public static boolean any(boolean arr[]) {
    for (int i = 0; i < arr.length; i++)
        if (arr[i])
            return true;
        return false;
} // end any
} // end class FlowProblem
```

Note that although we have maintained the arrays as they were specified in the algorithm, we could have eliminated the array *forward* by setting *precede[nd]* to a positive number in the case of a forward arc and to a negative number in the case of a backward arc. You are asked to pursue this possibility as an exercise.

For large graphs with many nodes, the arrays *improve* and *endPath* may be prohibitively expensive in terms of space. Furthermore, a search through all the nodes to find a node *nd* such that *endPath[nd]* = **true** may be very inefficient in terms of time. An alternative solution might be to note that the value of *improve* is required only for those nodes *nd* such that *endPath[nd]* = **true**. The graph nodes at the ends of semipaths may be kept in a list whose nodes are defined by:

```
public class ListNode {
        private int graphNode;
        private int improve;
        private int next;
};
```

When a node at the end of a semipath is required, remove the first element from the list. We can similarly dispense with the array *precede* by maintaining a separate list of nodes for each semipath. However, this suggestion is of dubious value because almost all the nodes will be on some semipath. You are invited to write the routine *maxFlow* as an exercise using these suggestions to save time and space.

EXERCISES

8.2.1   Find the maximum flows for the graphs in Figure 8.2.1 using the Ford-Fulkerson method (the capacities are shown next to the arcs).

8.2.2   Given a graph and a capacity function as in this section, define a **cut** as any set of nodes x containing S but not T. Define the **capacity of the cut x** as the sum of the capacities of all the arcs leaving the set x.

    a.   Show that for any flow function f, the value of the total flow v is less than or equal to the capacity of any cut.

    b.   Show that equality in (a) above is achieved when the flow is maximum and the cut has minimum capacity.

8.2.3   Prove that the Ford-Fulkerson algorithm produces an optimum flow function.

8.2.4   Rewrite the routine *maxFlow* using a linked list to contain nodes at the end of semipaths, as suggested in the text.

8.2.5   Assume that in addition to a capacity function for every arc, there is also a cost function, *cost. cost(a,b)*, which is the cost of each unit of flow from node a to node b. Modify the program in the text to produce the flow function that maximizes the total flow from source to sink at the lowest cost (i.e., if there are two flow functions, both of which produce the same maximum flow, choose the one with the least cost).

8.2.6   Assuming a cost function as in the previous exercise, write an application to produce the maximum cheapest flow—that is, a flow function such that the total flow divided by the cost of the flow is greatest.

8.2.7   A **probabilistic** directed graph is one in which a probability function associates a probability with each arc. The sum of the probabilities of all the arcs emanating from any node is 1. Consider an acyclic probabilistic digraph representing a tunnel system. A person is placed at one node in the tunnel. At each node, the person chooses to take a particular arc to another node with probability given by the probability function. Write an application to compute the probability that the person passes through each node of the graph. What if the graph were cyclic?

8.2.8   Write a Java application that reads the following information about an electrical network:

    1. n, the number of wires in the network.

    2.   The amount of current entering through the first wire and leaving through the nth.

    3.   The resistance of each of the wires 2 through $n - 1$.

    4.   A set of ordered pairs $<i,j>$ indicating that wire i is connected to wire j, and that electricity flows through wire i to wire j.

The program should compute the amount of current flowing through each of wires 2 though $n - 1$ by applying Kirchoff's law and Ohm's law. Kirchoff's law states that the amount of current flowing into a junction equals the amount leaving the junction. Ohm's law states that if two paths exist between two junctions, the sums of the current times the resistance over all the wires in the two paths are equal.

8.3   LINKED REPRESENTATION OF GRAPHS

The adjacency matrix representation of a graph is frequently inadequate because it requires advance knowledge of the number of nodes. If a graph must be constructed in the course of solving a problem, or if it must be updated dynamically as the program proceeds, a new matrix must be created for each addition or deletion of a node. This is prohibitively inefficient, especially in a real-world situation, where a graph may have a hundred or more nodes. Further, even if a graph has very few arcs, so that the adjacency matrix (and the weight matrix for a weighted graph) is sparse, space must be reserved for every possible arc between two nodes, whether or not such an arc exists. If the graph contains n nodes, a total of n^2 locations must be used.

As you might expect, the remedy is to use a linked structure, allocating and freeing nodes from an available pool. This is similar to the methods used to represent dynamic binary and general trees. In the linked representation of trees, each allocated node corresponds to a tree node. This is possible because each tree node is the son of only one other tree node and is therefore contained in only a single list of sons. However, in a graph an arc may exist between any two graph nodes. It is possible to keep an adjacency list for every node in a graph (such a list contains all the nodes adjacent to a given node), and a node might find itself on many different adjacency lists (one for each node to which it is adjacent). But this requires that each allocated node contain a variable number of pointers depending on the number of nodes to which it is adjacent. This solution is clearly impractical, as we saw in attempting to represent general trees with nodes containing pointers to each of its sons.

An alternative is to construct a multilinked structure in the following way. The nodes of the graph (hereafter referred to as **graph nodes**) are represented by a linked list of **header nodes**. Each header node contains three fields: *info, nextNode,* and *arcPtr.* If p points to a header node representing a graph node a, *info*(p) contains any information associated with graph node a. *nextNode*(p) is a pointer to the header node representing the next graph node, if any. Each header node is at the head of a list of nodes of a second type, called **list nodes**. This list is called the **adjacency list**. Each node on an adjacency list represents an arc of the graph. *arcPtr*(p) points to the adjacency list of nodes representing the arcs emanating from the graph node a.

Each adjacency list node contains two fields: *ndPtr* and *nextArc.* If q points to a list node representing an arc $<a,b>$, *ndPtr*(q) is a pointer to the header node representing the graph node b. *nextArc*(q) points to a list node representing the next arc emanating from graph node a, if any. Each list node is contained in a single adjacency list representing all the arcs emanating from a given graph node. The term **allocated node** is used to refer to either a header or a list node of a multilinked structure representing a graph. We also refer to an adjacency list node as an **arc node**.

Figure 8.3.1 illustrates this representation. If each graph node carries some information but (since the graph is not weighted) the arcs do not, then two types of allocated nodes are needed: one for header nodes (graph nodes), and the other for adjacency list nodes (arcs). These are illustrated in Figure 8.3.1a. Each header node contains an *info* field and two pointers. The first of these is to the adjacency list of arcs emanating from the graph node, and the second is to the next header node in the graph. Each arc node contains two pointers, one to the next arc node in the adjacency list, and the other

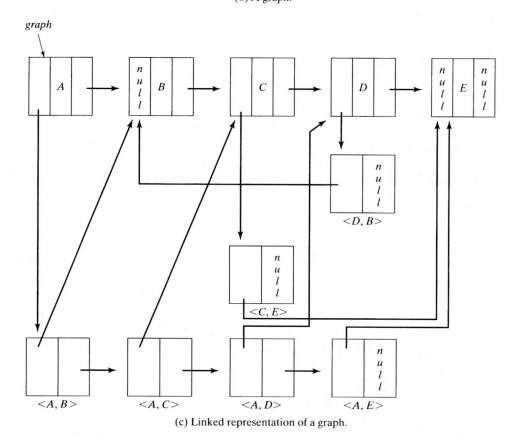

(a)

(b) A graph.

(c) Linked representation of a graph.

FIGURE 8.3.1 Linked representation of a graph.

to the header node representing the graph node that terminates the arc. Figure 8.3.1b depicts a graph, and 8.3.1c its linked representation.

The implementation of the primitive graph operations using the dynamic representation follows. We assume the existence of the *DynamicList* class, as defined in Section 4.3, to which we have added the following *ListEnumerator* class:

```
class ListEnumerator implements Enumeration {
    private DynamicNode current;

    public ListEnumerator(DynamicNode list) {
        current = list;
    }

    public boolean hasMoreElements() {
        if (current == null)
                return false;
        else
                return true;
    } // end hasMoreElements

    public Object nextElement() {
        DynamicNode tmp = current;

        if (current == null)
                return null;
        current = current.getNext();
        return tmp.getInfo();
    } // end nextElement
} // end ListEnumerator class
```

The *ListEnumerator* class implements the *Enumeration* interface of the *DynamicList* class that allows us to traverse the list of graph nodes. This interface which should be added to the *DynamicList* class is simply:

```
public Enumeration elements() {
  return new ListEnumerator(list);
}
```

Each node of the graph, referenced by one of the header nodes of the *DynamicList* class, is defined as:

```
public class GraphNode {
  private Object info;
  private DynamicList arcptr;

  public GraphNode(Object info) {
        this.info = info;
        this.arcptr = null;
  } // end GraphNode constructor

  public GraphNode(Object info, DynamicList arcptr) {
        this.info = info;
        this.arcptr = arcptr;
  } // end GraphNode constructor
```

```java
public Object getInfo() {
      return info;
}

public void setInfo(Object o) {
      info = o;
}

public DynamicList getArcptr() {
      return arcptr;
}

public void setArcptr(DynamicList n) {
      arcptr = n;
}

// returns true if the info fields are equal
public boolean equals(Object o) {
      if (!(o instanceof GraphNode))
            return false;
      GraphNode gn = (GraphNode) o;
      return info.equals(gn.info);
} // end equals
} // end GraphNode class
```

A node representing an arc is defined in a similar fashion.

```java
public class ArcNode {
  protected GraphNode ptr;

  public ArcNode() {
      ptr = null;
  } // end constructor

  public ArcNode(GraphNode gn) {
      ptr = gn;
  } // end constructor

  public GraphNode getPtr() {
      return ptr;
  }

  public void setPtr(GraphNode d) {
      ptr = d;
  }

  // Returns true if the ptr fields point to the same object
  public boolean equals(Object o) {
      if (!(o instanceof ArcNode))
            return false;
      ArcNode tmp = (ArcNode) o;
      return (ptr == tmp.ptr);
  } // end equals
} // end ArcNode class
```

The *Graph* class itself is defined as an ***abstract*** class. An abstract class is used when it is desirable to create a class with methods that may be further refined by classes that inherit the methods of the abstract class without implementing the base class itself. We wish to use the linked representation of graphs to implement both the unweighted *LinkedGraph* class and the weighted *WLinkedGraph* class. Rather than having to duplicate the methods common to both, we use the abstract *Graph* class to define such features. By specifying that the *LinkedGraph* and *WLinkedGraph* classes extend the *Graph* class (using the Java ***extends*** keyword), the methods of the abstract *Graph* class are inherited and implemented by these classes.

```java
public abstract class Graph {
    protected DynamicList graphNodes;

    public Graph() {
        graphNodes = new DynamicList();
    }

    // Adds the specified graph node to the graph. If another node
    // with the same name is already on the graph, the method does
    // nothing and returns false.
    public boolean add(Object name) {
        if (findNode(name) != null)
            return false;
        GraphNode gn = new GraphNode(name);
        graphNodes.insertLast(gn);
        return true;
    } // end add

    // Returns an Enumeration of the names of all the nodes in
    // this graph
    public Enumeration nodes() {
        Vector v = new Vector();
        Enumeration enum = graphNodes.elements();
        while (enum.hasMoreElements()) {
            GraphNode gn = (GraphNode)enum.nextElement();
            v.addElement(gn.getInfo());
        } // end while
        return v.elements();
    } // end nodes

    // Returns true if node1 is adjacent to node2
    public boolean adjacent(Object node1, Object node2) {
        GraphNode gn1 = findNode(node1);
        GraphNode gn2 = findNode(node2);
        DynamicList arcList = gn1.getArcptr();

        // if arcList is null, then node1 is not adjacent to
        // anything
        if (arcList == null)
            return false;
```

```
        // search the arcList for node2
        Enumeration e = arcList.elements();
        while (e.hasMoreElements()) {
                ArcNode an = (ArcNode)e.nextElement();
                if (an.getPtr() == gn2)
                        return true;
        }
        return false;
    } // end adjacent

    // Searches the list of graph nodes for one for which name ==
    // graphNode.info. If such a node cannot be found, the method
    // returns null.
    protected GraphNode findNode(Object name) {
        DynamicNode dn = graphNodes.search(new GraphNode(name));
        if (dn != null)
                return (GraphNode) dn.getInfo();

        else
                return null;
    } // end findNode
} // end Graph class
```

The dynamic list implementation of a weighted graph follows. *WLinkedGraph* implements all the methods of the abstract *Graph* class as well as the methods specific to a weighted graph. We leave the implementation of an unweighted graph as an exercise for the reader.

```
public class WLinkedGraph extends Graph {

    public WLinkedGraph() {
        super();
    } //  end constructor

    // Creates an arc between node1 and node2 with the given weight.
    public void join(Object node1, Object node2, int weight) {
        GraphNode gn1 = findNode(node1);
        GraphNode gn2 = findNode(node2);
        DynamicList arcList = gn1.getArcptr();
        WArcNode arcNode = new WArcNode(gn2, weight);

        // If the graph node is not connected to anything, create
        // the arc.
        if (arcList == null) {
                DynamicList list = new DynamicList();
                list.insertFirst(arcNode);
                gn1.setArcptr(list);
        }
        else if (arcList.isEmpty())
                  arcList.insertFirst(arcNode);
          else {
                Enumeration enum = arcList.elements();
```

```
                        while (enum.hasMoreElements()) {
                            WArcNode tmp = (WArcNode)enum.nextElement();
                            if (tmp.getPtr() == gn2) {
                                arcNode.setWeight(weight);
                                return;
                            }
                        }
                        // connect node1 and node2
                        arcList.insertLast(arcNode);
                    }
    } // end join

    // Removes an arc between node1 and node2; if one exists return
    // the weight. If node1 and node2 were not connected throws a
    // WlinkedGraphException.
    public int remove(Object node1, Object node2)
                                    throws WLinkedGraphException {
        // if node1 is not adjacent to node2, throw an exception
        if (!adjacent(node1, node2))
                throw new WLinkedGraphException(node1.toString() +
                    " is not" +" connected to " + node2.toString());
        int w = getWeight(node1, node2);    // get the weight
        GraphNode gn1 = findNode(node1);
        GraphNode gn2 = findNode(node2);
        DynamicList arcList = gn1.getArcptr();
        // node1 is not connected to anything, so there is
        // nothing to remove
        if (arcList == null || arcList.isEmpty())
                throw new WLinkedGraphException(node1.toString() +
                    " is not" + " connected to any other node.");
        arcList.removeX(new WArcNode(gn2, 0));
        return w;
    } // end remove

    // Returns the weight on the arc between node1 and node2.
    // If node1 is not connected to node2 throws a
    // WLinkedGraphException.
    public int getWeight(Object node1, Object node2)
                                    throws WLinkedGraphException {
        GraphNode gn1 = findNode(node1);
        GraphNode gn2 = findNode(node2);
        DynamicList arcList = gn1.getArcptr();
        Enumeration enum = arcList.elements();

        while (enum.hasMoreElements()) {
            WArcNode arcNode = (WArcNode)enum.nextElement();
            if (arcNode.getPtr() == gn2)
                    return arcNode.getWeight();
        }
        // node1 and node2 are not connected
```

```
        throw new WLinkedGraphException(node1.toString() + " is not" +
                                  " connected to " + node2.toString());
    } // end getWeight
} // end WLinkedGraph class
```

The use of the *super* keyword in the constructor of the *WLinkedGraph* class invokes the constructor of the abstract *Graph* superclass. When used by the constructor of the subclass, *super* must appear as the very first statement. Any statements that are specific to the constructor of the subclass and follow its invocation are then executed in turn.

Attempting to remove an arc or returning the weight of an arc between two nodes that are not adjacent throws a *WLinkedGraphException*. *WLinkedGraphException* may be implemented as a simple subclass of the general Java *Exception* class, as shown below:

```
public class WLinkedGraphException extends Exception {
    public WLinkedGraphException() {
            super();
    }

    public WLinkedGraphException(String msg) {
            super(msg);
    }
} // end WLinkedGraphException class
```

The *WArcNode* class extends the *ArcNode* class by including methods and fields to contain the weight of the arc. Note that the constructors of the subclass, *WArcNode*, override those of the superclass, *ArcNode*.

```
public class WArcNode extends ArcNode {
    private int weight;

    public WArcNode() {
            this(null, 0);
    }

    public WArcNode(int weight) {
            this(null, weight);
    }

    public WArcNode(GraphNode ptr, int weight) {
            super(ptr);
            this.weight = weight;
    }

    public int getWeight() {
            return weight;
    }

    public void setWeight(int w) {
            weight = w;
    }
} // end WArcNode class
```

The reader should be aware of another important difference between the adjacency matrix representation and the linked representation of graphs. Implicit in the matrix representation is the ability to traverse a row or column of the matrix. Traversing a row is equivalent to identifying all the arcs emanating from a given node. This can be done efficiently in the linked representation by traversing the list of arc nodes starting at a given header node. Traversing a column of an adjacency matrix, however, is equivalent to identifying all the arcs that terminate at a given node; there is no corresponding method for accomplishing this under the linked representation. Of course, the linked representation could be modified to include two lists emanating from each header node: one for the arcs emanating from the graph node, and the other for the arcs terminating at the graph node. However, this would require allocating two nodes for each arc, thus increasing the complexity of adding or deleting an arc.

Alternatively, each arc node could be placed on two lists. In this case, an arc node would contain four pointers: one to the next arc emanating from the same node, one to the next arc terminating at the same node, one to the header node at which it terminates, and one to the header node from which it emanates. A header node would contain three pointers: one to the next header node, one to the list of arcs emanating from it, and one to the list of arcs terminating at it. In choosing one or another of these representations, the programmer must examine the needs of the specific problem and considering both time and storage efficiency.

We invite the reader to write a method *Graph.RemNode(p)* that removes a header node referenced by *p* using the various graph representations outlined above. When a node is removed from a graph, all the arcs emanating and terminating at that node must also be removed. In the linked representation which we have presented, there is no easy way to remove a node from a graph because the arcs terminating at the node cannot be obtained directly.

Dijkstra's Algorithm Revisited

In Section 8.1, we presented an implementation of Dijkstra's algorithm for finding the shortest path between two nodes in a weighted graph represented by a weight matrix. The implementation was $O(n^2)$, where n is the number of nodes in the graph. We now show how the algorithm can be implemented more efficiently in most cases if the graph is implemented using adjacency lists.

We suggest a review of the algorithm described in Section 8.1. This algorithm may be outlined as follows. We seek the shortest path from *s* to *t*. *pd* is to be set to the shortest distance; *precede[i]* to the node preceding node *i* in the shortest path:

```
1.  for (all nodes i) {
2.       distance[i] = INFINITY;
3.       perm[i] = NONMEMBER;
4.  }
5.  perm[s] = MEMBER;
6.  distance[s] = 0;
7.  current = s;
8.  while (current != t) {
9.       dc = distance[current];
10.      for (all nodes i that are successors of current) {
```

```
11.                newDist = dc + weight[current][i];
12.                if (newDist < distance[i]) {
13.                      distance[i] = newDist;
14.                      precede[i] = current;
15.                }
16.          }
17.          k = the node k such that perm[k] == NONMEMBER and such that
                                        distance[k] is smallest;
18.          current = k;
19.          perm[k] = MEMBER;
20.   }
21.   pd = distance[t];
```

Review how this algorithm is implemented in Section 8.1. Note especially how finding the minimum distance (line 17) is incorporated into the *for* loop and how that loop is implemented.

The keys to an efficient implementation are lines 10 and 17. In Section 8.1, where we had access only to a weight matrix, there is no way to limit the access to the successors of *current* as specified in line 10. It is necessary to traverse all the n nodes of the graph each time the inner loop is repeated. We are able to increase efficiency by looking only at elements not in *perm*, but that cannot speed things up by more than a constant factor. Once an $O(n)$ inner loop is required, we may as well use it to compute the minimum as well (line 17).

However, given an adjacency list representation of the graph, it is possible to traverse directly all the nodes adjacent to *current* without examining all the graph nodes. Therefore, the total number of nodes i examined in the loop headed by line 10 is $O(e)$, where e is the number of edges (arcs) in the graph. [Note that we are not saying that each execution of the inner loop is $O(e)$, but that the total of all the repetitions of all the passes of the inner loop is $O(e)$.] In most graphs, e is far smaller than n^2, so this is quite an improvement.

However, we are not yet done. Since we are eliminating a traversal through all the nodes, we must find an alternative way of implementing line 17 to find the node with the smallest distance. If the best we can do in finding this minimum distance is $O(n)$, then the entire process remains $O(n^2)$.

Fortunately, there is a solution. Suppose that, instead of maintaining the array *perm*, we maintained its complement, *notPerm*. Then line 3 would become

```
3.   notPerm[i] = MEMBER;
```

line 5 would become

```
5.   notPerm[s] = NONMEMBER;
```

line 17 would become

```
17.   k = the node k such that notPerm[k] == MEMBER and such that
                               distance[k] is smallest;
```

and line 19 would become

```
19.   notPerm[k] = NONMEMBER;
```

The operations performed on the array *notPerm* are creation [line 5; this may be $O(n)$, but it is outside the ***while*** loop and therefore does not hurt the overall efficiency], finding the minimum element (line 17), and deleting the minimum element (line 19). But the latter two operations can be combined into the single *pqMinDelete* operation of an ascending priority queue, and by now we have a number of ways of implementing this operation in less than $O(n)$. In fact, we can implement *pqMinDelete* in $O(\log n)$ by using an ascending heap, a balanced binary tree, or a 2–3 tree. If the set *notPerm* is implemented as a priority queue using one of these techniques, the efficiency of n such operations is $O(n \log n)$. If a priority queue ordered by the value of distance is used to implement *notPerm*, the position of i must be adjusted in the priority queue whenever *distance*[i] is modified in line 13. Fortunately, this can also be done in $O(\log n)$ steps.

Thus Dijkstra's algorithm can be implemented using $O((e + n)\log n)$ operations, which is significantly better than $O(n^2)$ for sparse graphs (i.e., graphs with very few edges, as opposed to dense graphs that have an edge between almost every pair of nodes). We leave an actual Java implementation as an exercise for the reader.

Organizing the Set of Graph Nodes

In many applications, the set of graph nodes (as implemented by header nodes) need not be organized as a simple linked list. The linked list organization is suitable only when the entire set of graph nodes must be traversed and when graph nodes are being dynamically inserted. Both of these operations are highly efficient on a linked list.

If graph nodes must also be deleted, then the list must be doubly linked. In addition, as noted earlier, we must ensure that no arcs emanate from or terminate at a deleted node or that all such arcs are deleted as part of the node-deletion routine. If we choose merely to ensure that no arcs terminate in a node being deleted rather than to delete any such arcs, it is not necessary to keep with each node a list of arcs terminating at the node. It is only necessary to maintain a count field in the node to hold the number of arcs terminating at the node; when count becomes 0 (and no arcs terminate at the node), the node may be deleted.

If graph nodes are not being added or deleted, then the nodes can be kept in a simple array, where each array element contains any necessary information about the node plus a pointer to an adjacency list of arcs. Each arc need contain only an array index to indicate the position of its terminating node in the array.

In many applications, graph nodes must be accessed by their contents. For example, in a graph whose nodes represent cities, an application must find the appropriate node given the name of the city. If a linked list is used to represent the graph nodes, then the entire list must be traversed to find the node associated with a particular name.

The problem of finding a particular element in a set based on its contents, or value, is one that we have already studied in great detail: it is simply the searching problem. And we know a great many possible solutions; binary search trees, multiway search trees, and hash tables are all ways of organizing sets to permit rapid searching.

The set of graph nodes can be organized in any of these ways. Which organization is chosen depends on the detailed needs of the application. In Dijkstra's algorithm, for example, we have just seen an illustration where the set of graph nodes could be organized as an array that implements an ascending heap used as a priority queue. Let us now look at a different application. We introduce it with a frivolous example, but the application itself is quite important.

Application to Scheduling

Suppose a chef in a diner receives an order for a fried egg. The job of frying an egg can be decomposed into a number of distinct subtasks:

Get egg	Crack egg	Get grease
Grease pan	Heat grease	Pour egg into pan
Wait until egg is done		Remove egg

Some of these tasks must precede others (e.g., "get egg" must precede "crack egg"). Others may be done simultaneously (e.g., "get egg" and "heat grease"). The chef wishes to provide the quickest service possible and is assumed to have an unlimited number of assistants. The problem is to assign tasks to the assistants so as to complete the job in the least possible time.

Although this example may seem frivolous, it is typical of many real-world scheduling problems. A computer system may wish to schedule jobs to minimize turnaround time; a compiler may wish to schedule machine-language operations to minimize execution time; a plant manager may wish to organize an assembly line to minimize production time, and so on. All of these problems are closely related and can be solved by the use of graphs.

Let us represent the above problem as a graph. Each node of the graph represents a subtask, and each arc $<x,y>$ represents the requirement that subtask y cannot be performed until subtask x has been completed. This graph G is shown in Figure 8.3.2.

Consider the transitive closure of G. The transitive closure is the graph T such that $<x,y>$ is an arc of T if and only if there is a path from x to y in G. This transitive closure is shown in Figure 8.3.3.

In the graph T, an arc exists from node x to node y if and only if subtask x must be performed before subtask y. Note that neither G nor T can contain a cycle, because if a cycle from node x to itself existed, then subtask x could not be performed until after subtask x had been completed. This is clearly an impossible situation in the context of the problem. Thus G is a *dag*, a directed acyclic graph.

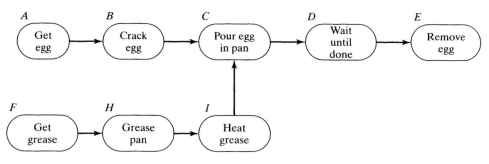

FIGURE 8.3.2   Graph G.

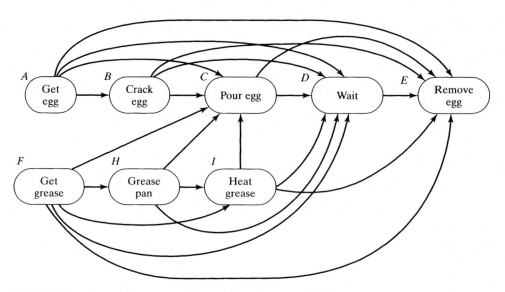

FIGURE 8.3.3   Graph *T*.

Since *G* does not contain a cycle, there must be at least one node in *G* which has no predecessors. To see this, suppose that every node in the graph did have a predecessor. In particular, let us choose a node *z* that has a predecessor *y*. *y* cannot equal *z* or the graph would have a cycle from *z* to itself. Since every node has a predecessor, *y* must also have a predecessor *x* which is not equal to either *y* or *z*. Continuing in this fashion, a sequence of distinct nodes

$$z, y, x, w, v, u, \ldots$$

is obtained. If any two nodes in this sequence were equal, a cycle would exist from that node to itself. However, since the graph contains only a finite number of nodes, two of the nodes must eventually be equal. This is a contradiction. Thus there must be at least one node without a predecessor.

In the graphs in Figures 8.3.2 and 8.3.3, the nodes *A* and *F* do not have predecessors. Since they have no predecessors, the subtasks they represent may be performed immediately and simultaneously without waiting for any other subtasks to be completed. Every other subtask must wait until at least one of these is completed. Once these two subtasks have been performed, their nodes can be removed from the graph. Note that the resulting graph does not contain any cycles, because nodes and arcs have been removed from a graph that originally contained no cycles. Therefore the resulting graph must also contain at least one node with no predecessors. In the example, *B* and *H* are two such nodes. Thus the subtasks *B* and *H* may be performed simultaneously in the second time period.

Continuing in this fashion, we find that the minimum time in which the egg can be fried is six time periods (assuming that every subtask takes exactly one time period), and that a maximum of two assistants need be employed, as follows:

Time Period	Assistant 1	Assistant 2
1	Get egg	Get grease
2	Crack egg	Grease pan
3	Heat grease	
4	Pour egg into pan	
5	Wait until done	
6	Remove egg	

The above process can be outlined as follows:

1. Read the precedences and construct the graph.
2. Use the graph to determine subtasks that can be done simultaneously.

Let us refine each of these steps. Two crucial decisions must be made in refining step 1. The first is to decide on the format of the input; the second is to decide on the representation of the graph. Clearly, the input must contain indications of which subtasks must precede others. The most convenient way to represent these requirements is by ordered pairs of subtasks; each input line contains the names of two subtasks where the first subtask on a line must precede the second. Of course, the data must be valid in the sense that no subtask may precede itself (no cycles are permitted in the graph). Only those precedences which are implied by the data and the transitive closure of the resulting graph are assumed to hold. A subtask may be represented by a character string, such as "*get egg*," or by a number. We choose to represent subtasks by character strings in order that the input data reflect the real-world situation as closely as possible.

What information should be kept with each node of the graph? Clearly, the name of the subtask that the node represents is needed to locate the node associated with a particular task and for output purposes. This name will be kept as an array of single characters. The remaining information depends on how the graph is used. This will become apparent only after step 2 is refined. Here is a good example of how the various parts of a program outline interact with each other to produce a single unit.

Step 2 can be refined into the following algorithm:

```
while (the graph is not empty) {
    determine which nodes have no predecessors;
    output this group of nodes with an indication that they
            can be performed simultaneously in the next time period;
    remove these nodes and their incident arcs from the graph;
}
```

How can it be determined which nodes have no predecessors? One method is to maintain a *count* field in each node containing the number of nodes that precede it. Note that we are not interested in which nodes precede a given node—only in how many.

Initially, after the graph has been constructed, we examine all the graph nodes and place those with zero count on an output list. Then, during each simulated time period, the output list is traversed, each graph node on the list is output, and the adjacency list of arcs emanating from that graph node is traversed. For each arc, the count in the graph node that terminates the arc is reduced by 1, and if the count thereby becomes 0, the terminating graph node is placed on the output list of the next time period. At the same time, the arc node is freed.

The refinement of step 2 may thus be rewritten as follows:

```
    // traverse the set of graph nodes and place all those nodes
    // with 0 count on the initial output list
1.    outp = null;
2.    for (all node(p) in the graph)
3.        if (count(p) == 0) {
4.            remove node(p) from the graph;
5.            place node(p) on the output list;
6.        }
    // simulate the time periods
7.    period = 0;
8.    while (outp != null) {
9.      ++period;
10.     System.out.println ("" + period);
          // initialize the next period's output list
11.     nextOut = null;
          // traverse the output list
12.     p = outp;
13.     while (p != null) {
14.       System.out.println("" + info(p));
15.       for (all arcs a emanating from node(p)) {
              reduce count in terminating node
16.           t = the pointer to the node that terminates a;
17.           count(t)--;
18.           if (count(t) == 0) {
19.               remove node(t) from the graph;
20.               add node(t) to the nextOut list;
21.           }
22.           free arc (a);
23.       }
24.       q = next(p);
25.       free node(p);
26.       p = q;
27.     }
28.     outp = nextOut;
29. }
30. if (any nodes remain in the graph)
31.     error - there is a cycle in the graph;
```

We have been purposely vague in this algorithm about how the graph is implemented. To efficiently process all the arcs emanating from a node (lines 15–23), an adjacency list implementation is desired. But what of the set of graph nodes? Only a single traversal is required (lines 3–7) to initialize the output list. Thus the efficiency of this operation is not very crucial to the efficiency of the program.

It is necessary in step 1 to be able to access each graph node from the character string that specifies the task the node represents. For this reason, it makes sense to organize the set of graph nodes in a hash table. While the initial traversal will require accessing some extra table positions, this is more than offset by the ability to access a node directly from its task name. The only impediment is the need (in line 19) to delete nodes from the graph.

However, further analysis reveals that the only reason to delete a node is to be able to check whether any nodes remain when the output list is empty (line 30) so that a cycle may be detected. If we maintain a counter of the number of nodes and implement the deletion by reducing this counter by 1, we can check for remaining nodes by comparing the counter with zero. (This is similar to using a count field rather than requiring a list of arcs terminating in a given node.) Having determined what data structures are required, we are ready to transform the algorithm into a Java application.

Java Program

Let us first indicate the classes that are required in order to represent the graph using the linked graph representation. The linked list consists of the following classes: *DynamicList*, *DynamicNode*, and the *Sortable* interface. As described in the previous section, the graph is implemented using the following classes: *LinkedGraph*, *Graph*, *GraphNode*, and *ArcNode*.

Each task on the graph is represented by a member of the *TaskNode* class, in which *name* is the name of the subtask represented by this node, and *count* denotes the number of predecessors of this graph node.

```java
public class TaskNode {

   private String name;
   private int count;

   public TaskNode(String name) {
          this.name = name;
          count = 0;
   } // end constructor

   public TaskNode() {
          this("");
   } // end constructor

   public String getName() {
          return name;
   } // end getName

   public int getCount() {
          return count;
   } // end getCount

   public void incCount() {
          count++;
   } // end incCount

   public void decCount() {
          count--;
   } // end decCount
```

```
    // returns true if the name fields are equal
    public boolean equals(Object o) {
        if (!(o instanceof TaskNode))
                return false;
        TaskNode tn = (TaskNode) o;
        return name.equals(tn.name);
    } // end equals

    // returns a hash code for this TaskNode
    public int hashCode() {
            return (name.hashCode() * 5 + count * 13);
    } // end hashCode
} // end TaskNode class
```

taskNodes is a hash table implemented using the *java.util.HashTable* class. The *HashTable* class requires that the *hashCode* method and the *equals* method be implemented by the object (*TaskNode*) stored in the table. The *get* and *put* methods of the *HashTable* class are used to store and retrieve items from the table.

We may now write a Java scheduling application.

```
import java.util.*;

public class Scheduling {
  public static void main(String args[ ]) {
      LinkedGraph graph = new LinkedGraph();      // precedence graph
      Hashtable taskNodes = new Hashtable();

      // construct the graph based on input
      System.out.println("Enter ordered pairs of tasks in the form:
      task1,task2");
      while (true) {
          String line = Console.readLine();       // read the next
                                                   // line of input
          if (line.length() == 0)                  // empty line means
                                                   // end of input
              break;
          // tasks are separated by a comma
          StringTokenizer st = new StringTokenizer(line, ",", false);
          if (st.countTokens() != 2) {
              System.err.println("Wrong number of subtasks entered.");
              System.exit(1);
          }

          // add the two tasks to the graph
          String task1 = st.nextToken();
          String task2 = st.nextToken();

          // look up the tasks in the hash table
          TaskNode tn1 = (TaskNode) taskNodes.get(task1);
          TaskNode tn2 = (TaskNode) taskNodes.get(task2);
```

```java
// if the task has not been seen previously, create a new
// TaskNode and add it to the graph
if (tn1 == null) {
    tn1 = new TaskNode(task1);
    graph.add(tn1);
    taskNodes.put(task1, tn1);
}
if (tn2 == null) {
    tn2 = new TaskNode(task2);
    graph.add(tn2);
    taskNodes.put(task2, tn2);
}

tn2.IncCount();
graph.join(tn1, tn2);
} // end while
// while the graph is not empty traverse the graph and
// remove all task nodes with a 0 count
int period = 0;
while (!graph.isEmpty()) {
    // determine which nodes have no predecesors
    System.out.println("Period " + period);
    Vector buffer = new Vector();
    Enumeration enum = graph.nodes();          // traverse the
                                               // graph

    boolean flag = false;                      // used for
                                               // error detection

    while (enum.hasMoreElements()) {
        TaskNode tn = (TaskNode) enum.nextElement();
        // if this task node has a 0 count, print out its
        // name, add it to the buffer, and set flag to true
        if (tn.getCount() == 0) {
            System.out.println(tn.getName());
            buffer.addElement(tn);
            flag = true;
        }
    }
    // if flag is false, then no task node has a 0 count --
    // graph has a cycle
    if (!flag) {
        System.err.println("error in input - graph contains a
        cycle.");
        System.exit(1);
    }
    // traverse the task nodes in the buffer, decrement the
    // count of all adjacent task nodes, and delete the
    // task nodes in the buffer from the graph
    Enumeration enum2 = buffer.elements();     // traverse the
                                               // buffer
```

```
            while (enum2.hasMoreElements()) {
                TaskNode tn2 = (TaskNode) enum2.nextElement();
                Vector v = graph.getAllAdjacent(tn2);
                Enumeration enum3 = v.elements();     // traverse
                                                      // adjacent nodes
                while (enum3.hasMoreElements()) {
                    TaskNode tn3 = (TaskNode) enum3.nextElement();
                    tn3.DecCount();
                }
                graph.delete(tn2);
            }
            period++;
        }
    } // end main
} // end Scheduling class
```

We assume the existence of the *Console.readLine*() method, which reads a series of characters terminated by a carriage return from the keyboard and returns a *String*. The *Console* class was presented in Section 4.5. Once an input string has been read, the *java.util.StringTokenizer* class is used to parse it.

EXERCISES

8.3.1 Using the abstract *Graph* class, implement the unweighted graph class *LinkedGraph*.

8.3.2 Implement a graph using linked lists so that each header node heads two lists: one containing the arcs emanating from the graph node, and the other containing the arcs terminating at the graph node.

8.3.3 Implement a graph so that the lists of header nodes and arc nodes are circular.

8.3.4 Implement a graph using an adjacency matrix represented by the sparse matrix techniques in Section 8.1.

8.3.5 Implement a graph using an array of adjacency lists. Under this representation, a graph of n nodes consists of n header nodes, each containing an integer from 0 to $n - 1$ and a pointer. The pointer is a reference to a list of list nodes each of which contains the node number of a node adjacent to the node represented by the header node. Implement Dijkstra's algorithm using this graph representation with the array formed into an ascending heap.

8.3.6 There may be more than one way to organize a set of subtasks in a minimum number of time periods. For example, the subtasks in Figure 8.3.2 may be completed in six time periods in one of three different methods:

Period	Method 1	Method 2	Method 3
1	A, F	F	A, F
2	B, H	A, H	H
3	I	B, I	B, I
4	C	C	C
5	D	D	D
6	E	E	E

Write a program to generate all the possible methods of organizing the subtasks in the minimum number of time periods.

8.3.7   Consider the graph in Figure 8.3.4. The application *schedule* outputs the following organization of tasks:

Time	Subtasks
1	A, B, C
2	D, E
3	F
4	G

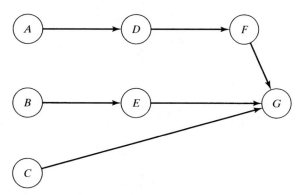

FIGURE 8.3.4

This requires three assistants (for time period 1). Can you find a method of organizing the subtasks so that only two assistants are required in any time period, yet the entire job can be accomplished in the same four time periods? Write an application that organizes subtasks so that a minimum number of assistants is needed to complete the entire job in the minimum number of time periods.

8.3.8   If there is only one worker available, then it will take *k* time periods to complete the entire job, where *k* is the number of subtasks. Write an application to list a valid order in which the worker can perform the tasks. Note that this application is simpler than *schedule*, since an output list is not needed; the task may be output as soon as the *count* field reaches 0. The process of converting a set of precedences into a single linear list in which no later element precedes an earlier one is called a ***topological sort***.

8.3.9   A ***PERT network*** is a weighted acyclic directed graph in which each arc represents an activity and its weight represents the time needed to perform that activity. If arc $<a,b>$ and $<b,c>$ exist in the network, then the activity represented by arc $<a,b>$ must be completed before the activity represented by $<b,c>$ can be started. Each node x of the network represents a time at which all activities represented by arcs terminating at x can be completed.

a.   Write a Java method that accepts a representation of such a network and assigns to each node x the earliest time that all activities terminating in that node can be completed. Call this quantity $et(x)$. [*Hint:* Assign time 0 to all nodes with no predecessors. If all the predecessors of a node x have been assigned times, then $et(x)$ is the maximum over all the predecessors of the sum of the time assigned to a predecessor and the weight of the arc from that predecessor to x.]

b. Given the assignment of times in part (a), write a Java method that assigns to each node x the latest time that all activities terminating in x can be completed without delaying the completion of all the activities. Call this quantity $lt(x)$. (*Hint:* Assign time $et(x)$ to all nodes x with no successors. If all the successors of a node x have been assigned times, then $lt(x)$ is the minimum over all the successors of the difference between the time assigned to a successor and the weight of the arc from x to the successor.)

c. Prove that there is at least one path in the graph from a node with no predecessors to a node with no successors such that $et(x) = lt(x)$ for every node x on the path. Such a path is called a ***critical path***.

d. Explain the significance of a critical path by showing that reducing the time of the activities along every critical path reduces the earliest time by which the entire job can be completed.

e. Write a Java method to find all the critical paths in a PERT network.

f. Find the critical paths in the networks in Figure 8.3.5.

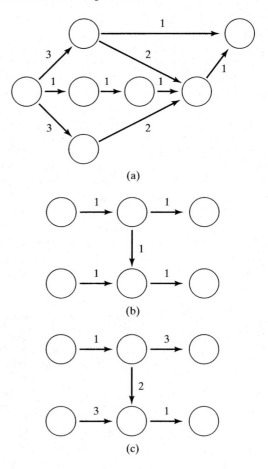

(a)

(b)

(c)

FIGURE 8.3.5   Some PERT networks.

8.3.10   Write a Java application that accepts a representation of a PERT network as given above and computes the earliest time in which the entire job can be finished if as many activities as possible may be performed in parallel. The application should also print the starting and ending times of each activity in the network. Write another Java application to schedule the activities so that the entire job can be completed at the earliest possible time subject to the constraint that at most *m* activities can be performed in parallel.

8.4   GRAPH TRAVERSAL AND SPANNING FORESTS

A great many algorithms depend on being able to traverse a graph. In this section, we examine techniques for systematically accessing all the nodes of a graph and present several useful algorithms that implement and use them. We also look at ways of creating a general forest that is a subgraph of given graph *G* and contains all its nodes.

Traversal Methods for Graphs

It is often desirable to *traverse* a data structure, that is, to visit each of its elements in a systematic manner. We have already seen traversal techniques for lists and trees; we now examine traversal techniques for graphs.

The elements of the graph to be visited are usually the graph nodes. It is always possible to traverse a graph efficiently by visiting the graph nodes in an implementation-dependent manner. For example, if a graph with *n* nodes is represented by an adjacency matrix or an array of adjacency lists, simply listing the integers from 0 to $n - 1$ "traverses" the graph. Similarly, if the graph nodes are maintained as a linked list, a search tree, a hash table, or some other structure, traversing the underlying structure might be considered a "traversal" of the graph. However, of greater interest is a traversal that corresponds to the graph structure of the object; not one for the underlying implementation structure. That is, the sequence in which the nodes are visited should relate to the adjacency structure of the graph.

Defining a traversal that relates to the structure of a graph is more complex than one for a list or a tree for three reasons:

1. In general, there is no natural "first" node in a graph from which the traversal should start, whereas there is a first node in a list or a root in a tree. Further, once a starting node has been determined and all the nodes reachable from it have been visited, there may remain other nodes in the graph that have not been visited because they are not reachable from the starting node. This is again unlike a list or tree, where every node is reachable from the header or the root. Thus, once all the reachable nodes in a graph have been visited, the traversal algorithm faces the problem of selecting another starting node.

2. There is no natural order among the successors of a particular node. Thus there is no a priori order in which the successors of a node should be visited.

3. Unlike a node of a list or a tree, a node of a graph may have more than one predecessor. If node *x* is a successor of both node *y* and node *z*, then *x* may be visited after *y* but before *z*. It is therefore possible for a node to be visited before one of its predecessors. In fact, if a graph is cyclic, every possible traversal must include some node that is visited before one of its predecessors.

To deal with these three complications, any graph traversal method incorporates the following three features:

1. The algorithm is either presented with a starting node for the traversal or chooses a random node at which to start. The same traversal algorithm produces a different ordering of the nodes depending on the node at which it starts. In the following discussion, *s* denotes the starting node.

We also assume a method *select* with no parameters that chooses an arbitrary unvisited node. The *select* method is usually dependent on the graph representation. If the graph nodes are represented by the integers 0 to $n - 1$, *select* maintains a class variable *last* (initialized to -1) that keeps track of the last node selected by *select*, and utilizes a flag *visited(i)* that is **true** only if *node(i)* has been visited. The following is an algorithm for *select*.

```
for (i = last + 1; i < n && visited(i); i++)
    ;
if (i == n)
        return -1;
last = i;
return I;
```

A similar *select* routine can be implemented if the graph nodes are organized as a linked list, with *last* being a reference to the last header node selected.

2. Generally, the implementation of the graph determines the order in which the successors of a node are visited. For example, if the adjacency matrix implementation is used, the node numbering (from 0 to $n - 1$) determines the order; if the adjacency list implementation is used, the order of the arcs on the adjacency list determines the order in which the successors are visited. Alternatively, and much less commonly, the algorithm may choose a random ordering among the successors of a node. We consider two operations: *firstSucc(x)*, which returns a pointer to the "first" successor of *node(x)*, and *nextSucc(x,y)*, where *node(y)* is a successor of *node(x)*, which returns a pointer to the "next" successor of *node(x)* following *node(y)*. Let us examine how to implement these functions under both the adjacency matrix and linked representations of a graph.

In the adjacency matrix representation, if *x* and *y* are indices such that *node(y)* is a successor of *node(x)*, the next successor of *x* following *y* can be computed as the lowest index *i* greater than *y* such that *adj(x,i)* is **true**. Unfortunately, things are not so simple for the linked representation. If *x* and *y* represent two graph nodes in a graph representation that uses adjacency lists (*x* and *y* can be either array indices or pointers to header nodes), there is no way to access the "next" successor of *node(x)* following *node(y)*. This is because, the ordering of successors in the adjacency list representation is based on the ordering of arc nodes. It is therefore necessary to locate the arc node following the arc node that points to *node(y)*. But there is no reference from *node(y)* to the arc nodes that point to it, and therefore no way to get to the next arc node. It is therefore necessary for the parameter *y* to point to an arc node rather than a graph node, although the pointer actually represents the graph node terminating that arc [i.e., *node(ndPtr(y))*]. The next successor of *node(x)* following that graph node can then be found as *node*(*ndPtr*(*nextArc*(*y*))), that is, the node that terminates the arc that follows the arc node *node*(*y*) on the adjacency list emanating from *node*(*x*).

To employ a uniform calling technique for *firstSucc* and *nextSucc* under all graph implementations, we present these methods as algorithms with similar headers:

- *firstSucc*(*x*,*yptr*,*ynode*) sets both *yptr* and *ynode* to the index of the first successor of *node*(*x*) under the adjacency matrix representation. Under the linked representation, *ynode* is set as a reference to the header node (or a node number) of the first successor of *node*(*x*), and *yptr* is set to point to the arc node representing the arc from *node*(*x*) to *node*(*ynode*).

- *nextSucc*(*x*,*yptr*,*ynode*) accepts two array indices (*x* and *yptr*) in the adjacency matrix representation and sets both *yptr* and *ynode* to the array index of the successor of *node*(*x*) that follows *node*(*yptr*). In the linked representation, *x* is an array index or a reference to a header node, *yptr* is a reference to an arc node and is reset to refer to the arc node that follows *node*(*yptr*) on the adjacency list, and *ynode* is set to point to the header node that terminates the arc node pointed to by the modified value of *yptr*.

In order to provide a Java implementation of these methods in both the adjacency matrix representation and the linked representation with similar headers, we define these methods as follows. Note that the parameters *yptr* and *ynode* are implemented as arrays of a single element so that they can be set to new values using a Java method.

Adjacency Matrix Representation

```
public void firstSucc(int[ ] x, int[ ] yptr, int[ ] ynode) {
  int[ ] beg = new int[1];

  beg[0] = -1;
  nextSucc(x, beg, ynode);
  yptr[0] = ynode[0];
} // end firstSucc

public void nextSucc(int[ ] x, int[ ] yptr, int[ ] ynode){
  int n = MAXNODES;

  for( int i = yptr[0] + 1; i < n; i++)
        if (adjacent(x[0], i)) {
              yptr[0] = ynode[0] = i;
              return;
        }
  yptr[0] = ynode[0] = -1;
  return;
} // end nextSucc
```

Linked Representation

```
public void firstSucc(GraphNode x, ArcNode[] yptr, GraphNode[]
ynode) {
```

```
    yptr[0] = x.arcPtr();
    ynode[0] = (yptr[0] == null) ? null : yptr[0].getPtr();

    if (yptr[0] != null)
            yptr[0].visit();
} // end firstSucc

public void nextSucc(GraphNode x, ArcNode[] yptr, GraphNode[] ynode) {
    yptr[0] = x.nextArc();
    ynode[0] = (yptr[0] == null) ? null : yptr[0].getPtr();

    if (yptr[0] != null)
            yptr[0].visit();
} // end nextSucc
```

Under each implementation, we assume a method *visit*() (see below) that marks a node as having been visited.

Traversing all of a node's successors in a graph of n nodes is $O(n)$ using the adjacency matrix representation. Under the linked representation, if e is the number of edges (arcs) in the graph and n the number of graph nodes, e/n is the average number of arcs emanating from a given node. Traversing the successors of a node by this method is therefore $O(e/n)$ on the average. If the graph is sparse (i.e., very few of the n^2 possible edges exist), this is a significant advantage of the adjacency list representation.

Given these methods, a method *traverse*() to visit all the successors of a node may be written as follows:

Adjacency Matrix Representation

```
public void traverse() {
  int[ ] yptr = new int[1];
  int[ ] ynode = new int[1];
  int[ ] x = new int[1];

for (x[0] = 0; x[0] < MAXNODES; x[0]++) {
      firstSucc(x,yptr,ynode);
      while (yptr[0] != -1) {
        visit(x, ynode);
        nextSucc(x, yptr, ynode);
      }
  } // end for
} // end traverse
```

Linked Representation

```
public void traverse() {
  GraphNode[ ] ynode = new GraphNode[1];
  ArcNode[ ] yptr = new ArcNode[1];

  Enumeration nodes = graphNodes.elements();

  while (nodes.hasMoreElements()) {
        GraphNode x = (GraphNode)nodes.nextElement();
```

```
        firstSucc(x, yptr, ynode);
        while (yptr[0] != null) {
                ynode[0].visit();
                nextSucc(x, yptr, ynode);
        }

        System.out.println();
    } // end while
} end traverse
```

3. If a node has more than one predecessor, it is necessarily encountered more than once during a traversal. Therefore, to ensure termination and to ensure that each node is visited only once, a traversal algorithm must check that a node being encountered has not been visited previously. There are two ways to do this. One is to maintain a set of visited nodes. The set would be maintained as a search tree or a hash table for efficient lookup and insertion. Whenever a node is encountered, the table is searched to see if the node has already been visited. If it has, the node is ignored; if it has not, the node is visited and added to the table. Of course, the lookup and insertion add to the traversal overhead.

The second technique is to keep a flag *visited* in each node. Initially, all flags are set off (***false***) via a quick nongraph traversal through the list of graph nodes. The *visit* method turns the flag on (***true***) in the node being visited. When a node is encountered, its flag is examined. If it is on, the node is ignored; if it is off, the node is visited and the flag is set on. The flagging technique is used more often, because the flag initialization overhead is less than the table lookup and maintenance overhead.

Spanning Forests

A ***forest*** may be defined as an acyclic graph in which every node has one or no predecessors. A ***tree*** may be defined as a forest in which only a single node (called the ***root***) has no predecessors. Any forest consists of a collection of trees. An ***ordered forest*** is one whose component trees are ordered. Given a graph G, F is a ***spanning forest*** of G if:

1. F is a subgraph of G containing all the nodes of G.
2. F is an ordered forest containing trees $T_1, T_2, \ldots, T_n$.
3. T_i contains all the nodes that are reachable in G from the root of T_i and are not contained in T_j for some $j < i$.

F is a ***spanning tree*** of G if it is a spanning forest of G and consists of a single tree.

Figure 8.4.1 illustrates four spanning forests for the graph in Figure 8.1.3. In each case, the arcs of the graph that are not included in the forest are shown as dotted arrows, and the arcs included in the forest are solid arrows. The spanning forests in Figures 8.4.1a and b are spanning trees, while those in Figures 8.4.1c and d are not.

Any spanning tree divides the edges (arcs) of a graph into four distinct groups: ***tree edges***, ***forward edges***, ***cross edges***, and ***back edges***. Tree edges are arcs of the graph that are included in the spanning forest. Forward edges are arcs of the graph from a node to a

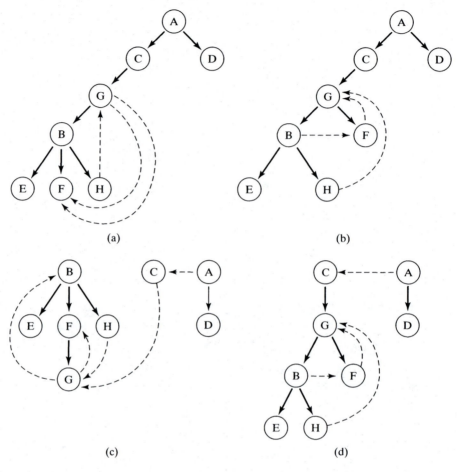

FIGURE 8.4.1

spanning forest nonson descendant. A cross edge is an arc from one node to another node that is not the first node's descendant or ancestor in the spanning forest. Back edges are arcs from a node to a spanning forest ancestor. The following table classifies the arcs of the graph in Figure 8.1.3 in relation to each of the spanning trees in Figure 8.4.1:

Arc	(a)	(b)	(c)	(d)
$<A,C>$	tree	tree	cross	cross
$<A,D>$	tree	tree	tree	tree
$<B,E>$	tree	tree	tree	tree
$<B,F>$	tree	cross	tree	cross
$<B,H>$	tree	tree	tree	tree
$<C,G>$	tree	tree	cross	tree
$<F,G>$	back	back	tree	back
$<G,B>$	tree	tree	back	tree
$<G,F>$	forward	tree	back	tree
$<H,G>$	back	back	cross	back

Consider a traversal method that visits all the nodes reachable from a previously visited node before visiting any node not reachable from a previously visited node. In such a traversal, a node is visited either arbitrarily or as the successor of a previously visited node. The traversal defines a spanning forest in which an arbitrarily selected node is the root of a tree in the spanning forest, and in which a node $n1$ selected as the successor of $n2$ is a son of $n2$ in the spanning forest. For example, the traversal *ACGBEFHD* defines the forest in Figure 8.4.1a, and the traversal *BEFGHCAD* defines the one in Figure 8.4.1c. While any particular traversal defines only a single spanning forest, a number of traversals may define the same forest. For example, *ACDGBEFH* also defines the spanning forest in Figure 8.4.1a.

Undirected Graphs and Their Traversals

Thus far, we have only considered directed graphs. An undirected graph may be considered a ***symmetric*** directed graph, that is, one in which an arc $<B,A>$ must exist whenever an arc $<A,B>$ exists. The undirected arc (A,B) represents the two directed arcs $<A,B>$ and $<B,A>$.

An undirected graph may therefore be represented as a directed graph using either the adjacency matrix or the adjacency list method. An adjacency matrix representing an undirected graph must be symmetric; the values in row i, column j and in row j, column i must be either both ***false*** [i.e., the arc (i,j) does not exist in the graph] or both ***true*** [the arc (i,j) does exist]. In the adjacency list representation, if (i,j) is an undirected arc, the arc list emanating from *node(i)* contains a list node representing directed arc $<i,j>$, and the list emanating from *node(j)* contains a list node representing directed arc $<j,i>$. In an undirected graph, if a node x is reachable from a node y (i.e., there is a path from y to x), then y is reachable from x as well along the reversed path.

Since an undirected graph is represented by a directed graph, any traversal method for directed graphs induces a traversal method for undirected graphs as well. Figure 8.4.2 illustrates an undirected graph and two spanning trees for it. The tree in Figure 8.4.2b is created by either of the traversals *ABEFKGCDHIJ* or *ABEFGKCHDIJ*, among others. The tree in Figure 8.4.2c is created by the traversal *ABEFGKDCJHI* or *ABDJECHIFGK*, among others. Note that the edges included and excluded from the spanning tree are all bidirectional.

Spanning forests constructed by undirected graph traversals have several special properties. First, there is no distinction between forward edges (or tree edges) and back edges. Since an edge in an undirected graph is bidirectional, such a distinction is meaningless. In an undirected graph, any arc between a node and its nonson descendant is called a back edge.

Second, in an undirected graph, all cross edges are within a single tree. Cross edges between trees arise in a directed graph traversal when there is an arc $<x,y>$ such that y is visited before x and there is no path from y to x. Therefore, the arc $<x,y>$ is a cross edge. In an undirected graph containing an arc (x,y), x and y must be part of the same tree, since each is reachable from the other via that arc at least. A cross edge in an undirected graph is possible only if three nodes x, y, and z are part of a cycle, and y and z are in separate subtrees of a subtree whose root is x. The path between y and z must then include a cross edge between the two subtrees. Confirm that this is the case with all the cross edges in Figure 8.4.2c.

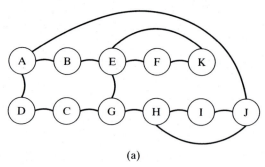

(a)

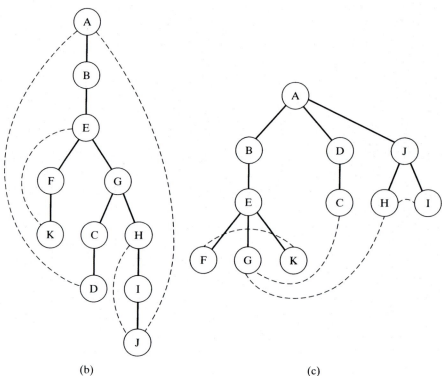

(b)   (c)

FIGURE 8.4.2

Because undirected graphs have "double" the edges of directed graphs, their spanning forests tend to have fewer, but larger, trees.

An undirected graph is termed **_connected_** if every node in it is reachable from every other. Pictorially, a connected graph has only one segment. For example, the graph in Figure 8.4.2a is a connected graph. The graph in Figure 8.1.1a is not connected because node E is not reachable from node C, for example. A **_connected component_** of an undirected graph is a connected subgraph containing all the arcs incident to any of its nodes such that no graph node outside the subgraph is reachable from any node in the subgraph. For example, the subgraph in Figure 8.1.1a has three connected components:

nodes A,B,C,D,F; nodes E and G; and node H. A connected graph has a single connected component.

The spanning forest of a connected graph is a spanning tree. Each tree in the spanning forest of an undirected graph contains all the nodes in a single connected component of the graph. Thus any traversal method that creates a spanning forest (i.e., one that visits all the nodes reachable from visited nodes before visiting any other nodes) can be used to determine whether an undirected graph is connected and to identify its connected components.

In traversing an undirected graph, it is not very important which node s is used as the starting node or how *select* chooses an arbitrary node (except perhaps in terms of the efficiency of *select*.) This is because all the nodes of a connected component will wind up in the same tree regardless of the choice of s or how *select* operates. This is not true in traversing a directed graph.

For example, the traversal in Figures 8.4.1a and b used $s = A$. Since all the nodes are reachable from A, the spanning forest is a tree, and *select* is never needed to choose an arbitrary node once that tree is built. In Figure 8.4.1c, however, B is the starting node, so only nodes reachable from B are included in the first tree. *select* then chooses C. Since only visited nodes are reachable from C, it is alone in its tree. *select* is then required again to choose A, whose tree completes the traversal. In Figure 8.4.1d, s equals C, and *select* is required only once, when it returns A. Thus, if it is desired to create as large and as few trees as possible, s should be a node with as few predecessors as possible (preferably none), and *select* should choose such a node as well. This may make *select* less efficient.

We now examine two traversal methods and their applications to both directed and undirected graphs.

Depth-First Traversal

The **depth-first** traversal technique is best defined using an algorithm *dfTraverse(s)* that visits all the nodes reachable from s. This algorithm will be presented shortly. We assume an algorithm *nd.visit()* that visits a node *nd*, and a method *nd.visited()* that returns **true** if *nd* has already been visited, and **false** otherwise. This is best implemented by a flag in each node. *visit* sets the field to **true**. To execute the traversal, the field is first set **false** for all nodes. The traversal algorithm also assumes the method *select* with no parameters to select an arbitrary unvisited node. *select* returns **null** if all the nodes have been visited.

```
for (every node nd)
    nd.visited() = false;
s = a reference to the starting node for the traversal;
while (s != null) {
    dfTraverse(s);
    s = select();
}
```

Note that a starting node s is specified for the traversal. This node becomes the root of the first tree in the spanning forest. The following is a recursive algorithm for *dfTraverse(s)*, using the methods *firstSucc* and *nextSucc* presented earlier:

```
// visit all nodes reachable from s
visit(s);
// traverse all unvisited successors of s
firstSucc(s,yptr,nd);
while (yptr != null) {
    if (nd.visited() == false)
        dfTraverse(nd);
    nextSucc(s,yptr,nd);
} // end while
```

If it is known that every node in the graph is reachable from the starting node s (as in the case of the graph in Figure 8.1.3, starting from node A, or in the case of a connected undirected graph like the one in Figure 8.4.2a), then the spanning forest is a single spanning tree, and the **while** loop and *select* are not required in the traversal algorithm because every node is visited in a single call to *dfTraverse*.

A depth-first traversal, as its name indicates, traverses a single path of the graph as far as it can go (i.e., until it visits a node with no successors or a node all of whose successors have already been visited). It then resumes at the last node on the path just traversed that has an unvisited successor and begins traversing a new path emanating from that node. Spanning trees created by a depth-first traversal tend to be very deep. Depth-first traversal is also sometimes called *depth-first search*.

Figures 8.4.1a and c are both depth-first spanning trees of the graph in Figure 8.1.3. In Figure 8.4.1a, the traversal started at A and proceeded as follows: *ACGBEFHD*. Note that this is the preorder traversal of the spanning tree. In fact, the depth-first traversal of a tree is its preorder traversal. In Figure 8.4.1c, the traversal starts at B and proceeds as follows: *BEFGH*. At that point, all the nodes reachable from B have been visited, so *select* is called to find an arbitrary unvisited node. Figure 8.4.1c assumes that *select* returned a reference to C. But no unvisited nodes are successors of C (G has already been visited), so *select* is called again and returns A. D is an unvisited successor of A and is visited to complete the traversal. Thus Figure 8.4.1c corresponds to the complete depth-first traversal *BEFGHCAD*.

This illustrates that there may be several depth-first traversals and depth-first spanning trees for any directed graph. The traversal depends very much on how the graph is represented (adjacency matrix or adjacency list), how the nodes are numbered, the starting node, and how the basic depth-first traversal is implemented (in particular, the implementation of *firstSucc*, *nextSucc*, and *select*). The essential feature of a depth-first traversal is that, after a node is visited, all its descendants are visited before its unvisited brothers. Figure 8.4.2b represents the depth-first traversal *ABEFKGCDHIJ* of the undirected graph in Figure 8.4.2a.

As usual, a stack can be used to eliminate the recursion in depth- first traversal. The following is a complete nonrecursive depth-first traversal algorithm:

```
for (every node nd)
    set visited to false;
s = a pointer to the starting node for the traversal;
ndStack = the empty stack;
while (s != null) {
    s.visit();
```

```
    // find first unvisited successor
    firstSucc(s,yptr,nd);
    while (nd != null && nd.visited() == true)
        nextSucc(s,yptr,nd);
    // if no unvisited successors, simulate return from recursive call
while (nd == null && ndStack.isEmpty() == false) {
    s = ndStack.popsub(yptr);
    // find next unvisited successor
    nextSucc(s,yptr,nd);
    while (nd != null && nd.visited() == true)
        nextSucc(s,yptr,nd);
}   // end while
if (nd != null) {
    // simulate the recursive call
    ndStack.push(s,yptr);
    s = nd;
}   // end if
else
    s = select();
} // end while (s != null)
```

Note that each stack element contains pointers to both a father node (*s*) and an incident arc or its son (*yptr*) to allow continuation of the traversal of the successors.

To use this algorithm to construct a spanning tree, it is necessary to keep track of a node's father when it is visited, as follows. First, change the *if* statement at the end of the algorithm to

```
if (nd != null) {
    // simulate the recursive call
    push(ndStack,s,yptr);
    f = s;                  // this statement is added
    s = nd;
}
else {
    s = select();
    f = null;               // this statement is added
}
```

Second, initialize *f* to *null* at the beginning of the algorithm. Third, change *visit(s)* to *addSon(f,s)*; *visited(s)* = *true*, where *addSon* adds *node(s)* to the tree as the next son of *node(f)*. [Recall that *visit(s)* was defined to set *visited(s)* to *true*.] If *f* is *null*, *addSon(f,s)* adds *node(s)* as a new tree in the forest (e.g., it calls *makeTree*. It is assumed that the tree roots are kept in a linked list managed by *makeTree* using two global variables pointing to the first and last trees in the forest.)

You are invited to apply this modified algorithm to the graph in Figure 8.1.3, with *s* initialized to *A*, and the successors of any node ordered alphabetically, to obtain the spanning tree in Figure 8.4.1a. Similarly, applying the modified algorithm to the same graph, with *s* initialized to *B*, and assuming that select chooses *C* before *A* and *D*, and *A* before *D*, yields the spanning forest in Figure 8.4.1c. Applying the algorithm to the graph in Figure 8.4.2a produces the tree in Figure 8.2.4b.

As illustrated by Figure 8.4.2b, a depth-first spanning forest of an undirected graph may contain tree edges and back edges but cannot contain any cross edges. To see why, assume that (x,y) is an edge in the graph, and that x is visited before y. In a depth-first traversal, y must be visited as a descendant of x before any nodes that are not reachable from x. Thus the arc (x,y) is either a tree edge or a back edge. The same is true in reverse if y is visited first, since the undirected arc (x,y) is equivalent to (y,x). In a directed graph, however, the arc $<x,y>$ but not $<y,x>$ may be in the graph. If y is visited first, then since x may not be reachable from y, x may not be in a subtree rooted at y, so the arc $<x,y>$ may be a cross edge even in a depth-first spanning tree. This is illustrated by the arcs $<A,C>$ and $<C,G>$ in Figure 8.4.1c.

Applications of Depth-First Traversal

Depth-first traversal, like any other traversal method that creates a spanning forest, can be used to determine whether an undirected graph is connected and to identify the connected components of an undirected graph. Whenever *select* is called, a new connected component of the graph is being traversed. If *select* is never called, the graph is connected.

Depth-first traversal can also be used to determine whether a graph is acyclic. In both directed and undirected graphs, a cycle exists if and only if a back edge exists in a depth-first spanning forest. It is obvious that if a back edge exists, the graph contains a cycle formed by the back edge itself and the tree path, starting at the ancestor head of the back edge, and ending at the descendant tail of the back edge. To prove that a back edge must exist in a cyclic graph, consider the node *nd* of a cycle that is the first node in its cycle visited by a depth-first traversal. There must exist a node x such that the arc (x,nd) or $<x,nd>$ is in the cycle. Since x is in the cycle, it is reachable from *nd*, so that x must be a descendant of *nd* in the spanning forest. Thus the arc (x,nd) or $<x,nd>$ is a back edge by definition.

Therefore, to determine whether a graph is acyclic, it is only necessary to determine that an edge encountered during a depth-first traversal is not a back edge. When considering an edge (s,nd) or $<s,nd>$ in the depth-first traversal algorithm, the edge can be a back edge only if *visited(nd)* is *true*. In an undirected graph, where there are no cross edges in a depth-first traversal, (s,nd) is a back edge if and only if *visited(nd)* is *true* and *nd! = father(s)* in the spanning forest.

In a directed graph, $<s,nd>$ can be a back edge even if *nd == father(s)* because $<s,nd>$ and $<nd,s>$ are distinct arcs. Thus, in a directed graph, a cycle may consist of only two nodes (e.g., s and *nd*), whereas at least three are required in an undirected graph. However, since a directed graph's spanning tree may contain cross edges as well as back edges, *visited(nd)* equaling true is not enough to detect a cycle. For example, the cross edges $<A,C>$, $<H,G>$, and $<C,G>$ in Figure 8.4.1c are not part of a cycle, although C has been visited by the time $<A,C>$ is considered, and G has been visited by the time $<H,G>$ and $<C,G>$ are considered. To determine that an arc $<s,nd>$ is not a back edge when *visited(nd)* is *true*, it is necessary to consider each ancestor of s in turn to ensure that it does not equal *nd*. We leave the details of an algorithm to determine whether a directed graph is acyclic (i.e., a dag) as an exercise for the reader.

In the previous section, we examined an algorithm to schedule tasks given a series of required precedences among them. We saw that the precedence relations among the tasks can be represented by a dag. The algorithm presented can be used to specify a linear ordering of the nodes in which no node comes before a preceding node. Such a linear ordering is called a ***topological sort*** of the nodes.

A depth-first traversal can be used to produce a reverse topological ordering of the nodes. Consider the inorder traversal of the spanning forest formed by a depth-first traversal of a dag. We now prove that such an inorder traversal produces a reverse topological ordering.

To repeat the recursive definition of inorder traversal of a forest from Section 5.5:

1. Traverse the forest formed by the subtrees of the first tree in the forest, if any.
2. Visit the root of the first tree.
3. Traverse the forest formed by the remaining trees in the forest, if any.

In the following discussion, to differentiate the depth-first traversal that creates the forest from the inorder traversal of the forest, we refer to DF-visits (and a DF-traversal) and IO-visits (and an IO-traversal) respectively.

An IO-traversal of the depth-first spanning tree of a dag must be in reverse topological order. That is, if x precedes y, then x is IO-visited after y. To see why this is so, consider the arc $<x,y>$. We show that y is IO-visited before x. Since the graph is acyclic, $<x,y>$ cannot be a back arc. If it is a tree arc or a forward arc, so that y is a descendant of x in the spanning forest, then y is IO-visited before x because an inorder traversal IO-visits the root of a subtree after traversing all its subtrees. If $<x,y>$ is a cross edge, then y must have been IO-visited before x (otherwise, y would have been a descendant of x). Consider the smallest subtrees, $S(x)$ and $S(y)$, containing x and y respectively whose roots are brothers. (Roots of trees in the spanning forest are also considered brothers in this context.) Then, since y was DF-visited before x, $S(y)$ precedes $S(x)$ in their subtree ordering. Thus $S(y)$ is IO-traversed before $S(x)$, which means that y is IO-visited before x.

Thus an algorithm to determine a reverse topological ordering of the nodes of a dag consists of a depth-first search of the dag followed by an inorder traversal of the resulting spanning forest. Fortunately, it is unnecessary to make a separate traversal of the spanning tree, since an inorder traversal can be incorporated directly into the recursive depth-first traversal algorithm. To do this, simply push a node onto a stack when it is DF-visited. Whenever *dfTraverse* returns, pop the stack and IO-visit the popped node. Since *dfTraverse* DF-traverses all the subtrees of a tree before completing the tree's DF-traversal, and traverses the first subtree of a set of brothers before DF-traversing the others, this routine yields an IO-traversal. The reader is invited to implement this algorithm nonrecursively.

Efficiency of Depth-First Traversal

The depth-first traversal routine visits every node of a graph and traverses all the successors of each node. We have already seen that, for the adjacency matrix implementation, traversing all the successors of a node using *firstSucc* and *nextSucc* is $O(n)$, where n is the number of graph nodes. Thus traversing the successors of all the nodes is $O(n^2)$. For this reason, depth-first search using the adjacency matrix representation is $O(n + n^2)$ (n node visits and n^2 possible successor examinations), which is the same as $O(n^2)$.

If the adjacency list representation is used, then traversing all the successors of all the nodes is $O(e)$, where e is the number of edges in the graph. Assuming that the graph nodes are organized as an array or a linked list, visiting all n nodes is $O(n)$, so that the efficiency of depth-first traversal using adjacency lists is $O(n + e)$. Since e is usually much smaller than n^2, the adjacency list representation yields more efficient traversals. (The difference, however, is somewhat offset by the fact that in an adjacency matrix, traversal of successors merely involves counting from 1 to n, while in an adjacency list, it involves successively accessing fields in nodes.) Depth-first traversal is often considered $O(e)$ because e is usually larger than n.

Breadth-First Traversal

An alternative traversal method, **breadth-first traversal** (or **breadth-first search**), visits all the successors of a visited node before visiting any successors of any of the successors. This is in contradistinction to depth-first traversal, which visits the successors of a visited node before visiting any of its "brothers." Whereas depth-first traversal tends to create very long, narrow trees, breadth-first traversal tends to create very wide, short trees. Figure 8.4.1b represents a breadth-first traversal of the graph in Figure 8.1.3, and Figure 8.4.2c represents a breadth-first traversal of the graph in Figure 8.4.2a.

In implementing depth-first traversal, each visited node is placed on a stack (either implicitly via recursion or explicitly), reflecting the fact that the last node visited is the first node whose successors will be visited. Breadth-first traversal is implemented using a queue, representing the fact that the first node visited is the first node whose successors are visited. The following is an algorithm *bfTraverse(s)* to traverse a graph using breadth-first traversal beginning at *node(s)*:

```
ndQueue = the empty queue;
while (s != null) {
    s.visit();
    ndQueue.insert(s);
    while (ndQueue.isEmpty() == false) {
        x = ndQueue.remove();
        // visit all successors of x
        firstSucc(x,yptr,nd);
        while (nd != null) {
            if (nd.visited(nd) == false) {
                    nd.visit(nd);
                    ndQueue.insert(nd);
            } // end if
            nextSucc(x,yptr,nd);
        } // end while
    } // end while
    s = select();
} // end while
```

We leave the modification of the algorithm to produce a breadth-first spanning forest as an exercise for the reader. Figure 8.4.1b illustrates a breadth-first spanning tree for the graph in Figure 8.1.3, representing the breadth-first traversal *ACDGBFEH*. Note that while the traversal differs significantly from the depth-first traversal *ACGBEFHD* that produced the spanning tree in Figure 8.4.1a, the two spanning trees themselves do not differ except for the position of node *F*. This reflects the fact that the graph in Figure 8.1.3 has relatively few arcs (10) compared to the total number of potential arcs ($n^2 = 64$). In a graph with more arcs, the difference in spanning forests is more pronounced.

A breadth-first spanning tree does not have any forward edges, since all the nodes adjacent to a visited node *nd* have already been visited or are spanning tree sons of *nd*. For the same reason, for a directed graph, all the cross edges within the same tree are to nodes on the same or higher levels of the tree. For an undirected graph, a breadth-first spanning forest contains no back edges, since every back edge is also a forward edge.

Breadth-first traversal can be used for some of the same applications as depth-first traversal. In particular, breadth-first traversal can be used to determine whether an undirected graph is connected and to identify its connected components. Breadth-first traversal can also be used to determine whether a graph is cyclic. For a directed graph, this is detected when a back edge is found; for an undirected graph, it is detected when a cross edge within the same tree is found.

For an unweighted graph, breadth-first traversal can also be used to find the shortest path (fewest arcs) from one node to another. Simply begin the traversal at the first node, and stop when the target node has been reached. The breadth-first spanning tree path from the root to the target is the shortest path between the two nodes.

The efficiency of breadth-first traversal is the same as that of depth-first traversal: each node is visited once, and all the arcs emanating from every node are considered. Thus its efficiency is $O(n^2)$ for the adjacency matrix graph representation, and $O(n + e)$ for the adjacency list graph representation.

Minimum Spanning Trees

Given a connected weighted graph *G*, it is often desired to create a spanning tree *T* for *G* such that the sum of the weights of the tree edges in *T* is as small as possible. Such a tree is called a ***minimum spanning tree*** and represents the "cheapest" way of connecting all the nodes in *G*.

There are a number of techniques for creating a minimum spanning tree for a weighted graph. The first of these, ***Prim's algorithm***, discovered independently by Prim and Dijkstra, is very much like Dijkstra's algorithm for finding the shortest paths. An arbitrary node is chosen initially as the tree root (note that in an undirected graph and its spanning tree, any node can be considered the tree root, and the nodes adjacent to it are its sons). The nodes of the graph are then appended to the tree one at a time until all the nodes of the graph are included.

The node of the graph added to the tree at each point is that node adjacent to a node of the tree by an arc of minimum weight. The arc of minimum weight becomes a tree arc connecting the new node to the tree. When all the nodes of the graph have been added to the tree, a minimum spanning tree has been constructed for the graph.

To see that this technique creates a minimum spanning tree, consider a minimum spanning tree *T* for the graph, and consider the partial tree *PT* built by Prim's algorithm at any point. Suppose that (*a*,*b*) is the minimum-cost arc from nodes in *PT* to nodes not in *PT*, and suppose that (*a*,*b*) is not in *T*. Then, since there is a path between any two graph nodes in a spanning tree, there must be an alternative path between *a* and *b* in *T* that does not include arc (*a*,*b*). This alternative path *P* must include an arc (*x*,*y*) from a node in *PT* to a node outside of *PT*. Let us assume that *P* contains subpaths between *a* and *x* and between *y* and *b*.

Now, consider what would happen if we replaced arc (*x*,*y*) in *T* with (*a*,*b*) to create *NT*. We claim that *NT* is also a spanning tree. To prove this, we need to show two things: that any two nodes of the graph are connected in *NT*, and that *NT* does not contain a cycle; that is, that there is only one path between any two nodes in *NT*.

Since *T* is a spanning tree, any two nodes, *m* and *n*, are connected in *T*. If the path between them in *T* does not contain (*x*,*y*), then the same path connects them in *NT*. If the path between them in *T* does contain (*x*,*y*), then consider the path in *NT* formed by the subpath in *T* from *m* to *x*, the subpath in *P* (which is in *T*) from *x* to *a*, the arc (*a*,*b*), the subpath in *P* from *b* to *y*, and the subpath in *T* from *y* to *n*. This is a path from *m* to *n* in *NT*. Thus any two nodes of the graph are connected in *NT*.

To show that *NT* does not contain a cycle, suppose it did. If the cycle does not contain (*a*,*b*), then the same cycle would exist in *T*. But that is impossible because *T* is a spanning tree. Thus the cycle must contain (*a*,*b*). Now consider the same cycle with arc (*a*,*b*) replaced by the subpath of *P* between *a* and *x*, the arc (*x*,*y*), and the subpath in *P* between *y* and *b*. The resulting path must also be a cycle and is a path entirely in *T*. But, again, *T* cannot contain a cycle. Therefore *NT* also does not contain a cycle.

NT has thus been shown to be a spanning tree. But *NT* must have lower cost than *T*, since (*a*,*b*) was chosen to have lower cost than (*x*,*y*). Thus *T* is not a minimum spanning tree unless it includes the lowest-weight arc from *PT* to nodes outside *PT*. Therefore any arc added by Prim's algorithm must be part of a minimum spanning tree.

The crux of the algorithm is a method for efficient determination of the "closest" node to a partial spanning tree. Initially, when the partial tree consists of a single root node, the distance of any other node *nd* from the tree, *distance*[*nd*], is equal to *weight*(*root*, *nd*). When a new node, *current*, is added to the tree, *distance*[*nd*] is modified to the minimum of *distance*[*nd*] and *weight*(*current*, *nd*). The node added to the tree at each point is the node whose distance is lowest. For nodes *tnd* in the tree, *distance*[*tnd*] is set to *infinity*, so that a node outside the tree is chosen as closest. An additional array *closest*[*nd*] points to the node in the tree such that *distance*[*nd*]= *weight*(*closest*[*nd*],*nd*); that is, the node in the tree closest to *nd*. If two nodes, *x* and *y*, are not adjacent, *weight*(*x*,*y*) is also *infinity*.

Prim's algorithm may therefore be implemented as follows:

```
root = an arbitrary node chosen as root;
for (every node nd in the graph) {
    distance[nd] = weight(root,nd);
    closest[nd] = root;
}
distance[root] = INFINITY;
current = root;
for (i = 1; i < number of nodes in the graph; ++i) {
    // find the node closest to the tree
    minDist = INFINITY;
```

```
for (every node nd in the graph)
        if (distance[nd] < minDist) {
                current = nd;
                minDist = distance[nd];
        }
// add the closest node to the tree and adjust distances
addson(closest[current],current);
distance[current] = INFINITY;
for (every node nd adjacent to current)
        if (distance[nd] < INFINITY && weight(current,nd) <
           distance[nd]) {
           distance[nd] = weight(current,nd);
           closest[nd] = current;
        }
}
```

If the graph is represented by an adjacency matrix, then each for loop in Prim's algorithm must examine $O(n)$ nodes. Since the algorithm contains a nested for loop, it is $O(n^2)$.

However, just like Dijkstra's algorithm, Prim's algorithm can be made more efficient by maintaining the graph using adjacency lists and keeping a priority queue of the nodes not in the partial tree. The first inner loop [*for*(*every node nd in the graph*) ...] can then be replaced by removing the minimum-distance node from the priority queue and adjusting the priority queue. The second inner loop simply traverses an adjacency list and adjusts the position of any nodes whose distance is modified in the priority queue. Under this implementation, Prim's algorithm is $O((n + e) \log n)$.

Kruskal's Algorithm

Another algorithm to create a minimum spanning tree is due to Kruskal. The nodes of the graph are initially considered as n distinct partial trees with one node each. At each step of the algorithm, two distinct partial trees are connected into a single partial tree by an edge of the graph. When only one partial tree exists (after $n - 1$ such steps), it is a minimum spanning tree.

The issue, of course, is what connecting arc to use at each step. The answer is to use the arc of minimum cost that connects two distinct trees. To do this, the arcs can be placed in a priority queue based on weight. The arc of lowest weight is then examined to see whether it connects two distinct trees. In order to determine whether an arc (x,y) connects distinct trees, we can implement the trees with a *father* field in each node. Then we can traverse all the ancestors of x and y to obtain the roots of the trees containing them. If the roots of the two trees are the same node, then x and y are already in the same tree, arc (x,y) is discarded, and the arc of next lowest weight is examined. Combining two trees simply involves setting the *father* of the root of one to the root of the other.

We leave the actual algorithm and its Java implementation for the reader. Forming the initial priority queue is $O(e \log e)$. Removing the minimum-weight arc and adjusting the priority queue is $O(\log e)$. Locating the root of a tree is $O(\log n)$. Initial formation of the n trees is $O(n)$. Thus, assuming that $n < e$, as is true of most graphs, Kruskal's algorithm is $O(e \log e)$.

Round-Robin Algorithm

Still another algorithm, due to Tarjan and Cheriton, provides even better performance when the number of edges is low. The algorithm is similar to Kruskal's except that there is a priority queue of arcs associated with each partial tree, rather than one global priority queue of all unexamined arcs.

   All partial trees are maintained in a queue, Q. Associated with each partial tree, T, is a priority queue, $P(T)$, of all the arcs with exactly one incident node in the tree, ordered by the weights of the arcs. Initially, as in Kruskal's algorithm, each node is a partial tree. A priority queue of all arcs incident to nd is created for each node nd, and the single-node trees are inserted into Q in arbitrary order. The algorithm proceeds by removing a partial tree, $T1$, from the front of Q; finding the minimum-weight arc a in $P(T1)$; deleting from Q the tree, $T2$, at the other end of arc a; combining $T1$ and $T2$ into a single new tree $T3$ [and at the same time combining $P(T1)$ and $P(T2)$, with a deleted, into $P(T3)$]; and adding $T3$ to the rear of Q. This continues until Q contains a single tree: the minimum spanning tree.

   It can be shown that this round-robin algorithm requires only $O(e \log \log n)$ operations if an appropriate implementation of the priority queues is used.

EXERCISES

8.4.1   Consider the following nonrecursive depth-first traversal algorithm:

```
for (every node nd)
      set visited to false;
s = a pointer to the starting node of the traversal;
ndStack = the empty stack;
while (s != null) {
     ndStack.push(s);
     while (ndStack.isEmpty() == false) {
          x = ndStack.pop();
          if (x.visited() == false) {
               x.visit();
               firstSucc(x,yptr,nd);
               while(nd != null) {
                    if (nd.visited() == false)
                         ndStack.push(nd);
                    nextSucc(x,yptr,nd);
               }
          }
     }
     s = select();
}
```

a. Apply the algorithm to the graphs in Figures 8.1.3 and 8.4.2a to determine the order in which the nodes are visited, if the successors of a node are assumed ordered in alphabetical order.

b. Draw the spanning trees induced by the traversal on each of the graphs. Modify the algorithm to construct a depth-first spanning forest.

    c. Would a modified ordering of successors produce the spanning trees in Figures 8.4.1a and 8.4.2b using this algorithm? Would a modified ordering produce the spanning trees in (b) using the algorithm of the text?

    d. Is either algorithm preferable?

8.4.2 Write an algorithm and a Java application to determine whether a directed graph is a dag.

8.4.3 Write a recursive Java application to print the nodes of a dag in reverse topological order.

8.4.4 Write a nonrecursive Java application to print the nodes of a dag in reverse topological order.

8.4.5 A node *nd* in a connected graph is an ***articulation point*** if removing *nd* and all the arcs adjacent to *nd* results in an unconnected graph. Thus the "connectedness" of the graph depends on *nd*. A graph with no articulation points is called ***biconnected***.

    a. Show that the root of the depth-first spanning tree of a biconnected graph has only a single son.

    b. Show that if *nd* is not the root of a depth-first spanning tree *t*, then *nd* is an articulation point if and only if *t* does not contain a back edge from a descendant of *nd* to an ancestor of *nd*.

    c. Modify the recursive depth-first traversal algorithm to determine whether a connected graph is biconnected.

8.4.6 Write a Java method to create a breadth-first spanning forest of a graph.

8.4.7 Write Java methods that use a breadth-first traversal to determine whether a directed and an undirected graph are cyclic.

8.4.8 Write a Java method to produce the shortest path from node x to node y in an unweighted graph, if a path exists, or an indication that no path exists between the two nodes.

8.4.9 Show that the algorithms to find a cycle using depth-first or breadth-first search must be $O(n)$.

8.4.10 Implement Prim's algorithm using an adjacency matrix, adjacency lists, and a priority queue.

8.4.11 Implement Kruskal's algorithm as a Java method.

C H A P T E R   9

Storage Management

A programming language that incorporates a large number of data structures must contain mechanisms for managing them and for controlling how storage is assigned to them. The previous chapters of this book illustrated some of these management techniques. As data structures become more complex and provide greater capabilities, the management techniques grow in complexity as well.

In this chapter, we look at several techniques for implementing dynamic allocation and freeing storage. Most of these methods are used in some form by operating systems to grant or deny user program requests. Others are used directly by individual language processors. We begin by expanding the concept of a list.

9.1   GENERAL LISTS

In Chapter 4 and in Section 7.1, we examined linked lists as a concrete data structure and as a method of implementation for such abstract data types as the stack, queue, priority queue, and table. In those implementations, a list always contained elements of the same type.

It is also possible to view a list as an abstract data type in its own right. As an abstract data type, a list is simply a sequence of objects called *elements*. Associated with each list element is a *value*. We make a very specific distinction between an *element*, which is an object as part of a list, and the element's *value*, which is the object considered individually. For example, the number 5 may appear on a list twice. Each appearance is a distinct element of the list, but the values of the two elements—the number 5—are the same. An element may be viewed as corresponding to a node in the linked list implementation, while a value corresponds to the node's contents. Note that the phrase "linked list" refers to the linked implementation of the abstract data type "list."

There is no reason to assume that the elements of a list must be of the same type. Figure 9.1.1 illustrates a linked list implementation of an abstract list *list*1 that contains both integers and characters. The elements of that list are 5, 12, 's', 147, and 'a'. The reference *list*1 is called an **external pointer** to the list (because it is not contained within a list node), whereas the other references in the list are **internal pointers** (because they are contained within list nodes). We often reference a linked list by an external pointer

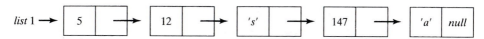

FIGURE 9.1.1 List of integers and characters.

to it. In this chapter, since the memory management system may be implemented at a level lower than the Java language, we use the terms "reference" and "pointer" interchangeably. Thus references may be implemented by pointers or by actual memory locations or offsets.

It is not necessary that a list contain only "simple" elements (e.g., integers or characters or, for that matter, objects of a type other than a list); it is possible for one or more of the elements of a list to themselves be lists. The simplest way to implement a list element e whose value is itself a list, l, is by representing the element by a node containing a pointer to the linked list implementation of l.

For example, consider the list $list2$ in Figure 9.1.2. This list contains four elements. Two of them are integers (the first element is the integer 5; the third is the integer 2), and the other two are lists. The list that is the second element of $list2$ contains five elements, three of which are integers (the first, second, and fifth elements) and two of which are lists [the third element is a list containing the integers 14, 9, and 3, and the fourth element is the null list (the list with no elements)]. The fourth element of $list2$ is a list containing the three integers 6, 3, and 10.

There is a convenient notation for specifying abstract general lists. A list may be denoted by a parenthesized enumeration of its elements separated by commas. For example, the abstract list represented by Figure 9.1.1 may be denoted by

$$list1 = (5, 12, \text{'s'}, 147, \text{'a'})$$

The null list is denoted by empty parentheses (e.g., ()). Thus the list in Figure 9.1.2 may be denoted by

$$list2 = (5, (3, 2, (14, 9, 3), (), 4), 2, (6, 3, 10))$$

We now define a number of abstract operations on lists. For now, we are concerned only with the definition and logical properties of the operations; we consider methods of implementing the operations later in this section. If $list$ is a nonempty list, then

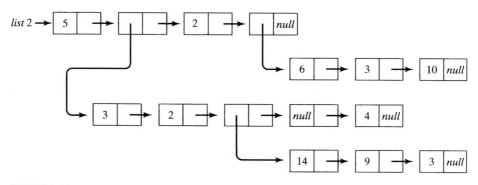

FIGURE 9.1.2

list.head() is defined as the value of the first element of *list*. If *list* is a nonempty list, *list.tail()* is defined as the list obtained by removing the first element of *list*. If *list* is the empty list, *list.head()* and *list.tail()* are not defined. For a general list, *list.head()* may be either a list (if the value of the first list element is itself a list) or a simple data item; *list.tail()* must be a (possibly null) list.

For example, if *list1* and *list2* are as in Figures 9.1.1 and 9.1.2, then:

$$list1 = (5, 12, \text{'s'}, 147, \text{'a'})$$

$$list1.head() = 5$$

$$list1.tail() = (12, \text{'s'}, 147, \text{'a'})$$

$$(list1.tail()).head() = 12$$

$$(list1.tail()).tail() = (\text{'s'}, 147, \text{'a'})$$

$$list2 = (5, (3, 2, (14, 9, 3), (), 4), 2, (6, 3, 10))$$

$$list2.tail() = ((3, 2, (14, 9, 3), (), 4), 2, (6, 3, 10))$$

$$(list2.tail()).head() = (3, 2, (14, 9, 3), (), 4)$$

$$((list2.tail()).head()).head() = 3$$

The *head* and *tail* operations are not defined if their argument is not a list. A **sublist** of a list *l* is a list that results from the application of zero or more *tail* operations to *l*.

The operation **list.first()** returns the first element (or node) of list *list*. (If *list* is empty, *list.first()* is a special **null element**, which we denote by *nullelt*.) The operation **elt.info()** returns the value of the list element *elt*. The *head* operation produces a value, while the *first* operation produces an element. In fact, *list.head()* equals *(list.first()).info()*. Finally, the operation **elt.next()** returns the element that follows the element *elt* on its list. This definition presupposes that an element can have only one follower.

The operation **elt.nodeType()** accepts a list element *elt* and returns an indication of the type of the element's value. Recall that an element is represented by a node in the linked list implementation. Thus if the enumerated constants *ch*, *intgr*, and *lst* represent the types character, integer, and list, respectively, then *(list1.first()).nodeType()* equals *intgr*, *(first((list1.tail()).tail())).nodeType()* equals *ch*, and *((list2.tail()).first()).nodeType()* equals *lst*.

Operations That Modify a List

head, *tail*, *first*, *info*, *next*, and *nodeType* extract information from lists already in existence. We now consider operations that build and modify lists.

Recall the *push* operation in Chapter 2 and its list implementation in Section 4.2. If *list* refers to a list, the operation *list.push(x)* adds an element with value *x* to the front of the list. To illustrate the use of the *push* operation in constructing lists, consider the list (5, 10, 8), which can be constructed by the operations:

```
list = null;
list.push(8);
list.push(10);
list.push(5);
```

Note that the abstract *push* operation changes the value of its invoking list to the newly created list. We introduce as a new operation the method

```
list.addOn(x)
```

which returns a new list that has *x* as its head and *list* as its tail. For example, if *l*1 = (3, 4, 7), then the operation

```
l2 = l1.addOn(5);
```

creates a new list *l*2 equal to (5, 3, 4, 7). The crucial difference between *push* and *addOn* is that *push* changes the value of its invoking list and *addOn* does not. Thus, in the example above, *l*1 retains the value (3, 4, 7). The operation *list.push*(*x*) is equivalent to *list* = *list.addOn*(*x*). Since *addOn* is more flexible than *push*, and since *push* is usually used only in connection with stacks, we henceforth use *addOn* exclusively.

Two other operations used to modify lists are **setInfo** and **setNext**. *elt.setInfo*(*x*) changes the value of a list element *elt* to the value *x*. Thus we may write (*list.first*()).*setInfo*(*x*) to reset the value of the first element of the list *list* to *x*. This operation is often abbreviated as *list.setHead*(*x*). For example, if *list* equals (5, 10, 8), then the operation

```
list.setHead(18)
```

changes *list* to (18, 10, 8), and the operation *list.setHead*((5, 7, 3, 4)) changes *list* to ((5, 7, 3, 4), 10, 8).

setHead is called the "inverse *head* operation" for an obvious reason. After the operation *list.setHead*(*x*) is performed, the value of *list.head*() is *x*. Note that *list.setHead*(*x*) is equivalent to

```
list = (list.tail()).addOn(x);
```

The operation *elt*1.*setNext*(*elt*2) is somewhat more complex. It modifies the list containing *elt*1 so that *elt*1.*next*() = *elt*2. *elt*1 cannot be the null element. *elt*2.*next*() is unchanged. Also, if *elt*3.*next*() had been equal to *elt*2 before execution of *elt*1.*setNext*(*elt*2), *elt*3.*next*() still equals *elt*2 after its execution, so that both *elt*1.*next*() and *elt*3.*next*() equal *elt*2. In effect, *elt*2 has become an element of two lists. The operation *list*1.*setTail*(*list*2) is defined as (*list*1.*first*()).*setNext*(*list*2.*first*()) and sets the tail of *list*1 to *list*2. *setTail* is sometimes called the inverse *tail* operation.

For example, if *list* = (5, 9, 3, 7, 8, 6), then *list.setTail*((8)) changes the value of *list* to (5, 8), and *list.setTail*((4, 2, 7)) changes its value to (5, 4, 2, 7). Note that the operation *list.setTail*(*l*) is equivalent to *list* = *l.addOn*(*list.head*()).

Examples

Let us look at some simple examples of algorithms that use these operations.

The first example is an algorithm to add 1 to every integer that is an element of a list *list*. Character or list elements remain unchanged.

```
p = list.first();
while (p != nullelt) {
    if (p.nodeType() == intgr)
```

```
                    p.setInfo(p.info() + 1);
                    p = p.next();
        }
```

The second example involves deletions. We wish to delete from a list *list* any character element whose value is 'w'. (Compare this example with the routine in Section 4.2). One possible solution is as follows:

```
        q = nullelt;
        p = list.first();
        while (p != nullelt)
           if (p.info() == 'w') {
                    // remove node(p) from the list
                    p = p.next();
                    if (q == nullelt)
                            list = list.tail();
                    else
                            q.setNext(p);
           }
           else {
                    q = p;
                    p = p.next();
           }
```

Before looking at a more complex example, we define a new term. An element (or a node) *n* is ***accessible*** from a list (or an external pointer) *l* if there is a sequence of *head* and *tail* operations, which, if applied to *l*, yields a list with *n* as its first element. For example, in Figure 9.1.2 the node containing 14 is accessible from *list2*, since it is the first element of (((*list2.tail()).head()).tail()).tail()*. In fact, all the nodes shown in that figure are accessible from *list2*. When a node is removed from a list, it becomes inaccessible from the external pointer to that list.

Now, suppose we wish to increase by 1 the value in every integer node accessible from a given list pointer *list*. We cannot simply traverse *list*, because it is also necessary to traverse all the lists that are elements of *list*, as well as all the lists that may be elements of elements of *list*, and so forth. One tentative solution is the following recursive algorithm *list.addOne2()*.

```
        p = list.first();
        while (p != nullelt) {
           if (p.nodeType() == intgr)
                    p.setInfo(p.info() + 1);
           else if (p.nodeType() == lst)
                    (p.info()).addOne2();
           p = p.next();
        }
```

It is simple to remove the recursion and use a stack explicitly.

Linked List Representation of a List

As previously noted, the abstract concept of a list is usually implemented by a linked list of nodes. Each element of the abstract list corresponds to a node of the linked list.

Each node contains fields *info* and *next*, whose contents correspond to the abstract list operations *info*() and *next*(). The abstract concepts of a "list" and an "element" are both represented by a pointer: a list by an external pointer to the first node of a linked list, and an element by a pointer to a node. Thus, a pointer to a node *nd* in a list, which represents a list element, also represents the sublist formed by the elements represented by the nodes from *nd* to the end of the list. The value of an element corresponds to the contents of the *info* field of a node.

Under this implementation, the abstract operation *list.first*(), which returns the first element of a list, is meaningless. If *list* is a pointer that represents a list, then it points to the first node of a linked list, and therefore it also represents the first element of the list. Since *list.first*() and *list* are equivalent, *list.head*(), which is equivalent to (*list.first*()).*info*(), is equivalent to *list.info*(). *setHead*(*list,x*), defined as *setInfo*(*first*(*list*),*x*), is equivalent to *setInfo*(*list,x*). Similarly, *setTail*(*list1,list2*), defined as *setNext*(*first*(*list1*),*first*(*list2*)), is equivalent to *setNext*(*list1,list2*) under the linked list representation.

We defer a discussion of the implementation of *nodeType* until we present the Java implementation of general lists later in this section.

There are two methods of implementing the *addOn* and *tail* operations. Consider the list *l1* = (3, 4, 7) and the operation *l2* = *l1.addOn*(5). The two possible ways of implementing this operation are illustrated in Figures 9.1.3a and b. In the first method, called the **pointer method**, the list (3, 4, 7) is represented by a pointer to it, *l1*. To create the list *l2*, a node containing 5 is allocated, and the value of *l1* is placed in its *next* field. Thus the list *l1* becomes a sublist of *l2*. The nodes of list *l1* are used in two contexts: as part of list *l1* and of list *l2*. In the second method, called the **copy method**, the list (3, 4, 7) is copied before the new list element is added to it. *l1* still points to the original version, while the new copy is made a sublist of *l2*. The copy method ensures that a node appears in only one context.

The difference between these methods becomes apparent when we attempt to perform the operation

```
l1.setHead(7)
```

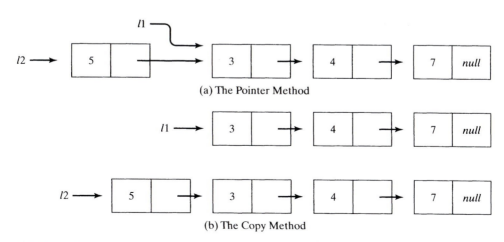

(a) The Pointer Method

(b) The Copy Method

FIGURE 9.1.3

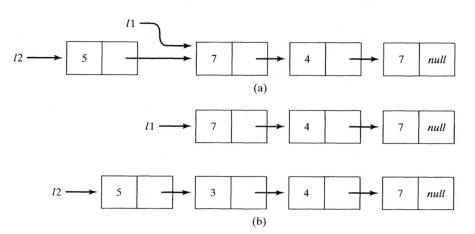

FIGURE 9.1.4

The resulting lists are shown in Figures 9.1.4a and b. If the copy method is used, then a change in list *l*1 does not affect list *l*2 (Figures 9.1.3b and 9.1.4b). If the pointer method is used, any subsequent change in list *l*1 also modifies *l*2 (Figures 9.1.3a and 9.1.4a).

The *tail* operation can also be implemented by either the pointer method or the copy method. Under the pointer method, *list.tail*() returns a pointer to the second node in the input list. After a statement such as *l* = *list.tail*(), the pointer *list* still points to the first node, and all the nodes from the second on are on both list *list* and list *l*. Under a strict copy method, a new list would be created containing copies of all the nodes from the second list node onwards, and *l* would point to the new list. Here, too, if the pointer method is used, then a subsequent change in either the input list (*list*) or the output list (*l*) causes a change in the other list. If the copy method is used, the two lists are independent. Note that, under the pointer method, the operation *list.tail*() is equivalent to *list.next*(): both return the pointer in the *next* field of the node pointed to by the pointer *list*. Under the copy method, however, an entirely new list is created by the *tail* operation.

The operation of the copy method is similar to an operation of the assignment statement *a* = *b*, and thus a subsequent change in *b* does not change *a*. This is because the assignment statement copies the contents of location *b* (the "value of *b*") into location *a*. A change in the value of *b* changes only the copy in location *b*. Similarly, in the copy method, although *l*1 is a pointer, it really refers to the abstract list being represented. When a new list is formed from the old, the value of the old list is copied. The two lists are then entirely independent. In the pointer method, *l*1 refers to the nodes themselves rather than the list they collectively represent. A change in one list modifies the contents of nodes that are also part of another.

For reasons of efficiency, most list-processing systems use the pointer method rather than the copy method. Imagine a hundred-element list to which nodes are constantly being added (using *addOn*) and from which nodes are being deleted (using *tail*). The overhead in time and space involved in allocating and copying one hundred list nodes (not to mention any list nodes on lists that appear as elements) each time an operation is performed is prohibitive. Under the pointer method, the number of oper-ations involved in adding or deleting an element is independent of the list size, since it involves only modification of a few pointers. However, in exchange for this efficiency, the user must be aware of possible changes to other lists. When the pointer method is used, list nodes are often be used in more than one context.

In list-processing systems that use the pointer method, an explicit copy operation is provided. The method

```
list.copy()
```

copies the list pointed to by *list* (including all list elements) and returns a pointer to the new copy. The user can use this operation to ensure that a subsequent modification to one list does not affect another.

Representation of Lists

So far, we have ignored a number of important implementation questions: When may list nodes be freed? When must new list nodes be allocated? How are list nodes allo-cated and freed? For example, *setTail* appends a new list to the first element of a list. But what happens to the previous tail of the list that was replaced?

These questions are related to another question: What happens when a node (or a list) is an element or a sublist of more than one list? For example, suppose the list (4, 5, 3, 8) occurs twice as an element of a list (i.e., it is the information field of two separate nodes of the list). One possibility is to maintain two copies of the list, as in Figure 9.1.5a. Or, suppose a list appears at the end of two lists, as does (43, 28) in Figure 9.1.5b. Al-though it is possible to duplicate each element whenever it appears, this often results in

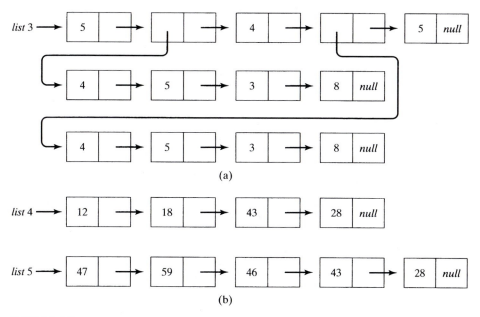

FIGURE 9.1.5

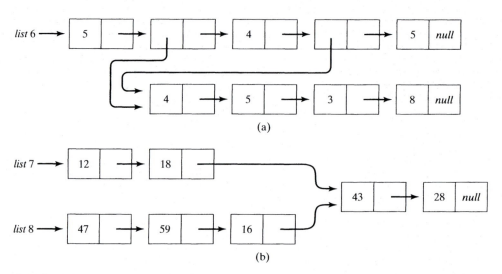

FIGURE 9.1.6

a needless waste of space. An alternative is to maintain the lists as in Figure 9.1.6. In this representation, a list appears only once, with all appropriate pointers pointing to the head of the single list. Under this method, a node is pointed to by more than one pointer.

If this possibility is allowed, then the recursive algorithm *addOne2* presented earlier to add 1 to each accessible element in a list does not work correctly. For example, if *addOne2* is applied to *list6* in Figure 9.1.6a, when 1 is added to the integer 4 as the first element of the second element of *list6*, the contents of that node are changed to 5. But the routine again adds 1 to that node, since the node is pointed to by the information field of another list element as well. Thus the final value in the node becomes 6 rather than 5. Similarly, the values of the nodes containing 5, 3, and 8 are changed to 7, 5, and 10 respectively. (Why?) This is clearly incorrect.

In general, modifying the contents of a node from 4 to 5 is equivalent to replacing the node containing 4 by a new node containing 5 and then freeing the node containing 4. But this assumes, possibly erroneously, that the node containing 4 is no longer needed. Whenever the contents of a node are changed or a node is deleted, it is first necessary to ensure that the old value is no longer required.

In Figure 9.1.6b, the list (43, 28) appears as a sublist of both *list7*, which is (12, 18, 43, 28), and *list8*, which is (47, 59, 16, 43, 28). Imagine the chaos that would result if an attempt were made to remove the third element of *list7*.

One solution to this problem is to disallow use of the same node in more than one context. That is, lists should be constructed as in Figure 9.1.5a rather than as in Figure 9.1.6a. Then, when a node is no longer needed in a particular context, it can be freed because no other internal pointers point to it.

crList Operation

Suppose that we wanted to create the list in Figure 9.1.6a. The following sequence of operations accomplishes this:

```
1 = null;
1 = 1.addOn(8);
1 = 1.addOn(3);
1 = 1.addOn(5);
1 = 1.addOn(4);
list6 = null;
list6 = list6.addOn(5);
list6 = list6.addOn(1);
list6 = list6.addOn(4);
list6 = list6.addOn(1);
list6 = list6.addOn(5);
```

Let us introduce the operation $l = crList(a_1, a_2, \ldots, a_n)$, where each parameter is either a simple data item or a reference to a list. This operation is defined as the sequence of statements:

```
1 = null;
1 = addOn(1,aₙ);

    . . .

1 = addOn(1,a₂);
1 = addOn(1,a₁);
```

That is, $crList(a_1, a_2, \ldots, a_n)$ creates the list $(a_1, a_2, \ldots, a_n)$. Then the sequence of operations above can be rewritten as

```
1 = crList(4, 5, 3, 8);
list6 = crList(5, 1, 4, 1, 5);
```

Note that this is not the same as the single operation

```
list6 = (5, crList(4, 5, 3, 8), 4, crList(4, 5, 3, 8), 5);
```

which creates two distinct copies of the list $(4, 5, 3, 8)$, one as its second element, and one as its fourth.

We leave as an exercise for the reader the task of finding a sequence of list operations that creates the lists *list*7 and *list*8 in Figure 9.1.6b.

If the pointer method is used to implement list operations, it is possible to create **recursive lists**. These are lists that contain themselves as elements. For example, suppose the following operations are performed:

```
1 = crList(2, crList(9, 7), 6, 4);
11 = (1.tail()).tail();
11.setHead(1);
12 = (1.tail()).head();
12 = 12.tail();
12.setHead(1);
```

Figure 9.1.7 illustrates the effect of each of these operations. At the end of the sequence (Figure 9.1.7e), the list *l* contains itself as its third element. In addition, the second element of *l* is a list whose second element is *l* itself.

Use of List Headers

In Chapter 4, list headers were introduced as a place to store global information about an entire list. In many general list-processing systems, header nodes are used for other purposes as well. We have already seen two ways of implementing general lists: the pointer method and the copy method. There is a third alternative, called the **header method**, that is widely used in list-processing systems. Under this method, a header node is always placed at the beginning of any group of nodes that is to be considered a

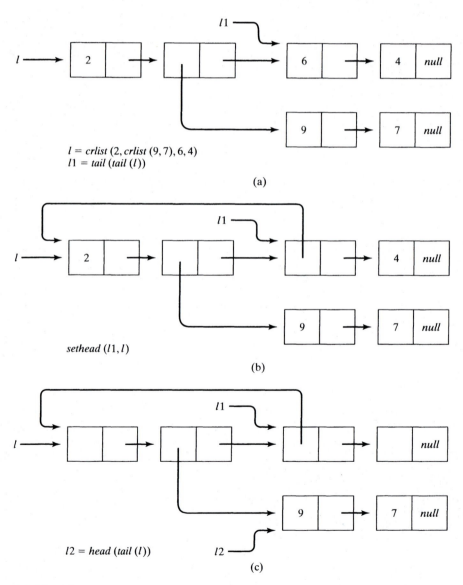

$l = crlist\,(2, crlist\,(9,7), 6, 4)$
$l1 = tail\,(tail\,(l))$

(a)

$sethead\,(l1, l)$

(b)

$l2 = head\,(tail\,(l))$ $l2$

(c)

FIGURE 9.1.7

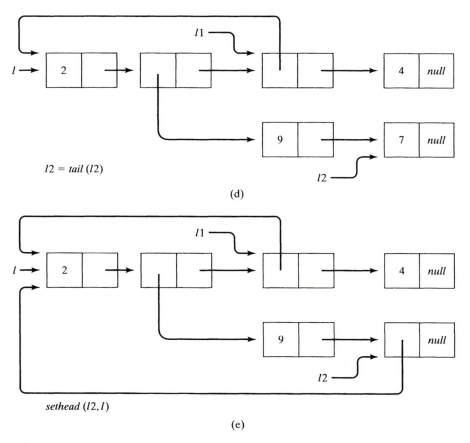

FIGURE 9.1.7 (*Continued*)

list. In particular, an external pointer always points to a header node. Similarly, if a list *l* is an element of another list, there is a header node at the front of *l*. Figure 9.1.8 illustrates the list from Figure 9.1.2 using the header method. The information portion of a header node holds global information about the list (e.g., the number of nodes in it, a pointer to its last node). In the figure, this field is shaded. Note that a null list is now represented by a pointer to a header node containing a null pointer in its *next* field rather than by the null pointer itself.

Any parameter that represents a list must be implemented as a reference to a header node for that list. Any method that returns a list must be implemented so as to return a reference to a header node.

The header method is similar to the pointer method in that a list is represented by a pointer to it. However, the presence of the header node causes significant differences (as we noted in Section 4.5, when we discussed linear, circular, and doubly linked lists with headers). For example, we made a distinction between the *push* and the *addOn* operations. If *l* is a reference to a list, the method *l.addOn(x)* adds a node containing *x* to the list referenced by *l*, without changing the value of *l*, and returns a reference to the new node. *l.push(x)* changes the value of the object to which *l refers* to the

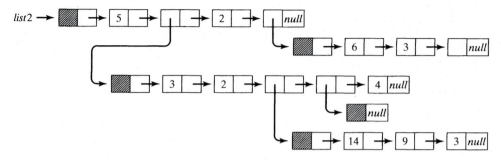

FIGURE 9.1.8

new node. Under the header method, adding an element to a list involves inserting a node between the header and the first list node. Thus, despite the fact that the value of *l* is not changed, the list that *l* represents has been altered.

Freeing List Nodes

Earlier in this section, we saw that a node or a set of nodes could be an element and/or a sublist of one or several lists. In such cases, it is difficult to determine when such a node can be modified or freed. Define a ***simple node*** as a node containing a simple data item (so that its *info* field does not contain a pointer). Generally, multiple use of simple nodes is not permitted. That is, operations on simple nodes are performed by the copy method rather than the pointer method. Thus any simple node deleted from a list can be freed immediately.

However, the copy method is highly inefficient when applied to nodes whose values are lists. The pointer method is the more commonly used technique when manipulating such nodes. Thus, whenever a list is modified or deleted as an element or a sublist, it is necessary to consider the implications of the modification or freeing of the list on other lists that may contain it. The question of how to free a deleted list is compounded by the fact that lists may contain other lists as elements. If a list is freed, it may also be necessary to free all the lists that are elements of it; however, if these lists are also elements of other lists, they cannot be freed.

As an illustration of the complexity of the problem, consider *list9* in Figure 9.1.9. The nodes in the figure are numbered arbitrarily so that we may refer to them easily in the text.

Consider the operation

```
list9 = null;
```

Which nodes can be freed, and which must be retained? Clearly, the list nodes of *list9* (nodes 1, 2, 3, 4) can be freed, since no other pointers reference them. Freeing node 1 allows us to free nodes 11 and 12, since they too are accessed by no other pointers. Once node 11 is freed, can nodes 7 and 8 also be freed? Node 7 can be freed because each of the nodes containing a pointer to it (nodes 11 and 4) can be freed. However, node 8 cannot be freed, since *list11* points to it. *list11* is an external pointer, and therefore the node to which it points may still be needed elsewhere in the program. Since

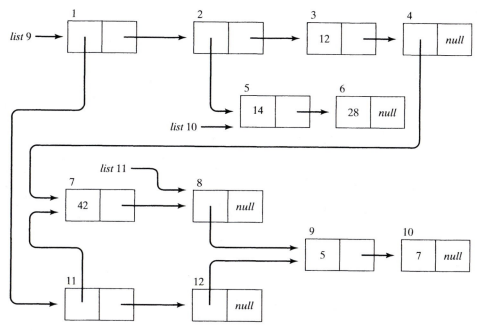

FIGURE 9.1.9

node 8 is kept, nodes 9 and 10 must also be kept (even though node 12 is being freed). Finally, nodes 5 and 6 must be kept because of the external pointer *list*10.

The problem to be addressed in the next section is how to determine algorithmically which nodes are to be kept and which are to be freed. However, before considering possible solutions, let us consider how lists can be implemented in Java and make some comments about list-processing languages and their design.

General Lists in Java

Because general list nodes can contain simple data elements of any type or references to other lists, the most direct way to declare list nodes is by declaring the data component of the node to be of the *Object* type. One possible implementation is as follows:

```java
class Data {
    public final static int INTGR = 1;
    public final static int CH = 2;
    public final static int LST = 3;

    Object info;
    int oType;      // oType equals INTGR, CH, or LST
      Data() {}
} // end Data class

public class Node {
    Data info;
    Node next;
```

```
public Node() {}

int nodeType() {
        return info.oType;
} // end NodeType

} // end Node class
```

Each list node has two elementary fields: an information field of type *Data*, and a pointer to the next node in the list. The *Data* class contains a flag (*oType*) to indicate the type of the information field, the actual information (*info*) defined to be of type *Object*. The operation *nodeType(p)* is implemented by a method which references *info.oType*.

The actual implementation of any list operation depends upon whether the system in question is implemented using the pointer method, the copy method, or the header method. In the implementation above we use the pointer method.

The *tail* operation always produces a reference to a list (possibly the **null** reference), assuming that its argument points to a valid list. Thus this operation may be implemented as a simple Java method of the class *Node*:

```
Node tail() {
  return next;
} // end tail
```

The *head* operation may similarly be implemented as a method of *Node* by simply returning the object in the *info* field of the node:

```
Data head() {
    return info;
} // end head
```

It is, of course, the responsibility of the programmer to invoke the *nodeType* method prior to accessing the object referred to by the *info* field.

In some applications, it may not be necessary to return the value of the contents of the information portion of the node; it may be sufficient to identify a reference to the desired node. In such a case, the value of the reference variable traversing the list may be used instead of the *head* method. Note that neither the *head* nor the *tail* operation changes the original list in any way. All fields retain the same values that they had before the routines were called.

Once the basic forms of *head* and *tail* have been implemented, other list operations can be implemented either in terms of these operations or by accessing list nodes directly. For example, the *addOn* operation may be implemented as follows:

```
Node addOn(Data pitem) {
  Node newPtr = new Node();

  newPtr.info = pitem;
  newPtr.next = this;
  return newPtr;
} // end addOn
```

Now that *addOn* has been implemented, *list.setHead(item)* can be implemented by the statement *list = tail(list).addOn(item)*, as we mentioned earlier. Alternatively, the *setHead* operation can be implemented directly by:

```
void setHead(Data item) {
    info = item;
} // end setHead
```

The *setTail* operation may be implemented similarly as follows:

```
void setTail(Node t) {
    next = t;
} // end setTail
```

Despite the fact that we are using the pointer method, there will probably be no need for the previous tail of the list. Once it is determined that there is no other reference to this portion of the list, the Java garbage collector will automatically free the previous tail of the list. Thus there is no need to call the *freeList* operation mentioned in the algorithm.

The implementation of the Java garbage collector highlights the problem of automatic list management and how to determine when a node should be freed if it may indeed appear in more than one context (as in the pointer method or if recursive lists are permitted). As mentioned, we examine these issues in Section 9.2.

Programming Languages and Lists

Throughout this text, we have been treating lists as a compound data structure (a collection of nodes) rather than as a native data type (an elementary item such as *int, char*). The reason for this is that we have been working closely with the Java language. In Java, one cannot make a declaration such as

```
list x;
```

and apply such methods as *head* and *tail* to *x* directly. Rather, to implement lists the programmer must write the necessary methods for their manipulation. Other languages, however, do contain lists as elementary data structures with the operations *crList, head, tail, addOn, setHead*, and *setTail* already built into the language. (A good example of such a language is LISP.)

As a consequence of the fact that Java does not include list-manipulation capabilities, a programmer who programs a list-manipulation application also has the responsibility to allocate the necessary list nodes. This problem is not at all trivial if lists are allowed in all their generality. However, any given application can usually be designed more easily using a specific type of list, tree, or graph, as we saw in Chapters 4, 5, and 8. Indeed, general list-manipulation techniques are more expensive in terms of both time and space than techniques designed specifically for a particular application. (This is a corollary to the axiom that a price is always paid for generality.) Thus the Java programmer will rarely have occasion to use general list-manipulation techniques.

However, a general list-processing system, in which the list is a native data type and list operations are built-in, must be able to deal with lists in all their generality. Since the fundamental objects are lists and data items rather than nodes, the programmer cannot be responsible for allocating and freeing individual nodes. Rather, when a program issues a statement such as

```
l1 = crlist(3, 4, 7);
```

the system is responsible for allocating sufficient list nodes and initializing the proper pointers. When the program later issues the command

```
l1 = null;
```

the system is responsible for identifying and freeing those nodes previously on list $l1$ that now become inaccessible. If such nodes are not freed, available space would rapidly become exhausted.

In some sense, languages that include lists as native data types are of "higher level" than Java because the programmer is freed from so much of the bookkeeping activity associated with storage management. Java may be thought of as a language of higher level than C in that Java includes data structures such as classes and stacks, whereas C does not. So too, a list-processing system is of higher level than Java in that it includes lists, whereas Java does not.

Another point that should be made concerns the implementation of lists. The implementation of lists as presented in this section is oriented toward Java. Because Java permits the use of *Objects* of indeterminate types, it was possible to define a type *infoType* to encapsulate any of the legal data types in our list system. Some languages (e.g., C) do not support objects. In such languages, the type of a node (with certain limited exceptions) is fixed in advance. In such languages it would be necessary to separate a list system into **list nodes** and **atomic nodes**. An atomic node is a node that contains no pointers—only a simple data item. Several different types of atomic nodes would exist, each with a single data item corresponding to one of the legal data types. A list node contains a reference to an atomic node and a type indicator indicating the type of atomic node to which it points (as well as a reference to the next node on the list, of course). When it is necessary to place a new node on a list, an atomic node of the appropriate type must be allocated, its value must be assigned, the list node information field must be set to point to the new atomic node, and the type field in the list node must be set to the proper type.

To understand how clumsy this situation is, suppose there are ten different types of atomic nodes (there is no reason that an atomic node may not be an array or a stack or a queue, for example). Each of these must have a unique typecode. Further, there must be a separate variable declared for each type of atomic node. Let us suppose that the typecodes used for the ten types are $t1, t2, \ldots, t10$, and that the atomic node variables are $node1, node2, \ldots, node10$. Then each time that an atomic node is processed, we would need code such as:

```
switch (typecode) {
  case t1:
        // do something with node1
        break;
  case t2:
        // do something with node2
        break;

  . . .
```

```
        case t10:
              // do something with node10
     }
```

This is a cumbersome organization, and one which we are able to avoid by using an object-oriented programming language.

In the next section of this chapter, we examine techniques incorporated into list-processing systems to recover storage that is no longer needed. We retain the list structure conventions of this section, but it should be understood that they are not absolute.

EXERCISES

9.1.1   How would you implement a general stack and queue in Java? Write all the methods necessary for doing so.

9.1.2   Implement the methods *addOn, setHead, SetTail*, and *crList* in Java.

9.1.3   Write a Java method *list.freeList()* that frees all the nodes accessible from a reference to a *list* object. If your solution is recursive, rewrite it nonrecursively.

9.1.4   Rewrite *addOne2* so that it is nonrecursive.

9.1.5   Write a Java method *list.dlt(n)* that deletes the *n*th element of a *list* object. If this *n*th element is itself a list, all the nodes accesible through the list should be freed. Assume that a list can appear in only one position.

9.1.6   Implement the method *list.copy()* in Java. This routine accepts a reference to a *list* object representing a general list and returns a reference to a copy of the list. What if the list is recursive?

9.1.7   Write a Java method that accepts a reference to a list object and prints the parenthesized notation for that list. Assume that list nodes can appear only on a single list, and that recursive lists are prohibited.

9.1.8   What are the advantages and disadvantages of languages in which the type of variables need not be declared, as compared to languages such as Java?

9.1.9   Write two sets of list operations to create the lists in Figures 9.1.4b and 9.1.9.

9.1.10 Redraw all the lists in this section that do not include header nodes so that they are now included.

9.1.11 Implement the methods *addOn, head, tail, setHead*, and *setTail* in Java for lists using the following methods:

   a. the copy method
   b. the header method

9.1.12 Implement the list operations for a system that uses doubly linked lists.

9.2   AUTOMATIC LIST MANAGEMENT

In the last section, we presented the need for algorithms to determine when a given list node is no longer accessible. In this section we investigate such algorithms. The philosophy behind incorporating such an algorithm into a programming system is that the programmer should not have to decide when a node should be allocated or freed. Instead, the programmer should code the solution to the problem with the assurance that the system will automatically allocate any list nodes that are necessary for the lists being created and will make available for reuse any nodes that are no longer accessible.

There are two principal methods used in automatic list management: the ***reference count*** method and the ***garbage collection*** method. We proceed to a discussion of each.

Reference Count Method

Under this method, each node has an additional *count* field that keeps a count (called the ***reference count***) of the number of pointers (both internal and external) to the node. Each time the value of some pointer is set to point to a node, the reference count in the node is increased by 1; each time the value of some pointer that had been pointing to a node is changed, the reference count in the node is decreased by 1. When the reference count in any node becomes 0, the node can be returned to the available list of free nodes.

Each list operation of a system using the reference count method must make provision for updating the reference count of each node that it accesses and for freeing any node whose count becomes 0. For example, to execute the statement

```
l = l.tail();
```

the following operations must be performed:

```
p = l;
l = l.next();
p.next() = null;
p.reduce();
```

where the operation *p.reduce()* is defined recursively as follows:

```
if (p != null) {
  p.count()--;
  if (p.count() == 0) {
          r = p.next();
          r.reduce();
          if (p.nodeType() == lst)
                  (p.head()).reduce();
          free node(p);
  }
}
```

reduce must be invoked whenever the value of a pointer to a list node is changed. Similarly, whenever we refer to a list node, the *count* field of the node must be increased by 1. The *count* field of a free node is 0.

To illustrate the reference count method, consider again the list in Figure 9.1.9. The following set of statements creates the list:

```
list10 = crList(14, 28);
list11 = crList(crList(5, 7));
l1 = list11.addOn(42);
m = crList(l1, list11.head());
list9 = crList(m, list10, 12, l1);
m = null;
l1 = null;
```

Figure 9.2.1 illustrates the creation of the list using the reference count method. Each part of the figure shows the list after an additional group of the above statements has been executed. The reference count is shown as the leftmost field of each list node. Each node in the figure is numbered according to the numbering of the nodes in Figure 9.1.9. Make sure that you understand how each statement alters the reference count in each node.

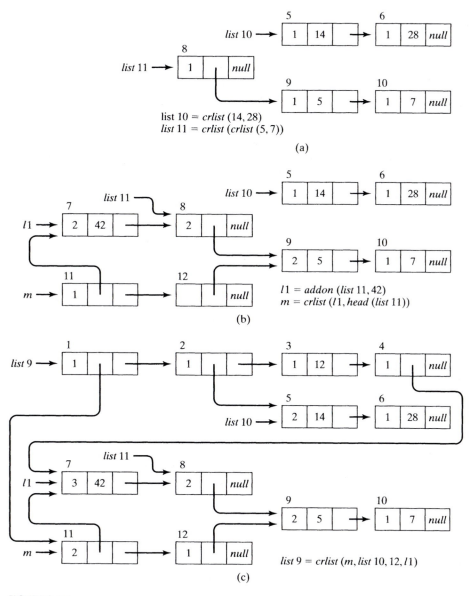

list 10 = crlist (14, 28)
list 11 = crlist (crlist (5, 7))

(a)

l1 = addon (list 11, 42)
m = crlist (l1, head (list 11))

(b)

list 9 = crlist (m, list 10, 12, l1)

(c)

FIGURE 9.2.1

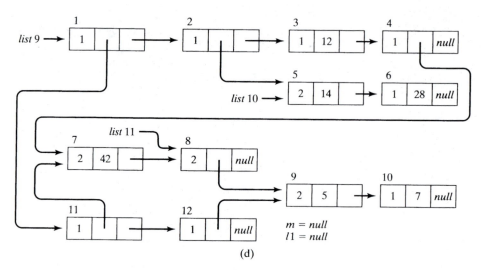

FIGURE 9.2.1 (*Continued*)

Let us now see what happens when we execute the statement

```
list9 = null;
```

The results are illustrated in Figure 9.2.2, where freed nodes are illustrated using dashed lines. The following sequence of events may take place:

	count of node 1 is set to 0.
	Node 1 is freed.
	*count*s of nodes 2 and 11 are set to 0.
	Nodes 2 and 11 are freed.
	*count*s of nodes 5 and 7 are set to 1.
(Figure 9.2.2a)	*count*s of nodes 3 and 12 are set to 0.
	Nodes 3 and 12 are freed.
	count of node 4 is set to 0.
	Node 4 is freed.
	count of node 9 is set to 1.
	count of node 7 is set to 0.
	Node 7 is freed.
(Figure 9.2.2b)	*count* of node 8 is set to 1.

Only those nodes accessible from the external pointers *list*10 and *list*11 remain allocated; all others are freed.

One drawback of the reference count method is illustrated by the above example. The amount of work that must be performed by the system each time a list manipulation statement is executed can be considerable. Whenever a pointer value is changed, all the nodes previously accessible from that pointer can potentially be freed.

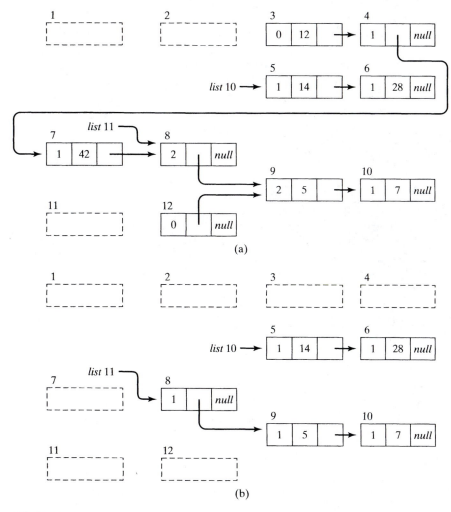

FIGURE 9.2.2

Often, the work involved in identifying the nodes to be freed is not worth the re-claimed space, since there may be ample space for the program to run to completion without reusing any nodes. After the program has terminated, a single pass reclaims all of its storage without any worry about reference count values.

One solution to this problem can be illustrated by a different approach to the previous example. When the statement

```
list9 = null
```

is executed, the reference count in node 1 is reduced to 0 and node 1 is freed—that is, it is placed on the available list. However, the fields of this node retain their original values, so that it still points to nodes 2 and 11. (This means that an additional pointer field is necessary to link such nodes on the available list. An alternative is to reuse the reference count field for this purpose.) The reference count values in these two nodes remain unchanged. When additional space is needed and node 1 is reallocated for some other use, the reference counts in nodes 2 and 11 are reduced to zero, and they are then placed on the available list. This removes much of the work from the deallocation process and adds it to the allocation process. If node 1 is never reused because enough space is available, then nodes 2, 11, 3, 4, 7, and 12 are not freed during program execution. In order for this scheme to work best, however, the available list should be kept as a queue rather than as a stack, so that freed nodes are never allocated before nodes that have not been used for the first time. (Once a system has been running for some time, so that all the nodes have been used at least once, this advantage no longer exists.)

There are two additional disadvantages to the reference count method. The first is the additional space required in each node for the count. This is not usually an overriding consideration, however. The problem can be somewhat alleviated if each list is required to contain a header node and a reference count is kept only in the header. However, then only a header node could be referenced by more than one pointer (i.e., a list like the one in Figure 9.2.3b would be prohibited). The lists in Figure 9.2.3 are analogous to those in Figure 9.1.6 except that they include header nodes. The counts are kept in the first field of the header node. When the count in a header node reaches 0, all the nodes on its list are freed, and the counts in header nodes pointed to by *info* fields in the list nodes are reduced.

If counts are to be retained in header nodes only, certain operations may have to be modified. For example, the *setTail* operation must be modified so that the situation in Figure 9.2.3b does not occur. One method of modification is to use the copy method in implementing these operations. Another method is to differentiate somehow between external pointers, which represent lists (and therefore must point to a header node), and "temporary" external pointers, which are used for traversal (and can point

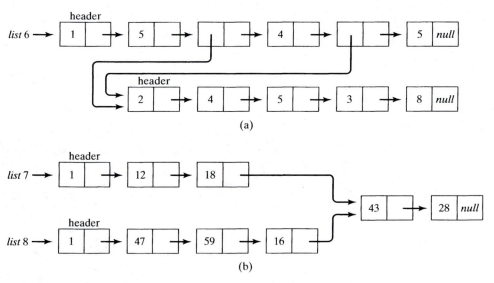

(a)

(b)

FIGURE 9.2.3

directly to list nodes). When the count in a header node becomes 0, references to its list nodes through temporary pointers are illegal.

The other disadvantage of the reference count method is that the count in the first node of a recursive or circular list will never be reduced to zero. Of course, whenever a pointer within a list is set to point to a node on the list, the reference count can be maintained rather than increased, but detecting when this is so is often a difficult task.

Garbage Collection

Under the reference count method, nodes are reclaimed when they become available for reuse (or under one version when they are needed). The other principal method of detecting and reclaiming free nodes is called *garbage collection*. Under this method, nodes no longer in use remain allocated and undetected until all available storage has been allocated. A subsequent request for allocation cannot be satisfied until nodes that were allocated but are no longer in use are recovered. When a request is made for additional nodes and there are none available, a system routine called the *garbage collector* is called. This routine searches through all of the nodes in the system, identifies those that are no longer accessible from an external pointer, and restores the inaccessible nodes to the available pool. The request for additional nodes is then fulfilled with some of the reclaimed nodes, and the system continues processing user requests for more space. When available space is used up again, the garbage collector is called once more.

Garbage collection is usually done in two phases. The first phase, called the *marking phase*, involves marking all the nodes that are accessible from an external pointer. The second phase, called the *collection phase*, involves proceeding sequentially through memory and freeing all the nodes that have not been marked. We examine the marking phase first, and then turn our attention to the collection phase.

One field must be set aside in each node to indicate whether it has or has not been marked. The marking phase sets the mark field to *true* in each accessible node. As the collection phase proceeds, the mark field in each accessible node is reset to *false*. Thus, at the start and end of garbage collection, all mark fields are *false*. User programs do not affect the mark fields.

It is sometimes inconvenient to reserve one field in each node solely for the purpose of marking. In that case, a separate area in memory can be reserved to hold a long array of mark bits, one bit for each node that may be allocated.

Garbage collection must run when there is very little space available. This means that there is little space available for auxiliary tables and stacks, so the garbage collector's need for them must be kept to a minimum. An alternative is to reserve a specific percentage of memory for the exclusive use of the garbage collector. However, this effectively reduces the amount of memory available to the user and means that the garbage collector will be called more frequently.

Whenever the garbage collector is called, all user processing comes to a halt while the algorithm examines all the allocated nodes in memory. For this reason, it is desirable that the garbage collector be called as infrequently as possible. For real-time applications, in which a computer must respond to a user request within a specific short time span, garbage collection has generally been considered an unsatisfactory method of storage management. We can picture a spaceship drifting off into the infinite as it waits for directions from a computer occupied with garbage collection. However, methods have recently been developed whereby garbage collection can be performed simultaneously with user processing. This means that the garbage collector must be called before all space has been exhausted, so that user processing can continue in whatever space is left while the garbage collector recovers additional space.

Another important consideration is that users must be careful to ensure that all lists are well formed and all pointers are correct. Usually, the operations of a list processing system are carefully implemented, so that the entire system still works correctly if garbage collection does occur in the middle of one of them. However, some users try to outsmart the system and implement their own pointer manipulations. In such cases, great care so is required to make the garbage collection work properly. In a real-time garbage collection system, we must ensure not only that user operations do not upset list structures that the garbage collector must have, but also that the garbage collection algorithm does not unduly disturb the list structures that are being used concurrently by the user. As we shall see, some marking algorithms do (temporarily) disturb list structures and are therefore unsuitable for real-time use.

Sometimes, when the garbage collection program is called, the users are actually using almost all the nodes that are allocated. Thus almost all the nodes are accessible and the garbage collector recovers very little additional space. After running for a short time, the system will again be out of space; the garbage collector will again be called, only to recover very few additional nodes, and the vicious cycle starts again. This phenomenon, in which system storage-management routines, such as garbage collection, are executing almost all the time, is called *thrashing*.

Clearly, thrashing is a situation to be avoided. One drastic solution is to impose the following condition. If the garbage collector is run and does not recover a specific percentage of the total space, then the user who requested the extra space is terminated and removed from the system. All of the user's space is then recovered and made available to other users.

Algorithms for Garbage Collection

The simplest method for marking all the accessible nodes is to mark initially all the nodes that are immediately accessible (i.e., those pointed to by external pointers) and then repeatedly pass through all of memory sequentially. On each sequential pass, whenever a marked node nd is encountered, all the nodes pointed to by a pointer within nd are marked. These sequential passes continue until no new nodes have been marked in an entire pass. Unfortunately, this method is as inefficient as it is simple. The number of sequential passes necessary is equal to the maximum path length to any accessible node (why?), and on each pass every list node in memory must be examined. However, this method requires almost no additional space.

A somewhat more efficient variation is the following: Suppose that a node $n1$ in the sequential pass has already been marked and includes a pointer to an unmarked node, $n2$. Then node $n2$ is marked and the sequential pass would ordinarily continue with the node that follows $n1$ sequentially in memory. However, if the address of $n2$ is less than the address of $n1$, the sequential pass resumes from $n2$ rather than from $n1$. Under this modified technique, when the last node in memory is reached, all the accessible nodes have been marked.

Let us present this method as an algorithm. Assume that all the list nodes in memory are viewed as a sequential array.

```
public final static int NUMNODES = ...;

public class NodeType {
    public final static int INTINFO = 1;
    public final static int CHARINFO = 2;
    public final static int LSTINFO = 3;

    boolean mark;
    Object info;
    int oType;      // oType equals INTINFO, CHARINFO, or LSTINFO
    int next;
}

NodeType node[] = new NodeType[NUMNODES];
```

An array *node* is used to convey the notion that we can step through all the nodes sequentially. *node*[0] is used to represent a dummy node. We assume that *node*[0].*info* and *node*[0].*next* are initialized to 0, *node*[0].*mark* to *true*, and *node*[0].*oType* to *LSTINFO*, and that these values are never changed throughout the system's execution. The *mark* field in each node is initially *false* and is set to *true* by the marking algorithm when a node is found to be accessible.

Now that we have defined the format of our nodes, we turn to the actual algorithm. Assume that *acc* is an array containing external pointers to immediately accessible nodes, declared by

```
public final static int NUMACC = ...;
int acc[] = new int[NUMACC];
```

The marking algorithm is as follows:

```
// mark all immediately accesible nodes
for (i = 0; i < NUMACC; i++)
    node[acc[i]].mark = true;
// begin a sequential pass through the array of nodes
// i points to the node currently being examined
i = 1;
while (i < NUMNODES) {
    j = i + 1;
    // j points to the node to be examined next
    if (node[i].mark) {
        // mark nodes to which i points
        if (node[i].oType == LSTINFO &&
                node[((Integer) node[i].info).intValue()].mark
                != true) {
            // the information portion of i points to an unmarked
            node node[((Integer) node[i].info).intValue()].mark
            = true;
            if (((Integer) node[i].info).intValue() < j)
                j = ((Integer) node[i].info).intValue();
        }
```

```
      if (node[node[i].next].mark != true) {
            /* the list node following node[i] is an unmarked node
            node[node[i].next].mark = true;
            if (node[i].next < j)
                  j = node[i].next;
      }
}
i = j;
}
```

Note that in order to extract the integer value stored within the *info* field, it is necessary to use the *intValue()* method of the *Integer* class. In the exercises you are asked to trace the execution of this algorithm on a list distributed throughout memory, such as *list*9 in Figure 9.1.9.

Although this method is better than successive sequential passes, it is still inefficient. Consider how many nodes must be examined if *node*[1] is immediately accessible and points to *node*[999], which points to *node*[2], and so on. Thus it is usually too slow to use in an actual system.

A more desirable method is one that is not based on traversing memory sequentially but traverses all accessible lists. Thus it examines only those nodes that are accessible, rather than all nodes.

The most obvious way to accomplish this is by use of an auxiliary stack and is very similar to depth-first traversal of a graph. As each list is traversed through the *next* fields of its constituent nodes, the *oType* field of each node is examined. If the *oType* field of a node is *LSTINFO*, then the value of the node's *info* field is placed on the stack. When the end of a list or a marked node is reached, the stack is popped and the list headed by the node at the top of the stack is traversed. In the algorithm that follows, we again assume that *node*[0].*mark* = *true*.

```
for (i = 0; i < NUMACC; i++) {
      // mark the next immediately accessible node and place it on the
      stack
      node[acc[i]].mark = true;
      push(stack, acc[i]);
      while (empty(stack) != true) {
            p = pop(stack);
            while (p != 0) {
                  if (node[p].oType == LSTINFO &&
                        node[((Integer)
                        node[p].info).intValue()].mark != true) {
                  node[((Integer) node[p].info).intValue()].mark =
                  true;
                  push(stack, ((Integer) node[p].info).intValue());
                  }
                  if (node[node[p].next].mark == true)
                        p = 0;
            else {
                        p = node[p].next;
```

```
                        node[p].mark = true;
                }
            }
        }
    }
```

This algorithm is as efficient as we can hope for in terms of time, since each node to be marked is visited only once. However, it has a significant weakness because of its dependence on an auxiliary stack. A garbage collection algorithm is called when there is no extra space available, so where is the stack to be kept? Since the size of the stack is never greater than the depth of the list nesting, and lists are rarely nested beyond some reasonable limit (such as 100), a specific number of nodes reserved for the garbage collection stack would suffice in most cases. However, there is always the possibility that a user would want to nest nodes more deeply.

One solution is to use a stack limited to some maximum size. If the stack is about to overflow, we can revert to the sequential method given in the previous algorithm. We ask the reader to work out the details in an exercise.

Another solution is to use the allocated list nodes as the stack. Since the extra space could be better used for other purposes, we do not want to add an additional field to each list node to hold a pointer to the next node on the stack. Thus either the *info* field or *next* field of the list nodes must be used to link the stack together. But this means that the list structure is temporarily disturbed. Provision must be made for the lists to be restored properly.

In the above algorithm, each list is traversed using the *next* fields of its nodes, and the value of each pointer *info* to a list node is pushed onto a stack. When either the end of a list or a section of the list which has already been marked is reached, the stack is popped and a new list is traversed. Therefore, when a pointer to a node *nd* is popped, there is no need to restore any of the fields within *nd*.

However, suppose the stack is kept as a list, linked by the *next* fields. Then, when a node is pushed onto the stack, its *next* field must be changed to point to the top node in the stack. This implies that the field must be restored to its original value when the node is popped. But the original value has not been saved anywhere. (It cannot be saved on the stack because, there is no extra storage available for it.)

A solution to this problem can be described by the following scheme. Let us first assume a list with no elements that are themselves lists. As each node in the list is visited, it is pushed onto the stack and its *next* field is used to link it onto the stack. Since each node preceding the current node on the list is also present on the stack (the top of the stack is the last-encountered element on the list), the list can be reconstructed easily by simply popping the stack and restoring the *next* fields.

The situation is only slightly different in the case where one list is an element of another. Suppose that *nd1* is a node on *list1*, *nd2* is a node on *list2*, and *node*[*nd1*].*info* = *nd2*. That is, *nd2* is the first node of *list2* where *list2* is an element of *list1*. The algorithm has been traversing *list1* and is now about to begin traversing *list2*. In this case, *node*[*nd1*].*next* cannot be used as a stack pointer because it is needed to link *nd1* to the remainder of *list1*. However, the *info* field of *nd1* can be used to link *nd1* onto the stack because it is currently being used to link to *nd2*.

In general, when a node *nd* is pushed onto the stack, either its *info* field or its *next* field is used to point to the previous top element. If the next node to be examined is pointed to by *node[nd].info*, then the *info* field is used to link *nd* onto the stack, while if the node is pointed to by *node[nd].next*, then the *next* field is used to link *nd* onto the stack. The remaining problem is how to determine for a given node on the stack whether the *info* or *next* field is used to link the stack.

If the *oType* field of a node indicates that the node is a simple node, then its *next* field must be in use as a stack pointer. (This is because the node has no *info* field that must be traversed.) However, a node with a *oType* field of *LSTINFO* is not so easily handled. Suppose that each time the *info* field is used to advance to the next node, the *oType* field in the list node is changed from *LSTINFO* to some new code (say *STKINFO* for stack) that is neither *LSTINFO* nor any of the codes that denote simple elements. Then, when a node is popped from the stack, if its *oType* field is not *STKINFO*, its *next* field must be restored, and if its *tag* field is *STKINFO*, its *info* field must be restored and the *oType* field restored to *LSTINFO*.

Figure 9.2.4 illustrates how this stacking mechanism works. Figure 9.2.4a shows a list before the marking algorithm begins. The pointer *p* points to the node currently being processed, *top* points to the stack top, and *q* is an auxiliary pointer. The mark field is shown as the first field in each node. Figure 9.2.4b shows the same list immediately after node 4 has been marked. The path taken to node 4 is through the *next* fields of nodes 1, 2, and 3. This path can be retraced in reverse order, beginning at *top* and following along the *next* fields. Figure 9.2.4c shows the list after node 7 has been marked.

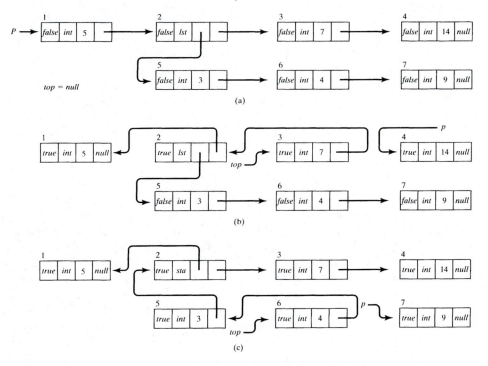

FIGURE 9.2.4

The path to node 7 from the beginning of the list was from node 1, through *node*[1].*next* to node 2, through *node*[2].*info* to node 5, through *node*[5].*next* to node 6, and then from *node*[6].*next* to node 7. The same fields that link the stack together are used to restore the list to its original form. Note that the *oType* field in node 2 is *stkinfo* rather than *lstinfo* to indicate that its *info* field, not its *next* field, is being used as a stack pointer. The algorithm that incorporates these ideas is known as the Schorr-Waite algorithm, after its discoverers.

Now that we have described the temporary distortions that are made in the list structure by the Schorr-Waite algorithm, we present the algorithm itself. We invite the reader to trace through the effects of the algorithm on the lists in Figure 9.2.4a and 9.1.9.

```
for (i = 0; i < NUMACC; i++) {
    // for each immediately accessible node, trace through its list
    p = acc[i];
    // initialize the stack to empty
    top = 0;
    again = true
    while (again) {
        // Traverse the list through its next fields, marking each node
        // and placing it on the stack until a marked node or the end
        // of the list is reached. Assume node[0].mark= true
        again = false
        while (node[p].mark != true) {
            node[p].mark = true;
            // place node[p] on the stack, saving a pointer to the
            // next node
            q = node[p].next;
            node[p].next = top;
            top = p;
            // advance to the next node
            p = q;
    } // end while
    // at this point trace the way back through the list, popping
    // the stack until a node is reached whose info field
    // points to an unmarked node, or until the list is empty
    while (top != 0 && again = false) {
        // restore info or next to p and pop the stack
        p = top;
        // restore the proper field of node[p]
        if (node[p].oType == STK) {
            // info was used as the stack link. Restore the tag
            // field
            node[p].oType = LST;
            // pop the stack
            top = (Integer) node[top].info).intValue()].;
            // restore the info field
            node[p].info = new Integer(q);
            q = p;
        }
```

```
                            else {
                                // next was used as the stack link. Pop the stack.
                                top = node[top].next;
                                // restore the next field
                                node[p].next = q;
                                q = p;
                                // check if we must travel down node[p].info
                                if (node[p].oType == LST) {
                                    // indicate that info is used as the stack link
                                    node[p].oType = STK;
                                    // push node[p] on the stack
                                    node[p].info = new Integer (top);
                                    top = p;
                                    // advance to next node
                                    p = q;
                                    again = true;
                                } /* end if (node[p].oType == LST)
                        } /* end if (node[p].oType == STK)
                } /* end while (top != 0 && again = false)
        } /* end while (again)
} /* end for
```

Although this algorithm is advantageous in terms of space, since no auxiliary stack is necessary, it is disadvantageous in terms of time because each list must be traversed twice: once in pushing each node in the list on the stack, and once in popping the stack. This can be contrasted with the relatively few nodes that must be stacked when an auxiliary stack is available.

Several methods of garbage collection can be combined into a single algorithm. For example, an auxiliary stack of fixed size can be set aside for garbage collection, and the algorithm can switch to the Schorr-Waite method when the stack is about to overflow. We leave the details as an exercise.

Collection and Compaction

The collection phase may begin once the memory locations of a given system have been marked appropriately. The purpose of this phase is to return to available memory all those locations that were previously garbage (not used by any program but unavailable to any user). It is easy to pass through memory sequentially, examine each node in turn, and return unmarked nodes to available storage.

For example, given the type definitions and declarations presented above, the following algorithm could be used to return the unmarked nodes to an available list headed by *avail*:

```
for (p = 0; p < NUMNODES; p++) {
    if (node[p].mark != true) {
        node[p].next = avail;
        avail = p;
    }
    node[p].mark = false;
}
```

After this algorithm has completed, all the unused nodes are on the available list, and all the nodes that are in use by programs have their *mark* fields turned off (for the next call to garbage collection). Note that this algorithm places nodes on the available list in opposite order of their memory location. If it were desired to return nodes to available memory in the order of increasing memory location, the *for* loop above could be reversed to read

```
for (p = NUMNODES - 1; p >= 1; p--)
```

Although at this point (following the marking and collection phases of the system) all the nodes that are not in use are on the available list, the system's memory may not be in an optimal state for future use. This is because the interleaving of the occupied nodes with available nodes may make much of the memory on the available list unusable. For example, memory is often required in blocks (groups of contiguous nodes) rather than as single discrete nodes one at a time. The memory request by a compiler for space in which to store an array would require the allocation of such a block. If, for example, all the odd locations in memory were occupied, and all the even locations were on the available list, then a request for even an array of size 2 could not be honored, despite the fact that half of memory is on the available list. Although this example is probably not very realistic, there are certainly situations in which a request for a contiguous block of memory could not be honored, despite the fact that sufficient memory does indeed exist.

There are several approaches to this problem. Some methods allocate and free portions of memory in blocks (groups of contiguous nodes) rather than in units of individual nodes. This guarantees that when a block of storage is freed (returned to the available pool), a block will be available for subsequent allocation requests. The size of these blocks and the manner in which they are stored, allocated, and freed are discussed in the next section.

However, even if storage is maintained as units of individual nodes rather than as blocks, it is still possible to provide the user with blocks of contiguous storage. The process of moving all the used (marked) nodes to one end of memory and all the available memory to the other end is called *compaction*, and an algorithm that performs such a process is called a *compaction* (or *compacting*) *algorithm*.

The basic problem in developing an algorithm that moves portions of memory from one location to another is to preserve the integrity of the pointer values to the nodes being moved. For example, if *node*(*p*) in memory contains a pointer *q*, then when *node*(*p*) and *node*(*q*) are moved, not only must the addresses of *node*(*p*) and *node*(*q*) be modified, but the contents of *node*(*p*) (which contained the pointer *q*) must be modified to point to the new address of *node*(*q*). In addition to being able to change the addresses of nodes, we must have a method of determining whether the contents of any node contains a pointer to some other node (in which case its value may have to be changed) or whether it contains some other data type (so that no change is necessary).

A number of compaction techniques have been developed. As in the case of marking algorithms, the process is required at precisely the time that little additional space is available, and in consequence, methods that require substantial additional storage (e.g., a stack) are not practical. Let us examine one compaction algorithm that does not need additional memory when it runs.

The compaction algorithm is executed after the marking phase and traverses memory sequentially. Each marked node, as it is encountered in the sequential traversal, is assigned to the next available memory location, starting from the beginning of available memory. When examining a marked node *nd*1 that points to a node *nd*2, the pointer in *nd*1 that now points to *nd*2 must be updated to the new location where *nd*2 will be moved. That location may not yet be known, because *nd*2 might be at a later address than *nd*1. *nd*1 is therefore placed on a list, emanating from *nd*2, of all the nodes that contain pointers to *nd*2, so that when the new location of *nd*2 is determined, *nd*1 can be accessed and the pointer to *nd*2 contained in it modified.

For now, let us assume that a new field *header* in each node *nd*2 points to the list of nodes that contain pointers to *nd*2. We call this list the **adjustment list** of *nd*2. We can reuse the field that pointed to *nd*2 (either *next* or *info*) as the link field for the adjustment list of *nd*2; we know that its "real" value is *nd*2 because the node is on the list emanating from *header*(*nd*2). Thus, its adjustment list (once it has been formed) can be traversed when *nd*2 is reached in a sequential traversal, and the values in the fields used to link the list can be changed to the new location assigned to *nd*2. Then, once all nodes that point to *nd*2 have had their pointers adjusted, *nd*2 itself can be moved.

However, one additional piece of information is required. The adjustment list of nodes pointing to *nd*2 can be linked via either the *next* pointer of a node *nd*1 (if *next*(*nd*1) = *nd*2) or the *info* pointer (if *info*(*nd*1) = *nd*2). How can we tell which it is? For this purpose, three additional fields in each node are necessary. The values of these fields can be either "N" for *none*, which indicates that a node is not on an adjustment list, "I" for *info*, which indicates that a node is linked onto the adjustment list using *info*, or "L" for *link*, which indicates that it is linked onto the adjustment list using *next*. The three fields are named *headPtr*, *infoPtr*, and *nextPtr*. *headPtr*(*nd*) defines the link field in the node pointed to by *header*(*nd*), *infoPtr*(*nd*) defines the link field in the node pointed to by *info*(*nd*), and *nextPtr*(*nd*) defines the link field in the node pointed to by *next*(*nd*).

Thus, we assume the following format for the nodes:

```
public class NodeType {
  boolean mark;
  int header;
  int next;
  char headPtr;
  char infoPtr;
  char nextPtr;
  int oType;
  Object info;

  public NodeType(){}
}
```

Now consider a single sequential pass of the algorithm. If a node *nd*1 points to a node *nd*2 that appears later in memory, *nd*1 will have already been placed on the adjustment list of *nd*2 by the time the algorithm reaches *nd*2 sequentially. When the algorithm reaches *nd*2, therefore, the pointers in *nd*1 can be modified. But if *nd*2 appears earlier in memory, then when *nd*2 is reached, it is not yet known that *nd*1 points to it, so the pointer in *nd*1 cannot be adjusted. For this reason, the algorithm requires two sequential passes. The first places nodes on adjustment lists and modifies pointers in nodes that it finds on adjustment lists. The second clears away adjustment lists remaining from the first pass and actually moves the nodes to their new locations. The first pass may be outlined as follows:

1. Update the memory location to be assigned to the next marked node, *nd*.
2. Traverse the list of nodes pointed to by *header(nd)*, and change the appropriate pointer fields to point to the new location of *nd*.
3. If the *oType* field of *nd* is *LSTINFO*, and *info(nd)* is not **null**, then place *nd* on the list of the nodes headed by *header(info(nd))*.
4. If *next(nd)* is not **null**, then place *nd* on the list of the nodes headed by the *header(next(nd))*.

Once this process has been completed for each marked node, a second pass through memory will perform the actual compaction. During the second pass, we perform the following operations:

1. Update the memory location to be assigned to the next marked node, *nd*.
2. Traverse the list of nodes pointed to by *header(nd)*, and change the appropriate pointer fields to point to the new location of *nd*.
3. Move *nd* to its new location.

The following algorithm performs the actual compaction. (We assume an auxiliary variable *source* that will contain an "N", "I", or "L", as explained before, for use in traversing the lists.)

```
// initialize fields for compaction algorithm
for (i = 1; i < MAXNODES; i++) {
    node[i].header = 0;
    node[i].headPtr = 'N';
    node[i].infoPtr = 'N';
    node[i].nextPtr = 'N';
}
//                          Pass 1
// Scan nodes sequentially. As each node nd is encountered
// perform the following operations:
// 1. Determine the new location of the node
// 2. For all nodes that were previously encountered on this
//    pass that point to nd, adjust the appropriate pointer to
//    point to the new location of nd.
// 3. If any of the fields of nd point to some other node, p,
//    place nd on the list headed by node[p].header

newLoc = 0;
for (nd = 1; nd < MAXNODES; nd++)
    if (node[nd].mark == true) {
        // nodes that are not marked are to be ignored.
        newLoc++;    // operation 1
        // operation 2
        p = node[nd].header;
        source = node[nd].headPtr;
        while (p != 0)
```

```
                        // traverse the list of nodes encountered
                        // thus far that point to nd
                        if (source == 'I') {
                                q = ((Integer) node[p].info).intValue();
                                source = node[p].infoPtr;
                                node[p].info = new Integer(newLoc);
                                node[p].infoPtr = 'N';
                                p = q;
                        }
                        else {
                                q = node[p].next;
                                source = node[p].nextPtr;
                                node[p].next = newLoc;
                                node[p].nextPtr = 'N';
                                p = q;
                        }
                        node[nd].headPtr = 'N';
                        node[nd].header = 0;
                        // operation 3
                        if (node[nd].oType == LSTINFO &&
                                        ((Integer) node[nd].info).intValue() != 0) {
                                // place node[nd] on a list linked by node[nd].info
                                p = ((Integer) node[nd].info).intValue();
                                node[nd].info = new Integer(node[p].header);
                                node[nd].infoPtr = node[p].headPtr;
                                node[p].header = nd;
                                node[p].headPtr = 'I';
                        }
                        // place node[nd] on a list linked by node[nd].next
                        p = node[nd].next;
                        node[nd].next = node[p].header;
                        node[nd].nexPtr = node[p].headPtr;
                        if (p != 0) {
                                node[p].header = nd;
                                node[p].headPtr = 'L';
                        }
                } /* end if node[nd].mark == true

//*                    Pass 2
// This pass examines each node nd in turn, updates all nodes on
// the adjustment list of nd, and then moves the contents of nd
// to its new location.
newLoc = 0;
for (nd = 1; nd < MAXNODES; nd++)
                if (node[nd].mark) {
                        newLoc++;
                        p = node[nd].header;
                        source = node[nd].headPtr;
                        while (p != 0)
                                if (source == 'I') {
                                        q = ((Integer)node[p].info).intValue();
```

```
                              source = node[p].infoPtr;
                              node[p].info = new Integer(newLoc);
                              node[p].infoPtr = 'N';
                              p = q;
                        }
                        else {
                              q = node[p].next;
                              source = node[p].nextPtr;
                              node[p].next = newLoc;
                              node[p].nextPtr = 'N';
                              p = q;
                        }
                  node[nd].headPtr = 'N';
                  node[nd].header = 0;
                  node[nd].mark = false;
                  node[newLoc] = node[nd];
      // end if node[nd].mark
```

Several points should be noted with respect to this algorithm. First, *node*[0] is suitably initialized so that the algorithm need not test for special cases. Second, the process of adjusting the pointers of all the nodes on the list headed by the header field of a particular node is performed twice: once during the first pass, and once during the second. This process could not be deferred entirely to the second pass, when all the pointers to a particular node are known. The reason for this is that when a field in a node *nd2* in the adjustment list of node *nd* is changed to *nd*, it must be changed before *nd2* is moved to a new location, since no record of the new location is maintained in *nd2*. Thus nodes on the adjustment list of *nd* that precede *nd* sequentially must have their fields modified before they are moved. But since they are moved before we reach *nd* in the second pass, and they have already been placed on the adjustment list by the time we reach *nd* in the first pass, we must clear the adjustment lists and modify the pointer fields at that point. We must also modify the pointer fields in the second pass for nodes on the adjustment list of *nd* that are sequentially after *nd* and were put on the adjustment list of *nd* during the first pass after having already passed *nd*.

The algorithm seems to require several additional fields for each node. In reality, these additional fields are not required. Most systems have at least one field in each node that cannot take on a pointer value during the ordinary course of processing. This field can be used to hold the *header* pointer to the adjustment list, so that an additional *header* field is not necessary. The value that was held in this field can be moved to the last node in the adjustment list, and placed in either the *next* or *info* field, depending on which of the two held the pointer to the target node. We assume that it is possible to distinguish between a pointer and a nonpointer value so that we can detect when we reach the end of the adjustment list by the presence of a nonpointer value in the last node.

We therefore see that our compaction algorithm can be modified so that it does not require any additional storage in the nodes. Such an algorithm is called a ***bounded workspace algorithm***.

The time requirements of the algorithm are easy to analyze. There are two linear passes throughout the complete array of memory. Each pass through memory scans each node once and adjusts any pointer fields to which the nodes point. The time requirements are obviously $O(n)$.

With respect to the actual compaction, it is not necessary to invoke the compaction routine each time the garbage-collection routine is called. The garbage-collection routine is called when there is little (or no) space available. The amount of space reclaimed by the algorithm may or may not provide sufficient contiguous blocks. The compaction algorithm ensures that the space reclaimed is contiguous at one end of memory. If the memory returned by the garbage-collection algorithm is not sufficiently fragmented to warrant a call to the compaction routine, there will be several calls to the collection routine before it is necessary to call the compaction algorithm.

On the other hand, if the compaction routine is not called often enough, then the system may indicate that insufficient space is available when in fact there is sufficient space but it is not contiguous. Failure to invoke the compaction routine may then result in additional calls to the garbage-collection routine. Deciding when to invoke the compaction algorithm in conjunction with the garbage-collection algorithm is difficult. Nonetheless, since compaction is usually more efficient than garbage collection, it is usually not too inefficient to invoke them at the same time.

Variations of Garbage Collection

There are a number of recently discovered variations of the garbage-collection systems presented above. In the traditional schemes we have considered, the applications programs function as long as the space availability of the system satisfies certain criteria (e.g., the total amount of free space available, the number and size of contiguous memory locations available, the amount of memory requested since the last garbage-collection phase). When these criteria are no longer met, all applications programs halt and the system directs its resources to garbage collection. Once the collection has completed, the applications programs may resume execution from the point at which they were interrupted.

In some situations, however, this is not satisfactory. Applications that are executing in real-time (e.g., computing the trajectory of a spaceship, monitoring a chemical reaction) cannot be halted while the system is performing garbage collection. In these circumstances, it is usually necessary to dedicate a separate processor devoted exclusively to the job of garbage collection. When the system signals that garbage collection must be performed, the separate processor begins executing concurrently with the applications program. This simultaneous execution makes it necessary to guarantee that nodes in the process of being acquired for use by an application program are not mistakenly returned to the available pool by the collector. Avoiding such problems is not a trivial process. Systems that allow the collection process to proceed simultaneously with the applications program use "on-the-fly" garbage collection.

Another subject of interest deals with minimizing the cost of reclaiming unused space. In the methods we have discussed, the cost of reclaiming any portion of storage is the same as the cost of reclaiming any other portion (of the same size). Recent attention has been directed toward designing a system in which the cost of reclaiming a portion of storage is proportional to its lifetime. It has been shown empirically that some portions of memory are required for smaller time intervals than others, and that requests for portions of memory with smaller lifetimes occur more frequently than requests for portions of memory with longer lifetimes. Thus, by reducing the cost of retrieving portions of memory required for short time periods at the expense of the cost of retrieving portions of memory with longer lifespans, the overall cost of the garbage-collection process will be reduced. Exactly how one classifies the lifetimes of portions of memory and the algorithms for retrieving portions of memory will not be considered further.

The process of garbage collection is also applied to reclaiming unused space in secondary devices (e.g., a disk). While the concept of allocation and freeing space is the same (i.e., space may be requested or released by a program), algorithms that manage space on such devices often cannot be translated efficiently from their counterparts that manipulate main memory. The reason for this is that accessing any location in main memory costs the same as accessing any other location in main memory. In secondary storage, on the other hand, the cost depends on the location of the storage currently being accessed as well as the location we desire to access. It is very efficient to access a portion of secondary storage that is in the same block that is now being accessed; to access a location in a different block may involve expensive disk seeks. For this reason, device management systems for offline storage try to minimize the number of such accesses. The interested reader is referred to the literature for a discussion of the relevant techniques.

EXERCISES

9.2.1   Implement each of the following list operations from Section 9.1 in Java assuming that the reference count method of list management is used.

    a. *head*
    b. *tail*
    c. *addOn*
    d. *setHead*
    e. *setTail*

9.2.2   Rewrite the methods in the previous exercise under the system in which the reference counter in a node *nd1* is decremented when a node *nd2* pointing to *nd1* is reallocated, rather than when *nd2* is freed.

9.2.3   Implement the list operations in Exercise 9.2.1 in Java assuming the use of list headers, with reference counts in header nodes only. Ensure that illegal lists are never formed.

9.2.4   Write an algorithm to detect recursion in a list, that is, whether or not there is a path from some node on the list back to itself.

9.2.5   Write an algorithm to restore all the nodes on a list *list* to the available list. Do the same using no additional storage.

9.2.6   In a multiuser environment where several users are running concurrently, it may be possible for one user to request additional storage and thus invoke the garbage collector while another user is in the middle of list manipulation. If garbage collection is allowed to proceed at that point (before the lists of the second user have been restored to legal form), the second user will find that many list nodes have been freed.

Assume that there exist two system methods, *noGarbage* and *okGarbage*. A call to the first inhibits the invocation of garbage collection until after the same user calls the second. Implement the list operations in Exercise 9.2.1, using calls to these two methods to ensure that garbage collection is not invoked at inopportune moments.

9.2.7 Trace the actions of the three garbage-collection algorithms in the text on the lists in Figures 9.2.4a and 9.1.9, assuming that the integer above each list node is the index of that node in the array *node*. Trace through the algorithms on the list in Figure 9.1.9, after executing the statement

```
list9 = null;
```

9.2.8 Given pointers p and q to two list nodes, write an algorithm to determine whether *node(q)* is accessible from *node(p)*.

9.2.9 Assume that each node contains an arbitrary number of pointers to other nodes rather than just two, so that the lists now become graphs. Revise each of the marking algorithms presented in this section under this possibility.

9.2.10 Revise each of the marking algorithms presented in this section under the assumption that the lists are doubly linked, so that each list node contains a *prevPtr* field to the previous node on the same list. How do each of the algorithms increase in efficiency? What restriction on the list structure does the presence of such a field imply?

9.2.11 Write two marking algorithms that use a finite, auxiliary stack of size *STKSIZE*. The algorithms operate like the second marking algorithm presented in the text until the stack becomes full. At that point, the first of the two algorithms operates like the sequential algorithm presented in the text, and the second operates like the Schorr-Waite algorithm.

9.3   DYNAMIC MEMORY MANAGEMENT

In the previous sections, we assumed that storage is allocated and freed one node at a time. There are two characteristics of nodes that make the previous methods suitable. The first is that each node of a given type is of fixed size, and the second, that each node is fairly small. In some applications, however, these characteristics do not apply. For example, if a program requires a large amount of contiguous storage (e.g., a large array), it would be impractical to attempt to obtain such a block one node at a time. Similarly, if program requires storage blocks in a large variety of sizes, the memory management system must be able to process requests for variable-length blocks. In this section we discuss some systems of this type.

As an example, consider a small memory of 1024 words. Suppose a request is made for three blocks of storage of 348, 110, and 212 words, respectively. Let us further suppose that these blocks are allocated sequentially, as shown in Figure 9.3.1a. Now suppose that the second block, of size 110, is freed, resulting in the situation depicted in Figure 9.3.1b. There are now 464 words of free space; yet, because the free space is divided into noncontiguous blocks, a request for a block of 400 words could not be satisfied.

Suppose block 3 were now freed. Clearly, it is not desirable to retain three free blocks of 110, 212, and 354 words. Instead, the blocks should be combined into a single

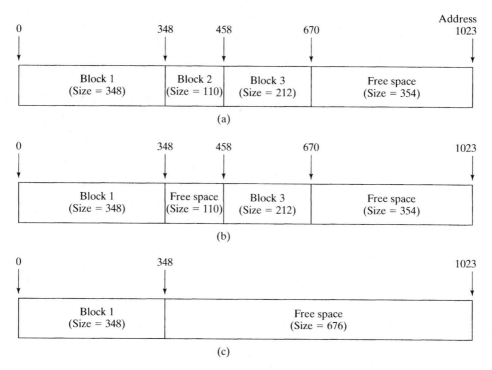

FIGURE 9.3.1

large block of 676 words so that further large requests can be satisfied. After combination, memory will appear as in Figure 9.3.1c.

This example illustrates the need to keep track of available space, allocate portions of space when allocation requests are presented, and combine contiguous free spaces when a block is freed.

Compaction of Blocks of Storage

One scheme that is sometimes used involves compaction of storage as follows: Initially memory is one large block of available storage. As requests for storage arrive, blocks of memory are allocated sequentially, starting from the first location in memory. This is illustrated in Figure 9.3.2a. A variable *freePoint* contains the address of the first location following the last block allocated. In Figure 9.3.2a, *freePoint* equals 950. Note that all the memory locations between *freePoint* and the highest address in memory are free. When a block is freed, *freePoint* remains unchanged and no combinations of free spaces take place. When a block of size n is allocated, *freePoint* is increased by n. This continues until a block of size n is requested and $freePoint + n - 1$ is larger than the highest address in memory. The request cannot be satisfied without further action being taken.

At this point, user routines come to a halt and a system compaction routine is called. Although the algorithm in the previous section was designed to address uniform

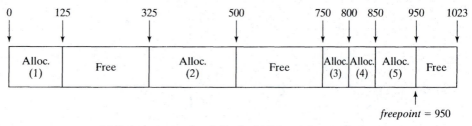

(a) Before compaction. A block of 150 words is requested.

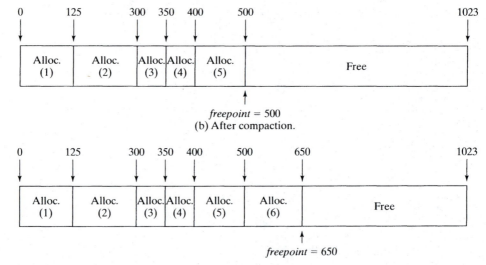

freepoint = 500
(b) After compaction.

(c) The request for 150 words has been granted.

FIGURE 9.3.2

nodes, it could be modified to compact memory consisting of blocks of storage. Such a routine copies all the allocated blocks into sequential memory locations starting from the lowest address in memory. Thus the free blocks that were interspersed with the allocated blocks are eliminated, and *freePoint* is reset to the sum of the sizes of all the allocated blocks. One large free block is created at the upper end of memory, and the user request may be filled if there is sufficient storage available. This process is illustrated in Figure 9.3.2 on a memory of 1024 words.

When allocated blocks are copied into lower portions of memory, special care must be taken to keep the pointer values. For example, the contents of memory location 420 in allocated block 2 in Figure 9.3.2a might contain the address 340. After block 2 is moved to locations 125 through 299, location 140 contains the previous contents of location 340. In moving the contents of 420 to 220, those contents must be changed to 140. Thus, in order for compaction to be successful, there must be a method to determine whether the contents of a given location is an address.

An alternative is a system that computes addresses as offsets from some base address. In this case, only the contents of the base address must be changed, while the offset in memory need not be altered. For example, in the previous instance, location 420 would contain the offset 15 before compaction, rather than the address 340. Since the base address of the block is 325, the address 340 would be computed as the base address 325 plus the offset 15. When the block is moved, its base address is changed to 125, while the offset 15 is moved from location 420 to location 220. Adding the new base address 125 to the offset 15 yields 140, which is the address to which the contents of 340 have been moved. Note that the offset 15 contained in memory has not been changed at all. However, such a technique is useful only for intrablock memory references; interblock references to locations in a different block must still be modified. A compaction routine requires a method by which the size of a block and its status (allocated or free) could be determined.

Compaction is similar to garbage collection in that all user processing must stop as the system takes time to clean up its storage. For this reason, and because of the pointer problem discussed above, compaction is not used as frequently as the more complicated schemes presented below.

First-Fit, Best-Fit, and Worst-Fit

If it is undesirable to move blocks of allocated storage from one area of memory to another, then it must be possible to reallocate memory blocks that have been freed dynamically as user processing continues. For example, if memory is fragmented, as shown in Figure 9.3.1b, and a request is made for a block of 250 words of storage, locations 670 through 919 would be used. The result is shown in Figure 9.3.3a. If memory is as shown in Figure 9.3.1b, then a request for a block of 50 words could be satisfied by either words 348 through 397 or words 670 through 719 (see Figures 9.3.3b and c). In each case, part of a free block is allocated, leaving the remaining portion free.

Each time a request is made for storage, a free area large enough to accommodate the size requested must be located. The most obvious method for keeping track of the free blocks is to use a linear linked list. Each free block contains a field containing the size of the block and a field containing a pointer to the next free block. These fields are in some uniform location (say, the first two words) in the block. If p is the address of a free block, the expressions $size(p)$ and $next(p)$ are used to refer to these two quantities. A global pointer *freeBlock* points to the first free block on this list. Let us see how blocks are removed from the free list when storage is requested. We then examine how blocks are added onto this list when they are freed.

Consider the situation in Figure 9.3.1b, reproduced in Figure 9.3.4a to show the free list. There are several methods of selecting the free block to use when requesting storage. In the *first-fit* method, the free list is traversed sequentially to find the first free block whose size is larger than or equal to the amount requested. Once the block is found, it is removed from the list (if it is equal in size to the amount requested) or split into two portions (if it is greater than the amount requested). The first of these portions remains on the list, and the second is allocated. The reason for allocating the second portion rather than the first is that the free list *next* pointer is at the beginning of each free block. By leaving the first portion of the block on the free list, this pointer

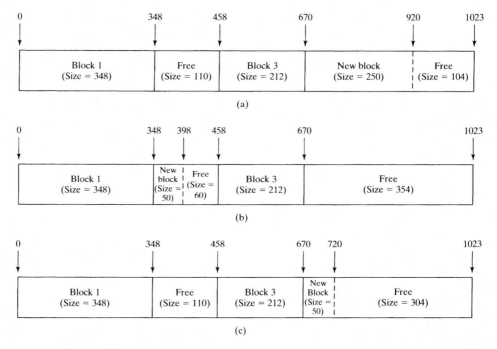

FIGURE 9.3.3

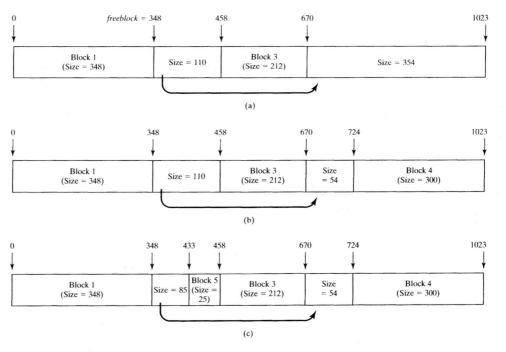

FIGURE 9.3.4

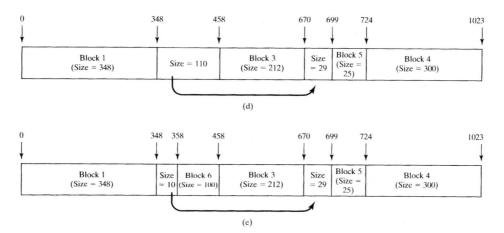

FIGURE 9.3.4   (*Continued*)

need not be copied into some other location, and the *next* field of the previous block in the list need not be changed.

The following first-fit allocation algorithm returns the address of a free block of storage of size *n* in the variable *alloc* if one is available, and sets *alloc* to the null address if no such block is available.

```
p = freeBlock;
alloc = null;
q = null;
while (p != null && size(p) < n) {
    q = p;
    p = next(p);
}
if (p != null) {                 // there is a block large enough
    s = size(p);
    alloc = p + s - n;   // alloc contains the address of the desired
                         // block
  if (s == n)
            // remove the block from the free list
            if (q == null)
                    freeBlock = next(p);
            else
                    next(q) = next(p);
    else     // adjust the size of the remaining free block
            size(p) = s - n;
}
```

The ***best-fit*** method obtains the smallest free block whose size is greater than or equal to *n*. An algorithm to obtain such a block by traversing the entire free list follows. We assume that *memSize* is the total number of words in memory.

```
p = freeBlock;              // p is used to traverse the free list
q = null;                   // q is one block behind p
```

```
        r = null;                  // r points to the desired block
        rq = null;                 // rq is one block behind r
        rsize = memSize + 1;       // rsize is the size of the block at r
        alloc = null;              // alloc will point to the block selected
        while (p != null) {
           if (size(p) >= n && size(p) < rsize) {
                    // we have found a free block closer in size
                    r = p;
                    rq = q;
                    rsize = size(p);
           }
           // continue traversing the free list
           q = p;
           p = next(p);
        }
        if (r != null) {
                // there is a block of sufficient size
                alloc = r + rsize - n;
                if (rsize == n)
                        // remove the block from the free list
                        if (rq == null)
                                freeBlock = next(r);
                        else
                                next(rq) = next(r);
           else
                size(r) = rsize - n;
        }
```

To see the difference between the first-fit and best-fit methods, consider the following examples. We begin with memory fragmented, as in Figure 9.3.4a. There are two blocks of free storage, of sizes 110 and 354. If a request is made for a block of 300 words, the block of 354 is split, as shown in Figure 9.3.4b, under both the first-fit and best-fit methods. Suppose a block of size 25 is then requested. Under first-fit, the block of size 110 is split (Figure 9.3.4c), while under best-fit the block of size 54 is split (Figure 9.3.4d). If a block of size 100 is then requested, the request can be fulfilled under best-fit because the block of size 110 is available (Figure 9.3.4e), but it cannot be fulfilled under first-fit. This illustrates an advantage of the best-fit method: very large free blocks remain unsplit, and thus requests for large blocks can be satisfied. In the first-fit method, a very large block of free storage at the beginning of the free list is nibbled away by small requests and thus is severely shrunken by the time a large request arrives.

However, it is also possible for the first-fit method to succeed where the best-fit method fails. As an example, consider the case in which the system begins with free blocks of size 110 and 54 and then makes successive requests for 25, 70, and 50 words. Figure 9.3.5 illustrates that the first-fit method succeeds in fulfilling these requests, while the best-fit method does not. The reason is that remaining unallocated portions of blocks are smaller under best-fit than under first-fit.

Yet another method of allocating blocks of storage is the ***worst-fit method***. In this method, the system always allocates a portion of the largest free block in memory. The

		Blocks remaining using	
	Request	First-fit	Best-fit
Initially		110, 54	110, 54
	25	85, 54	110, 29
	70	15, 54	40, 29
	50	15, 4	cannot be fulfilled

FIGURE 9.3.5

philosophy behind this method is that the repeated use of a small number of very large blocks to satisfy the majority of requests will leave many moderately sized blocks unfragmented. Thus, this method is likely to satisfy a larger number of requests than the other methods, unless most of the requests are for very large portions of memory. For example, if memory consists initially of blocks of sizes 200, 300, and 100 then the sequence of requests 150, 100, 125, 100, 100 can be satisfied by the worst-fit method but not by either the first-fit or best-fit method. (Convince yourself that this is the case.)

The main reason for choosing one method over the other is efficiency. In each of the methods, the search can be made more efficient. For example, a true first-fit method, which allocates the block at the lowest memory address first, will be most efficient if the available list is maintained in the order of increasing memory address (as it should be for reasons to be discussed shortly). On the other hand, if the available list is maintained in the order of increasing size, then a best-fit search for a block becomes more efficient. And finally, if the list is maintained in the order of decreasing size, then a worst-fit request requires no searching, as the largest-size block is always the first on the list. However, for reasons we shall discuss shortly, it is not practical to maintain the list of available blocks in size order.

Each of the methods has certain characteristics that make it either desirable or undesirable for various request patterns. In the absence of any specific consideration to the contrary, the first-fit method is usually preferred.

Improvements in the First-Fit Method

The first-fit method can be improved in several ways. If the size of a free block is only slightly larger than the size of the block to be allocated, the portion of the free block that remains free is very small. This remaining portion is often so small that there is little likelihood of its being used before the allocated portion is freed and the two portions are recombined. Thus little benefit is achieved by leaving the small portion on the free list. Also, recall that any free block must be of some minimum size (in our case, two words) so that it may contain *size* and *next* fields. What if the smaller portion of a free block is below this minimum size after the larger portion has been allocated?

The solution to these problems is to insist that no block may remain free if its size is below some reasonable minimum. If a free block is about to be split, and the remaining portion is below this minimum size, the block is not split. Instead, the entire free block is allocated as though it were exactly the right size. This allows the system to remove the entire block from the free list and does not clutter up the list with very small blocks.

The phenomenon in which there are many small noncontiguous free blocks is called **external fragmentation** because free space is wasted outside allocated blocks. This contrasts with **internal fragmentation**, in which free space is wasted within allocated blocks. The above solution transforms external fragmentation into internal fragmentation. The choice of what minimum size to use depends on the pattern of allocation requests in the system. It is reasonable to use a minimum size such that only a small percentage of the allocation requests (say 5 percent) is less than or equal to that size. Since the possibility of small slivers remaining is even greater under the best-fit method than under first-fit, the establishment of a minimum size is of correspondingly greater importance under that method.

Another significant improvement in the first-fit method can be made. As time goes on, smaller free blocks will tend to accumulate near the front of the free list. This is because a large block near the front of the list is reduced in size before a large block near the back of the list. Thus, the small blocks near the front cannot be used in searching for a large or even a moderate-size block. The algorithm would be more efficient if the free list were organized as a circular list whose first element varies dynamically as blocks are allocated.

Two ways of implementing this dynamic variance suggest themselves. In the first, *freeBlock* (the pointer to the first free block on the list) is set to *next(freeBlock)*, so that the front of the list advances one block each time a block is allocated. In the second, *freeBlock* is set to *next(alloc)*, where *alloc* points to the block just chosen for allocation. Thus all the blocks that were too small for this allocation request are, in effect, moved to the back of the list. The reader is invited to investigate the advantages and disadvantages of both techniques.

Freeing Storage Blocks

Thus far, nothing has been said about how allocated blocks of storage are freed and combined with contiguous free blocks to form larger blocks of free storage. Specifically, three questions arise:

1. When a block of storage is freed, where is it placed on the free list? The answer to this question determines how the free list is ordered.
2. When a block of storage is freed, how can it be determined whether the blocks of storage on either side of it are free (in which case the newly freed block should be combined with an already existing free block)?
3. What is the mechanism for combining a newly freed block with a previously free contiguous block?

The term **liberation** is used for the process of freeing an allocated block of storage; an algorithm to implement this process is called a **liberation algorithm**. The free list should be organized to facilitate efficient allocation and liberation.

Suppose that the free list is organized arbitrarily, so that a freed block is placed at the front of the list. Perhaps the block just freed is adjacent to a previously free block. It should be combined with the adjacent free block in order to create a single large free block. There is no way, short of traversing the entire free list, to determine whether such an adjacent free block exists. Thus each liberation would involve a traversal of the free list. For this reason it is inefficient to maintain the free list this way.

An alternative is to keep the free list sorted in order of increasing memory location. Then, when a block is freed, the free list is traversed in a search for the first free block *fb* whose starting address is greater than the starting address of the block being freed. If a contiguous free block is not found in this search, no such contiguous block exists, and the newly freed block can be inserted into the free list immediately before *fb*. If *fb* or the free block immediately preceding *fb* on the free list is contiguous to the newly freed block, it can be combined with the newly freed block. Under this method, the entire free list need not be traversed. Instead, only half of the list must be traversed, on the average.

The following liberation algorithm implements this scheme, assuming that the free list is linear (not circular), and that *freeBlock* points to the free block with the smallest address. The algorithm frees a block of size *n* beginning at address *alloc*.

```
q = null;
p = freeBlock;
// p traverses the free list. q remains one step behind p
while (p != null && p < alloc) {
    q = p;
    p = next(p);
}
// At this point, either q = null or q < alloc and either p = null
// or alloc < p. Thus if p and q are not null, the block must be
// combined with the blocks beginning at p or q or both, or must be
// inserted in the list between the two blocks.
if (q == null)
    freeBlock = alloc;
else if (q + size(q) == alloc) {
    // combine with previous block
    alloc = q;
    n = size(q) + n;
}
else
    next(q) = alloc;
if (p != null && alloc + n == p) {
    // combine with subsequent block
    size(alloc) = n + size(p);
    next(alloc) = next(p);
}
else {
    size(alloc) = n;
    next(alloc) = p;
}
```

If the free list is organized as a circular list, the first-fit allocation algorithm begins traversing the list from varying locations. However, traversing the list from the lowest location during liberation requires an additional external pointer, *lowBlock*, to the free block with the lowest location. Ordinarily, traversal starts at *lowBlock* during liberation. However, if it is found that *freeBlock* < *alloc* when the block that starts at *alloc* is about to be freed, traversal starts at *freeBlock* so that even less search time is used during liberation. The reader is urged to implement this variation as an exercise.

Boundary Tag Method

It is desirable to eliminate all searching during liberation to make the process more efficient. One method of doing this comes at the expense of keeping extra information in all blocks (both free and allocated).

A search is necessary during liberation to determine whether the newly freed block may be combined with some existing free block. There is no way of detecting whether such a block exists or which block it is without a search. However, if such a block exists, it must immediately precede or succeed the block being freed. The first address of the block that follows a block of size *n* at *alloc* is *alloc* + *n*. Suppose every block contains a field *flag* which is **true** if the block is allocated, and **false** if the block is free. Then, by examining *flag*(*alloc* + *n*), it can be determined whether or not the block immediately following the block at *alloc* is free.

It is more difficult to determine the status of the block immediately preceding the block at *alloc*. The address of the last location of the preceding block is, of course, *alloc* − 1. But there is no way of finding the address of its first location without knowing its size. Suppose, however, that each block contains two flags, *fFlag* and *bFlag*, both of which are **true** if the block is allocated, and **false** otherwise. *fFlag* is at a specific offset from the front of the block, and *bFlag* is at a specific negative offset from the back of the block.

Thus, to access *fFlag*, the first location of the block must be known; to access *bFlag*, the last location of the block must be known. The status of the block following the block at *alloc* can be determined from the value of *fFlag* (*alloc* + *n*), and the status of the block preceding the block at *alloc* can be determined from the value of *bFlag* (*alloc* − 1). Then, when a block is to be freed, it can be determined immediately whether it must be combined with either of its two neighboring blocks.

A list of free blocks is still needed for the allocation process. When a block is freed, its neighbors are examined. If both of them are allocated, the block can simply be appended to the front of the free list. If one (or both) of the neighbors is free, it (or they) can be removed from the free list and combined with the newly freed block, and the newly created large block can be placed at the head of the free list. Note that this would tend to reduce search times under first-fit allocation as well, since a previously allocated block (especially if it has been combined with other blocks) is likely to be large enough to satisfy the next allocation request. Since it is placed at the head of the free list, the search time is reduced sharply.

In order to remove an arbitrary block from the free list (to combine it with a newly freed block) without traversing the entire list, the free list must be doubly linked. Thus each free block must contain two pointers, *next* and *prev*, to the next and previous free blocks on the free list. It is also necessary to be able to access these two pointers from the last location of a free block. (This is needed when combining a newly freed block with a free block that immediately precedes it in memory.) Thus the front of a free block must be accessible from its rear. One way to do this is to introduce a *bSize* field at a given negative offset from the last location of each free block. This field contains the same value as the *size* field at the front of the block. Figure 9.3.6 illustrates the structure of free and allocated blocks under this method, which is called the ***boundary***

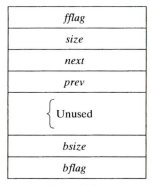

Free block

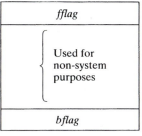

FIGURE 9.3.6   Allocated block

tag method. Each of the control fields, *fFlag*, *size*, *next*, *prev*, *bSize*, and *bFlag* is shown as occupying a complete word, although in practice they may be packed together, several fields to a word.

We now present the liberation algorithm using the boundary tag method. For clarity, we assume that *fFlag* and *bFlag* are logical flags, ***true*** indicates an allocated block, and ***false*** indicates a free block. [We assume that *bFlag*(0) and *fFlag*(*m*), where *m* is the size of memory, are both ***true***.] The algorithm frees a block of size *n* at location *alloc*. It makes use of an auxiliary routine *remove* that removes a block from the doubly linked list. The details of the routine are left as an exercise for the reader.

```
// check the preceding block
if (bFlag(alloc - 1) != true) {
    // the block must be combined with the proceeding block
    start = alloc - bSize(alloc - 1);       // find the initial address
                                            // of the block
    remove(start);                          // remove the block from
                                            // the free list increase
                                            // the size and combine the
                                            // blocks
    n = n + size(start);
    alloc = start;
}
```

```
    // check the following block
    if (fFlag(alloc + n) != true) {
        // the block must be combined with the following block
        start = alloc + n;
        n = n + size(start);
        remove(start);
    }
    // add the newly free, possibly combined block to the free list
    next(alloc) = freeBlock;
    prev(freeBlock) = alloc;
    prev(alloc) = null;
    freeBlock = alloc;
    // adjust the fields in the new block
    fFlag(alloc) = false;
    bFlag(alloc + n - 1) = false;
    size(alloc) = n;
    bSize(alloc + n - 1) = n;
```

Of course, the newly freed block can be inserted into the list based on its size, so that one of the other methods (e.g., best-fit, worst-fit) can also be used.

Buddy System

An alternative method of handling the storage management problem without frequent list traversals is to keep separate free lists for blocks of different sizes. Each list contains free blocks of only one specific size. For example, if memory contains 1024 words, it might be divided into fifteen blocks: one block of 256 words, two blocks of 128 words, four blocks of 64 words, and eight blocks of 32 words. Whenever storage is requested, the smallest block whose size is greater than or equal to the size needed is reserved. For example, a request for a block of 97 words is filled by a block of size 128.

There are several drawbacks to this scheme. First, space is wasted due to internal fragmentation. (In the example, 31 words of the block are totally unusable.) Second, and more serious, a request for a block of size 300 cannot be filled because the largest size maintained is 256. Also, if two blocks of size 150 are needed, the requests cannot be filled even if sufficient contiguous space is available. Thus, the solution is impractical. The impracticality results from the fact that free spaces are never combined. However, a variation of this scheme, called the **buddy system**, is quite useful.

Several free lists consisting of various sized blocks are maintained. Adjacent free blocks of smaller size may be removed from their lists, combined into free blocks of larger size, and placed on the larger-size free list. These larger blocks can then be used intact to satisfy a request for a large amount of memory or be split once more into their smaller constituent blocks to satisfy several smaller requests.

The method outlined below works best on binary computers in which the memory size is an integral power of 2, and multiplication and division by 2 can be performed very efficiently by shifting. Initially, the entire memory of size 2^m is viewed as a single free block. For each power of 2 between 1 (which equals 2^0) and 2^m, a free list containing blocks of that size is maintained. A block of size 2^i is called an **i-block**, and the free list containing i-blocks is called the **i-list**. (In practice, it may be unreasonable to keep free blocks of sizes 1, 2, and 4, so that 8 is the smallest free block size allowed; we will ignore this possibility.) However, it may be the case (and usually is) that some of the free lists are empty. Indeed, initially all the lists except the m-list are empty.

Blocks may be allocated only in sizes 2^k for some integer k between 0 and m. If a request for a block of size n is made, an i-block is reserved where i is the smallest integer such that $n <= 2^i$. If no i-block is available (the i-list is empty), an $(i + 1)$-block is removed from the $(i + 1)$-list and split into two equal-size buddies. Each of these buddies is an i-block. One of the buddies is allocated, and the other remains free and is placed on the i-list. If an $(i + 1)$-block is also unavailable, an $(i + 2)$-block is split into two $(i + 1)$-block buddies, one of which is placed on the $(i + 1)$ list, and the other of which is split into two i-blocks. One of these i-blocks is allocated, and the other is placed onto the i-list. If no $(i + 2)$-block is free, this process continues until either an i-block has been allocated or an m-block is found to be unavailable. In the former case, the allocation attempt is successful; in the latter case, a block of proper size is not available.

The buddy system allocation process can best be described as a recursive method, $getBlock(n)$, that returns a reference to the address of the block to be allocated, or null if no block of size n is available. An outline of this method follows:

```
find the smallest integer i such that 2^i >= n;
if (the i-list is not empty) {
        p = the address of the first block on the i-list;
        remove the first block from the i-list;
        return p ;
}
else  // the i-list is empty
     if (i == m)
                return null;
     else {
                p = getBlock(2^i + 1);
                if (p == null)
                        return null;
                else {
                        put the i-block starting at location p on the
                        i-list;
                        return p + 2^i;
                }
        }
}
```

In this outline, if an $(i + 1)$-block starts at location p, then the two i-blocks into which it is split start at locations p and $p + 2^i$. The first of these remains on the free list, and the second is allocated. Each block is created by splitting a block of one size higher. If an $(i + 1)$-block is split into two i-blocks, $b1$ and $b2$, then $b1$ and $b2$ are **buddies** of each other. The buddy of an i-block at location p is called the **i-buddy** of p. Note that a block at location p can have several buddies but only one i-buddy.

If an i-block is freed and its i-buddy is already free, the two buddies are combined into the $(i + 1)$-block from which they were initially created. In this way, a larger free block of storage is created to satisfy large requests. If the i-buddy of a newly-freed i-block is not free, then the newly freed block is placed directly on the i-list.

Suppose a newly freed i-block has been combined with its previously free i-buddy into an $(i + 1)$-block. It is possible that the $(i + 1)$-buddy of this recombined $(i + 1)$-block is also free. In that case, the two $(i + 1)$-blocks can be recombined further into an $(i + 2)$-block. This process continues until a recombined block is created whose buddy is not free or the entire memory is combined into a single m-block.

The liberation algorithm can be outlined as a recursive method, *liberate*(*alloc*, i), that frees an i-block at location *alloc*.

```
if (i == m) or (the i-buddy of alloc is not free)
     add the i-block at alloc to the i-list
else {
     remove the i-buddy of alloc from the i-list;
     combine the i-block at alloc with its i-buddy;
     p = the address of the newly formed (I + 1)-block;
     liberate(p, I + 1);
}
```

Let us refine the outline of *liberate*; we leave the refinement of *getBlock* as an exercise for the reader.

There is one obvious question that must be answered. How can the free status of the i-buddy of *alloc* be established? Indeed, how can it be determined whether an i-buddy of *alloc* exists at all? It is quite possible that the i-buddy of *alloc* has been split and part (or all) of it is allocated. Additionally, how can the starting address of the i-buddy of *alloc* be determined? If the i-block at *alloc* is the first half of its containing $(i + 1)$-block, then its i-buddy is at *alloc* $+ 2^i$; if the i-block is the second half of its containing block, then its i-buddy is at *alloc* $- 2^i$. How can we determine which is the case?

At this point, it would be instructive to look at some examples. For illustrative purposes, consider an absurdly small memory of $1024(=2^{10})$ words. Figure 9.3.7a illustrates this memory after a request for a block of 100 words has been filled. The smallest power of 2 greater than 100 is $128(=2^7)$. Thus, the entire memory is split into two blocks of size 512; the first is placed on the 9-list, and the second is split into two blocks of size 256. The first of these is placed on the 8-list, and the second is split into two blocks of size 128, one of which is placed on the 7-list, and the second of which is allocated (block $b1$). The starting addresses of the blocks on each nonempty i-list are indicated at the bottom of the figure. Make sure that you follow the execution of the methods *getBlock* and *liberate* on this and succeeding examples.

Figure 9.3.7b illustrates the sample memory after filling an additional request for 50 words. There is no free 6-block, so the free 7-block at location 768 is split into two 6-blocks. The first 6-block remains free, and the second is allocated as block $b2$. In Figure 9.3.7c, three additional 6-blocks have been allocated in the order $b3$, $b4$, and $b5$. When the first request is made, a 6-block at location 768 is free, so that no splitting is necessary. The second request forces the 8-block at 512 to be split into two 7-blocks, and the second 7-block at 640 to be split into two 6-blocks. The second of these is allocated as $b4$, and when the next request for a 6-block is made, the first is also allocated as $b5$.

Note that the block beginning at 768 is a 7-block in Figure 9.3.7a, while in Figure 9.3.7b it is a 6-block. Similarly, the block at 512 is an 8-block in Figures 9.3.7a and b, but a 7-block in Figure 9.3.7c. This illustrates that the size of a block cannot be determined from its starting address. However, as we shall soon see, a block of a given size can start only at certain addresses.

Figure 9.3.7d illustrates the situation after blocks $b4$ and $b3$ have been freed. When block $b4$ at location 704 is freed, its buddy is examined. Since $b4$ is a 6-block that is the second half of the 7-block from which it was split, its buddy is at location $704 - 2^6 = 640$. However, the 6-block at location 640 (which is $b5$) is not free, so no combination can take place. $b3$ is a 6-block, and was the first half of its containing 7-block, so when it is freed, its 6-buddy at $768 + 2^6 = 832$ must be examined. However, that 6-buddy is allocated, so, again, no combination can take place. Note that two adjacent blocks of the same size (6-blocks $b4$ and $b3$ at 704 and 768) are free but are not combined into a single 7-block. This is because they are not buddies; that is, they were not originally split from the same 7-block. $b4$ can be combined only with its buddy $b5$, and $b3$ can be combined only with its buddy $b2$.

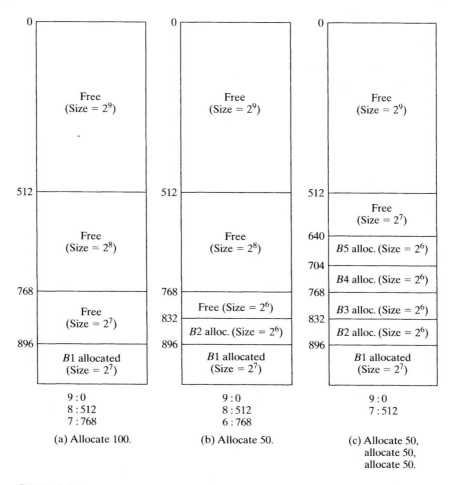

FIGURE 9.3.7

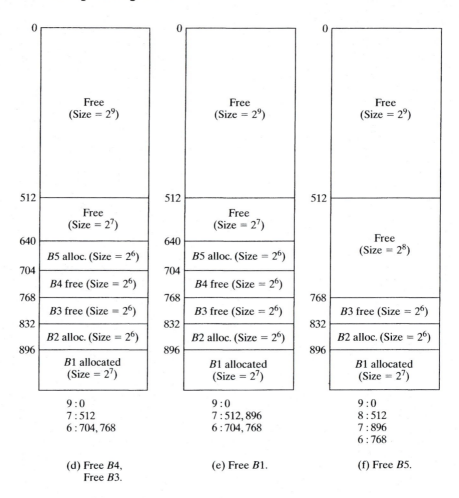

9 : 0
7 : 512
6 : 704, 768

(d) Free $B4$,
Free $B3$.

9 : 0
7 : 512, 896
6 : 704, 768

(e) Free $B1$.

9 : 0
8 : 512
7 : 896
6 : 768

(f) Free $B5$.

FIGURE 9.3.7   *(Continued)*

In Figure 9.3.7e, the 7-block $b1$ has been freed. $b1$ is the second half of its 8-block, so its 7-buddy is at $896 - 2^7 = 768$. Although block $b3$, which starts at that location, is free, no combination can take place. This is because block $b3$ is not a 7-block, but only a 6-block. This means that the 7-block starting at 768 is split and therefore partially allocated. We see that it is not yet ready for combination. Both the address and the size of a given free block must be considered when making a decision as to whether or not to combine buddies.

In Figure 9.3.7f, the 6-block b5 at location 640 is freed. $b5$ is the first half of its containing 7-block, so its 6-buddy is at $640 + 2^6 = 704$. That 6-buddy (block $b4$) is already free, so the two can be combined into a single 7-block at 640. That 7-block is the second half of its containing 8-block, so its 7-buddy is at $640 - 2^7 = 512$. The 7-block at that location is free, so that the two 7-blocks can be combined into an 8-block at 512. That 8-block is the first half of its containing 9-block, so its 8-buddy is at $512 + 2^8 = 768$. But the block at location 768 is a 6-block rather than an 8-block, so no further combination can take place.

These examples illustrate that it is necessary to be able to determine whether a given i-block is the first or second half of its containing $(i + 1)$-block in order to compute the location of its i-buddy.

Clearly, there is only one m-block in memory, and its starting location is 0. When this block is split, it produces two $(m - 1)$-blocks starting at locations 0 and 2^{m-1}. These split into four $(m - 2)$-blocks at locations $0, 2^{m-2}, 2^{m-1}$, and $3 * 2^{m-2}$. In general, there are 2^{m-i} i-blocks starting at locations that are integer multiples of 2^i. For example, if $m = 10$ (memory size is 1024), there are $2^{10-6} = 16$ 6-blocks starting at locations $0, 64, 128, 192, 256, 320, 384, 448, 512, 576, 640, 704, 768, 832, 896$, and 960. Each of these addresses is an integral multiple of 64 (which is 2^6), from $0 * 64$ to $15 * 64$.

Note that any address that is the starting location of an i-block is also the starting location of a k-block for all $0 <= k < i$. This is because the i-block can be split into two $(i - 1)$-blocks, the first of which begins at the same location as the i-block. This is consistent with the observation that an integral multiple of 2^i is also an integral multiple of 2^{i-1}. However, the reverse is not necessarily true. A location that is the starting address of an i-block is only the starting address of an $(i + 1)$-block if the i-block is the first half of the $(i + 1)$-block, but not if it is the second half. For example, in Figure 9.3.7, addresses 640 and 768 begin 7-blocks as well as 6-blocks, and 768 begins an 8-block as well. However, addresses 704 and 832 begin 6-blocks but not 7-blocks.

After making these observations, it is easy to determine whether a given i-block is the first or second half of the $(i + 1)$-block from which it was split. If the starting address p of the i-block is evenly divisible by 2^{i+1}, then the block is the first half of an $(i + 1)$-block, and its i-buddy is at $p + 2^i$; otherwise it is the second half of an $(i + 1)$-block, and its buddy is at $p - 2^i$.

We can therefore introduce a method $buddy(p, i)$ that returns the address of the i-buddy of p [we use the standard $java.lang.Math$ method $pow(a, b)$ that computes a^b]:

```
if (p % pow(2, i + 1) == 0)
    return p + pow(2, i);
else
    return p - pow(2, i);
```

Now that the address of a newly freed block's i-buddy can be found, how can we determine whether or not the buddy is free? One way of making this determination is to traverse the i-list to see whether a block is present at the desired address. If it is, then it can be removed and combined with its buddy. If it is not, then the newly freed i-block can be added to the i-list. Since each i-list is generally quite small [because as soon as two i-buddies are free they are combined into an $(i + 1)$-buddy and removed from the i-list], this traversal is fairly efficient. Furthermore, to implement this scheme, each i-list need not be doubly linked, since a block is removed from the i-list only after the list is traversed so that its list predecessor is known.

An alternative method that avoids list traversal is to have each block contain a flag to indicate whether or not it is allocated. Then, when an i-block is freed, it is possible to determine directly whether or not the block beginning at the address of its buddy is already free. However, this flag alone is insufficient. For example, in Figure 9.3.7e, when 7-block $b1$ at location 896 is freed, its buddy's starting address is calculated as 768. The block at 768 is free, and its flag would indicate this fact. Yet the two blocks at 768 and 896 cannot be combined because the block at 768 is not a 7-block, but a 6-block whose 6-buddy is allocated. Thus an additional *power* field is necessary in each block. The value of this integer field is the base-2 logarithm of its size (i.e., if the block is of size 2^i, the value of *power* is i). When an i-block is freed, its buddy's address is calculated. If the *power* field at the address is i, and if the flag indicates that the buddy is free, the two blocks are combined.

Under this method, a block of proper size can be found efficiently because the i-lists are required only for the allocation algorithm. However, since blocks are removed from the i-lists without traversing them, the lists must be doubly linked. Thus each free block must contain four fields: *free*, *power*, *prev*, and *next*. The last two are pointers to the previous and next blocks on the i-list. An allocated block need contain only the *flag* field.

We present the second method of liberation, leaving the first to the reader as an exercise. We assume an array of pointers, *list[m]*, where *list[i]* points to the first block on the i-list. We also replace the recursive call to *liberate* by a loop in which successively larger blocks are combined with their buddies until a block is formed whose buddy is not free. The algorithm *liberate(alloc, i)* frees an i-block at location *alloc*. For completeness, let us establish that *buddy(p, m)* equals 0. The flag *free* is **true** if the block is free, and **false** otherwise.

```
p = alloc;
bud = buddy(p, i);
while (i < m && free(bud) == true && power(bud) == i) {
        // remove i-buddy of p from the i-list
        q = prev(bud);
        if (q == null)
                list[i] = next(bud);
        else
                next(q) = next(bud);
        if (next(bud) != null)
                prev(next(bud)) = q;
        // combine the i-block at p with its buddy
        if (p / pow(2, i + 1) != 0)
                // the combined block begins at bud
                p = bud;
        i++;
        bud = buddy(p, i);
        // attempt to combine the larger block with its buddy
}
// add the i-block at p to the i-list
q = list[i];
prev(p) = null;
next(p) = q;
list[i] = p;
if (q != null)
    prev(q) = p;
```

```
// adjust the fields on the i-block
power(p) = i;
free(p)= true;
```

Other Buddy Systems

The buddy system that we have just considered is called the **binary buddy system**, based on the rule that two equal sized $(i - 1)$-blocks are created when an i-block (of size 2^i) is split. Similarly, two i-blocks that are buddies can be joined into a single $(i + 1)$-block.

There are, however, other buddy systems in which a large block is not necessarily split into two equal-sized smaller blocks. One such system is called the **Fibonacci buddy system**. The sizes of the blocks in this system are based on the Fibonacci numbers first introduced in Section 3.1. Instead of blocks of size 1, 2, 4, 8, 16, ..., as in the case of the binary buddy system, the Fibonacci buddy system uses blocks of size 1, 2, 3, 5, 8, 13, ... When an i-block is split into two blocks (the size of an i-block in this system is the ith Fibonacci number), one of the blocks is an $(i - 1)$-block, and the other is an $(i - 2)$-block. Thus, for example, a 9-block (of size 34) may split into an 8-block (size 21) and a 7-block (size 13). Similarly, the buddy of an i-block may be either an $(i + 1)$-block or an $(i - 1)$-block. In the former case, recombination produces an $(i + 2)$-block, while in the latter case, an $(i + 1)$-block is produced.

Another alternative buddy system is the **weighted buddy system**. In this scheme, a block of size 2^k is split into two blocks, one of size 2^{k-2} and the other of size $3 * 2^{k-2}$. For example, a block of size 64 splits into two buddies of sizes 16 and 48. The rules for recombination are similar.

The philosophy behind such schemes, in which blocks are split into unequal subblocks, is that requests for storage are usually not for sizes that match those of the blocks in the system. Thus, the next-larger size block must be used, with the result that space is wasted within the block. For example, in the binary buddy system, when a request is made for a block of size 10, a block of size 16 will be allocated (resulting in six wasted bytes); in the Fibonacci buddy system, however, a block of size 13 may be allocated (resulting in only three wasted bytes); while in the weighted buddy system, a block of size 12 will be sufficient (resulting in only two wasted bytes). It is not always the case that the Fibonacci system results in less wasted space than the binary system (i.e., a request for a block of size 15), but in general, allowing blocks of varying sizes is more likely to produce a close fit than requiring groups of blocks to be of uniform size.

An alternative to the above approach is to combine smaller blocks into larger ones only when necessary. In such a scheme, called a **recombination delaying buddy system**, when a block is freed, it is returned to the list of blocks of its size. When a block of a particular size is required, the list of blocks of that size is searched. If a block of the required size is found, then the search halts successfully; otherwise a search is made for a pair of blocks of the next-smaller size that are buddies. If such a pair exists, then the two blocks are combined to form a single block of the required size. If no such pair exists, then the process is repeated recursively with successively smaller blocks until either a block of the required size can be formed from smaller blocks, so that the search is successful, or until it is determined that the required block cannot be formed from smaller blocks. Blocks of larger sizes will also be searched to determine whether a split is feasible. If a block of the desired size cannot be found either by splitting larger blocks or by combining smaller blocks, then the search ends in failure.

The philosophy behind this scheme is that smaller blocks are often returned to the available pool only to be called for again. Instead of recombining the smaller blocks into a larger block only to decompose it again, the smaller blocks are retained and are recombined into larger blocks only when blocks of the larger size are necessary. The disadvantage of this approach is that blocks of larger sizes may not be available when there is, in fact, enough memory to satisfy their requests. For example, there may be three i-blocks available, two of which are buddies. If a request for an i-block arrives and one of the i-buddies is used to satisfy it, then a subsequent request for an $(i + 1)$-block cannot be satisfied. If, on the other hand, the two i-blocks were recombined into an $(i + 1)$-block first, then the request for an i-block would be satisfied from the isolated i-block before an attempt was made to break up an $(i + 1)$-block. (Of course, it is possible to place the i-block on the i-list in such a way that i-buddies are always at the rear of the list. This prevents the allocation of one of a pair of buddies before an isolated block of the required size is allocated. However, when it is necessary to allocate one of several pairs of buddies, it may be difficult to select the pair that will allow subsequently larger recombinations.)

Yet another variation of the buddy system is the ***tailored list buddy system***. In this system, instead of maintaining the lists in blocks as large as possible (the standard system), and instead of not combining buddies until blocks of a larger size are necessary (the recombination delaying system), the blocks are distributed on the various lists in preassigned proportions.

If the relative frequency of requests for blocks of the possible block sizes is known, then memory may be divided initially into blocks of the different sizes according the given distribution. As blocks are called for and returned to the pool, a record is kept of the actual number of blocks of each block size. When a block is returned to the pool and the number of blocks of that size is at or greater than the number specified by the distribution, then an attempt is made to combine the block into a block of the next-larger size. This process is repeated successively until no such recombination is possible or until the number of blocks of each size is not exceeded.

When a block of a particular size is requested and there is no block of the required size, then a block may be formed either by splitting a block of larger size or by recombining several blocks of smaller size. Various allocation strategies can be used in this case. Very often the distribution of requests is not known in advance. In such a case, it is possible to allow the distribution of blocks to stabilize slowly, by maintaining a record of the actual distribution of requests as they arrive. The desired distribution will probably never be achieved exactly, but it can be used as a guide in determining whether and when to recombine blocks.

There are two primary disadvantages to buddy systems. The first is internal fragmentation. For example, in the binary buddy system, only blocks whose sizes are integral powers of 2 can be allocated without waste. This means that a little less than half the storage in each block could be wasted. The other disadvantage is that adjacent free blocks are not combined if they are not buddies. However, simulations have shown that the buddy system does work well, and that once the pattern of memory allocations and liberations stabilizes, splitting and combinations take place infrequently.

EXERCISES

9.3.1   Let s be the average size of an allocated block in a system that uses compaction. Let r be the average number of time units between block allocations. Let m be the memory size, f the average percentage of free space, and c the average number of time units between calls on the compaction algorithm. If the memory system is in equilibrium (over a period of time, equal numbers of blocks are allocated and freed), derive a formula for c in terms of s, r, m, and f.

9.3.2   Implement the first-fit, best-fit, and worst-fit methods of storage allocation in Java as follows: Write a method $getBlock(n)$ that returns the address of a block of size n that is available for allocation and modifies the free list appropriately. The method should utilize the following variables:

   a. $memSize$, the number of locations in memory.

   b. $memory[memSize]$, an array of integers representing the memory.

   c. $freeBlock$, a pointer to the first location of the first free block on the list.

   The value of $size(p)$ may be obtained by the expression $memory[p]$, and the value of $next(p)$ by the expression $memory[p + 1]$.

9.3.3   Revise the first-fit and best-fit algorithms so that, a block on the free list is less than x units larger than a request, the entire block is allocated as is, unsplit. Revise the Java implementations in Exercise 9.3.2 in a similar manner.

9.3.4   Revise the first-fit algorithm and its implementation (see Exercise 9.3.2) so that the free list is circular and is modified in each of the following ways:

   a.   The front of the free list is moved up one block after each allocation request.

   b.   The front of the free list is reset to the block following the block that satisfied the last allocation request.

   c.   If a block is split in meeting an allocation request, its remaining portion is placed at the rear of the free list.

   What are the advantages and disadvantages of these methods over the method presented in the text? Which of the three methods yields the smallest average search time? Why?

9.3.5   Design two liberation algorithms in which a newly freed node is placed on the front of the free list when no combinations can be made. Do not use any additional fields other than $next$ and $size$. In the first algorithm, when two blocks are combined, the combined block is moved to the front of the free list; in the second, the combined block remains at the same position in the free list as its free portion was before the combination. What are the relative merits of the two methods?

9.3.6   Implement the liberation algorithm presented in the text in which the free list is ordered by increasing memory location. Write a Java method $liberate(alloc, n)$ that uses the variables presented in Exercise 9.3.2, where $alloc$ is the address of the block to be freed, and n is its size. The procedure should modify the free list appropriately.

9.3.7   Implement a storage management system by writing a Java application that accepts inputs of two types: An allocation request contains an 'A', the amount of memory requested, and an integer that becomes the identifier of the block being allocated (i.e., block 1, block 2, block 3, etc.). A liberation request contains an 'L' and the integer identifying the block to be liberated. The program should call the methods $getBlock$ and $liberate$ programmed in Exercises 9.3.2 and 9.3.6.

9.3.8 Implement the boundary tag method of liberation as a Java method, as in Exercises 9.3.2 and 9.3.6. The values of $size(p)$ and $bSize(p)$ should be obtained by the expression $abs(memory[p])$, $fFlag(p)$, and $bFlag(p)$ by $(memory[p] > 0)$, $next(p)$ by $memory[p + 1]$, and $prev(p)$ by $memory[p + 2]$.

9.3.9 How could the free list be organized to reduce the search time in the best-fit method? What liberation algorithm would be used for such a free list?

9.3.10 A storage management system is in **equilibrium** if as many blocks are allocated as are liberated in any given time period. Prove the following about a system in equilibrium.

a. The fraction of total storage that is allocated is fairly constant.
b. If adjacent free blocks are always combined, then the number of allocated blocks is half the number of free blocks.
c. If adjacent free blocks are always combined, and the average size of an allocated block is greater than some multiple of the average size of a free block, then the fraction of memory that is free is greater than $k/(k + 2)$.

9.3.11 Present allocation and liberation algorithms for the following systems:

a. Fibonnaci buddy system
b. Weighted buddy system
c. Recombination delaying buddy system
d. Tailored list buddy system

9.3.12 Refine the outline of *getBlock*, which is responsible for allocation in the buddy system, into a nonrecursive algorithm that explicitly manipulates free lists.

9.3.13 Prove formally (using mathematical induction) that in the binary buddy system:

a. There are 2^{m-i} possible i-blocks.
b. The starting address of an i-block is an integer multiple of 2^i.

9.3.14 Implement the binary buddy system as a set of Java applications.

Index